RICELANDS

RICELANDS

The World of South-east Asian Food

Michael Freeman

REAKTION BOOKS

Published by Reaktion Books Ltd
33 Great Sutton Street
London EC1V 0DX

www.reaktionbooks.co.uk

First published 2008
Copyright © Michael Freeman 2008

Printed and bound in China by C&C Offset Printing Co., Ltd

British Library Cataloguing in Publication Data
Freeman, Michael, 1945–
    Ricelands : the world of South-East Asian food
    1. Food habits – South East Asia   2. Cookery, Southeast Asian
    I. Title
    394.1'2'0959

ISBN-13: 978 1 86189 378 9

CONTENTS

1 THE PADDY FIELD

Even on a quiet night, the village dogs would finish their last, crazed barking about four hours before sunrise. This left some three hours of relative silence, a chance for uninterrupted sleep before the next event. This, which never failed to wake me, but which also gave me a strange sensation of comfort, began with a single beat, a sound between a clack and a thud, definitely of wood, repeated every few seconds. After some minutes it was joined by another beat from a distance. Soon there was a chorus of clacking-thudding from across the several close hillsides that supported this Akha hill-tribe village in the far north of Thailand. It took up from where the dogs had left off. It was also the sound of breakfast, lunch and dinner – the daughters of the households pounding rice in hollowed-out upright logs.

I was on an assignment from the publishers Time-Life to make a book documenting the life of this ethnic group, which at that time, in the late 1970s, was almost pristine in its culture, and remote. Many of the settlements had quite recently arrived in Thailand from Burma and from Laos, a long-marginalized people pushed into the hills, always at the receiving end of political turmoil and the encroachment of more powerful lowland cultures. During the several weeks I spent living in this community, this was the sound that reminded me just how much rice dominated the cycle of life, as indeed it did also in the rural lowlands at the foot of our small mountain. Rice is not only the staple across South-east Asia, it fills more of the diet than does any other staple anywhere else in the world. The Akha invitation to eat is to 'eat rice', *haw dza*, and sometimes even *haw haw*, meaning 'rice rice'. When I walked down the forest trail to the road and caught a passing *song taeo*, a 'two-bencher' truck, to take me to Chiang Mai, one of the typical Thai greetings was *giin khao reu yang?* or 'have you

My Akha village in the hills above Chiang Rai, northern Thailand. Morning mist covers the slopes as a woman returns from the forest with cut banana stems, with which she will feed the family pigs.

7

Apö, the 14-year-old second daughter of her Akha household, preparing the day's rice before dawn.

eaten rice yet?'. To eat is to eat rice. Never just 'eat' on its own. You hear the same in the Burmese *sa tamin*, the Cambodian *si bai*, in the Vietnamese *an com*. In the region's semantics, 'rice' and 'food' are largely one and the same. Rice in Thai is *khao*, everything else is simply *kap khao*, meaning '[things] with rice'. The Burmese, world record-holders in rice eating, consume on average more than 200 kilograms of rice a year, which frankly doesn't leave much room for anything else. From Burma in the west to the Philippines in the east, these are cultures and landscapes shaped by rice.

Nuns in one of the large Buddhist convents in Sagaing, near Mandalay, preparing a large midday meal for visiting monks at the annual robe-presentation ceremony.

Rice of varying qualities and prices, for sale in Chiang Mai, Thailand.

There are about twenty species of rice of the *Oryza* type, but only two have agricultural value: the Asian *Oryza sativa* and *Oryza glaberrima* in West Africa. The Asian species had its wild origins in the foothills of the Himalayas, and around two to three million years ago, as animals migrated across the still-passable proto-Himalayas, the rice went with them and gradually diverged into *O. sativa japonica*, on the northern side of the mountains, and *O. sativa indica* on the Indian side. *Japonica* is called a round grain – short to medium in length – while *indica* has long, thin and slightly flattened grains. Most of the cultivated varieties belong to *indica*. After millennia of cultivation, there is now a huge number of varieties. Although there is no direct evidence of when and where domestication began, the wild forms from which the cultivars were developed are the most varied in South-east Asia, if we extend the region westward to eastern India and north-eastward into southern China. In 1996, at a site in north-east Thailand called Non Nok Tha, pottery shards were found that carried the imprint of rice grains and husks; carbon-14 and thermoluminescence tests dated these to around 4,000 BC. The heartland of South-east Asia was certainly one of the oldest centres of rice cultivation, sharing this distinction with sites such as Hemu Du in China, where there is evidence of rice crops from around 5,000 BC.

Ceremonial seed rice at an Akha ritual, used for seeking fertility for the coming year's crops.

Although cities like Bangkok, Saigon, Singapore and Jakarta hog the news, the politics and visitors' first impressions, the population of South-east Asia remains hugely rural, and the principal rural activity remains the growing of *Oryza sativa*. This is the landscape with its millions of lives that passes under the aircraft carrying tourists from Europe and America to Phuket, Bali and the beaches of central Vietnam, little noticed by these millions of visitors that South-east Asia attracts. I'm tempted to say that this is the *real* South-east Asia, but that would be both over-simplification and skewed, even though in my heart I believe it. But essential it certainly is. The planting, growing and tending of the rice crop goes on from first to last light and across the seasons. Indeed, the annual rhythm probably gives the best insight into its complexities. But where to start?

There are many beginnings to the South-east Asian year. The first rains are one beginning, the first planting is another. Across much of the mainland, the official New Year is a water festival, held in the hot season, a propitiatory rite calling for the monsoonal rains on which the crop depends. But rice production is a continuous cycle, and because the grain from one harvest is the seed for the next planting, harvest time can perhaps lay claim to being the main point at which everything begins anew. The crop is safely gathered, there is a brief period for the farmer to relax, or at least tend to matters other than the fields, and a general sense of accomplishment. The exact dates vary according to the climate, the terrain, the variety of rice and the local techniques, but across the mainland, from Burma to Vietnam, November and December see the fields turn golden, and the cutting, threshing and winnowing begins.

In the shadow of the tenth-century temple of East Mebon at Angkor, a Khmer farmer sharpens his scythe, sitting on the edge of a pristine field of rice, yellow-gold in the early morning sunlight, ready to begin the first cutting. He works unnoticed by a group of tourists arriving by bus to view the ruins on their tour of the Grand Circuit, even though later in the morning, when they visit the temple of Bayon, they will study in fascination a succession of scenes carved in bas-relief on the outer wall depicting the daily life of Khmers in the twelfth century, farming and hunting and eating in exactly the same way as today.

The scene changes to a northern Thai valley, on the day before Loy Krathong, the lunar festival at which candles placed in lotus leaves are floated down the rivers. A group of farmers from the village of Ban Maesuk, north of the provincial capital of Lampang, are threshing by hand, slowly accumulating a pile of the loosened grains in an enormous, two-metre-wide woven basket. They are smiling, not just for my camera, but because this is always a popular time in a farming community. When the job is done today and the crop is safely in, there will be time to celebrate the full moon festival. The year is 1988 and the date is 23 November, the full moon of the twelfth lunar month. In the north of Thailand this is called Yi Peng rather

than Loy Krathong, and from one of the neighbouring fields which has already been cut, they will perform a local variation on the floating candles, launching a hot-air balloon made of paper. These balloons, known as *khom loy*, are candle-powered, and the light will float into the sky rather than down the river.

Eighty kilometres due north, in the last straggling foothills of the Himalayas that finger their way into Thailand, a lone Akha man on his hillside plot dances barefoot on a bamboo mat to winnow his crop of hill rice. Here too there is a general sense of well-being, because soon there will be some free time, to celebrate and do household essentials such as re-thatching and repairs. It is also, however, a physically hard time here in the hills as the rice fields are always some distance from the village. The winnowing is done

Northern Thai farmers thresh sheaves of rice into a large basket, on the eve of Loy Krathong.

In the hills above my Akha village, a man winnows rice with a large fan, blowing the chaff away from the large woven mat where he stands.

on the spot to lighten the burden, and the men use a large bamboo fan to blow away the chaff, performing a kind of dance on the large mats that have been laid out on the hillside for the purpose. As he whisks the fan, this man calls out the words 'Jeu, jeu', meaning 'Increase, increase!', a call echoed occasionally from across the steep valley by other farmers. The way back, up and down, is hard, but this is normal Akha life, so normal that there is no simple word for 'to go'; instead, in the Akha language, you either 'go up' or 'go down'. And you do, all day. Paul and Elaine Lewis, with whom I worked, recorded the song for carrying the rice home:

> If you are strong, let ten baskets be full,
> Going to and from the fields ten times in a day

With a full basket on your back,
Carrying the youngest child in front;
Carrying a basket, pointing to heaven on your back.

On the island of Java, on the outskirts of Yogyakarta, an Indonesian woman in a conical hat painted eggshell blue is still using an ancient and very particular technique for cutting the ears of rice. Held in one hand, almost secretively, is a small hand-blade set into a bodkin-shaped bamboo holder, known as an *ani-ani*. This special cutting tool, used only for rice, was designed to be used in a way that could not be seen. Rice was by tradition supposed to grow on the grave of the goddess Dewi Sri, and there was therefore a taboo on harvesting it with large farm tools like the sickle. She removes only the heads, leaving the stalks untouched, and the whole operation is discreet, in deference to the rice goddess. Alas, the year is 1985 and this must have been one of the last occasions on which the *ani-ani* could be seen in use. Beginning in the 1970s, the Indonesian government started to introduce chemically intensive farming methods, and the sickle began to replace the much slower, more intimate *ani-ani*. By the time I photographed this, only a handful of traditionalists were using it, and by now, as I write, it has become a part of history, a collector's item.

The harvest everywhere is the end of one crop cycle and the beginning of the new. The grains are the seeds for the coming year. The harvest is then either stored if the farmer is self-

An *ani-ani*, a hand-held blade used in a Javanese field to harvest the rice stalks one by one.

14

Two Burmese young men load their bullock cart with rice from harvested fields near Maymyo.

supporting (an increasing rarity), or sold and delivered to a mill. One of the incidental cultural side-effects of the rice harvest is the special architecture of rice barns. These have the appearance of miniature houses, usually raised high to protect the grain from insects and water, and frequently express great individuality. In the case of the Balinese, for example, the granaries, known as *lumbung*, are tall and narrow, with curved tapering thatch roofs shaped like a gothic arch. But as more and more rice enters the market system, the need for these lovely little buildings is disappearing, and they are either dismantled, with the decorative parts ending up in antique shops, or else are converted to other uses.

15

For the farmer, the respite from work is brief. Almost imme-diately, preparations must be made for the new year, and chief among these is maintaining the paddy fields. What gives rice its huge importance, as we'll soon see in more detail, is that it is capable of being intensively cultivated more than any other staple. In particular, it will grow in standing water, and as long as it has this, at the right depth, the soil does not need to be very fertile. In any case, this can be enhanced by manure and fertiliz-er. Rice can be grown dry, or by following the flood retreat on gently sloping land, or even floating, but the classic Far Eastern technique is in a paddy field, meaning a levelled plot surrounded by a low mud wall, or *bund* (the term comes from India).

The prime paddy lands of South-east Asia are the most man-made and intensively altered landscapes in the world. Every square inch has been considered, worked and re-worked for generations. The great European landscape gardeners of the eighteenth century such as as Capability Brown may have moved hills and re-routed small rivers, but for sheer attention to detail, the paddy field is the ultimate craft. This is landscape as sculpture. There are four kinds of paddy *bund*, which relate to the type of terrain. In the lowlands, the walls are made of packed earth, on average about half a metre high, but when the slopes are steeper, the lower part of the wall is constructed with stones, and these topped with packed earth. On much steeper slopes in the moun-tains, earth would be useless to resist the pressure of water and slippage, so stone is used exclusively. On the steepest slopes of all, the stone walls are canted inwards for even greater structural stability, and may also have a projecting or concave inner lip to help contain the water better.

The ultimate expression of sculpting the landscape is the rice terracing in hills and mountains, a technique that probably origi-nated in China. The amount of work taken to transform a hillside into a staircase of water shelves beggars the imagination, and the most spectacular are in the central highlands of the Philippines' main island of Luzon. In the central cordillera, the ancestors of the indigenous Batad people began carving these steps out of the mountainsides some 2,000 years ago. On the upper slopes, but below the rainforest peaks that provide the source of water, the terraces are generally at around 1,500 metres, and cover a stag-gering 10,000 square kilometres. The greatest concentration is at Banaué, now a UNESCO World Heritage Site. I spent a week driving across the cordillera in a jeepney, the flamboyant Filipino evolution

A line of farmers planting rice seedlings, dwarfed by the cascading rice terraces at Banaué, in the highlands of Luzon.

of the jeeps introduced during the Second World War by the United States. The hand-painted sign on this one read: 'God knows Judas not pay. thank you. Ride again.' For some reason, the landscape reminded me of an exercise at school, in geography class, one in which we traced out the contours from a map, drawing each line individually onto tracing paper, then cut these out to make a series of ascending patterns. Then we cut sheets of cardboard to these exact shapes, and stuck them together to create a model in perfect relief. The stepped series of rice terraces looked exactly like this from a distance: a cartographer's landscape.

The most abiding impression as we drove around was one of constant labour and effort, and for all its visual charms (because these are truly spectacular landscapes to travel through), there is a palpable sense of century after century of grinding, unrelieved work. At the end of it, the reward is simply a meal, just enough to keep a family fed, but with no possibilities or time for anything else. No square foot of land is wasted in these hills, as was driven home on one day, when we drove from Mount Polis to Banaué. The road, unpaved of course, followed the contours of the mountainside in exactly the same way as the terraces, for the minimum disruption. But not only this, it was a single-track road for about twenty kilometres. Widening it would just have lost valuable rice land, so instead, the solution was something I've never seen before or since – a manned post at each end, with a telephone. And not just a regular telephone, but a hand-cranked set. You arrive in your jeep, the man with the telephone cranks it up and speaks to his colleague at the other end of the road. If no vehicle has passed through in your direction recently, you can go. Otherwise, you sit and wait, as does any new vehicle arriving at the *other* end, as you are now next in line. Sometimes you may have to wait for an hour, which gives time to reflect on the value of rice. Unfortunately, though inevitably, the static life of tending and rebuilding rice terraces does not appeal greatly to the younger Bontoc, Kalinga and other groups. They, as else-where, move to the towns, and the terraces are at risk of falling into disrepair. In this sense, rice terraces are a living landscape, and capable of dying.

When the livelihood of every farmer is so closely connected to that of his neighbour, it makes considerable demands on the social organization, not least because the building and re-building of terrace walls and waterways offers all kinds of opportunity for disputes. Moreover, the steeper and larger the terracing, the more complex the distribution of water. In fact, what determines the building of terraces such as those at Banaué is the water source, not the difficulty of re-shaping the mountainside. Probably the most sophisticated of all communal water distribution systems is in Bali, where the terraces bear Ubud vie with those of Luzon for sheer spectacle. It goes by the name of *Subak*, and works quite independently of local government.

And it is entirely necessary because of Bali's climate and mountainous terrain. The island's long dry season runs from April to October and leaves no choice but to irrigate. Yet Bali is largely volcanic, and the soft rock has been cut through by the 162 rivers and streams into deep valleys and gorges, which makes the usual irrigation dams and channels impossible. Instead, the water is conveyed from field to field by an elaborate series of tun-nels (some as long as three kilometres), aqueducts and bamboo pipes, from top to bottom. The only way to organize this equit-

Rice terraces near Ubud, Bali. The farmer is re-planting.

ably is to link all the communities into an elaborate social system. Community organizations known as *Subak* control this, with water-temples and priests at the heart. There are some 1,500 *Subaks*, each with around 200 members, and each covering part of a watershed. Within each *Subak* area are smaller units called *Tempek*, which each cover a planting area bounded naturally, such as by rocky outcrops and streams.

The entire system is about collaboration, both in allocating water and in co-ordinating planting, and is tightly bound by custom and the Hindu religion (which itself stresses the importance of the individual's relationship to the community). What makes this particularly necessary is that the physical advantage is with upstream farmers. On the face of it at least, there is not much incentive for them to release water in a cooperative way with their downhill neighbours. However, as one study points out, coordinating the planting over an entire watershed helps control pests by creating a wide, dry fallow area, a kind of insect fire-break. But really, the consequences of upstream–downstream conflict are so serious that avoiding an extreme conflict is its own reward. On a much larger scale, this is the problem now being faced on rivers such as the Nile and the Mekong, where upriver nations either want to implement, or are actually implementing, dams and irrigation schemes which will reduce the flow to the countries lower down. The *Subak* principles might well be salutary. Interestingly, in Bali, almost all the attempts by government agencies to in some way use the *Subaks* for their own purposes have backfired in one way or another, proving the strength of this home-grown community system.

Much of what I've been writing about makes rice growing seem, if not idyllic, at least comfortable and pleasant and stable. Certainly, driving or walking through a typical South-east Asian rice landscape, particularly with the thought in mind of a delicious meal of rice with something, it is hard to escape the feeling that this is all beautiful and fitting. Yet rice has helped to create over the centuries a culture of hard labour and, in many areas, a rural poverty that was almost impossible to escape. There is no significant leisure time if you grow rice and only rice. Increasing the yield means spending ever more time and back-bending effort, so that while there is enough food (natural disasters apart), there is only *just* enough. The life of rural peasants across a large swathe of Asia was for centuries locked into an intimate relationship with the soil, so intimate that it left little time for anything else. There is a couplet in Vietnamese, translated by Huu Ngoc:

> *Ai oi bung bat com day*
> *Deo thom mot hat, dang cay muon phan?*

> You who taste a bowl of rice
> Do you feel in the fragrant grains all the pains
>   I've taken to grow them?

Rice growing has created some of the densest concentrations of rural humanity in the world. The calculations become a little fuzzy because of the difficulty of defining 'rural' exactly, and also deciding how large an area of land to include, but the rice farming region of central Java has long been considered about the densest in the world. Indonesia itself is the fourth most heavily populated country in the world, and set against a world average of 43 people per square kilometre, Java as a whole reaches 890. Even taking the city of Jakarta out of the equation brings this down only to 830 people for each square kilometre. In fact, rural densities were higher before the attraction of the cities began siphoning them off, and back in 1930, the very highest was in the district of Adiwerno on the north coastal plain of Java, an area of 93 square kilometres, where there were 1,640 persons to the square kilometre.

The land is dense in another way, because all of this has gone on for generations. Pierre Gourou, whose fieldwork in the 1930s in the Red River Delta of Vietnam was one of the foundations of tropical geography, had a somewhat macabre take on this historical depth when he described the implications of 'ten or twenty centuries' of shaping the land: 'Millions of dead bodies have rotted in this earth, for so long overpopulated; the dust and the alluvium are charged with impalpable human remains.' The entire mass of Riceland and its population is indeed really composed of more corpses than living beings.

With December there is extra work for farmers who grow a second crop. Because most of the region's rice is grown in standing water – paddy rice – the extent to which this can be controlled by the farmers, as well as the variety of rice they plant, is a major factor in the number of crops in a year. A single crop is still the norm. Thailand, for example, the world's largest exporter of rice, still produces three-quarters of its output from a single harvest. Elsewhere there may be the opportunity to plant and irrigate a second crop. In The Red River Delta in Vietnam, the lowest lands are too flooded to be cropped in the rainy season, as would be normal, and instead are planted some months before a May harvest, just in advance of the rains. In Thailand, this 'off-season rice', or *khao naa prang*, gets planted earlier, straight after the main November harvest. In northern Vietnam, this is known as 'fifth-month' rice.

After a few weeks, in the Red River Delta in January, the seedlings of this second crop are ready for re-planting. This technique is typical of the intensiveness of rice growing, and is a way of getting the most out of the land and also of limiting the effects of weeds. The seeds, which are pre-germinated, are sown close together, and after a few weeks the young rice stalks are uprooted and re-planted, by which time they are too tall to be at risk from weeds. February and March are taken up with caring for the

fifth-month rice and other secondary crops, with weeding, manuring and *bund* maintenance the principal work.

By April, across the mainland, the hot season is in full blast. Temperatures rise to the high thirties and the pace of life slows noticeably. To leave the shade is to be instantly stunned by the heat, and this, naturally, is the time of year for water festivals. Burma, Thailand, Laos and Cambodia make the most of this. By tradition, water should simply be sprinkled from a bowl on passers-by, but in recent years things have got out of hand, and these days in cities like Chiang Mai you are much more likely to receive a bucketful of iced water in the face thrown from a speeding pickup than the former genteel welcome of a few drops to relieve the heat. The Burmese in the cities developed a penchant for hose pipes, so that the Thingyan water festival in Rangoon has come to resemble the quelling of a street demonstration with water cannon. Ice, of course, helps to make the modern hot season bearable, not to mention air-conditioning, but in former days there were a few subtle recipes for cooling off. In Thailand there was, still is, *khao chae*, a cold rice dish designed

Up to his knees in mud, a Burmese farmer re-planting seedlings in December, near Bhamo in the north.

for the hot weather, originally an ethnic Mon creation but adopted by the Palace. Normal rice is too soft, so old, harder rice is used (*khao taa haeng*). The rice is first soaked in alum water for a few hours, then washed well to remove all the starch and leave the rice grains shiny; traditionally the grains were then polished in cloth. The rice is then parboiled for a few minutes, then rinsed in a sieve under cold water. Meanwhile, the special ingredient, jasmine water, is prepared. A large pot is filled with water, ideally rainwater, and handfuls of jasmine blossoms added. A small flower-scented candle is then floated on top, lit, and the pot is half-covered with its lid. After 15 minutes the process is repeated, and then a third time. This jasmine water is then sprinkled liberally over the polished rice, which is wrapped tightly in a piece of cheesecloth so that it will not swell, then steamed over boiling water, then left to cool completely.

When the rice is quite cold, it is placed in serving bowls to which the jasmine water is added, and eaten with a selection of small dishes that include green peppers stuffed with ground pork and chopped shrimp; shallots stuffed with dried and pounded

Songkran, the Thai water festival, in Chiang Mai. A young woman, traditionally dressed for the occasion, is the recipient (or rather target) of cooling water.

salt fish, chillies, garlic, lemon grass and other ingredients; shrimp paste balls dipped in batter and fried; crispy fried sugar beef; and salted fish balls deep fried until golden. Nowadays, ice is added to the jasmine water in the serving-bowls. The climatic engine across the region is the monsoon, which ultimately depends on the differences in temperature between the sea and land masses. The air above the oceans cools and heats more slowly, and as winter sets in, the low temperatures over central Asia create a large zone of high pressure from December to early March. The jet stream splits into two, the polar jet and the southern subtropical jet, and the latter directs northerly winds from the cold, dry interior of the continent to blow across South-east Asia and India, although the mass of the Himalayas blocks the coldest air. As the land temperatures gradually rise in the following months, the situation is reversed, and low pressure over the land draws moisture-laden air in from the southern oceans, and the rainy season begins around May. The monsoon over Indonesia and Malaysia is complicated by their being surrounded by water, which generally means that south-facing coasts receive their rain during the May to September monsoon, while north-facing coasts receive most of theirs from the November to March winds. During the changeover, there are a few weeks of transition, as the intertropical convergence zone, also known as the Doldrums, drifts slowly across the islands.

By the end of May or the beginning of June (again, the dates vary, but this is the average for the mainland), the scene is set for planting. This is, naturally, the key time for making propitiations and for attempting to divine the success or otherwise of the harvest. In Cambodia, there is the *Pithi Chrat Neanng Korl*, the Royal Ploughing Ceremony, or the opening of the Sacred Furrow. This is the first of the year's agrarian festivals, and originally it was the king who ploughed the first furrows in a sacred rice field. Nowadays, at the auspicious time, a man, King Meakh, leads the yoked royal oxen and plough, followed by a woman, Queen Me Hour, who casts the sacred seeds. The oxen are then unyoked and led to seven golden trays containing rice, corn, sesame seeds, beans, grass, water and wine. What they choose is interpreted as a forecast of the harvest. In 1995, for instance, they fed mainly on rice and corn, which promised well for the main and secondary crops, and because they only sniffed at the water and turned away from the wine, the prediction was that there would be no serious floods.

'Celestial maidens' carry seed rice in gilded baskets in front of the King at the annual Ploughing Ceremony outside the Grand Palace, Bangkok.

This ploughing ceremony, like so many aspects of Khmer culture, was adopted by the Thais, and is substantially the same. I attended this one year in the Sanam Luang, the open ground in front of the Grand Palace, Bangkok. In front of the King, two oxen, harnessed to a traditional plough, were led to the site, a small oval of ground. Accompanying them were four 'celestial maidens' (from the Agriculture Department), carrying gilded panniers filled with unhusked rice, and the Lord of the Festival,

Phaya Raek Na, who in real life is the Minister of Agriculture. He sows the seed by hand, while the entire procession is led by Brahmin priests. At the end, as in the Cambodian original, the two oxen are presented with a choice of trays. The ceremony complete, the barriers are removed, at which point the crowd surges forward to scramble for the sacred rice grains. Following this public ceremony is another, private ceremony, at the royal Chitrlada Palace. There, in front of a small tented pavilion for the King, his son and second daughter, Princess Sirindhorn, more of the blessed rice is sown on a small plot of land.

But the most elaborate and colourful of all the rice propitiation ceremonies is, without a doubt, the Garebeg in central Java, although the climatic differences of the archipelago put it two or three months later. This is a court ritual centred on the palaces, or Kraton, of Yogyakarta and Solo, and goes back, probably, to the twelfth century and the Majapahit kingdom. Over the centuries it has acquired many layers of history and adaptations, not the least being that since 1756 it has been spread over three separate annual state ceremonies, all tied to Islam. One is the Garebeg Maulud, on the birthday of the Prophet Muhammad, another on the Muslim holiday celebrating the return of pilgrims from Mecca, Idul Ad'ha, and a third at the end of the fasting month of Ramadan, Idul Fitri. The second of these, the Garebeg Besar, has the strongest elements of the original rice festival, during which huge constructions of rice known as *gunungan* are paraded through the palace and the crowds outside.

The pre-Islamic myths of Java attribute the origin of rice to the dead body of a woman, who then becomes Dew Sri, the Rice Goddess. In one of the central Javanese myths, a young man comes across a group of sky nymphs bathing in a forest spring, and hides the dress of the most beautiful one. This, unfortunately, she needs not just for modesty but to be able to fly home, so she is forced to stay and marry him. She feeds her new family from a single stalk of rice, but forbids her husband to look into the rice steamer to see how this works. Of course, he eventually disobeys, which breaks the spell, and the granary empties of rice. The nymph finds her clothing hidden under the rice steamer and leaves him. To this day, farmers have to work hard to grow their rice in the fields.

In another version, a beautiful maiden, Retna Jumilah, is born from an egg and adopted by the principal Hindu god of

One of the oxen at the Thai Ploughing Ceremony attempts to divine the success of the year's harvest.

In Yogyakarta, Java, the Sultan leads the procession that carries rice mountains from the palace to the mosque, accompanied by ceremonial guards.

Java and his wife. But the god begins to desire her. She refuses his advances, but he imposes himself on her and she dies. He has her buried in the fields, from where, after forty days, plants sprout from her body – significantly, rice from her womb.

Commemorating this, the centrepieces of the modern Garebeg are a number of rice mountains (*gunungan* comes from the word *gunung*, meaning mountain). Arriving in Yogyakarta at the end of August to photograph the Garebeg Besar, I first watch the preparations, which are at the stage of making the female *gunungan*. The foundation, inside a bamboo frame, is sticky rice, and five different colours of this also adorn the top. The assembly happens at some speed, to the accompaniment of the rhythmic beating of a large, empty rice pounder, which has become a drum for the occasion. More of the sticky rice is shaped into separate offerings, and the several handfuls that are left over from the construction are passed through the railings of the small building to the small crowd outside. Distributing the

One of the offerings of sticky rice prepared in the palace, accompanied by small dishes presented in banana leaves, at the Garebeg festival.

Rice mountains, or *gunungan*, being carried in the Garebeg procession.

gunungan rice is an essential part of the Garebeg, and at the end of the ceremony, in three days' time, these elaborate rice mountains will be broken up. The final wrapping of its base in sheets of banana stem will take place without ceremony tomorrow.

Two days later, the Muslim festival of Idul Adl-ha takes place in the Alun-Alun Lor, the North Palace Square that lies between the Kraton and the Great Mosque, and the day after that is the turn of the Garebeg. For this, the five *gunungan* are taken by the sultan, with a guard of 800 men, through the palace and across the square to the Great Mosque. Prince Poeroeboyo, whom I first met manning the ticket counter, greets us in the early morning and takes us through to the Keben Courtyard where all the *gunungan* are already laid out. There are two principal 'mountains', one male (cone-shaped) and one female (also round, but with a narrow base and a top vaguely resembling a parasol). A third *gunungan* is made up of small individual offerings covered with a cloth, and the remaining two are smaller, slimmer versions of the female.

The honorary palace guard have assembled already, and at about nine o'clock they move into formation as the bearers take up the *gunungan*. This palace guard, honorary and unpaid, is a spectacle. There are ten units, drawn from the surrounding villages, each with its own distinctive uniform. The origin of the uniforms is a mixture of ancient Javanese and Napoleonic, and all are colourful. The Wirobrojo are clad all in red, with hats shaped like red chillies. The Daheng have soft white trouser suits trimmed with red, and a black cocked hat adorned with red and white feathers. The Bugis wear black top hats, the Patangpuluh have black boots, grey pinstripe and a long white apron, while the Nyutra, with fez-like hats in black and gold and knee-length black trousers, go barefoot, their commanding officer carrying a bow and arrow. With drums and muskets, the entire contingent proceeds at a slow march through the several courtyards of the

Kraton, to emerge at the North Gate, where the riflemen fire volleys into the air. The parade then crosses the North Palace Square through the waiting crowd to the Great Mosque, After all this pomp and solemnity, it comes as a surprise to see what happens to the sacred *gunungan*. Inside the Mosque they are taken to a small dusty courtyard and set down. At this, the crowd – those who have been able to squeeze into this little space, attack them in a frenzy. Total pandemonium amid swirling dust as everyone tries to grab a handful of the sticky rice. Within a couple of minutes all that is left of the ravaged rice mountains are broken bamboo frames. Those streaming away from the courtyard clutching handfuls of the rice consider that these have magical powers, enhanced by the sultan's blessing, which will guarantee them well-being and a successful harvest.

Among the hill-tribes, the role of the supernatural is even more specifically tied to rice. The Akha believe that rice has a soul. Two of the anthropologists with whom I worked were Paul and Elaine Lewis. Over their long career as missionaries in Burma and Thailand they recorded the legends, songs and poetry of these societies which had only an oral tradition. They maintain that to the Akha 'rice is much more than merely food: it is Life', and they recount one Akha legend, in which a poor widow with a young daughter had to go daily to dig up wild tubers and yams near a large river in order to survive. One day, the daughter disappeared, but later, when the mother, alone, was digging again near the river she heard her daughter call out from the water. She had married the Lord Dragon and now lived in the river. The Lord Dragon gave the mother some magical rice as seed, which if planted would always provide her with enough to eat. The promise came true, but to such an extent that the woman was unable to carry all of the huge harvest home. She returned to the river to ask the Lord Dragon what she should do, and he replied that if there was too much rice, all she had to do was stand in her field, then whistle and clap her hands three times. She returned to the field and did this, whereupon there remained only the quantity of rice that could be carried home in one day. The lesson, learned by all Akha, is never to whistle or clap in a rice field. There is, of course, no such thing in South-east Asia as too much rice. This makes it all the more impressive when large quantities of rice are offered for rites of passage, as the Akha do on death. I attended the funeral of a village elder one bright clear week in the hills above Chiang Rai,

In the grounds of the Yogyakarta mosque, the rice mountains are finally attacked by spectators who will carry the blessed grains back to their homes.

On the spur of the highlands in northern Thailand, a water buffalo sacrificed to accompany the soul of a deceased Akha elder is laid out and covered with unhusked rice.

a three-day affair that ended with a buffalo being sacrificed so that it could guide the deceased along the right path to the land of his ancestors. After the animal's death, it was laid out on the ridge of a hill, feet tethered and on its side, and basketfuls of unhusked rice were poured over the body.

In northern Cambodia and on the neighbouring Khorat plateau, there are more urgent practical needs. Here, frequent droughts and a constant uncertainty over rainfall have kept this large area in the centre of mainland South-east Asia impoverished for centuries. Prayers and invocations for abundant rainfall are common across the region, but here the action is focused and specific. Since at least the eighth century, through trade along the sea routes from southern India, Hindu gods have gained a following, in particular at Angkor, the capital of the once-great Khmer Empire. Indra is the god of the sky, and it is to him that the Khmers pleaded for rain by firing huge ceremonial rockets. In the annals of Angkor there is an exact account that has survived, written by Zhou Daguan (Chou Ta Kuan), a member of a Chinese diplomatic mission. He arrived in August 1296 and stayed a year. In the observations he wrote, titled *Records of the Natural Environs and Social Customs of Chen La*, is the following reference to an annual festival:

> In front of the royal palace, a great platform is erected, sufficient to hold more than 1000 persons, and decorated from end to end with lanterns and flowers. Opposite this, some 120 feet rises a lofty scaffold, put together of light pieces of wood shaped like the scaffolds used in building stupas . . . Every night from 3 to 6 of these structures rise. Rockets and firecrackers are placed on top of these – all this at great expense to the provinces and the noble families. As night comes on, the king is besought to take part in the spectacle. The rockets are fired, and the crackers touched off. The rockets can be seen at a distance of 13 kilometres; the fire-crackers, large as swivel guns, shake the whole city with their explosions. Mandarins and nobles are put to considerable expense to provide torches and areca-nuts [used for betel chewing]. Foreign ambassadors are also invited by the King to enjoy the spectacle, which comes to an end after a fortnight.

One of the city gates of Angkor Thom, where 13th-century accounts record the early launching of rockets to call on the gods for rain.

Any north-eastern Thai would recognise this ancient description, particularly if he or she were from the area around Yasothon, because the ceremony has persisted to this day, although not in Cambodia itself. Towards the end of April, teams of men, usually working in the grounds of their local temple, begin the process of building rockets from scratch for the annual festival *Ban Bung Fai*. By this time of the year the temperature has soared, and the land is parched. I drive into Yasothon and meet Khun Veeravat, who works at the Tessaban (the municipality offices). He takes me to see the construction of one of the largest rockets, four metres long. The body has already been finished, bright blue PVC tubing six inches in diameter bound tightly with coiled rope, and fitted inside with zinc sheeting, and is now being filled with black powder – 150 kilos of it! PVC in this standard blue is a relatively new addition (this was in 1987), a local government regulation imposed two years ago for safety. It and the binding, which can be rope or steel wire, limits the fragmentation if the rocket explodes, as many do. Formerly, and still for shorter rockets, the casing was always bamboo, and this frequently caused injuries as the splinters and shards flew off. Indeed, it was just such an accident three years ago, with one fatality, that prompted the Tessaban to impose the PVC ruling. One of the team, an associate of Veeravat called Pornchai, says that while safer and lighter, the new rockets are not as powerful, despite the improved power-to-weight ratio.

These home-made rockets, *bung fai*, may look like oversized fireworks, with their 10-metre-long bamboo tails lashed on, but the engineering is sound and sophisticated. Pornchai, who has been involved in making them for ten years, explains. At the top, a wooden plug is bolted to the tube, and this is strengthened with a plug of clay and sugar mixed together and rammed down hard from inside. A hole is drilled through both the wood and clay for the fuse. The powder is then packed in, slowly, over at least a day, and this is the stage that this team is at when I arrive. This rocket is attached vertically to a metal frame, and buckets of black

Packing home-made gun-powder into a rocket casing on the outskirts of Yasothon, northeastern Thailand.

powder are hauled to the top, where one man empties them in, half a kilo at a time. A hydraulic jack then rams the powder down.

It takes twenty days on average to build one of these rockets. When the powder is finally packed in, the bottom end is sealed with clay-and-sugar and wood, exactly as at the top end. Then the hard part begins, which is boring out the packed gunpowder in increasingly wide sections. Using long steel rods, some with sharpened blade tips, others with screw tips, the borer aims to make four sections with different diameters. At the top, a 25-mm hole will penetrate the 100-mm diameter section of gunpowder; lower down the hole is widened to 50 mm, below this to 75 mm, while the last section is 90 mm, leaving just a thin, 10-mm jacket of packed powder. This technique ensures an even, progressive burn; with ignition at the top, the widening central hole carries the exhaust gases from the combustion safely through to the end.

I had assumed that the powder was bought ready-made, but no, everything except the PVC tubing is hand-built. A couple of days later we go to a house where, in the front garden, the explosive mixture is being cooked. I say 'cooked' advisedly, because as I arrive, one man, stripped to the waist and dripping with sweat, is toiling over a large wok over a charcoal fire. What he's doing is dissolving saltpetre in water, then stirring in the charcoal granules until the liquid is all absorbed. I love this; it takes me back to my own, always unsuccessful, attempts to make gunpowder as a boy. The best I could ever do, thankfully, was

34

achieve a slow intense burn. The cook insists it isn't dangerous, though it seems to me that inattention and over-cooking might create more than the usual kitchen disaster.

Explosions are on my mind, and I ask more. There are three reasons for launching pad accidents. One is using the wrong proportions of mixture, specifically too much saltpetre. Another is irregularities in the bored hole. A third is a crack in the casing, easy to do by ramming the powder too hard. We will see on the day of ceremony.

The real business of launching the rockets takes place in the afternoon, after a morning of parades, dancing and increasing inebriation. The rockets that are drawn through the town accompanied by musicians and dancers are the decorative only, and there is a kind of beauty contest separate from the serious contest later. This also allows plenty of time for the young men, including some of those who will launch the rockets, to get thoroughly plastered on rice liquor, both the branded Mekong and home-made *lao kao*. This informs the proceedings with a quality of chaos, and by mid-afternoon, when the contest begins, the majority are plastered in another sense also, having fallen, been pushed or wrestled in pools of mud. The minority are adorned with brightly coloured mineral powder, this year's fashionable hue apparently being blue. The launching towers, recalling those at thirteenth-century Angkor, are tall wooden frames, the active side inclined slightly to achieve the optimum parabolic flight for height. One at a time, the rockets are lashed lightly into

Mineral blue is the fashionable colour this year for drunken revellers at the Yasothon Rocket Festival.

35

position, and the long trailing fuse fitted. The length of the fuse, punctuated with small firecrackers for dramatic effect, gives the launch crew time to climb down and retire to a safe distance – in theory at least.

No-one knows how high the rockets go, although Pornchai guesses between 1,000 and 2,000 feet. What counts is airtime, from launch through parabola to impact, and the record stands at 70 seconds. That is, *when* they go. There are many failures of one kind or another, some burn short and land in the next field, others crash with more spectacle, tail and flames first, and others fail to ignite. This last is what happens to rocket number four, simply because the fuse burns out a couple of metres short. One of the crew members either volunteers or is deputed to return to the tower, but he is so paralytic that, having re-lit the fuse and made it back down to one of the lower rungs, he decides to sit and sway for a while. The crowd in the distance shout and wave for him to get a move on, and he dutifully waves back. Some seconds before the fuse ignites the monster rocket, he somehow recalls why he is where he is, and scuttles, stumbling across the field away from the tower as a gout of flame lifts the *bung fai* into the air. Occasionally, mid-air explosions happen, and the worst in recent years was in 1999, when a 120-kilo rocket exploded 50 metres above the ground, two seconds after launch, killing five people and injuring another eleven. Calling for rains, as in any dealing with the gods, carries a certain risk.

A well-fuelled and over-staffed ground crew fix one of the rockets to its angled launching tower.

By the month of June, with luck, the monsoon has hit most of the mainland, and with it the time for planting. In those areas with a second crop of off-season rice, the work is even harder, as this must be harvested before the new, main planting. In the cordillera of central Luzon, with its intricate and demanding system of steep rice terraces, the rains serve another valuable purpose, as the Bontoc use water as a tool, to help with lifting and transport. Impounded water, when released, is used to shift rocks, debris and soil. The details of planting are more intricate and localized than most people would imagine, because after years of stamping down mud, weeding and watching the different rates of growth in different parts of the paddy, farmers know every idiosyncrasy of every foot of their fields. They adapt accordingly, not only by planting a variety of strains depending on the soil and water, but with endless ingenious techniques.

The Bontoc, whose yields are outstandingly high (over six tons a hectare without fertilizers, in contrast to the two-and-a-half ton national average) make terraces that are significantly longer and with rounded river stones instead of angular rocks. The long stone perimeters absorb more heat than usual, while the rounded stones are said to conserve the heat better, and it is certainly true that the edges of the paddies produce more tillers and filled grains. Most of this is empirical, without the benefit of agricultural science.

After planting, the crop must be watched and tended almost continuously. Pests and diseases are a particular concern during the early growing period, with many locally developed treatments. The Bontoc, for example, have a pragmatic solution for one of the plant diseases, known as *Lisao*. This is related to continuous flooding, and is thought to be due to a zinc deficiency, and the answer is to grind up the contents of spent batteries and spread these over the diseased fields. The Akha from my village had other techniques for dealing with their insect pests. Thirty-six days after planting, someone from each household finds a white grub from the rice field. All of them then meet, wrapping the grubs in leaves which they squeeze into the split ends of bamboo stakes driven into the soil. They then say to the trapped grubs, 'You who ate the roots before, now try eating the leaves!' They perform a similar ceremony around August for grasshoppers, which they catch and trap, telling them, 'You who ate the leaves before, now try eating the roots!'

But rice rituals continue in one form or another throughout the year. In Thailand, the spirit in charge of rice, the Protector of the Fields and Paddies, is one of nine with territorial responsibilities, including the Protector of the House, Protector of the Gates and Stairways, Protector of the Bridal Chamber and so on. These are not just spirits of place but masters – *jao* – of their particular patch of the natural environment. As such they must be propitiated so that they will not be offended by the humans who must

share the habitat with them. Propitiation is by giving gifts, and these always include some rice. Every morning, in countless homes across Thailand, some grains are placed on the front porch of miniature Thai houses, usually perched on a stand. These little constructions are spirit houses, built as dwellings for the real owners of the land that has been usurped by humans moving in. There is always the risk that the guardian spirit of the land, *phra phum*, will not accept the continued presence of the householder and his family, who are, by spiritual reckoning, squatters. They were, after all, in principle usurping the spirit by moving in and erecting a building. The full title of the guardian spirit is *phra phum jao thi*, the final two words meaning 'master of the place'.

Monsoon clouds gather over Sumatra at the beginning of the rainy season.

One of the daughters of the house in Lap Lae, central Thailand, place the morning offering of rice and other morsels at the spirit house.

overleaf:
Rice offerings wrapped in banana leaf containers at a village shrine in Thailand.

Novice monks from a Rangoon monastery make the morning rounds with their black lacquered alms bowls.

In the monastery of Wat Prathat Haripunchai, in Lamphun, Thailand, monks eat their midday meal, composed of the offerings they have collected on their morning alms round.

The rains continue through June, July, August and, depending on the region, into September and even October. This is also the time in the Buddhist societies of Burma, Thailand, Laos and Cambodia for the 'rains retreat', the three-month period when monks remain in the monastery to concentrate on their studies of the Buddhist texts, and the time when novices are initiated. Monks are supported by the lay community, and indeed every male should spend at least one rainy season, the Buddhist equivalent of Lent, as a novice monk. This, of course, is on the decline, particularly in cities, but the tradition continues in the poorer rural areas. Support includes feeding, and still a common sight in much of mainland South-east Asia is the early morning round of alms-collection. The monks, individually and in groups, walk through the town or village, barefoot and carrying their bowls, pausing outside houses and shops where the owner is waiting with offerings of rice and other food. When they return to the monastery, they will eat this as their last and main meal of the day, just before noon.

Areas with second rice crops, such as the Red River delta, have much more work, as fields need to be ploughed immediately after the smaller harvest in time for the main planting. Irrigation

water has to be added if necessary, and after about four weeks the young plants from the main planting have to be gathered from their seed beds and re-planted in the main paddies.
As the crop matures, and flowers, irrigation must be monitored carefully, the water stirred, the fields weeded and manured. Even among the many varieties of rice there are differences in the ripening period. The Thai farmers distinguish between early ripening rice (*khao bao*, 'light rice'), regular (*khao klang*, 'middle rice') and late ripening (*khao nak*, 'heavy rice'). The descriptions acknowledge the yield, but even though early rice is less productive, it has its uses, and is a safer bet if there is danger of a crop being harmed by drought or flood. This early rice is usually reaped beginning in September.

Two Khmer girls near Siem Reap, Cambodia, slap sheaves of young rice stalks against their legs to shake the water off during transplanting.

Glass mosaic scenes set into the plastered wall of Wat Xien Thong, one of Luang Phrabang's best-known temples, depict scenes from the agricultural year.

As the rains come to an end – again, a variable date depending on the location and the year, sometime between October and November on the mainland – and the cool dry season begins, it is time once more for the harvest, and another cycle of South-east Asian life. The techniques vary according to the degree of mechanization and the social organization, but the sheaves must first be beaten to loosen the ears, the seed grain taken more carefully by hand, the rest winnowed and gathered.

Rice bags being unloaded at Bangkok's port for export.

In those communities lacking harvesting machines, the sheaves may be threshed by hand, or beaten with a flail, trodden under-foot, even placed on the road for passing traffic to do the job. Where the crop is commercial, it goes to the mills, and from there to shipping warehouses. Trains of rice barges still ply the Chao Phaya river, towed by tugboats past the five-star hotels and high-rise apartment blocks of Bangkok, the water washing over their gunwales on the way down, riding high in the water on their way back up to the central plains for a fresh load.

Rice is the second largest cereal in the world after wheat, but even this high ranking masks its true importance, because more than 90 per cent of the production and consumption of rice is in Asia. Indeed, most rice is eaten in the country in which it is grown, and that means an Asian average of more than 80 kilograms a year. The Burmese, as I mentioned earlier, are the world's rice trenchermen, putting away more than 200 kilograms a year each. Think of what most westerners would consider a normal helping – a hand-sized regular Chinese serving bowl – and multiply it by one and a half thousand. This may be the record, but the average throughout South-east Asia is still very respectable: Indonesia, for example, consumes 150 kilograms, respectably higher than even China's 90 kilograms, while the average in the West is only 10 kilograms. This gives an immediate clue as to the role of rice at the South-east Asian table. Quite simply, it dominates everything. At a Thai or Vietnamese restaurant you may well enjoy a succession of

Raking over rice at one of the large mills in Thailand's central plains.

varied, tasty dishes, with a little rice on the side, but a farmer in the Cambodian countryside, for example, will be eating a mound of rice with just a few additions for flavouring and protein, sometimes little more than condiments. This goes a long way to explaining the crucial role of spices and herbs in so much South-east Asian cooking, about which more in the next chapter.

2 SPICE AND SAVOUR

'Place sour fruit and salt together', goes an old Burmese proverb, 'and the tip of the tongue cannot contain itself'. It means that two people of the opposite sex cannot help but attract each other, but the analogy is one of the fundamentals of South-east Asian cooking. The juxtaposition of opposing flavours underlies everything: sweet combined with salt, hot and sour, bitter and sweet, and so on. Perhaps the single most identifying feature of South-east Asian cuisines, and the one that has made them so popular in the West, is the range and complexity of the spices and aromatic seasonings that they use. Lemon grass, galangal, basil, coriander, turmeric, ginger, cumin and kaffir lime are just some of the better-known ingredients. There are hundreds more. In particular, cooks of the region use spices in combinations that tend to stimulate rather than to match. And they use them liberally.

After all, wasn't it the Spice Islands of the Indonesian archipelago that first brought South-east Asia to the attention of a wide European audience in the seventeenth century (and much earlier to the Romans)? Well, yes and no. Nutmeg, cloves and mace were the spices coveted in Europe, and the former became a fabulously expensive luxury when Elizabethan physicians declared it to be a cure for the plague. But it was not these spices that contributed to the regional cooking. Indeed, they are conspicuous by their absence, and the plantations of nutmeg trees on the remote island of Run, which caused so much conflict between England and the Netherlands and eventually led to the Dutch ceding Manhattan in return for keeping Run at the Treaty of Breda in 1667, are now forgotten. As for the spices and seasonings that give South-east Asian dishes their distinctiveness, they have actually been added to by imports, including black pepper

A traditional northern Thai kitchen, fully stocked with a meal in preparation, the raised hearth used for open fires.

47

from India, coriander from the eastern Mediterranean or Asia Minor and tamarind from Eastern Africa, not to mention the subject of the next chapter, chilli.

But what exactly is a spice? It turns out that this is one of those words that everyone *thinks* they know the meaning of, and has a universal currency, but under close inspection is rather vague and definitely changeable. The word comes from species, which was used in the Middle Ages to refer to exotic food-stuffs, principally aromatic plant products used for flavouring and for incenses and perfumes, and mainly imported from Asia. The passion for spices, which stimulated a trade centered in Arabia, began with the Greeks and Romans, and continued into the Middle Ages and the Renaissance. It was a luxury business, associated with banquets and status. The liberal use of rare, exotic flavourings was a statement about wealth and power. It was also, for those who could afford it, a means to improve health and treat illness. Medieval medical philosophy recognized four humours (blood, phlegm, yellow and black bile) and four corresponding moods (sanguine, phlegmatic, choleric and melancholic), and the important spices of the day – ginger, clove, nutmeg, peppercorn and cinnamon – were believed to affect these. There is no evidence, by the way, that these rare spices were used as preservatives. Given the cost, it would have been incredibly wasteful, particularly as there were other, local alternatives, such as garlic, honey and pickling in vinegar, and the quantities needed to retard decay would have made the food unpalatable.

The source of these expensive spices was South and Southeast Asia. Ginger originated in southern China and spread southwards. Clove and nutmeg grew in the group of islands in the Moluccas that became known as the Spice Islands and black pepper and cinnamon were first grown in southern India,

Haw mok, a Thai steamed dish that features coconut milk, spices and chopped seafood, resembling a chunky mousseline.

A street stall in northeastern Thailand where one of the region's best-known dishes, *som tam*, is being prepared by pounding together shredded unripe mango (from the tall glass jar), fish sauce, lime juice and chillies.

but spread to South-east Asia. The sources were jealously guarded, but the immensely valuable trade was eventually wrested from Arab control, first by the Venetians between the twelfth and sixteenth centuries, then by the Portuguese, Dutch and British in the seventeenth century.

Eventually and inevitably, the cultivation of tradeable spices spread beyond their origins and the demand was more easily met. What was once exotic and rare became commonplace and inexpensive, changing forever the essential meaning of the word spice. Today, although there is still some lingering notion of the idea of exotic, the term refers to flavourings that are strong and aromatic – though even so this is still vague. In South-east Asia, where spices are important for their regular culinary use rather than for luxury and status, the range used is very different from that in Medieval and Renaissance Europe. Of those mentioned above, only black pepper and ginger play a significant role in food, notwithstanding the famous Indonesian *kretek* – clove-scented cigarettes (for which cloves now have to be imported from Zanzibar).

Ironically, it is the overwhelming importance of rice, and its blandness, that has created the reputation for intense and varied flavours across a large swathe of South-east Asia. People who love rice, and I'm one of them, may not immediately think of it as somewhat lacking in flavour, and generally take a more complimentary view, but this is because rice is rarely by choice eaten on its own. Yes, connoisseurs wax lyrical about the flavour merits of Thai jasmine rice versus Indian basmati, and of new season rice and the rice grown in this field rather than that, but these are very fine points when it comes to normal eating. Rice needs other flavours to make it palatable as a staple dish, day in and day out, and it has been the search for these

that, more than anything else, has created the intricacy of the classic South-east Asian cuisines.

The search for flavour is also, as we'll soon see, intimately connected to the provision of other essential components of the diet. The object of growing rice is to produce carbohydrates which, as Pierre Gourou points out in *The Tropical World*, 'are the basis of human food'. Rice, particularly if unmilled, also provides niacin, thiamin, magnesium, zinc, iron, the B vitamins, and is an antioxidant. But alone it cannot supply the total nutrition necessary for a human being, and certainly not enough proteins. In fact, rice has less protein than most other plant foods: just 8 per cent of its total calories, as opposed to, say, 17 per cent for wheat, 29 per cent for lentils and 45 per cent for broccoli. And, like most plant proteins, it is deficient in essential amino acids. A study undertaken in the southern province of Salavan in Laos, mentioned by Natacha Du Pont De Bie in her book exploring the roots of Laotian food, found that glutinous rice made up 70 per cent of the diet. This meant, of course, that there was a constant problem for the villagers in taking enough protein, vitamins A and C, iron, calcium and iodine. For these Laotian farming families

Rice cooking in the traditional manner in northern Thailand, represented in a nineteenth-century mural on the walls of Wat Buk Khrok Luang, Chiang Mai.

carbohydrate makes up 85 per cent of their diet, with only 10 per cent protein and 2 per cent fat.

Searching for protein is one of the consequences of living in a rice culture, because the most efficient source, meat, is less available than in other societies. However, it is highly unlikely that societies developed their tastes and diets in the direct knowledge of nutritional value. That is a very recent phenomenon. Yet food systems do evolve towards an optimal use of the possible foodstuffs and as good a balance as is possible of the nutrients that the body needs. The messenger for many of these is flavour. As a rice-growing region, South-east Asia is essentially a vegetal culture, with little access to animal products, and the search for the necessary nutrients lacking in rice has generally been among plants and in the sea. If, like me, you subscribe to the view that there is a reason behind every choice of food, however illogical it might at first seem, this goes a long way towards explaining why strong sauces and pastes, some of them startlingly so, feature so much in most South-east Asian cuisines.

The dominance of rice, and its enhancement with a vibrant mix of strong flavours, has led to a very specific way of eating the staple. The standard meal throughout the region is a substantial

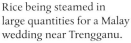

Rice being steamed in large quantities for a Malay wedding near Trengganu.

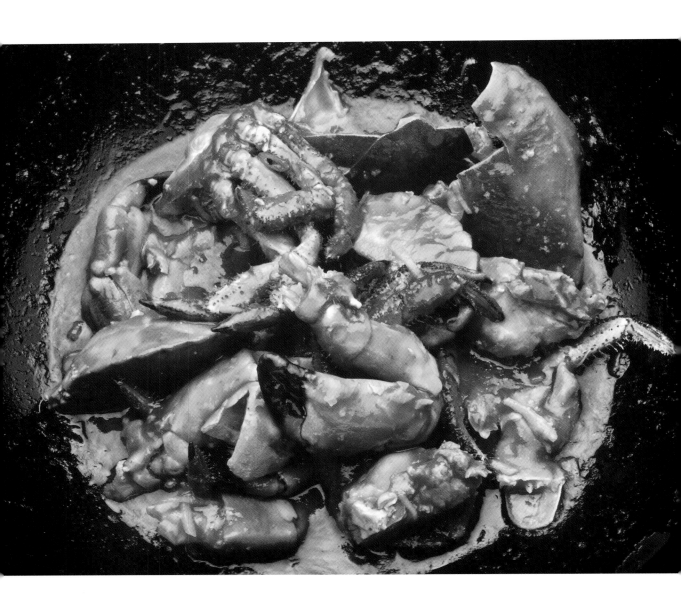

Chilli crab, a Singapore signature dish, which is eaten messily with the fingers.

A Padaung woman, wearing a traditional brass coiled neck ring that deforms the shoulders, shopping in a village market in Kayah State, Burma.

plate of plain white rice, together with one or more strongly flavoured preparations in much smaller quantities. Naturally, this is a gross over-simplification, but still, this is the median. Rice does not accompany the meal; everything else accompanies the rice.

There are a few and particular exceptions to this treatment of rice. One is fried rice, of which there are many similar variations on a common theme throughout the region. There is nothing complicated to it; the rice is stir-fried with any of a number of chopped ingredients, from shrimps to shallots, and seasoned according to local custom. The point of fried rice is that it uses old, already cooked rice. It is a practical dish of leftovers. Another Chinese-inspired use of rice, popular for breakfast, is rice gruel of one kind or another. Sticky rice, being cooked by steaming, lends itself to a range of interesting 'steamed-packet' recipes, using leaves as the wrapping and incorporating various ingredients that suffuse their flavour through the mix. Additions to the rice include blanched peanuts, lotus seeds, peas, sesame, red beans and coconut flesh, though not all together! A banana leaf usually provides the wrapping for steaming. The Vietnamese *banh*

53

chung, stuffed with mung beans, fatty pork and black sesame seeds is one example, a particular favourite for *Tet*, the Lunar New Year.

This applies as much to sticky, or glutinous rice, as the now much more common white, 'fluffy' rice with separated grains. Sticky rice is the same species, but is distinctly different in its cooking and eating experience. The grains are white and opaque uncooked, but become slightly translucent after cooking, and adhere to each other. Sticky rice in fact embraces a range of varieties with a waxy appearance, short grain and a very low amylose content. Amylose represents the amount of starch in the grain, and determines its eating and cooking quality. The dry, fluffy appearance of regular rice is due to a high amylose content, whereas sticky rice has less than two per cent in its endosperm and pollen starch. Alan Davidson, former British Ambassador to Laos and a noted food writer, explains that there is no clear-cut distinction between the two; instead, 'there is a more or less continuous spectrum of varieties of rice from the markedly non-glutinous to the markedly glutinous'.

The technique for cooking sticky rice is to steam it, never boil, and the secret of success is to soak it beforehand for a few hours. The technique for eating it is to use your fingers. Specifically, you take a small lump of the sticky grains, about as much as you can conveniently catch between one thumb and the first two or three fingers, and knead it into a concave pad with which to scoop food from another dish. The thumb and fingers of the right hand, that is. This stricture applies all the more to communal eating from common bowls. I once stayed for a week at an elephant training camp in northern Thailand, and on the first day sat down to eat with the mahouts. As the sticky rice and the accompanying dishes were all in the middle of the table, to be shared by all, they were noticeably anxious that I might not know the etiquette, which included, naturally, washing the right hand before the meal. Sticky rice is the staple in Laos and adjoining north-eastern Thailand, and also among most of the hill-tribe groups. Historically it was indeed the principal form of rice consumed, but over the centuries has lost ground across most of Asia to the regular variety. The famous bas-reliefs at the temple of Bayon in the heart of Angkor, showing on the lower register scenes from daily life in the twelfth century, include many small tableaux of cooking and eating, among them what is clearly sticky rice being eaten from individual woven baskets – exactly as in north-east Thailand and Laos today. Yet the rice now grown is the regular hard variety.

Lunch in an upper-class Malaysian household, the women of the family seated around a floor mat.

A village family in north-eastern Thailand taking lunch. The cylindrical woven containers are filled with sticky rice, the staple to which relishes and dips are added.

But back to the main event, the mound of rice on the table and its accompaniments. Throughout South-east Asia, the foundation of most of the ancillary dishes is a 'base' of pounded ingredients, a paste that is prepared before anything else and in essence defines the dish. Quite often there is a choice of meat or principal vegetable upon which this base will work its effect, and more often than not this takes the form of a 'curry'. Although this is not exactly like the 'curry' with which we are most familiar from India, and the flavourings are different, this is the standard term in English for any spicy, more-or-less liquid dish containing roughly chopped and sliced ingredients. So, to take one of the best known of this type in the West, a Thai green curry, *gaeng kihew waan*, it is perfectly legitimate and traditional to make it with chicken, pork, beef or fish balls, and also sits well with local versions (such as duck) or modern inventions. What counts is the base. There are many basic styles to suit different types of food, from fish to chicken to vegetarian, and countless individual 'bases' devised by individual cooks and housewives. This merits some further explanation, because South-east Asia retains something that has been largely lost by anxious and uncertain

By a *klong* on the outskirts of Bangkok, a Thai woman prepares steamed-rice packets wrapped in banana leaves.

Sweetened and with coconut milk added, sticky rice becomes the basis for several popular Thai desserts, here prepared at a roadside stall.

western cooks – the idea of cooking by taste rather than by measurement and recipe.

The French chef and food writer Marcel Boulestin (and also the first television chef, in 1937 on the BBC) wrote that 'the most dangerous person in the kitchen is the one who goes rigidly by weights, measurements, thermometers and scales'. This is never more true than when talking about a South-east Asian kitchen, where one of the crucial skills is balancing flavours and the other is exercising your own judgement. There is little that can go mechanically wrong in these cuisines – no soufflés that fail to rise, pastry that goes soggy, or other clear and indisputable disasters. Instead, there is a framework of taste within which each cook exercises discretion. I thought this worth mentioning because while there are recipes included here, I've deliberately avoided unnecessary and unrealistic precision.

In chapter Five, where we look at the characteristics of the eight national cuisines, I list the main flavour biases into which each one drifts, but in fact there is more held in common than separate. Among the citrusy and sour tastes are lime, kaffir lime, the Filipino *calamansi*, lemon grass or citronella, palm vinegar

Bas-reliefs on the walls of Bayon, in the centre of the Khmer temple of Angkor Thom, depict daily life in the 12th century, including a meal of sticky rice, eaten as it still is today in Lao-speaking areas of the continent.

and tamarind. Lemony flavours and undertones are popular throughout the region, and the subtle distinctions between them are correspondingly more important than in the West. The leaves of the kaffir lime, for example, have a mild, lime-lemon flavour with a strange, lingering aftertaste, and are highly aromatic, while the citrus notes from lemon grass could be described as clean and with a hint of ginger. Normal food vocabularies falter with these unfamiliar distinctions.

Then there is a group of rhizomes (the creeping rootstocks of certain plants) of which the most well-known is ginger, but which also includes galangal, turmeric and fingerroot. Galangal, known also as *laos* or *kha* (in Thailand), has comphorous notes added to the gingery components, and is a 'de-fisher' which, like turmeric and ginger, helps to remove 'fishiness' from seafood dishes. Fingerroot, also known in the West as Chinese keys, often mistaken for lesser galangal or lesser ginger, is, in addition to being gingery, aromatic, peppery and uniquely woody and earthy.

Various mints, coriander and basil are among the more aromatic herbs, and these always need to be fresh. The leaves are usually added at the end of cooking to allow their sweetness and fragrance to balance the other, already cooked spices. Coriander is an import, originating in Greece, where its name, incidentally, comes from the word *koris*, meaning bedbug, a reference to the smell from crushed unripe seeds and leaves, which some people find offensive. Three principal varieties of basil are used,

58

A northern Thai cook prepares a curry base by pounding, using the fermented shrimp paste *kapi*, here in the small dish.

Ocimum basilicum, similar to European sweet basil, with a sweet, liquorice flavour; *O. canum*, with a lemony scent and pungency; and *O. sanctum*, or holy basil, which has a heady, permeating aroma and is lightly lemon-scented.

The onion family is represented by small reddish onions (*Allium cepa*), shallots, spring onions (scallions) and garlic. Shallots have a more intense flavour than onions, with specific differences between the varieties, some being sweeter and less pungent than others. Bitter notes in regional cooking come from a huge variety of dark green leafy plants and from bitter gourd, while the many cultivars of chillies bring pungency to varying degrees, as does black pepper. Sweetness, often used for contrast with sour and salty flavours, comes traditionally from palm sugar, or jaggery.

Spices and aromatic seasonings, however, are only a part of the story. Returning briefly to nutritional matters, the key deficiency that has to be made up in a rice culture is protein. Some plants can supply some of this, for instance soy bean and spinach, but for high-quality protein, meaning protein with the essential amino acids, only animal or fish products will really do. With very little of the agricultural land given over to stock-raising, meat has traditionally been in short supply, and South-east Asians have turned more to the sea, the rivers and lakes for protein. Fish and shrimps do the job well; for example, tilapia is 18 per cent protein, tiger prawn 20 per cent, squid 16 per cent, but in this sub-tropical to tropical climate they have the grave disadvantage of going off quickly. And there are few things more unpleasant in the kitchen than rotting fish.

Or are there? What about turning this into a benefit? What about deciding actually to *like* fish and shrimps that are long past their sell-by date? Sounds rather weird, it's true, but it brings us to the very necessary South-east Asian process of fermentation. This is the food area which, chillies apart (the subject of the next chapter), causes people not accustomed to it the most 'difficulty'. All South-east Asian cuisines are full of fermentation products, yet these are the first ingredients to be ditched in restaurants in the West and hotel restaurants in general. Their lack is the single most important reason why so many South-east Asian restaurants outside the region are such a complete waste of time. Let me pursue my admittedly extreme argument a little further.

There are three principal members in the family of fermented ingredients in the region. There is fish sauce, fish or shrimp paste and a class of fermented fish which is generally so repugnant to westerners that it doesn't even have a western term, but which consists of bits of putrid fish floating in their own juices. Does it sound as if I don't care for this last one? Far from it, though like most Cambodians, Laos and others, I prefer it kept out of nostril range until it is finally used, and that sparingly. The key to the use of all these products is indeed 'sparing', because a few drops or a small spoonful can create a very different taste experience from what you might expect from meeting the same thing in industrial quantities.

First, fish sauce. From west to east, in Burma it is called *ngan-pya-ye*, Thailand *nam plaa*, Laos *nam pa*, Cambodia *tuk trei*, Malaysia *budu*, Vietnam *nuoc mam*, Indonesia *kecap-ikan* and the Philippines *patis*. It appears as a rich and clear amber liquid, and is made by pressing, salting and fermenting small fish to extract their juice. The fish used are nowadays nearly always saltwater, principally anchovies and other species of around 5–12 cm long that can be caught in large shoals.

While all of these countries make their own similar version, the Vietnamese can probably lay claim to making the *premier cru* of fish sauce. Within Vietnam there are, as you might expect, places

A selection of Akha vegetables collected from the fields, including ginger and varieties of aubergine.

60

with higher reputations for the quality of their *nuoc mam*, than others, and the island of Phú Quoc, off the southernmost part of Vietnam, is the country's most famous producer, with a history of several centuries. Phú Quoc's production is based on the long-jawed anchovy. The secret to making good fish sauce, here as throughout the region, is freshness and purity. As soon as the catch is landed, the fish are rinsed, drained, and a layer of them placed in large wooden barrels each with a bamboo strainer at the bottom. Coarse sea salt is then sprinkled over the anchovies, then another layer of fish added, more salt, and so on until the barrel is full. Finally, another bamboo strainer is placed over the top layer. A heavy wooden block goes over this, and presses the fish for one year. The precious liquid is removed from the bottom. From time

The spring shallot harvest near Lap Lae, in Thailand's north-central Uttaradhit province.

Shallots for sale in one of the floating markets in the Chao Phraya delta, east of Bangkok.

to time, the anchovies are uncovered and exposed to sunshine, which helps the fermentation process, and the drained liquid also is aired in the sun for a week or two, during which time any fishy odour dissipates.

And not only does it taste rich and strong (and obviously very good to South-east Asians), but it has an even higher protein content than regular fish – as high as 80 per cent of its calories, meaning around 2 grams for every tablespoon. Add this to zero fat, zero cholesterol, good levels of B vitamins, calcium, phosphorous, iodine and iron and all in all, fish sauce is a remarkable food concentrate that could hardly have been better designed to go with a massive rice diet. Among other things, it is also a salt substitute. One tablespoon has around 1,200 mg of sodium, half of

63

most people's daily needs, while its iodine content makes it a valuable export to the interior of the mainland. The figure of a man clearly suffering from goitre among the late nineteenth-century murals of Wat Phumin in the northern Thai town of Nan (page 66) recalls the problem of iodine deficiency from lack of salt that was a constant in the heart of the South-east Asian mainland, far from the sea. Across a nearby mountain pass, in the village of Bo Luang, meaning 'Great Well', salt is still extracted by a couple of families by boiling saline well water, as it has been since at least the fifteenth century, when it was a significant royal tribute.

Going up a notch on the ladder of what for want of a better term we could call the *intensity* of fermentation, is paste made from shrimp or fish. This is more of a challenge to the western-trained palate than the fish sauce. I particularly like the description of this by Sir George James Scott, a nineteenth-century Colonial Administrator in Burma. Scott was a true Victorian individualist, who loved Burma, learned its language and customs, and adopted the Burmese name Shway Yoe. Under this sobriquet, he wrote *The Burman: His Life and Notions* in 1882, a title which sets the tone for his imperialist, yet engaged and engaging observations. He also, by the way, introduced soccer to Burma. He wrote:

> There are few articles of food which meet with more energetic denunciation than the favourite Burman condiment, ngapi, which means literally pressed fish. The frogs of France, the rats and puppy dogs of China, the diseased liver of the Strasburg patês, the 'ripe' cheeses of most European countries, and the peculiar character of game in England, with its occasional garniture of 'rice', all meet with condemnation from those who dislike such dainties. The smell of ngapi is certainly not charming to an uneducated nose, but the Backsteiner or Limburger cheese of southern Germany is equally ill-calculated to evoke approbation on a first experience. An old herring barrel smells strong, but there is nothing in nature that more than ngapi hath an ancient and fish-like smell. Travellers on the steamers of the Irrawady Flotilla Company are wont to rail in no measured terms at the fish-paste which forms an invariable and obtrusively evident part of the cargo, yet no Burman would think a dinner complete without his modicum of ngapi.

What for want of a better term could be called a fish sauce distillery, in central Vietnam, where the *nuoc mam* ferments slowly in tightly bound wooden barrels.

Much earlier than Scott, Father Nicolas Gervaise, who was a missionary in Siam from 1683 to 1687, wrote in his *The Natural and Political History of the Kingdom of Siam*, published the year after his return,

> They mix with all their stews a certain paste made of rotten prawns, called capy in Thai . . . which has a pungent smell that nauseates anyone not accustomed to it.

65

It is said to give meat a certain zest which whets the appetite . . . so that to make a good sauce in the Siamese manner salt, pepper, ginger, cinnamon, cloves, garlic, white onions, nutmeg and several strongly flavoured herbs must be mixed in considerable quantities with this shrimp paste.

Note, by the way, and by way of digression, that in this seventeenth-century account, nutmeg and cloves, the famous exports of the Spice Islands, were apparently being used for cooking, at least at banquets for foreigners. If this were true, the custom did not persist.

There is more variety among these pastes than there is in fish sauces, and the different techniques can produce degrees of saltiness, sweetness, pale or dark colour, semi-liquid to almost dry texture. The Burmese are particular aficionados, and as Scott noted, there are three main kinds of pastes. The Myanmar Women's Affairs Federation in Rangoon takes up the story. There is first *ngapi gaung*, consisting of whole fish pressed, dried and later eaten baked; *ngapi seinsa*, made from the squeezed and fermented juices of shrimp, which is stored in the earthen pots, not dissimilar to anchovy paste; and third, they say, and the most pungent, is 'ngapi yecho – this is made from small fish which are left unclean in the sun for a day or two, (by which time "their condition is better imagined than closely investigated") then they are salted, pounded and stored in clay pots.'

During the colonial period, there were the beginnings of a riot in the town of Yandun as a result of, according to Scott, 'a crusade against the condiment by a young civil officer with more zeal than discretion'. It was 1880, and cholera was rife in the area, which also happened to be one of the principal *ngapi* producers in Burma. The Assistant Commissioner was convinced by his nose that the cause must be the paste, and banned its manufacture. The uproar was so great that he had to be removed to another station.

Across the region, every country has its version of *ngapi*. In Thailand it is *kapi*, Cambodia *kapik*, Malaysia *belacan*, Vietnam *mam tom*, Indonesia *terasi* and the Philippines *bagoong*. Overall, small shrimp are the most common ingredient, and these are first rinsed and drained before being salted and dried, on mats or raised racks. After several days of fermentation, the mixture darkens and turns into a thick mash. If the shrimp used are really

Iodine deficiency, resulting in goitres such as this, depicted in a nineteenth-century mural at a temple in the northern Thai town of Nan, used to be a common condition in inland communities far from the sea and a supply of salt.

small, the paste is ready to be used quite quickly, but larger shrimp call for extra pounding and a longer fermentation, often repeatedly, until the final smooth consistency and mature flavour is achieved. Once dried into cakes, the paste needs no refrigeration. The paste is used in cooking, to make spicy dips for eating with raw and blanched vegetables when combined with ingredients such as chillies, garlic, lime, aubergine (as in the many varieties of Thai *nam phrik*) and simply for spreading lightly on green mangoes (as in the Philippines). Even so, it is hard to imagine the events described in the early nineteenth-century Vietnamese book on the history of Saigon, *Gia Dinh thanh thong chi*, which relates how 'salty food eating contests were usually held in which winners would break a record by eating over ten kilos of *mam*'.

Having got as far as shrimp paste, there is a major step still to go. Actually, it is an unsurpassable hurdle for many people. This is variously known as *pla raa* in Thai, *prahok* in Cambodia and *padek* in Laos. Made from freshwater fish, this is fermentation taken to extremes, yet is essential to many dishes from areas far from the sea, in particular land-locked Laos. I watched it being made in Cambodia, not far from the ruins of Angkor – or rather, watched a small part of the process, because it typically takes up to half a year to reach perfection. A smelly string of entire villages lining the banks of the Tonlé Sap, Cambodia's seasonally expanding and contracting Great Lake, make their living from the production of *prahok*. The season begins with the swelling of the lake during the rains, and such an explosion of the fish population of 300 species that it has traditionally supplied three-quarters of the country's protein consumption. The fish catch for *prahok* concentrates on just a few of these species, notably *trei ros*, or snakehead fish, a *kamplienh* that is chopped into pieces, and *trei*, smaller and used gutted and whole.

First, the oil has to be expressed from the fish catch, and this is done over a number of days, the fish, having been gutted, poured into baskets or pits, then trodden down by foot. Every so often the fish are rinsed in water, then the pressing continues. After this, sea salt is added and the fish packed into tubs, which are then sealed and left to mature, sometimes for months. When finally ready for use, the product is a greyish liquid with rotted chunks of fish floating in it. In Laos and Thailand, rice dust and husks are added to give it extra body. Used very sparingly, this seemingly objectionable concoction imparts a subtle (yes, really) yet deep flavour to a dish. For example, in the Recipes section of

Basket after basket of dried shrimps line the tables of stalls in Bangkok's weekend market.

Dried seafood – one of the most easily preserved forms – plays an essential part in all of the region's cuisines.

Nam prik ong, a spicy dip that includes tomatoes, popular in the north, is one of many similar Thai relishes, typically eaten in small quantities with vegetables and rice. Crispy pork crackling is a specific accompaniment to this dish.

this book there is a recipe from northern Thailand for a spicy mixed vegetable dip called *yam phak*, which means simply 'spicy vegetable salad'. The *pla raa* plays a small part in quantity, but the dish just doesn't taste right without it.

The love of this kind of flavour is almost universal across the region, and it definitely plays a major role in setting South-east Asian cooking apart from others. But what class of flavour is it, exactly? And are there really no western equivalents? Like most

Like silver leaves, small fry are pinned to dry in the sun in a Manila market.

people, I suppose, I vaguely thought there were four or five basic flavours for all foods, but when I began to look into this in detail, I discovered that it is by no means so simple, and that theories of taste are evolving. Also, flavour is the combination of taste and smell, although most of us fail to separate the two when it comes to food and drink, and simply take it as a single sensory package. Our sense of smell is much more acute than our tasting abilities. Taking into account the difference in volume (more air sniffed than food swallowed), it is around 10,000 times more sensitive, and Dr Alan Hirsch of the Taste Treatment and Research Foundation in Chicago flatly states that 'ninety per cent of what is perceived as taste is actually smell'.

Well, back to tastes, or flavours. Aristotle distinguished between two basic tastes, 'sweet' and 'bitter', and held another six as elaborations, namely 'succulent', 'salt', 'pungent', 'harsh', 'astringent' and 'acid'. There has traditionally been a general acceptance in the West of four basic tastes – sweet, sour, salty, bitter – while the Chinese make this up to five by adding spicy or hot, in the sense of chilli 'heat'. The Chinese approach accords with their basic Five Elements philosophical principle, in which there are five classes of natural phenomena, and these are correlated with several other fields, including taste. The pairings between the elements and tastes make little practical sense, but they do help the Chinese idea of order, thus wood/sour, fire/bitter, earth/sweet, metal/spicy, water/salty.

But things have been moving along on this front. To begin with, there is now no clear agreement on whether taste belongs exclusively to the realm of biochemical reactions (taste buds, basically), or whether it is partly psychological – a matter of how we perceive, in other words. Not only that, but there seem not to be such clear divisions between the basic tastes. And, beyond that, there are new tastes, one in particular. This goes under the somewhat specialized Japanese name of *umami*. The nearest we can get to it in English is 'savoury' in a 'meaty' kind of way, but its origins and implications are interesting. It was first defined by a Japanese researcher in 1908 at Tokyo Imperial University, Kikunae Ikeda, while he was studying the strong flavour in stock made from kelp (*kombu*). After further work, he managed to isolate the substance responsible, and it was monosodium gluta-mate. In this way, MSG was born, and was manufactured and dis-tributed by the Ajinomoto company (the name means 'essence of taste' in Japanese). More recently, *umami* receptors on the tongue

A Chiang Mai kitchen, with the charcoal-fired stove built in to a concrete block, with typical essential ingredients that include, from front to back, fresh green chillies, ginger, fermented whole freshwater fish, fermented shrimp paste, salt, lemon grass, a variety of fruits, vegetables and leaves, two packets of fermented soy paste and in the background a bottle of fish sauce.

have been isolated, and it has been shown that they respond to the presence of glutamates in food. Glutamates are one kind of amino acid, and abundant in protein-rich foods such as meat, cheese and yes – fish sauce and its brothers in fermentation.

This creates a puzzle, because every food culture enjoys 'savouriness', yet many people are repelled by other cultures' sources of *umami*. A ripe gorgonzola, gamey meat, fish sauce and seaweed broth. What do they have in common? A lot, but people who favour one are unlikely to accept another. Their glutamates fit into the same taste receptors on the tongue, but somewhere on the way to the brain they suffer discrimination. Also odd is that a prime concentrated source of *umami* is the sodium salt of glutamic acid, otherwise known as the by now roundly demonized monosodium glutamate. But why demonized? MSG without dispute enhances 'savoury' flavour and is used hugely in processed foods around the world. It is also believed by many people to be responsible for burning and tingling sensations, headaches, nausea and a whole raft of symptoms generally described under the term Chinese Restaurant Syndrome. The evidence for this, though, is anecdotal, and backed by no quantitative studies. There is a pro-MSG industry camp and an anti-MSG camp, slugging it out in some of the most unlikely places, including my most recent source of information, Wikipedia.

Fascinating though I find this on-going spat between two opposing food-and-health camps, it is drifting away from fermented fish and the flavour of South-east Asian food. Suffice to say that fish sauce, fish and shrimp paste, and the grey stuff with the nasty floating bits are all supremely tasty because they hit the

umami button. There are other recent taste contenders, one being for fatty substances submitted by some French researchers in 2005, and another for something called *kokumi* by a Japanese team, which translates more or less as a 'full-bodied' taste but mixed up with connotations of 'thickness', 'depth of flavour' and 'mouthfulness'. It seems that once the classic set of four (or for the Chinese five) basic tastes has been breached, it is now open season on new taste definitions. And on top of all this is a quality that the Chinese call *kougang*, or 'mouthfeel', the sensation that explains why some people like the specific crunchiness of jellyfish, however tasteless it may be.

With this vocabulary of taste, South-east Asian food can be seen to have a distinct tonal scale. In particular, the most characteristic and memorable of South-east Asian flavours are a result of pitching three, four or even five basic flavours against each other in the same dish. This is high-vibrance, technicolour cooking, composing with the primary colours of flavour rather than restrained modulations. And the reason, I submit, is that rice is the basic vehicle. To make this large fluffy (or sometimes sticky) plateful thoroughly palatable, South-east Asian cooks have spent centuries searching for strong flavour, usually in relatively small quantities of sauces, pastes and soups accompanied by many, many species of plants, often leafy. The result is a cooking ethic of intense opposing flavours, held together by the concept of balance.

Kombu, Japanese kelp, used for its very particular *umami* flavour. Reserach into its flavour led to the discovery of monosodium glutamate, better known as MSG and marketed as Aji no Moto.

Key fermented products throughout South-east Asia, but here shown as Thai varieties, are, from top to bottom, *kapi*, fermented shrimp paste, *pla raa*, fermented whole shunks of freshwater fish in their own juices, and *tua nao*, fermented soybean paste.

3 FIRE AND FIXINGS

Chillies to me are a genuine food mystery, not least because I love them yet am unsure exactly why. Many people don't, and that seems sensible, given that far from hitting the obvious pleasure buttons, chillies frequently cause the kind of pain that most of us take care to avoid. The mystery deepens when you consider that in much of South-east Asia chillies have been one of the most welcome imports, all the way from Latin America, where I first tried them and where they are indigenous. Chillies take on a cultural dimension as well as being a sensory puzzle. One country in particular, Thailand, has incorporated them so thoroughly into its cuisine that it has become a defining quality (think of all those Thai menus for westerners that append little red chilli symbols to dishes as if a Michelin guide to discomfort).

This raises almost too many questions at once, following the initial I-didn't-know-they-came-from-Latin-America (a common reaction, by the way, among less formally educated South-east Asians). Why did so many South-east Asians adopt them? What did they do before? What's the pleasure? Why do they add so much? Why am I eating this?

Chillies arrived with the Portuguese in the early sixteenth century, but the how and why of their integration, and the eagerness of South-east Asians for them, is undocumented. Here was a food culture puttering away with pepper and precious little else to give that kind of kick, yet when introduced to the *Capsicum* chilli, the Thais (in particular) changed their eating habits with hardly a pause. Was this in the genes somewhere? A need waiting to be fulfilled? The social history of the chilli is an intriguing study, as is its science.

Chillies, fresh and dried, are shown prominently in the market in Lashio, in north-eastern Burma.

77

The chief sources of pungency in South-east Asian cooking are chillies, both fresh and dried in various colours and varieties, and pepper, here shown both as fresh green peppercorns still on the stalk and dried white pepper.

First, definitions. English, for once, is unusually the least precise language for any chilli discussion. The word 'pepper' is used liberally, but this can mean any of three different plants. There is pepper as in salt and pepper, also known as *piper nigrum*, or black pepper. Then there are bell peppers which, although they *look* like oversized chilli peppers, have not one molecule of 'heat' effect. And then there are chillies, small, fiery, and for want of a better word, piquant. Indeed, most European and Asian languages refer to chillies in terms of something else, usually the nearest foodstuff that had a similarly biting effect. Variations and qualifications of black pepper are the most common, thus, *poivre rouge* in French and *peperoncino* in Italian, *pimienta picante* in Spanish and *fulful har* in Arabic). These last two mean 'hot pepper', and the same term crops up in parts of Asia, as in the Chinese *la jiao*. The New World languages of chilli-cultures suffer from none of this secondhand reference, which is no surprise.

Things on the definition front get worse when we come to the *effect* of eating chillies. Oddly enough, there is no generally agreed specific word for this burning effect in English, even though many other languages do, quite precisely. The most common term is hot, but this gets confused with temperature, so that it sounds strange to say, though perfectly accurate, that much Thai food is not served hot. You could distinguish between the two as heat-hot versus chilli-hot, but that sounds just clumsy. Fiery, for the same reason, doesn't get us very far either. The most recognized food-academic word is pungent, but this too has its own confusion, as pungent can also mean (and I quote from a range of sources) acrid, astringent, strong, assertive, biting, aromatic, earthy, brisk. Part of the problem is that it is used in the terminology of wine, tea and coffee, in each of which it has different connotations. One wine-tasters' glossary, for example, has it as 'very aromatic or earthy. It is a good or bad term depending on the style of wine; it's a good term in Sauvignon Blanc, for example.' Not, I fear, if we are talking about chilli pungency.

Chillies are native to South America, and it is believed that they were being eaten as early as the seventh millenium BC. Between the fifth and third millennia they were cultivated, and by 2300 BC they were being grown by the Incas. By 1500 BC they had reached Mexico where, under the Olmecs, and later the Zapotecs, Mayans and Aztecs, they were adopted as an important

A Chiang Mai housewife drying chillies in the winter sun.

part of the cuisine, not only for their pungency, but also for their flavour. The idea of chillies having identifiable flavours may strike non-addicts as strange, and the popular view is that, whatever other merits a chilli may have, it actually destroys flavour. This, though, is a subjective view, and you'll excuse me for stating the obvious that it's an *uninformed* view. As the chemistry of chillies suggests (about which more in a minute), people who eat them regularly become inured to the heat-and-pain component, and this enables them to discern taste differences between cultivars and species. Among the several excellent websites devoted to chillies, all run by informed obsessives, I like the argument given by Gernot Katzer on his website at Graz University against chilli's flavour-killing reputation: 'I do not doubt that novices really feel this way, and that chiles really spoil a dish for them, but the argument is not directed against chile use, but against untrained taste buds. After some experience with fiery but tasteful food, most people develop the ability to discern subtle flavours behind the chiles' heat, and actually I feel that chiles *enhance* and *amplify* the taste of other food ingredients.' In par-

80

ticular, the key chilli-using American cuisines, Mexican, Peruvian and Bolivian, use specific chillies for specific dishes. As Katzer comments, 'It is absolutely no sin to employ Thai chiles for Indonesian or Tamil food, whereas a Mexican *mole Poblano* prepared from Bolivian *ají amarillo* would probably terrify Mexicans and Bolivians alike.'

It was the Spanish court physician Diego Alvarez Chanca who, accompanying Columbus' second expedition to the Caribbean in 1493, brought chillies back to Spain. The South-east Asian love affair with chillies and pungency began in the sixteenth century, no more than two decades later. The first Portuguese envoy to Siam arrived in 1511, and while there are no records that the first chillies arrived with his delegation, it cannot have been long after, because from what sparse accounts survive, chillies were taken up rapidly. It was not only the Thais who fell in love with them. In 1553, the *O Chau Reports* written by the then Vietnamese Prime Minister Duong Van An listed chillies among the produce of the southern province of Quang Tri.

The adoption, however, was and remains patchy. Beyond their American source, the main strongholds of chillies' pungency are southern India, central China and Korea (outside our scope), Thailand, Laos and Burma. While they appear in every South-east Asian country's repertoire, the other nations tend not to be quite so fixated on them. Moreover, there are regional patches, such as Padang, which is the largely curry-based cuisine of the Minangkabau in western Sumatra. There are five cultivated

A little milder than the 'mouse-shit chillies' illustrated on the previous pages are these long *prik chi faa* or 'chillies pointing to the sky', another cultivar.

species of *Capsicum* – *C. annuum*, *C. baccatum*, *C. chinense* (absolutely nothing to do with China), *C. frutescens* and *C. pubescens* – with close to thirty wild species in addition. Of the chillies imported into South-east Asia, most are *C. annuum*, although there are by now many cultivars of this.

But down to the effect. The active ingredients in chillies are a class of compounds called capsaicinoids, which are concentrated in the placental tissue that holds the seeds (rather less in the seeds themselves, contrary to popular opinion). The most common capsaicinoid is known simply as capsaicin, and its chemical description is N-Vanillyl-8-methyl-6-(E)-noneamide. As its name suggests, it is a vanilloid, of which others are the compound that gives vanilla its flavour, but also zingerone, which gives the distinctive 'hot' flavour in ginger and mustard. The reason why chillies taste 'hot', or pungent as I'd better start calling it, is simply that these capsaicinoids bind to the same receptor sites on the tongue and in the lining of the mouth that register 'real', high-temperature heat. They do not actually burn the mouth, but the nerve endings certainly get the full impression that this is happening. Significantly, more and more exposure to capsaicinoids actually depletes the receptors and so increases the taster's tolerance.

There is even a scale of pungency, invented by one Wilbur Scoville in 1912, and Scoville units are still very much in use today, although the modern measurements are by chromatography rather than the subjective tests that he originally used. A panel of tasters was asked to say when an increasingly dilute solution of chilli peppers no longer produced a burning sensation. Approximately, one part per million of chilli pungency is rated as 1.5 Scoville units. Classic red Tabasco sauce, an easily tasted standard, is between 2,500 and 5,000 units. A basic New Mexican chilli, so widely touted in the United States for its pungency, is actually only a miserable few thousand units. The serious stuff starts in the tens of thousands, with a typical Thai *prik kii noo* (literally, 'mouse-shit chilli' because of its size and shape) scoring around 60,000. Pure capsaicin, thankfully not encountered outside the laboratory, rates 16 million Scoville units.

The increasing tolerance of the blistering heat of capsaicin explains why chilli users can go on eating more and with higher doses, but why start in the first place? The answer, or maybe just part of the answer, lies in the body's chemical reaction to the sensation. It releases a class of neurotransmitter known as endorphins, which act as a pain-killer. Specifically, they bind to certain receptors in the brain in the same way as do opiates, and have an analgesic effect as well as creating a sense of well-being and happiness. Other activities for noticing endorphins at work are sex and concentrated physical exercise (the 'runner's high'). On the pain side, there has to be a balance between the amount of heat in the mouth and the size of the neurological reward, and most people will still not think the experience worth it. There is, of course, the 'manliness' component of how-hot-can-you-take-it, which encourages certain western males to prove themselves by demonstrating pain tolerance. This recalls the old Burmese proverb, 'A real chilli, seven fathoms under water, will still taste hot', meaning that an outstanding person will rise to any occasion.

And the solution for quelling the heat sensation if you've just gone a chilli too far? Not that glass of beer or water on the table in front of you, despite what you may think you need. As it turns out, the most efficient way to ease the pain is to drink milk or take any other dairy product. This is because the casein in dairy foods acts like a detergent at molecular level, and strips away the offending capsaicin from its receptor binding site on your tongue. Ironically, though, this is the very region of the world where you are least likely to find milk on the table, for genetic reasons. South-east Asians on the whole are genetically intolerant of milk. What we in the west have been brought up to think of as one of the best things for children to consume tends to make many Asians feel somewhere between mildly uncomfortable and violently sick, with flatulence, abdominal pain and diarrhoea the main symptoms. The cause of this reaction is the lack of the enzyme needed to digest lactose, which is milk's natural sugar. The enzyme is lactase, and if your body doesn't have it, dairy products become indigestible.

A 1972 survey found that 98 per cent of Thais were lactose intolerant. I almost wrote 'suffer from', but of course, in a culture where livestock for consumption has traditionally been a rarity, it hardly matters. It has become significant only since economic growth and westernization of habits have created a demand for things like ice cream. There are ways around the problem, if it can be considered one, such as milk processed to contain little lactose, and dairy product companies have been quick to adopt measures like this. And lactose tolerance appears to be on the increase. A 2004 study by Mahidol Univeristy in Bangkok concluded this after tests showed that almost half of a sample of adults showed no significant gastrointestinal upset. The interesting assumption in most of the literature written on lactase deficiency is that it is in some way abnormal. But really, the reverse is true. Worldwide there are many more people averse to milk than there are milk-drinkers. Genetically, lactase was originally acquired as an enzyme by Scandinavians, and then spread through northern and western Europe.

I digress. The question of why some cultures took to fiery pungency with such alacrity while most kept it at arms length has never been satisfactorily explained. Nevertheless, it seems reasonable to think that chillies were taken up where there was already a predisposition to foodstuffs containing compounds that also bind to the tongue's heat receptors. Black pepper, for example, does this through its compound piperine, and has a related 'bite' or 'kick'. So do some gingers, and if we look for evidence of what was eaten *before* the sixteenth century, we ought to find foods like this being used significantly. The problem for South-east Asia, however, is lack of early written records on culinary matters. In Thailand, the former Prime Minister and writer Kukrit Pramoj claimed to be 'reasonably sure' that Thai

Fresh green peppercorns on the stalk.

food in the Sukhothai era (the twelfth to thirteenth centuries) was very similar to modern northern Thai, featuring 'hot' sauces and condiments known as *nam prik*, made with garlic, salt and peppercorns and various native gingers. The modern Thai word for chillies is *prik*, while peppercorns are distinguished by being called *prik Thai*, meaning 'Thai pepper' and suggesting that these were the original 'hot' ingredient.

There is a further piece of evidence to support this from outside the region – Szechuan, another epicentre of volcanic pungency. This central Chinese province is home to the Szechuan pepper, quite different botanically and effectively from black pepper. Once, in Tibet, I landed up very happily in a Han Chinese restaurant. The sign painted on the window – 'Customer is God' – had that no-nonsense appreciation of the dynamics of catering that filled me with confidence. To be honest, I can't remember the meal, other than that it hit the spot, but the menu had an entry that afterwards I loved to quote. The item was 'Hot and Anaesthetic Pig Tribe', which I thought a cute but odd way of describing the destructive effect of chillies on the tongue. Strangely, it was years later that I had the chance to taste real Szechuan food in China, and then I got it. Anaesthetic is the perfect description for the blend of those unique Szechuan peppers and chilli – a totally numbing effect laced with hints of the dentist's chair. The Szechuan pepper produces a unique sensation of tingling numbness known to the Chinese as *má*. Combined with chillies it creates *málá* – 'numbing-and-hot'. Very different from the Thai version, more powerful, especially with the quantities used.

The complexities of spice and pungency do more than any other ingredients to define South-east Asian cuisine, and this, as I hope I'm managing to show, is the logic of a rice culture. If rice dominates your diet, you need to find strong flavours to accompany its essential blandness. Thus far, I've deliberately concentrated on the search for flavour rather than food ingredients, which with other cuisines might seem an about-face way of doing things. Spices, savoury fermented concoctions and the fire from chillies are indeed hallmarks of South-east Asian. Rice dominates, but why exactly? And what are the other food ingredients, the 'fixings', on which all these flavour ideas work?

Elsewhere in the world, variety comes from other sources, notably animal products. But here in South-east Asia there has traditionally been a problem with meat. For a start, tropical grassland is

nutritionally quite poor for raising livestock, with the additional scourge of a wide range of diseases. And in any case, it is the sheer ability of rice to sustain a higher population that has made it so dominant here, and against its yield, animals raised for their meat are a very poor option. Cattle can convert only 6 per cent of their grazing into weight, and humans eat only about two-thirds of this, meaning that 96 per cent of plants grown to raise livestock is wasted. Put another way, a hectare of food crops in Asia can produce around 10 million calories, but if used for dairy pasture, the same land would deliver only 1.7 million calories. The result is that traditionally, meat plays a very small part in the South-east Asian diet and the culture. This might not seem so obvious to most westerners, but then our normal experience of these cuisines is in restaurants, not homes in the countryside.

Ducks, cooked and hanging, waiting to be served.

None of this means that South-east Asians don't like meat. Far from it, with the exception of devout Buddhists. The religious constraints of Islam shift the preference in much of Indonesia and Malaysia towards beef and chicken, but across the region meat is popular when affordable. This has caused one of the great recent shifts in South-east Asian cuisine. Back say fifty

A Burmese poultry farmer near Ava drives his flock of ducks homeward.

86

One of Chiang Mai's best-known duck restaurants does a roaring lunchtime trade.

years, the great majority of the population was agricultural at a level that varied from subsistence to moderately comfortable, but with little surplus for luxury. The national cuisines were established under these conditions. Now that the economies are either booming or about to boom, meat is much less of a luxury.

No doubt one result of meat being traditionally rare on the table is the love of all parts of the animal. And I do mean all parts. Calf's brains, sweetbreads (the thymus gland), intestines and other offal have a precarious position in western cooking, and are generally considered mildly adventurous food. Mild, certainly, compared with a tasty stew that I discovered in northern Thailand – made from water buffalo's penis. The local name for this is a charming euphemism, *tua dio, ahn dio*, translating as 'one body, one thing'. From a culinary point of view, there is very little else but stewing that can be done with this impressive organ (about two-and-a half feet long as sold, flaccid, in the market). Only long, slow cooking can make it tender enough to eat. I had the dish prepared in a friend's restaurant. As I photographed the preparation, watching the girl in the kitchen doing the necessary chopping with a meat cleaver produced a slight feeling of disquiet,

88

particularly as she was grinning. I ate the results with reduced enthusiasm, despite the fact that it did, indeed, taste very good. I'm not sure how much the penis contributed, other than the texture – the Chinese *kougang* or 'mouthfeel'.

Not far from here, the northern Thai town of Phayao is especially known for its culinary use of all possible parts of cattle and buffalo, including, in the plastic bag, the cloudy green liquid called *phia*, from the second ruminant sac. Locals call it *khi phia*, the prefix being the word for excrement, and use it to flavour dishes such as spicy salads. Holding the clear plastic bag, tied up with a rubber band, to the light, I tried my best to imagine the cloudy pea-green liquid, with floating bits of what I imagined were the remains of grass, as a tasty kitchen resource.

And it's not just that all parts of animals are used, they are used in all ways. You would not think that chickens and eggs would lend themselves much

Khi phia, the liquid contents of a cow's second ruminant sac, occupies pride of place in a plastic bag among other offal offerings in Phayao market.

Vivid blocks of coagulated pig's blood at a market in Luang Phrabang, Laos.

A Thai sous-chef enthusiastically chops a flaccid but impressive water-buffalo penis in preparation for a stew.

to inventive cooking, or even repulsive cooking. But yes, there is a South-east Asian oddity, and while it is found across much of the region, the country that specializes in it is the Philippines. I first came across it as I was just about to leave the small town of Pulilan, some way north of Manila, at the end of a local festival. My driver, Romeo, ducked out of the car and headed for a road-side stall. As far as I could see, he was buying a boiled egg, and I called out to add one for me as I felt rather peckish.

Balut, the immensely popular Filipino eggs containing a duck embryo, achieved by allowing the eggs to go half-term before being boiled.

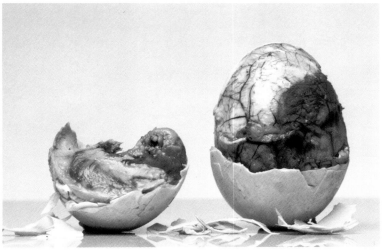

'Are you sure?' he asked. 'Better come and see first.' He cracked a small hole in the top of the shell, placed it to his lips and tipped his head back. Having drunk some liquid, he began to peel off bits of shell. I peered inside. Instead of a reassuring yolk nestling in white albumen, what I saw was a melange of grey and dirty yellow, with unmistakable wisps of bedraggled feathers. 'This is *balut*,' Romeo went on. 'Surely you've heard of our famous national delicacy.' Despite having the shape of a hard-boiled egg, this was the half-formed embryo of a duck. I couldn't help wincing at the thought of biting into a convoluted mixture of egg and small bird, but Romeo was so obviously enjoying the treat that I decided to risk a taste. Preferring not to examine the hard bits too closely, I settled for a morsel of what seemed closest to a yolk. Not at all bad: a strong flavour and a little chewy. Later, back in London, I found some in a local Asian supermarket, and took a few home to dissect, the result being the photograph on page 91. Filipinos swear by its invigorating effect, as well as its ability to enhance virility. The duck embryo is allowed to mature for sixteen days – half the time it would take to hatch out as a chick. As dusk falls in Manila and other cities, the *balut* vendors appear on the streets, most of them carrying wicker baskets. Inside, a padded cloth lining and lid keep the eggs hot for as long as possible, and they do a brisk trade. Yet to anyone brought up on the virtues of three-minute eggs for breakfast with buttered soldiers, *balut* does seem a rather perverse treatment.

Pla tu, dried mackerel, in an Issaan market.

Notwithstanding these strange ways with animals, as a way of making up for so little land being given over to producing meat, the South-east Asian passion for fish comes as little surprise. As Alan Davidson says in his seminal *Seafood of South-East Asia* (written while he was British Ambassador to land-locked Laos), 'Fish play a more important role as food in S. E. Asia than in most other parts of the world.' Indeed, they contribute more than half of the animal protein eaten in Indonesia and the Philippines, and not a great deal less than that in the other countries.

Davidson goes on to stress that 'Freshwater fish are abundant and more commonly eaten, except in the coastal areas, than marine fish.' In total, between rivers and the sea, the number of species that finds its way to the table is huge, and uncounted. Among marine species, herring-like fish of the order *Clupeiformes* dominate, but beyond them is a bewildering variety that includes sea bass, groupers, sea perch, mullet, snappers, scad, bream, croakers, parrotfish, mackerel, tuna and flatfish, not to mention crustaceans – shrimp, prawns, lobsters and crabs. And then the molluscs, bivalves, squid, cuttlefish and octopus. Freshwater species include barbs, carps, catfish, loaches and snakeheads, with more than a thousand species in total. Aquaculture is major, with almost a tenth of the world's production in the region. Ninety-nine per cent of aquaculture is freshwater, but fishing over the centuries has developed into a rich tradition. The techniques have changed little, although as a social event it no longer compares to the communal fish-drives that once took place. Sir William Maxwell, writing in 1907, described one such fish-drive in the Malay state of Perak, the most important event of the year, organized when the river was at its lowest. A huge

A wet market in the northern Burmese town of Bhamo, selling freshwater fish that is mainly from the Irrawaddy River.

enclosure of split bamboo and rattan took some thirty to forty men to build on an island in mid-stream, while the drive would begin seven or eight miles upriver. The fish were driven by means of a *relap* – Maxwell wrote: 'It was merely a long line of native rope; at intervals of about a foot strips of thin yellow palm-leaf were threaded into the line at right-angles to it, – and that was all. When the line was dragged through the water the palm-leaves whirled madly round, like windmill arms, and the unnatural appearance and weird glitter that were due to the sparkle of the river and the rapid revolution, were well calculated to strike panic into any fish.' The fish, nearing the enclosure and then once inside it, were caught with a hand-casting net, standard throughout South-east Asia. As these were colonial

Floating fish farms at Songkhla, southern Thailand.

Fishermen in Phnom Penh working a lift net at sunrise to catch Mekong fish.

times, English government officials joined in the catch, and Maxwell marvels at the sight. 'When one considers that these men were with one exception Government officials and remembers the extent to which their race owes its position to its prestige, this schoolboy frolic without loss of dignity cannot but be striking. Not a single one of them could throw a net even moderately well, and the majority had only the barest notion of how it should be done. And of course every one of them knew that, judged by Malay standards, he was making an exhibition of himself.' But the Malays, generous to a man, take it all with extraordinary grace, applauding even the worst flops. As well they might, because when *they* began the catch, it was with supreme elegance. 'As he stands ready and poised in act to cast,

Mosaic scenes from Laotian rural life on the exterior walls of Wat Xieng Thong in Luang Phrabang include the catching and carrying of large Mekong catfish.

he is a magnificent subject for a sculptor. The curve of the movement starts from the waist, and a sweeping line of action rises to the right shoulder; then simultaneously there is a swing of the right arm, a turn of the left hand, and a swooping lateral movement of the right shoulder; straightaway the part of the net that had been held in the right hand flies out horizontally over the water, followed by the part that had hung on the right forearm and elbow. As they fly out the left hand moves forward, and when held out in front of the body gives a fan-wise lateral motion to the meshes and checks them as they slip over the fingers, and thus gives the net its full spread.'

Steering his boat through the shallows of Lake Inlé, Burma, a Burmese leg-rower searches for a likely fishing spot. The method here is to sink a large cone trap in water only a few feet deep.

In an inlet on the coast of the Indonesian island of East Flores, a fisherman displays his prowess at spearing in the shallows.

And there are some very particular ways of catching seafood. Some years ago, returning to Phuket from the Similan Islands in the Andaman Sea, I had the helm of our sailing boat as dusk fell. As it became darker, I could see the glow of lights ahead, below the horizon, which puzzled me as we were still hours away from land. Gradually, these resolved themselves into a string of bright lights across a good arc of the horizon. Still a mystery, and it wasn't until we were almost sailing past them that they became obvious as fishing boats festooned with lights. Each one was like a floating fairground, in its own bright pool, visible for miles around. These were squidders, using strings of electric lamps powered by generators to attract the squid shoals. It was so unexpected in the middle of the ocean that I was entranced. It stayed in the back of my mind as something I'd like to learn more about, and earlier this year I finally had the opportunity, shooting on a book project that involved sending fifty-five photographers around Thailand on different assignments in the course of a week. I decided to go out for one night on a squidder, and as we had an assignment team to organize such things, it seemed easy to fix. What I hadn't realized, or at least hadn't thought through as it should have been fairly obvious, was that fishing by light works only when there isn't a moon. However, by good luck, it was, as it turned out, around the new moon.

Accompanied by my Thai friend Pong Skuntnaga, we took the slow train down to Hua Hin (the railways were also an assignment for the book), passing the town of Petchburi, famous

Hauling in the nets on Koh Samui in the Gulf of Thailand at sunrise. During the night, the boats trawl towards shore, carrying the large nets between them.

for its many delicious sweets concocted from the local palm sugar. We then drove in a hired car to a small creek to meet the captain of our already-booked fishing boat. Lung Jhong (Lung means 'Uncle' and is used to show politeness and respect for men who are experienced and getting on in years) was a short, stocky man, face and arms dark brown from the sun, who spoke incredibly rapid Thai that I really could not follow. Before heading out, he recommended that we eat, and there was a place, hardly a restaurant, that served the local fishermen. As normal, there was no menu; you were expected to know what might be available and ask for it cooked the way you liked it. I tried the usual 'mee alai aloy?' or 'what have you got that's tasty?' and received the predictable stock reply of '*everything's* tasty'. So that

didn't help in the way of suggestions, but Lung Jhong proposed that simplest of quick dishes, *phad thai*, stir-fried leftover rice with additions. Here this became *phad thai thalae*, with all kinds of seafood, from squid to prawns and fish.

Replete, we walked along the lane that passed sheds and jetties perched out on stilts over the muddy creek. There were, as I had expected, a few dozen of the brightly painted, sturdy wooden fishing vessels, though none seemed to have strings of lights, and more ominously, few showed any signs of life. The fact that it was low tide and they were all lying tilted at different angles in the mud clearly had something to do with this. But there was worse to come, as our captain led us down to a boat that was floating quite easily, which it could because it was all of 14 feet long. The lighting, moreover, consisted of one medium-sized fluorescent strip-light painted green and strapped vertically to the small mast. This was not exactly what I had expected, and we were now about an hour from sunset.

We explained our evident disappointment, and Lung Jhong took it without blinking. He understood perfectly, and proposed heading out to find some larger vessels that were already

A squid boat in the Gulf of Thailand, using bright lights suspended on booms over the water to attract the catch on moonless nights.

at sea. We set off, having taken the precaution of finding some life jackets first. More conversation as we headed downstream past mangrove swamps revealed that there were not that many squid around right now, and most of these little boats were simply mooring off mudbanks to collect cockles. I was becoming less and less enthusiastic, and when, after some radio conversations, it seemed that the nearest real boats were at least 20 nautical miles out in the Gulf, I called it a day. The next morning, Pong and I went down to the quayside at Hua Hin where catches are landed and found the harbour master. 'Ah,' he said, 'there are very few squid around now on this coast. They're all on the other side of the Gulf.' Right.

And so, a couple of days later, on to the good ship *Improving Business*, which is approximately the meaning of the Thai name *S. Kit Charoeun*, painted in old-fashioned, highly cursive Thai script. We board this 60-foot wooden fishing vessel with its crew of seven from a wooden jetty at a rivermouth a little south of Rayong on the eastern seaboard of the Gulf of Thailand. After the communications failures that led us on a wild squid chase over on the other side of the Gulf, today we are taking no chances, and have called in advance from Bangkok to book the ship and crew for a night's fishing. Other fishing boats are moored along the opposite bank of the small, muddy river, and with minor structural variations they all fit the same pattern, which has changed hardly at all in the last century (the *Improving Business* was in fact built only ten years ago). With the engine filling the hold, and the long foredeck reserved for the nets, ice and plastic barrels to take the catch, a single wooden superstructure in the stern houses everything else – captain's cabin, galley, crew's recreation room, this last less than three feet in height, just enough room for about three men lying down to watch the small television set. But the most striking feature of these Gulf fishing boats is the forest of poles and booms that they carry, mainly in wood and bamboo. The two main booms on the port side carry the net, and the several others carry rows of huge electric lamps for the night fishing – which is my ultimate photographic goal.

It takes about a quarter of an hour to reach the river mouth, then line up with the two channel lights that lead out to sea. There's been some rain, and there still is cloud, uncharacteristically for January, but we can see patches of blue sky beginning to clear as the light slowly fades towards evening. Even if it were clear, tonight would be dark, as we are a few days from the new moon.

Indeed, this is how this style of fishing works, as I'm about to see. After nearly two hours at eight knots, we anchor, and wait for nightfall. First though, we need to be fed. Pong and I are seen to first, the cook predictably concerned about how to deal with a foreigner. We persuade him to do what he normally does, which turns out to be slowly stir-fried pork with plain rice and a sauce, which I watched being pounded in a granite mortar, composed of two handfuls of dried red chillies, four cloves of garlic and a half handful each of sugar and monosodium glutamate. Very tasty, not least because we were starving and because we ate it squatting on the foredeck, just happy to be at sea. Political correctness apart, I think MSG has had a bad press. I know it gives some people headaches and the like, but as an invention it was a genuine attempt at enhancing flavour, which it does very well, and our cook, like countless others across Asia, chooses to use it because he likes the result. But this is re-treading old ground.

Of course, we get the raw end of the deal, as the crew, waiting for dark, start line-fishing for *pla daeng* and later, deeper, for squid, and these end up as their clearly more delicious meal. Never mind, we're here to work. Eventually, the daylight fades, and the crew get busy. First out are the light booms, the six long poles that carry over-sized, high-wattage lamps.

The captain powers up the generator, and the lamps light up. Each one is 300 watts, and there are about forty of them, so within a minute the ship is suddenly ablaze and the centre of a pool of intense light. That's 12,000 watts, and I can feel the heat from the deck. The idea is, this being the couple of dark weeks of the month around the new moon, meaning with no real moon for competition, we have become an artificial moon for the squid and fish below us. Like any romantics, I suppose, they come to the surface to gaze at the full moon, and are then, or shortly will be in our case, cruelly deceived and hauled out for cooking. The lighting set-up, which naturally as a photographer intrigues me, is sophisticated, and offers the captain a number of choices. At the end of one boom is a cluster of five silver-backed reflector bulbs, which provide a concentrated 'moon' if the general circle of light fails to work. Also, on each boom are two different lamps, metal halide I think, though I don't quite get round to asking, which emit a blue-green light. This wavelength penetrates the water deeper, because water selectively absorbs light, first the reds, then the yellows, until finally, way down, everything looks blue. Blue-green reaches the depths that squid inhabit. I'm also surprised to learn that using lights as a lure became popular in the Gulf only in the 1970s.

As it turns out, even though we are moored over a wreck ('usually means squid', says one of the crew), the radar shows no schools at squid depth, so we switch to the lighter fish net. Squid are tough and aggressive (indeed, man is their only significant predator) and merit a stronger mesh. But before the net goes down, we have to redistribute the ballast. In action, the ship is heavily lopsided, listing to port where the net is, and this needs to be balanced with barrels of seawater on the opposite side. This done, the crew slip the net, folded along the length of the deck, into the water, then winch out the two booms fore and aft from which the far end of the net is hung. Technically, this is known as a stick-held dip-net, an evolution of the traditional lift-net in which the net is allowed to sink and remain underwater long enough for the fish, or squid, to forget about it and swim over it. Our crew lower it on pulleys, then wait. All around us, on the still sea on this sultry night, other pools of night occupy their own little territories, none closer than about a kilometre. After about fifteen minutes, we begin hauling in. This pulls in

Racks of *pla meuk*, squid, drying in the sun, near Krabi, Thailand.

the booms, until finally, with effort, the catch at the bottom of the net appears.

Not a great first catch tonight, but as we have hired the boat and are paying for it, no-one minds that much. The fish go into a barrel, and are topped with ice, and the whole process starts again. The crew, most of whom are ethnic Khmers, displaying complex magical tattoos as they strip for action, work with boundless energy. This is tough work, all through the night. Actually, as I *am* paying for the boat, and the catch is not all that great, there seems to be no compelling reason to stay out until dawn, so we head back. My final lesson in deep-sea fishing is to learn why the fishing boats come back in the early morning, as for years I've seen them do. With one of the two channel lights out of order, no-one has any idea where the sandbanks are, and we wander around for an hour, shining lights into the water and shifting between forward and reverse before we finally make it to the landing. A new experience for the crew, finishing at night.

Coconuts from the east coast of the Malay peninsula being landed at Trengganu port for sale in the market.

Even with the region's love of fish, the cuisines are still weighted towards vegetables. After rice, coconut is probably the most widely used ingredient in most South-east Asian cooking, though concentrated in the south of the region. Indeed, every part of the palm, including the leaf, trunk, nut and husk, finds a use in daily rural life. The wood from the trunk, combined with the hardened shell, provides a dense material for constructing implements such as spoons and scoops. In cooking, the prime contribution of the coconut is its milk, which is used to thicken and flavour different curries, meat, vegetable and fish dishes, and in creating a range of sweets and desserts. This milk is *not* the water that sloshes around inside a young green coconut, which makes a refreshing drink. Instead, it is the liquid that is expressed from the white meat of a ripe coconut, and for extracting and shredding this there is, in parts of the mainland, a unique kitchen implement, the coconut scraper, known as *khood maprao*. It is basically a low wooden seat into which is firmly attached an iron grater so that it sticks out in front. In use, the person grating cracks open the coconut and, squatting on the wooden scraper to stabilize it, deftly rotates one half of the coconut around the sharp end of the grater to extract the flesh inside. In one motion, the flesh is removed and shredded.

The next step in the operation is to steep the grated meat in boiling water, and then, after it has cooled, squeezing it to express the milky liquid. It is important to distinguish between two kinds of coconut milk: 'thick' and 'thin'. The first pressing of the moist shreds is 'thick', and this is set aside because it is used at different stages in cooking, and for different dishes. Repeated soakings of the shreds in water produce 'thin' milk.

No doubt the original scraper was a simple block of wood that allowed the user to sit in a more-or-less comfortable position while scraping, but over the years, the Laos, Khmers and Thais have elaborated the implement, usually to represent an animal. By far the most common animal is the rabbit, which is what this implement is often called, sometimes by its full name of 'grating rabbit', even when the scraper is a plain block. The reasons for choosing this animal are quite obscure. One theory is that the sharp protruding iron grater recalls the rabbit's prominent front teeth.

Actually collecting the coconuts is, however, another matter, and down the Malay peninsula, the owners of plantations, which on average are quite small, have recruited some unusual help. It was my agent in Paris who first sent me a newspaper clipping about a Thai school for training monkeys. I had become used to the quirkiness in the national character that made such an idea perfectly plausible. In any case, it appealed immediately to magazine editors, and on my next visit to Thailand I drove down the coast to Surat Thani, where Khun Sumporn, a pleasant, stocky man in his forties had hit on the idea of training the local macaques (*Macaca nemestrina*, the pig-tailed macaque) in the skills needed to collect coconuts. Here in the south, and on down through the Malay peninsula, this is coconut palm country, especially on the east coast, with plantation after

A traditional rabbit-shaped coconut grater in a Chiang Mai household. The wooden body of the rabbit functions as a stool on which one sits while grating the coconut halves on the protruding iron grater.

Tom kaa gai, a Thai soup-like dish made with a coconut milk base and cooked with galangal and chicken, among other ingredients.

Novice nuns at a Sagaing convent near Mandalay shred and squeeze coconut flesh for a ceremonial meal.

plantation. Now the thing about coconuts is that if you wait for them to fall, they may be too dry and old. On the other hand, many of these palms are uncomfortably tall to climb, up to 25 metres, and in any case this is a rather dangerous profession, even for the agile young boys who learn to climb by gripping the trunk with the soles of their feet (a cord tied to both ankles helps to lock the feet into place). But really, monkeys do it better and faster, and while not generally as bright as human beings (though I did meet exceptions on both sides during the course of this story), can be trained to choose the just-ripe fruit, twist it off and throw it down.

I find Sumporn's 'Monkey Training College' a little out of town, among coconut groves. In reality, the title is too grand. Sumporn simply teaches local coconut plantation owners how to train their own monkeys. Nevertheless, he is an expert trainer, and his three monkeys, aged four years, one year and six months, are quite special. This becomes even more obvious when I later see how other local macaques perform, and one obvious differ- ence is that Sumporn loves his monkeys and takes good care of them. Many of the others are in a sorry state of neglect and are pretty well unapproachable. I think it is Sumporn's intention to highlight this contrast when he takes me on a tour of the neighbourhood.

The star of the college is four-year-old Nooey (which means 'mouse' and in this context means, roughly, 'youngster'). It's a sort of affectionate diminutive that an adult would use when calling a child. Nooey has been trained to walk on his hindlegs, though not for circus-like reasons. It frees up his hands to help Sumporn when he's working on the ground, and there's an undeniable charm to watching the two of them loading a hand cart with coconuts and splitting them for copra. Sumporn splits them on a spear-like spike of iron planted in the ground, while Nooey hands him new coconuts one at a time.

But a trained monkey's real forté is collecting ripe coconuts from the trees. No human can match it for speed and agility, not to mention the amount of time saved by leaping from one palm to another, rather than climbing down and up. A regular monkey can collect about 500 coconuts in a day, but a special animal like Nooey can manage 700 or 800. Because of its training, a macaque will always go first for the ripe nuts – brownish or yellow in colour. It picks them by rotating the coconut rapidly, so twisting its stem until this breaks. The major hazard from the macaque's point of view is that red ants love to build their nests among the coconuts, and poor Nooey's work is interrupted constantly while he stops to dash the furious insects out of his hair.

Sumporn begins training a macaque at about six months, and his first stage is to hold an old coconut between the palms of his hands and show the young animal how to spin it, using its hands and feet. He always uses ripe, old coconuts for this, so that the macaque gradually learns to pick only these, not the green ones. The next stage, when the macaque is aged about seven months, is to hang nuts from their stems on a wooden frame, teaching the young animal to twist them while they hang vertically. Finally, the macaque learns to work up in the tree, with a long cord attached to its neck chain. Sumporn stands below, encouraging it with shouts of 'Ao! Ao!' ('Get! Get!').

My own problem is how to get shots of the macaques up among the coconuts at the top of a palm tree, and the solution, which ends up taking a couple of days, is to build a wooden tower right next to a palm, with a platform on top higher than the tree. I don't want it appearing in the shot, so we site it a

Nooey, star pupil at Sumporn's academy for coconut-gathering macaques, climbs one of the palms on the plantation to select ripe fruit.

couple of metres to one side of the trunk. One of the younger macaques is not too happy with this arrangement, having to climb up towards a white-skinned photographer in addition to his normal duties, but Nooey is an old pro, and just gets on with it. But it makes me think that it would be nice to find a more candid way of being up in the tree with the macaque.

Almost a year later I unexpectedly get the chance. Having just delivered the Monkey Training College pictures to the magazine in Washington, I'm handed essentially the same story the following day by the Smithsonian magazine. Caroline, the picture editor, is unfazed by the first assignment, and this new one is set further down the peninsula, on the east coast of Malaysia. Here the macaques are called *berok*, and by now I'm familiar with what goes on. My new plan, because I do need to find a different approach, is to set up a remotely controlled camera on its own tower overlooking a palm tree, and operate it from below. These

Nooey's work continues with collecting and transporting the collected coconuts.

are pre-digital days, so this involves fixing a small security video camera next to the still camera, and lots of wires and batteries.

There is even an unlikely moral to the tale. Training your monkey properly can avoid accidents, as happened a number of years after I photographed this story. In Kelantan, just up the coast from Trengganu, in 2001, a fifty-nine-year-old man hired a macaque from its owner to help harvest his coconuts. Whether by accident or design, the macaque dropped a coconut on the man's head, killing him instantly. Also, incidentally, inspiring some black humour based on the linguistic confusion in Malay between head (*kepala*) and coconut (*kelapa*).

4 WILD ABOUT WILD

With meat and proteins traditionally in short supply, gathering foodstuffs from the wild became ingrained in the farming communities throughout South-east Asia. The immediate location was the paddy field itself and its surrounding irrigation system, home to small fish, crabs and shrimps, as well as frogs and various amphibious insects. Gourou, writing about Vietnamese rice farmers, describes the many techniques, from rod and line to fish traps in ditches, casting-nets, dipnets or nets that scrape the bottom of ponds. Children and adolescents go netting for shrimps and crabs, or catch crabs by hand. Of course, in the Buddhist parts of the region it is improper to take life, even so lowly – or perhaps especially the lowly forms of life, given the snakes-and-ladders way in which reincarnation can work. However, as Norman Lewis recounts about the Cambodian view, people 'got round moral objections by "rescuing fish from drowning", and it was agreed that if they subsequently happened to die there could be no harm in consuming their flesh.'

A study conducted in 1995 by Thailand's Khon Kaen University into wild-food gathering and hunting activities in the northeast of the country looked first at twenty villages scattered over three provinces, and then, using this information, in depth at the specifics in one village. The results showed that rural people did indeed depend on locally gathered or hunted wild food, which included fish, crabs, snails, shrimps, birds, red ants' eggs, frogs, toads, rabbits, rats, insects and many kinds of plants. The knowledge and techniques have been handed down from generation to generation. As one woman remembered, 'When I was young my mother took me to gather wild plants and animals with her. She taught me how to recognize and gather them, and when to find them in each season. I remembered helping her

Two young Akha hunters pause for lunch to barbecue the small woodland birds they have just shot with their homemade small-bore muzzle-loading shotguns.

gather *dork grajaew* and mushrooms in the forest. It's fun. We would dig for crabs in the paddy in the hot season. We went to gather red ants' eggs together. I also helped her scoop for shrimp and water insects (*maeng langum*). I watched my mom make nets for scooping and my grandfather make and mend fishing nets. He also made *khong* from bamboo to put fish in.'

The division of labour tends to be along gender lines, with women mainly responsible for gathering forest plants and fungi, and men for hunting, using traps, nets, slingshots, blowpipes and guns (often homemade). The study listed sixty-six different wild plants and mushrooms, including yam, lotus root, wild mango, caladium, morning glory, bitter cucumber, various tubers and a large number of leaves with no English names. A high proportion of the last of these are to some extent bitter, which no doubt helps account for the relatively strong place of this flavour in much South-east Asian cooking.

But this kind of scavenging went beyond necessity to outright preference, and even today, in the countryside of Vietnam or Burma or any of the countries nearby, small game and forest plants give local cuisines their character. They are sought after eagerly, and relished. Small frogs, rice birds, obscure bitter leaves found nowhere else, certain insects; it would be quite wrong to see these as in any way desperate measures to supplement a diet. Far from eating *in extremis*, the wild component is of great culinary importance in rural South-east Asia. One of the conclusions of the Khon Kaen study was that 'Most people, both rich and poor, preferred wild food to cultivated food. Therefore, wild foods were not only for the poor. People who did not hunt or gather wild foods purchased them from those who did.' Natacha du Pont de Bie in her investigations in Laos, discovered that the favourite dish of the King, who died in captivity following the Communist revolution of the 1970s, had been *or lam nor kor*, a spiced stew made with a jungle fowl from around Luang Prabang. The bird was hung until high, then smoked. Not only this, but the King insisted it be cooked by the Kha, his tribal palace guard, in the old manner of cooking it slowly over a fire in a piece of bamboo tube. When she talks about this to one of the exiled Lao aristocracy, he describes 'real Lao food' as 'the simple wild food of our country made the same way for centuries.'

From a western point of view, wild food poses some cultural problems, largely because this is something we have lost. Few

Fat and meaty frogs for sale in a Singapore market.

people in Europe and America eat anything remotely wild, and as our food sources become increasingly farmed, sanitized and organized, we began to look askance at creatures running around unwrapped and without a barcode. Frogs and toads are borderline in this respect, but in South-east Asia are snapped up whenever possible, which tends to be from the rainy season until the beginning of winter. Immediately after rain, it's time for a frog hunt in the paddy fields or swamp, and the best time to catch them is at night, using lights.

Following the French practice, many people are familiar with large frogs, the legs and thighs in particular, but there are hundreds of species of all sizes, and when it comes to the smallest, they fry up nicely to a morsel that can be eaten whole, crunchy little bones and all. The American Consul in Chiang Mai told me once of a related incident. He was visiting an upcountry town on official business. In the evening he dined in an open-air restaurant, of which one speciality was a tiny variety of frog dropped into hot oil and deep-fried. The name of the dish, as described by the waiter, was *sukaydaywer*. The Consul spoke good Thai, but

Eviscerating a lizard in north-eastern Thailand, prior to grilling over a charcoal fire. The eggs will also be eaten.

could make no sense of this, and asked his companion, who lived in the town, to explain.

'Well', the man said, 'a few years ago there was an air display here, in front of the governor of the province and other dignitaries at the local sports field. A part of the show was a parachute drop, but then a disaster occurred. One of the parachutes failed to open. It was very messy, and happened right in front of everyone.' He went on to say that it had not taken the locals long to see that the splayed posture of these little frogs had more than a passing resemblance to the hapless parachutist. Hence the name.

'Yes', said the Consul, 'but I still don't understand. What is the name?'

The man replied, slightly puzzled, 'But the word is English. I thought you'd understood.' Taking rather more care over his pronunciation than had the waiter, he repeated, 'It's "Skydiver Frog".'

The wild menu extends beyond frogs to lizards and the like. These, in all their varieties, feature prominently on the menus of many so-called 'Jungle Food' restaurants. This kind of establishment is generally on the outskirts of town, has a rough-and-ready 'rustic' appearance, promises a list of endangered species that resembles the IUCN Red Data Book, but in practice has available a very tame selection of game. Invariably, at least three quarters of the menu is unavailable, but lizard is usually a reliable bet, while snake is less frequently available.

Insects get very short shrift in culinary writings, which is a pity, because as food they have their own lore and are, besides, nutritious. Unfortunately, these days they cause a certain amount of revulsion in most societies (though not if we delve back far enough into our own food histories). Before I go any further, and I do intend to go into some obscure foodways, can we agree that we all like honey? There will always be a few dissenting voices, but in the long list of human food, honey from the bee ranks pretty high as desirable and cross-cultural. So, given that most of us actively like partially digested bee regurgitation (vomit, if you like), it seems fairly clear that there is more psychology at work here than actual taste and mouthfeel sensations.

I once came across a book – a short tract, really – written in 1885 by an Englishman, one Vincent M. Holt, titled 'Why Not Eat Insects?'. In the confident, moralizing tone of Victorian social reformers, he clearly believed in the nutritious value of insects – especially for those less fortunate than himself.

> What a pleasant change from the labourer's unvarying meal of bread, lard, and bacon, or bread and lard without bacon, or bread without lard or bacon, would be a

good dish of fried cockchafers or grasshoppers. "How the poor live!" Badly, I know; but they neglect wholesome foods, from a foolish prejudice which it should be the task of their betters, by their example, to overcome.

How curious, but also, how logical. It was on my mind because South-east Asia is full of insectivory, and one part in particular, from the north-east of Thailand up into Laos, seemed to me to lead the way. At least, I can think of nowhere else where so many insects are displayed and sold for food. When I travelled around the region with Madhur Jaffrey, the actress and food writer, for a book on South-east Asian cooking, we strolled through the covered market in Khon Kaen, one of the regional capitals. There must have been a dozen different species of bugs on sale next to the usual vegetables, dried fish, chillies and spices. There were large grasshoppers, fat round

During the Cambodian civil war, when the temples at Angkor were left untended, this local farmer supplemented his family's diet by collecting bats from inside the towers of Angkor Wat.

cockchafers and many others that I couldn't easily put a name to, including a pile of small, shiny black beetles, looking from a distance like over-sized spiky water melon seeds. For some reason these caught my eye, and I asked the stallholder about them.

The woman called them *maeng* (the general word for insect) *chiu chee*, and later research revealed these to be *Onitis virens*), which occur in abundance in, of all things, buffalo and cattle dung. She assured us they were tasty when roasted with salt. These are by no means the only species found in and collected from piles of dung, and not just in Thailand, but in at least Burma also. Several species of the genus *Copris*, about one to one-and-a-half centimetres in length, are active at night, and collected from the dung piles early in the morning by digging them out and placing them in a bucket of water to soak overnight. In some villages, piles of dung are 'posted' by sticking signs in them to

Copris beetles, which hatch in mounds of buffalo dung, making them easy to find in northeastern Thailand, on sale in Khon Kaen market.

show that they are reserved. It took me a little while to work out why these dung beetles should be so popular. The reason is simple logistics – they are easy to find. If you want to eat insects, it wastes less time if you go to known concentrations of them. Fascinating as this was, I tried to get Madhur to eat a handful, but she made some excuse.

Indeed, insects are widely eaten all across South-east Asia (and into China), to an extent not realized by visitors, and perhaps not even by many urban residents. Professor Gene DeFoliart, in his comprehensive and continuing survey *The Human Use of Insects as a Food Resource: A Bibliographic Account in Progress*, records more than ninety species of insects eaten in the region. Spiders not being insects, this excludes the edible tarantula popular in Cambodia and surrounding countries, though most westerners would file them under the same general category of being small, repulsive and skin-crawling. I have to admit I was a little shocked to learn that there were so many species, because until then I thought I had more or less covered the spectrum with my own oral investigation. Funnily enough, even I may not seek out the seventy-odd that I've missed.

For the time being, however, back to the north-east of Thailand, because this is indeed the culinary heartland for insectivory. The Khorat Plateau is known to the Thais as Issan, and is mainly Lao speaking. The Mekong River in the north separates it from Laos itself, but the cuisine is largely the same, and among other qualities Laotians are particular insect gourmets. On another visit, I drove along the country roads, parched rice fields containing nothing but stubble stretching away to the horizon on either side. This was the height of the dry season, and one of the few signs of activity was an occasional figure carrying a bucket in one hand and a long pole topped with a small net in the other. April and May are the months to collect the large, juicy eggs of the red ant (*Oecophylla smaragdina*). I stopped to watch one girl, using the net to scoop ants and their eggs from a nest high in a tree. She emptied her harvest into a bucket half-filled with water, hopping and slapping at her legs as furious escapees took revenge.

The girl explained that the water would drown the ants, making it painless to pick out the eggs. I walked back with her to the village, where her mother set about making a spicy salad, using the white eggs and the pale gold bodies of the few winged females that had been caught. She called it *goy kai mot daeng*, though the more usual term is *yam kai mot daeng* (*yam* is a spicy salad, *kai* is egg, *mot* ant and *daeng* red) by mixing them, uncooked, with fermented fish sauce, lime juice, chilli paste and mint. This is just one of several popular preparations. They can also be steamed, cooked in a curry, or simply popped straight into the mouth if you really can't wait. They can be preserved by pickling the ants, their larvae and pupae in salt water, tamarind juice, ginger, onion, a little sugar and the *bai makrut* leaf (*Citrus hystrix*). I actually liked the spicy salad I was offered sufficiently to search out other recipes. One from Laos itself that a friend cooked for me is *mok kai mod*. A *mok*, which makes its appearance more familiarly in central Thai cuisine as *haw mok thalae*, the seafood version, is a type of steamed curry prepared and served in banana leaves, with a custard-like consistency. In this Laotian version, my hostess, Gaeo Everingham, added the eggs to a paste of minced pork, pounded shallots and a hen's or duck's egg, with chopped spring onion and ground black pepper, wrapped the mixture in pieces of banana leaf to make little packets and steamed them.

Staying in Washington a little while later, I went out for a Thai dinner in Bethesda with an old friend who had lived many years in Cambodia and Thailand, and who recommended the Bangkok Garden. Rather against the odds in Maryland, the food was good and authentic, he said, and to test this we tried asking the waitress for things off the menu, searching our memories for ever more recondite dishes. She remained unfazed; the kitchen

A spicy salad made with the eggs of the red ant makes a typical and tasty lunchtime meal and is eaten with sticky rice, at a farm near Yasothon, northeastern Thailand.

could do it all. They even had sticky rice, which triggered an association and I finally asked if they had *yam kai mot daeng*. 'Raw *suk kru*' ('Please wait') she said, asking us to wait a minute, and she went back to the kitchen. And yes they could do that too. They did, and it was delicious, although how the red ants made it through customs I have no idea. When we left to pay the bill, we asked how red ants' eggs happened to be available. 'The owner likes them', was the answer.

The eggs have a soft skin and a creamy filling, and are considered to have a slightly sour taste, which comes from the formic acid better known to most people in its painful application as a bite. Another term for this ant is *mot som,* or 'sour ant', and locals who particularly relish this sourness also occasionally eat the colony's worker ants, which are supposed to have an even more sour flavour. To my own palate, the flavour and texture hinted at a soft Brie that is beginning to flow over the cheeseboard.

This made me think a bit harder about the difficulty of describing the taste of insects. Unfamiliarity means searching for similarities elsewhere in our taste experiences. Just to say that insects have a nutty flavour (the usual description) is true as far

121

as it goes, but conveys no more than saying that reptiles taste of chicken or that beef, lamb and pork all taste meaty. I collected the following from a variety of papers and books on insects in the region, and they make surprising reading.

W. S. Bristowe, writing in the 1930s, noted that insects in general 'for the most part . . . were insipid, with a faint vegetable flavour', and 'dragonflies are said to taste like crayfish'. Acknowledging that for the most part 'Flavour is exceptionally hard to define', he goes on to say, 'but lettuce would, I think, best describe the taste of termites, cicadas and crickets; lettuce and raw potato that of the giant *Nephila* spider, and concentrated Gorgonzola cheese that of the giant waterbug (*Lethocerus indicus*).' A Thai researcher, L. Jonjuapsong, claims that 'the flesh of praying mantis is very similar to that of shrimp mixed with fresh mushrooms', and that in eating termites, the 'flavor is nutty and delicious, although some people believe that if you eat too many they can make you groggy'. Other Thais, Jintana Yhoung-aree and P. Puwastien, clearly equally in thrall, found that 'Deep-frying is the main technique used to prepare bamboo caterpillars. This dish is delicious and tastes much like french fries.' T. Cahill, found that the sago beetle was unique in flavour: 'They were unlike anything I'd ever eaten before; the closest I can come to describing the taste is 'creamy snail'.' Van der Burg in Indonesia thought the roasted queen termite, *ratoe rajap*, a 'special delicacy', tasted like almonds. A Japanese researcher, Y. Hirashima, declared of cricket 'It was well edible, having a taste somewhat similar to shrimp.'

An odd collection of parallels, and perhaps some inconsistencies, but then in general we do not have much of a useful vocabulary for describing the flavour of food. Try describing the difference in flavour between beef and lamb, for instance – that is, without referring to texture and appearance. But the variety in the insect world is undeniable. Ants, grubs, locusts, beetles: all offer unique taste sensations. Insects also have that other quality essential in an appetizing food: interesting textures. 'Crisp on the outside, soft on the inside' has always been a sure formula for success in the food industry, and has helped establish the popularity of all kinds of favourites, from liqueur chocolates to roast suckling pig. Most insects give this sensation ready packaged. The opinion of one British writer who studied insect-eating in the region in the 1930s was that 'a toasted dungbeetle or soft-bodied spider has a nice crisp exterior and soft interior of soufflé consistency which is by no means unpleasant.' Quite.

Little wonder, then, that seasonal grasshoppers are one of the choicest sidewalk snacks in many parts of the region. Deep-fried in a wok until they are crisp and golden-brown, they compare favourably with Japanese soy snacks, and are very much cheaper. The Thais refer to them as 'flying shrimp', not as a euphemism but lauding their attraction as a food (echoes of the Greek Aristophenes calling grasshoppers 'four-winged fowl', alluding to their use as food by the poor of Athens). They are still offered for sale in huge mounds on sidewalk stalls in parts of Bangkok, although their popularity was dented for a while by the use of pesticides. Swarming grasshoppers are a major pest for rice farmers, and while in the words of one report 'villagers have fought back with their own appetites, instead of the more expensive and dangerous chemicals', massive government spraying programmes in the 1980s had the effect of causing some human deaths by poisoning. In some districts, the local authorities responded by holding grasshopper-catching competitions, with health and culinary experts demonstrating the best ways to clean and prepare them. Indeed, in the ten years from 1983, when this initiative began, the price rose from 12 US cents per kilogram to US$2.80 per kilo, while in local restaurants they cost the equivalent of US$6.00 per kilo. Ironically, at up to US$120 per half-acre, this makes the insects more profitable than some of the crops they attack, and the trade in grasshoppers is now worth about US$6 million a year. The Thai government has even promoted a number of grasshopper recipes. In the Philippines, a plague of locusts in 1994 prompted a similar initiative, with cooking contests in some areas and prizes awarded for recipes. These include *locust adobo*, in which the de-winged and de-legged insects are boiled for a few minutes, then fried in oil until crisp, and served with tomatoes, local red onions (*lasona*) and *bagoong*.

Like other wild foods, insects are the most popular in poorer areas, for the obvious reason that they supply missing protein. So, Laos, north-eastern Thailand, the deep countryside of Burma and Laos, and the highlands of the Philippines are the heartlands of entomophagy. Nevertheless, as W. S. Bristowe, who published the first definitive paper on this in the region in 1932, found, 'As regards their reasons for eating insects, I found that without question the Laos like them. Some fetch high prices and the capture of others is fraught with considerable risk.' Subsequent researchers, and my own experiences, backs this up, that where insects are eaten, they are actively enjoyed.

One of the most prized insects in South-east Asian cooking is the giant waterbug, *Lethocerus indicus*. The male secretes a fragrant liquid from two abdominal glands, and this is used to flavour dishes. In Vietnam, and in particular in Hanoi, it is a costly ingredient used in dishes such as *cha ca la vong*, and the custom is to serve a few drops from a medicine dropper. The whole insect can also be eaten, although it has only a little flesh, either by steaming or grilling over charcoal. Or it can be chopped and sautéed, chitin and all.

It is used even more widely in Thailand, in the form of a spicy dipping paste, *nam prik maeng da*. Bearing a superficial resemblance to a well-fed cockroach (and often wrongly referred to as such), the *maeng-da*, as it is called, secretes a remarkably pleasant aroma. One method of using this beetle is to squeeze the liquid out between thumb and forefinger; another is simply to pound the insect, minus legs and wings, in a mortar. The strangest thing about the *maeng-da* is that the smell and taste confounds everyone's first expectations. The paste is highly scented, a perfumed aroma with a hint of pears (to me at least), and very little is needed to flavour a dish.

Deep-fried large grasshoppers are a popular roadside snack in Bangkok, an Issaan speciality that has found favour among city dwellers.

Pounding *Lethocerus indicus* water beetles to release flavour and aroma from their highly prized and delicately perfumed guts, here to make a spicy dip.

Far from being considered an odd cooking ingredient, this water beetle is so highly regarded that it appears not only in country markets, but in big city department stores, and there is even a cheaper synthetic version of the liquid. To make a *maeng-da dip*, take 1 or 2 male *Lethocerus* (they sell for twice the price of the females), 10g of shrimp paste, 3–5g of crushed garlic, lemon, soybean or fish sauce, and pepper. Pound all together in a mortar. If you include the entire beetle, as the cook in my photograph is doing, it may take some time to reduce the chitin, so an alternative is first to squeeze out the insides of the insect using your thumbs. The term *maeng-da*, incidentally, is used to refer to a pimp in Thai. The origin is actually twice-removed. Down in the Gulf, the horseshoe crab makes an occasional appearance at the table, chiefly for its eggs. Its primeval, bug-like appearance has earned it the name *maeng-da talae*, meaning 'sea water-beetle'. One of its observed habits is that the male horseshoe crab spends a great deal of time hitched to the back of the female, along for the ride as it were. This appeals to the well-developed Thai sense of humour.

Central Thais, particularly those living in cities, tend to look down on this Lao entomophagy as being uncouth, although, and certain kinds of ant and ant grub are pickled for the consumption of good family Siamese in Bangkok.' Yet in the latest *Nutrient Composition Table of Thai Foods*, published by the Nutrition Division of the Thai Department of Health, there is no information on the nutritional value of insects. An academic survey undertaken in the early 1980s in one district of Issan found that 20–60g of insects are consumed daily, providing 1–5g of protein, 1–50g of fat, 1–5g of carbohydrate and 10–350 kcal of energy. The authors, Sungpuag and Puwastien, concluded that insects are a good source of protein and high in several minerals (calcium, phosphorus, sodium and potassium), although low in iron. Vitamin B_2 and niacin were at higher levels than vitamin B_1.

The list goes on and on, not surprising given how many insect species there are. Bamboo caterpillars go by the amusing name in Thailand of *rot duan*, meaning 'express bus', possibly to do with the speed at which they crawl, and are found in large numbers in deep bamboo forests. One bamboo section can contain up to a thousand caterpillars, and they are cooked by stir-frying in a little oil with garlic – a popular snack everywhere. Cockchafers have more substance, at least the ones that were cooked up for me – pale brown, large chunky bugs that rolled and crawled incessantly around the basket in which they had come from the market. These are such big, solid insects that they need more careful preparation than most. The wings, wing-cases and entrails are all removed first, and then the cockchafer is dry-roasted in a pan. Cooked to perfection, it should be rather more chewy than crisp on the outside, with plenty of the rich, gravy-like liquid remaining inside.

A stranger use of insects as flavouring is the practice of putting them in bottles of alcohol. The most well-known is the small worm that lives in maguey plants in Mexico, put into bottles of some brands of mescal, a fiery spirit distilled from the same plant, but a similar idea is behind the way that some hill-tribes spice up their home-made rice whisky. The giant Scolopendra centipede is both malevolent and greatly feared for its bite. Although not fatal, its venom causes excruciating pain, and in the wild is treated with great caution and respect. Ironically, its aggressive nature is the insect's occasional undoing, for the fear it generates also makes it a worthy candidate for embalming. Some of the qualities of the centipede are considered to infuse the alcohol, making it a more manly drink. Certainly, taking a shot of the colourless rice whisky is not for the faint-hearted: the Scolopendra, which can almost match the bottle in length, stays alive and angry for a considerable time. The approach of a hand reaching for the bottle sends it into paroxysms, battering noisily against the glass. Another method of infusion is as a tea. Excrement of the giant phasmid, *Eurycnema versirubra*, is apparently used to make a flavourful tea, according to French entomologist Pierre Jolivet. It feeds on the guava tree (*Psidium quajava*) and consequently the excrement is quite fragrant, somewhat resembling the scent of Chinese jasmine tea. And in Malaysia, according to Chinese medicinal belief, the dried excreta of a large species of stick insect (*Eurycnema versifasciata*) mixed with herbs is supposed to cure asthma, stomach upsets and muscular pains.

Dragonflies seem an unlikely choice of insect food, given their slim proportions and general aerodynamic agility, but they are

A giant *Scolopendra* centipede embalmed in locally made rice spirit adds a virility-inducing element to this Akha drink.

indeed hunted, and one of the places most given over to this sport is Bali. I had read of it in Wallace's book *The Malay Archipelago*, and though this was written in 1869, I'd heard that the practice continued. Wallace wrote:

> Every day boys were to be seen walking along the roads and by the hedges and ditches, catching dragon-flies with bird-lime. They carry a slender stick, with a few twigs at the end well anointed, so that the least touch captures

127

Two young Balinese men 'fishing' for dragonflies with a rod tipped with a sticky paste.

the insect, whose wings are pulled off before it is consigned to the small basket. The dragon-flies are so abundant at the time of the rice-flowering that thousands are caught in this way.

A friend arranged for me to see the process, and we drove to a nearby village. The boys had already prepared their catching equipment, which was a long thin strip of bamboo coated with the sticky sap of the jackfruit tree. This strip was then inserted into the end of a long bamboo stick. The operation resembled a kind of aerial fishing, and the object was to wield the rod so as to touch the dragon-fly just as it alighted on a blade of grass. When they had accumulated a large handful of dragon-flies, the legs and wings were removed, and the insects added to a pounded mixture of coconut paste, fermented fish paste, garlic, chillies, tamarind juice, basil leaves, ginger and the juice of a lime. This mixture was then wrapped in banana leaf packets to make a variety of the common dish known as *pepes* – the packets cooked over an open grill.

According to entomologist R. W. Pemberton, 'Given the ingenuity and fun involved in the capture of dragonflies, the customs seem to relate as much to sport as to food', adding, 'The many Asian customs relating to dragonflies and other insects reflect a more positive attitude toward insects than generally occurs in the West.'

Pepes, a familiar method of cooking in Indonesia in which a spicy paste is grilled or steamed in a leaf packet, here made with the dragon-flies, less their wings, caught in the operation on the facing page.

The American anthropologist Marvin Harris, noted for his work on food habits, considers that insectivory is rejected in the West because there are so many other food sources and because insects bite, sting and itch. In direct contact with humans they are not needed as food and are harmful. When circumstances make them useful as a food source, attitudes change. The circumstances in the poorer agricultural parts of South-east Asia, are quite straightforward – poverty and insufficient protein. But does this explain the genuine enthusiasm that many South-east Asians have for insects? One writer on food habits, a native of Burma, Dr Delphin, concludes his survey with 'I come from a culture where insects are traditionally eaten because we like the taste of them. If I have written this account with my heart and soul, I have also written it with my stomach, so to speak.' A Thai researcher, Chaiya Uisoognern, in his book *Malaeng Daa Naa* ('Of Edible Insects'), gets carried away with such enthusiasm that, 'blissfully unaware of the revulsion experienced by those from other cultures' as one reviewer put it, he declares one dish made with the giant waterbug, fish, shrimp sauce, small aubergine and the infamous *pla raa* described in chapter Two, as being 'too tasty to tell anyone about' (*aroi ya bork khrai*). And going back to the Victorian writer, Vincent Holt, with unassailable naivety, he managed to 'foresee the day when a dish of grasshoppers fried in butter (will be) as much relished by the English peasant as a similarly treated dish of locusts is by an Arab or Hottentot.'

I think not, and perhaps it makes more sense to look, not at why South-east Asians can be enthusiastic about insectivory, but at why Europeans and Americans regard insects with such peculiar loathing when the question of food arises. To most, even the sight of an insect scuttling around is repellant: a cockroach in the pantry, an earwig on a bedspread, or a spider just about anywhere. The idea of serving them at the table (intentionally, that is; flies in soup do not count) is one of the most disgusting possible to the western mind.

Personally, I can't deny a lifelong fascination with strange and unusual food, which goes back at least to early experiments with earthworm sandwiches. What I and my childhood friends were doing there, of course, was experimenting with the idea of being revolting, not savouring the delights of a wriggling flesh-coloured tube (they were alive, simply because worms are rather difficult to kill, and chopping them up didn't immediately seem to do the trick). Dare I eat this? But more recently, as I hunted out things that were nominally peculiar and sometimes loathsome, my interest shifted to the differences in opinion between food cultures. When you have sat having a drink with someone who is clearly enjoying each mouthful of crispy fried tarantula, especially the gooey bit in the thorax (Cambodia), or watched the eyes light up of someone about to eat freshly plucked dragonflies steamed in banana leaves (Bali), you begin to realize that your own prejudices and lack of appetite in the matter have no priority. Strangeness in food is entirely relative.

This led me to the psychology of disgust. This – disgust – is a reaction which crops up regularly when many westerners get to things like insects and fermentation food. Marvin Harris has a theory that creatures are either apotheosized or abominated according to whether or not they have residual utility. Thus, as he says, 'A horse not eaten wins battles and plows fields. It is a noble creature.' But insects not eaten (in situations as in the West where there are other sources of protein) are not only useless but harmful. They eat crops, bite, sting, suck blood. Moreover, they lead 'a furtive existence in close proximity to humans', as Harris puts it. They hide by day and emerge by night. The net result is phobia, us for them.

Food psychologist Paul Rozin considers that disgust derives from the food rejection system of mammals, but centred not on the sensory aspects of a food, but on knowledge of its nature or origin. Worms, therefore, are disgusting because of what they are, rather than what they might taste like (they don't taste all that bad). At the heart of this is the idea of offensiveness, and Danish psychoanalyst Andras Angyal defined disgust as 'fear of oral incorporation of an offensive object'. Worms, cockroaches, rotten fish and so on are just such offensive objects, so much so that they have the strange ability to contaminate in the mind of a disgusted person; if they touch something edible, they make it inedible.

5 CROSSROADS

Adding hugely to the variety for which South-east Asian food is known is the meeting of two great neighbouring cuisines, Chinese and Indian. As you might expect, the inroads they have made and the extent of their influence has to do with proximity and the migration routes. The Indian influence is at its strongest in Burma, and also in the Malay Peninsula, where Indians settled during British colonial rule. Chinese influence is stronger and wider, reflecting the much greater penetration of settlement as well as the much longer border that China shares with South-east Asia. The most 'Chinese' of national cuisines is, again not surprisingly, Vietnam, which is the only one in which chopsticks are central to eating; elsewhere, eating by hand was the major tradition, gradually becoming refined into spoon and fork, with chopsticks used for pre-eminently Chinese dishes and by the Chinese communities that became embedded in South-east Asian societies. There are, indeed, substantial Chinese communities in every country in the region, notably in the major cities, and one particular community, that of the Peranakan or Straits Chinese of Singapore, Malacca and Penang, that has evolved its own unique cuisine. Called 'Nyonya' after the honorific term for the women, this cuisine is an early fusion, an invention that combines mainly Chinese ingredients with Malay spices.

Chinese and Indian are not the only major influences to have met at the South-east Asian crossroads. Religion too, in varying degrees has left its mark. The most powerful influences, because of their strict dietary laws, have been Islam and Hinduism, and principally these have been prohibitory ones, one abjuring pork, the other beef. The archipelago is the Islamic stronghold, although there are Muslim communities from Burma to the Philippines. Hindu influences spread through the region much

Shan villagers eat noodles at a wedding dinner. The use of chopsticks signifies the cultural proximity of this part of Burma to neighbouring China.

133

earlier than Islam, being an essential part of the great empires of the Khmer and the Cham, as well as in Java, but now exist in pockets, notably the island of Bali. Many of the Cham, centred in the middle of Vietnam, converted to Islam, and traces of both culinary traditions from the Indian sub-continent are evident in the spices and curries.

The regional patterns of flavour, ingredients and the styles of cooking and eating are, as we'll see, very largely a result of the complex interaction of these outside influences. But perhaps even more noticeable are the immigrant foodstuffs, most of which we've already seen, and which include chillies, noodles, potatoes and coffee. Chilli probably remains the oddest of all, having been so thoroughly and enthusiastically absorbed into many of the cuisines that it is sometimes difficult to remember that it is not indigenous. This easily happens.

More Chinese culinary influence in evidence in the neon sign over a Bangkok restaurant, featuring a steaming bowl with chopsticks.

As time passes, foods that were exotic become embedded, often so thoroughly that their origins are completely forgotten. I remember one embarrassing interchange, in Bangkok. I was travelling with Madhur Jaffrey, making a book on the cuisines of South-east Asia, and in Thailand we had been invited for dinner to the house of a judge – an introduction from a friend. The conversation turned to food sources, and the question of potatoes came up. Madhur explained that they came from South America, but the Thai judge would have none of it. Madhur insisted, the judge dug his heels in, and the evening soured. Odd, really, considering that potatoes appear hardly at all in Thai cooking, just in the Muslim dishes of the south. Yet another example of how people tend to identify themselves by their food, and many don't like being challenged on their preconceptions.

Coffee is another introduction from the European trade routes, although its ultimate origin is Ethiopia and the practice of drinking coffee developed in the Arab world. It spread from the Middle East to Europe in the seventeenth century, and by 1690 the Dutch had managed to ship seeds to their colonies in the East

134

The market in Lashio. Potatoes have become embedded in the cuisine of certain parts of the region, including the highlands of Burma's northern Shan State but only arrived as an import following the Spanish and Portuguese colonization of South America.

Indies, where Javanese plantations became important exporters. More recently, Vietnam has expanded its production to the point where it is the world's second largest producer after Brazil. And one South-east Asian coffee is by far and away the most expensive in the world. *Kopi luwak*, as it is known in Indonesia, sells for up to US$600 a pound, which comes to about $10 a cup, and the reason for this outrageous price premium is the special pre-processing that the bean receives. *Luwak* is the Indonesian term for the Palm Civet, a mongoose-like animal, *Paradoxurus hermaphroditus*, that is perhaps best known for its scent glands near the anus from which it defensively sprays a noxious secretion. Less well known is its predilection for just-ripe coffee cherries, for which it scouts among the plantations in Java, Sumatra, Sulawesi and also in Vietnam and the Philippines. The inner bean, however, is not digested, and ends up among the civet's faeces, subtly yet significantly altered chemically. Studies at the University of Guelph in Canada have shown that part of the digestive process breaks down some of the proteins within the bean that contribute bitterness to coffee flavour. But the reason that the study was carried out at all is that for a long time it has been local knowledge that these excreted beans, when washed (as you would) and roasted, make coffee with a superb flavour. Now that within the last few years the secret has emerged, thanks to the internet, *kopi luwak* is enjoying something of an international boom among coffee aficionados. There may be another reason for the high reputation in which this coffee is held, which is the natural selective judgement of the civet. In any plantation, there are variations in the time of ripening, with some berries almost mature, some a bit over, some just right. A local belief is that the civet naturally chooses the best of the crop, rather like the coconut monkeys but without the need for training.

Overwhelmingly, however, it is China that has made the strongest impression on South-east Asia. In particular, two ways of dealing with rice are indisputably Chinese – noodles and gruel. Noodles have been thoroughly adopted almost everywhere, sometimes served in a recognizably Chinese way, often altered and made into a dish unique to the country in which it is cooked. There are five common kinds of noodles, with variations, three of them made purely from rice, one with egg and another made from soy. The standard trinity of rice noodles are thin round (often referred to as rice vermicelli), medium flat and broad flat. Variations include the long skeins used in the Thai dish *kanom chin* and the somewhat thicker round *laksa* noodles of Malaysia and Singapore. Egg noodles are more spaghetti-like in appearance, and have added egg (or just colouring in the cheaper varieties). Cellophane noodles are extremely thin and transparent, and made from soy beans; a Vietnamese variety, *mien*, uses a mixture of rice and manioc flour.

Noodles, and their European iteration, pasta, have always encouraged a trend towards fanaticism, but in noodle obsession it is hard to beat the northern Vietnamese feelings for *pho*, a noodle soup in beef broth. This is a quintessential Hanoi dish (though some claim that its origins are in Nam Dinh province some hundred kilometres to the south-east), and in essence is simplicity itself. There are five elements: rice noodles, beef broth, pieces of beef, fresh herbs and the proper condiments. However, as with many dishes constructed from a very few basic ingredients, the simplicity tends to be deceptive. *Pho* joins the legion of preparations that include omelette, sashimi and a martini – all seemingly so straightforward that the step between good and excellent is impossible to take by recipe alone. They require skill of a high order, experience, confidence and even art. The distinctions are fine, but to the Vietnamese *pho* gourmet, the difference is between real and false. *Pho* has stimulated endless writings, discussions, poems and proverbs. 'Oh my beloved', enthuses one, 'life without you is like *pho* without its broth.'

A Malay Muslim woman shopping in a Kuala Lumpur market. The largest concentration of Muslims outside the Middle East is in this region, which maintains Islamic dietary customs.

Wide flat noodles being cooked on a boat in a floating market near Bangkok. Noodles are a direct Chinese culinary import.

Food writer Hoang Hai gives some clues as to what to look for in *pho* (and here we are talking about *only* in Hanoi; the general gourmet opinion is that searching anywhere else for good *pho* is a waste of time). First, the restaurant, which will always be plain and unpretentious, with low tables so that diners can hover over the bowls, should specialize in *pho* only. If there is a choice, go for one that serves either beef or chicken, not both. Next, examine 'the cooking pot used for simmering the beef bones. The

137

Noodles of another kind being served at a roadside stall in Ho Chi Minh city. In culinary terms, Vietnam is the South-east Asian nation with the closest links to China.

more bones there are, the better the quality of the broth', and so 'serious *pho* restaurants use a pot about one metre tall and two metres across'. Naturally, the noodles must be steeped in boiling water only as required for each bowl and never in advance, but if you see bean sprouts or large vegetable leaves, the dish is not the real thing. In a genuine Hanoi *pho*, only spring onions and aromatic leaves 'the size of a fingernail' are allowed (yes, many Vietnamese men have long fingernails). The condiments served on the side should be just lemon, chilli, chilli sauce, pepper and pickled garlic.

The broth and the beef are where the secrets lie, in choice of cut, preparation, timing, proportion and so on. According to one *pho* restaurauteur who has been in operation for fifty years, *pho* needs, as well as the bones, five or six different cuts of beef, including flank, haunch, shoulder and thigh, each being cooked to a particular and different degree. Additions include fish sauce, ginger, cinnamon, black cardamom and leaves of *lang* mint. It is served in the way familiar to anyone who knows the other noodle dishes of Chinese origin: typically, the cook puts a handful of noodles into a small basket and plunges them into boiling water, then drains them and tips them out into the diner's bowl. On top he places pieces of beef (or chicken), chopped spring onions or shallots. Finally, he ladles the clear beef broth over everything to fill the bowl.

> Rice gruel or porridge is the standard Chinese breakfast, and while it has never and probably will never catch on in the West for this most conservative of the day's meals, it can be found in any market in the region. Although the term used in English is congee, taken from the Tamil, many of the South-east Asian names derive from the Chinese (Mandarin) *zhou*. In Burmese it is *san byouk*, in Thai *jok* and in Vietnamese *chao*. The Malays call it *bubur*, the Khmers *babar* and the Filipinos *lugao*. Prepared by cooking rice slowly and for a long time in many times its volume of water, until it becomes viscous, it is a savoury dish with variety of condiments added to it, and sometimes meat and egg. As well as a breakfast dish, it is also a kind of comfort food and frequently given to invalids. As with so many food imports, congee is given different culinary twists according to the culture it is found in. In the northern highlands of Vietnam, the colder weather makes it particularly popular, and the Tai ethnic groups of the hills have adapted it to their preferences for gathering food wild. As related by Vietnamese writer Doan Lu, there are three typical kinds of *chao* from the region: with eels, with bee pupae and with chameleon. As he remarks, 'Rice gruel by itself is delicious, but the added flavour of chameleon makes it truly wonderful, a treasure of Vietnamese cuisine.'

The ethnic minority cuisines of the highlands, from Burma to Vietnam, are in fact repositories of some ancient Chinese culinary traditions, albeit neither sophisticated nor elegant ones. Almost all of this highland region borders China, and many of the ethnic groups have spread outwards from southwest China, in particular southern Yunnan. This brings me back to my Akha village, where one of the favourite winter dishes is, as in China, dog. Meat of any kind is relatively rare, in the traditional way of rice cultures, as already mentioned, and this is usually a celebratory dish, or at least reserved for special occasions. The Akha are ardent dog fanciers, though in a different sense from canine breeders in the West, and this tale will almost certainly provoke a sense of outrage in many readers. Both sides of the argument are understandable, if incompatible. The dog lover sees the pet as almost human, with a personality and sensibilities. The dog gourmet sees the animal as an attractive source of meat, in the same category as pig or chicken, and feels no more sentimentality about it than a westerner would about cattle. Few westerners, of course, have the opportunity to see the food that they eat actually being slaughtered, and it is fortunate for a large section of the fast food industry that cattle are not thought of in the same way as cocker spaniels and fox terriers.

Nevertheless, one of my meals in the village turned out to be quite difficult, even for my reasonably strong stomach. I had been invited for breakfast to one home. This bears a little explanation. For the book I was doing with the writer Fred Grunfeld, because it was part of a series, the publishers, Time-Life, wanted to include a standard feature covering a day in the life of one person in the community. Fred told me, 'You're the photographer, so choose whoever you think will look good', and I chose a photogenic fourteen-year-old girl called Apö. The day of photography went fine, but later, it turned out that the parents thought I might like to marry her. I explained, through the translation services of one of our consultant anthropologists, Nina, that I was already married, but that carried no weight. Apö could be my second wife. Nor did the age difference seem to figure in this. I tried to let the matter disappear through inactivity, but one day shortly afterwards I was invited for breakfast *chez* Apö. Unlike the usual affairs, with many people crowded around the low dining tables, this was a select gathering: the host, his daughter, my anthropologist companion Nina and myself. This immediately presented a problem. On any of the usual special occasions, if you didn't fancy a nibble from one of the dishes, no-one minded at all – meals were communal, everyone using chopsticks, so there was no issue with what you did or did not pick to eat. Here, however, I was very much the guest of honour and under scrutiny, so refusing food was not an option. And I pretty well knew what to expect. Dog was very much in order for an occasion to promote marriage.

The meal arrived, and yes it was dog, but it was not as expected. Peering at the dish as it was brought to the low table, I soon discovered that the meat, chopped almost to a mince, was uncooked. Mixed with a few spices and vegetables, this was a kind of Asian Dog Tartare. I was already thinking wistfully of coffee, juice and scrambled eggs when Apö's father held his right hand over the meat and began to dribble on to it what looked, in the flickering light of an oil lamp, like a dark liquid. I turned to Nina and said quietly but resignedly, 'Aha, blood again.' This was perfectly normal procedure, to reserve the blood taken by slitting the animal's throat, and serve it as a side-dish. It didn't bother me much, because blood, in one way of looking at it, is pretty much uncooked gravy. But no. 'It's worse than that, I'm afraid', replied Nina, 'The blood is already in those small bowls on the table. *That* is the dog's bile.'

'And', she added, 'you're on your own!' With that, she deftly made the kind of polite excuse that only fluency in the language permits, and left me to it. The taste sensations of the next several minutes were quite varied, and funnily enough the bile was not the worst part. It actually gave an interesting accent to the dish, in a bitter, back-of-the-throat kind of way. On later trips, to Laos and north-east Thailand, I found that bile (of water buffalo) was quite commonly sold in meat markets, and even, in country towns like Buriram, appeared as a standard condiment on a restaurant table. Not at all bad if you didn't think about it deeply.

Not only was China a huge influence on the cuisines of the region, but it was also a market for certain foodstuffs unique to South-east Asia. None is stranger than the trade in the world's most valuable food – edible bird's nests. Indeed, this is arguably the oddest food of importance anywhere in the world, for not only is it the most expensive food by weight, but it is one of the most impractical. At the time that I became professionally interested, in the 1980s, the retail price for the finest quality nests was the same as that of gold, yet the nutritive value is hardly worth mentioning. This has not deterred the Chinese for centuries from believing in its aphrodisiac and health-giving properties (it is supposed to improve skin tone, balance *qi* and reinforce the immune system). It does certainly have a gelatinous texture, which you could, if feeling generous, call velvety, and this gives it originality in the all-important 'mouth-feel' that is admired in Chinese cuisines. Of the three species of swiftlet, it is the Brown-rumped (Edible Nest) Swiftlet, *Aerodramus fuciphagus*, that produces the 'white gold' for the Chinese trade. It creates its nests from pure dried saliva, and nests high, generally above 200 feet and often at 500–600 feet, choosing the most inaccessible parts of caves on the most remote islands.

A simple plastic sign in Bangkok's Chinatown reads 'Bird's Nests' in both Thai script and Chinese characters.

The trade in edible nests probably began with the Chinese admiral Zheng He's expeditions to these southern waters in the 15th century, and possibly even earlier, in the T'ang Dynasty (AD 618–907). As to why, there are no completely logical reasons, as I was about to find out.

The story came to me courtesy of the *Smithsonian* magazine. Caroline Despard, the Picture Editor, had sent me the typescript, from a well-known and respected food writer, Roy Andries de Groot. It was a fabulous tale, of a thoroughly improbable foodstuff that most people had heard of or seen in passing while flicking through the menu in higher-class Chinese restaurants, yet the details of which were a mystery. As de Groot put it, 'From remote islands in the South China Sea and the Indian Ocean they are distributed, in an atmosphere of secrecy like that of the drug trade, by operatives who sometimes have high connections and invariably make equally high profits.' The story developed into a saga and became, without a doubt, the most intriguing food investigation I ever did.

On the trail of the nests, I started in Bangkok at the end of September. My first visit is to the Tourist Authority of Thailand, to meet Khun Manoon, the Director of Marketing. He makes a call to one of the major concessionaries, the Laem Tong Company. I can see an expression of surprise cross his face partway through the conversation. When he finally puts the phone down, he has unwelcome news; there are no birds at this season! Added to this is the fact that this year the monsoon is still raging in the south, around Chumphon and Phang Nga, where the collecting

Freshly scrubbed valuable white nests wait for packing in the offices of the Laem Tong Company in Bangkok.

takes place. This clearly upsets my plans, but as I'm here anyway I might as well drive down to the south and make a reconnaissance. Writing this now, I'm struck by how much we now take for granted internet information searches, cellphones and efficient telecommunications. This was the early 1980s, not exactly distant history, but doing this kind of undocumented research usually meant groundwork.

So, with my driver Pichai, I headed off in the rain, down the long isthmus of Kra that leads eventually to Malaysia. As we near the west coast and the Andaman Sea, we see for the first time the limestone formations that give the south its most spectacular and characteristic scenery. Limestone in the tropics weathers strangely, helped by a simple chemical reaction that I learned in school chemistry class. Rainwater, already slightly acidic, combines with carbon dioxide in the atmosphere to form the mild carbonic acid, which can slowly dissolve some limestones (which are calcium carbonate). So, $CaCO_3$ (calcium carbonate) + CO_2 (carbon dioxide) + $H2O$ (water) —> $Ca++$ (calcium ion) + $2HCO_3$ (bicarbonate). The result is sheer cliffs that help to create steep and isolated sugar-loaf hills, and even slim, tall pillars, festooned with forest

143

and creepers. Moreover, the interiors of these hills and mountains are frequently riddled with caves as water slowly percolates through cracks and gently dissolves the rock. Even the exterior cliffs are raggedly decorated with oddly-shaped dewlaps and fins of limestone, in pendulous fringes.

The island with reputedly the largest caves inhabited by the swiftlets, is Koh Phi Phi, some 40 kilometres east of Phuket, and it seems that there is also some basic accommodation. Many years have passed since I stood on the shore at Rawai Beach looking out towards the small and hazy outline of the island, and in that time Koh Phi Phi has gone from being remote and largely unvisited to becoming an unfortunate symbol of over-exploitation and despoliation. Its rare and fragile beauty was quickly seized upon by local tour operators, and its fate was sealed when it was chosen as the location for the Hollywood movie *The Beach* with Leonardo diCaprio. Thai environmental activists took this opportunity to protest the filming, which involved re-landscaping one of the beaches, while the film-makers must have wondered what hit them, given that they were having to clean up an already garbage-infested environment.

But long before this, in 1983, it was just very difficult to reach, and there were no boat services from Phuket. Better, we were told by the local T.A.T. office, to go to the other side of the Andaman Sea to Krabi, and sail from there. The boatman who takes us snorkelling says that we could reach the island in about three hours, but I'm not sure how much I would like to be out there when an afternoon storm blows up.

The next day we drive north to Phang Nga, the small town at the head of Phang Nga Bay, dotted with towering sugar-loaf islands. At a small landing stage we negotiate a price for a long-boat, and set off to explore. The boatman follows a muddy creek for about a mile to where this joins a shallow river flowing between low, swampy banks. After two more miles winding through the swamp we are in open water, and directly ahead of us is the first of the sheer limestone islands jutting out from the bay.

The boatman insists that he knows some small caves where the swiftlets nest, and takes us first to one that cuts right through a great slab of cliff, making a short natural tunnel with a low roof hung with stalactites. It looks rather exposed for a nest site to me, but he claims that nests are collected here. His judgement seems vindicated at the next cave, on one of a pair of tiny islets a mile away. Here we land, painfully as the rock is covered with small, sharp oyster shells, and wade inside a low entrance to a small tidal cave. Its walls are slimy and the floor is a great thickness of glutinous, malodorous mud, which makes for a thoroughly unpleasant experience as we try to balance, sinking in it to our knees. Overhead, roughly lashed bamboo scaffolding is a clear sign that some collecting goes on, or at least did. Right now, however, all is silent except for the lapping of the waves and the gurgling of the mud under our feet; no birds, and of course, no nests. Our boatman admits, grinning, to doing a little poaching here, which I later learn is far from healthy.

From Phang Nga we drive south towards Krabi, a fishing port and administrative centre. Here we eventually find a couple of local businessmen who are just starting to run tours to Koh Phi Phi. They confirm that the birds will not start to return until the end of January, and that the nests are collected by about a half-dozen local fishermen who live on the island, under contract to whoever the license-holders are at the time.

Five months later, almost to the day, we are back. Meanwhile, in Bangkok, Khun Manoon of the T.A.T. has succeeded in getting a letter from the elusive Laem Tong Company allowing me to photograph the processing stages of their bird's nest operation. I telephone Khun Somsak in Krabi, and all still seems well. He sounds very relaxed about the whole matter, and while he and his partners have lost the concession to some people in Phuket, he still says that for me there is 'no problem', a phrase that I always enjoy hearing in Thai, even when people are just being polite.

Early on a Saturday morning we join about twenty other Thai day-trippers on a converted fishing boat. Somsak and his cousin Suwat are with us, checking up on their thatched bungalows, and we leave a couple of hours after sunrise, the sea as calm as a lake. It takes two and a half hours to cross the 50 miles to the small group of islands, and the boat enters the broad bay of the main island, Phi Phi Don, and ties up at the wooden jetty by the fishing hamlet. To the south, a few miles away, rises the smaller island with the cave, Phi Phi Lae, its cliffs sheer and jagged. After a short stop, the boat continues there, mooring by the cave entrance. Poles are wedged into all kinds of crevices and there is not a rope in sight. The entire web of scaffolding looks organic. In fact, much of the scaffolding is there only by grace of existing natural roots and lianas that gave the original nest

collectors something to build on. Since then, new scaffolding is installed each year, the old being left to bleach and rot. At other parts of the cliff faces we can see fragments of broken scaffolding high up on the sheer rock; they have been abandoned for too long and there is now no way of ever reaching them again.

After scrambling over the rocks to enter the cave, I look around. It seems surprisingly bright, as the broad entrance illuminates most of the floor area of packed earth as far as the opposite wall, about 200 feet away. A slim, dark-skinned muscular man in his thirties approaches. Somsak introduces me to Haem, from the fishing village. He is nominally in charge of collecting. He, his father, brother and other relations, all Muslim fishermen, have been doing this for some forty years, an unusual family profession started by the father, who is now around sixty (people hereabouts are characteristically vague about time, dates and ages). According to Haem, the cave has been worked for nests for five or six hundred years, though this may be part of the vagueness and I doubt that there are records.

More bamboo scaffolding, sprouting like giant weeds from the ground, rises to odd holes and tunnels, with a large clump

The nest-collecting family from Koh Phi Phi sail towards the cave on the smaller of the two islands shortly after sunrise.

reaching up into the main shaft from the centre, close to a little shrine. I peer up, shading my eyes from the daylight streaming horizontally through the entrance. The dimensions are awesome; lianas hang some 200 feet from the darkness above. I ask Haem when he and his family will start work. 'There are already four men up there', he replies. I don't see how, as I've just been looking, but Haem points out that what I thought was the ceiling is in fact just the base of the main shaft, which rises 600 feet. I look back up and wait for my eyes to adjust better to the dark. There, much, much higher and only faintly visible, is a delicate lattice of bamboo. Beyond that, absolute darkness. Even from here, it needs little imagination to feel intense vertigo, and I have an unpleasant feeling in my gut when I try and think of going up there. The idea of climbing that creaking bamboo (let alone building it) with only a hand torch and candle, in bare feet and among slippery limestone rocks, is not one I care to contemplate. As far as I can tell, the entire cave is shaped like the cast of a giant *stupa*, or an elongated bell, dark, damp and echoing. Galleries and tunnels lead off from this basic shape, some of them, Haem says, leading to exits elsewhere on the island.

Haem's father squats on the floor of Payanak cave, displaying prime nests just collected from the heights above.

Nesting here are the three species of swiftlet, including the Brown-rumped Swiftlet that makes the prized white nest. The nest is built up as the bird weaves its head to and from, drawing the spaghetti-like strands of whitish saliva from side to side. The result is a thin, shell-like cup of great architectural delicacy. The other species of birds build black nests, full of feathers and twigs, which are consequently much less valuable. However, there is a height problem. The white nests are mainly built much higher than the black, above 200 feet at least. How strange that these birds have done everything imaginable to keep their eggs and brood safe from predators, only to find that for the most illogical of reasons, men find it worthwhile going to such extreme lengths to search them out.

The collecting season has just started, although the majority of the birds will be nesting next month. According to Haem, the birds do *not* migrate as I had thought; they are here the whole year round. Nest-building begins at the end of February, and they are collected for a few days. The birds are then allowed to build a second and a third time before they are finally left alone (this at the end of April). The hatchlings then stay in their costly nests for about two months until finally, in August, when all the young have left, Haem and his family make a final collection. When they are not collecting nests they fish, although about four months of the year are taken up with collecting bamboo and lianas and repairing and extending the scaffolding.

Two days later, at sunrise, we leave the fishing hamlet with Haem, his father, brother and another man (armed with a revolver, he is the guard). The sight of the revolver reminds me that there are supposed to be murky and dangerous elements to this business. In fact, I've been extraordinarily lucky to reach this point of access to the nest collection. At US$300 per ounce for

The three-pronged tool for prising the nests off the wall.

the best quality, yet found on remote islands, the nests are a commodity needing serious protection. Of course the Laem Tong Company didn't want photographers and writers wandering around. They were never under ordinary circumstances going to give permission. De Groot, the writer, had learned something of this in Hong Kong, when he finally got to meet one of the Chinese license holders. He had asked about the barbed wire samples in the office, and was told this was just a part of the protection service offered to contractors. And, the man added, 'every time we move a shipment . . . we face the danger of hijacking.' Much later – this year in fact – I met another photographer, Eric Valli, who had shot the caves after me, for *National Geographic.* We compared notes. He had had all kinds of difficult dealings with the Chinese concessionaries. At one of the islands, where the guards had m-16s, he asked them about poachers. 'Oh', they said, 'there's no problem with them. We killed them all.'

At Payanak Cave, Haem has kindly set aside the entire day for me to shoot. He moves around the rocks and scaffolding with graceful ease, but I find it hot, dirty and strenuous. We start with the main cluster of bamboo rising from the centre of the cave, me first to photograph Haem climbing up. Actually, I feel like Jack on the Beanstalk, and even at the miserable height of about 60 feet I feel distinctly insecure on the creaking, sagging poles. Freeing one hand to hold and focus the camera makes me feel even more exposed.

I watch his feet as he climbs up. Splayed and powerful, they can grip a liana between the first and second toes, *and* support his full weight like this. At times they look like a second pair of hands. He uses a special collecting tool, three-pronged and made of iron, that fits into the hand or else is lashed to the end of a long bamboo pole. One of the chisel-bladed prongs is longer than the other two, and this is used to prise the nest off the wall from underneath. The other two prongs then form a support for the delicate nest as it is lifted away. The only other piece of equipment, apart from a torch and candles, is a cloth bag tied to the waist for storing the gathered nests. I watch his feet as he climbs up. Splayed and powerful, they can grip a liana between the first and second toes, *and* support his full weight like this. At times they look like a second pair of hands. He uses a special collecting tool, three-pronged and made of iron, that fits into the hand or else is lashed to the end of a long bamboo pole. One of the chisel-bladed prongs is longer than the other two, and this is used to prise the nest off the wall from underneath. The other two prongs then form a support for the delicate nest as it is lifted away. The only other piece of equipment, apart from a torch and candles, is a cloth bag tied to the waist for storing the gathered nests.

After a few days we leave, my one regret being that I have no close views of the elusive swiftlet. There seem not to be so many, and they nest very high, beyond my climbing abilities. Also, they leave the cave during daylight hours, returning in the evening, which poses further problems of lighting, not to mention getting down in pitch darkness. I have to find another way.

Two months later, I'm in Hong Kong, following the writer's footsteps. These, however, seem to lead down different alleyways from mine. There is a particular dish in the story that features snake venom in a special form of the soup – 'Nests of Sea Swallows with Venomous Snake and Chrysanthemum Petals with Lemon Grass and Lotus Petals in Soup'. A mouthful in every sense, and there is a scene in which an old Chinese gentleman shuffles in, with a leather bag hanging from his wrist. As he reaches the soup tureen, the head of a snake darts out from the bag. 'With a quick motion, the old man grasped the snake behind the head and, deftly squeezing, appeared to spritz into the soup just a drop or two of the venom.' Not one of my contacts in Hong Kong has heard of such a thing, and even when we set up an interview with the owner of a snake shop, the helpful owner is nonplussed. He says that only the meat is eaten, and the gall bladder used in medicine. I suppose he should know. Ultimately, I have to give up on what I imagine would be an interesting photograph and a unique dining experience.

Returning to Bangkok, I find that I am now clear to photograph at the Laem Tong offices, where teams of girls squat on a cloth-covered floor cleaning nests with small hand-brushes, packing them into boxes. Here also I learn that this company now has the new concession for, guess where – Koh Phi Phi! I silently congratulate myself for having made my arrangements through the local Thais. Laem Tong might well have stopped me going. In any case, I still have the practical matter of getting close to the nesting birds. I managed on my last visit to Washington to persuade the magazine that the story was worth a trip to Borneo, where de Groot visited the Gomanton Caves. One thing that makes me optimistic is that his description suggested a far more sophisticated, even hi-tech, operation than I've so far seen.

Bird's nest soup as a dessert, sweetened and served with melon balls, in a Hong Kong restaurant. The meticulously carved water melon, its interior scooped out to act as a container for presenting the soup, hints that this is not a cheap dish to order.

150

He writes of steel scaffolding and, which sounds wonderful, steel hawser trapezes on which collectors swing out hundreds of feet in the air to snatch the most inaccessible nests with long special tongs. It sounds like the set of an early James Bond movie, with the arch-villain's operations centre concealed in a remote cave. Come to think of it, Christopher Lee's lair in *The Man with the Golden Gun* was exactly in Phang Nga Bay.

We land in Kota Kinabalu, the capital of Sabah, and I make contact with Thomas Willie, from Hornbill Tours. He seems to have everything under control, including permissions and transport. The more we talk, however, the less confident I become in de Groot's information. Willie insists that the Gomanton Caves are absolutely prohibited to foreigners, and that he knows of no-one else in a number of years who has visited, at least not through his office. And then, something I had not even thought to ask, he knows nothing of the writer. Curiouser and curiouser.

Five days later we are on the flight to Sandakan, on the north-east coast of Borneo, the town nearest the caves. The next morning we meet Dr Patrick Andau, Game Warden at the Forestry Department, in the grandest offices in town. Fittingly so, as the department's major business is lumber, contributing three-quarters of Sabah's GNP. We thought, back in Bangkok, that collecting would start three days from now, but Patrick says this was probably invented by Thomas Willie, as they are never that precise, and in any case the ranger at the caves, Ismail, has the final say. There are still birds on the nests, which is good for me, but generally, Patrick says, they like to wait until 95 per cent of them are empty before they start collecting. This sounds way too precise to me, and it does turn out to be more casual.

We take Patrick's four-wheel drive and set off down the pitted road west that eventually leads to Kota Kinabalu. After an hour we turn left and south along an unmade forest road, past cacao and oil palm plantations. Gradually these die out and we are in primary forest. The road turns, and turns again, and finally, after three hours, there is a rutted track that leads to the mountain that holds the caves. Our first sign of our destination is an enormous number of swiftlets, darting in front of us over the track and through the trees in pursuit of insects. At the camp, a Canadian ornithologist, Charles Francis, greets us and after we unload equipment and baggage, we follow him down the path towards the entrance. This is only a hundred yards long, but so completely infested with mosquitoes, of a daytime variety, that we arrive heavily bitten.

Fortunately, the mosquitoes do not relish the cave, and it is a welcome relief to step inside. The entrance is broad and high, about 100 by 50 feet, and the interior is huge, some 300 feet high and more than 500 feet deep. Better still from my point of view, there are two huge shafts leading up from the roof of the cave, and light streams down from them. Here at last, I can see the scale of one of these vast interiors in one glance. Free from mosquitoes, we smile and relax, but not for long.

As my eyes adjust to the dimness, I can see the ground stretching ahead in what looks, and feels, like large soft mounds of loose soil. It is not. This is a thick carpet of guano – a mixture of bird and bat droppings – that gives off an appallingly strong ammoniac smell. How deep it is I can only guess, and while no doubt compacted at lower levels, on the surface it is spongy and moist. I think inappropriately of Black Forest gateau as I sink up to my calves as I wade forward. Not only this, but in the light from the entrance, the dark brown mass is flecked attractively with gold specks that glitter and seem to move. A closer look reveals that they are indeed moving – a sea of predatory carnivorous cockroaches burrowing through the guano and patrolling the surface for anything that falls. I can feel them tickling my feet, or is that nibbling?

A chick or injured adult that falls from the nest stands no chance down here; if the fall from more than 200 feet hasn't been fatal, they soon die under the onslaught of these golden-backed roaches, which emerge from the shiny moist ground and attack immediately. Any seething ball of cockroaches invariably conceals a chick. I even see them fighting to get into one of the tiny broken eggs that litter the floor like mushroom caps. This is not all that the swiftlets have to contend with, as a commotion high up near an open shaft turns out to be hordes of swiftlets taking to their wings as a pair of white helmeted hornbills swoop in on a raid.

But something is missing. To my surprise (yet why, after all this travelling around, should I be surprised?), there is no steel scaffolding and none of the paraphernalia, such as trapezes, described in such detail. I ask Charles, and several of the collectors, and all think it very peculiar. No-one knows of such a system, or can think of any reason why it should exist. Here, as in any other cave, local materials from the forest are used, and in Gomanton these are principally rattan and bamboo. What I'd been expecting to photograph now turns out to be a piece of fiction.

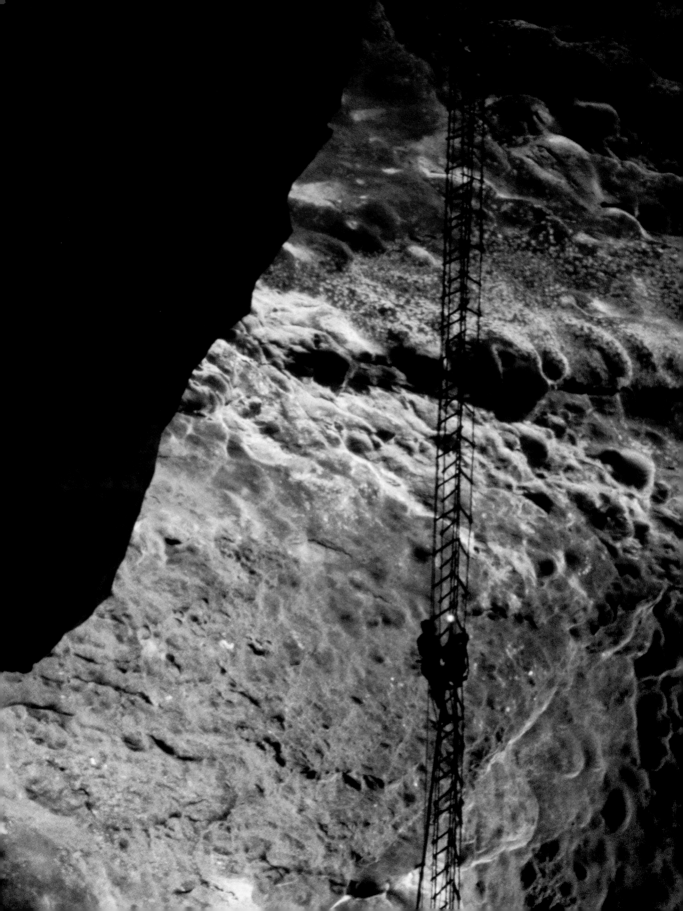

And the odd thing is that the cave and the methods of collection are completely fascinating in their own way, without this mechanistic nonsense. Suspended from the larger of the two shafts that penetrate the roof of the cave, close to the centre, is a ladder woven from rattan, flexible like rope. About 250 feet of this is visible, hanging right to the ground. The top must be tied somewhere higher up the shaft. These ladders, called *gugulog*, are the standard climbing aid, and other, shorter ones hang around the cave, tied to wooden staves wedged tightly into crevices in the roof. It's hard to imagine how the first men to attach these were able to climb there unaided. For every climber, there are between a few and several ground crew, who pull and manoeuvre the *gugulog* to help the collector into position. The other climbing structure is a rigid, bamboo ladder known as a *patau*. For low sites, short *patau* may simply be leaned against a wall, but most are used vertically, with four guy ropes to hold it steady. These are attached to hoops around the ladder so that they don't interfere with the climbing.

The next day we investigate the upper cave, which has even more of the Brown-rumped Swiftlets. Access to this, however, is only from above. On the top of the mountain is an opening, like a well, and this drops 500 feet to the floor of Himut Puteh, or 'White Cave'. A thickly woven rattan ladder protrudes and is secured to rocks and trees; I'm told it takes an experienced climber an hour to descend, and that his immediate difficulty is that the ladder hangs down in a curve, which has the collector leaning backwards as he begins his descent into the darkness. Better him than me. A little lower down the mountain another shaft enters from the side. We rest here in the shade, a relief from the stifling heat of the forest, and then edge forward for a better view. The rock floor disconcertingly slopes down at a steadily increasing angle, so that there is no lip, and I have to decide for myself at which point I might start to slide down. The darkness below is absolute. Charles takes a pebble and tosses it forward, and we wait for the impact. And wait. I count seven seconds before we hear a dull echo from below. From a limestone projection at the right-hand edge of the shaft, a chain hangs several feet, and from here we have a good view of clusters of white nests, about 20 feet across from us on the vertical wall.

For Charles, who has to check sample nests of each species, this is more than a little dangerous. He climbs down the chain a few feet and then edges along the vertical wall on a thick but

In the Gomanton caves in Sabah, Borneo, one of the collectors climbs a 500-foot rattan rope ladder to reach the upper walls.

narrow mat of bamboo and rattan. If it were to give way, there's nothing below for at least seven seconds! There are only a few birds on their nests – the late layers – and I will have to come out to this ledge tonight when the others return from their day's feeding.

Ismail the ranger brings me back just before sunset to this high shaft facing the white nests. Armed with the old-fashioned but powerful flash bulbs, and the camera and long lens set up as far down the sloping ledge as seems safe, we wait. At dusk, the birds begin to swoop into the shaft, over our heads and around us, their chirruping echoing around the shaft. In fact, as I learned from Charles, they use echo-location, in much the same way as do the bats. The numbers increase, and they put on fancy displays of aerobatics, pulling over and down like old-fashioned fighter pilots doing wing-overs and diving turns, rattling their echo-locating calls to find their way in the hollow darkness. Within an hour, the nests are full, and I start shooting, until I exhaust my supply of bulbs. Using flashlights to find our

Brown-rumped, edible-nest swiftlets nesting at 500 feet up a sheer wall of the Gomanton caves. The nests, woven purely from the birds' saliva, adhere to the surface of the rock. Perched with my camera and tripod on a rock surface sloping down to the abyss between us, this was one of my least favourite moments.

way out, we reach the side of the mountain just as a storm erupts, flashes of lighting taking up where my own ended.

When I next arrived in Washington, the story complete, I met Caroline, only to find a tragic end to the whole affair. 'I have some terrible news about the Bird's Nest Soup story', she began. 'The writer just shot himself'.

I was stunned. For one horrified yet ludicrous moment, I wondered whether my spilling the beans on the fictitious parts of the story had had anything to do with it. 'Why?' I asked Caroline, 'What on earth happened?' She told me that it went back a long time, to the Second World War, when he had been injured during the Blitz in London.

'That's when he started to go blind, and I think he never got used to it'.

'Blind?' I asked, incredulously.

'Didn't I tell you?', she asked. 'I thought you knew'.

I never guessed. And was someone with him in those huge caves in Borneo, someone who embellished the sight? Though it was wonderful and unpleasant enough without being added to. Or had he never gone? I would never find out.

Well, that was just a part, albeit an extreme part, of the huge Chinese interaction with the food of South-east Asia. The total effect of all these external influences, not just China but also India, the Arab world and Europe, has been to create a complex interweaving of cuisines. Defining them is problematic, because there are so many overlapping layers of immigration and culture. If we include the prehistory of the region, the term indigenous becomes almost meaningless. Who were the original inhabitants of, say, Thailand? Were they the Mon, who predated the Tai who moved down from what is now south-western China in the twelfth and thirteenth centuries? Or, in the north, for example, other Austro-Asiatic groups such as the Lawa, who pre-dated the Mon, or hunter-gatherers like the Mlabri? Research into the prehistory of the region is uneven and fragmentary, but indicates early migrations from the east and south – Melanesia, Polynesia, Australia. During the historical period, the major waves of migration were from the north, mainly China. Other movements on different scales were from southern India, which had a great religious and cultural influence on what is now Cambodia, from where Khmer rule fanned out across the mainland, and from the Middle East, which brought Islam through Arab traders. Western colonialism had a profound effect, in translocating Indians into Burma and Malaysia, and easing Chinese settlement into the cities.

One of the results of this complex historical pattern of settlement is that present national boundaries may not be the most accurate way of subdividing the cuisines of South-east Asia. They do, of course, exert a powerful influence, but less than many people imagine. In general, it is easier to point to the similarities across borders than to the differences. How, for example, would you distinguish between the cooking of peninsular Malaysia and that of western Indonesia? An unfair question (answer: not by much), perhaps, because the traditional trading status of both areas has helped them both to accumulate roughly the same ethnic mix – Malay, Indian, Chinese, with Islam superimposed – and they share most of the same dishes. But consider northern and

north-western Thailand, adjacent to the Shan states of Burma. A dish like *gaeng hang lay* is more or less identical on either side of the national border, and in both countries carries a distinct flavour from the dishes at the national heart – Bangkok or Rangoon. Or the food of the southern Philippines, which in its use of coconut milk, aromatic spices and chillies shows far more affinity to the the rest of South-east Asia than it does to the cuisine in the north. Here, the Ilocano diet favours boiled and steamed vegetables and seasonal foods flavoured strongly with fermented fish paste, while the Igorots of the Luzon Cordillera prefer roasted meats.

We've seen much of what ties the countries of South-east Asia together in culinary unity. Rice as the central dish, many aromatic spices, fermentation products, especially from fish, forest products and sparse amounts of meat. But what divides them? This is not a question that tends to exercise South-east Asian cooks too much, not least because relatively few study the cuisines of their neighbours. My friend Vatch, who has owned a number of successful restaurants in England and in Thailand, and on whose books I've worked as photographer, recounted in one of them exploring the food of Burma. At the home of a Burmese friend, a businesswoman, he finds that dinner at home is a mixture of what looks like Indian and Chinese dishes, and asks if this is 'real' Burmese food. This provokes laughter and the enigmatic response 'You could say that while there are some Indian flavours, they are used in ways much closer to Chinese techniques.'

'So what is real Burmese food?' Vatch asks.

'Ah', says one neighbour, 'Real Burmese food is what real Burmese eat. This is Rangoon, you'll have to look elsewhere.' He does, and finds dishes specific to the regions he visits, and some specific ingredients, like turmeric, but more than that is a sense of the unity of mainland South-east Asian cuisine. In a village near Mandalay, 'I felt very much at home. If this was "real" Burmese food, it was clearly part of that central South-east Asian tradition that I had seen all through my travels.' There are certain identifiable dishes that are found only in Burma, but many more hints of Thailand, of India, of China, and a coherent summation of Burmese cuisine is never forthcoming.

Ultimately, many of the differences, maybe even most of the differences, are across a smaller scale than countries. And you can keep on going down in scale, to a valley, a town, a stretch of coastline. The idea of a national cuisine has a ring of artificiality

Gaeng hang lay, a Shan dish that has entered northern Thai cuisine, featuring pork and tamarind.

159

to it, something imposed at times by politics, more recently by marketing. We all like Thai food! We know what Thai food is – *tom yam gung* and half a dozen other dishes! This kind of idea, all too common, just masks the incredible diversity of food. I stayed a night with a friend and his fiancée at her parents' home in Phayao in northern Thailand. Among the home-cooked dishes that evening was a *laab* made with the bark of a tree found in the local forest. I couldn't get enough of a description to be able to identify it, and I never will. Nor does it matter, because this dish is made just there, maybe only by a few households. Cooking that has not had a marketing makeover is like that. It is different little by little, mile by mile. Like ethnicity, the cuisines of these countries merge and intertwine.

Nevertheless, I'll attempt a kind of summary, with the warning that it hinges on a few characteristic dishes and ingredients. To begin in the west, the cuisine of Burma is noted for an exceptionally wide range of flavours mixed together, a heavy use of herbs and vegetables, and of course an especial fascination with shrimp and fish paste (possibly even more so than in neighbouring countries). Indian influences are felt except in the eastern

Wedding guests in a small town on the Irrawady eat *mohinga*, a noodle soup made with fish, arguably the Burmese national dish.

and north-eastern hills of Shan and Kachin states, and appear not only as outright Indian imports such as *chapatis* and *biryanis*, but also in the many rich curry sauces, liberal addition of pickles, and the practice of frying in oil (sesame and peanut, mainly). The unofficial national dish is *mohinga* – rice noodles in a fish broth – and other very Burmese dishes include *lahpet thouk*, a Shan salad of pickled tea leaves, served with fried peas, peanuts and garlic, toasted sesame, fresh garlic, tomato, green chilli, crushed dried shrimps and preserved ginger and dressed with peanut oil, fish sauce and lime; also *oun no hkauk swè*, a curried chicken with wheat noodles in a coconut milk broth, similar to the Malaysian *laksa* and Chiang Mai's *khao soi*. Notably, the Burmese traditionally drink nothing with the meal, not even water, but light soups are usually served. Scott, already quoted on the subject of the powerful Burmese shrimp and fish paste, described a family meal:

> The staple article of food is plain boiled rice, which is piled up in a heap on a huge platter, round about which the household arrange themselves, sitting, like pit-men, on

Poo ja, meaning 'dear crab', a Thai dish in which shredded crabmeat and minced pork are mixed together, a variety of spices added, the mixture is returned to the shell and then steamed.

As in most South-east Asian countries, Thailand has a tradition of street food, and itinerant food-sellers patrol the city with their panniers, often carrying small stools for customers.

their heels. The curry which is taken with it is placed in little bowls, and each one of the party has his own plate, and helps himself. Knives are unnecessary; spoons and forks and celestial chopsticks are unknown . . . Ordinarily, the curry consists of a soup, or thin concoction of vegetables, in which chillies and onions figure largely. The other ingredients are very various. Young shoots of bamboo are very delicate in their flavour, if not overpowered by too much garlic. Wild asparagus, the succulent stems of a number of aquatic plants and fleshy arums are constantly used, and may be seen exposed for sale in every bazaar. Tamarind leaves and those of the mango-tree are used by the very poor. The former have a somewhat acrid taste, the latter are curiously aromatic. Along with the curry, which has always a large amount of oil and salt in it, there are a variety of condiments, notably the strongly-flavoured *nga-pi*, without which no Burman would consider his meal complete.

Thai cooking, which has become the best known of South-east Asian cuisines in the West, features above all a vigorous counter-balancing of two or three of the major flavour groups, with a pronounced use of chillies, fish sauce and lemon grass. The elongated shape of the country helps to create some pronounced regional differences, as the cooking becomes more Laotian in the north and north-east, more Malay and Muslim in

Another Thai favourite, *gaeng kiew waan*, ('sweet green curry'), whch can be made with almost any meat, coconut milk and small aubergines.

163

the south. Famous Thai dishes include *tom yam*, a hot and sour soup with meat or seafood (such as *tom yam gung* with shrimp), a range of colour-specific curries such as *gaeng phet* (red), *gaeng khiew waan* (green) and *gaeng massaman* (yellow, often with beef), many noodle dishes such as *pad thai, rad na* and *khanom cheen nam ya*, and a variety of relishes and dips known collectively as *nam prik*, based around chillies and eaten with raw and blanched vegetables. Also very Thai are the wide range of sweets, based on rice flour, palm sugar and coconut.

Yet all of this varies regionally. In the north of the country, around Chiang Mai and its adjacent valleys, the cooking has strong affinities with the neighbouring Burmese Shan States. Carl Bock,

A relatively simple dish by Thai standards, charcoal-grilled seafood served with a dip of lime juice spiced with chopped garlic, ginger and chilies, at one of Bangkok's many riverside restaurants.

A northern Thai family meal in a simple household, with sticky rice, fresh leaves and *laab*, the spicy chopped meat dish made here from water buffalo.

the nineteenth century Norwegian explorer and naturalist, described a meal in Chiang Mai in 1884:

> They sit in a circle on the floor, or on mats, with a lacquer or brazen tray before them, on which were placed a number of saucers or small bowls containing dried or boiled fish, bits of buffalo-meat stewed, a salted egg, or a piece of the favourite pork: all these meats are invariably served with rice and curry. For vegetables they eat stewed bamboo shoots – not at all a bad substitute for asparagus – beans, plantains, tamarinds, and powdered capsicums. Pervading everything is the inevitable fishy flavour, which, like the

Vegetables including carrot, cucumber and red cabbage, carved in the Thai Palace style.

garlic among the Spaniards, is never absent. This is imparted by adding to the dishes a small quantity of rotten fish – the *ngapee* of the Burmese – the preparation of which is as much an art among the Laosians and Siamese, Burmese and Malay, as the anxious endeavour on the part of the European housewife to keep her fish fresh. The rice, simply boiled or steamed, is served separately to each person in a small basket . . . from the basket of dry rice a small quantity is taken with the fingers and rolled between the hands into a ball, which is then dipped into one or more of the various curries and flavouring dishes.

Bock is clearly describing sticky rice, which suggests that he did not pay too much attention to the goings on in the kitchen, as this is always steamed, never boiled.

Thailand's long-surviving aristocracy and royalty are responsible for a refined 'palace' cuisine, with an emphasis on subtle combinations and flavours and on presentation. Notwithstanding the love of King Chulalongkorn, the country's reforming nineteenth-century monarch, for simple farmer's food (which he liked

166

to cook for himself in the grounds of Dusit Palace in Bangkok), this royal cuisine stands apart from the more robust cooking of the countryside and the common people. One of its best known features is the intricate carving of vegetables and fruit into the form of flowers and other shapes. Indeed, there remains a royal vegetable carver with accommodation inside the Grand Palace.

Further east from here, although this is not a direct journey that most people make, is the part of the country that borders Laos. Here in Issaan, the north-eastern region of Thailand inhabited by mainly Lao-speaking people, favourite dishes include *som tam*, a pounded salad featuring slivers of young papaya, and *laab*, chopped spicy meat. This area of the Khorat plateau has many close ties with Laos, on the opposite, northern bank of the Mekong. Here, fresh herbs, leaves and raw vegetables are served in great abundance, and a good deal of grilling. *Padek*, which we sniffed in passing in chapter Two, is a recurring signature, chillies are used liberally, and everything is eaten, as in north-eastern Thailand, with sticky rice. There is a preference for bitter, herbal and astringent flavors, including mint, dill and galangal, and no tradition of sweet with savoury, unlike Thailand. There is a

The Royal vegetable carver at work at his accommodation inside the Grand Palace, Bangkok.

The Mekong River at Vientiane, a major food source for Laotians.

saying in Lao cuisine, *van pen lom; khom pen ya*, which translates as, 'sweet makes you dizzy; bitter makes you healthy'. *Or lam* is a famous green vegetable stew in the style of the old capital, Luang Prabang, while *tam mak houng* is the Laotian term for *som tam*. The unofficial national dish is *laab*, made from a variety of meats (water buffalo, village chicken, duck) and river fish.

I'll make a diversion here to investigate *laab* in some more depth, because, setting dog aside (please), it is a firm favourite of mine. *Laab* is indeed a standard dish throughout not only Laos, but also the seven northern provinces of Thailand, still sometimes referred to by their old name as Lanna, and the Thai north-east. The recipe here is from Chiang Mai, and is for a buffalo meat *laab*. The differences between northern and north-eastern *laab* are mainly that in Lanna ground roasted rice is absent, there is a preference for red meat, very finely chopped,

168

The ancient Royal capital of Luang Phrabang, where Lao cuisine developed in its most refined and intense form.

overleaf:
Four representative Lao dishes (clockwise from top left): *or lam nok kho* (quail stew with vegetables), *mok kheuang nai kai* (mashed chicken giblets steamed in banana leaf packets), *hoy khong* (steamed apple snails), *jaew mak len* (spicy dip made with tomatoes).

Laab, chopped meat spiced and with chillies, has spread in popularity from its origins in Laos into north and north-eastern Thailand. It is accompanied by sticky rice and raw or parboiled vegetables and leaves.

and there are more bitter flavours, not just from forest leaves and herbs but also from bile, an under-rated condiment in the West as mentioned earlier. There is also, as I remembered from my memorable Akha breakfast, a particular liking for raw meat, which Lanna shares with Laos rather than Issaan.

Moving south and east, we find that Cambodian cuisine is similar in many respects to Thai, though rather plainer, more country-style and not as spicy. Or rather, not spicy through

169

the heavy Thai and Lao use of chillies, but through the more old-fashioned way of adding pungency, relying on pepper, salt and lime juice. More than most South-east Asian countries, Cambodian cooking suffers from being described in terms of how it compares with that of its neighbours. *Banh chiao* and *naem* become the Cambodian versions of the Vietnamese *bánh xeo* and *nem*; *amok* and *bok l'hong* become simply versions of Thai *haw mok* and *som tam*; *kuytheav* is Chinese noodle soup, *mee katang* is the Chinese *chow fun*, and so on. Unfair though this may seem, it reflects Cambodia's history of dependence and invasion. Despite its glorious period of rule from Angkor from the ninth to the fourteenth centuries, by the middle of the nineteenth century it had almost been squeezed out of existence between the Thais and the Vietnamese, and was rescued from extinction by the French.

Nevertheless, some distinct traits can be discerned. There is a more than usually strong repertoire of soups, and also a bias towards sour flavours, hence one of the most identifiable of all Khmer dishes is *somlar machou banle*, a sour fish soup. Other noted Cambodian dishes are *amok*, a pounded steamed thick curry paste

Partly inundated ricefields near Siem Reap, Cambodia. The annual flooding of the Tonlé Sap has long supported a flood-retreat system of irrigation.

Bok l'hong, made with shredded green mango mixed with fish sauce, lime juice, chillies and basil leaves, served here in a rather fancy way with prawns, is the Cambodian equivalent of the Issaan *som tam*.

A modest Phnom Penh restaurant aims at an unexpected elegance with its signage.

with fish and coconut milk, and *bok l'hong*, the Khmer style of *som tam* and *tam mak houng*, shredded unripe papaya pounded with lime juice and fish sauce, sometimes with tomatoes. There is a great love of fish from the Great Lake of the Tonlé Sap, with its annual bounty as the waters from the Mekong reverse and flow up into the heart of the country to expand the lake and fill it with millions of fish. There is also a great enthusiasm for *prahok*, the local version of the Lao *padek*. Indeed, the population of Laos being even smaller, Cambodian cuisine might pin its hat on this gloriously smelly concoction, described earlier, in chapter Two. The Khmers might even argue on circumstantial grounds that they invented it and distributed it around mainland South-east Asia during the years of the Khmer empire, which stretched at its peak as far west as Burma, north into Laos, and east to the Annamese coast. Funnily enough, the ancient Romans had something

173

Rice transplanting in the coastal plains of central Vietnam.

similar, a staple condiment called *garum,* made by crushing and fermenting the intestines of a variety of fish. The ancient Khmer empire, militaristic, conquering and with straight highways fanning out from the capital, is often compared to the Roman Empire.

Vietnam, to the east, has undeniably a more distinctive cuisine, heavily influenced, as is the culture, by China. Or rather three cuisines, because climate and geography here combine to make a very definite division, one that has been felt throughout its history. The central Annamite chain runs parallel to the coast, squeezing the centre of Vietnam into a long narrow strip, doing more to separate than unite the north and the south. The shape of the country is often likened to two rice panniers on a shoulder pole, an apt analogy given that the Red River delta in the north and the Mekong delta in the south are both rice bowls. Overall, there is a strong Chinese influence, but adapted with the addition of different ingredients, especially fish sauce. There are many dips, served with an abundance of fresh herbs and vegetables. Northern cooking is less flamboyant than southern or central, with grills and stir-fries, and soy sauce featuring quite prominently. Southern cooking is more influenced by Khmer cuisine (shrimp paste, chillies, lemon grass, palm sugar), and by French food, and has a strong repertoire of seafood.

These are the two rice 'panniers', while the central, Annamese, cuisine is the richest and most colourful of all, with a strong influence from the court at Hué giving it more sophistication, and an Indian curry influence from the Chams. One Vietnamese writer identified 1,700 national dishes, of which 1,400 originated from the area around Hué. Among notable dishes are many noodle soups, including *pho* in the north around Hanoi, and *bun bo hue* from Hué

A Vietnamese village street breakfast.

175

(thicker, reddish broth from long simmering of bones). There is also *nem rán* or *chả giò*, deep-fried spring rolls filled with pork meat, Vietnamese yam, crab, shrimp, rice vermicelli, mushrooms and other ingredients, and *gâi con*, the fresh and unfried variety in which rice paper is filled with shrimp, herbs, thin rice noodles and other ingredients, and dipped in *nuoc mam* (a dipping sauce made from fish sauce, chillies, sugar, garlic and lime or vinegar) or peanut sauce. *Chao tom* is a minced prawn paste wrapped around sugar cane and grilled, while *nem nuong* are meat balls made with fish sauce, skewered and grilled. Among the dishes showing French influence is *bánh xèo*, crepes made out of rice flour, coconut milk and spring onions, pan-fried and stuffed with pork, shrimp and bean sprouts among other ingredients, then served wrapped with lettuce leaves, mint and other herbs, and dipped in *nuoc mam*.

Banh, of which there are many varieties, are steamed 'cakes', which can be of rice or tapioca flour and which in style vary from translucent sheets to sticky buns reminiscent of Japanese *mochi*. Hué, regarded as the culinary epicentre of the country (at least by the people who live there) has the greatest variety and sophistication of *banh*. *Banh khoai* is the Hué version of the southern *banh xeo*, the crepe-like stuffed crispy pancake, but there is also *banh beo*, silver-dollar translucent discs of rice flour, *banh bot loc*, similarly translucent but made with tapioca flour, *banh it*, and many more. And while the court dishes have given the old capital much of its culinary reputation, simple dishes such as Hué beef soup (*bun bo hué*) are quintessential.

As a reminder that here, as elsewhere in South-east Asia, the significant differences are often local rather than national, one central Vietnamese noodle dish, *cau lau*, served with slices of pork (marinated and simmered for up to six hours), bean sprouts and herbs, is unique to the old port town of Hoi An, little more than a hundred kilometres from Hué. These noodles can be made only with water drawn from one of the town's wells, and some purists claim that of these, only the ancient Ba Le well will do. Here again, the depth of history informs such a seemingly simple dish. According to tradition, *cau lau* noodles are descended from recipes introduced by the sixteenth-century Japanese traders who, together with the Chinese, founded Hoi An as a trading port. It is the sweetness of the Hoi An well water, together with, apparently, ashes from local lacquer trees (*cay son* in Vietnamese), that have established its reputation.

177

Delving into the cuisine of the region does this kind of thing. You begin in a known universe of commonly understood dishes – the standard repertoire picked up and reinforced by lazy restaurants – and before you know it you are talking about *that* field over *there*. The journalistic ambition to make things conform to a known list, or at least to make it all understandable, comes face to face with specifics that seem to make a nonsense of generalization.

Perhaps one exception to this might be the Philippines, due partly to the relative isolation of the string of 7,000 islands, and more so to their unique experience of having been colonized by first the Spanish and then the Americans. The addition of Chinese and Malay adds to the multicultural mixture, but this is the one

Basligs, Filipino fishing craft from the south equipped with outriggers, in the Sulu Sea close to Zamboanga.

Chicken *adobo*, the classic Filipino dish, cooked slowly with a marinade of soy sauce, vinegar and garlic.

nation in the region with a significant New World culinary heritage. Except for the south, which tends to follow the Malay-Muslim food culture, most Filipino cooking uses fewer spices than other countries. There is a preference for sour, though concentrated more in the north and centre of the islands than in the south, and this comes through from palm vinegar, which shows itself in the very characteristic class of dish called *adobo* – chicken or pork braised in garlic, soy sauce and vinegar – and in *sinigang*,

a sour soup using tamarind. This desire for sour has even helped create an important fruit, the *calamansi*. Very characteristic of the Philippines, it looks like a small, soft-skinned lime, but is in fact a hybrid, unknown in the wild, created so long ago that its origins are obscure. It has the aroma of a tangerine, but a flavour that is distinctly sour (one of its western names is acid orange). Generally, Filipino treatment of flavours tends to be less subtle, more flamboyant than that of its neighbours, with many sweet, sour and spicy combinations. One of the most memorable dishes is *lechon*, or whole roasted suckling pig. At restaurants specializing in this, the *lechon* are stacked on their poles in rows outside.

If South-east Asia as a region is a crossroads of culture and food, the heart of the exchange has traditionally been the Strait of Malacca, one of the world's most important shipping lanes, running 500 miles along the southern coast of the Malay

Lechon, barbecued piglet, in preparation in Manila.

Fishing boats in an inlet near Marang, on the east coast of the Malay peninsula.

Peninsula. This alone exposed Malaysia to the long-distance influences of China, India, the Middle East and Europe, but being colonized by the British ensured the settlement of large numbers of different ethnic groups, with the result that more cuisines co-exist here than anywhere else. There is Malay, Chinese, Indian, and variations that include Mamak (Indian Muslim) and Nyonya (Chinese Malaysian). Overall, there is an emphasis on sweet and pungent, and the cuisines are pervaded by coconut meat and milk. Grilling, frying and slow braising are common techniques. *Satay*, grilled meat on skewers served with a mildly spicy peanut sauce, was introduced by Arab traders, and is essentially a version of kebab. Beef and goat are more common than in mainland South-east Asia because of Islam, while chicken is ubiquitous (and in particular *kampung*, or free-range village chicken). The unofficial national dish, vying with *satay* in popularity, is *nasi*

lemak, a dish of rice soaked in rich coconut milk and steamed, often with pandanus leaves added for flavour, and served with accompaniments which can include small dried fish, pickled vegetables, egg and stir-fried water convolvulus.

Nyonya cuisine is particularly distinctive, an invention of the early Chinese, mainly Hokkien, settlers. Following Admiral Zheng He's visit in the early fifteenth century, a Chinese princess, Hang Li Po, was presented to the then Sultan of Malacca. Her retinue were the ancestors of a class of Straits-born Chinese who became known as the Peranakan (meaning 'descendants' in Malay). Male descendants are known as Babas, and female descendants Nyonya, which gave the name to the unique cuisine that evolved, blending Chinese ingredients with South-east Asian spices and coconut; one of its signature dishes is *ayam buah keluak*, using nuts from the Kepayang tree (*Pangium edule*).

And accompanying almost any Malaysian meal is *sambal*, in small dishes. *Sambal* is a paste or sauce with chillies as a base and

Preparations for a wedding feast near Trengganu, with coconut being pounded and rice already steamed.

182

Food stalls at a night market in Malacca, on Malaysia's west coast.

the addition of any of a variety of other flavours. *Sambal belacan*, for example, includes a small quantity of the fermented fish paste. Other ingredients, according the cook's taste, can be garlic, ginger, onion, galangal, lime juice, lemon grass and tamarind. *Sambal* is used both for cooking (in preparing the *rempah*, or curry base) and as a condiment, and any serious Malaysian cook takes great pride in the flavour of individually prepared *sambal*. Florence Caddy, writing in 1889 in the wonderfully titled *To Siam and Malaya in the Duke of Sutherland's Yacht 'Sans Peur'*, described eating at the court of the Sultan of Johore:

> Sometimes we had a Malay breakfast, beginning with a capital mayonnaise of fish and capers, and then a ponderous

183

Malay curry, twenty courses in one, of about twenty-six dishes and 'sambals', which are grated, shredded, chopped, or powdered preparations of seven little dishes in each sambal-tray, of which you are expected to select several of nearly all . . . This masterpiece is compounded by the Babu – the Sultan's chef – under the Sultan's own eyes. Like a domesticated Frenchman, Sultan Abubekir likes poking about doing his housekeeping, looking after the 'perfectionating' of the sambals.

Sir Spenser St John, writing in 1863 in his journal *Life in the Forests of the Far East*, details some of the varieties prepared by his cook in Borneo:

The one he made was of the sliced cucumber, and green and red chillies cut into fine threads; others are of dried salt fish finely powdered, or fish roes, or hard-boiled eggs, or the tender shoots of bamboo, but with all, or nearly all, red or green chillies are added. The most delicious I have ever seen put on a table was made of

A Javanese farmer ploughing furrows with a pair of reluctant water buffalo, near Yogyakarta.

prawns about an inch long, partly boiled, then seasoned with freshly prepared curry mixture, and at last slightly moved over the fire in a frying-pan, taking care not to burn it; if chillies are added judiciously, so as not to render it too fiery, it causes a keen appetite to all but a confirmed invalid.

Indonesia, spanning over 5,000 kilometres and with 6,000 populated islands (17,508 in total), is definitely too large to have a truly national cuisine. In the west, parts of Sumatra and Java share many of their most popular dishes with Malay culture across the Strait, such as *nasi goreng* (rice stir-fried with a variety of ingredients) and *rendang* (a slow-cooked meat curry with coconut milk), but towards the east habitat and tastes change, until eventually, in Irian Jaya, there is little resemblance in the indigenous cooking.

Javanese cuisine has the reputation within Indonesia for a measure of refinement, mirroring the Javanese pride in the concept of *halus*, meaning refined in the sense of gracious, polite and soft-spoken, contrasting with *kasar*, meaning crude, boorish and coarse. It tends towards more sophisticated and more varied dishes, with

A fisherman in Cirebon harbour on Java's north coast baling water from his boat.

Cumi-cumi, an Indonesian dish of stuffed chilli-fried squid.

fewer chillies than elsewhere, more sauces, and sweetness (*manis*). The sweetening for Javanese dishes (more popular in the centre and east of the island than in the west), comes from the Palmyra palm, and also, more specially, from the coconut palm. Certain flavours and ingredients mark the island's cuisine. The fruit of the *bilimbi*, related to the *carambola* and hardly known in the West (where its English names 'cucumber tree' and 'tree sorrel' give little idea of what it is), is a traditional souring agent, while the *salam* leaf (*Eugenia polycantha*), a kind of laurel, known confusingly and inaccurately in the West as Indian bay-leaf, is delicately aromatic and slightly sour. Distinctive Javanese dishes include a sweet stew of jackfruit known as *gudeg*, and a stew of mixed vegetables in coconut milk called *sayur lodeh*. Tofu and *tempe* (a fermented soybean cake invented in Java) are common substitutes for meat. Java is predominantly Muslim, but pork still puts in an occasional appearance, particularly around Semarang and Surakarta, underlining once again the significance of local differences in South-east Asian cooking.

As across the Malacca Strait, *sambal* sauces and condiments play a key role. Writing in 1912, Augusta de Wit, in *Java facts and fancies*, wrote of,

> 'sambals' of fowl's liver, fish-roe, young palm-shoots, and the gods of Javanese cookery alone know what more, all strongly spiced, and sprinkled with cayenne. There is nothing under the sun but it may be made into a sambal; and a conscientious cook would count that a lost day on which he had not sent in at the very least twenty of such nondescript dishes to the table of his master, for whose digestion let all gentle souls pray!

One of the most popular sauces, distinctive and now used widely beyond Java, is *kecap manis*, with a base of soy sauce to which is added sugar, anise, *salam* leaf and galangal. The name, which means 'sweet soy sauce' has the pronunciation 'ketchup', and this is indeed the origin of the widely used smothering agent typical of American cuisine. Soy sauce betrays Chinese influence in Java, and it fulfils much of the role of fish sauce elsewhere in

Balinese rice terraces, just turning golden-brown the week before harvest.

South-east Asia. Even though they have *kecap-ikan* (fish sauce), the Indonesians are generally less committed to fermented fish than most of the other South-east Asian countries. This said, the fish paste known as *trassi* or *terasi*, is popular in Java and Bali.

Sumatrans tend to eat more meat than do most Indonesians, and the cooking lacks the sweetness and, perhaps, subtlety of its neighbouring island Java. Yet Sumatra has the most successful food export within Indonesia – Padang cuisine from the Minangkabau people of west Sumatra, notable for its many curries cooked in large vessels with extensive use of chillies. Padang 'restaurants' abound across the island; they are popular, if somewhat downmarket, and known for chilli-hot, slow-cooked meat dishes. A favourite Padang dish is *rendang*, a special cooking technique in which meat (typically beef, although traditionally buffalo) is cooked slowly in coconut milk and spices for several hours, beginning with boiling and ending with frying, so that the final dish is without liquid but thoroughly coated and infused with the spicy ingredients, which can include ginger, galangal, turmeric, lemon grass and chillies.

Balinese food, like the religion and culture, is highly individual, featuring, for instance, pounded fresh rhizomes. Islam, which supplanted Hindusim in Java, gained no purchase here. Balinese Hinduism bears scant resemblance to that practised in India, but the dietary laws are similar, and in place of beef there is pork, served enthusiastically in many ways. Perhaps most famous among visitors is *babi guling*, suckling pig, as popular here as *lechon* is in the Philippines. Family ceremonies, of which there are many, are usually accompanied by *lawar babi*, shredded spicy pork. *Lawar* means 'thinly sliced', and the slicing is men's work, usually in a group. By tradition, the pig's organs and blood are incorporated, though this is less common nowadays.

Sulawesi to the north-east is different yet again. The predominantly Christian population in the north of the island, the Minahasa, also eat pork, and indeed have dishes for which the meat is first marinated in alcohol. Chillies are heavily used, possibly more so than anywhere else in Indonesia. Typical dishes of Manado cuisine, as it is called after the capital, are *ayam rica-rica*, a grilled chicken topped with chilli and onion paste, the local variety of *ikan pepes* (fish wrapped and cooked in banana leaf) made with red snapper, chilli (again), shallots and basil, and *bubur manado*, a porridge made with rice, corn, smoked fish, greens and chillies. Minahasans are also known for their predilection for exotic meats, including dog, cat, forest rat and fruit bat. Esoteric euphemisms apply to the first two. Dog is called 'RW', the acronym for 'fine hair' in the local language, while cat is known as 'everready', after its appearance in the logo of the well-known make of battery.

From here eastwards, other staples begin to predominate over rice, principally sago palm flour, sweet potatoes and cassava (the last an import from South America). Indeed, the Wallace Line, named after the naturalist Alfred Russell Wallace, which demarcates the flora and fauna of Asia from that of Australasia, runs just west of Sulawesi. The division is a sharp one, and in the southern islands this happens in the space of just 35 kilometres, the stretch of water separating the islands of Bali and Lombok. Indonesia continues as a nation for some 3,400 kilometres to the east of here, but this is the culinary limit for South-east Asia, Padang restaurants notwithstanding. Rice is no longer indigenous, although its use has spread from the west. The sago palm takes over first. Wallace himself, writing in his 1869 account of his travels in the islands, *The Malay Archipelago*, describes the making of flour from the sago palm in lengthy detail:

> When sago is to be made, a full-grown tree is selected just before it is going to flower. It is cut down close to the ground, the leaves and leaf-stalks cleared away, and a broad strip of the bark taken off the upper side of the trunk. This expresses the pithy matter, which is of a rusty colour near the bottom of the tree, but higher up pure white, about as hard as a dry apple . . . This pith is cut or broken down into a coarse powder . . . Water is poured on the mass of pith, which is kneaded and pressed against the strainer till the starch is all dissolved and has passed through . . . The water charged with sago starch passes on to a trough, with a depression in the centre, where the sediment is deposited . . . When the trough is nearly full, the mass of starch, which has a slight reddish tinge, is made into cylinders of about thirty pounds' weight, and neatly covered with sago leaves, and in this state is sold as raw sago.
>
> Boiled with water this forms a thick glutinous mass, with a rather astringent taste, and is eaten with salt, limes and chillies. Sago-bread is made in large quantities, by baking it into cakes in a small clay oven containing six or

eight slits side by side . . . The raw sago is broken up, dried in the sun, powdered and finely sifted . . . The hot cakes are very nice with butter, and when made with the addition of a little sugar and grated cocoa-nut are quite a delicacy. They are soft, and something like cornflour cakes, but have a slight characteristic flavour which is lost in the refined sago we use in this country . . . Soaked and boiled they make a very good pudding or vegetable, and served well to economize our rice, which is sometimes difficult to get so far east.

Even further east, the sweet potato takes over, until in the heart of Irian Jaya, Indonesia's furthest territory and the western half of the island of New Guinea, it is almost the full diet for many of the Melanesian communities. Photographing a story on malaria research, I found myself in the central highlands of New Guinea, and staying in a remote village. From the nearest town, Wamena, this was a half-hour helicopter ride (which I had taken on the way out) but a three-day hard walk (which I was hoping not to have to take on the way back and so was somewhat anxious for the clouds to clear). Earlier in the day, I had been impressed by the scarcity of vegetables in the impromptu market that gathered on the hillside, but at dinner, I was for once quite taken aback. I and the doctor with whom I was travelling joined a family for dinner, which took place in the low-ceilinged ground floor of the house, straw-covered and lit by an oil lamp. A simple fire was burning in the centre of the room, the only ventilation being the single low doorway, so the atmosphere was thick and choking. We squatted around the fire against the damp mountain cold, and our hosts threw sweet potatoes, just as they were, into the ashes. After around half an hour, we fished them out, juggling them in our hands because of the heat, and bit into them. That was the complete dinner. It felt very far from South-east Asia.

6 SOUTH-EAST BY WEST

'In reading the books of explorers I have been very much struck by the fact that they never tell you what they eat and drink.' This is Somerset Maugham writing in 1935 about a journey he made from Rangoon to Haiphong, and much the same thought occurred to me as I trawled through the writings of western authors on South-east Asian matters, searching for what I assumed would be an easy catch, accounts of what the local cuisines used to be like. He qualified this statement with 'unless they are driven to extremities and shoot a deer or a buffalo that replenishes their larder when they have drawn in their belts to the last hole'. In fact, I was after lesser game than this kind of explorer. I simply wanted to know how more ordinary travellers, expatriates and novelists had described in the past the foods I knew well from my own experience, but it was proving hard going.

My original intention, way too optimistic, was to use the accounts of outsiders as a clue to if and how the cuisines had changed. Was Thai food always so diverse and rich in flavours, or had the cuisines developed with increasing prosperity? One problem was, as we saw in the last chapter, that there had never been much written in the languages of these countries. There have, nevertheless, been many western writers giving accounts of South-east Asia, from diplomats to anthropologists, dilettante travellers to those who, for one reason or another, had decided to settle in one of these exotic cultures. Yet accounts and opinions of the food are conspicuous by their rarity. There is Gervaise, an exception, a French missionary in the late seventeenth century, mentioning the shrimp paste 'made of rotten prawns' with its nauseating smell, and some observations on how dinner was served at the Thai court: 'At banquets the dishes are served all higgledy-piggledy and in no particular order, with fruit and rice

193

in vessels of gold, silver and porcelain.' Scott in Burma relates a nineteenth-century temple festival, at which 'Mountains of cooked rice send out spurs of beef and pork, with flat lands of dried fish and outlying peaks of roasted ducks and fowls', all pervaded by the 'malodorous varieties' of fish paste, which 'loads the air with suggestions of a fish-curing village, or an unclean fishmonger's in the dog days.' Generally, however, the South-east Asian table was ignored.

And, of course, there were the novelists and storytellers, notable among whom are Conrad, Maugham, Greene, Orwell, Le Carré and Burgess. Actually, I had remembered nothing to do with food from the first time I had read books such as *Almayer's Folly*, *The Quiet American*, *Burmese Days* or *Time for a Tiger*. This didn't surprise me, as culinary matters have rarely been seen as important enough to be the central theme of fiction (although Maugham has a disgusting little story about what some Chinese cook does to an obnoxious passenger's food on board a ship), but I did expect some asides which might be useful. However,

Afternoon tea at the Carcosa and a vintage limousine waiting at the entrance to the E&O in Penang have become part of the *faux* experience of the British Empire.

194

it seems that Lord Jim was not a gourmet, neither Pyle nor Fowler were much engaged by Vietnamese *gôi cuon*, while Flory, despite having some empathy for Burmese culture, seems not to have relished *mohinga*, and Nabby Adams did not care for much else other than warm Tiger beer. As far as I could tell, there is no South-east Asian food in fiction.

So when I came across Maugham's complaint at the beginning of a chapter of his non-fiction account, I thought I was on to something, particularly as he went on, 'But I am no explorer and my food and drink are sufficiently important matters to me to persuade me in these pages to dwell on them at some length.' Me too, wholeheartedly. He had just completed a three-week journey on horseback from Taungyii across the difficult hill country of the Shan States to Keng Tung, and Shan food has some delicious dishes, such as *gaeng hang ley*, popular in Chiang Mai, where Shan influence is felt. However, what Maugham goes

A Burmese monk approaches one of the stilted temples lining the margins of Lake Inlé, close to Taungyi in the Shan States, from where Somerset Maugham began his trek to Thailand.

on to discuss is 'two large cabbages. I had eaten no green vegetables for a fortnight and they tasted to me more delicious than peas fresh from a Surrey garden or young asparagus from Argenteuil.' Then duck 'with mashed potatoes and abundant gravy'. Professing little knowledge of cooking himself, he nevertheless taught his Burmese cook how to make a corned beef hash, trusting 'that after he left me he would pass on the precious recipe to other cooks and that eventually one more dish would be added to the scanty repertory of Anglo-Eastern cuisine. I should be a benefactor of my species.'

Well, Maugham was something of a snob and more than a little condescending, so this shouldn't have been a surprise. After the main course he received trifle one day and cabinet pudding the next, which, as he says, 'are the staple sweets of the East, and as one sees them appear at table after table, made by a Japanese at Kyoto, a Chinese at Amoy, a Malay at Alor Star or a Madrassi

At Sinbyugyun, downriver from Mandalay, a classic Burmese landscape of rice-fields studded with pagodas at sunrise, encapsulates the romantic view expressed by Kipling.

196

at Mulmein, one's sympathetic heart feels a pang at the thought of the drab lives of those English ladies in country vicarages or seaside villas (with the retired Colonel their father) who introduced them to the immemorial East.' This, of course, in a continent where there are, by tradition, almost no desserts at all.

Anthony Burgess, who began his writing career in Malaya after the Second World War while a teacher there, and who wrote about Malay life as much as that of the expatriates, was resentful of the high opinion in which Maugham was held. When his first novel, *Time for a Tiger*, was published in 1956, he wrote, 'The book was sometimes compared unfavourably with the Eastern stories of Somerset Maugham, who was considered, and still is, the true fictional expert on Malaya. The fact is that Maugham knew little of the country outside the very bourgeois lives of the planters and the administrators. He certainly knew none of the languages. Nor did Joseph Conrad.'

The title that Maugham gave his book is a clue. He called it *The Gentleman in the Parlour* after a passage by the early nineteenth-century English essayist Willian Hazlitt which celebrates the freedom and independence of travel. It's interesting how little this means nowadays; almost incomprehensible as a visitor from afar waiting downstairs to be introduced. But Maugham's idea of a traveller, like many of his contemporaries, was moving from one drawing room to another – visiting the outposts of western civilization dotted around various imperial holdings. In the north Vietnamese port of Haiphong, he was invited to the rooms of an Englishman who was outside colonial society and who had married a Vietnamese woman, and the man advised Maugham to come *after* dinner, as 'We only eat native food and I don't suppose you'd care for that.' When he did chance to eat Asian, in Bangkok, he found that 'the insipid Eastern food sickened me.' Now this is a little strange, because whether you like Thai food or not, it could hardly properly be described as insipid. However, Maugham was talking of the dining room of the Oriental, so goodness knows what they were giving him. Hotels, of course, are known to be bastions of bastardizing local cuisines, given that they think their first duty is toward the prejudices of their guests, and the menus are usually devised by foreign Executive Chefs.

So perhaps Burgess, then. I always found him more generally sympathetic than Maugham to local culture. By contrast to the great old story-teller, Burgess omnivorously consumed the Malay language, culture and sex, but if he also enjoyed *laksa lemak* or *ikan bekar*, he didn't find it worth exploring in his novels or autobiography. I was disappointed in this, because Burgess was as enthusiastic in his way for Malaya as was Scott for Burma, and even considered taking Malay citizenship when his teaching contract expired. One lesson from this comparison is that differences in class entered into the western experience of food in the region much less than expectancy and creature comforts.

In fact, so much has changed in the relationship between the West and Asia since the early and mid-twentieth century that at times it's difficult to remember that long-haul tourism, huge numbers of ethnic restaurants in western cities and even the interest in travel experience that makes a book like this one possible are all recent phenomena. Take Thailand, the most popular destination of the region. In 2006 there were 13.4 million foreign visitors, but in 1990 there were 5.3 million, and in 1980 just 1.8 million. In 1970 there were less than a quarter of a million, and in 1960 only a hundred thousand. Before that, most westerners in South-east Asia were not adventurers or travellers, let alone ordinary tourists. They were, for the most part, traders, functionaries of empire or, like rubber planters in Malaya, caretakers of various

Cheroots, untapered (and therefore inexpensive) cigars clipped at both ends, for sale in a Shan market.

A Shan woman 'a-smokin' of a whackin' white cheroot', in Kipling's words. The Burmese made their own, individual cultural symbol from tobacco.

parts of the imperial economy. For their personal lives they simply wanted as many as possible of the personal comforts from home. Take, for example, the Vocabulary section in a traveller's guide to the East Indies published in 1912, *Isles of the East: An Illustrated Guide*, by one W. Lorck. Prominent among the useful phrases for eating are 'Let me have some rice but none of the hot dishes [*maoe sambal*]', followed by 'Boy, I want some bread' and then 'Bring me a bottle of Claret No. 10'. Wine, as you might imagine, did not penetrate very far into South-east Asian society. There were, of course, many varieties of locally produced alcohol, distilled from rice or sugarcane or palm. But such rituals as a stengah (a small whisky and soda poured over ice, from the Malay word for 'half') or a gin pahit (gin and bitters, Malay for 'bitter') on the verandah at sundown, and Bordeaux with supper, remained firmly and exclusively within the expatriate community of the time.

For the wives living abroad meant taking charge of the cook and kitchen to make sure that they could produce reasonable facsimiles of home dining. This did not mean that westerners in those days were completely immune to the attractions of local tastes, but rather that they cherry-picked their way through the recipes, drawing a firm line above the 'difficult' components that included anything fermented and hot chillies. An institution widespread

199

An East Flores man scales a palm tree to collect sap for the making of *tuak*, a local liquor.

around the region was a Sunday lunch that was based, though often loosely, on local dishes. In the British colonies it was typically a curry tiffin, both words needing explanation for different reasons. Tiffin comes from the days of the British Raj, meaning a light meal taken during the day and derived from an old English slang word, *tiffing*, for taking a little sip of something. The term curry seems at first glance to come from the Tamil word *kari*, meaning sauce and applied to various spiced dishes eaten with rice, but in fact it was

Tobacco, a South American import, was embraced enthusiastically by all the societies to which it was introduced, including northern Burma, where a Shan man enjoys a smoke in a characteristically Chinese pipe.

used in English before the days of the Raj to refer to a stew, and was adopted as a blanket term for all Indian-spiced, fairly liquid, sauce-based dishes. The term is rarely used by Indians. Its use spread with the expansion of empire to Burma and Malaya, and its meaning changed drastically in the hands of the British housewife. First, it was generally considered sufficient to cook the meat with curry powder, which consisted mainly of ground turmeric with a very little chilli. Then, this being an exotic dish and therefore an occasional treat, some sweet ingredients were added, in particular sultanas, with perhaps some chopped banana and possibly a sprinkling of coconut powder. I remember my mother's curry, which I always looked forward to as a child, especially the sultanas and bananas (I could have done without the meat, or even the rice, come to think of it). There was a dish known as coronation chicken, invented by Constance Spry in 1953, the principal flavouring of which came from, in order of importance, curry paste, tomato pureé, red wine and chopped apricot. The English curry, which made even Anglo-Indian cuisine seem authentic by comparison, was perfectly pleasant, even though it was nothing like any South or South-east Asian dish known to man. In the same way that processed peas and tinned salmon can be tasty without bearing any resemblance to their fresh counterparts, it had its own unique identity, although on its way to nowhere.

In the East, with access to local products and in the hands of a local cook, the curry was more authentic, but still reflected western conservatism. Nancy Madoc, quoted by Charles Allen in his wonderfully researched book *Tales from the South China Seas*, recounts the occasion in Malaya:

> When you went in you started off with mulligatawny soup, and then a really good hot curry with a lot of

sambals, which were little side dishes like coconut, banana and fruit and all sorts of things like that to put on your curry, which was sometimes almost too hot but very good, a huge meal generally. After that you were expected to have your sweet, which was always a thing called *gula Malacca*, a cold sago with two sauces, one coconut cream and the other *gula*, which was palm-tree sugar of a very dark colour, an absolutely delicious sweet. After you'd had all that all you could do was long to get away and pass out on your bed for the rest of the day.

While sweet dishes like this are authentic, the idea of a dessert to finish the meal is definitely not South-east Asian. Nor Asian in general. The normal ending to a meal, if it is special enough to have an ending, is fruit. Sweets, which enjoy a rich tradition in the region, occupy a different place in the eating day, as snacks and treats. Nevertheless, for the western palate that feels something is missing after dinner, some of these sweets fit in rather well. My particular favourite is the Thai seasonal sweet of *Khao niaow ma muang*, mango slices with sweetened sticky rice. The success of this lies in the contrast between the texture and taste of the sticky rice that has been mixed with sweet coconut milk, and the slightly tart yellow mangoes, quite different from the typical Indian varieties. I include a recipe for this at the end.

The Americans, in their early South-east Asian colonial adventure in the Philippines, were less adventurous. Remarking on the unpalatability of bread 'baked by native bakers', William Freer, an American teacher recounting in 1906 his experiences, wrote that 'Thus it is that all American teachers in the Islands except in Manila and the large centres, eat boiled rice in place of bread, often three times a day, as the natives do', but somewhat spoiling the effect of mucking in by adding, 'With fresh or tinned sausages or devilled ham, it makes a particularly delicious blend.'

The Dutch version of the curry tiffin acquired rather more gravity as it was developed by the planters and colonial administrators into an elaborate banquet with political overtones. This was *rijstafel*, meaning literally 'rice table', and was successfully exported back to Holland, where restaurants would serve it as an authentic Indonesian experience. Although its name is simple, the occasion was anything but. It originated toward the end of the eighteenth century among Dutch landlords in Central and East Java as a pompous colonial feast. According to Indonesian historian

Desserts, or puddings as the English prefer to call them, generally occupy an inter-meal place in South-East Asia. Clockwise from top left: *halo-halo*, a frozen Filipino dessert with clear western colonial underpinnings; sweet marinated fruits near Petchburi, Thailand; *luk chub*, ornamental Thai desserts in the form of miniature fruit and vegetables; and mangoes with sticky rice, a dish that successfully crosses the East-West cultural divide.

Ong Hok Ham, it was a demonstration of affluence, luxury and power. 'It was not at all about flavours since the ambience, the ceremony and the service was more important.' In a classic *rijstafel* banquet, guests were served samples of what were considered to be Javanese dishes, in conspicuously large numbers. For each dish, and there could be as many as forty at one of the grander ceremonies, there was a male waiter, a *jongo*, barefoot but dressed in a white uniform with a traditional Javanese cap (*blangkon*) and batik waist sash.

Plain rice was served first in the main dish at each place setting, then soup, followed by a succession of small dishes, adapted and altered to Dutch taste. Three key dishes, without which the *rijstafel* was not considered authentic, were *pisang goreng* (fried banana), *serundeng* (a crisp, shredded coconut topping made by slowly frying with a variety of spices and shrimp paste) and *telor ceplek* (fried egg). The idea of eating fruit with rice, much less a common fruit like banana, was strange to the Javanese, and on one occasion the Sultan of Surakarta even complained to the Dutch about this unseemly practice. Dutch desserts followed. The *rijstafel* spread throughout the colony, to the grand hotels, the passenger liners plying to Europe, and to the Netherlands.

Baden Baden-Powell, younger brother of the founder of the Boy Scouts, described rather disparagingly this Dutch *grande bouffe* in his *In Savage Isles and Settled Lands: Malaysia, Australasia and Polynesia, 1888–1891* (being 'merely a short account of my impressions during a journey of some 50,000 miles, and extending over three years'). Having first established that, 'The Dutch way of life is decidedly peculiar', he goes on to describe

> a truly alarming meal. The basis is one only soup-plate. On this you successively place piles of rice, hot stewed chicken, tropical fried fish, curry of butcher's meat, omelets, and other delicacies, the number ordinarily amounting to ten or twelve – I have known more. Dozens of chutneys and condiments flow, and it is strict etiquette to take and pile up on the same plates portions of everything handed round. One is overwhelmed with all the variety, and internally feels quite content to confine one's attention to two or three, at the most, of the dishes brought round. But then it transpires, to one's stomachic horror, that this great 'rystafel' is only the

preliminary to an ordinary course of beefsteak, and after that one is supposed to partake of banana or pineapple fritters.

The French, with more confidence in their own cuisine than the Dutch or English, did the opposite. Instead of incorporating their colonies' food into their table, they left behind a legacy of French dishes, as indeed they did all around the world. One constant reminder of the French overseas empire is bread and bakery products. I've bought baguettes in the Comoros (in the market in Moroni), in villages in Vietnam, Laos and Cambodia, and they have absolutely nothing to do with tourism and western visitors, but are simply an addition to the local staples. Across Indochina, the market presentation is a sandwich, the baguette split down its length and filled with, typically, a paté, varieties of ham, cucumber, pickled carrot and daikon, sliced chillies and coriander.

Underlying this is the persistent conservatism of human beings where food is concerned, which shows itself in the unwillingness of most people everywhere (not just in the West) to experiment with the opposite side of their own food spectrum. I intend no criticism, even though at times throughout this book I've been guilty of promoting the one-upmanship of food travel adventure. I've made it a practice to try whatever I can wherever I travel, and if I come across something which at first seems distinctly unappetizing or even stomach-churning, my first thought nowadays is not 'how can anyone eat this?' but 'what am I missing?' Nevertheless, there are limits for everyone, and there are indeed some things even I would not put in my mouth. Still, within reason, there is a principle involved which is relevant to all who see themselves as travellers by inclination. As food psychologist Paul Rozin points out, apart from breathing, eating is the occasion on which we open our otherwise hermetically-sealed bodies to taking in something of the environment. Some have argued that sex does much the same (I'm thinking in particular of Anthony Burgess and his novel *Beds in the East*), but with food we *incorporate* the surroundings into our bodily make-up. Put simply, what's the point of attempting to travel if we stick to the food from home and don't listen to the advice of cooks from the cultures we visit? In an ideal world, we should all learn the language and the customs of where we travel to, and eat the food. The first is rarely an option for travellers on a short visit,

the second demands effort and application, but eating is available to everyone who can find the door out of the hotel. You could see it as the fast-track way of absorbing local culture.

I wonder if there was always such food conservatism. I take as just one specific example, Greater Galangal, a member of the ginger family sometimes called *laos* in cookery books or *kha* by the Thais, that is very localized to South-east Asia. It looks very much like a ginger, and indeed is of the same family, but it has a distinctive aroma and flavour. In addition to being gingery and pungent, it has a camphorous, more aromatic quality, and it is one of those spices that helps to define a dish as being from South-east Asia. It is in fact indigenous to the region, and nowadays is not used significantly elsewhere. Yet it was well-known in medieval Europe as a culinary ingredient, and is described by Chaucer in the prologue to *The Canterbury Tales*, begun in 1387: 'A Cooke they hadde with hem for the nones / To boille the chiknes with the marybones / And poudre-marchant tart and galyngale.' 'Poudre-marchant' was the Norman French for spice, and galangal was worthy of mention by itself. So what happened there? It was widely used six and more centuries ago within European cuisine, yet it became obsolete. I suspect that there are swings and shifts in how we feel about the foreign and the exotic, and that we are at a lower point now than during the Middle Ages. I don't even trust what now passes for food exploration. There may be fads, but strong exotic flavours tend not to last in the West. Their individualism gets ironed out, chefs play safe, and international hotel rules tend to, well, rule.

I've saved for last what is for me one of the most peculiar examples of South-east Asian food discrimination, instructive in how we tend to approach the unfamiliar. Many people will, of course, disagree with my enthusiasm for the king of South-east Asian fruits, the durian, but I'm determined to press my case. Fortunately, this is one local foodstuff which, contrary to the general poverty of historical food writing, has attracted endless comment. Up to 40 centimetres long and 30 centimetres wide, covered with large sharp spikes and containing soft, large flesh-covered seeds, durian has two diverging reputations, one in the East where it is eaten, and another in the West where it is not but yet still attracts a following because of its perceived strangeness. How you think about durian (and there are dozens of websites devoted to it, to establish its international credentials) depends very much on which reputation you choose as a starting point.

South-East Asian cuisine targeted at the well-heeled western traveller includes (clockwise from top left): a *nouvelle* oyster concoction with Thai references; the kitchen on the Orient Express (Singapore to Bangkok line); fruit cocktail at the refurbished Grand Hotel, Siem Reap, formerly *the* hotel for Angkor visitors; a 'seafood market' restaurant in Bangkok that combines assisted supermarket shopping with freshly cooked fish, lobsters and so on.

As someone who sought it out eagerly because of its scent, I'll take the Asian point of view. Make no mistake that this really is the most highly regarded fruit of the region. In Thailand, where there are 133 cultivars, the cost of the tastiest, known as *mon thong* or 'golden pillow') can reach as much as 2,000 baht in Thai currency, or about £30 at present rates. To put this in context, an entire meal in a simple, local Bangkok restaurant for Thais would set you back about 60 baht (£1).

What makes it so special? Oddly, one of the most enthusiastic advertisements for it came from an Englishman, Alfred Russell Wallace, writing in 1869:

> A rich butter-like custard highly flavoured with almonds gives the best general idea of it, but intermingled with it come wafts of flavour that call to mind cream-cheese, onion sauce, brown sherry and other incongruities. Then

there is a rich glutinous smoothness in the pulp which nothing else possesses, but which adds to its delicacy. It is neither acid, nor sweet, nor juicy, yet one feels the want of none of these qualities, for it is perfect as it is. It produces no nausea or other bad effect, and the more you eat of it the less you feel inclined to stop. In fact to eat Durian is a new sensation, worth a voyage to the East to experience.

Praise indeed, but this was before the growth of the durian-phobia among foreigners that is largely responsible for its being banned on regional airlines, on the Singapore subway system and in most four- and five-star hotels. Wallace also quoted the Dutch explorer Jan Huygens van Linschoten from 1599 saying, 'It is of such an excellent taste that it surpasses in flavour all the other fruits of the world, according to those who have tasted it.' The Dutch collector Bernardus Paludanus, whom van Linschoten supplied with specimens, wrote 'This fruit is of a hot and humid nature. To those not used to it, it seems at first to smell like rotten onions, but immediately they have tasted it they prefer it to all other food. The natives give it honourable titles, exalt it, and make verses on it.' The issue with durian is partly that it does taste like nothing else, a unique fruit experience, but even more that it has an unusually cloying smell. By the time we get to the early twentieth century, the conservatism of regular western visitors has overtaken the enquiring minds of the explorers and naturalists, and the first reaction of Nancy Madoc, newly married to a British colonial police officer, on her arrival in Penang in the 1930s, was of a smell 'so frightful that I couldn't believe it. I said in a horrified voice to Guy, "What is that terrible smell?" And he said, "Oh, that's durian. That's this wonderful fruit that they all think so much of."'

I too came across durian unwittingly by its smell, and I remember the occasion well. I was riding a motorcycle around the moat at Chiang Mai on a warm night at the beginning of the hot season, and caught a waft of heavy scent that reminded me of something between vanilla and musk, very compelling. I was approaching Sompet market by the moat and slowed down. Parking the bike, I followed my nose and came to a stall piled with green spiky fruits, the largest about the size of a misshapen football. Two of them had been split open, revealing, nestled in the very thick pithy skin, pale yellow pulpy flesh. I was surprised

at how expensive they were, but buying one and eating it
on the spot, found that it tasted even better than it smelled.
Wallace's description, which I read later, could hardly be
bettered, although for some reason I've never been able to
find the onion component.

This, of course, is just my opinion, and while it is shared
by many, there are also those who find the smell of durian as
acceptable as that of a fart. I know a number of Thais who can't
stand either the smell or taste, which persuades me that it isn't
just a matter of familiarity. Years of continuing to sample durian
whenever possible, yet also listening to other people's views,
have made me realize that durian really polarizes attitudes.
You love it or hate it; there seems to be no neutral ground.

However, I'm also convinced that there is more to this polar-
ization of opinion over its smell than a simply natural reaction.
As in so many sensory experiences, we also tend to fall in with
what we are primed to expect. If you like strong cheeses, such as a
ripe Camembert, the smell accords with what you can see on the
plate in front of you. But what if, instead, you came across this
smell while standing outside a door in an unfamiliar house? What
if you were unsure that this was a larder, and thought that it might
be a toilet instead? Just the question alone seems revolting.

Not only is durian associated *in advance* with 'stink' (no need
to type both words into an internet search; you are guaranteed
to find the two together in every article), but it is regularly
referred to in terms of the smell of sewage. I couldn't find an
original attribution for this idea, so I did some research in my
own collection of books. It turns out that it comes from none
other than the eccentric Victorian Sir George James Scott, great
lover of all things Burmese. He wrote in *The Burman: His Life and
Notions*,

> In the same way [as for *ngapi*, the fermented fish paste]
> there are equally various opinions with regard to the
> celebrated Durian, a fruit found as abundantly in the
> Tenasserim province as in the islands of the East Indian
> Archipelago, and equally highly prized by Burmans.
> Some Englishmen will tell you that the flavour and the
> odour of the fruit may be realised by eating 'garlic cus-
> tard' over a London sewer; others will be no less positive
> in their perception of blendings of sherry, noyau, deli-
> cious custards, and the nectar of the gods, while a some-

what objectionable smell is regarded as doing no more than suggest, or recall, a delightful sensation.

Unfortunately, it was the first part that stuck in the collective imagination and was passed along. Three scientific studies were carried out in the last three decades, each returning a different mix of volatile compounds, but without any agreement on what is responsible for the aroma. I suppose there's one reason to be grateful that most non-Asians are primed to find durian disgusting, which is that it's expensive enough already without having foreigners adding to the demand.

Alfred Russell Wallace, writing in *The Malay Archipelago* in 1869, noted that in Borneo the dyaks liked durian as a savoury accompaniment to their rice, and preserved the fruit salted in jars. Perhaps it was Wallace's account of the durian's occasionally deadly nature that resulted in the apocryphal tale of its use as a weapon. He wrote,

> The Durian is, however, sometimes dangerous . . . When a Durian strikes a man in its fall, it produces a dreadful wound, the strong spines tearing open the flesh, while the blow itself is very heavy; but from this circumstance death rarely ensues, the copious effusion of blood preventing the inflammation which might otherwise take place. A Dyak chief informed me that he had been struck down by a Durian falling on his head, which he thought would certainly have caused his death, yet he recovered in a very short time.

This continues to happen, the latest recorded incident being in 2003 on the west coast of the Malay Peninsula, when a fifty-nine-year-old grandmother from Kampung Batu Laut was felled by a 5 kilogram fruit and knocked unconscious.

For several years there went around the story that there was an obscure Thai law that banned the offensive use of this heavy spiked fruit, and the seeming plausibility of this idea allowed the legend to linger in the collective imaginations of journalists. A friend of mine, a *Time* stringer at the time in Bangkok, searched high and low for this, but concluded that it was a fiction. The clincher is the sheer impossibility of wielding a durian as a weapon. Short of hiding in a tree and waiting for your victim to walk underneath before dropping the fruit on his head, there is no

211

way of inflicting harm with it. While a durian on its long stem does surely look like a vegetable mace, you wouldn't be able to manage half a swing before the stem would part from the heavy fruit. Even throwing it wouldn't work; you'd puncture your own hands in the process.

Yet durian can and does kill, in a rather more subtle way. Henri Mouhout, the French explorer who brought the ruins of Angkor to the attention of the West, wrote, 'By an odd freak of nature, not only is there the first repugnance to it to overcome, but if you eat it often, though with ever so great moderation, you find yourself next day covered with blotches, as if attacked by measles, so heating is its nature.' In 2004, Thailand's Ministry of Public Health issued a warning against excessive consumption, following the death by surfeit of a civil servant in the town of Singburi. He had eaten four of the fruit in quick succession. The problem is its energy value, as a long-stemmed durian has on average 181 calories for every 100 grams. As the peeled weight of a 2-kilogram *mon thong* durian is around 600 grams, the over-zealous civil servant must have taken 4,000 calories in one go. 'People who are already overweight or obese, together with people with high blood pressure, heart conditions and diabetes, should eat durians in limitation and with caution', said a Ministry spokeswoman, and went on to recommend exercise after eating, and to accompany the durian with another fruit, the mangosteen, as a traditional method of avoiding stomach ache.

As it happened, the one time that the law was invoked against the durian in Thailand was when one enterprising contraceptive manufacturer began selling durian-flavoured condoms. They were indeed popular, and certainly attracted publicity, until the government put a stop to them. Even then, the ban was on the grounds that the condoms encouraged sexual promiscuity, and not, as some journalists preferred to think, that this was an obscene use of a noble fruit. Advertising them, said the Consumer Protection Committee, was 'encouraging sexual misconduct in young people', in a ruling that fined the manufacturer and its advertising agency in 1996, for breaking a law prohibiting advertisements which are 'directly or indirectly detrimental to national culture'. The idea was taken up a few years later in the Philippines and Indonesia, where condom use is being promoted in the face of growing HIV infection. Strawberry and mint, however, are reportedly still the favourite flavours.

A variety of ill-conceived South-East Asian products based on durian, including condoms flavoured and perfumed with the notorious fruit.

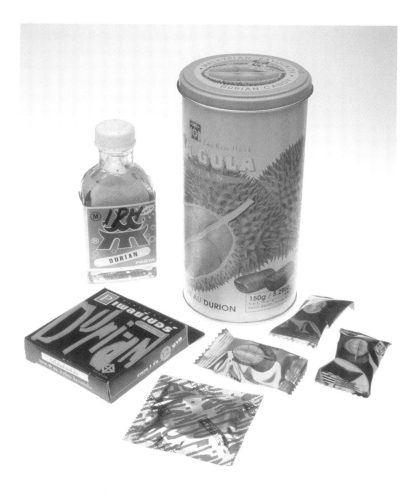

I seem on the verge of ending this book with something weird, and I was just thinking why. Nothing in my upbringing primed me for durian, but then neither did it for the whole South-east Asian food experience, and the appeal of the exotic probably figures largely in all of this. Clearly, I'm not alone. Within the last twenty years or so, South-east Asian food has become the most exported group of cuisines to the West, with Thai and Vietnamese foods leading the pack, but some of the others catching up. This is a recent and rapid development. Until the middle of the last century it was hardly known. The wars in Indochina drove refugees first to France, then to America, and many of them did the obvious thing, which was to open a restaurant, but the great boom happened later. No doubt the inspiration was mass tourism, which really took off in the 1980s, but that alone was no guarantee that South-east Asian food would be a hit in the West in the way that it has. Nor can it be down to such a matter-of-fact, logical matter that a South-east Asian diet is healthy and low in fat. I think the answer lies somewhere in the complexity and richness of intense flavours – flavours that also happen to be exotic.

At the same time as being highly stimulating to the palate, this relatively new (to the West) range of flavours also happens to be a vernacular cuisine rather than the invention of a class of super-chefs. The irony is that this is actually a kind of social inequality. This is food that has become desirable because of wealth. South-east Asian dishes are tasty because we can consume them in what would seem to a peasant farmer to be excess. The taste components were invented out of necessity, to make palatable what would be otherwise an extremely boring carbohydrate diet of rice. However refined your discrimination may be over varieties and harvests of rice, I defy anyone to get through a large bowl of it meal after meal without something to alleviate its blandness. The intense flavours of fermented fish, spices, chillies, forest leaves and so on also accompanied the proteins, vitamins and minerals that the body needs. This was a solution born of poverty, but when taken and developed by the chefs of royal palaces and noble houses within the region, and now more recently by restaurants, this exquisite complexity became a pleasure and even sometimes an art.

And yet, I can't help feeling that the heart of South-east Asian cuisine lies in the traditional and robust rather than in the elegant and refined. The ingredients are almost all affordable and available to all, and with very few exceptions (durian is one, but more as a fruit outside meals) there is no cult of the expensive. Truffles, Kobe beef, Beluga and *foie gras* do not have their equivalents here, unless they are the Chinese imports of abalone, shark's fin and bird's nests, which featured at the imitative banquets of royalty (where according to the *Da Nam thuc luc*, the 'Veritable Records of Viet Nam', a typical banquet to welcome foreign envoys would have sixty-one dishes). Take the Vietnamese *pho*, for example, almost the national dish, which is never served in style. It is a daily food, unpretentious, a food of the people, and yet is treated with respect and rigour. The same applies to a Burmese *mohinga*, a Cambodian *bok la hong* or a Malayan *nasi lemak*. These are dishes that have been perfected over centuries in homes and in small unpretentious restaurants, while allowing, perhaps even insisting

South-East Asian food at its least pretentious and, outside the region, unfortunately the least known – a well-regarded stall close to Bangkok's Grand Palace.

on, the latitude for special secret techniques of preparation. Refinement in the sense of elegance and impeccable presentation has little place here, despite the entirely understandable attempts of expensive restaurants aimed largely at western audiences to 'elevate' dishes. This is, first and last, vernacular cooking, born of necessity and honed in rural kitchens. Also – a heresy in our food-nation culture – inherently unimprovable. And why should it be improved when the best of it is so good?

RECIPES

BURMA *La phet thoke* – Fermented Tea-leaf Salad
Mohinga – Noodles with Freshwater Fish and Fish Sauce

THAILAND *Yam phak* – Spicy Vegetable Dip Flavoured with Fermented Fish
Hoy tod – Oyster Crêpes with Bean Sprouts
Chiang Mai *laab*
Gaeng paa moo paa – Wild Boar Jungle Curry
Khao niao ma muang – Mangoes with Sweet Sticky Rice

LAOS *Or lam nok kho* – Luang Phrabang-style Quail Stew with Vegetables

CAMBODIA *Samla mchou banle* – Sour Fish Soup
Amok trey – Steamed Spicy Fish Mousseline
Loc lac – Marinated Stir-fried Beef with Pepper Lime Sauce

VIETNAM *Pho* – Noodles in Beef Broth
Chao tom – Mashed Prawn on Sugar Cane

PHILIPPINES *Chicken adobo* – Slow-cooked Chicken Marinated in Soy Sauce, Vinegar and Garlic
Fish sinigang – Sour Fish Soup

MALAYSIA *Laksa asam*
Satay ayam – Chicken Satay

SINGAPORE Chilli Crab

INDONESIA *Gudeg* – Young Jackfruit Sweet Stew
Nasi goreng – Fried Rice
Pepes – Marinated Fish Steamed in Banana Leaves

La phet thoke – Fermented Tea-leaf Salad

This recipe is from a friend, Cherie Aung-Khin, owner of three restaurants, in Yangon, Mandalay and Pagan, all called Green Elephant. The tea-leaves, a Shan speciality, are picked young, mixed with salt and pressed in wooden barrels or terracotta jars for two to three months. The principal suppliers, and there are many brands, are in Mandalay.

Ingredients
4 tbsp fermented tea-leaves
3 tbsp peanut or sesame oil
dash of fish sauce (*nganpyaye*) (only if mixed, see below)
1/2 tbsp lime juice (only if mixed)
2 small chillies (optional, only if mixed)

Accompaniments
3 cloves garlic
2 tbsp sesame seeds
2 tbsp peanuts
2 tbsp mung beans
2 tbsp green peas
2 tbsp dried shrimp

Preparation
La phet is served in two ways: either as a snack at any time during the day, or as a dish served with others at mealtimes. If the former, the dried and roasted accompaniments are served separately in small dishes; if as part of a meal, mix all ingredients together to make a salad.

Slice the garlic, then fry in a little oil until golden in colour, and set aside (to remove the pungency, some Burmese cooks first soak the slices in lime-water for an hour).
    In a wok or pan over a slow-to-medium heat, roast the seeds, peanuts, beans and peas, each separately, until crisp, and set aside.
    Pound the dried shrimp until fluffy, and also set aside.
    Place the tea-leaves in a small dish and add the oil to soften them.

Serving
As a snack, place each of the accompaniments in a small dish on a tray surrounding a central dish of tea-leaves. Guests eat with their fingers, taking a little from each dish as they wish. According to the Burmese, *la phet* is meant to be chewed slowly for the full flavour to be released. As a main dish for a meal, mix all together in a serving dish, adding a dash of fish sauce and lime juice. The temperature is unimportant.

Mohinga – Noodles with Freshwater Fish and Fish Sauce
Essentially, the Burmese national dish.

Ingredients
750g catfish
2 tbsp fish sauce
2 stalks lemon grass, crushed
½ tsp turmeric
1 litre water
2 tbsp peanut or sesame oil
800g coconut milk
50g ground rice, roasted until pale golden
50g ground lentils, roasted until golden
200g young banana trunk, sliced and chopped
500g rice noodles (and 6–8 litres of water for cooking)

Paste
300g onions, sliced
4 cloves garlic, roughly chopped
2 cm fresh ginger, shaved and chopped
1 stalk lemon grass, lower half only, finely sliced
3 fresh chillies, seeded and sliced
1 tsp shrimp paste (*ngapi*)

Accompaniments
3 eggs (ideally duck, otherwise hen), hard-boiled and cut into quarters
1 onion, cut into rings and fried
2 lemons, cut into wedges

Preparation
Bring the water to the boil in a pan, add the crushed lemon grass stalks, turmeric, and the fish (better taste if the head is still on), and boil gently for 5 minutes.

Remove the fish, allow a few minutes to cool, then cut off the flesh in small (2-cm) chunks. Set aside.

Pound the paste ingredients in a mortar until smooth.

In a wok or large pan, heat the oil until it begins to smoke, add the paste, mix well, then simmer for several minutes.

Add to this paste the coconut milk and the banana trunk (if available), and continue simmering for several minutes until the banana softens.

Add the rice and lentil powder to thicken, then the fish and fish sauce, and simmer for another 3–4 minutes over medium heat. Remove from the heat.

In a large saucepan, bring 6–8 litres of water to the boil.

Plunge the noodles into the water and stir for no more than 1 minute. Remove and drain.

Serving
Serve in individual bowls, each ideally with a capacity of ½ litre. Divide the noodles equally between the bowls, then add the fish pieces and plenty of liquid. Set out the eggs, onion rings and lemon on side plates, one for each diner. Diners then squeeze the lemon over the noodles and soup to taste, and add pieces of egg and fried onion rings on top as desired. Eat with chopsticks and a spoon.

THAILAND   *Yam phak* – Spicy Vegetable Dip Flavoured with Fermented Fish

Ingredients
200g small round aubergines (*makheua pro* in Thai)
100g long green beans
100g snap or snow peas
100g button mushrooms
about 15 dried red chillies
1 fingertip of galangal
1–2 tsp *kapi* (shrimp paste)
2 tsp *plaa raa* liquid plus one small piece of the fish
1 tsp salt
3 cloves garlic (about 15 if the small Thai variety) plus 2 more for garnish
2 stalks coriander for garnish
2 spring onions for garnish

Preparation
Steam the vegetables until cooked but firm. Chop vegetables finely and put in a bowl.

Finely slice then chop the galangal. Finely chop the coriander (including stalks) and spring onions.

Roast the chillies over medium heat until blackened. De-stalk.

In a mortar, pound together the salt, garlic, chillies, galangal, *kapi* and the fish piece from the *pla raa*. Add the *pla raa* liquid and pounded mixture to vegetables in bowl and mix thoroughly.

Pound the 2 garlic cloves for garnish. Heat 2 tsp of oil in a wok over medium heat until it begins to smoke, then add the just-pounded garlic and fry until just beginning to turn golden. Set aside.

In the same oil, fry the vegetables over medium heat for 5 minutes.

Serving
Serve in a dish, garnished with the fried garlic, chopped coriander and spring onion. This dish should be accompanied by sticky rice. To eat, mould a small ball of the rice into a flattened pad and use this to scoop up some of the dip.

Hoy tod – Oyster Crêpes with Bean Sprouts

Ingredients
500g small oysters, shucked
300g tapioca floor
200g rice flour
400g bean sprouts
1 egg
6 sprigs coriander, leaves only, roughly chopped
¼ litre water
3 tbsp vegetable oil

Sauce
Sriracha sauce, sweet and hot, is made from chillies, vinegar, garlic, sugar and salt. There are several proprietary brands (Sri Racha is a town, not a manufacturer). If unavailable, add a little sugar to a regular chilli sauce.

Preparation
Chop the coriander, and set aside a third as garnish.

Beat the egg in a bowl.

Mix the two kinds of flour with the water to make a thin batter (adjust the quantity of water as necessary).

In a wok or large frying pan, add the oil and turn the heat to medium high. Dribble the batter all across the pan, then sprinkle half of the oysters on top. Sprinkle most of the chopped coriander on top, cook for 1–2 minutes, then divide the crêpe in half and flip over the two pieces to fry the other sides for another 1–2 minutes, until light brown and partly crispy.

Depending on the size of the pan, when the crêpe halves are flipped, push to one side, tilt the pan and in the free space add the remaining oysters and beaten egg and cook these for 1–2 minutes (otherwise, divide the operations).

Tip the crêpes out onto a serving dish and sprinkle the separately cooked oysters over them.

Add a teaspoon of oil if the pan is quite dry, and over the same medium-high heat, stir in the bean sprouts and move around for under a minute; they should be just crisped and slightly browned, not cooked, and remain crunchy.

Serving
Place the bean sprouts next to the crêpes on the serving dish. Add the remaining coriander leaves as garnish, and serve with *Sriracha* sauce.

Chiang Mai *laab*

The idea is to serve this dish with some rice (ideally sticky rice), a mound of mixed, fresh leaves and raw green vegetables, and to choose these for their interesting and contrasting flavours, with several of them slightly bitter. Possibilities include the small round crunchy aubergines known as *makheua pao*, tasty cabbage, cucumber, spring onions, coriander, mint and young mango leaves. Served with this *laab* in Chiang Mai were some local leaves unlikely to be found in the West, including *fuak lid mai, sadao* (neem), *yod ma'yoh* and *ki hood*. I'm all for searching out local western leaves and herbs to give it that desirable local character.

Ingredients
500g good quality buffalo steak (could be beef)
100g tripe
100g liver
$^1/_2$ cup blood from same animal
3 tsp bile from same animal
6 small red chillies
2 stalks lemongrass
$^1/_4$ cup galangal
3–4 cloves garlic (but up to 20 if the very small Thai variety)
6 spring onions (of which 2 reserved for garnish)
6 stalks coriander (of which 2 reserved for garnish)
20–30 mint leaves
1 tsp salt
1 tsp coriander seeds
several stalks of local forest leaves

Preparation
Roast chillies over medium heat until blackened. De-stalk. Pound in mortar.

Chop lemon grass and galangal into thin slices. Peel garlic and chop finely.

Roast the lemon grass, galangal and garlic over medium heat until just beginning to brown. Add to chillies in mortar.

Roast coriander seeds over a low to medium heat for 2 minutes. Add to ingredients in mortar.

Pound ingredients in mortar, adding salt.

Boil tripe and liver in just enough water to cover over medium heat for 10 minutes. Set aside but reserve liquid.

Chop meat very finely on a chopping board, using a sharp heavy blade. Do not use a blender, as this will destroy the texture of the meat into a mush. Add blood, a little at a time, and continue chopping in to blend.

Cut tripe and liver into thin strips. In a bowl, mix the chopped meat, tripe, liver and pounded spices. Add $^1/_2$ to 1 cup of liquid stock from the boiled tripe and liver (according to how liquid or dry you want the *laab* to be).

Bring the bile to a boil, add to the bowl and mix thoroughly with the other ingredients. Finely chop the coriander (including stalks), spring onions and mint. Mix into bowl.

Serving
Scoop onto a serving dish and surround with leaves and vegetables. Garnish with chopped spring onion and coriander.

If you prefer the dish cooked rather than raw, at the end, after the final step, simply heat 1 tbsp oil (or lard) and fry the mixture over a medium heat for 1 minute. Add 1 cup water and continue stirring for 2 minutes.

Gaeng paa moo paa – Wild Boar Jungle Curry

Wild boar, even if farm-raised, is tastier than pork, but pork will do fine. The key ingredient in this coconut-free curry is the *krachai*, a rhizome of the ginger family that has a distinctively woody taste. This curry is intended to be very hot in a chilli sense (pungent).

Ingredients
400g wild boar or lean pork, the best cut possible
6 fingers of *krachai*, chopped diagonally lengthwise into 3 or 4 slivers
1 clove garlic, finely chopped
100g thin green beans, chopped into 5-cm lengths
100g baby corn, chopped diagonally into 2 or 3 pieces
100g small, crunchy round aubergines (*makheua pro*), cut into 2-cm
    chunks (but cut at the last minute to prevent them going brown)
3 sprigs fresh green peppercorns, on the stalk
4–5 kaffir lime leaves, finely shredded
12 holy basil leaves, roughly torn
2–3 tbsp fish sauce
2 tbsp vegetable oil
½ litre water

Paste
5 shallots, chopped
2 cloves garlic, chopped
8–10 red chillies (the variety that is about 8-cm long, not the small *prik kii noo*), seeded and sliced
1 stalk lemon grass, finely sliced then chopped (the lower two thirds)
1 tsp galangal (*kaa*), finely chopped
1 tsp coriander root, finely chopped
1 finger of krachai, finely chopped

1 tbsp shrimp paste
1 tsp salt

Preparation
Prepare the *gaeng paa* paste by pounding all the ingredients together until smooth. (This differs from the regular red curry paste (*gaeng pet*) in that it adds shallots and *krachai* and misses out cumin and white pepper).

Slice the meat into thin (about 0.5-cm) strips; that is, bite-sized pieces.

Heat the oil in a wok or frying pan and add the garlic; fry until golden. Add the paste, briefly mix and stir with the oil and garlic.

Add the meat and stir-fry over a medium heat until well-coated and no longer pink; this should only take a few minutes. Add the fish sauce, water, *krachai* and lime leaves. Stir. Add the peppercorns, basil leaves, green beans and baby corn. Continue simmering for 15–20 minutes.

Add the aubergines and continue cooking for another 5 minutes (no longer, or the aubergines will become too soft).

Serving
Pour into a serving bowl and serve with boiled rice. As this is a pungent dish, take small amounts at a time and add to the mound of rice on each plate.

Khao niao ma muang – Mangoes with Sweet Sticky Rice

Ingredients
200g sticky rice (dry weight)
2 tbsp coconut milk
2 tbsp sugar
1/2 tsp salt
sprinkling of mung beans, lightly roasted
2 mangoes, sliced

Preparation
Steam the rice until just cooked.

Roast the mung beans until they begin to give off an aroma.

Stir the sugar and salt into the coconut milk in a bowl until all is dissolved. Add the rice and mix well. Set aside.

Peel the mangoes, then slice as follows. Hold a peeled mango in the palm of one hand. Start to cut from the far narrow end towards you with the blade horizontal, following by feel the upper surface of the stone, and remove the upper almost-half in one piece. Slice this piece crossways into four. Turn the mango over and do the same for the other side. There will be two narrow pieces of pulp remaining on the sides; carve these off, again staying close to the stone.

Serving

Shape the sticky rice into a flattish mound on a plate, sprinkle with the mung beans and arrange the mango slices around it.

LAOS   *Or lam nok kho* – Luang Phrabang-style Quail Stew with Vegetables

Probably the most famous recipe for this traditional Laotian dish from the ancient capital is by the late Phia Sing, chef at the Royal Palace, which was collected and published by Alan Davidson. This is an adaptation, as the local quail is larger than the European species normally available in shops. What is needed is any medium-sized game bird, preferably hung and so somewhat 'high'. Wood pigeon, partridge or grouse do well.

Ingredients

800g of game bird (see above), separated into legs, wings and the body cleaved in half

8 round crunchy aubergines, the same as the Thai *makheua pro* (see the Thai recipes above for *yam phak* and *gaeng paa moo paa*), quartered but cut at the last minute to avoid them turning brown

6 long (8–10 cm) fresh green chillies, roughly chopped

4 spring onions, roughly chopped

1 stalk lemon grass, crushed

1 *sakhan* (stem of a woody aromatic forest plant of the Piper species), cut into 5-cm sections – probably unavailable in the West and without a substitute (but if at all possible, worth asking for)

2 cowpeas (*Vigna unguiculata*), which are long, cut into 5-cm sections

100g coriander leaves, roughly torn

1 tbsp black peppercorns, roughly crushed in a mortar

½ cup *phak tam nin* leaves (an edible forest climber, *Melothria heterophylla*), also probably unavailable, though possibly as a medicinal plant.

½ cup dill, cut into short pieces

1 tbsp fermented fish of the type known in Lao as *padek* and in Thai as *pla raa*, and described in chapter Two, with a little of the liquid. If unavailable, use 2–3 tbsp of fish sauce

1 cup pork rind, deep-fried until puffed-up and crunchy

pinch of salt

(It may seem perverse to include such difficult wild leaves, but this is the nature of Lao regional cooking. You might substitute any interesting-tasting leaves, preferably with a slightly bitter flavour.)

Accompaniments

handful of salad leaves

1 cup watercress

6 spring onions, whole

Preparation

Bring the water to the boil in a saucepan, then lower the heat. Add the bird, 4 of the chopped aubergines, chillies, spring onions, lemon grass, a pinch of salt and the *sakhan* if available. Allow to return to the boil, then reduce the heat to simmer.

When the aubergines have softened a little but are not yet shapeless (about 15 minutes), remove them and the chillies and put in a mortar. Pound to a paste, and return this to the saucepan, stirring. Add the cowpeas and *phak tam nin* if available and simmer for 10–15 minutes.

Add the remainder of the aubergines and continue to simmer for 5 minutes.

Finally, add the pork crackling and torn coriander leaves, and transfer everything immediately to a deep serving bowl.

Serving

Serve with rice, and the accompaniments on the side. Laos would use sticky rice.

CAMBODIA   *Samla mchou banle* – Sour Fish Soup

This is probably the most popular soup in Cambodia, and is characterized by its use of sour and citric notes. Freshwater fish is normally used.

Ingredients
400g white fish (such as catfish or tilapia), cut into bite-sized pieces, about 2 cm
2 tbsp fish sauce (*tuk trey* in Khmer)
1 tbsp fermented fish (*prahok* in Khmer but essentially the *pla raa* of Thailand and *padek* of Laos)
2 cloves garlic, finely chopped
4 round aubergines (as the Thai *makheua pro*), quartered but chopped at the last minute to avoid turning brown
200g small tomatoes, chopped into wedges
100g shallots, finely chopped
1 stalk lemon grass, crushed
6 kaffir lime leaves, chopped
4–6 coriander stalks; leaves only, roughly torn
6 small chillies, finely chopped
several holy basil leaves
1 spring onion, finely sliced
lime wedges
1 litre water
1/2 tsp salt
1 tbsp vegetable oil

Paste
2 pods tamarind
2 stalks lemon grass, finely sliced and chopped
4 cm galangal, thinly sliced
several stalks of rice paddy herb (*Limnophila aromatica*), known as *ma-am* in Khmer and *ngò ôm* in Vietnamese. It has a lemony aroma and flavour
1 clove garlic

Preparation
Prepare the tamarind by soaking the fruit in a little hot water, then mashing and removing the seeds. Pound this and the other paste ingredients in a mortar until smooth.

Bring the water to the boil in a saucepan and add the salt. Add the paste to the water and mix well; turn heat down to simmer.

In a frying pan, heat the oil and fry the garlic until just golden; add to the water.

Add the lemon grass, kaffir lime leaves and shallots; simmer for 5 minutes.

Add the tomatoes and basil leaves; continue to simmer for another 5 minutes.

Add the fish and aubergines; continue to simmer for 5 minutes or until fish is just cooked.

Serving
Ladle into individual bowls. Sprinkle coriander, spring onion slices and chopped chillies on top as a garnish. Serve with lime wedges.

Amok trey – Steamed Spicy Fish Mousseline

This is similar to the probably better-known Thai *haw mok*.

Ingredients
400g white freshwater fish, cut into 2-cm pieces
200 ml coconut cream
1 egg
4 kaffir lime leaves, finely chopped
2 banana leaves

Paste
2 stalks lemon grass, with the lower halves finely sliced and chopped
5 cm galangal, finely sliced and chopped
10–12 long (about 8 cm) dried red chillies, soaked in hot water for 20 minutes to soften, de-seeded and chopped
rind of 1 lime
1 tsp salt

Preparation
Make the banana leaf cups as follows: soak the leaves in hot water for
10 minutes to soften them. Take any circular form, such as a small
bowl, about 10 cm in diameter, place this on a leaf and cut around it,
repeating for each leaf. Take 2 pieces together, dull sides facing inward;
twist and fold them about 1 cm at one edge and staple (or more traditionally skewer with a bamboo sliver) Repeat this twist, fold and staple
at 3 other points equally spaced around the circumference. The result is
a cup. Make 4 of these.

Pound the paste ingredients in a mortar until smooth.

Knead the fish in a bowl, adding the paste, coconut cream, egg and
kaffir lime leaves until it all becomes a smooth mixture.

Fill the 4 cups with the mixture, place in the top compartment of a
steamer and steam for 15–20 minutes.

Serving
Serve the cups individually.

Loc lac – Marinated Stir-fried Beef with Pepper Lime Sauce

This dish is also popular and similar in Vietnam.

Ingredients
300g good quality beef, ideally fillet, cut into 3-cm cubes
handful lettuce leaves or salad leaves
2 tbsp vegetable oil

Marinade
5 cloves garlic, finely chopped
2 tbsp soy sauce
1 tbsp sugar
1 tsp ground black pepper

Tuk Marij Dipping Sauce
8 tbsp lime juice, freshly squeezed
1 tbsp freshly ground black pepper
1 tsp salt

Preparation
Prepare the marinade by mixing all the ingredients in a bowl.

Add the cubes of beef and stir around until fully coated. Allow to
marinate for 30–40 minutes.

Prepare the dipping sauce by mixing all the ingredients together and
put in small individual bowls for each diner.

Heat the oil in a wok or large frying pan, and over a high heat stir-fry the beef for a few minutes until browned but no more than medium rare.

Serving
Place the lettuce or salad leaves on a serving platter. Tip the beef cubes on top. Wrap a piece of meat in a leaf and dip in the dipping sauce.

VIETNAM   *Pho* – Noodles with beef broth

This soup is all about the quality of the stock, and the best *pho* resataurants in Hanoi go to enormous lengths to use the right selection of bones and meat.

Ingredients
200g flat, wide rice noodles
200g good cut of beef (e.g., fillet), thinly sliced and cut into bite-sized pieces
2 spring onions, finely sliced, including green parts
handful of bean sprouts

Stock
2 kilos beef bones
1 kilo oxtail, chopped
1 kilo brisket
8 shallots
8 cm ginger, cut into 2-cm pieces
4 cm cinnamon
2 star anise
3 litres water
2 tbsp fish sauce

Accompaniments
12 stalks coriander
12 stalks mint
12 stalks holy basil
4 tbsp white vinegar
2 fresh chillies, de-seeded and finely sliced
2 limes, cut into wedges

Preparation
In a deep stockpot or pan, place the bones, add the water and bring to the boil; turn the heat down and simmer very slowly for 3–4 hours. Every so often, skim off the bits and pieces floating on the surface to keep the stock clear. Remove the bones and add the oxtail and brisket; continue simmering.

In a wok or frying pan, dry roast the ginger and shallot, tossing until they are lightly browned. Add to the stockpot, together with the cinnamon and star anise. Continue to simmer for 1–2 hours.

Remove the brisket and set aside. Continue to simmer for 1 hour. Cut the brisket into thin slices.

Remove the bones and oxtail, strain the stock through a sieve and return the liquid, which should now be clear and brown with a good aroma, to the stockpot. Bring back to a simmer. Add the fish sauce.

Prepare the accompanying pungent vinegar by chopping the chillies and sprinking into the white vinegar in a small, shallow bowl.

Bring a large pan of water to the boil. Plunge the noodles into it for no more than 1 minute. Remove and drain.

Cut the raw beef into paper-thin slices.

Serving
Divide the noodles into individual bowls, then place on top the sliced brisket, bean sprouts and spring onion slices. Ladle over this the stock. Place the raw beef slices and green leaves on side plates. Diners can add these and squeeze lime into their bowls as they wish.

Chao tom – Mashed Prawn on Sugar Cane

These are sometimes just grilled over charcoal, but steaming them first ensures that they are properly cooked through without unnecessary burning.

Ingredients
500g raw prawns, peeled and de-veined
45 cm sugar cane
1 tbsp sticky rice dry-roasted until golden, then pounded to a powder in a mortar
20–30g pork fat, rendered
2 cloves garlic
1 tbsp tapioca flour
2 cm ginger, peeled and finely chopped
1 tsp sugar
1 tsp salt

Nuoc Cham Dipping Sauce
2 cloves
3 small fresh chillies
1 tbsp sugar
4 tbsp fish sauce (*nuoc mam*)
1 tbsp white vinegar
1 tbsp water

50 ml freshly squeezed lime juice

Accompaniments
12 salad leaves or lettuce leaves
12 fresh rice paper roundels
12 stalks coriander
12 stalks mint

Preparation
Mix together the ingredients for the *nuoc cham* dipping sauce.

Cut the sugar cane into 3 sections 15 cm long, and split each into 4 lengthwise, making 12 'skewers'.

Mash together the prawns, pork fat, garlic, flour, ginger, sugar and salt to make a smooth paste. Mould a handful of this paste around the middle section of each stick, leaving the ends of the sugar cane exposed.

Steam the coated sticks (ideally in a Chinese bamboo steamer) over boiling water for 4–5 minutes.

Pat the cooked prawn sticks dry with a paper towel and grill for a few minutes over a charcoal fire until the surface is lightly blackened.

Serving
Place the prawn sticks on a serving dish and the accompaniments on another plate. Each diner takes a stick, eases the mashed prawn off the sugarcane, and wraps it in a rice paper roundel together with a few fresh leaves, then dips this into the *nuoc cham* dipping sauce.

PHILIPPINES *Chicken adobo* – Slow-cooked Chicken Marinated in Soy Sauce, Vinegar and Garlic

This dish from the north of the Philippines has a combined Spanish and Chinese heritage, and its name comes from the Spanish *adobar,* to marinate.

Ingredients
1 kilo chicken, chopped into thighs, legs and wings
2 tbsp dark soy sauce
100 ml white wine vinegar
6 cloves garlic, chopped
8 black peppercorns
3 bay leaves
2 tbsp oil
pinch of salt

Preparation
Heat the oil in a large saucepan or wok and stir-fry the garlic, pepper-

corns and bay leaves over a low heat until the garlic begins to brown. Add the soy sauce, vinegar and a pinch of salt.

Add the chicken pieces, stirring until coated.

Cover and simmer slowly for 30–40 minutes, basting occasionally.

Serving
Place the chicken pieces on a serving dish and pour the sauce from the pan over it. Serve with plain boiled rice.

Fish sinigang – Sour Fish Soup

One of the dishes that best characterizes the Filipino love of slightly sour flavours.

Ingredients
750g marine fish, with head and bones for the stock, the flesh cut into small fillets
1 litre rice water (the water usually discarded when washing starch from rice before cooking; in this case, reserve this water when preparing the rice)
5 tbsp tamarind water from 5 pods
2 tbsp lime juice (or *calamansi* if available)
2 tomatoes, quartered
2 onions, sliced
200g sweet potato, peeled, cut into 2-cm pieces
1 tbsp fish sauce
200g fresh greens, such as spinach, mustard greens, watercress or morning glory
salt and pepper to taste

Preparation
Pour the rice water into a saucepan, add the fish head and bones and simmer, covered, for 30–40 minutes. Remove the fish head and bones, strain and return the stock to the pan.

Add the tomatoes, onions, sweet potato, fish sauce, tamarind water and lime juice. Simmer for 10 minutes, covered.

Add the greens and tomatoes and continue simmering for 5 minutes, covered.

Add the fish fillets and continue simmering for 2–3 minutes or until the fish is opaque.

Serving
Serve with rice. Diners ladle soup onto a mound of rice on their plates.

MALAYSIA   *Laksa asam*

A popular noodle dish for which Penang is particularly well-known, which relies for its flavour on a gravy-like soup.

Ingredients
800g mackerel
800g laksa noodles
1 litre water

Soup or 'Gravy'
6 candlenuts
6 dried red chillies, finely chopped
6 fresh red chillies, finely chopped
6 shallots, chopped
4 cloves garlic
2 lemon grass stalks, finely sliced and chopped
1 stem and pink bud of ginger plant
4 sprigs *daun kesom* (*Polygonum sp.*), sometimes called Vietnamese
    coriander or hot mint
1/2 litre tamarind water
1 tbsp shrimp paste (*blachan*)
1 tsp sugar
1 tsp salt
1 tbsp coconut oil

Accompaniments
1/2 cucumber, chopped roughly
4 shallots, chopped
lime wedges from 3 limes
1 tsp dark shrimp paste (*patis udang*)
small red chillies
mint leaves

Preparation
Bring 1 litre of water to the boil, add the fish and continue to boil gently for 20 minutes.
    Remove the fish, allow to cool and then shred into small pieces. Sieve the stock until clear.
    Heat the oil in a wok or saucepan and stir-fry the shallots until they turn golden. Set aside.
    Pound together the candlenuts, chillies, shallots, garlic, lemon grass and shrimp paste in a mortar to a smooth paste. Put the paste into the wok or pan, mix thoroughly with a little of the stock, then add the rest of the stock and the tamarind water and bring to the boil. Add the ginger stem and bud and the *daun kesom* and cook for 20 minutes.

Add the fish flakes, sugar and salt and simmer for 30 minutes, until the 'gravy' is lightly creamy in consistency.

In a large saucepan, bring 6–8 litres of water to the boil. Plunge the noodles into the water and stir for about 2–3 minutes. Remove and drain.

Serving
Serve in individual bowls, each ideally with a capacity of $^1/_2$ litre. Divide the noodles between the bowls, then ladle the soup or 'gravy' over them. Place the accompaniments separately in small dishes. Diners sprinkle these over their noodles as desired.

Satay ayam – Chicken Satay

These skewered small kebabs, served with a distinctive spicy peanut sauce, can be traced back to Arab traders from the Middle East, but are now widely served as street food around South-east Asia.

Ingredients
500g chicken breasts, cut into strips about 10 cm by 1 cm
16 satay sticks made from bamboo slivers, soaked in water for 30 minutes before use

Marinade
4 shallots, chopped
2 cloves garlic, chopped
2 cm ginger, chopped
2 tsp coriander seeds, ground
2 tbsp light soy sauce
1 tbsp vegetable oil

Sambal Kacang (Peanut Sauce)
200g shelled peanuts
4 shallots, chopped
3 cloves garlic, chopped
3 medium-length chillies, de-seeded and chopped
1 tsp shrimp paste
1 tsp palm sugar or brown sugar
1 tbsp soy sauce
1 tbsp tamarind water from 1 pod
200 ml thin coconut milk
200 ml water
2 tbsp vegetable oil
$^1/_2$ tsp salt

Preparation
First prepare the marinade, beginning with pounding the shallots, gar-

lic, ginger and coriander seeds in a mortar. Mix in the soy sauce and oil. Pour the mixture into a bowl, add the chicken strips and stir to coat. Leave for 1–2 hours.

Prepare the peanut sauce for dipping, beginning with pounding the shallots, garlic, chillies and shrimp paste in a mortar until smooth.

In a wok, heat the oil and stir-fry the peanuts for 4–5 minutes. Remove from the oil. When cool, pound the peanuts into a powder.

Re-heat the oil in the wok and fry the pounded paste for the sauce for 1 minute.

Add to the wok the sugar, soy sauce, coconut milk and water and bring to the boil, then turn down the heat to simmer for 6–8 minutes to thicken. Finally, add the tamarind water, mix and allow to cool.

Take the marinated chicken strips, skewer one on each stick and grill (preferably over charcoal) for about 5 minutes.

Serving
Place the skewers on a serving dish and the sauce in a small dish. Diners dip the chicken skewers into the sauce.

SINGAPORE   Chilli Crab

One of Singapore's signature dishes.

Ingredients
2 large or 4 medium crabs, cooked (boiled for 2 minutes)
6 medium-length fresh chillies, finely chopped
3 cm ginger, shaved and finely chopped
3 cloves garlic, finely chopped
1 tsp shrimp paste
1 tbsp fish sauce
2 tbsp tomato purée
1 tbsp light soy sauce
2 tbsp vegetable oil
100 ml water
1 tsp sugar
1 egg
2 stalks coriander to garnish

Preparation
Remove the undershell, feathery gills and abdominal sac. Break off the claws and crack them. Quarter each crab with a cleaver.

Pound together the chillies, ginger, garlic and shrimp paste. Heat the oil in a wok and stir-fry the paste until it gives off a good aroma, then add the tomato purée and 100 ml water.

Add the crab pieces, fish sauce, soy sauce and sugar and stir-fry over a medium-high heat for 4–5 minutes, until the crab pieces are orange in colour.

Serving
Place the crab pieces in a serving dish. Diners eat with their hands. This is a messy dish for the table and a tablecloth is not recommended.

INDONESIA   *Gudeg* – Young Jackfruit Sweet Stew

This is a little-exported Javanese dish, a speciality of Yogyakarta, and an acquired taste, as it not only uses jackfruit but is also eaten sweet.

Ingredients
300g jackfruit
500g chicken on the bone, chopped roughly
5 cm galangal, roughly crushed
2 tbsp tamarind water, from 2 pods
4 *salam* leaves (*Eugenia polycantha*); these are aromatic and a little sour.
    Bay leaves are a possible substitute.
1 tsp cumin
700 ml thick coconut milk
1 litre thin coconut milk
6 eggs

Bumbu paste
6 shallots, chopped
8 cloves garlic, chopped
8 candlenuts
1 tbsp coriander seeds, crushed
1 tsp shrimp paste (*terasi*)
1 tbsp sugar
1 tsp salt
1 tsp ground white pepper

Preparation
Cut the jackfruit flesh into 2–3-cm chunks.
    Prepare the paste by pounding the ingredients in a mortar. Add several tbsp of the thick coconut and stir until smooth.
    Transfer to a saucepan, bring almost to the boil, and then turn down to simmer for 5 minutes, stirring continuously.
    Add 1 litre of thin coconut milk, the tamarind, galangal, *salam* (or bay) leaves. Return to the boil, and reduce to a simmer for 10 minutes.
    Add the jackfruit. Simmer for at least 4 hours, until the colour is brown (admittedly unappetizing in appearance in western experience). Some Javanese cooks add teak leaves to further enhance this brown colour.

Meanwhile, grill the chicken pieces slowly until the skin is browned and they are cooked about halfway through. Hard-boil the eggs; remove shells.

Add the remaining thick coconut milk, the chicken and the hard-boiled eggs to the stew. Continue simmering for about 30 minutes.

Serving
Serve as a stew with rice and prawn crackers.

Nasi goreng – Fried Rice

This is the Indonesian and Malay version of the Chinese dish devised for making use of leftover rice. Pork, common in the Chinese version, is replaced by chicken or beef. Prawns are added, and a fried egg topping. Thai *kao pad* is another regional variation.

Ingredients
400g leftover, cold cooked rice
150g raw prawns, peeled
150g chicken, cut into 5-cm pieces
4 shallots, chopped
3 cloves garlic, chopped
3 tbsp vegetable oil
1–2 tbsp light soy sauce

Garnish
2 spring onions, sliced to include some of the green stalks
3 medium-length fresh chillies, de-seeded and chopped
1 tbsp parsley, chopped
3 stalks coriander, leaves torn and chopped
pinch salt
pinch ground pepper
4 eggs

Preparation
In a wok, heat the oil until almost smoking, then add the garlic and cook over a medium heat until it begins to turn golden-brown. Add the shallots and stir-fry until they begin to brown. Add the prawns, chicken and soy sauce and stir-fry until the prawns turn pink and the chicken loses its pinkness.

Add the rice and stir continuously, mixing thoroughly with the prawns and chicken, for a few minutes, until hot. Cover and set aside.

Fry the eggs in oil without breaking the yolks. Remove and set aside

Serving
Scoop the rice out onto individual dishes, sprinkle the spring onions, chillies, coriander and parsley leaves on top, add salt and pepper and finally place a fried egg on top of each.

Pepes – Marinated Fish Steamed in Banana Leaves

Ingredients
1 kilo white fish
2 tbsp coconut cream
1 stalk lemon grass, crushed
4 kaffir lime leaves

Marinade
3 tbsp tamarind water, from 3 pods
1 tsp sugar
pinch salt

Paste
6 shallots, chopped
6 cloves garlic, chopped
2 cm ginger, chopped
4 medium sized chillies, chopped
1 tsp shrimp paste
8 black peppercorns, crushed

Preparation
Clean and scale the fish, making several deep diagonal cuts on both sides.

Mix the marinade ingredients together and stir until the sugar is dissolved.

Pound the paste ingredients together in a mortar. Smear the paste over both sides of the fish and place in the marinade. Leave to marinate for 30 minutes, turning occasionally.

Transfer the fish and paste onto a banana leaf, then pour the coconut cream over the fish, add the lemon grass stalk and lime leaves, and wrap into a packet, using other banana leaves as necessary to seal it.

Steam (or alternatively, bake high over a charcoal grill) for 30–40 minutes.

Serving
Place the banana leaf packet on a serving dish, unwrap at the table and serve.

BIBLIOGRAPHY

Allen, C., *Tales from the South China Seas* (London, 1985)
'Asian Rice Culture and its Terraced Landscapes',
    http://whc.unesco.org/archive/rice95.htm (Manila, 1995)
Bellringer, M., 'The Chemistry of Chilli Peppers',
    http://www.chemsoc.org/exemplarchem/entries/mbellringer/
Bhumichitr, V., *The Taste of Thailand* (London, 1991)
Burgess, A., *Little Wilson and Big God* (London, 1987)
—, *Malayan Trilogy* (London, 1972)
Davidson, A., *Seafood of South-east Asia* (Singapore, 1976)
DeFoliart, G., 'Insects as Food', http://www.food-insects.com
Du Pont De Bie, N., *Ant Egg Soup* (London, 2004)
'Durian OnLine', http://www.ecst.csuchico.edu/~durian/
Espejo-Hermes, J., 'EC-Cambodia Project on Standards, Quality and
    Conformity Assessment: Manual on Fish Handling and Processing'
    (Phnom Penh, 2006)
Giles, M., *Nathaniel's Nutmeg* (London, 2000)
Gourou, P., *The Tropical World* (London, 1953)
—, *Man and Land in the Far East* (London, 1975)
Harris, M., *Good To Eat* (London, 1986)
Jackson, A., H. Chau and V. Chi, *The Cuisine of Viet Nam: Nourishing a
    Culture* (Hanoi, 2005)
Jaffrey, M., *The Taste of the Far East* (London, 1993)
Katzer, G., 'Gernot Katzer's Spice Pages', http://www.uni-
    graz.at/~katzer/engl/index.html
Maugham, S., *The Gentleman in the Parlour* (London, 2001)
McPeck, C., 'Causes of Endorphin Addiction',
    http://pages.prodigy.net/unohu/endorphins.htm
Rozin, P., 'Food is Fundamental, Fun, Frightening, and Far-reaching',
    Social Research, 66 (1999) pp. 9–30
Scott, G. J., *The Burman: His Life and Notions* (London, 1910)
Sing, P., *Traditional Recipes of Laos* (London, 1981)
Thaitawat, N., *The Cuisine of Cambodia* (Bangkok, 2000)
Thompson, D., *Thai Food* (London, 2002)

Toko, K., *Biomimetic Sensor Technology* (Cambridge, 2000)
Wallace, A. R., *The Malay Archipelago* (London, 1928)
Yen Ho, A., *At the South-East Asian Table* (Kuala Lumpur, 1995)

ACKNOWLEDGEMENTS

It's difficult to know where to begin, and even more so where to stop. The events in this book span thirty years and a large number of trips, some focused on the subject at hand, others just touching on it. Over the course of this time many people helped me in many ways. There were my companions, friends and helpers, including in particular Pichai Suranantsri, John Wallingford, Tanistha Dansilp, Yeang Sokhon, Chris Burt, Danny and Kurt Kahrs, Saing Poukwan, Kyaw Swar and Pong Skuntanaga. Travelling with Madhur Jaffrey, Vatcharin Bhumichitr and Chuck Williams, on different occasions, was especially rewarding; all of them are experts in their respective fields. Dinner with Alan Davidson, unarguably the authority on the fish and fish dishes of the region, and on Laotian cooking, was memorable. Various friends and acquaintances inducted me into their authentic regional and local cuisines, including Supadee Ruangsakvichit, Cherie Aung-Khin, Gaeo Everingham, Siriporn Puranabhandu and Paisarn Piammattawat.

As a documentary photographer I have always relied on the the generosity of my publishing clients as a source of so many absorbing and entertaining assignments, from the search for birds' nests to the exploration of strange foods. These were Pamela Marke of Time-Life Books, Caroline Despard of the Smithsonian magazine, Eric Oey of Periplus Editions, John Owen of Weldon Owen and Didier Millet of Editions Didier Millet. The writer Jerry Hopkins, with whom I did an earlier book, *Strange Foods*, for Eric, deserves my special thanks for his insights, researches and sense of humour.

On these many assignments, I received help and assistance from so many people that it is with some concern over omission that I mention Prince G. P. Poeroeboyo, M. R. Narisa Chakrabongse, John Hoskin, Somphon Saekhon, Haji Angullia, Sabi Zakaria, Nina Kammerer, Leo Alting von Geusau, W. Manoon, Nopakun Tangchitnob, Somsak Kittidhrakul, Suwat Boonchanawiwet, Thomas Willie, Dr Patrick Andau, Charles Francis and Philip Round.

And finally, given that the theme of this book is that South-east Asian cooking is essentially vernacular, my thanks to all the cooks and chefs in homes, farms, village restaurants, street and market stalls, even on fishing boats, who fed me and changed my somewhat orthodox Lancashire palate into a much more adventurous one.

WHY?

The first question on everybody's lips must be "Why on earth would a dealer write a price guide?"

Well, that's a very good question, and one I've pondered a great deal while compiling this book, which to say the least has been a labour of love. Over the last ten years, I have logged and cross-referenced every response to any listing, together with how often a particular record has become available and its condition. This has enabled the production of both a 'pricing system' for my own use and a reference guide for the market at the current time. But to get a true picture we have to start at the beginning......

Back in 1968 my Mother had the foresight to add a record player to our living room furniture. Although I wasn't quite sure what to do with it, I went straight out and bought a Supremes record to test the "sound". On reflection the sound must have been extremely poor as the records were stacked eight-high on a central spindle waiting to crash down one after another, every so often one would get stuck or start to slip and I would help it along - but within week I had caught the bug, the record-buying bug to be precise.

It was true to say that in my family, as in many others, my big brother the "Mod" fell about laughing and asked " haven't you *heard Little Piece of Leather" by* Donnie Elbert? 'Who the hell's Donnie Elbert??' I thought. Next day though, I went straight down to see Sandra at W.H.Smith, a pretty cute mid-twenties blonde who promptly told me WIP matrix was Island records and sorry, but all Sue 45's were deleted now.
WHAT!!! Unavailable, ..a record I want can't be unavailable, a record I want but can't buy? What is this? Are the record companies stupid? Well, they've lost out on a 17/6p sale. Aagh, come on guys just give the record to me.

Well, as we all know the record never came and it was a good 2 years later before I even heard the record, let alone owned it. By that time I thought I had amassed the greatest, greatest, greatest soul collection in the whole wide world ever! .... But then I met "Decky".

Decky Stevens was a real together hip sort of guy, and as it happened my girlfriend at that time was also hip and particularly beautiful, so when he suggested he take 'me' to a soul club in Nottingham, as he thought I'd like the music I was kinda pleased. So on a Saturday night in 1970 me and my gal caught a bus with Decky Stevens to Trent Bridge in Nottingham. The Club for the evening was "The Brit". I remember it vividly, a young guy who had been launched into the 'Soul Big Time' with a 30 minute bus journey to the big city to listen and dance to Soul music. "I hope they play *Stoned Love*" I liked that one, " or what about *Give Me Just A Little More Time*" I was good at moving to that, after hours of practice in the bathroom.

Anyone who visited 'The Brit' will remember those wooden stairs leading to the Pay Desk, but as we queued I heard a new sound..... a rather smooth vocal over an altogether different beat.

"I got a funny funny funny feeling, there's something you're trying to hide, I got funny funny funny feeling you've found yourself another guy." For the first time in my life, the hairs on the back of my neck stood up!!

" When you love somebody baby, as much as I love you it's the little things in life that count. What you say and do.. But the way you've been acting lately, I think you've found someone new 'cause you just ain't satisfied no matter what I do for you"

WOW!! Every part of my skin came alive, as we climbed the stairs the sound became louder and louder, a drum roll was followed by girls...oooooh.oooh What or Who the hell was that??

Later I was treated to *Jackie Edwards "I feel so bad" Jimmy McCracklin "The Walk" Len Barry "Somewhere."* Then, the best moment of my seventeen year old life - ...*Leon Haywood "Baby Reconsider".* Shit!! I had the worst record collection anywhere in the world. I was THE nerd of Soul music. ..I had never even heard any of these records EVER!!

Little did I know that a Soul Scene had sprouted in England from teenagers so bored of guys with one-drum-and-three- guitars from Liverpool or Oldham trying to sing "Money, that's what I want", when money was what they'd got, but no soul. The mods had discovered American 60's soul and boy had they discovered it!

Fortunately for the whole of the 60's teenage generation Emi Music Co. had released various USA soul 45's on their Stateside/Capitol/Liberty labels, with sounds that were so totally different to anything being produced in England that a cult following emerged in almost every major city in England. To make this whole new movement even more interesting to music fans these UK release 45's were quickly deleted and became almost impossible to track down. As a result another faction of the soul record scene emerged, it wasn't just the dancing, it wasn't just the emotion that soul music stirred inside these kids it was now the thrill of the chase, the hunt for discs rare and exclusive. In order to be hip, the most desirable items in any self respecting Mods 'wardrobe' were his records, it got to the stage where your Street-Cred was based on the fact of whether or not you owned a copy of Alexander Patton, Incredibles, or Mary Love, not how many mirrors your Vespa had, or whether your hand stitched suit was tailored. Your passport was your record collection, and your knowledge of these records and so it was from this hip, chic, vibrant mod club scene that the NORTHERN SOUL scene was born.

Most Saturdays collectors were taken up with travelling to a different city or town to 'check out that little old lady's music shop' in the hope that she might just have some Stateside, some Tamla Motown, or Sue 45's still left on her shelves and so the first Soul Record Hounds were born. Most Saturday evenings were spent in your choice of Soul Club, either to dance, but more likely to talk about your day's finds, rather like a fisherman in the pub boasting about his catch - these soul children of the Sixties were truly hooked.

By early 1970 explorers of soul 45's had started to make regular trips to the USA to search for new sounds. John Anderson in particular was responsible for bringing to the UK hundreds of thousands of soul records that until now nobody in Great Britain knew existed and nobody in the USA even cared. It was heaven. The USA was giving us the greatest music we could ever have dreamed of, and nobody in that country wanted any of it. Maybe, it was God's way of paying back those early settlers who found gold, which the Indians weren't too bothered about either. Those 'golden nuggets' lay the foundations of, what is today, the largest underground collecting music scene in the world. Whole weekends are dedicated to soul festivals in the UK, all-night clubs playing rare soul music are springing up in France, Spain, New York, California, Australia, Sweden, Italy, even Germany has got turned onto black music in the Northern Soul fever. More recently Japan has played host to DJ's such as Mark Dobson and Keb Darge in an effort to entertain huge crowds of soul fans.

So from its humble beginnings in the mid-sixties with hip kids searching for a hip sound grew this scene of dedicated and highly knowledgeable music fans.

Let's go back to my starting point, the PRICING of soul 45's. Of course, years of such passion have seen a rise in the price of from 50p or a £1.00 to a place where a £1000 sale is almost common.

However, in order to be qualified to take on the task of producing a guide that truly reflects this complex scene, one would need at least three credentials:-

1) Soul music would have to be your full time job, dealing with record queries on the phone every day for at least eight hours a day is the only way to understand the current demand for any 45 single;

2) You would have to be a time-served craftsman that is to have been operating long enough to know that if someone suggests 'Epitome Of Sound' is a rare record, you know it's extremely common because I had & sold Ten 100 count boxes of the titlet in 1978 and other dealers had just as many from various other sources. If it's suggested that a Michael & Raymond black issue is only one of three copies, well perhaps not, as I can remember having a 25 count box of that same title. Along with so many other titles, that have lined my and other dealers walls especially in the early years in quantities of one, two or even three hundred copies of a title that are now considered "rare" were common at one time or another. Les Moss told me he used to have boxes and boxes of the Cashmeres on Hem – at what price!!

It's also useful to have travelled to every USA State, as what is rare on the West Coast can be common on the East, what is rare in Detroit can be common in New Orleans and vice-versa;

3) Lastly, but perhaps most importantly, you cannot be a collector and hope to produce an unbiased price guide. It is amazing just how much collectors overvalue their records. If someone owns the record, then it's worth £1000's, if they don't , well it's probably a white singer, or it's rare but not that rare - 'although he did have the chance to buy it for much less than the current value but he turned it down!'

Many dealers will have heard these stories. Only yesterday someone said to me a record he has he wouldn't sell for less than £6000, when I auction the record 18 months ago, I recieved a single bid!
So it is not always true to say that just because you own it someone else will give you a sky-high price for it.

However those 'Pie in the Sky" prices are occasionally paid, but to the owner of that record it's the price he wanted to pay. And maybe no one else in the world wide world would have paid anything like that price. This happens, so I've tried to hit a current going sensible price. But beware as well as maybe getting more, at auction you may find some three figure records just don't sell at all!! It is certainly a truism that prices don't have so much to do with what the last guy paid, but definitely about what the next guy will pay!

PRICING POLICY

Within the record collecting fraternity, there are not just Northern Soul collectors, for example, consider these groupings, Deep Soul, Funk, Sweet Soul, Group Harmony, Girl Groups, Crossover, 70's & 80's, Jamaican Soul, Spector, etc etc. Jeff Beckman wrote in his introduction to the Soul Harmony Singles: *"Soul music presents it's own, unique problems. Soul collectors are segmented into two almost mutually exclusive groups. Collectors in the US and Japan generally favour Sweet Soul, the dreamy, mellow, smooth midtempo and, often-falsetto led, ballad recording. While in England and other areas in Europe collectors favour Northern Soul the brassy, uptempo, barnstorming stompers..."*

How true, but actually there are many totally different scenes, you've only got to go to Great Yarmouth Soul Essence weekends to see that there are more than three different collecting scenes just within the inner circle of soul fans.

This book is merely a Price Guide, not a pricing bible. The prices within the soul scene are particularly volatile as, unlike any other collectable vinyl market, the whole pricing structure is influenced by DJ's. A 45 that is a current in-demand sound will command more money than when it is dropped from play lists. I recently saw The Brothers - *Are You Ready For This* - RCA listed at £25.00 but six months ago you would not have had a buyer at £5.00.

The prices quoted are based on Set Sale or Auction and because this is taken from a data base, it is what I would expect to sell these 45's for, but as we have discovered, the Scene is constantly changing so Edition II will not only contain many different titles but the prices may have changed too. Some records contained within this guide I've listed for 10 years or more and never sold a single copy. Yep, we've all done that!!

PRICES ARE IN USA $$ and UK ££

USA prices do not include State sales tax.
UK prices include VAT "Value Added Tax" @ 17.5%. (All list prices in Europe include Tax)

MORE INFORMATION

No matter how much time you spend on a project like this, it is unavoidable to miss titles, artists, b-sides etc. Your help is most welcome to making this Guide more complete. If you know a missing label number or missing B-side, or you may have a record in your own collection that you feel should be within this guide. please let me know, I'd be pleased to hear from you.

Prices are relative to mint minus vinyl condition with no label defects.

I've tried to be concise in all areas and I've included one, perhaps the most important point, rare soul titles that have been bootlegged or counterfeited using the *original label* design have been noted as **northerB**.
If you need to know how to detect the bootleg copy from the original.
MANSHIP'S GUIDE TO NORTHERN SOUL BOOTLEGS Edition 3 is available see the advert .

northern	= Northern Soul 45
northerB	= Northern Soul 45 bootlegged using the original label design
funk	= Funk 45
ballad	= Soul 45 either deep/ballad/collectable artist/collectable label
group	= Group harmony soul
70's	= 70's dance soul 45
motown	= Tamla Motown related 45
NI (after serial #)	= Most Probably never released
PS	= Price with a Picture Cover

Some 45's obviously fall into more than one category, so I've picked the one in which it is easiest to sell. Remember each scene may have different price, a group collector may value a Northern Soul record at $30 , but it could be sold for $300 and visa versa. For example, Magicians on Vila is scarce in New York but common in England.

ACKNOWLEDGEMENTS

A great deal of the information contained in this Guide has been drawn from my trusty computer database, but without the support and help of my friends this book would have been much less informative and much harder to produce. So grateful thanks go to :-

Andy Rix, Ian Wright, John Dixon, Stella Morris, Ella Calver, Michelle Greet, Karen Kemp, Jeff Beckman, Jim Hunt, Tom Kline for their marvellous book "Soul Harmony Singles". Heidi for the artwork.

And my Mother for buying that record player in 1968.

Copyright and Disclaimer

The information contained herein is the property of John Manship
Records and iis suipplied without liability for errors or omissions.
No part of the book maybe reproduced in any form what so ever
without the prior consent in writing of John Manship. The
Information contained in the material is subject to change without notice.

John Manship
45 Dalby Road, Melton Mowbray, Leics, LE 13 0BG
Tel. (44) 1664 464526
Fax (44) 1664 464155
E.mail Info@raresoulman.co.uk
Web Site WWW.raresoulman.co.uk
June 2001

JOHN MANSHIP'S PRICE GUIDE

When the first 45rpm records were made nobody could ever have imagined the impact it would have on the generations to come. For many people collecting records is a way of life and the desire to own elusive pieces of vinyl drives individuals to invest significant amounts of time, energy and money in realising their dreams.
The Brits have always been staunch collectors and few have been more loyal or tireless in their pursuits than those who collect the music of Black America. Our fascination with Soul music, and all of its associated genres, has now spanned more than four decades.

Collectors of obscure, and often extremely rare, soul 45s have long battled to keep what they have discovered a secret from the rest of the world so that they can continue to pillage untapped sources without fear of apprehension. But times change and life moves on and the knowledge that used to be exclusive to a few is now available to many.

It goes without saying that the value of a record is directly related to demand. When that demand only existed in clubs specialising in playing that style of sound it seemed only right and proper that the patrons who had given that record its status were allowed first call on the copies that were in circulation. Those outside the specialist clubs merely dismissed the music as trash and of no interest in any case.

The UK collectors always knew that the vinyl they purchased was something special and it may have taken years for the rest of the world to recognise that but slowly and surely the conversion has happened.

Access to the music has been the real turning point and the advent of compilation CDs and the world wide web has made the world a very small and affordable place indeed. There is little to be gained in trying to pretend that the treasures we seek are worthless as there is no real secret any more. Collectors now exist in increasing numbers across the major continents and regular publications, both magazines and record lists, which focus on selling their wanted 45s are as easy to get as bread from a shop.

Record price guides have always been part of the collecting scene although the publications dealing with more popular forms of music have been more realistic and accurate in both content and valuations. Given the scenarios alluded to it would seem to be the right time to publish a guide that focuses on the rare side of soul and that such a guide is compiled by somebody who has years of experience in the market.

John Manship had been buying and selling records for thirty years and for the last ten has actually committed information to paper as opposed to keeping it in his head. This guide is a result of that commitment and whilst not claiming to be definitive it does lay a very solid foundation upon which future revisions and updates can be built.
For collectors like myself who have never quite got organised it should mean an end to trawling through piles of paper to locate the title of that long forgotten B side. For others it will mean having a degree of confidence when buying or selling items that may not be that familiar to them.

Andy Rix

A

A BROTHER'S GUIDING LIGHT

GETTING TOGETHER	SWEET STUFF	MERCURY 73389	100.00	70's

A FACINATING MUSICAL EXPERIENCE

THE MONSTER	1-2-3	HONEY 216	50.00	funk

A.A.B.B.

PICK UP THE PIECES ONE BY ONE	C.O.L.D.	I DENTIFY 8003	20.00	funk

ABRAHAM AND HIS SONS

I CAN'T DO WITHOUT YOU	YOUR MOTHER UNDERSTOOD	REVUE 11059	25.00	northern

ABRAHAM, J.D.

DOCTOR OF LOVE	LET ME TELL YOU WHAT I WANT	REENA 1028	150.00	northern

ABSTRACT REALITY

LOVE BURNS LIKE A FIRE INSIDE	SAME: INSTRUMENTAL.	SPORT 0104	100.00	northern

ACCENTS

NEW GIRL	DO YOU NEED A GOOD MAN	M-PAC 7216	15.00	northern
ON THE RUN	HE'S THE ONE	KARATE 529	20.00	northern
YOU BETTER THINK AGAIN	WHO YOU GONNA LOVE	ONEDERFUL 4833	85.00	northern

ACE SPECTRUM

DON'T SEND NOBODY ELSE	DON'T LET ME BE LONELY	ATLANTIC 3012	20.00	70's
LIVE AND LEARN	JUST LIKE IN THE MOVIES	ATLANTIC 3353	10.00	70's
TRUST ME	I JUST WANT TO SPEND THE NIGHT	ATLANTIC 3281	8.00	70's

ACE, BUDDY

BEGGIN FOR YOUR LOVE	BEGGIN FOR YOUR LOVE Pt.2	A&B 12172	30.00	funk
COLOR MY LOVE		MIND TRIPPER 100	150.00	northern
IT'S GONNA BE ME	NOTHING IN THE WORLD CAN HURT	DUKE 397	15.00	northern
TRUE LOVE MONEY CAN'T BUY	MY LOVE	DUKE 381	20.00	northern

ACKLIN, BARBARA

RAINDROPS	HERE YOU COME AGAIN	CAPITOL 3892	10.00	70's
AM I THE SAME GIRL	BE BY MY SIDE	BRUNSWICK 55399	8.00	northern
LOVE MAKES A WOMAN	COME AND SEE BABY	BRUNSWICK 55379	8.00	northern
AFTER YOU	MORE WAYS THAN ONE	BRUNSWICK 755421	8.00	northern
I DID IT	I'M LIVING WITH A MEMORY	BRUNSWICK 55440	10.00	northern
LOVE MAKES A WOMAN	COME AND SEE ME BABY	DAU 1015	30.00	northern
THE OLD MATCHMAKER	I'VE GOT YOU BABY	BRUNSWICK 55355	10.00	northern
AM I THE SAME GIRL	BE BY MY SIDE	BRUNSWICK 55399	8.00	northern
I'M NOT MAD ANYMORE	NOBODY CARES	SPECIAL AGENT 203	800.00	northern

ACUNA, SAMMY

I NEVER FOUND A GIRL	SAME: INSTRUMENTAL	NEW WAVE 3	30.00	70's

AD LIBS

I DON'T NEED NO FORTUNE TELLER	SPRING AND SUMMER	PASSION 1	300.00	70's
NOTHING WORSE THAN BEING ALONE	IF SHE WANTS HIM	SHARE 106	10.00	northern
THE BOY FROM NEW YORK CITY	KICKED AROUND	BLUE CAT 102	8.00	northern
LOVE ME	KNOW ALL ABOUT YOU	CAPITOL 2944	20.00	northern
DON'T EVER LEAVE ME	YOU'RE IN LOVE	PHILIPS 40461	20.00	northern
NEIGHBOR, NEIGHBOR	LOVELY LADIES	INTERPHON 7717	10.00	northern
NEW YORK IN THE DARK	HUMAN	A.G.P. 100	200.00	**northerB**
NEW YORK IN THE DARK	HUMAN	ESKEE 1003	300.00	northern
THINK OF ME	EVERY BOY AND GIRL	KAREN 1527	50.00	northern

ADAMS APPLES

DON'T TAKE IT OUT ON THIS WORLD	DON'T YOU WANT ME HOME	BRUNSWICK 55330	200.00	northern
YOU ARE THE ONE I LOVE	STOP ALONG THE WAY	BRUNSWICK 78025	30.00	northern

ADAMS, ALBERTA

I GOT A FEELING	WITHOUT YOUR LOVE	THEMLA 82363	100.00	motown

ADAMS BOBBY

THAT'S THE KIND OF MAN I AM		BIG BEE 778	500.00	northern

ADAMS, ARTHUR

CAN'T WAIT TO SEE YOU	IT'S PRIVATE TONIGHT	CHISA 8011	10.00	70's

ADAMS, BILLY

YOU AND ME	GO (GO ON GET OUT OF HERE)	AMY 893	15.00	northern

ADAMS, BOBBY

BE CAREFUL WITH MY HEART	A NEW WAY TO HURT ME	BO-AD 101	20.00	northern
SIXTEEN YEARS IN THE MAKING	BETTER DAYS AHEAD	BATTLE 45914	25.00	northern
YOU GOT NEXT TO ME BABY	HOME DOESN'T SEEM LIKE HOME	PILMA 887	20.00	northern

ADAMS, JOHNNY

YOUR KIND OF LOVE	ONE DAY (YOU'RE GONNA COME MY	MODERN 1044	20.00	northern

7

ADAMS, JUNE

THE HUMAN RACE	I'M NOT THAT KIND OF GIRL	ROULETTE 4660	30.00	northern

ADAMS, KERRY

FAST TALKING LOVER	I JUST FOUND LOVE	CALLA 103	25.00	northern

ADAMS, LINDY

A BIRD IN THE HAND	SUPRISE PARTY	TRI DISC 108	15.00	northern

ADAMS, MARIE

FOOLIN' AROUND	OLD FEELIN'	SURE PLAY 1001	40.00	northern
FOOLIN' AROUND	OLD FEELING	VENDED 1003	30.00	northern

ADAMS, NATE

I'M GONNA BE GOOD	WHY IS IT TAKING SO LONG	ATLANTIC 2466	30.00	northern

ADAMS, RITCHIE

I CAN'T ESCAPE FROM YOU	ROAD TO NOWHERE	CONGRESS 256	150.00	northern

ADAMS, VIKI

I'M DROWNING	SO GLAD YOU'RE HOME	STOP 244	15.00	northern

ADAMS, VINNY

WHILE WE'RE STILL YOUNG	LISTEN HEART	HOLTON 2566	20.00	northern

ADENO, BOBBY

THE HANDS OF TIME	IT'S A AD WORLD	BACK BEAT 552	15.00	northern

ADMIRAL ICE

MY CAROLINA GIRL	BEACH BUM	ADMIRAL ICE 3219	30.00	70's

ADMIRATIONS

DON'T LEAVE ME	ALL FOR YOU	ONEDERFUL 4851	15.00	northern
LONELY STREET	HEY MAMMA	BRUNSWICK 55332	30.00	northern
WAIT TIL I GET TO KNOW YOU	SAME: INSTRUMENTAL.	ONEDERFUL 4849	10.00	northern
YOU LEFT ME	I WANT TO BE FREE	PEACHES 6721	1000.00	northern

ADORABLES

BE	SCHOOL'S ALL OVER	GOLDEN WORLD 10	15.00	motown
DEEP FREEZE	DADDY PLEASE	GOLDEN WORLD 4	15.00	motown
DADDY PLEASE	DEEP FREEZE	GOLDEN WORLD 5	15.00	northern
OOH BOY	DEVIL IN HIS EYES	GOLDEN WORLD 25	50.00	northern

ADVENTURERS

SOMETHING BAD (IS HAPPENING)	NOBODY CAN SAVE ME	BLUE ROCK 4071	20.00	northern
EASY BABY	A GOOD GIRL IS SO HARD TO FIND	COMPASS 7010	100.00	**northerB**
I'VE CAUGHT YOU CHEATING	DARLIN' (YOU SAUD YOU LOVED ME)	MUSIC WORLD 110	100.00	northern

AGEE, RAY

I'M LOSING AGAIN	HARD LOVING WOMAN	SOUL TOWN 104	1000.00	northern

AGE OF BRONZE

I'M GONNA LOVE YOU	EVERYTHING SEEMS TO CHANGE	GUAVA 102	150.00	northern

AGENTS

TROUBLE	THE LOVE I HOLD	LIBERTY BELL 3260	500.00	northern
YOU WERE MEANT FOR ME	YOU'RE EVERYTHING	P&L 1001	25.00	northern

AIKEN, BEN

BABY YOU MOVE ME	THANKS TO YOU	LOMA 2100	10.00	northern
CALLIN'	GOD BLESS THE GIRL AND ME	LOMA 2076	15.00	northern
HURRY ON HOME BABY	STAY TOGETHER, YOUNG LOVERS	SQUIRE 504	30.00	northern
HURRY ON HOME BABY	STAY TOGETHER, YOUNG LOVERS	ROULETTE 4649	10.00	northern
SATISFIED	THE LIFE OF A CLOWN	LOMA 2084	60.00	northern
YOU WERE MEANT TO BE MY BABY	IF I TOLD YOU ONCE	LOMA 2069	10.00	northern

AKENS, JEWEL

I'M GOIN' BACK HOME	NAKED CITY	AS-WANA 2176	20.00	ballad
A SLICE OF THE PIE	YOU BETTER BELIEVE IT	ERA 3156 DJ	15.00	northern
HE'S GOOD FOR ME	HELPLESSLY IN L.OVE	WEST-ONE 109	15.00	northern
I'VE ARRIVED	YOU DON'T NEED A CROWN	ERA 3154	30.00	northern
WHAT WOULD YOU DO	SINCE I DON'T HAVE YOU	ICEPAC 303	30.00	northern
MY FIRST LONELY NIGHT	MAMA TAKE YOUR DAUGHTER BACK	ERA 3164 DJ	200.00	northern

AKINS, AUDREY

DOWN CAME MY TEARS	I STILL LOVE YOU	PETAL 1030	30.00	northern
WHAT CAN YOU LOSE (BUT THE BLUES)	THAT'S THE MAN THAT'S MINE	KARATE 515	20.00	northern

AL AND JET

NOTHING TO HIDE	LUCKY US	PHILIPS 40425	10.00	northern

ALAIMO, STEVE

EVERY DAY I HAVE TO CRY	LITTLE GIRL	CHECKER 1032	10.00	northern
SO MUCH LOVE	TRUER THAN TRUE	ABC 10805	8.00	northern

ALAN, LEE AND THE VENDELLAS

SET ME FREE	SAME:	ZTSC 94422	50.00	motown

ALCON SHADES

ALL IS FORGIVEN	MIDNIGHT LIGHT	BLUE ROCK 4068	50.00	northern

ALEONG, AKI

GIVING UP ON LOVE	LOVE IS FUNNY	VEE JAY 527	45.00	northern

ALEXANDER TECHNIQUES, RAY

LET'S TALK	SAME: INSTRUMENTAL	LU JUN 2001	25.00	funk

ALEXANDER, ARTHUR

ANNA	YOU BETTER MOVE ON	DOT 126	8.00	northern
KEEP HER GUESSING	WHER DID SALLY GO	DOT 16554	70.00	northern
SHOW ME THE ROAD	TURN AROUND (AND TRY ME)	SS7 2572	20.00	northern

Artist / Title	B-side	Label	Price	Genre
ALEXANDER, BRANDI				
DO RIGHT MAN	LIFE HAS NO MEANING	TRC 996	20.00	northern
ALEXANDER, J.W.				
KEEP A LIGHT IN THE WINDOW UNT	BABY, IT'S REAL	MIRWOOD 5518	15.00	ballad
ALEXANDER, REGGIE				
IT'S BETTER	MY CONFESSION (TO YOU)	BOSS 102	400.00	northern
ALFROS BAND				
RIGHT ON RIGHT OF	WHY DID YOU LEAVE	LYNDELL 883	300.00	funk
ALGERE, RAY				
IN MY CORNER	YOU'RE DRIVING ME CRAZY	TOU-SEA 126	30.00	northern
ALL NIGHT WORKERS				
DON'T PUT ALL YOUR EGGS IN ONE	WHY DON'T YOU SMILE	ROUND 1	50.00	northern
ALL STARS				
DISINTEGRATED PT.1	DISINTEGRATED PT.2	MOTOWN 1018 NI	400.00	motown
ALL THE PEOPLE				
CRAMP YOUR STYLE	WHATCHA GONNA DO ABOUT IT	BLUE CANDLE 1496	15.00	funk
ALLEN GROUP, RANCE				
REASON TO SURVIVE	GOT TO BE READY	CAPITOL 4443	30.00	70's
ALLEN, BOBBY AND THE GEE PEES				
HERE SHE COMES AGAIN	YA YA SONG	UPPP 101	20.00	ballad
ALLEN, CHRISTY				
WALK TALL LIKE A MAN	ANY MOMENT	DIAMOND 209	15.00	northern
ALLEN, LAINEY				
I CAN'T TAKE IT		J.W.J. 22917	75.00	northern
ALLEN, L.				
CAN'T WE TALK IT OVER	SOMEWHERE THERE IS PARADISE	GREEN DOLPHIN 115	200.00	northern
ALLEN, LARRY				
CAN'T WE TALK IT OVER	SOMEWHERE THERE IS PARADISE	GREEN DOLPHIN 115	300.00	northern
ALLEN, NA				
I'M IN LOVE WITH YOU	I'M MY OWN MAN	JANUS 182	10.00	ballad
EVERYTIME IT RAINS	LAY IT ON ME RIGHT NOW	RONN 47	30.00	northern
THANKS FOR NOTHING	NO EASY WAY DOWN	ATCO 6753	100.00	northern
ALLEN, NICK				
HARD WAY TO GO	DON'T MAKE ME BE WHAT YOU DON'	WALAS 1	20.00	northern
ALLEN, RICKY				
SKATE BOOGALOO	IT'S A MESS I TELL YOU	BRIGHT STAR 150	15.00	northern
NOTHING IN THE WORLD CAN HURT	WHAT DO YOU DO	BRIGHT STAR 147	15.00	northern
ALLEN, SHERLI				
THINK IT OVER		X-TRA 120	75.00	northern
ALLEN, SONNY				
YOUR LOVE IS SO WONDERFUL	YOUR LOVE IS SO WONDERFUL PT.2	HIT PACK 42747	200.00	northern
ALLEY, PATRICK				
GROOVE FEELING	GROOVE FEELING PT. 2	PERSIST 1006	30.00	70's
ALLISON, LEVERT				
I WANT TO GIVE MY HEART TO YOU	SHAPE I'M IN	PONCHELLO 7004	20.00	northern
ALLISON.				
OOH BABY CAN'T EXPLAIN THE FEE	I'VE GOT THE PLACE IF YOU'VE GOT	ANSAP 1101	20.00	northern
ALSTON, RON				
SOMETHIN' AIN'T RIGHT	ONE MORE TEAR	PHILIPS 40416	20.00	northern
ALVON, TONY AND THE BELAIRS				
SEXY COFFEE POT	BOOM-BOOM-BOOM	ATLANTIC 2632	50.00	funk
AMAR, CHARLES				
I'M GONNA GET YOU YET	A TENDER KISS IN THE DARK	LAMAR 101	20.00	northern
AMARO, TONY AND THE CHARIOTS				
HEY BABY	RUNNIN' AROUND	LOMA 2068	20.00	northern
AMAZERS (AMAZORS)				
WITHOUT A WARNING	IT'S YOU FOR ME	THOMAS 1638	10.00	northern
WITHOUT A WARNING	IT'S YOU FOR ME	THOMAS 1638 black lbl	15.00	northern
IT'S YOU FOR ME	COME BACK BABY	BREAD 74	10.00	group
AMBASSADORS				
I'M SO PROUD OF MY BABY	I'VE GOTTA FIND HAPPINESS	ATLANTIC 2442	15.00	northern
(I'VE GOT TO FIND) HAPPINESS	GOOD LOVE, GONE BAD	ATLANTIC 2491	15.00	northern
DO YOU EVER THINK ABOUT ME	I LOVE YOU	DEBROSSARD 827D5831	50.00	northern
STORM WARNING	I DIG YOU BABY	ARCTIC 153	25.00	northern
AIN'T GOT THE LOVE OF ONE GIRL	MUSIC (MAKES YOU WANNA DANCE)	ARCTIC 150	10.00	northern
I CAN'T BELIEVE YOU LOVE ME	I REALLY LOVE YOU	ARCTIC 147	10.00	northern
TOO MUCH OF A GOOD THING	WHOLE LOTTA SOUL	PEE VEE 1000	200.00	**northerB**
AMBERS				
DON'T GO	SOUL IN ROOM #401	JEAN 727	8.00	70's
BLUE BIRDS	BABY (I NEED YOU)	NEW ART 104	20.00	group
NEVER COULD YOU BE MY GIRL	DON'T GO	JEAN 729	20.00	group
I LOVE YOU BABY	NOW I'M IN TROUBLE	VERVE 10436	25.00	northern
POTION OF LOVE	ANOTHER LOVE	SMASH 2111	30.00	**northerB**
AMBROSE, SAMMY				
THEY'LL BE COMING	RAM RAM	CRAZY HORSE 1315	20.00	northern
THIS DIAMOND RING	BAD NIGHT	MUSICOR 1061	80.00	northern

9

WELCOME TO DREAMSVILLE	MONKEY EE MONKEY DO	MUSICOR 1072	100.00	northern
AMERICAN YOUTH CHIOR				
KEEP YOUR FINE SELF NEAR ME	TOGETHER WE CAN MAKE IT	POLYDOR 14020	20.00	northern
AMES, NANCY				
I DON'T WANT TO TALK ABOUT IT	CRY SOFTLY	EPIC 10056	10.00	**northerB**
AMES, STEWART				
ANGELINA, OH ANGELINA	KING FOR A DAY	J&W 1000	300.00	**northerB**
ANDANTES				
LIKE A NIGHTMARE	IF YOU WERE MINE	V.I.P. 25006	4000.00	northern
ANDEREGG, CALLEEN				
FOOL'S PARADISE	DON'T CRY ON MY SHOULDER	RBE 112	150.00	northern
ANDERSON BROS.				
I CAN SEE HIM LOVING YOU	SAME:	GSF 6914 DJ only	300.00	**northerB**
ANDERSON, ANITA				
SECRECTLY	LITTLE BIT LONGER	CONTACT 502	400.00	northern
ANDERSON, CAROL				
HOLDING ON	IT SHOULDN'T HAPPEN TO A DOG	MID-TOWN 270	20.00	northern
HOLDING ON	YOU BOY	MID-TOWN 271	15.00	northern
I'M NOT WORRIED	TAKING MY MIND OFF LOVE	WHIP 347	125.00	northern
SAD GIRL	I'LL GET OFF AT THE NEXT STOP	FEE 101	50.00	northern
ANDERSON, CURTIS				
RUNNING AWAY FROM LOVE	THE LOVELY FEELING	TEMPRE 100	8.00	ballad
THE HARDEST PART		BROWN BAG	800.00	70's
ANDERSON, ERNESTINE				
KEEP AN EYE ON LOVE	CONTINENTAL MIND	SUE 793	30.00	northern
YOU'RE NOT THE GUY FOR ME	I PITY THE FOOL	SUE 115 .	30.00	northern
ANDERSON, GAIL				
MY TURN NOW	IT'S SO EASY TO SAY	EARLY BIRD 49662	30.00	northern
THEY'RE LAUGHING AT ME	SAME:	SHELL 102	20.00	nortern
BE PROUD YOU'RE IN LOVE		SALVADOR 999	20.00	northern
LET'S FALL IN LLOVE ALL OVER	SAME:	GMBLE 206 DJ	20.00	northern
ANDERSON, GENE				
THE GIGILO	THE LONELIEST ONE	ROYAL-TONE 1005	40.00	funk
BABY I DIG YOU	WHAT'S WRONG WITH YOU GIRL	ROYAL-TONE 1000	20.00	northern
ANDERSON, JESSE				
MIGHTY MIGHTY	I GOT A PROBLEM	THOMAS 805	15.00	funk
ANDERSON, JOE				
YOU AND I	SAME: (Long Version)	BUDDAH 480	15.00	70's
DON'T YOU KNOW	I CAN'T GET ENOUGH OF YOU	HEIDI 112	40.00	northern
I'M SO GLAD	HOW LONG WILL IT LAST	HEIDI 110	30.00	northern
ANDERSON, KIP				
I DONE YOU WRONG	THAT'S WHEN THE CRYING BEGINS	ABC 10578	25.00	northern
I GET CARRIED AWAY	HERE I AM, TRY ME	TOMORROW 501	40.00	northern
ANDERSON, VICKI				
ANSWER TO MOTHER POPCORN	I'LL WORK IT OUT	KING 6251	20.00	funk
BABY, DON'T YOU KNOW	LET IT BE ME	KING 6293	15.00	funk
I'M TOO TOUGH FOR MR. BIG STUF	SOUND FUNKY	BROWNSTONE 4202	15.00	funk
IN THE LAND OF MILK AND HONEY	DON'T THROW YOUR LOVE IN THE GARBAGE	BROWNSTONE 4207	15.00	funk
IN THE LAND OF MILK AND HONEY	I'LL WORK IT OUT	BROWNSTONE 4204	15.00	funk
MESSAGE FROM THE SOUL SISTER	YESTERDAY	KING JAMES 6377	20.00	funk
WIDE AWAKE IN A DREAM	NOBODY CARES	DELUXE 6201	25.00	northern
ANDRE, TOMMY				
ONE MORE TRY	BLUEPRINT	BROADWAY 503	20.00	northern

* Some DJ copies have a different mix, Alt.Mix 50.00

ANDREA, JOHN				
COME ON IN	MY FOOL OF A HEART	MGM 13378	15.00	northern
ANDREWS, DEE				
STOP! YOU'RE HURTING MY HEART	I'LL DO WHAT YOU WANT ME TO	TRC 992	30.00	northern
ANDREWS, ERNIE				
FINE YOUNG GIRL	THEN I'LL KNOW	CAPITOL 5530	10.00	northern
WHERE WERE YOU (WHEN I NEEDED YOU)	WHAT DO I SEE IN THE GIRL	CAPITOL 5448	15.00	northern
ANDREWS, H.				
STEPPIN' OUT	I'D LIKE TO SCHOOL YOU	BALANCE 2030	20.00	70's
I'M SO TIRED OF BEING LONELY	I LIKE MUSIC	BALANCE 2000	100.00	northern
ANDREWS CONGREGATION, H.				
CHITLIN CIRCUIT		BALANCE	100.00	funk
ANDREWS, HAROLD				
WE GOT TO GET BACK TOGETHER	YOU'RE A WINNER	EARLY BIRD 9663	30.00	ballad
SINCE I TALK TO MY BABY	SINCE I TALK TO MY BABY PT.2	HLS 500	10.00	northern

This record was especially "recorded" for Bob Catteneo for the Northern Soul scene circa 1977

ANDREWS, JIMMY				
BIG CITY PLAYBOY	HAPPY GUY	BLUE JAY 5003	1000.00	northern
ANDREWS, LEE AND THE HEARTS				
I'VE HAD IT	LITTLE BIRD	CRIMSON 1015	100.00	northern
NEVER THE LESS	ISLAND OF LOVE	CRIMSON 1009	20.00	northern
QUIET AS IT'S KEPT	YOU'RE TAKING A LONG TIME COMING	RCA 8929	20.00	northern

ALL YOU CAN DO	COLD GREY DAWN	LOST NITE 1001	20.00	northern
CAN'T DO WITHOUT YOU	OH MY LOVE	LOST NITE 1004	15.00	northern
QUIET AS IT'S KEPT	ISLAND OF LOVE	LOST NITE 1005	30.00	northern

ANDREWS, RUBY

I GOT A BONE TO PICK WITH YOU	I DON'T KNOW HOW TO LOVE YOU	ABC 12215	10.00	70's
CASANOVA (PLAYING DAYS ARE OVER)	I JUST DON'T BELIEVE IT	ZODIAC 1004	8.00	northern
GOTTA BREAK AWAY	YOU OLE BOO BOO YOU	ZODIAC 1020	10.00	northern
HELP YOURSELF (LOVER)	ALL THE WAY	ZODIAC 1016	10.00	northern
HEY BOY (LET'S TAKE A CHANCE)	COME TO ME	ZODIAC 1006	20.00	northern
I JUST CAN'T GET ENOUGH	JOHNNY'S GONE AWAY	ZODIAC 1003	75.00	northern
JUST LOVING YOU	I LOVE I NEED	ZODIAC 1010	75.00	northern

ANDRIANI, BOBBY

TO BE IN LOVE WITH YOU	I'VE GOT TO FIND A WAY	ATCO 6374	30.00	northern

ANGEL, JIMMIE

DON'T FALL IN LOVE	WHAT'S HAPPENING TO OUR WORLD	MAJESTIC 206	20.00	northern

ANGELENOS

(DOWN IN) EAST L.A.	LORI	HIGHLAND 1169	50.00	northern

ANGELLE, BOBBY

I'M BEGGING	I LOVE THE OLOVE YOU LOVE	MONEY 123	10.00	group
LIVING LIE	I WANNA GO BACK HOME	MONEY 125	20.00	northern
TOO MUCH FOR YOU	SOMEONE IS GONNA HURT YOU	MONEY 128	20.00	northern

ANGELS

WHAT TO DO	I HAD A DREAM I LOST YOU	RCA 9129	15.00	northern

ANGLOS

INCENSE	STEPPING STONE	ORBIT 201	30.00	northern
SINCE YOU'VE BEEN GONE	SMALL TOWN BOY	SHIPTOWN 009	40.00	northern
SINCE YOU'VE BEEN GONE	SMALL TOWN BOY	SCEPTER 12204	20.00	northern

ANKA, PAUL

I CAN'T HELP LOVING YOU	CAN'T GET ALONG VERY WELL WITH	RCA 8893	40.00	**northerB**
WHEN WE GET THERE	CAN'T GET YOU OUT MY MIND	RCA 9457	30.00	northern

ANN, BEVERLEY

HE'S COMING HOME	HE WON'T SEE THE LIGHT	RCA 9269	40.00	northern
YOU'VE GOT YOUR MIND ON OTHER THINGS	UNTIL YOU	RCA 9468	40.00	northern

ANN, CHERYL

I CAN'T LET HIM	GOODBYE BABY	PATTY 52	200.00	northern
I CAN'T LET HIM	GOODBYE BABY	PATTY 52 PS	300.00	northern

ANSWERS

THINKING OF YOU		SCORPION 1005	300.00	northern

ANTELLECTS

LOVE SLAVE		FLODAVIEUR 804	8500.00	northern

ANTHONY AND THE AQUA LADS

I REMEMBER	THE HEART THAT'S TRUE	GOLD BEE 1650	150.00	northern

ANTHONY AND THE DELSONICS

EVERY TIME	NEVER HAD A GIRL SO SWEET	EMERGE 1106	250.00	northern

ANTHONY, CHARLES

I CAN DIG IT	THIS I CAN GIVE TO YOU	FILMTOWN 51768	500.00	northern

ANTHONY, EL

WILL YOU WAIT	SWEET JO-ANN	STAR-VUE 1001	8.00	ballad
WE'VE BEEN IN LOVE TOO LONG	I WANT TO BE TOGETHER WITH YOU	LA CINDY 1002	40.00	northern

ANTHONY, LA MONT

JUST TO BE LOVED	I DIDN'T KNOW	CHECK MATE 1001	75.00	motown
LET'S TALK IT OVER	BENNY THE SKINNY MAN	ANNA 1125	25.00	motown
POPEYE	LET'S TALK IT OVER	ANNA 1125 stock	200.00	motown
POPEYE	LET'S TALK IT OVER	ANNA 1125 DJ	100.00	motown

ANTHONY, RICHARD

WHAT NOW MY LOVE	I DON'T KNOW WHAT TO DO	V.I.P. 25022	20.00	motown
NO GOOD		SWAN 4257	30.00	northern
KEEP ON LIVING ON		VIRTUE 189	200.00	northern

ANTHONY, SHELIA

LIVIN' IN LOVE	WOMAN TO WOMAN	BUTTERCUP 7	25.00	northern

ANTHONY, WAYNE

BLOW ME A KISS	GO GO WEDDING	WALANA 102	300.00	northern
YOU AIN'T WRAPPED TOO TIGHT	LITTLE MISS LONELY	ROULETTE 4672	10.00	northern

ANTHONY AND THE IMPERIALS (also see Little Anthony)

WHAT GREATER LOVE	IN THE BACK OF MY HEART	VEEP 1283	8.00	northern
YESTERDAY HAS GONE	MY LOVE IS A RAINBOW	VEEP 1285	8.00	northern
DON'T TIE ME DOWN	WHERE THERE'S A WILL THERE'S A	VEEP 1255	10.00	northern
IT'S NOT THE SAME	DOWN ON LOVE	VEEP 1248	15.00	northern

ANTHONY AND THE SOPHOMORES

ONE SUMMER NIGHT	WORK OUT	JAMIE 1340	20.00	group
IT DEPENDS ON YOU	GEE (BUT I'D GIBVE YOU THE WOR	ABC 10737	20.00	northern
HEARTBREAKER	I'LL GO THROUGH LIFE LOVING YOU	ABC 10844	40.00	northern

ANTIQUES

GO FOR YOURSELF	PENANCE	LA SALLE 0069	1200.00	northern

APOLLAS

JUST CAN'T GET ENOUGH OF YOU	NOBODY'S BABY (AM I)	LOMA 2025	15.00	northern
PRETTY RED BALOONS	YOU ALWAYS HURT ME	LOMA 2039	10.00	northern
SORRY MAMA	MY SOUL CONCERTO	LOMA 2053	15.00	northern

YOU'RE ABSOLUTELY RIGHT	LOCK ME IN YOUR HEART	LOMA 2019	15.00	northern
MR. CREATOR	ALL SOLD OUT	WB 5893	75.00	northern

APOLLIS
WHAT IT IS		SOUL SET	60.00	funk

APOLLO, AL
I'M WALKING	I LAUGHED	CUB 9121	100.00	northern

APOLLO, VINCE
I BEAR WITNESS	I CAN'T TURN MY BACK	PENTAGON 1112	40.00	northern

APOSTLES
SIX PACK	SOUL FIESTA	KAPP 2011 DJ	20.00	funk

APPLE AND THE 3 ORANGES
FREE AND EASY	FREE AND EASY PT.2	STAGE MUSIC 101	50.00	funk

APPOINTMENTS
I SAW YOU THERE	KEEP AWAY	DELITE 520	600.00	northern

APPRECIATIONS
AFRAID OF LOVE	FAR FROM YOUR LOVE	JUBILEE 5525	40.00	northern
I CAN'T HIDE IT	NO NO NO	AWARE 1066	500.00	**northerB**
IT'S BETTER TO CRY	GIMME BACK MY SOUL	SPORT 111	500.00	northern
SHE NEVER REALLY LOVED ME	THERE'S A PLACE IN MY HEART	SPORT 108	50.00	northern
THERE'S A PLACE IN MY HEART	SHE NEVER REALLY LOVED ME	SPORT 108	60.00	northern

APRIL, MAY AND JUNE
HE WENT AWAY	I LOVE THE GUY	RCA 8696	50.00	northern

ARABIANS
(PLEASE) TAKE A CHANCE ON ME	YOU UPSET ME BABY	LE MANS 2	150.00	northern
LET ME TRY	TODAY I KISSED MY NEW LOVE	STAFF 1808	250.00	northern

ARCADES
THERE'S GOT TO BE A LOSER	THE SOUL P.W.	TRIAD 502	100.00	northern

ARGIE AND THE THE ARKETTS
YOU'RE THE GUY	HEY BABY	RONNIE NO #	50.00	northern

ARISTOCRATS
LET'S GET TOGETHER NOW	IP SLIPPIN DIPPIN	WB 7736	150.00	70's
DON'T GO		RONDO NO#	300.00	funk

ARMSTEAD, JO
GOT MY TASTE (OF THE HONEY)	WON'T YOU JOIN THE BAND	PREACHER ROSE 1	8.00	70's
I'VE BEEN TURNED ON	I'M GONNA SHOW YOU	GIANT 710	15.00	northern
I FEEL AN URGE COMING ON	I WHO LOVE YOU SO	GIANT 701	15.00	**northerB**
I'VE BEEN TURNED ON	NEVER HAD IT LIKE THIS BEFORE	GIANT 707	15.00	northern
THE URGE KEEPS COMING	A STONE GOOD LOVER	GIANT 704	15.00	northern
I GOT THE VIBES	RIDE OUT THE STORM	GOSPEL TRUTH	15.00	70's
1207				

ARMSTEAD, JOSHIE
SITTING HERE THINKING	LOOKING FOR A LOVER BOY	INFINITY 28	100.00	northern

ARMSTRONG, JIMMY
CLOSE TO YOU	HANGING OUT WITH EARLY BIRD	STOP 105	150.00	ballad
I'M GOING TO LOCK MY HEART	COUNT THE TEARS	ENJOY 1016	15.00	ballad
YOU'RE GETTING NEXT TO ME, BAB	GOING TO THE WELL TOO MANY TIM	BROTHERS THREE	300.00	ballad
I WON'T BELIEVE IT UNTIL I SEE IT		JET SET 768	40.00	northern
I BELIEVE I'LL LOVE ON	IT'S GONNA TAKE LOVE	SHRINE 105 NI	1000.00	northern
MYSTERY	I'M ABOUT TO SAY GOODBYE	SHRINE 102	100.00	northern

ARMSTRONG, TAL.
YOU'VE GOT SO MUCH FEELING	YOU'VE GOT SO MUCH FEELING Pt2	LOVE 1001	50.00	70's

ARMSTRONG, TALMADGE AND THE ESCOTTS
GIGI	GIVE IT UP	SPINDLETOP 15	70.00	northern

ARNELL, BILLY
TOUGH GIRL	SAME: INSTRUMENTAL	HOLLY. 101	750.00	northern

ARNELLS
HEART REPAIR SHOP	TAKE A LOOK	ROULETTE 4519	75.00	northern

ARRIVALS
WOMAN AND CHILD	THE GRANNY DRESS	LUMMTONE 118	20.00	northern

ARTER SET
SERMON		MUSICLAND USA 20005	80.00	northern

ART-FORMS LTD
I'M A BAD MAN	APPLE TREES AND BUTTERFLIES	RCA 354	20.00	group
WHAT DID I DO WRONG	TIME TO CALL IT A DAY	RCA 411	20.00	group

ARTISTICS
HOPE WE HAVE	I'M GONNA MISS YOU	BRUNSWICK 55301	10.00	**northerB**
JUST ANOTHER HEARTACHE	AIN'T IT STRANGE	BRUNSWICK 755431	8.00	northern
YESTRDAYS' GIRL	PRICE OF LOVE	BRUNSWICK 755416	15.00	northern
YOU LEFT ME	LONELY OLD WORLD	BRUNSWICK 55384	15.00	northern
GET MY HANDS ON SOME LOVIN'	I'LL LEAVE IT UP TO YOU	OKEH 7193	30.00	**northerB**
GLAD I MET YOU	GIRL I NEED YOU	BRUNSWICK 55315	10.00	**northerB**
I'LL ALWAYS LOVE YOU	LOVE SONG	BRUNSWICK 55326	10.00	northern
IN ANOTHER MAN'S ARMS	PATTY CAKE	OKEH 7217 DJ	20.00	northern
JUST ANOTHER HEARTACHE	AIN'T IT STRANGE	BRUNSWICK 55431	10.00	northern
NOTHING BUT HEARTACHES	YOU MAKE ME HAPPY	BRUNSWICK 55353 DJ	10.00	northern
SO MUCH LOVE IN MY HEART	LOVELAND	OKEH 7243	20.00	northern
THIS HEART OF MINE	I'LL COME RUNNING	OKEH 7232	75.00	northern
WHAT HAPPENED (*TO THE LOVE WE	WALKING TALL	BRUNSWICK 55404	10.00	northern

Title	B-side	Label	Price	Category
WHAT'LL I DO	I NEED YOUR LOVE	OKEH 7177	15.00	northern
YOU LEFT ME	LONELY OLD WORLD	BRUNSWICK 55384	10.00	northern
ARTISTS b / w TAYLOR, TEDTHIS HEART OF MINE	STAY AWAY FROM MY BABY	OKEH 111809 DJ only	50.00	northern

ASCOTS

Title	B-side	Label	Price	Category
MISS HEARTBREAKER	THIS OLD HEARTACHE	MBS 106	10.00	northern
ANOTHER DAY	LOVE	MIR-A-DON 1004	250.00	northern
ANYTIME	SOMETIMES I WONDER	MIR-A-DON 1001	200.00	northern
MISS HEARTBREAKER	THIS OLD HEARTACHE	MIR-A-DON 1000	100.00	northern
MOTHER SAID	YES IT'S ALL RIGHT	MIR-A-DON 1002	50.00	northern

ASHFORD, NICK

| WHEN I FEEL THE NEED | YOUNG EMOTIONS | VERVE 10493 D | 15.00 | northern |

ASHLEY, TONY

| I CAN'T PUT YOU DOWN | WE MUST HAVE LOVE | DECCA 32342 | 20.00 | northern |

ASHLEY, TYRONE

| I WANT MY BABY BACK | LET ME BE YOUR MAN | PHIL LA SOUL 342 | 20.00 | northern |

ASPIRATIONS

| YOU LEFT ME | I WANT TO BE FREE | PEACHES 6721 | 1200.00 | northern |

ASTOR, JIMMY (Jimmy Castor)

| IT'S OK | | JETSET 1001 | 200.00 | northern |

ASTORS

JUST ENOUGH TO HURT ME	WHAT CAN IT BE	STAX 139	150.00	group
CANDY	I FOUND OUT	STAX 170	15.00	northern
IN THE TWILIGHT ZONE	MYSTERY WOMAN	STAX 179	30.00	northern

ATHENS ROGUE

| SHE COULD LOVE ME | SALLY SALLY FROM TIN PAN ALLEY | STOP 185 | 250.00 | northern |

ATKINS, BEN AND THE NOMADS

| COME ON OVER | BURNING | YOUNGSTOWN 609 | 200.00 | northern |
| LOVE IS A BEAUTIFUL THING | SAME: INSTRUMENTAL | GOLDWAX 336 | 20.00 | northern |

ATKINS, LARRY

| AIN'T THAT LOVE ENOUGH | HAVE MERCY ON ME | ROMARK 115 | 250.00 | northern |
| LIGHTEN UP | AIN'T THAT LOVE ENOUGH | HIGHLAND 1193 | 40.00 | northern |

ATLANTICS

| WHAT'S SO GOOD ABOUT GOODBYE | BABY I NEED YOU | MARQUEE 444 | 300.00 | northern |

ATTRACTIONS

BURN UP SOME ROAD (BACK TO MY BABY)	TIME GOES BY SO SLOWLY	DE TO 1	75.00	northern
FIND ME	DESTINATION YOU	RENFRO 1	20.00	northern
FIND ME	DESTINATION YOU	BELL 659	10.00	northern
THAT GIRL IS MINE	NEW GIRL IN THE NEIGHBORHOOD	BELL 674	20.00	northern
DID I DO THE RIGHT THING	GOT TO SAY WHAT YOU MEAN	NATION-WIDE 104	50.00	northern
YOU DON'T KNOW BOY	THINK BACK	JUNE BUG 697	200.00	northern

AUBURN, JI

| NOTHING COULD BE WORSE | PUSH, SWEEP | MALA 452 | 40.00 | northern |

AUDIO ART STRINGS

| THERE IS NOTHING ELSE TO SAY 60028 | I CAN'T GET OVER LOSING YOUR LOVE | AUDIO ARTS | 10.00 | northern |

AUGER, BRIAN

| BLACK CAT | IN AND OUT | ATCO 6611 | 15.00 | mod |
| RED BEANS AND RICE | GEORGE BRUNO MONEY | ATCO 4536 | 20.00 | mod |

AUGUST AND DENEEN

| WE GO TOGETHER | CAN'T GET YOU OUT OF MY HEAD | ABC 11082 | 100.00 | northern |

AUGUST MOON

| WASTED YEARS | YOU'RE TOGETHER BABY | O-GEE 100 | 100.00 | northern |

AUSTIN, PATTI

MUSIC TO MY HEART	LOVE 'EM & LEAVE 'EM KIND OF L	ABC 11104	150.00	northern
ARE WE READY FOR LOVE	NOW THAT I KNOW WHAT LONELINES	COLUMBIA 45337	30.00	northern
CAN'T FORGET THE ONE I LOVE	GOD ONLY KNOWS	COLUMBIA 45499	25.00	northern
DIDN'T SAY A WORD	DAY BY DAY	COLUMBIA 45592	15.00	northern
GOT TO CHECK YOU OUT	WHAT A DIFFERENCE A DAY MAKES	CORAL 62511	15.00	northern
HE'S GOOD ENOUGH FOR ME	EARL	CORAL 62455	125.00	northern
I WANNA BE LOVED	A MOST UNUSUAL BOY	CORAL 62471	20.00	northern
LEAVE A LITTLE LOVE	MY LOVELIGHT AIN'T GONNA SHINE	CORAL 62500J	125.00	northern
ONLY ALL THE TIME	OH HOW I NEED YOU JOE	CORAL 62518	30.00	northern
SOMEONE'S GONNA CRY	YOU BETTER KNOW WHAT YOU'RE GE	CORAL 62478	85.00	northern
TAKE AWAY THE PAIN STAIN	TAKE YOUR TIME	CORAL 62491	100.00	northern
YOU'RE TOO MUCH A PART OF ME	I'LL KEEP ON LOVING YOU	CORAL 62541	50.00	northern

AUTOGRAPHS

I CAN DO IT	I'M GONNA SHOW YOU HOW TO LOVE	OKEH 7293	25.00	northern
LOVE'S GONNA DO YOU IN	ON A HOT SUMMER DAY	JOKER 714	75.00	northern
SAD SAD FEELING	SAME: INSTRUMENTAL	LOMA 2040	10.00	northern
SAD SAD FEELING	SAME: INSTRUMENTAL	JOKER 719	40.00	northern

AUTOMATIONS

| GOING OUT OF MY MIND | WORLD OF MAKE BELIEVE | GAYE 5006 | 500.00 | group |

AVONS

SINCE I MET YOU BABY	HE'S MY HERO	EXCELLO 2296	15.00	northern
TELL ME BABY (WHO WOULD I BE)	A SAMPLE OF MY LOVE	REFOREE 700	20.00	northern
TONIGHT KISS YOUR BABY GOODBYE	WHATEVER HAPPENED TO OUR LOVE	GROOVE 39	20.00	northern

B

Artist / Title	B-side	Label	Price	Style
B, MARY				
SOMETHING FOR YOU, BABVY	SINCE I FELL FOR YOU	FLING 725	30.00	northern
B.G. SOUL BROTHERS (see Benny Gordon)				
THE HOLD BAG		ESTILL 1000	25.00	funk
B.W. AND THE NEXT EDITION				
CHOSEN ONE	WORK, WORK, WORK	DAKAR 4540	25.00	70's
B.W.SOULS				
MARVIN'S GROOVE	GENERATED LOVE	ROUND 1038	30.00	funk
BABY DOLLS				
NOW THAT I'VE LOST YOU	I WILL DO IT	BOOM 60002	20.00	group
GOT TO GET YOU INTO MY LIFE	WHY CAN'T I LOVE HIM LIKE YOU:	HOLLYWOOD 1111	25.00	northern
BABY GEORGE				
GONNA LOBE YOU AND LEAVE YOU		WORLD WIDE NO#	200.00	funk
BABY HUEY AND THE BABY SITTERS				
JUST BEING CAREFUL	MESSIN' WITH THE KID	USA 801	100.00	northern
JUST BEING CAREFUL	MESSIN' WITH THE KID	SHANN 73924	250.00	northern
BACKYARD HEAVIES				
EXPO 83	SOUL JUNCTION	SCEPTER 123'4	25.00	funk
KEEP ON TRUCKIN'	NEVER CAN SAY GOODBYE	HOT LINE 102	25.00	funk
BAD BOYS				
WHAT TOOK YOU SO LONG	YOU'RE NOT ALONE ANYMORE	BELL 840	20.00	northern
BAD MEDICINE				
TRESPASSER PT.1	TRESPASSER PT. 2	ENYX 2	100.00	funk
BAD WEATHER INC:				
I NEVER KNEW	YOU REALLY GOT A HOLD ON ME	BAD WEATHER 100	200.00	northern
BAGS AND BEANS (also see UNFORGETABLES)				
TRUST YOUR LUCK	GYPSEY	SAMONE 100	600.00	northern
BAILEY, AARON (CHICO)				
THE POINT	THE POINT II	KRIS 8097	60.00	funk
BAILEY, HORACE				
DOWN THRU THE YEARS	COOL MONKEY	DELENE 700	100.00	ballad
BAILEY, J.R.				
THE EYES DON'T KNOW THE FEELIN	SAME: Long version	RCA 10799	20.00	70's
LOVE WON'T WEAR OFF	SAME	CALLA 158	30.00	northern
TOO LATE	HOLD BACK THE DAWN	MALA 12015	15.00	northern
BAILEY, JIMMY				
EVERYTIME	STOP, WAIT A MINUTE	COLUMBIA 43260	15.00	northern
IF GOODBYE MEANS GONE	HUSH	COLUMBIA 43408	30.00	northern
BAILEY, ROGER				
LOST GENERATION		AUDIO FORTY 60001	50.00	northern
BAILEY, THOMAS				
FRAN	JUST WON'T MOVE	FEDERAL 12559	300.00	ballad
I WISH I WAS BACK	PERCY'S PLACE	FEDERAL 12567	300.00	ballad
BAINES, VICKIE				
GOT TO RUN	LOSING YOU	PARKWAY 957	20.00	northern
COUNTRY GIRL	ARE YOU KIDDING	PARKWAY966	750.00	northern
SWEETER THAN SWEET THINGS	WE CAN FIND THAT LOVE	SYMBOL 222	100.00	northern
SWEETER THAN SWEET THINGS	WE CAN FIND THAT LOVE	LOMA 2078	25.00	northern
BAITEY, PAMALA				
YOU CAN'T LET THE GIRL OVER PO	ACTION SPEAKS LOUDER THAN WORD	SY-ROC 1001	30.00	northern
BAKER, BILL				
ANOTHER SLEEPLESS NIGHT	IT SHOULDN'T HAPPEN TO A DREAM	PARNASO 110	150.00	northern
BAKER, BUTCH				
WORKING AT THE GO GO	FATMAN AT THE GO GO	ST. LAWRENCE 1011	20.00	**northerB**
BATMAN AT THE GO GO	ROBIN AT THE GO GO	ST. LAWRENCE 1010	100.00	northern
BAKER, ERNEST				
ALONE AGAIN	DO IT WITH FEELING	BLUE SOUL 10	300.00	70's
BAKER, JOAN				
EVERYBODY'S TALKING	SATISFY ME	DIAMOND 164	100.00	northern
BAKER, JOHNNY				
OPERATOR OPERATOR	PLEASE ACCEPT ME AS I AM	CISCO 1000	8.00	70's
FOG CITY (AND YOU BABE)	PRACTICE WHAT YOU PREACH	FOG CITY 800	10.00	northern
SHY GUY	DONNIE-O	FOG CITY 80004	10.00	northern
BAKER, LAVERN				
BABY	ONE MONKEY (DON'T STOP NO SHOW	BRUNSWICK 55291	20.00	northern
I'M THE ONE TO DO IT	BABY	BRUNSWICK 755408	50.00	northern
WRAPPED TIED AND TANGLED	NOTHING LIKE BEING IN LOVE	BRUNSWICK 55311	50.00	northern

BAKER, LITTLE BETTY
JUST WHAT THE DOCTOR ORDERED	STOP BOY	ALL PLATINUM 2327	15.00	northern

BAKER, SAM
I'M NUMBER ONE	I BELIEVE IN YOU	SS7 2590	15.00	northern

BAKER, YVONNE
EYES	THAT'S MY DESIRE	ARGO 5412	10.00	northern
MEND THE TORN PIECES	I CAN'T CHANGE	JUNIOR 1071	10.00	northern
MEND THE TORN PIECES	I CAN'T CHANGE	JUNIOR 1010	20.00	northern
YOU DIDN'T SAY A WORD	TO PROVE MY LOVE IS TRUE	PARKWAY 140	250.00	**northerB**

BALL, BILLY AND THE UPSETTERS
POPCORN 69		APOLLO. no#	250.00	funk

BALLAD, KENNY
DOWN TO MY LAST HEARTBREAK	THERE WILL NEVER BE ANOTHER YO	DYNAMO 106	150.00	northern
I'M LOSING YOU	YOUR LETTER	ROULETTE 4716	20.00	northern
MR. MAGIC	OH! HOW I CRIED	KAPP 602	30.00	northern

BALLADS
BUTTERFLY	CONFESSING ATHE FEELING	MUSIC CITY 897	20.00	70's
I'M GONNA SHOW YOU	LOVING YOU ISN'T ENOUGH	MUSIC CITY 896	30.00	70's
I WISH I KNEW	GIFT OF LOVE	VENTURE 637	10.00	northern
CONFESSING A FEELING	BUTTERFLI	BALJA 1001	10.00	group
I LOVE YOU.. YEAH	YOU'RE THE ONE	VENTURE 625	15.00	group
THIS IS MAGIC	WE KNOW	TINA 102	40.00	group
I CAN'T SEE YOUR LOVE	I CAN'T SEE YOUR LOVE Pt.2	WEE 714	75.00	northern
MY BABY KNOWS HOW TO LOVE HER	GOD BLESS OUR LOVE	VENTURE 615	15.00	northern

BALLARD, FLORENCE
IT DOESN'T MATTER HOW SAY IT	GOIN' OUT OF MY HEAD	ABC 11074	20.00	motown
LOVE AIN'T LOVE	FOREVER FAITHFUL	ABC 11144	15.00	motown
LOVE AIN'T LOVE	FOREVER FAITHFUL	ABC 11144 PS	30.00	motown

BALLARD, KENNY
I WANNA LOVE YOU	IT SURE LOOKS GOOD	TOY 105	30.00	ballad

BALTIMORE AND THE OHIO BAND
CONDITION RED	LAPLAND	JUBILEE 5592	10.00	**northerB**

BANBARRA
SHACK UP	SAME:	UA 734	25.00	funk

BANDS OF GOLD
IT'S OVER	YOU WON'T CHANGE ME	SMASH 2058	20.00	northern

BANKS, BARBARA
AIN'T I WORTH A DIME	LIVING LONG	SMASH 2011	40.00	northern
THE NIGHT TIME FEELING	SONNY BOY	MGM 13786	15.00	northern
RIVER OF TEARS	LIVING IN THE PAST	VEEP 1247	30.00	northern

BANKS, BESSIE
BABY YOU SURE KNOW HOW TO GET TO	SAME:	QUALITY 508 DJ	10.00	70's
DON'T YOU WORRY BABY THE BEST IS	SAME:	QUALITY 503	100.00	70's
TRY TO LEAVE ME IF YOU CAN	SAME:	VOLT 4112 DJ	15.00	ballad
GO NOW	IT SOUNDS LIKE MY BABY	TIGER 102	10.00	northern
GO NOW	IT SOUNDS LIKE MY BABY	BLUE CAT 106 DJ	40.00	northern
I CAN'T MAKE IT	NEED YOU	VERVE 10519	40.00	northern

BANKS, BOBBY
READ IT AND WEEP	I'M A BACHELOR	GIL 101	20.00	ballad

BANKS, DARRELL
BEAUTIFUL FEELING	NO ONE BLINDER	VOLT 4026	15.00	northern
I'M THE ONE WHO LOVES YOU	JUST BECAUSE YOUR LOVE HAS GONE	VOLT 4014	50.00	northern
I'VE GOT THAT FEELING	HERE COME THE TEARS	ATCO 6471	20.00	northern
OPEN THE DOOR TO YOUR HEART	OUR LOVE (IS IN THE POCKET)	REVILOT 201 pink	15.00	northern
OPEN THE DOOR TO YOUR HEART	OUR LOVE (IS IN THE POCKET)	REVILOT 201 grey	20.00	northern
SOMEBODY (SOMEWHERE) NEEDS YOU	BABY WHAT'CHA YOU GOT (FOR ME)	REVILOT 203 grey	20.00	northern
SOMEBODY (SOMEWHERE) NEEDS YOU	BABY WHAT'CHA YOU GOT (FOR ME)	REVILOT 203 pink	15.00	northern

BANKS, DOUG
I JUST KEPT ON DANCING	BABY SINCE YOU WENT AWAY	ARGO 5483	100.00	northern

BANKS, DOUGLAS
AINT' THAT JUST LIKE A WIOMA\N	NEVER SAY GOODBYE	GUYDEN 2082	150.00	northern

BANKS, GEORGETTA
SWEETLY AND COMPLETELY	AUTOGRAPH MY PHOTOGRAPH	DOT 16716	150.00	northern
SWEETLY AND COMPLETELY	AUTOGRAPH MY PHOTOGRAPH	G-NOTE 1001	300.00	northern

BANKS, HOMER
HOOKED BY LOVE	LADY OF STONE	MINIT 32020	10.00	northern
60 MINUTES OF YOUR LOVE	DO YOU KNOW WHAT	MINIT 32008	10.00	northern
A LOT OF LOVE	FIGHTING TO WIN	MINIT 32000 DJ	15.00	northern
SWEETIE PIE	LADY OF STONE	GENIE 101	100.00	northern

BANKS, LARRY
I'M COMING HOME	I DON'T WANNA DO IT	DCP 1133	20.00	northern
I'M NOT THE ONE	MUDDY WATER	KAPP 865	20.00	northern

BANKS, ROBERT
A MIGTHY GOOD WAY	SMILE	VERVE 10545	30.00	northern

BANKSTON, T.W.
YOU ARE THE ICING ON MY CAKE	SAME: INSTRUMENTAL	STRAIGHT UP 12948	30.00	70's

BARBARA AND BRENDA
HURTIN' INSIDE	THAT'S WHEN YOU'VE GOT SOUL	HEIDI 104	15.00	northern

NEVER LOVE A ROBIN	SALLY'S PARTY	DYNAMO 108	10.00	northern
IF IM HURT YOU'LL FEEL THE PAIN	TOO YOUNG TO BE FOOLED	DYNAMO 103	10.00	northern
NEVER LOVE A ROBIN	SALLY'S PARTY	DYNAMO 108	15.00	northern
DON'T WAIT UP FOR ME MAMA		DYNAMO 120	20.00	**northerB**

BARBARA AND THE BELIEVERS

WHAT CAN HAPPEN TO ME NOW	WHEN YOU WISH UPON A STAR	CAPITOL 5866	15.00	northern

BARBARA AND THE THE CASTLES

STONEY FACE	DON'T HURT ME BABY	RUBY-DOO 12	200.00	northern

BARBARA AND THE UNIQUES

I'LL NEVER LET YOU GO	YOU'RE GONNA MAKE ME CHEAT ON	ARDEN 3002	10.00	northern

BARBOUR, LEROY

I AIN'T GOING NOWHERE		FRONTERSMAN	200.00	northern

BARKLEY, TYRONE

MAN OF VALUE	SOME KIND OF WONDERFUL	MIDSONG 1016	20.00	70's

BARLOW, DEAN

DON'T LET HIM TAKE MY BABY	I DIDN'T SEE NOBODY DANCE	RUST 5068	75.00	northern
YESTERDAY'S KISSES	THE NIGHT BEFORE LAST	LESCAY 3010	100.00	northern
3RD WINDOW FROM THE RIGHT		LESCAY	100.00	northern

BARNES, DEE DEE

DON'T WHAT YOU WANNA DO	I'M YOURS AND YOU'RE MINE	ARCTIC 138	100.00	northern

BARNES, BETTY

WALKING DOWN BROADWAY	THE SKY WITHOUT THE SUN	RCA 9274	40.00	northern

BARNES, BILLY

TO PROVE MY LOVE	UNTIL	LIBERTY 55421	25.00	northern

BARNES, DENA

IF YOU EVER WALK OUT OF MY LIF	WHO AM I	INFERNO 2002	200.00	**northerB**

BARNES, J.J.

GOT TO GET RID OF YOU	SNOWFLAKES	VOLT 4027	30.00	northern
I'LL KEEP COMING BACK	EVIDENCE	BUDDAH 120	20.00	northern
DEEPER IN LOVE	SAY IT	RIC TIC 117	8.00	motown
DON'T BRING ME BAD NEWS	DAY TRIPPER	RIC TIC 115 DJ	10.00	motown
PLEASE LET ME IN	I THINK I FOUND A LOVE	RIC TIC 106	10.00	**northerB**
REAL HUMDINGER	I AIN'T GONNA DO IT	RIC TIC 110	10.00	motown
BABY PLEASE COME BACK HOME	CHAINS OF LOVE	GROOVESVILLE 1006	15.00	northern
FORGIVE ME	NOW THAT I GOT YOU BACK	GROOVESVILLE 1008	15.00	northern
I'LL KEEP COMING BACK	SAD DAY A COMING	REVILOT 218	10.00	northern
JUST ONE MORE TIME	HEY CHILD, I LOVE YOU	SCEPTER 1266	30.00	northern
JUST ONE MORE TIME	HEY CHILD, I LOVE YOU	MICKAYS 3004	50.00	northern
LONELY NO MORE	GET A HOLD OF YOURSELF	MICKAYS 4471	400.00	northern
NOW SHE'S GONE	HOLD ON TO IT	REVILOT 216	10.00	northern
OUR LOVE IS IN THE POCKET	ALL YOUR GOODIES ARE GONE	REVILOT 222 multi	120.00	northern
OUR LOVE IS IN THE POCKET	ALL YOUR GOODIES ARE GONE	REVILOT 222 pink	100.00	northern
POOR UNFORTUNATE ME	SHE AIN'T READY	RING 101	15.00	northern
THESE CHAINS OF LOVE	COLOR GREEN	MICKAYS 300	30.00	northern

BARNES, J.J.AND THE DELL FI'S

MY LOVE CAME TUMBLING DOWN	WON'T YOU LET ME KNOW	KABLE 437	30.00	motown
MY LOVE CAME TUMBLING DOWN	WON'T YOU LET ME KNOW	RICH 1005	20.00	motown

BARNES, JIMMY J.

I THINK I'VE GOT A GOOD CHANCE	I THINK I'VE GOT A GOOD CHANCE	ORGANIC 1	150.00	70's

BARNES, JOHNNY

REAL NICE	IT MUST BE LOVE	CAP CITY 122	15.00	northern

BARNES, LARRY

RAGS IS RAGS	I FEEL LOVE COMIN' ON	SMASH 2004	20.00	northern

BARNES, MYRA

MESSAGE FROM THE SOUL SISTERS	MESSAGE FROM THE SOUL SISTERS: PT.2	KING 6334	15.00	funk
SUPER GOOD	SUPER GOOD PT.2	KING 6344	10.00	funk

BARNES, ORTHEA

YOUR PICTURE ON THE WALL	SAME AS BEFORE	ABC 10434	40.00	northern
YOUR PICTURE ON THE WALL	SAME AS BEFORE	MICKAY'S 350	70.00	northern
I'VE NEVER LOVED NOBODY	WAITING FOR JOEY	CORAL 62529	30.00	northern
TAKE MY HEART AND SOUL	HEARTBREAKER SOULSHAKER	CORAL 62552	20.00	northern

BARNES, SIDNEY

NEW YORK CITY	TALKIN' BOUT A SHINDIG	BLUES TONE 402	15.00	mod
I HURT ON THE OTHER SIDE	SWITCHY WALK	BLUE CAT 125	150.00	northern
WAIT	I'M SATISFIED	GEMINI 101	60.00	northern
I HURT ON THE OTHER SIDE	SWITCHY WALK	RED BIRD 10054	350.00	northern
YOU'LL ALWAYS BE IN STYLE	I'M SO GLAD	RED BIRD 10039	100.00	northern

BARNES, TOWANDA

IF I'M GUILTY	OH DARLING	GROOVY 3003	10.00	northern
YOU DON'T MEAN IT	(YOU BETTER) FIND SOMEONE TO L	A&M 1141	25.00	**northerB**

BARNETT, JAMES

KEEP ON TALKING	TAKE A GOOD LOOK	FAME 1001	100.00	**northerB**

BARNETT, MATTHEW

IF YOUR LOVE IS REAL	MY ONLY LOVE	PUFF 1005	400.00	northern

BARNUM, EVE

WE GO TOGETHER	PLEASE NEWSBOY	CHECKER 1215	10.00	northern

BARNUM, H.B.

HEARTBREAKER	SEARCHIN' FOR MY SOUL	CAPITOL 5932	75.00	northern

IT HURTS TOO MUCH TO CRY	LONELY HEARTS	RCA 8112	75.00	northern
THE RECORD	I'M A MAN	CAPITOL 5391	10.00	northern
THREE ROOMS WITH RUNNING WATER	CALYPSO BLUES	IMPERIAL 66063	15.00	northern
IT HURTS TOO MUCH TO CRY	LONELY HEARTS	RCA 8112 PS	100.00	northern

BARON, ELLIOTT

MAN TO MAN	THE SPARE RIB	GOLDEN WORLD 11	100.00	motown

BARONS

THAT'S HOW LOVE IS	WE SHOULD BE TOGETHER	GAMMA 1150	10.00	70's
A TEARDROP FEEL FOR ME	SWIM, TINY SWIM	LAMAR 2811	200.00	northern
I'VE GOT A FEELING	CLAP YOUR LITTLE HANDS	ETAH 102	40.00	northern
SINCE YOUR GONE	MY SMILE IS BIGGER	RCA 9034	40.00	northern

BARRACUDAS

NO MATTER WHAT YOU DO	WAIT FOR TOMORROW	CRITIQUE 1075	30.00	northern

BARRETT, SUSAN

A GRAIN OF SAND	SHE GETS EVERYTHING SHE WANTS	RCA 8888	10.00	northern
WHAT'S IT GONNA BE	IT'S NO SECRET	RCA 9296	50.00	northern

BARRETTO, RAY

RIGHT ON	Y DICEN	FANIA 555	20.00	mod
SOUL DRUMMERS	MERCY, MERCY BABY	FANIA 454	25.00	mod

BARRY, LEE

I DON'T NEED IT		DOWNEY 134	40.00	northern

BARTEL, JOHNNY

MORE THAN EVER BEFORE	STATE OF MIND	SOLID STATE 2519	10.00	northern
IF THIS ISN'T LOVE	I WAITED TOO LONG	SOLID STATE 2514	100.00	northern

BARTLEY, CHRIS

THE SWEETEST THING THIS SIDE OF HEAVEN	LOVE ME BABY	VANDO 101	8.00	northern
I KNOW WE CAN WORK IT OUT	ONE WONDERFUL GIRL	BUDDAH 115	15.00	northern
I'LL TAKE THE BLAME	FOR YOU	BUDDAH 93	15.00	northern
BABY IT'S WONDERFUL	I'LL BE LOVING YOU	VANDO 3000	10.00	northern
I FOUND A GOODIE	BE MINE FOREVER	VANDO 14001	15.00	northern
TOMORROW KEEPS SHINING ON ME	A MAN, A WOMAN	MUSICOR 1437	15.00	northern
TRUER WORDS WEERE NEVER SPOKEN	THIS FEELING YOU GIVE ME	VANDO 14000	10.00	northern
YOU GET NEXT TO MY HEART	FOR YOU	VANDO 3002	10.00	northern

BARTON, EILEEN

THE JOKE (IS NOT ON ME)	THAT OLD FEELING	UA 206	40.00	motown

BASIC BLACK AND PEARL

THERE'LL COME A TIME, THERE'LL	HE'S A REBEL	POLYDOR 15111	15.00	70's

BASIL, TONI

BREAKAWAY	I'M 28	A&M 791	200.00	northern

BASKERVILLE, BOBBY

GOTCHA WHERE I WANCHA	SOUL TALK	DOT 17066	15.00	northern

BASS, FONTELLA

RECOVERY	LEAVE IT IN THE HANDS OF TIME	CHECKER 1131	8.00	northern
RESCUE ME	SOUL OF A MAN	CHECKER 1120	8.00	northern
SAFE AND SOUND	YOU'LL NEVER EVER KNOW	CHECKER 1147	8.00	northern
I CAN'T REST	I SURRENDER	CHECKER 1137	10.00	northern
LUCKY IN LOVE	SWEET LOVIN' DADDY	CHECKER 1183	15.00	northern

BASS, FONTELLA AND THE MCCLURE, BOBBY

YOU'LL MISS ME (WHEN I'M GONE)	DON'T JUMP	CHECKER 1111	10.00	northern
DON'T MESS UP A GOOD THING	JERK LOOSE	CHECKER 1097	8.00	northern

BASS, TOMMY

THIS IS MY THING	I GOTTA LEARN TO LIVE WITH THE	SOULFUL. 1004	25.00	northern

BASSEY, SHIRLEY

DON'T TAKE THE LOVERS FROM THE	TAKE AWAY	UA 50031	10.00	northern

BATAAN, JOE

GYPSY WOMAN	SO FINE	FANIA 447	25.00	mod
SPECIAL GIRL	MAGIC ROSE	FANIA 457	20.00	mod

BATES SISTERS

SYMPHONY FOR THE BROKEN HEARTE	SO BROKEN HEARTED	NOLA 736	10.00	northern

BATES, LEE

WHY DON'T YOU WRITE	GONNA MAKE YOU MINE	INSTANT 3310	25.00	northern
YOU WON'T DO RIGHT	THREE TRIP AROUND THE WORLD	INSTANT 3316	20.00	northern

BATISTE, ROSE

SWEETHEART DARLING	THAT'S WHAT HE TOLD ME	GOLDEN WORLD 33	15.00	motown
I STILL WAIT FOR YOU	COME BACK IN A HURRY	REVILOT 206	50.00	northern
HIT & RUN	I MISS MY BABY	REVILOT 204	100.00	**northerB**
HOLDING HANDS	THAT'S WHAT HE TOLD ME	RIC TIC 105	150.00	**northerB**

BATTLE, JEAN

I'VE GOT TO COME IN	UNSATISFIED WOMAN	CLINTONE 4	40.00	northern
LOVE MAKING	WHEN A WOMAN LOVES A MAN	RED LITE 119	15.00	northern

BAXTER, DUKE

I AIN'T NO SCHOOL BOY	EVERYBODY KNOWS MATILDA	VMC 740	8.00	northern

BAXTER, RON

THIS IS IT	I'VE GOT KNOW	OLE-9 1003	250.00	northern

BAXTER, TONY

I'LL COME TO YOU	WHEN DID I GET MARRIED	CHUBBY 711	30.00	northern

17

BAY BRIDGE

I CAN'T GET HER OUT OF MY MIND	BACKTRACK	ATLANTIC 2431	10.00	northern

BAY BROTHERS

WHAT DOES IT TAKE (TO WIN YOUR	ONE AND ONLY	MILLENIUM 11810	100.00	70's

BEACH GIRLS

SKIING IN THE SNOW	GOIN' PLACES	DYNOVOX 202 DJ	30.00	northern

BEAN BROTHERS

SHING A LING	HEY THERE	CASH SALES 10001	25.00	northern

BEAS

WHERE DO I GO FROM YOU	DOCTOR GOLDFOOT ETC.	DEE GEE 3010	15.00	northern

BEATY, PAMELA

TALKING EYES		TIP 1018	200.00	northern

BEAU DOLLAR

WHO KNOWS	WHERE THE SOUL TREES GROW	KING 6286	125.00	funk

BEAUMONT, JIMMY

I NEVER LOVED HER ANYWAY	YOU GOT TOO MUCH GOING FOR YOU	BANG 525	100.00	northern
THERE'S NO OTHER LOVE	PLEASE SEND ME SOMEONE TO LOVE	GALLANT 3007	20.00	northern

BEAUMONT, JIMMY AND THE SKYLINERS

I COULD HAVE LOVED YOU SO WELL	WHERE HAVE THEY GONE	CAPITOL 3979	40.00	70's

BEAVER (S) , JACKEY

I NEED MY BABY	LOVE THAT NEVER GROWS OLD	REVILOT 208	850.00	northern
LOVE COME BACK	I HATE TO SEE A MAN CRY	JABER 7111	500.00	northern
SILLY BOY	JACK A RUE	CHECKER 1102	15.00	northern
LOVER COME BACK	SOMEDAY WE'LL BE TOGETHER	SS7 1502	20.00	70's
TRYING TO GET BACK TO YOU GIRL	SAME: Pt. 2	DADE 2041	10.00	70's
HOLD ON	HEY GIRL	SS7 2649	10.00	northern
WE'RE NOT TOO YOUNG TO FALL IN	WHEN SOMETHING IS WRONG WITH M	MAINSTREAM 713	50.00	northern
BRING ME ALL YOUR HEARTACHES	DON'T WANNA LOSE YOU	GRANDLAND 19000	30.00	northern
HOLD ON	HEY GIRL (I CAN STAND TO SEE YOU)	JABER 7114	20.00	northern
SLING SHOT	I WANT SOMEBODY	CHECKER 1119	15.00	northern

BECK, FLOYD

GOT TO BE A MAN	WHAT BELONGS TYO SOMEONE ELSE	F&M 5060	50.00	northern

BEE GEE STANS

FRONT PAGE LOVE	WHERE IN MY HEART	TAL-VERT 1802	40.00	northern

BEE JAYS

PLEASE DON'T SAY WE'RE THROUGH	I'LL FIND YOU YOU	PRIME 10001	150.00	northern

BEE, JACKIE

FOR SOMEONE TO LOVE	WHAT ABOUT ME BABY	SALEM 61065	15.00	northern

BEE, JIMMY

IF IT WASN'T FOR LOVE	WHY DID I LOVE YOU BABY	20th. CENTURY 6673	20.00	northern
TALKIN' 'BOUT LOVE	A PRAYER	20th. CENTURY 6664	15.00	northern
WANTING YOU	I ONLY HAVE EYES FOR YOU	KENT 4531	10.00	northern
WANTING YOU	I ONLY HAVE EYES FOR YOU	KIMBEREY 1001	15.00	northern

BEEFUS, BARRY BAREFOOT

GO AHEAD ON BABY	BAREFOOT BEEFUS	LOMA 2058	15.00	northern

BEERY, DOROTHY

DON'T GIVE ME LOVE	SOUL POWER	BIG THREE 401	20.00	northern

BELAIRES

I GOT THAT FEELIN'	THE RABBIT	PALMER 5026	150.00	northern
I GOT THAT FEELIN'	WHY DID YOU CALL	PALMER 5026	200.00	northern

BELGIANETTS

THE TRAIN	MY BLUE HEAVEN	OKEH 7172	50.00	northern

BELGIANS

PRAY TELL ME	CHANGED	TEEK 4824	150.00	group

BELIEVERS

ACROSS THE TRACKS		BROWNSTONE	200.00	funk

BELL BOYS

I DON'T WANT TO LOSE YOU	WOMAN I LOVE	JAMAR 31968729	100.00	**northerB**

BELL BROTHERS

GIVE IT UP	SUPER LADY...SUPER GIRL	BELL-O-SOUL 1002	50.00	70's
PITY ME	LOOK AT ME	SURE SHOT 5023	15.00	ballad
THROW AWAY THE KEY	TELL HIM NO	SURE SHOT 5038	20.00	ballad
DON'T YOU KNOW SHE'S ALRIGHT	NOT YOUR KIND OF LOVE	SURE SHOT 5012	15.00	northern

BELL, ARCHIE AND THE DRELLS

SHE'S MY WOMAN, SHE'S MY GIRL	THE YANKEE DANCE	OVIDE 222	20.00	ballad
ON IN ONE	A SOLDIERS PRAYER 1967	OVIDE 226	15.00	mod
TIGHTEN UP northern	DOG EAT DOG	OVIDE	228	50.00
HERE I GO AGAIN	A WORLD WITHOUT MUSIC	ATLANTIC 2693	10.00	northern

BELL, ARLENE

THIRE TWO SIDES TO EVERY COIN	IT'S ABOUT TIME I MADE A CHANG	VELVET 19	30.00	70's
DID YOU MEAN IT	MY LOVER	VELVET 18	20.00	funk
IT AIN'T EASY	LOVE AIN'T SUPPOSED TO BE LIKE	VELVET 21	75.00	northern

BELL, ARLENE AND THE KENYATTAS

THERE'S SOMETHING WRONG WITH Y	WHATS-A-TEAR MORE OR LESS	VELVET 16	30.00	funk

BELL, BOBBY
DON'T COME BACK TO ME	DROP ME A LINE	RCA 9040	30.00	northern

BELL, JAMES AND THE HIGHLIGHTERS
AMAZING LOVE	POPPIN' POP CORN	ROJAM 1	500.00	northern

BELL, MADELINE
DON'T CROSS OVER (TO MY SIDE OF THEV TRACKS)	YOU DON'T LOVE ME NO MORE	ASCOT 2156 DJ	8.00	northern
PICTURE ME GONE	I'M GONNA MAKE YOU LOVE ME	PHILIPS 40517	8.00	northern
PICTURE ME GONE	I'M GONNA MAKE YOU LOVE ME	MOD 1007	10.00	northern

BELLES
DON'T PRETEND	WORDS CAN'T EXPLAIN	MIRWOOD 5505	20.00	northern

BELLINE, DENNY
OUTSIDE THE CITY	GREY CITY DAY	RCA 9041 DJ	15.00	northern

BELMONTS
YOU'RE LIKE A MYSTERY	COME WITH ME	UA 50007	25.00	northern

BELOYD
TODAY ALL DAY 2353	GET INTO MY LIFE	20th. CENTURY	50.00	70's

BEN, LA BRENDA AND THE BELL JEANS
THE CHAPERONE	CAMEL WALK	GORDY 7009	60.00	motown
JUST BE YOURSELF	I CAN'T HELP IT I GOTT'A DANCE	GORDY 7021	40.00	motown

BEN AND THE CHEERS
SINCE YOU CAME INTO MY LIFE	I KNOW YOU NEED A FRIEND	MOCHA 10001	10.00	70's

BENNETT, BOBBY GUITAR
YOU DID IT AGAIN		JUNIOR 1009	250.00	northern

BENNETT, BOBBY
BABY TRY ME	BIG NEW YORK	PHIL LA SOUL 326	20.00	northern

BENNETT, JOYCE
THE NEW BOY	MR. D.J.	FRAN-ETTE 11	30.00	northern
THE NEW BOY	MR. D.J.	JAGUAR 100	15.00	northern

BENSON, GEORGE
MY WOMAN'S GOOD TO ME	JACKIE, ALL	A&M 1076	30.00	70's

BENTON, BROOK
BETTER TIMES	MAKIN LOVE IS GOOD FOR YOU	OLDE WORLD 1100	8.00	70's
GLOW LOVE	SOFT	OLDE WORLD 1107	8.00	70's
WHERE DOES A MAN GO TO CRY	THE ROACH SONG	RCA 8944	20.00	northern

BERDELL, CHERYL
GIVING IT ALL TO YOU	FALL IN LOVE	EM.T 3846	10.00	**northerB**

BERKSHIRE, SEVEN
STOP AND START OVER		STOP 255	150.00	northern

BERNAL, GIL
CAN YOU LOVE A POOR BOY	TO MAKE A BIG MAN CRY	RCA 9390	30.00	northern
THIS IS WORTH FIGHTING FOR	THEY SAY (I DON'T SEE)	RCA 9261	15.00	northern

BERNARD, CHRIS
MOTHER	COLD HEARTED WOMAN	MCVOUTIE 7817	30.00	northern
MOTHER	GOOD HEARTED WOMAN	REVUE 11053	15.00	northern

BERNARD, CHUCK
EVERY HURT MAKES YOU STRONGER	FUNNY CHANGES	SATELLITE 2008	30.00	northern
GOT TO GET A HOLD OF MYSELF	EVERYBODY'S GOT THEIR OWN THI	ZODIAC 1050	15.00	northern
LOVE CAN SLIP AWAY	BESSIE GIRL	ZODIAC 1014	15.00	northern
SHE'S ALREADY MARRIED	MY BABY	SATELLITE 2012	20.00	northern
THE OTHER SIDE OF MY MIND	EVERYTHING IS ALRIGHT NO	ZODIAC 1018	15.00	northern
WASTED	LET'S GET STONED	SATELLITE 2003	15.00	mod
WASTED	LET'S GET STONED	ST.LAWRENCE 1023	15.00	mod
INDIAN GIVER	DIAL MY NUMBER	SATELILITE 2005	10.00	northern
SEND FOR ME	I CAN'T FIGHT IT	ST.LAWRENCE 1025	15.00	northern

BERNARD, KENNY
AIN'T NO SOUL (LEFT IN THESE O	HEY WOMAN	COMPASS 7002	15.00	**northerB**

BERRY, CHARLES
NEIGHBOR, NEIGHBOR	TIME	JETSTREAM 708	40.00	northern

BERRY, DELORISE
NO OTHER GIRL	CRYING WON'T HELP ME NOW	COTILLION 44008	15.00	northern

BERRY, DOROTHY
YOU BETTER WATCH OUT	AIN'T THAT LOVE	PLANETARY 101	50.00	northern

BERRY, GORDON (also see Tony Daniels)
HOW LONELY	SAME: INSTRUMENTAL	SPORT 103	40.00	northern

BERRY, JOAN
JUST LIKE MY BABY	HUMPTY DUMPTY	CHATEAU 159	100.00	northern

BERRY, MINZI
I DON'T WANT YOU NO MORE	THE HURT IS GONE	SCORE 1004	45.00	northern
DON'T LET A TEAR FALL	THOSE TEARDROPS IN YOUR EYES	SCORE 1006	100.00	northern
DON'T YOU DARE CRY	THOSE TEARDROPS IN YOUR EYES	SCORE 1007	100.00	northern

BERRY, RICHARD
DOIN' IT	TRACKIN' MACHINE	JONCO 51	10.00	funk
AIN'T THAT SOMETHING	AIN'T THAT SOMETHING PT.2	C-RAY 6706	15.00	mod
HAVE LOVE WILL TRAVEL	LOUIE LOUIE	FLIP 321	35.00	northern
HAVE LOVE WILL TRAVEL	NO ROOM	FLIP 349	20.00	northern

BEST, BILLY AND THE DITALIANS

BABY THAT TAKES THE CAKE	TIMES GETTING HARD (JOSEPHINE)	MERCURY 72923j	40.00	funk

BETHEA AND THE MASKMAN AND THE AGENTS

I WOULDN'T COME BACK	GET AWAY DREAMS	DYNAMO 136	15.00	northern

BETTY AND TERRI

YOU KILLED THE THRILL IN MY HE	LAVA	PROVIDENCE 414	40.00	northern

BEVERLEY, FRANK AND THE BUTLERS

I WANT TO FEEL I'M WANTED	BECUASE OF MY HEART	FAIRMOUNT 1017	650.00	northern
IF THAT'S WHAT YOU WANTED	LOVE (YOUR PAIN GOES DEEP)	GAMBLE 220	200.00	northern
SHE TRIED TO KISS ME	THE SUN'S MESSAGE	LIBERTYY BELL 1024	25.00	northern
IF THAT'S WHAT YOU WANTED	LOVE (YOUR PAIN GOES DEEP)	SASSY 1002	100.00	northern
IF THAT'S WHAT YOU WANTED	JUST A B-SIDE	SASSY 1002	75.00	northern
SHE KISSED ME	DON'T CRY LITTLE SAD BOY	FAIRMOUNT 1012	100.00	northern
LAUGH, LAUGH, LAUGH	BUTLER'S THEME	PHILA 1836 red logo	15.00	**northerB**
BEVERLEYWHERE THE GOOD TIMES ARE	HAPPY NEW YEAR	DERAM 7502	10.00	northern

BEVERLEY AND THE DEL-CAPRIS

MAMA I THINK I'M IN LOVE	MILDRED	COLUMBIA 43107	200.00	northern

BEVERLEY'S RAW SOUL, FRANK

COLOR BLIND	MOTHER NATURE'S BEEN GOOD TO YOU	GREGAR 108	100.00	funk
TOMORROW M\AY NOT BE YOUR DAY	SAME:	GREGAR 115	10.00	northern

BEVERLY AND DUANE

WE GOT TO STICK TOGETHER	GLAD I GOTCHA BABY	ARIOLA 7728	15.00	70's

BEY, SLOAN

TENDERNESS	LOOK AT YOUR BROTHER	JONAH 100	10.00	ballad

BIG AL AND THE STARTREKS

FUNKY FUNK		DOUBLE M NO#	100.00	funk

BIG BOE AND THE NIGHT HAWKS

MY THING		BIG BOE NO#	50.00	funk

BIG DON'S REBELLION

IT WAS TRUE	SMOKIN'	ETHON 101	100.00	northern

BIG ELLA

TOO HOT TO HOLD		SALEM NO#.	20.00	funk
IT TAKES A LOT OF LOVING	I NEED A GOOD MAN	LO LO 2101	15.00	northern

BIG FRANK AND THE ESSENCES

I WON'T LET HER SEE ME CRY	THE SECRET	PHILIPS 40283	200.00	northern
I WON'T LET HER SEE ME CRY	THE SECRET	BLUE ROCK 4012	250.00	northern

BIG GUYS

HANG MY HEAD AND CRY	MR. CUPID	WB 7047	30.00	northern

BIG JOHN'S SWING

TOSSING MY HEART AROUND	LILA CHA CHA	J.F.J. 600	150.00	motown

BIG MAYBELLE

96 TEARS	THAT'S LIFE	ROJAC 112	15.00	northern
I CAN'T WAIT ANY LONGER	TURN THE WORLD AROUND THE OTHE	ROJAC 115	15.00	northern
I CAN'T WAIT ANY LONGER	QUITTIN' TIME	ROJAC 118	10.00	northern
LET ME GO	NO BETTER FOR YOU	PORT 3002	40.00	northern
OH LORD WHAT RU DOING TO ME	SAME OLD STORY	SCEPTER 1279	25.00	northern
YESERDAY'S KISSES	I DON'T WANNA CRY	SCEPTER 1288	25.00	northern

BIGGER SAM AND THE COPY CATS

I'M READY FOR LOVE	BLOWING IN THE WIND	20th. CENTURY 6666	15.00	northern

BIGGIE RATT

ESCAPE	WE DON'T NEED NO MUSIC	REEM	30.00	funk
ESCAPE	WE DON'T NEED NO MUSIC	APT 26001	10.00	funk

BILEO

YOU CAN WIN	LET'S GO	WATTS CITY 101 orange	20.00	**northerB**

BILL

SPACE LADY	I FEEL GOOD WITH YOU	DOLLAR BILL 42480	20.00	70's

BILLUPS, EDDIE

SHAKE OFF THAT DREAM	TRY SOMETHING NEW	SEVENTY 7 127	50.00	70's
I WON'T BE AROUND	FEEL IT	JOSIE 971	15.00	ballad
MY FAITH IN YOU (WILL NEVER DIE)	N.Y. KANGAROO	MAXX 336	10.00	ballad
MY GIRL	NO LOVE HAVE I	SHURFINE 20 blue	30.00	ballad
MY GIRL	NO LOVE HAVE I	SHURFINE 20 pink	40.00	ballad
MY GIRL	NO LOVE HAVE I	JOSIE 960	20.00	ballad
ASK MY HEART	SOLDIER'S PRAYER	PEACHTREE 104	1000.00	northern
SHAKE OFF THAT DREAM	MRS M	GARPAX 123	100.00	northern

BILLY

PUT YOUR OWN WORDS TO IT	YOU MOVE ME	SNIFF 395	100.00	funk

BILLY AND THE ESSENTIALS

MY WAY OF SAYING	BABALU'S WEDDING DAY	SMASH 2045	10.00	northern

BINDERS

YOU DON'T HAVE TO CRY ANYMORE	SAVE THE LAST DANCE FOR ME	ANKH 7772	30.00	group
WHEN WE WERE YOUNG	MOJO HANNAH	SARA 7771	40.00	group
YOU DON'T HAVE TO CRY ANYMORE	SAVE THE LAST DANCE FOR ME	SARA7772	60.00	group

BINGHAM, J.B.

ALL ALONE BY THE TELEPHONE	SAME:	UA 816 DJ	100.00	70's
SHE'S GONE	SAME:	UA 872 DJ	20.00	70's
PEEK A BOO	SUNSHINE	WB 7775	20.00	ballad

Artist / Title	Track	Label	Price	Genre
BINGO				
WE CAN'T GET ENOUGH	MUMBLIN' MAN	SILVER BLUE 803	20.00	70's
BINNS, CLIFFORD				
YOU'VE GOT TO HELP ME	TAKE IT FROM ME	CARRIE 14 green	20.00	northern
YOU'VE GOT TO HELP ME	TAKE IT FROM ME	CARRIE 6501 orange	300.00	northern
BISCAYNES				
MIS-BEAT	OUT OF ORDER	RIDGE 6601	200.00	motown
BISHOP TRIO, JOHN				
WADE IN THE WATER	ALL DAY LONG	TRC 991	15.00	mod
BISHOP, ROMY				
YOU GAVE ME BACK MY PRIDE	BAD GIRL	HERITAGE 806	30.00	northern
BISHOPS				
OUT OF SIGHT	THEY CAN'T MAKE ME STOP LOVING	CAPITOL 5487	30.00	northern
BIT OF HONEY				
HE'S THE ONE	LIVE IN MAID	SHOUT 250	10.00	northern
BITS AND PIECES				
YOU SHOULD HAVE TOLD ME	I BET'CHA DON'T KNOW	PARAMOUNT 284	30.00	70's
KEEP ON RUNNING AWAY	SINNER HAVE YOU BEEN THERE	NASCO 33	20.00	northern
SMOKE STREAM	DID I SCARE YOU	NASCO 31	10.00	northern
BITTER AND THE SWEET				
I WON'T HAVE ANY BABIES FOR YOU				
EVERYTHING 32	P.O.W.	ANYTHING,	200.00	70's
BLACK AND BLUE				
OF ALL THE HEARTS TO BREAK	GOOD MORNING NEW DAY	GAME 395	20.00	70's
WHAT I GOT	GOING BACK O MISS ANNIE	MERCURY 73011	125.00	70's
BLACK , MARION				
WHO KNOWS	GO ON FOOL	CAPSOUL 20	20.00	northern
BLACK EYED PEAS				
SMALLEST MAN ALIVE	GO THRU THE MOTIONS	ULTRA CITY 70317	100.00	northern
BLACK FUR				
FEEL THE SHOCK		BAR-TONE	100.00	funk
BLACK ICE				
GIRL, THAT'S WHAT I CALL LOVE	MAKING LVE IN THE RAIN	AMHERST 706	8.00	70's
BLIND OVER YOU	I FEEL THE WEIGHT	HDM 505	10.00	group
BLACK NASTY				
CUT YOUR MOTOR OFF	KEEP ON STEPPING	BIG HIT 129	10.00	funk
HIP DROP	MAMA DIDN'T LIE	TANK 503	30.00	funk
TALKING TO THE PEOPLE	I MUST BE IN LOVE	ENTERPRISE 9098	10.00	funk
BLACK, CODY				
I STILL LOVE YOU	ICE CREAM SONG	STON-ROC 3378	20.00	ballad
I'M SORRY	FOOL ON THE WILD	CAPITOL 2807	50.00	northern
KEEP ON TRYING	STEPPIN' ON TOES	RENISSANCE 1001	20.00	northern
WHAT GOES ROUND	SWEET LOVE	RENISSANCE 2	25.00	northern
(THE NIGHT) A STAR WAS BORN	LIFE GOES ON	RAM-BROCK 2003	20.00	northern
GOING GOING GONE	SOMEBODY"S GONNA END UP CRYIN	RAM-BROCK 2002	10.00	northern
I'M SLOWLY MOULDING		KING 6148	300.00	northern
IT'S OUR TIME TO FALL IN LOVE		GIG 201	1000.00	northern
MR. BLUE	YOU'LL BE SORRY	D-TOWN 1057	300.00	northern
THE NIGHT ASTAR WAS BORN	YOU MUST BE IN LOVE	GROOVE CITY 9601	100.00	northern
TOO MANY IRONS IN THE FIRE	BECAUSE YOU FIRST LOVED ME	D-TOWN 1066	60.00	northern
I WILL GIVE YOU LOVE	WOULD YOU LET ME KNOW	WHEELSVILE 107	50.00	ballad
	I AM PATRICULAR			
BLACK, DOROTHY				
MIRACLE MAN		RIPE	100.00	funk
BLACK, MARION				
YOU'RE NOT ALONE	I'M GONNA GET LOADED	PRIX 7102	30.00	ballad
BLACK, MARJORIE				
ONE MORE HURT	YOU STILL LOVE HER	SUE 132	25.00	northern
BLACKNELL, EUGENE				
GETTIN' DOWN		SEASIDE	150.00	funk
THE TRIP	THE TRIP (Pt.2)	BOOLA BOOLA 6942	30.00	funk
WE KNOW WE GOT TO LIVE TOGETHER	SAME: Pt. 2	SEASIDE 4112	100.00	funk
BLACK'S COMBO, BILL				
LITTLE QUEENIE	BOO-RAY	HI 2079	10.00	northern
BLACKWELL, GEORGE				
CAN'T LOSE MY HEAD	DON'T WANT TO LET YOU GO	SMOKE 200	400.00	**northerB**
MISTER LOSER		SMOKE 100	40.00	northern
BLACKWELL, OTIS				
IT'S ALL OVER ME	JUST KEEP IT UP	EPIC 10654	20.00	northern
BLADES				
HEY GIRL	SUMMERTIME	KAM 100	100.00	northern
BLAIR, ARNOLD				
TRYING TO GET NEXT TO YOU	SAME:	GEMIGO 504	150.00	70's
BLAIR, LITTLE JOHNNY				
MOMMA'S GONE	EASIER TO SAY THAN TO DO	HOUSE OF THE FOX 5	10.00	northern
BLAKE, CICERO				
DON'T DO THIS TO ME	SEE WHAT TOMORROW BRINGS	SUCCESS 108	20.00	northern
IF I HAD MY WAY	STEP BY STEP	BRAINSTORM 119	50.00	northern

21

SHING-A-LING	LOVING YOU WOMAN IS EVERYTHING	BRAINSTORM 123	15.00	northern
TAKE IT FROM ME	SOUL OF PAIN	RENEE 106	10.00	northern
YOU'RE GONNA BE SORRY	SAD FEELING	RENEE 109	20.00	northern
YOU'RE GONNA BE SORRY	SAD FEELING	MAR-V-LUS 6004	20.00	northern
HERE COME THE HEARTACHE	FACE THE CASE	TOWER 454	10.00	ballad
DON'T WAIT UNTIL TOMORROW	BAD, BUT BEAUTIFUL BOY	TOWER 494	10.00	ballad

BLAKE, COREY

HOW CAN I GO ON WITHOUT YOU	YOUR LOVE IS LIKE A BOOMERANG	CAPITOL 4057	300.00	70's

BLAKELY, CORNELL

I WANT MY SHARE	I'VE GOT THAT FEELING	RICH 1801	20.00	motown
WAITING FOR MY LOVE	NO OTHER LOVE	SHENITA 733	50.00	motown
YOU AIN'T GONNA FIND	WHO KNOWS	RICH 1853	25.00	motown
YOU BROKE MY HEART	DON'T DO IT	SHENITA 731	50.00	motown

BLAKLY, VIRGINIA

LET NOBODY LOVE YOU	BUTTERFLIES AND MISTY EYES	Mojo 101	500.00	northern

BLANCHARD, BONNIE AND AARON, ANDY

YOU'RE THE ONLY ONE	RIGHT ON TIME	CRS 2	100.00	northern

BLAND, BILLY

ALL I WANNA DO IS CRY	BUSY LITTLE BOY	OLD TOWN 1114	40.00	northern
I CROSS MY HEART	STEADY KIND	OLD TOWN 1098	40.00	northern
MY HEART'S ON FIRE	CAN'T STOP HER FROM DANCING	OLD TOWN 1105	40.00	northern

BLAND, BOBBY

GOOD TIME CHARLIE	SAME: INSTRUMENTAL	DUKE 402	10.00	northern
YUM YUM TREE	I'M SORRY	DUKE 466	10.00	northern
BLUE MOON	WHO WILL THE NEXT FOOL BE	DUKE 347	10.00	mod
CALL ON ME	THAT'S THE WAY LOVE IS	DUKE 360	10.00	northern
CHAINS OF LOVE	ASK ME BOUT NOTHING	DUKE 449	8.00	northern
GETTING USED TO THE BLUES	THAT DID IT	DUKE 421	10.00	northern
HONEY CHILD	A PIECE OF GOLD	DUKE 433	8.00	northern
HONEY CHILD	AIN'T NOTHING YOU CAN DO	DUKE 375	10.00	northern
I AIN'T MYSELF ANYMORE	BACK IN THE SAME OLD BAG	DUKE 412	10.00	northern
LOVER WITH A REPUTATION	IF LOVE RULED THE WORLD	DUKE 460	8.00	northern
SHOES	A TOUCH OF THE BLUES	DUKE 426	15.00	northern
THESE HAND (SMALL BUT MIGHTY)	TODAY	DUKE 385	10.00	northern
TURN ON YOUR LOVELIGHT	YOU'RE THE ONE THAT I NEED	DUKE 344	10.00	northern
YIELD NOT TO TEMMPTATION	HOW DOES A CHEATING WOMAN FEEL	DUKE 352	10.00	northern

BLANDING, GIL

RULES	LA TA TA	READY 102	30.00	northern

BLANDING, VIRGIL

YOU TURN ME AROUND	THE GIRL WASN'T BORN	VERVE 10428	15.00	northern

BLANDON, CURTIS

IN THE LONG RUN	PUSH COMES TO SHOVE	WAND 11241	40.00	northern

BLAST, C.L.

LOVE DON'T FEEL LIKE LOVE NO M	BEAUTIFUL LOVER	JUANA 3412	15.00	70's
DOUBLE UP	I'M GLAD TO DO IT	STAX 229.	20.00	northern
WHAT CAN I DO	I'M IN A DAZE	UNITED 224	8.00	northern

BLENDELLS (BLENDELS)

DANCE WITH ME	GET YOUR BABY	REPRISE 340	10.00	northern
LA LA LA LA LA	HUGGIE'S BUNNIES	REPRISE 291	10.00	northern
NIGHT AFTER NIGHT	THE LOVE THAT I NEEDED	COTILLION 44020	10.00	group
NIGHT AFER NIGHT	THE LOVE THAT I NEEDED	CAP TOWN 4029	20.00	group
BEWARE	SAME: INSTRUMENTAL	DONTEE 104	1000.00	northern

BLENDERS

NOTHIN' BUT A PARTY		COBRA	150.00	funk
YOUR LOVE HAS GOT ME DOWN	LOVE IS A GOOD THING	MARVLUS 6010	600.00	northern
TALE OF SADNESS	FUNKY FUN IN THE GHETTO	DJO 1007	50.00	northern

BLEU LIGHTS

I GUESS I'M IN LOVE	AS LONG AS YOU'RE IN LOVE WITH	BAY SOUND 67013	70.00	northern
THEY DON'T KNOW MY HEART	FOREVER	BAY SOUND 67003	100.00	northern
YES I DO	THE END OF MY DREAM	BAY SOUND 67010	20.00	northern

BLISS, MELVIN

SYNTHETIC SUBSTITUTION	REWARD	SUNBURST 527	20.00	funk

BLOCKER, DAVE

JUST LIKE A SHIP	RIVER WHERE DO YOU GO	VERVE 10613	20.00	northern

BLOOD BROTHERS

BLACK IS SO BAD	SUPER COOL	TURBO 29	20.00	funk

BLOOM, BOBBY

LOVE, DON'T LET ME DOWN	BLOOM, BOBBY	KAMA SUTRA 223	20.00	northern

BLOSSOMS

DEEP INTO MY HEART	GOOD, GOOD LOVIN'	REPRISE 639	20.00	northern
GOOD, GOOD LOVIN'	DEEP INTO MY HEART	REPRISE 639	20.00	northern
THAT'S WHEN THE TEARS START	GOOD, GOOD LOVIN'	REPRISE 436	30.00	northern

BLU, NIKKI

(WHOA WHOA) I LOVE HIM SO	SAME: INSTRUMENTAL	PARKWAY 931	30.00	northern

BLUE BEATS

EXTRA GIRL	ASHE'S THE ONE	COLUMBIA 43790	20.00	northern

BLUE EYED SOUL

ARE YOU READY FOR THIS	WHEN SOMETHING'S WRONG WITH MY BABY	SAND CITY 2101	300.00	northern

Artist / Title A	Title B	Label	Price	Genre
BLUE GREEN				
CAN'T HIDE IT (SWEET BABY)	BLUE OVER LOSING YOU	EASTERS 4793	40.00	70's
BLUE JAYS				
POINT OF VIEW	THAT FEELIN'	JAY. 4815	200.00	northern
BLUENOTES				
STANDING BY YOU GIRL	IT'S OVER	GLADES 1746	10.00	70's
BLUES BUSTERS				
INSPIRED TO LOVE YOU	I CAN'T STOP	SHOUT 235	15.00	northern
LOVE IS THE ANSWER		MINIT 32090	20.00	northern
I'VE GOTTA BE THERE	IRREPLACEABLE YOU	CAPITOL 5959	20.00	northern
BLUES GROOVE				
I BELIEVE IN YOU	MAKIN' IT	VERVE 10417	25.00	northern
BLUES IMAGE				
PARCHMANT FARM	CAN'T YOU BELIVE IN FOREVER	IMAGE 5833	15.00	mod
BO, EDDIE				
CAN YOU HANDLE IT	DON'T TURN ME LOSE	BO SOUND 5116	15.00	funk
CHECK YOUR BUCKET	CHECK YOUR BUCKET PT.2	BO SOUND 5551	10.00	funk
HOOK AND SLING	HOOK AND SLING PT.2	SCRAM 117	15.00	funk
IF IT'S GOOD TO YOU	IF IT'S GOOD TO YOU PT.2	SCRAM 119	10.00	funk
SHOWDOWN		BO SOUND	50.00	funk
THE RUBBER BAND	THE RUBBER BAND Pt.2	KNIGHT 303	15.00	funk
WE'RE DOING IT	WE'RE DOING IT Pt.2	BO SOUND 5005	100.00	funk
GOTTA HAVE MORE	COME TO ME	BLUE JAY 154	20.00	mod
SKATE IT OUT	ALL I ASK OF YOU	SEVEN B 7011	10.00	mod
LUCKY IN LOVE	OUR LOVE (WILL NEVER FALTER)	BLUE JAY 157	50.00	northern
WHAT YOU GONNA DO	FALLIN' IN LOVE AGAIN	SEVEN B 7002	40.00	northern
BOATWRIGHT, HENRY				
I CAN TAKE OR LEAVE YOUR LOVIN	I'M HUNG UP ON A DREAM	CAPITOL 2131	20.00	northern
BOB AND EARL				
OH BABY DOLL	DEEP DOWN INSIDE	TEMPE 104	15.00	northern
OH YEA (HAVE YOU EVER BEEN LON	AS WE DANCE	TIP 1013	15.00	northern
BOB AND FRED				
I'LL BE ON MY WAY	INSTRUMENTAL: BAHA STRINGS	BIG MACK 6101	800.00	northern
BOB AND GENE				
IF THIS WORLD WERE MINE	IT WON'T GO	MO DO 11138	6.00	70's
SAILBOAT	I CAN BE COOL	MO DO 108	100.00	northern
BOBBETTES				
HAPPY GO LUCKY, ME	IT'S ALL OVER	RCA 8983	40.00	northern
I'VE GOT TO FACE THE WORLD	HAVING FUN	RCA 8832	20.00	northern
BOBBY AND BETTY LOU				
SOUL STIRRER	SUGAR	OLD TOWN 1194	10.00	northern
BOB-WHEELS				
LOVE ME (JUST A LITTLE BIT)	SHE'S GONE	TARX 1008	25.00	northern
BOGIS CHIMES				
I THINK YOU'LL FIND		CHAMP 3403	20.00	northern
BOGUS, ANN				
DON'T ASK ME TO LOVE AGAIN	YOU GOT IT WRONG	STATUE 256	100.00	northern
BOND, LOU				
YOU SHAKE ME UP	DON'T START ME CRYING	BRAINSTORM 124	15.00	northern
BONGALIS				
UNDERCOVER	COVER-UP	M-S 201	40.00	northern
BONNETS				
YA GOTTA TAKE A CHANCE	YA GOTTA TAKE A CHANCE (Inst.)	UNICAL 3010	20.00	northern
BONNIE AND CLYDE (Brenda Holloway)				
I WANT A BOYFRIEND	I GET A FEELING	IN SOUND 405	30.00	motown
BONNIE AND LEE				
THE WAY I FEEL ABOUT YOU	I NEED YA (GOTTA HAVE YOU FOR	FAIRMOUNT 1024	15.00	northern
BONNY, WILLIAM				
LOVE, LOVE, LOVE	JUST ONE MORE CHANCE	MERCURY 72594	10.00	**northerB**
BOOGIE KINGS				
TELL IT LIKE IT IS	PHILLY WALK	PAULA 260	10.00	group
I'VE GOT YOUR NUMBER	BONY MORONIE	PAULA 272	20.00	northern
BOOK OF LIFE				
I DON'T KNOW YOU	LOVE WILL RISE	SONSTAR 100	15.00	70's
BOOKER, JAMES				
GONZO	COOL TURKEY	PEACOCK 1697	10.00	mod
SMACKSIE	KINDA HAPPY	PEACOCK 1900	10.00	mod
BOOMER, BILLY				
YOU CAN'T HIDE	I LIKE WHAT SHE'S DOIN'	BLAST. 336	50.00	70's
BOONE, JESSE AND THE ASTROS				
I'M IN NEED OF YOU	YOU CAN'T BE A MONKEY WOMAN	BRUBOON 103	20.00	ballad
I GOT TO LOVE YOU	YOU CAN DEPEND ON THAT	SOUL-PO-TION 119	20.00	northern
BOOTHE, BETTE				
TEARDROP AVENUE	RIGHT ON TIME	FALEW 103	30.00	northern
BOOTLEGGERS				
DON'T COUNT ON TOMORROW	SOUL OF A SORT	DISCOVERY 1766	300.00	northern

BORDERS, TONY

YOU BETTER BELIEVE IT	WHAT KIND OF SPELL	SOUTH CAMP 7009	20.00	ballad
LOVES BEEN GOOD TO ME	STAY BY MY SIDE	TFC 125	20.00	northern

BOSEMAN, BOBBY

ANOTHER MAN'S WOMAN	CHEATERS NEVER WIN	EVEJIM 1941 pink lbl	20.00	ballad

BOSS FOUR

WALKIN' BY	SPACE MOOD	RIM 2025	15.00	northern

BOSS MAN

YOU'RE TAKING TOO LONG	WHEN I HADS MONEY	GAMBLE 222	50.00	northern

BOSTIC, WILLIAM

WHAT YOU DO TO ME	YOU WERE ALL I NEEDED	SOR 102946	20.00	70's

BOSTON HITESMEN

CAN'T LET IT RIDE	MY BABE	MTA 104	200.00	northern

BOTTOM AND COMPANY

GONNA FIND A TRUE LOVE	YOU'RE MY LIFE	MOTOWN 1291	75.00	70's
SPREAD THE NEWS	LOVE PAINS	MOTOWN 1309	15.00	70's

BOUNTY, JAMES

ACTION SPEAKS LOUDER THAN WORD	RAGS TO RICHES	COMPASS 7011	15.00	northern
AUCTION ON LOVE	GOIN' GOIN' GONE	REDDOG 4002	10.00	northern
PROVE YOURSELF A LADY	LIFE WILL BEGIN AGAIN	COMPASS 7005	50.00	**northerB**

BOUQUETS

I LOVE HIM SO	NO LOVE AT ALL	MALA 472	30.00	northern
WELCOME TO MY HEART	AIN'T THAT LOVE	BLUE CAT 115	20.00	northern

BOWE, TOBY

I CAN FEEL HIM SLIPPING AWAY	GROOVY FEELING	PATHEWAY 101	200.00	northern

BOWEN, HAROLD

FAITH	HOSANNA	BO-MAC 574	30.00	northern

BOWEN, JEFFERY

I'LL GET BY (ALL BY MYSELF)	I'VE GOT A BRAND NEW FEELING	MERCURY 72383	200.00	northern

BOWENS, JAMES

BABY I WANT YOU	THIS BOY AND GIRL	ROOSEVELT LEE	20.00	northern
21832				

BOWIE, JOHN

YOU'RE GONNA MISS A GOOD THING	AT THE END OF THE DAY	MERBEN 503	100.00	northern

BOWIE, LITTLE JOHN

MY LOVE, MY LOVE	GO GO ANNIE	PHIL LA SOUL 307	20.00	northern

BOWIE, SAM

(THINK OF)THE TIMES WE HAD TOGETHER	SWOOP, SWOOP	WINGATE 2	10.00	northern

BOYD, BOBBY

WHATCHA' GONNA DO ABOUT IT	SAME:	BANG 562 DJ	20.00	northern

BOYD, MELVIN

EXIT LONELINESS, ENTER LOVE	THINGS ARE GETTING BETTER	ERA 3167	30.00	northern

BOYD, OSCAR

LITTLE SWEET THINGS YOU DO	WHEN THINGS GET A LITTLE BETTE	HERMES 107	10.00	northern

BOYKIN, WAYNE

MAKE ME YOURS	HEART OF A POOR MAN	ATLANTIC 2670	10.00	northern

BOYS

THERE'S NOTHING I CAN DO	PT. 2	FLY BY NITE 1	30.00	70's

BOZE, ED

MEMORIES	LONELY	AVCO 4622	30.00	70's

BRACELETS

YOU'RE JUST FOOLING YOURSELF	YOU BETTER MOVE ON	20th. CENTURY 539	75.00	northern

BRACKENRIDGE, JOE AND THE KASCADES

GIRL FOR ME		USA 829	200.00	northern

BRADFORD, CLEA

SUMMERTIME	MY LOVES A MONSTER	CADET 5602	15.00	mod

BRADLEY, PATRICK

JUST ONE MORE CHANCE	SAME: INSTRUMENTAL	DECCA 32148	100.00	northern

BRADLEY, JAN

BABY WHAT CAN I DO	THESE TEARS	CHESS 1851	20.00	northern
BACK IN CIRCULATION	LOVE IS THE ANSWER	ADANTI 1051	15.00	northern
BEHIND THE CURTAINS	PACK MY THINGS (AND GO)	NIGHT OWL 1055	100.00	northern
I'M OVER YOU	THE BRUSH OFF	CHESS 1919	10.00	northern
MAMA DIDN'T LIE	LOVERS LIKE ME	FORMAL 1044	30.00	northern
MAMA DIDN'T LIE	LOVERS LIKE ME	CHESS 1845	10.00	northerB
WE GIRLS	CURFEW BLUES	FORMAL 1014	20.00	northern
YOU GAVE ME WHAT'S MISSING	NIGHTS IN NEW YORK CITY	CHESS 2043	10.00	northern
YOUR KIND OF LOVIN'	IT'S JUST YOUR WAY	CHESS 2023	10.00	northern

BRADSHAW, BOBBY

MAKE SOMEONE HAPPY	IT'S A MIRACLE	JAMIE 1366	15.00	northern

BRADY, BOB AND THE CON CHORDS

GOODBYE BABY	TELL ME WHY	CHARIOT 100	40.00	northern
I STAND REJECTED	MORE MORE MORE OF YOUR LOVE	A&M 1382	10.00	northern
MORE MORE MORE OF YOUR LOVE	IT'S A BETTER WORLD	CHARIOT 101	8.00	northern
EVERYBODY'S GOING TO A LOVE-IN	IT'S BEEN A LONG TIME BETWEEN	CHARIOT 526	10.00	northern

BRAGG, JOE
I'VE GOTTA MAKE IT	VOICE IN THE NIGHT	BOCART 101	100.00	northern

BRAGG, JOHNNY
THEY'RE TALKING ABOUT ME	IS IT TRUE	ELBEJAY 1	20.00	**northerB**
THEY'RE TALKING ABOUT ME	IS IT TRUE	ELBEJAY 1 PS	30.00	northern

BRAGGS, AL TNT
EARTHQUAKE	HOW LONG (DO YOU HOLD ON)	PEACOCK 1945	15.00	northern
GIVE IT UP	RUNNING OUT OF LIVES	PEACOCK 1967	15.00	northern
HOME IN THAT ROCK	THAT'S ALL A PART OF LOVING YO	PEACOCK 1957	15.00	northern
I JUST CAN'T GET OVER YOU	HOOTENANNY HOOT	PEACOCK 1931	15.00	northern
I'M A GOOD MAN	I LIKE WHAT YOU DO TO ME	PEACOCK 1962	15.00	northern
OUT OF THE PAN (INTO THE FIRE)	JOY TO MY SOUL	PEACOCK 1936	20.00	northern

BRAITHWAITE, MITCHELL
YOU'VE BEEN A LONG TIME COMIN'	MY WOMAN NEEDS ME	PROBE 465	25.00	northern

BRAMLETT, DELANEY
YOU HAVE NO CHOICE	LIVERPOOL LOU	GNP CRESCENDO	15.00	northern
339				

BRAND NEW
THOUSAND YEARS	PARTY TIME	DU-VERN 4176	250.00	70's

BRANDON, BILL
THE STREETS GOT MY LADY	TAG TAG	PIEDMONT 78	300.00	70's
RAINBOW ROAD	(YOU'VE GOT THAT) SOMETHING WRONG	TOWER 430	70.00	ballad
FULL GROWN MAN	SELF PRESERVATION	SOUTH CAMP 7006	25.00	northern
SINCE I FELL	FOR YOU	QUINVY 7007	50.00	ballad
STOP THIS MERRY GO ROUND	I'M A BELIEVER NOW	MOONSONG 9001	10.00	ballad
WHATEVER I AM, I'M YOURS	II'M A BELIEVER NOW	MOONSONG 9003	200.00	70's

BRANDON, BILL AND JOHNSON, LORRAINE
LET ME BE YOUR FULL TIME GROOV	LET'S MAKE A NEW LOVE SOMETHIN	MOONSONG 1	40.00	**northerB**

BRAND NEW FACES
BRAND NEW FACES	I DON'T WANNA CRY	LUJUNA 10655	700.00	northern

BRANDY, CHARLES
I CAN'T GET ENOUGH	WITHOUT YOU LOVE	BLUE CAT	700.00	northern

BRANTLEY, DAN
IT MUST BE LOVE	GET IT RIGHT, OR LEAVE IT ALON	DELUXE 119	15.00	northern

BRASSEAUR, ANDRE
THE KID	HOLIDAY	CONGRESS 271	10.00	**northerB**

BRASWELL, JIMMY
THIS TIME IT'S GOT TO BE REAL	TIME WAITS FOR NO MAN	JAR-VAL 15	20.00	northern
I CAN'T GIVE YOU MY HEART		KING 6374	100.00	northern

BRAXTON, P. AND THE AND THE SCACY SOUND SERVICE
SUNSHINE PT.1	SUNSHINE PT.2	SCACY 2200	100.00	funk

BREAKERS
LONG WAY HOME	BALBOA MEMORIES	MARSH 206	20.00	group

BREEDLOVE, JIMMY
I CAN'T HELP LOVING YOU	I SAW YOU	ROULETTE 7010	15.00	northern

BREEN, BOBBY
BETTER LATE THAN NEVER	HOW CAN WE TELL HIM	MOTOWN 1053	25.00	motown
HERE COMES THAT HEARTACHE	YOU'RE JUST LIKE ME	MOTOWN 1059	30.00	motown

BRENDA AND HERB
SWEET DREAMER	TONIGHT I'M GONNA MAKE YOU A S	H&L 4699	10.00	70's

BRENDA AND THE TABULATIONS
HEY BOY	JUST ONCE IN A LIFETIME	DIONN 503	10.00	northern
ONE GIRL TOO LATE	MAGIC OF YOUR LOVE	EPIC 10954	10.00	northern
THAT'S IN THE PAST	I CAN'T GET OVER YOU	DIONN 509	20.00	northern
THAT'S THE PRICE YOU HAVE TO PAY	I WISH I HADN'T DONE WHAT I DI	DIONN 512	10.00	northern
SCUSE UZ Y'ALL	A CHILD NO ONE WANTED	TOP & BOTTOM 406	10.00	funk
A LOVE YOU CAN DEPEND ON	WHY DIDN'T I THINK OF THAT	TOP & BOTTOM 411	8.00	northern

BRENT, BRYAN
VACATION TIME	FOR ETERNITY	PENNY 2201	100.00	motown

BREWER, DEANNA AND THE TITANS
I'VE GOTTA KNOW	HOW LONG (MUST I WAIT)	LEMCO 885	50.00	northern

BREWSTER CREW
I'M ONE WHO KNOWS	OUTTA MY LIFE	LIFELINE 2	75.00	70's

BREWTON, BETTY
PERSHING SQUARE	HEAVY, HEAVY LOVIN'	SUE 1	30.00	northern

BRIDGE
BABY DON'T HOLD YOUR LOVE BACK	SAME:	ATLANTIC 89565	15.00	70's

BRIDGES, CHUCK
KEEP YOU FAITH BABY	BAD SAM	VAULT 958	10.00	northern
DON'T YOU MAKE ME CRY	I LOVE HER I NEED HER	SCOOP 4	70.00	northern

BRIDGES, LAVON
WITH A SMILE (ON MY FACE)		GLORECO 1003	100.00	northern

BRIEF ENCOUNTER
HUMAN	TOTAL SATISFACTION	SOUND PLUS 2179	20.00	70's
I'M SO SATISFIED	DON'T LET THEM TELL YOU	SEVENTY 7 123	8.00	70's

BRIGGS, FRED
SOUND OFF	I'M SO SORRY	GROOVE CITY 202	200.00	ballad

BRIGGS, KATIE				
WHY DO YOU DO THIS TO ME		MOS-RAY 3101	500.00	northern
BRIGHT, CAL				
MY LOVE IS GOOD FOR YOU BABY	GOT TO GET MYSELF TOGETHER	AZETTA 1001	20.00	northern
BRIGHTLIGHTS				
MOTOR CITY FUNK Pt.1	MOTOR CITY FUNK Pt.2	SILVER FOX 16	20.00	funk
BRILLIANT KORNERS				
THREE LONELY GUYS	CHANGE IN ME	MODERN 1059	150.00	northern
BRILLIANTS				
WHAT YOU GONNA DO	SLOW LOVIN'	FRISCO 3221	30.00	group
BRIMMER, CHARLES				
THE FEELING IS IN MY HEART	MR. TEARDROPS	BROADMOOR 201	85.00	northern
BRINSON, JIMMY				
IT'S ALL OVER GIRL	SAME:	BRIN 1001	300.00	70's
BRISKER, BONNIE				
SOMEONE REALLY LOVES YOU (GUES	SO MUCH LOVIN' (DEEP INSIDE OF ME)	MAGIC CITY 3	75.00	northern
BRITT, MEL				
SHE'LL COME RUNNING BACK	LOVE INVENTED MISERY	FIP 650	450.00	**northerB**
BRITT, SHARON				
GUESS WHO I BELONG TO	RESCUE WILL COME	AVCO 4627	8.00	70's
BRITT, TINA				
SOOKIE, SOOKIE	KEY TO THE HIGHWAY	VEEP 1298	15.00	northern
THE REAL THING	TEARDROPS FELL (EVERY STEP OF	EASTERN 604	10.00	northern
YOU'RE ABSOLUTELY RIGHT	LOOK	EASTERN 605	15.00	northern
BRITTON, LEROY				
YOU'RE NEVER TOO YOUNG	RAIN FALLS ON HARLEM	SOUND RECORDS 101	25.00	northern
BROADWAYS				
GOIN' GOIN' GONE	ARE YOU TELLING ME GOODBYE	MGM 13486	15.00	northern
YOU JUST DON'T KNOW	SWEET HEAVENLY MELODY	MGM 13592	20.00	northern
BROCKINGTON, ALFREDA				
YOU MADE ME A WOMAN	CRUSHING ME	PHIL LA SOUL 338	10.00	ballad
YOUR LOVE HAS GOT ME CHAINED AND BOUND	I'LL WAIT FOR YOU	PHIL LA SOUL 334	15.00	**northerB**
BROCKINGTON, SANDY				
GIRL IN DISTRESS	IT WAS YOU	BENGEE 1002	15.00	northern
BRODY, MARSHA				
RIGHT COMBINATION	I CRIED	HOT SHOT 1000	10.00	**northerB**
BRONC-GLOWS				
CHARGE	SANDMAN	BULL CITY SOUNDS 1	20.00	funk
BRONZETTES				
RUN, RUN, YOU LITTLE FOOL	HOT SPOT	PARKWAY 929	20.00	northern
BROOKS AND JERRY				
I GOT WHAT IT TAKES	I GOT WHAT IT TAKES Pt.2	DYNAMO 114	15.00	northern
BROOKS BROTHERS				
LOOKING FOR A WOMAN	TWO GREAT LOVERS	TAY 501	800.00	northern
BROOKS, DALE				
WHAT IS THERE TO TELL	MY FOOLISH PRIDE	TWIRL 2028	40.00	northern
BROOKS, DIANE				
IN MY HEART	I JUST DON'T KNOW WHAT 2DO WIT	VERVE 5036	15.00	northern
BROOKS, HENRY				
GREATEST DEBT TO MY MOTHER	MINI SKIRTS	P&P 333	30.00	northern
BROOKS, KARMELLO				
TELL ME, BABY	YOU'RE BREAKING MY HEART	MILESTONE 7107	300.00	northern
BROOKS, ROSA LEE				
UTEE	MY DIARY	REVIS 1013	100.00	northern
BROOKS, ROSE				
I'M MOANING	THEY'RE COMING TO TAKE ME AWAY	SOUL CITY 750	200.00	northern
BROOKS, SMOKEY				
SPIN IT JIG	ETERNAL	NOW 101	15.00	funk
BROTHER SOUL				
COOKIES		LEO MINI NO#	50.00	funk
FEELIN FUNKY	LIFE IS LIKE A MAZE	ELMCOR 103 blue	15.00	funk
TRAIN SONG		JANION NO#	50.00	funk
BROTHER WILLIAMS				
RIGHT ON BROTHER		SAADIA NO#	100.00	funk
BROTHERHOOD.				
WHEN YOU NEED ME	EXPRESSING MY LOVE	TESSERACT 1	100.00	70's
BROTHERS AND SISTERS				
DON'T LET 'EM TELL YOU	DON'T LET 'EM TELL YOU PT. 1	NICKEL 1005	15.00	funk
MAKE ME SAD	FOR BROTHERS ONLY	TODDLIN TOWN 120	10.00	mod
BROTHERS BY CHOICE				
HOW MUCH I FEEL	SHE PUT THE EASE BACK	ALA 110	10.00	70's
OH DARLIN'	WHY CAN'T YOU MAKE UP YOUR MIN	ALA 108	20.00	70's
SHE PUTS THE EASE BACK INTO EA	SAME: INSTRUMENTAL	ALA 103	10.00	70's
BROTHERS GRIMM				
LOOKY LOOKY	A MAN NEEDS LOVE	MERCURY 72512	30.00	northern

BROTHERS OF SOUL

CANDY
CAN'T GET YOU OFF MY MIND
CANDY
CANDY
CAN'T GET YOU OFF MY MIND
A DREAM
COME ON BACK
COME ON BACK
HURRY, DON'T LINGER
I'D BE GRATEFUL

Title	Label	Price	Genre
DREAM	SHOCK 1313 orange	30.00	70's
HURRY DON'T LINGER	CRISS-CROSS 1001	50.00	northern
DREAM	SHOCK 131 yellow	60.00	northern
TRY IT BABE	SHOCK 1314	30.00	northern
HURRY DON'T LINGER	BOO 1001	15.00	northern
SAME: INSTRUMENTAL	BOO 1002	25.00	northern
THE LOVE I FOUND IN YOU	BOO 1005 yellow	80.00	northern
THE LOVE I FOUND IN YOU	BOO 1005	60.00	northern
I GUESS THAT DON'T MAKE ME A LOSER	BOO 1004	15.00	northern
WAIT FOR ME	BOO 1006	100.00	northern

BROTHERS SEVEN

Song	Title	Label	Price	Genre
EVIL WAYS		GOOD LUCK NO#	300.00	funk

BROTHERS SOUL

Song	Title	Label	Price	Genre
I SHALL BE RELEASED	LOOK AHEAD	OKEH 7322	20.00	ballad

BROTHERS TWO

Song	Title	Label	Price	Genre
MY SWEETNESS	HOPING	JONAH 99	15.00	northern

BROTHERS.

Song	Title	Label	Price	Genre
ARE YOU READY FOR THIS	EVERYBODY LOVES A WINNER	RCA 10243	10.00	70's

BROUSARD, VAN

Song	Title	Label	Price	Genre
FEED THE FLAME	NOTHING SWEET AS YOU	MALA 12021	15.00	ballad

BROWN BROTHERS OF SOUL

Song	Title	Label	Price	Genre
CHOLO	POQUITO SOUL	RAZA 1027	15.00	funk
CHOLO	POQUITO	SPECIALTY 698	10.00	funk

BROWN, ALEX

Song	Title	Label	Price	Genre
I'M NOT RESPONSIBLE	SOMETHING	SUNDI 316	300.00	70's
I'M IN LOVE	WHAT WOULD U DO WITHOUT SOMEON	TRC 1001	10.00	northern

BROWN, BARBARA

Song	Title	Label	Price	Genre
PITY A FOOL	IF IT'S GOOD TO YOU	MGM SOUNDS OF MEMPHI S 709	40.00	70's
SO IN LOVE	FORGET HIM	CARNIVAL 508	20.00	northern

BROWN, BEVERLY

Song	Title	Label	Price	Genre
TAKE MY LOVE	DON'T BREAK MY HEART	BRIMCO 100	30.00	northern

BROWN, CHARLIE (COLE BLACK)

Song	Title	Label	Price	Genre
I JUST CAN'T GET OVER YOU	I'VE GOT YOUR LOVE	JEWEL 838	15.00	70's

BROWN, ESTELLE

Song	Title	Label	Price	Genre
STICK CLOSE	YOU GOT JUST WHAT YOU ASKED FO	UA 727	75.00	northern

BROWN, GARY AND SOUL MACHINE 2

Song	Title	Label	Price	Genre
GET DOWN		COTCH NO#	50.00	funk

BROWN, HERBY

Song	Title	Label	Price	Genre
ONE MORE BROKEN HEART	BLUE ASH	181	500.00	northern

BROWN, J.T.

Song	Title	Label	Price	Genre
LIKE TAKING CANDY (FROM A BABY	UNDER LOCK AND KEY	MAHOGANY 1177	15.00	70's

BROWN, JAMES

Song	Title	Label	Price	Genre
PEOPLE WAKE UP AND LIVE	GIVE ME SOME SKIN	POLYDOR 14409	10.00	70's
MONEY WON'T CHANGE YOU	SAME: PT 2.	KING 6048	10.00	northern
NIGHT TRAIN	WHY DOES EVERYTHING HAPPEN TO	KING 5614	10.00	northern
ESCAPE-ISM	ESCAPE-ISM PT.2	PEOPLE 2500	8.00	funk
FUNKY DRUMMER	FUNKY DRUMMER Pt.2	KING 6290	10.00	funk
IN THE MIDDLE	LET'S UNITE THE WHOLE WORLD AT	KING 6205	10.00	funk
THE DRUNK	A MAN HAS TO GO BACK TO THE CR	BETHLEHEM 3098	15.00	funk
SHHHHHH (FOR A LITTLE WHILE)	HERE I GO	KING 6164	15.00	mod

BROWN, JAMES AND COLLINS, LYNN

Song	Title	Label	Price	Genre
WHAT MY BABY NEEDS NOW IS A LITTLE MORE LOVIN'	THIS GUY-THIS GIRL'S IN LOVE	POLYDOR 14157	8.00	70's

BROWN, JOCELYN

Song	Title	Label	Price	Genre
IF I CAN'T HAVE YOUR LOVE	SAME:	POSSE 5011	30.00	70's

BROWN, KEISHA

Song	Title	Label	Price	Genre
THE DANCE MAN		LULU NO#	200.00	funk

BROWN, LARRY

Song	Title	Label	Price	Genre
BREAKIN' TRAINING	BREAKIN' TRAINING PT. 2	FIREWORKS 1000	30.00	70's

BROWN, LATIMORE

Song	Title	Label	Price	Genre
SO SAYS MY HEART	EVERYDAY I HAVE TO CRY SOME	SS7 2616	20.00	northern

BROWN, MAGICA

Song	Title	Label	Price	Genre
A WHOLE LOTTA LOVIN' LEFT IN ME	I WON'T BE BACK	20th. CENTURY 553	20.00	northern

BROWN, MATT

Song	Title	Label	Price	Genre
EVERY DAY		JAR-VAL 4	750.00	70's
THANK YOU BABY	SWEET THING	JAR-VAL 6	600.00	70's

BROWN, MAXINE

Song	Title	Label	Price	Genre
ALWAYS AND FOREVER	MAKE LOVE TO ME	AVCO 4585	10.00	70's
I.O.U.	TREAT ME LIKE A LADY	AVCO 4604	8.00	70's
IT'S GONNA BE ALRIGHT	YOU DO SOMETHING TO ME	WAND 173	8.00	northern
I CAN'T GET ALONG WITHOUT YOU	REASON TO BELIEVE	COMMONWEALTH 3008	10.00	northern
SEEMS YOU'VE FORSAKEN MY LOVE	PLUM OUTA SIGHT	EPIC 10334	10.00	northern
AM I FALLING IN LOVE	PROMISE ME ANYTHING	ABC 10370	60.00	northern
LET ME GIVE YOU MY LOVING	WE CAN WORK IT OUT	WAND 1128	10.00	northern
OH NO NOT MY BABY	YOU UPSET MY SOUL	WAND 162	10.00	northern
ONE IN A MILLION	ANYTHING YOU DO IS ALRIGHT	WAND 1117	15.00	northern
ONE STEP AT A TIME	ANYTHING FOR A LAUGH	WAND 185	10.00	northern
THE SECRET OF LIVING	I DON'T NEED ANYTHING	WAND 1145	10.00	northern

YESTERDAY'S KISSES	ASK ME	WAND 135	15.00	northern
YESTERDAY'S KISSES	ASK ME	WAND 135 PS	30.00	northern

BROWN, MELVIN AND THE MATHEWS, JAMES

LOVE STORMY WEATHER	SOUL MAN	PHILMORE SOUND 607121	1000.00	70's

BROWN, NEAL

IF BY CHANCE	SHE'S A FINE WOMAN	CHART SOUND 129	10.00	northern

BROWN, NORMAN

EVERYBODY LIKES IT	SUGAR	SOUND TOWN 47663658	20.00	70's

BROWN, OTIS

WILL YOU WAIT	WHAT WOULD YOU DO	OLE 102	15.00	northern

BROWN, PAT

THE GOOD GOT TO SUFFER FOR THE BAD	HE'S A WONDERFUL GUY	SEVEN B 7009	40.00	northern

BROWN, PEP

I AM THE ONE WHO LOVES YOU	DON'T BLAME ME	POLYDOR 14204	100.00	70's

BROWN, PHYLLIS

OH BABY	WHY	RAINBO 1001	75.00	northern

BROWN, PINEY

EVERYTHING BUT YOU	(I'M TIRED OF) RUNNING	DEEP GROOVE 20931	100.00	funk

BROWN, RANDOLF AND COMPANY

IT AIN'T LIKE IT USED TO BE	YOU CAN BE CURED	IX CHAINS 7012	40.00	70's

BROWN, RANDY

I'M ALWAYS IN THE MOOD	I'D RATHER HURT MYSELF	PARACHUTE 506	10.00	70's

BROWN, ROCKIE

WITHOUT A WARNING	SAME: INSTRUMENTAL	PENNTOWNE 100	10.00	northern

BROWN, ROY

BABY IT'S LOVE	GOING HOME	GERT 11123	500.00	northern

BROWN, SAMMY

SOME DAY	HEAD ON COLLISON	PUGET 701	15.00	70's

BROWN, VEDA

SHOUTIN' OUT LOVE	BRAND NEW TOMORROW	RAKEN 1	10.00	70's
I HAD A FIGHT WITH LOVE				

BROWNER, DUKE (see also KADDO STRINGS)

CRYING OVER YOU	SAME: INSTRUMENTAL	IMPACT 1008	200.00	**northerB**

BROWNE'S ORCH., AL

THE GRAND CENTRAL SHUTTLE		SAXY	50.00	funk

BRUCE, ALAN

I FEEL BETTER	WHERE DO WE GO FROM HERE	GARRISON 3002	100.00	northern

BRUCE, ED

SEE THE BIG MAN CRY	I WON'T CRY ANYMORE	WAND 140	25.00	northern
I'M GONNA HAVE A PARTY		WAND 156	200..00	northern

BRUNO, TONY

SMALL TOWN, BRING DOWN	WHAT'S YESTERDAY	CAPITOL 2105	15.00	northern
SMALL TOWN, BRING DOWN	WHAT'S YESTERDAY	BUDDAH 43	10.00	northern

BRYANT GROUP, SAMMY

GRAPEVINE	POPEYE DANCE	ROULETTE 4569	100.00	northern

BRYANT, JAMES

HEY THERE YOU GIRL	THREE STEP	RENEE 108	20.00	northern

BRYANT, JAY DEE

STANDING OVATION FOR LOVE	I WANT TO THANK YOU BABY	ISLAND 6273	10.00	northern
YOU'RE HURTING ME	GET IT	ENJOY 2017	20.00	northern

BRYANT, JD

I WON'T BE COMING BACK	WALK ON IN	SHRINE 108	3000.00	northern

BRYANT, LILLIE

MEET ME HALFWAY	MAMA	TAYSTER 6016	800.00	**northerB**

BRYANT, TERRI

(YOU BETTER) STRAIGHTEN UP & F	EVERYTHING'S WONDERFUL	VERVE 10553	8.00	northern
GENI	WHEN I'M IN YOUR ARMS	VERVE 10508	40.00	northern

BRYANT, TOMMY

I WANNA COME HOME TO YOU BABY	HEADING HOME	T NECK 916	15.00	northern

BUBBA LOU AND THE HIGHBALLS

OVER YOU	LOVE ALL OVER THE PLACE	AMBITION 101 PS	20.00	70's

BUCKINS, MICKEY AND THE NEW BREED

BIG BOY PETE	REFLECTIONS OF CHARLES BROWN	SOUTH CAMP 7007	15.00	ballad
LONG LONG TIME	SEVENTEEN YEAR OLD GIRL	SOUTH CAMP 7004	15.00	ballad
SILLY GIRL	LONG LONG TIME	NORALA 6603	500.00	northern

BUCKMAN, JOE

RIGHT NOW	TILL THE END OF TIME	SEPIA 3	30.00	northern

BUENA VISTAS

HERE COME DA JUDGE	BIG RED	MARQUEE 443	15.00	mod
SOUL CLAPPIN	RAPPIN	MARQUEE 445	10.00	mod
SUGAR	KNOCK ON WOOD	LA SALLE 71	15.00	mod
T.N.T.	HOT SHOT	SWAN 4255	15.00	mod

BUFORD, RON

DEEP SOUL	DEEP SOUL Pt.2	CAMELOT 127	100.00	funk

BULL AND THE CAPALARAS

GIRL OF MY HEART	NO SIGHN OF MADNESS	BELL 975	20.00	northern

BYGONES | IN THE MEANTIME | BELL 45186 | 75.00 | northern

BULL AND THE MATADORS
IF YOU DECIDE | LOVE COME DOWN | TODDLIN TOWN 123 | 15.00 | northern

BULLET
WILLPOWER WEAK TEMPTATION STRO | HITTIN' ON YOU | BIG TREE 131 | 8.00 | northern

BURDICK, DONI
I HAVE FAITH IN YOU | OPEN THE DOOR TO YOUR HEART | SOUND PATTERNS 6807 | 350.00 | northern
I HAVE FAITH IN YOU | BARI TRACK | SOUND IMPRESSIONS | 250.00 | northern
OPEN THE DOOR TO YOUR HEART | IF YOU EVER WALK OUT OF MY LIFE | SOUND IMPRESSIONS | 50.00 | northern

BURKE, JOHNNIE
LOVE ON A LEASE PLAN | ME AND MY BABY | JOANNE 3001 | 10.00 | northern

BURKE, SOLOMAN
CRY TO ME | I ALMOST LOST MY MIND | ATLANTIC 2131 | 15.00 | northern

BURKES, DONNIE
SATISFACTION GUARENTEED | WHY DON'T YOU SMILE NOW | DECCA 32134 | 20.00 | northern
YOU NEVER KNOW WHAT YOU HAVE | I WAS SATISFIED | METROMEDIA 102 | 20.00 | 70's

BURKES, MAJOR
YOU'RE GONNA NEED ME | I'M IN LOVE | GULF 2541 | 300.00 | northern

BURKS, GENE
YOU DON'T LOVE ME | YOU GOT IT | CHRIS CRAFT 501 | 10.00 | ballad

BURNETT, CARL
JERK BABY JERK | SWEET MEMORIES | CARMAX 102 | 30.00 | northern

BURNETT, FRANCES
COME TO ME | SO MANY TEARS | CORAL 62092 | 50.00 | motown
HOW I MISS YOU SO | PLEASE REMEMBER ME | CORAL 62127 | 75.00 | motown
SHE WAS TAKING MY BABY | SWEETIE | CORAL 62214 | 50.00 | motown
TOO PROUD | I LOVE HIM SO | CORAL 62164 | 50.00 | motown

BURNETTE, DORSEY
EVER SINCE THE WORLD BEGAN | LONG LONG TIMEW AGO | MELODY 118 | 15.00 | motown
JIMMY BROWN | EVERYBODY'S ANGEL | MELODY 116 | 15.00 | motown
LITTLE ACORN | COLD AS USUAL | MELODY 113 | 15.00 | motown

BURNING BUSH
KEEPS ON BURNING | EVIL EYE | MERCURY 72657 | 75.00 | northern

BURNING EMOTIONS
THE NEW WORLD | THE WHATCHAMA CALL IT | BANG 553 | 10.00 | northern

BURNS, EDDIE
ORANGE DRIVER | (DON'T BE) MESSING WITH MY BREAD | HARVEY 118 | 20.00 | motown

BURNS, JACKIE AND THE BO-BELLS
I DO THE BEST I CAN | HE'S MY GUY | MGM 13182 | 50.00 | northern

BURNS, JIMMY
GIVE HER TO ME | POWERFUL LOVE | TIP TOP 2012 | 40.00 | northern
I REALLY LOVE YOU | I LOVE YOU GIRL | ERICA 2 | 1000.00 | northern

BURNS, JIMMY AND FANTASTIC EPICS
IT USE TO BE | YOU'RE GONNA MISS ME WHEN I'M GONE | TIP TOP 14 | 75.00 | northern

BURNS, LINDA (also see THE DOLLS)
THE REASON WHY | AND THAT REMINDS ME | TY TEX 121 | 40.00 | northern

BURRAGE, HAROLD
GOT TO FIND A WAY | HOW YOU FIX YOUR MOUTH | M-PAC 7225 | 15.00 | northern
MASTER KEY | FAITH | M-PAC 7201 | 30.00 | northern
MORE POWER TO YOU | A LONG WAY TOGETHER | M-PAC 7229 | 15.00 | northern
YOU MADE ME SO HAPPY | TAKE ME NOW | M-PAC 7234 | 15.00 | northern

BURRELL, ELOISE
CREAM ALWAYS RISES | (SHOULDA BEENA) SINGER | SCINTILLA 101 PS | 15.00 | 70's

BURRIS, DAISY
FOUR STRONG WINDS | IN LOVE TO STAY | DEESU | 200.00 | northern
TAKE THE SAME THING | | PORT 3007 | 70.00 | northern

BURTON, DEBBIE
BABY, IT'S OVER | THE NEXT DAY | CAPITOL 5666 | 20.00 | northern

BURTON, JOHNNY
SLAVE GIRL | COME ON, DANCE WITH ME | BROADWAY 401 | 150.00 | northern

BURTON, PAUL
SO VERY HARD TO MAKE IT | SAME: PT.2 | MUSIC-GO-ROUND 3 | 75.00 | northern

BURTON, WARD
SWEET TEMPTATION | | PANTHER 5 | 700.00 | northern

BURTON, WILLARD
LET ME BE YOUR PACIFIER | WARM THE POT | MONEY 2031 | 20.00 | 70's

BUSH, BILL
I'M WAITING | | RONN 17 | 100.00 | northern

BUSH, LITTLE DAVID
YOU AND I | RELIEVE ME | VEGA 1002 | 150.00 | motown

BUSH, OLIVER
I'LL MAKE IT UP TO YOU | SOUL IN MOTION | GAMBLE 234 | 50.00 | northern
PLEASE COME BACK MY LOVE | SAME: PT. 2 | JUBILEE 5603 | 40.00 | northern

BUSH, TOMMY
I DON'T LIKE IT (BUT I LOVE YOU) | AIN'T NO GUESSING GAME | RIKA 108 | 100.00 | **northerB**
COME ON NOW | | BOXER 3001 | 100.00 | northern

BUSTER AND EDDIE

CAN'T BE STILL	THERE I WAS	CLASS 1518 stock	50.00	**northerB**
CAN'T BE STILL	THERE I WAS	CLASS 1518 DJ	250.00	northern

BUTERA, SAM

THE RAT RACE	THE RAT RACE PT. 2	DOT 16080	8.00	northern

BUTLER BROTHERS

A REPUTATION	RATS IN MY \ALLEY	ACADEMY 119	50.00	northern

BUTLER, AALON AND NEW BREED BAND

GETTIN' SOUL		PKC	200.00	funk

BUTLER, ANDY

UP TO MY NECK IN ,LOVE	ONE PART, TWO PART	TRC 998	10.00	ballad
COMING APART AT THE SEAMS	HOLD BACK THE NIGHT	TRC 988	10.00	northern

BUTLER, BILLY

RIGHT TRACK	BOSTON MONKEY	OKEH 7245	15.00	**northerB**
(YOU MAKE ME THINK)YOU AIN'T READY	YOU'RE GONNA BE SORRY	OKEH 7227	20.00	northern
CARELESS HEART	I'LL BET YOU	BRUNSWICK 55347	15.00	northern
COME ON OVER TO MY SIDE	LOVE GROWS BITTER	BRUNSWICK 55323	30.00	**northerB**
FOUND TRUE LOVE	LADY LOVE	OKEH 7178	75.00	northern
GOTTA GET AWAY	I'M JUST A MAN	OKEH 7192	20.00	northern
HELP YOURSELF	SWEET DARLING	BRUNSWICK 55306	10.00	northern
I CAN'T WORK NO LONGER	TOMORROW IS ANOTHER DAY	OKEH 7221	20.00	northern
I'LL BET YOU	CARELESS HEART	BRUNSWICK 55347	10.00	**northerB**
I'M JUST A MAN	GOTTA GET AWAY	OKEH 7192	20.00	northern
LOVE GROWS BITTER	COME OVER TO MY SIDE	BRUNSWICK 55323	15.00	**northerB**
MY HEART IS HURTIN'	CAN'T LIVE WITHOUT HER	OKEH 7201	20.00	**northerB**
NEVERTHELESS	MY SWEET WOMAN	OKEH 7207	15.00	**northerB**
RIGHT TRACK (INSTRU.)	BOSTON MONKEY (INSTRU.)	OKEH 7245	15.00	**northerB**
YOU AIN'T READY	YOU'RE GONNA BE SORRY	OKEH 7227	15.00	northern

BUTLER, FREDDIE

SAVE YOUR LOVE FOR ME	ALL IS WELL	WHEELSVILLE 10001	1000.00	northern

BUTLER, FREDDY

I TOLD YOU SO	THIS ROAD	STAR MAKER 1930	40.00	northern
THERE WAS A TIME	THIS THING	KAPP 819	20.00	northern
I'M NOT AFRAID	THE SIGNIFYING MONKEY	SAMO 449	30.00	northern

BUTLER, JERRY

HIGH STEPPER	TAKE THE TIME TO TELL	MERCURY 73495	10.00	70's
JUST FOR YOU	BELIEVE IN ME	VEE JAY 707	8.00	northern
MOODY WOMAN	GO AWAY - FIND YOURSELF	MERCURY 72929	8.00	northern
YOU CAN RUN (BUT YOU CAN'T HIDE)	I'M THE ONE	VEE JAY 463	15.00	northern

BUTLER, ROY (CORTEZ)

A DREAM	SAME: INSTRUMENTAL	BOO 1002	100.00	northern
MARY'S HOUSE	MARY'S HOUSE PT.2	BOO 1003	10.00	mod

BUTLER, SAM

I CAN'T GET OVER (LOVING YOU)	I CAN TELL	SRI 17	150.00	70's

BUTLER, TOMMY

RIGHT ON UP TO THE WEEKEND		CHATTAHOOCHEE 688	20.00	northern

BUTLERS

SHE'S GONE (IT'S ALL OVER NOW)	LOVE IS GOOD	GAMBLE 233	25.00	northern
LAUGH, LAUGH, LAUGH	BUTLERS THEME	PHILA. 1836 red	30.00	**northerB**
SHE TRIED TO KISS ME	THE SUN'S MESSAGE	LIBERTY BELL 1024	25.00	northern

BUTLERS with FRANK BEVERLY

BECAUSE OF MY HEART	I WANT TO FEEL I'M WANTED	ROUSER 1017	2000.0	northern

BUTTERBALL

BUTTERBALLS	BUTTERBALLS Pt.2	FAST EDDIE 101	10.00	funk

BUTTERWORTH, JOHN

THIS LOVE CAN'T BE DENIED	I LOVE YOU JUST THE SAME	SABTECA 11	10.00	northern

BUTTS TRIO, HINDAL

BACK UP BABY	WALTZING WITH THE PARSON	WHEELSVILLE 108	15.00	mod
GIGIN'	HAPPINESS	KOOL KAT 1003	25.00	mod

BUTTS, NANCY

YOU'RE GONNA NEED SOMEBODY	GO ON TO HER	FLAMING ARROW 38	10.00	funk
I WANT TO HOLD YOUR HAND BABY	YOUR FRIEND WILL TAKE THE MAN	FLAMING ARROW 19	25.00	northern
LETTER FULL OF TEARS	ONLY ONE I LOVE	KING 6405	10.00	northern

BYERS, ANN

DEAD END	WHERE OH WHERE CAN I FIND MY BABY	ACADEMY 109	20.00	northern
I'M HAPPY WITHOUT YOU	SAME: INSTRUMENTAL.	ACADEMY 124	150.00	northern

BYNUM, JAMES

TIME PASSES BY	LOVE YOU	PHILLY CITY 1320	30.00	northern

BYRD, BOBBY

HANG UPS WE DON'T NEED	YOU GAVE MY HEART A BRAND NEW	KING 6289	8.00	funk
HOT PANTS-I'M COMING, COMING,	HANG IT UP	BROWNSTONE 4203	10.00	funk
I KNOW YOU GOT SOUL	IT'S I WHO LOVE YOU (NOT HIM..	KING 6378	10.00	funk
I NEED HELP (I CAN'T DO IT ALONE)	SAME: Pt.2	KING 6323	10.00	funk
KEEP ON DOIN' WHAT YOU'RE DOIN'	LET ME KNOW	BROWNSTONE 4205	10.00	funk
NEVER GET ENOUGH	MY CONCERTO	BROWNSTONE 4208	8.00	funk
NEVER GET ENOUGH	SAYIN' IT & DOIN' IT ARE TWO DIFFERENT	BROWNSTONE 4209	8.00	funk
THE WAY TO GET DOWN	BACK FROM THE DEAD	INTER. BROS. 901	8.00	funk
YOU'VE GOT TO CHANGE YOUR MIND	IF YOU GOT A LOVE YOU BETTER	BROWNSTONE 4206	10.00	funk

I FOUND OUT (with *Strings*)	I'LL KEEP PRESSING ON	KING 6069	20.00	northern
I FOUND OUT	THEY ARE SAYIN'	FEDERAL 12486	50.00	northern
LOST IN THE MOOD OF CHANGES	OH, WHAT A NIGHT	SMASH 2018	20.00	northern

BYRD, GEORGE

I'M AVAILABLE	YOU BETTER TELL HER SO	PAY-TONS 1001	150.00	northern
I KNOW I'M IN LOVE WITH YOU	LOVING YOU	PAY-TONS 1002	75.00	northern
I'M AVAILABLE	YOU BETTER TELL HER SO	TRC 1002	15.00	northern

BYRD, JOHN

I CAN'T STOP LOVING YOU, GIRL 2108	DIBBLIN' & DABBLIN'	20th. CENTURY	10.00	70's

BYRD, RUSSELL

HITCH HIKE	HITCH HIKE PT.2	SYMBOL 915	15.00	mod

BYSTANDERS

GIRLS ARE MADE TO LOVE northern	LUCKY TO HAVE YOUR LOVE	ON TAP 1001	30.00	

C

C, FANTASTIC JOHNNY

DON'T DEPEND ON ME	WAITING FOR THE RAIN	PHIL LA SOUL 361	10.00	**northerB**

C, NICKY AND THE CHATEAUX

THOSE GOOD TIMES	TRY SOME SOUL	BAY SOUND 67012	100.00	northern

C, ROY

GONE GONE	STOP WHAT YOU'RE DOING	SHOUT 206	30.00	northern
SHOTGUN WEDDING	I'M GONNA MAKE IT	BLACK HAWK 101	8.00	northern
SHOTGUN WEDDING	HIGH SCHOOL DROPOUT	UPTOWN 731	8.00	northern

CADILLACS

FOOL	THE RIGHT KIND OF LOVING	ARCTIC 101	80.00	northern

CAESARS

GIRL I MISS YOU	DESPERATE FOR YOUR AFFECTIONS	LANIE 2002	100.00	northern
GET YOURSELF TOGETHER	(LALA) I LOVE YOU	LANIE 500	25.00	northern

CAGER, WILLIE

HE'S A PLAYER	WHAT CAN YOU DO	CONTACT 504	10.00	northern

CAILLIER, J.J.

PUSHERMAN	LOUISIANA RAPPER	JAY-CEE 1001	40.00	70's

CAIROS

STOP OVERLOOKING ME	DON'T FIGHT IT	SHRINE 111	1500.00	**northerB**

CAITON, RICHARD

I SEE LOVE GIRL IN YOUR EYES	I WONDER WILL YOU ALWAYS LOVE	CAIBUT 3041	150.00	70's
YOU LOOK JUST LIKE A FLOWER	LISTEN TO THE DRUMS	GNP 327	40.00	group
OUR LOVE IS TRUE	WITHOUT YOUR LOVE	UP TIGHT 101	300.00	northern
I'D LIKE TO GET NEAR YOU		UP TIGHT 151	300.00	northern
TAKE A HOLD BROTHER AND SISTER		UPTIGHT 151	20.00	northern

CAJUN HART

GOT TO FIND A WAY	LOVER'S PRAYER	WB 7258	150.00	northern

CALDWELL, HARRY

NOBODY LOVES ME (LIKE MY BABY)	PLEASE COME BACK	CARNIVAL 516	30.00	northern

CALIF. MALIBUS

LOVE IN MY LIFE	I STAND ALONE	M&M 633	10.00	70's

CALIFORNIA ROCK CHIOR

WHOEVER YOU ARE	AIN'T NO MOUNTAIN HIGH ENOUGH	CYCLONE 75002	15.00	70's

CALLENDER, BOBBY

MY BABY CHANGES LIKE THE WEATHER	I WANT A LOVER	BAMBOO 101	100.00	northern

CALLIER, TERRY

I JUST CAN'T HELP MYSELF	GOTTA GET CLOSER TO YOU	CADET 5697	50.00	70's
LOOK AT ME NOW	YOU GONNA MISS YOUR CANDY	CADET 5623	150.00	northern

CALLOWAY, CHRIS

YOU'RE SOMETHING ELSE	I DON'T NEED ANOTHER BABY	CUB 9154	10.00	northern

CALLOWAY, RICKY

GET IT RIGHT		CAMARO	200.00	funk
TELL ME, PART 1	TELL ME, PART 2	JAYVILLE 5988	500.00	funk

CALVERT, DUANE

I THINK IT'S GONNA BE SOMEONE	IN THE FLESH TO FEEL.	DMD 106	250.00	northern
I THINK IT'S GONNA BE SOMEONE	DOES LOVE PAY.	DMD 107	200.00	northern

CALVIN AND THE TWILITES

BASHFUL BOY	MOMENTS LIKE THIS	HAR-LOW 705	100.00	northern

CAMACHO, RAY AND THE TEARDROPS

SHE'S SO GOOD TO ME	SUNSHINE SUPERMAN	ARV 5018	200.00	northern

CAMARO'S

WE'RE NOT TOO YOUNG	LOVER COME BACK	DAR CHA 1151	800.00	northern

CAMBRIDGE, DOTTIE

CRY YOUR EYES OUT	PERFECT BOY	MGM 13846	40.00	**northerB**

CAMERON, DEBBIE

SOMEDAY BABY	SAME: INSTRUMENTAL	LOCK 724	100.00	northern

CAMERON, CAM

THEY SAY	I'M A LONELY MAN	CAPRI 101	25.00	northern

CAMERON, GEORGE

MY HEART TELLS ME SO	TOY OF LOVE	PORTRAIT 104	150.00	northern

CAMERON, JIMMY AND VELA

LOVIN' YOU IS SUCH A GROOVE	I KNOW A PLACE	REPRISE 483	50.00	northern

CAMERON, JOHNNY AND CAMERONS

FUNKY JOHN		LOCK CENTRAL	30.00	funk

CAMERON, WYNN

WHERE CAN I GO	WHAT GOOD WOULD IT DO	MOMENTUM 664	40.00	northern

CAMILLE BOB AND THE LOLLIPOPS

BROTHER BROWN		SOUL UNLIMITED	25.00	funk

CAMPBELL, CHOKER

COME SEE ABOUT ME	PRIDE AND JOY	MOTOWN 1072	15.00	motown

CAMPBELL, CHRIS

YOU GOTTA PAY DUES	LI'L LIZA JANE	USA 885	100.00	northern

CAMPBELL, DON

CAMPBELL LOCK	SAME: INSTRUMENTAL	STANSON 509	15.00	funk

CAMPBELL, EDDIE

CONTAGIOUS LOVE	WHY DO YOU TREAT ME	ARTCO 103	1000.00	northern

CAMPBELL, SAMMY

I NEVER THOUGHT	S.O.S. FOR LOVE	QUEEN CITY 1601	200.00	northern
LISTEN TO MY RADIO	S.O.S. FOR LOVE	VISION 607	500.00	northern

CANDI-BARS

I BELIEVE IN YOU	YOU'RE THE ONE	CANDY-STIX 100	45.00	70's

CANDY AND THE KISSES

KEEP ON SEARCHIN'	TOGETHER	SCEPTER 12106	15.00	northern
CHAINS OF LOVE	SOMEONE OUT THERE	DECCA 32415	20.00	northern
OUT ON THE STREETS AGAIN	SWEET AND LOVELY	SCEPTER 12125	30.00	northern
THE 81	TWO HAPPY PEOPLE	CAMEO 336	15.00	northern
TONIGHT'S THE NIGHT	THE LAST TIME	SCEPTER 12136	30.00	northern

CANNON, LONZINE

QUIT WHILE I'M AHEAD	COLD AT NIGHT	PHILIPS 40240	60.00	northern

CANNON, P.W.

HANGING OUT MY TEARS TO DRY	HEY, HEY	HICKORY 1412	15.00	ballad
BEATING OF MY LONELY HEART	IT'S A WOMAN'S WORLD	HICKORY 1396	20.00	northern
TAKE THE BITTER WITH THE SWEET		PAPA JOE	100.00	ballad

CANOISE

OH NO NOT MY BABY	THERE'S SOMETHING ABOUT YOU BA	SONIC 141	20.00	northern
RIGHT TRACK	YOU'RE NO GOOD	SONIC 153	30.00	northern

CAPER BROTHERS

AIN'T GOT THE NERVE	GIVE ME SOUL	ROULETTE 4637	30.00	northern

CAPITALAIRS

ONE OF THESE MORNINGS	I WILL NEVER TURN MY BACK ON T	BOS 14	500.00	group

CAPITALS.

I CAN'T DENY THAT I LOVE YOU	OOH WHAT YOU'RE DOING TO ME	OMEN 5	700.00	northern

CAPITOLS

COOL JERK (Instrumental)	AFRO TWIST	KAREN 1537	10.00	northern
TAKE A CHANCE ON ME BABY	PATTY CAKE	KAREN 1534	10.00	northern
AIN'T THAT TERRIBLE	SOUL BROTHER, SOUL SISTER	KAREN 1543	10.00	northern
COOL JERK	HELLO STRANGER	KAREN 1524	10.00	northern
DON'T SAY MAYBE BABY	COOL PEARL	KAREN 1536	30.00	northern
TIRED RUNNING FROM YOU	WE GOT A THING THAT'S IN THE GROOVE	KAREN 1526	10.00	northern
WHEN YOU'RE IN TROUBLE	SOUL SOUL	KAREN 1546	20.00	group
I THOUGHT SHE LOVED ME	WHEN YOU'RE IN TROUBLE	KAREN 1549	50.00	northern

CAPREEZ

HOW TO MAKE A SAD MAN GLAD	IT'S GOOD TO BE HOME AGAIN	SOUND 149	30.00	**northerB**

CAPRELLS

I BELIEVE IN THE STARS	WHAT EVER GOES UP	BANO 103	10.00	70's
DOTTY'S PARTY	WHAT YOU NEED BABY	BANO 102	20.00	funk

CAPTAIN ZAP AND THE MOTORTOWN CUT-UPS

THE LUNEY LANDING	SAME:	MOTOWN 1151 DJ	15.00	motown

CAP-TANS

TIGHT SKIRTS & CRAZY SWEATERS	I'M AFRAID	ANNA 1122	25.00	motown

CAPTIONS

DON'T TAKE YOUR ARMS AWAY FROM	HIT IT	MILLAGE 102	50.00	northern

Artist / Song	Song Title	Label	Price	Genre
TURN OUT THE LIGHTS	NICOTINE SCENE	KAYHAM 8	200.00	northern
CARBO BROTHERS				
WHAT CAN I GIVE HER	SOUL SERENADE	CENCO 109	200.00	northern
CARBO, CHIC				
BIGGEST FOOL IN TOWN	TOUCH ME	INTERNATIONAL	20.00	ballad
CITY 7101				
CARBO, CHUCK				
CAN I BE YOUR SQUEEZE	TAKE CARE OF YOUR HOMEWORK	CANYON 47	30.00	funk
CARBO, HANK				
BAD LUCK	FUNNY (HOW TIME SLIPS AWAY)	HCP 973	40.00	funk
HOT PANTS	HOT PANTS, TOO	ALA 1172	25.00	funk
CARBO, HANK AND CLAUDE				
FOX IN A MINI SKIRT	MISTY	CASTLE 1	20.00	northern
BE PREPARED	I STILL LOVE HER	CASTLE 2	20.00	northern
CARESSORS				
I CAN'T STAY AWAY	WHO CAN IT BE	RU-JAC 20	250.00	northern
CAREY, VINCE				
DON'T WORRY	HULLABALOO	TURNTABLE 712	10.00	northern
CARL, DONNIE				
IT HAPPENED TO ME	IT HAPPENED TO ME Pt.2	TY TEX 113	40.00	northern
CARL, GARY AND THE ORCHIDS				
BABY STAY AND MAKE ME HAPPY	YOU'LL GET YOURS SOMEDAY	PHILIPS 40476	75.00	northern
CARLEEN AND THE GROOVERS				
CAN WE RAP		CJB NO#	300.00	funk
RIGHT ON		MUSIC WORLD NO#	200.00	funk
CARLETTES				
I'M GETTING TIRED	LOST WITHOUT YOUR LOVE	BR 101	150.00	northern
I'M GETTING TIRED	LOST WITHOUT YOUR LOVE	CAPITOL 2775	20.00	northern
CARLOS AND THE RIVINGTONS				
MIND YOUR MAN	I LOST THE LOVE (THAT I FOUND)	AGC 5	40.00	northern
REACH OUR GOAL	TEACH ME TONIGHT	BATON MASTER 202	40.00	northern
CARLSON, CHARLES				
SHE'S NOT TO BLAME		BOLD 1002	200.00	northern
CARLTON, CARL (LITTLE)				
YOU CAN'T STOP A MAN IN LOVE	YOU TIME ME PLUS LOVE	ABC 11378	8.00	70's
COMPETITION AIN'T NOTHIN'	THREE WAY LOVE	BACK BEAT 588	20.00	northern
NOTHIN' NO SWEETER THAN LOVE	I LOVE TRUE LOVE	GOLDEN WORLD 23	50.00	motown
DON'T YOU NEED A BOY LIKE ME	I'LL LOVE YOU FOREVER	LANDO 3046	25.00	northern
SO WHAT	I LOVE ONLY YOU	LANDO 8527	25.00	northern
CARLTON, EDDIE				
WAIT	KOKOMO	CRACKERJACK 4009	20.00	northern
IT WILL BE DONE	MISERY	SWAN 4218	150.00	northern
CARLTON, KENNY				
LOST AND FOUND	WAIT TILL I GET YOU IN MY ARMS	BLUE ROCK 4054	150.00	northern
CARLTON, LEROY				
I NEED YOU	SAME: INSTRUMENTAL.	CC7 1885	100.00	70's
CARLTONS				
CAN'T YOU HEAR THE BEAT	OOO BABY	ARGO 5470	15.00	northern
I'M A MAN	KEEP ON HOPING	ARGO 5517	25.00	northern
CARMEL				
I CAN'T SHAKE THIS FEELING	LET MY CHILD BE FREE	MGM 13869	15.00	northern
CARMEL STRINGS				
I HEAR A SYMPHONY	A LOVER'S CONCERTO	WORLD PACIFIC	15.00	**northerB**
77817				
CARN, JEAN				
DON'T LET IT GO TO YOUR HEAD	I BET SHE WON'T LOVE YOU LIKE	PIR 3654	10.00	70's
IF YOU WANNA GO BACK	YOU'RE ALL I NEED	PIR 3628	8.00	70's
CARNABY STREET RUNNERS				
WHILE YOU'RE OUT LOOKING FOR S	MAKING LOVE IN A TREEHOUSE	SUPER K 11	15.00	northern
CARNEGIE AND CO., ROSS				
OPEN UP YOUR MIND	CAN I BE YOUR FRIEND	EL-CON 50	40.00	funk
CAROL AND GERRI				
HOW CAN I EVER FIND THE WAY	ON YOU HEARTACHE LOOKS GOOD	MGM 13568	75.00	**northerB**
CAROL, VIVIAN				
OH YEAH, YEAH, YEAH	YOUR THE BOY	MERBEN 502	500.00	northern
CAROLL, YVONNE AND THE ROULETTES				
STUCK ON YOU	GEE WHAT A GUY	DOMAIN 1018	30.00	northern
CARPETS				
I JUST CAN'T WIN	WHAT CAN YOU DO FOR ME	VIJ 9732	1000.00	northern
KEEP PUSHING ON	YOU DON'T HAVE TO BUY ME	SHOW ME 1218	200.00	northern
CARR, BILLY				
IT'S MAD	THE ODYSSEY	CAPITOL 2238	10.00	northern
CARR, JAMES				
LET ME BE RIGHT	BRING HER BACK	RIVER CITY 1940	15.00	70's
COMING BACK TO ME BABY	LOVE ATTACK	GOLDWAX 309	10.00	northern
A LOSING GAME	LET IT HAPPEN	GOLDWAX 323	10.00	northern

LOVER'S COMPETITION	I CAN'T MAKE IT	GOLDWAX 112	15.00	northern
ONLY FOOLS RUN AWAY	YOU DON'T WANT ME	GOLDWAX 108	30.00	northern
TALK TALK	SHE'S BETTER THAN YOU	GOLDWAX 119	15.00	northern
THAT'S WHAT I WANT TO KNOW	YOU'VE GOT YOUR MIND MESSED UP	GOLDWAX 302	10.00	**northerB**

CARR, LINDA
AH! YOU AE MY WORLD TO ME	I CAN'T REALLY TELL YOU GOODBY	RANWOOD 828	20.00	northern
IN MY LIFE	I FEEL LOVE COMING ON	RANWOOD 806	20.00	northern
TRYING TO BE GOOD FOR YOU	EVERYTIME	BELL 658	15.00	northern

CARR, TIM
WORKIN		KEE 001	600.00	northern

CARR, TIMOTHY
LOVE MY LOVE	GONE	HOT BISCUIT DISC	20.00	northern
CO. 1456				

CARRINGTON, SUNNY
THE GIRL EVERY GUY SHOULD KNOW	NOW I NEED HER	DEEP 4	10.00	northern

CARROL, SCOTTY
TELL ME MORE	DO YOU ALWAY BELIEVE WHAT YOU	DUEL 524	50.00	northern

CARROLL, YVONNE
MISTER LOVEMAN	LAUGH OR CRY	CHALLENGE 59297	30.00	northern
PLEASE DON'T GO	THERE HE GOES	VEE JAY 592	100.00	northern

CARROW, GEORGE
ANGEL BABY (YOU DON'T EVEN LOVE ME)	SAME:	COLUMBIA 44161	30.00	**northernB**

CARSTAIRS
IT REALLY HURTS ME GIRL	THE STORY OF OUR LOVE	RED COACH 802 DJ	50.00	**northerB**
IT REALLY HURTS ME GIRL	THE STORY OF OUR LOVE	RED COACH 802	20.00	northern
HE WHO PICKS A ROSE	YESTERDAY	OKEH7329	30.00	**northerB**

CARTER, BLANCH
HALOS ARE FOR ANGELS	SAME:	GSF 6881	30.00	**northerB**

CARTER, CAROLYN
(DON'T YOU KNOW) IT HURTS	I' THRU	JAMIE 1294	15.00	northern

CARTER, CHUCK
PRETTY LITTLE BROWN SKIN GIRL	I CAN'T HELP MYSELF	BRUNSWICK 55295	15.00	northern

CARTER, CLARENCE
MESSIN' WITH MY MIND	I WAS IN THE NEIGHBORHOOD	ICHIBAN 101	30.00	70's
LOOKING FOR A FOX	I CAN'T SEE MYSELF	ATLANTIC 2461	8.00	northern

CARTER, EARL AND THE FANTASTIC 6
SHAKE A POO POO		PRINCESS	200.00	funk

CARTER, GENE
RING AROUND MY ROSIE	MARY MACK (THE ESSENCE)	JOCOY 93	100.00	northern

CARTER, J.T.
CLOSER TO YUR HEART	THE WILD ONES	DECCA 31785	75.00	northern

CARTER, JEAN
I BET YOU		SUNFLOWER 101	75.00	northern
LIKE ONE	THAT BOY AIN'T NO GOOD	DECCA 31965	100.00	northern

CARTER, KENNY
DON'T GO	HOW CAN YOU SAY GOODBYE	RCA 8970	40.00	northern
I'VE GOT TO FIND HER	BODY AND SOUL	RCA 8791	30.00	northern
I'VE GOTTA GET MYSELF TOGETHER	SHOWDOWN	RCA 8841	45.00	northern

CARTER, MELVIN
MIDNIGHT BREW	WELFARE CADILLAC	TRIP UNIVERSAL 26	150.00	northern
TEACHER OF LOVE	SOMETHING REMINDS ME	PEACOCK 1934	20.00	northern

CARTER, PENNY
HE CAN'T HURT ME NO MORE	WHY DID I LOSE YOU	VERVE 10405	15.00	northern
WE GOTTA TRY HARDER	SOMETIMES YOU WIN SOMETIMES YO	VERVE 10445	10.00	northern

CARTER, WAYNE
MAD MOUTH WOMAN	WAHOO WAHOO WAHOO	MOOTREYS 1258	50.00	funk

CARTWRIGHT, JONATHAN
I'M WALKING BEHIND YOU	SO TIRED OF BEING ALON E	VEEP 1260	20.00	ballad

CARVELS
DON'T LET HIM KNOW	SEVENTEEN	TWIRL 2022	10.00	northern

CARVER HIGH
NOT TONIGHT	CALL US COOL	CHALLENGER 72001	50.00	70's

CASANOVA TWO
WE GOT TO KEEP ON	I WAS A FOOL	EARLY BIRD 49658	25.00	**northerB**

CASCADES
BLUE HOURS	HEY LITTLE GIRL OF MINE	SMASH 2083	20.00	northern

CASHMERES
AIN'T NO COMING BACK	BACK TO SCHOOL AGAIN	HUBBA HUBBA 100	800.00	northern
FINALLY WAKING UP	FAIRY TALES JUST AIN'T TRUE	NINANDY 1013	50.00	northern
SHOWSTOPPER	DON'T LET THE DOOR HIT YOU IN THE BACK	HEM 1000	700.00	northern

CASINO ROYALE(S)
GET YOURSELF TOGETHER	LIVE AND LEARN	KEY-LOC 1043	30.00	northern
HURRY ON BACK TO ME	UP ON THE ROOF	KAYMAR 1333	100.00	northern

CASINOS
IF I TOLD YOU	EVERYBODY CAN'T BE PRETTY	DEL VAL 1002	25.00	northern
THAT'S THE WAY	TOO GOOD TO BE TRUE	AIRTOWN 2	15.00	northern

CASSADONS				
TWO SIDED LOVE	48 HOURS A WEEK	BELTONE 1025	30.00	northern
CASSIDY, TED				
THE LURCH	WESLEY	CAPITOL 5503	20.00	northern
CASTLES ROYAL BAND				
THE LITTLE FLORIDY	MISTY	CASTLE 3	20.00	northern
CASTOR, JIMMY				
HAM HOCKS ESPANOL	HEY, LEROY YOUR MAMA'S CALLIN'	SMASH 2069	10.00	mod
IN A BOOGALOO BAG	IN A BOOGALOO BAG PT. 2	DECCA 31963	10.00	mod
BLOCK PARTY	IT'S WHAT YOU GIVE	JET SET 1002	15.00	northern
JUST YOU GIRL	MAGIC SAXAPHONE	SMASH 2085	10.00	northern
CASTRO, BERNADETTE				
GET RID OF HIM	A GIRL IN LOVE FORGIVES	COLPIX 759	15.00	**northerB**
CASUALEERS				
DANCE, DANCE, DANCE	THERE'S SOMETHING ABOUT THIS GIRL	ROULETTE 4722	50.00	northern
YOU BETTA BE SURE	OPEN YOUR EYES	LAURIE 3407	10.00	northern
CASUALS ON THE SQUARE				
END OF TIME	TEARDROP A SAD FACE	LSP 1000	50.00	northern
CASWELL, JOHNNY				
YOU DON'T LOVE ME ANYMORE	I.O.U.	DECCA 32017	200.00	northern
CATALINAS				
LAUGHIN' THROUGH TEARS	SUMMER'S GROOVE	PAGODA 4839	20.00	northern
YOU HAVEN'T THE RIGHT	TICK TOCK	SCEPTER 12188	20.00	northern
CATO, JOE				
I'M SO GLAD	SAVE OUR LOVE	CHESS 2026	10.00	northern
CAUTIONS				
NO OTHER WAY	POOR LOSER	SHRINE 115	700.00	northern
WATCH YOUR STEP	IS IT RIGHT	SHRINE 104	600.00	northern
CAVALIERS				
DO WHAT I WANT	TIGHTEN UP	SHRINE 119	1000.00	northern
HOLD TO MY BABY	DANCE LITTLE GIRL	RCA 9054	50.00	northern
I'VE GOTTA FIND HER	I REALLY LOVE YOU	RCA 9321	20.00	northern
CELEBRITIES				
I CHOOSE YOU BABY	SAME: INSTRUMENTAL	BOSS 503	1200.00	northern
YOU DIDN'T TELL THE TRUTH	GOOD NIGHT	BOSS 502	100.00	northern

Most copies of this title have the labels reversed, copies that are correctly labelled add 25%

CELESTRIALS				
CHECKERBOARD LOVER	I FEEL IT COMING ON	DON-EL 126	40.00	northern
CHAIN REACTION	KEEP YOUR HANDS OFF MY BABY	RCA 9016	40.00	northern
CERF, CHRISTOPHER				
SWEET MUSIC	THE BOAT OF NOAH	AMY 954	30.00	northern
CHACHERE, LOUIS				
THE HEN		PAULA	30.00	funk
CHALFONTES				
HE LOVES ME	CONFESSIN' MY LOVE TO YOU	MERCURY 72474	40.00	**northerB**
MUCH TOO MUCH FOR COMFORT	HE'S THE RIGHT KINDA GUY	MERCURY 72424	40.00	northern
CHALLENGERS (III)				
STAY	HONEY HONEY HONEY	TRI-PHI 1012	20.00	motown
EVERY DAY	I HEAR AN ECHO	TRI-PHI 1020	40.00	motown
CHAMPION, MICKIE				
WHAT GOOD AM I (WITHOUT YOU)	THE HURT STILL LINGERS ON	MUSETTE 9151	100.00	**northerB**
CHANCE, NOLAN				
I'LL NEVER FORGET YOU	I'M LOVING NOTHING	THOMAS 802	30.00	northern
IF HE MAKES YOU	SHE'S GONE	CONSTELLATION 144	25.00	northern
JUST LIKE THE WEATHER	DON'T USE ME	CONSTELLATION 161	150.00	northern
JUST LIKE THE WEATHER	DON'T USE ME	BUNKY 161	700.00	**northerB**
CHANCELLORS				
ALL THE WAY FROM HEAVEN	SAD AVENUE	CAP CITY 107	100.00	northern
EVERYBODY'S GOT TO LOSE SOMETI	IT WAS A VERY GOOD YEAR	EL CID 2132	30.00	northern
CHANCES				
ONE MORE CHANCE	IT TAKES MORE LOVE ALONE	BEA & BABY 130	20.00	northern
CHANDELIERS				
DOUBLE LOVE	IT'S A GOOD THOUGHT	LOADSTONE 1601	15.00	northern
STOP DRAGGING MY HEART AROUND	FADING DAY	LOADSTONE 1607	30.00	northern
CHANDLER, DENIECE (DENISE)				
I DON'T WANNA CRY	GOOD BYE, CRUEL WORLD	TODDLIN TOWN 118	20.00	northern
I'M WALKING AWAY	LOVE IS TEARS	LOCK 1245	10.00	northern
CHANDLER, E.J.				
TEARS OF LOVE	AIN'T THAT RIGHT	GRAY SOUNDS 1	15.00	ballad
I CAN'T STAND TO LOSE YOU	BELIEVE IN ME	S.O.S. 1001	15.00	ballad
CHANDLER, GENE				
DON'T HAVE TO BE LYING BABE	DON'T HAVE TO BE LYING BABE PT	CURTOM 1979	10.00	70's
I'LL MAKE THE LIVING IF YOU MAKE THE TIME	TIME IS A THIEF	CHI SOUND 1001	8.00	70's
LET ME MAKE LOVE TO YOU	DOES SHE HAVE A FRIEND?	20th. CENTURY 2451	10.00	70's
NOTHING CAN STOP ME	THE BIG LIE	CONSTELLATION 149	8.00	northern
AFTER THE LAUGHTER	TO BE A LOVER	CHECKER 1165	10.00	northern
BET YOU NEVER THOUGHT	BABY THAT'S LOVE	CONSTELLATION 166	10.00	northern

CHECK YOURSELF	FORGIVE ME	VEE JAY 511	10.00	northern
FROM DAY TO DAY	IT'S NO GOOD FOR ME	CONSTELLATION 104	15.00	northern
I CAN TAKE CARE OF MYSELF	I CAN'T SAVE IT	CONSTELLATION 169	15.00	**northerB**
IF YOU CAN'T BE TRUE	WHAT NOW	CONSTELLATION 141	8.00	northern
MAN'S TEMPTATION	WONDERFUL, WONDERFUL	VEE JAY 536	15.00	northern
MR. BIG SHOT	I HATE TO BE THE ONE TO SAY	CONSTELLATION 172	20.00	**northerB**
PRETY LITTLE GIRL	A LITTLE LIKE LOVIN'	CONSTELLATION 110	100.00	northern
SUCH A PRETTY THING	I FOOLED YOU THIS TIME	CHECKER 1155	10.00	northern
TEAR FOR TEAR	MIRACLE AFTER MIRACLE	VEE JAY 461	10.00	northern
THERE WAS A TIME	THOSE WERE THE GOOD OLD DAYS	BRUNSWICK 55383	10.00	northern
THINK NOTHING ABOUT IT	WISH YOU WERE HERE	CONSTELLATION 112	10.00	northern
YOU THREW A LUCKY PUNCH	RAINBOW	VEE JAY 468	15.00	northern

CHANDLER, GENE AND ACKLIN, BARBARA

LOVE WON'T START	SHOW ME THE WAY TO GO	BRUNSWICK 55366	10.00	northern
WILL I FIND LOVE	LITTLE GREEN APPLES	BRUNSWICK 55405	10.00	northern
FROM THE TEACHER TO THE PREACHER	ANYWHERE BUT NOWHERE	BRUNSWICK 55387	15.00	northern

CHANDLER, KENNY

BEYOND LOVE	CHARITY	TOWER 405	20.00	northern

CHANDLER, LORRAINE

I CAN'T CHANGE	OH HOW I NEED YOUR LOVE	RCA 9349	75.00	**northerB**
I CAN'T HOLD ON	SHE DON'T WANT YOU	RCA 8980	75.00	**northerB**
TELL ME YOU'RE MINE	WHAT CAN I DO	RCA 8810	50.00	northern
TELL ME YOU'RE MINE	WHAT CAN I DO	GIANT 703	75.00	northern

CHANDLERS

YOUR LOVE KEEPS DRAWING ME CLOSER	I LOVED YOU, GIRL	BLEU ROSE 100	100.00	**northerB**
YOUR LOVE MAKES ME LONELY	I NEED YOUR LOVE	COL SOUL 1152	350.00	northern

CHANEY, KEN

KEEP ON GETTIN' UP	SUMMER SONG	BEN-L 1001	30.00	funk

CHANGING SCENE

WHEN THE CITY SLEEPS	YOU CAN'T DESTROY MY LOVE	JO-VEE-JO 5192	600.00	northern

CHANGING TIMES

A NEW DAY BEGINS	BLANK:	BOY WONDER	2000.00	northern

CHANNEL 3

THE SWEETEST THING	SAME:	DAKAR 4520 DJ	150.00	70's

CHANNEL, BRUCE

THAT'S WHAT'S HAPPENIN'	SATISFIED MIND	MELODY 112	15.00	motown
YOU NEVER LOOKED BETTER	YOU MAKE ME HAPPY	MELODY 114	15.00	motown

CHANNELS

I'VE GOT MY EYES ON YOU	ANYTHING YOU DO	GROOVE 46	30.00	northern
YOU CAN COUNT ON ME	OLD CHINATOWN	GROOVE 61	30.00	northern

CHANTEURS

YOU'VE GOT A GREAT LOVE	THE GRIZZLY BEAR	VEE JAY 519	20.00	northern

CHANTIQUE

I KNOW I'M FALLING IN LOVE	TOO MUCH OF ANYTHING (IT AIN'T)	AIP INTER 1001	30.00	70's

CHAPMAN, ANDY

DOUBLE YOUR SATISFACTION	HAPPY IS THE MAN	ATCO 6558	10.00	northern

CHAPRON, WILL AND THE STONED GUMBO

JEALOUS	HEY GIRL	MARQUEE 177	100.00	70's

CHARADES

I DON'T WANT TO LOSE YOU	NEVER SET ME FREE	MGM 13584	50.00	northern
THE KEY TO MY HAPPINESS	WEEPING CUP	MGM 13540	150.00	northern
YOU BETTER BELIEVE IT	DARLING BELIEVE HIM	HARLEM HIT PAR.	15.00	northern
YOU'RE WITH ME ALL THE WAY	POWER OF LOVE	MERCURY 72414	30.00	northern
CAN'T MAKE IT WITHOUT YOU	LOVE OF MY LIFE	OKEH 7195	50.00	northern

CHARISMA

LOVE LOVE IN YOUR LIFE	GONNA NEVER GIVE UP	ROCK MILL 8267	40.00	70's

CHARISMA BAND

AIN'T NOTHING LIKE YOUR LOVE	CHARISMA ROAD	BUDDAH 483	200.00	70's

CHARLENE AND THE SOUL SERENADERS

LOVE CHANGES	CAN YOU WIN	VOLT 4052	20.00	northern

CHARLES, DAVE

AIN'T GONNA CRY NO MORE		DONNIE 702	350.00	northern
SHE'S A WOMAN	THIS IS GONNA HURT	COLUMBIA 44223	20.00	northern

CHARLES, LEE

GIRL YOU TURNED YOUR BACK ON ME	YOU CAN'T GET AWAY	BAMBOO 117	25.00	northern
I GET HIGH ON MY BABY'S LOVE	YOU GOT TO GET IT FOR YOURSELF	BAMBOO 119	50.00	northern
I'LL NEVER EVER LOVE AGAIN	WRONG NUMBER	BRUNSWICK 55401	10.00	northern
STANDING ON THE OUTSIDE	IF THAT AIN'T LOVING YOU	REVUE 11007	10.00	northern
THEN WOULD YOU LOVE ME	IT'S ALL OVER BETWEEN US	DAKAR 601 DJ	15.00	northern
WHY DO YOU HAVE TO GO	I NEVER WANT TO LOSE MY GOOD THING	BAMBOO 111	15.00	northern
WRONG NUMBER	SOMEONE, SOMEWHERE	REVUE 11022	10.00	northern

CHARLES, RAY

BOOTY BOOT	SIDEWINDER	TRC 1015	10.00	mod
COMPARED TO WHAT	NOW THAT WE'VE FOUND EACH OTHE	ATLANTIC 3762	8.00	mod
I CHOSE TO SING THE BLUES	HOPELESSLY	ABC 10840	8.00	mod
THE TRAIN	LET'S GO GET STONED	ABC 10808	8.00	mod
I DON'T NEED NO DOCTOR	PLEASE SAY YOU'RE FOOLING	ABC 10865	10.00	northern
SOMETHING INSIDE OF ME	I WANT TO TALK ABOUT YOU	ABC 10901	8.00	northern

CHARMAINE				
YOUNG GIRL	DON'T YOU KNOW	SEROCK 2000	20.00	northern
CHARMAINES				
ETERNALLY	IF YOU EVER	DATE 1518	25.00	northern
CHARMELS				
LOVING MATERIAL	I'LL GLADLY TAKE YOU BACK	VOLT 153	15.00	northern
CHARMETTES				
SUGAR BOY	STOP THE WEDDING	WORLD ARTISTS 1053	15.00	northern
CHARTERS				
TROUBLE LOVER	SHOW ME SOME SIGN	MELODY 104	1500.00	motown
CHARTS				
DESIREE	FELL IN LOVE WITH YOU BABY	WAND 1112	10.00	northerB
LIVIN' THE NIGHTLIFE	NOBODY MADE YOU LOVE ME	WAND 1124	350.00	northern
CHAUMONTS				
I NEED YOUR LOVE	LOVE IS THE THING	BAY SOUND 67002	40.00	northerB
NOW YOU'VE GONE	BROADWAY WOMAN	BAY SOUND 67004	40.00	northern
LOVING SOFT SOUL	PART 2	BAY SOUND	10.00	group
WHEN YOU LOVE SOMEONE	ALL OF MY LIFE	BAY SOUND 67011	25.00	northern
CHAVEZ, FREDDIE				
THEY'LL NEVER KNOW WHY	BABY I'M SORRY	LOOK 5010	300.00	northerB
CHECKER, CHUBBY				
CU MA LA BE-STAY	EVERYTHING'S WRONG	PARKWAY 959	10.00	northern
(AT THE) DISCOTHEQUE	DO THE FREDDIE	PARKWAY 949	10.00	northerB
(DO THE) DISCOTHEQUE	DO THE FREDDIE	PARKWAY 949	15.00	northern
HEY YOU! LITTLE BOO-GA-LOO	PUSSY CAT	PARKWAY 989	10.00	northern
YOU BETTER BELIEVE IT BABY	SHE WANTS TO SWIM	PARKWAY 922	10.00	northern
YOU JUST DON'T KNOW (what you do to me girl)	TWO HEARTS MAKE ONE LOVE	PARKWAY 965	600.00	northerB
YOU BETTER BELIEVE IT BABY	SHE WANTS T'SWIM	PARKWAY 922 PS	15.00	northern
CHECKERBOARD SQUARES				
DOUBLE COOKIN'	A DAY SAUSALITO	VILLA 705	400.00	northerB
CHECKMATES LTD.				
ALL ALONE BY THE TELEPHONE	BODY LANGUAGE	POLYDOR 14313	40.00	70's
TAKE ALL THE TIME YOU NEED	LET'S DO IT	FANTASY 800	10.00	70's
KISSIN' HER AND CRYING FOR YOU	I CAN HEAR THE RAIN	CAPITOL 5753	50.00	northern
MASTERED THE ART OF LOVE		CAPITOL 5814	20.00	northern
CHEERS				
I'M NOT READY TO SETTLE DOWN	MIGHTY, MIGHTY, LOVER	PENNY 109	15.00	group
TAKE ME TO PARADISE	I MADE UP MY MIND	OKEH 7331	25.00	northern
CHEERS, LITTLE BEN AND THE				
I'M GONNA GET EVEN WITH YOU	NEVER MORE	PENNY 1206	30.00	northern
CHEFS				
MR. MACHINE		PRO-GRESS	300.00	funk
CHEKKERS				
LACK OF LOVE	PLEASE DON'T GO	LOOK 5007	100.00	northern
CHELL-MARS				
ROAMIN' HEART	FEEL ALRIGHT	JAMIE 1266	50.00	northern
CHEQUES				
DEEPER	FUNKY MUNKY	HEATWAVE 4000	40.00	northern
CHERRY PEOPLE				
AND SUDDENLY	IMAGINATION	HERITAGE 801	10.00	northern
CHESSMEN				
WHY CAN'T I BE YOUR MAN	NOTHING BUT YOU	CHESS 1950	20.00	northern
CHESTNUT, MORRIS				
TOO DARN SOULFUL	YOU DON'T LOVE ME ANYMORE	AMY 981	200.00	northern
CHEVELLS				
IT'S GOODBYE	ANOTHER TEAR MUST FALL	BUTANE 777	15.00	northern
CHI CHI				
IF YOU'RE GONNA LOVE ME	LOVE IS	KAPP 749	20.00	northern
JUST LET IT HAPPEN	SOMEWHERE THERE'S SOMEONE	KAPP 776	20.00	northern
CHICAGO ALL STARS				
NOWHERE TO RUN	THE BLOOD	TRI-EM 101	30.00	northern
CHICO AND BUDDY				
CAN YOU DIG IT	A THING CALLED THE JONES	TAYSTER 6025	15.00	funk
CHIFFONS				
KEEP THE BOY HAPPY	JUST FOR TONIGHT	LAURIE 3423	10.00	northern
KEEP THE BOY HAPPY	IF I KNEW THEN	LAURIE 3377	15.00	northern
CHILD OF FRIENDSHIP TRAINROBBERS				
WILL YOU ANSWER	GIVING UP	SA. 1001	30.00	group
CHI-LITES				
LIVING IN THE FOOTSTEPS OF ANTHER MAN	WE NEED ORDER	BRUNSWICK 55489	10.00	70's
PRETTY GIRL	LOVE BANDIT	DARAN 012	50.00	northern
(UM, UM) MY BABY LOVES ME	THATA'S MY BABY FOR YOU	REVUE 11018	10.00	northern
LOVE IS GONE	LOVE ME	REVUE 11005	1.00	northern
WHAT DO I WISH FOR	GIVE IT AWAY	BRUNSWICK 55398	10.00	northern
YOU DID THAT TO ME	I WON'T CARE ABOUT YOU	ORETTA 888	15.00	northern
I'M SO JEALOUS	THE MIX MIX SONG	BLUE ROCK 4007	20.00	northern
SHE'S MINE	NEVER NO MORE	BLUE ROCK 4037	150.00	northern

CHIMES				
THE BEGINNING OF MY LIFE	COMING CHANGES	DOWN TO EARTH	15.00	northern
CHIPS				
MIXED UP SHOOK UP GIRL	BREAK IT GENTLY	PHILIPS 40520	15.00	northern
CHOCOLATE COMPANY				
IN ONE SMALL MOTION	WALK ON BY	EUREKA 100	10.00	northern
CHOCOLATE GLASS				
JOSEPH HOLLY	FOR I LOVE YOU	JUDNELL	25.00	funk
CHOCOLATE SYRUP				
JUST IN THE NICK OF TIME	YOU'VE GOT A LOT TO GIVE	BROWN DOG 9000	10.00	70's
STOP YOUR CRYING	THE GOODNESS OF LOVE	AVCO 4567	15.00	70's
YOU'RE OFF AN RUNNIN'	ALL I EVER DIO IS DREAM ABOUT	IRA 8503	40.00	70's
STOP YOUR CRYIN	THE GODDESS OF LOVE	AVCO 45667	10.00	group
CHOICE OF COLOURYOUR LOVE	YOU'RE TWENTY ONE TODAY	APT 26011	50.00	northern
CHOSEN 3				
SOUL BAGG	YOU ARE MY SUNSHINE	LA VIC DA MAR	20.00	mod
CHOSEN FEW				
LIFT THIS HURT	YOU BEEN UNFAIR	BANDIT 2521	40.00	northern
BIRTH OF A PLAYBOY	TAKING ALL THE LOVE I CAN	MAPLE 1000	20.00	northern
FOOTSEE	YOU CAN NEVER BE WRONG	ROULETTE 7015 DJ	10.00	northern
FOOTSEE	SAME: INSTRUMENTAL	ROULETTE 7015	10.00	northern
TAKING ALL THE LOVE I CAN	I CAN'T TAKE NO CHANCES	MAPLE 9000	10.00	northern
CHOSEN LOT				
TIME WAS	IF YOU WANT TO	SIDRA 9004	30.00	northern
CHISTIAN, AL				
I'M A LONELY MAN	NOTHING GONNA CHANGE THE WAY I FEEL	CHANT 527	200.00	northern
CHRISTIAN, BARBARA				
NOT LIKE YOU BOY	I WORRY	BROWNIE 102	50.00	northern
CHRISTIAN, DIANE				
WONDERFUL GUY	IT HAPPENED ONE NIGHT	BELL 610	15.00	northern
CHRISTIE, RUTH				
MYSTERY OF A MIRACLE		TIDE 452011	200.00	northern
CHRYSLERS WITH THE MONARCHS BAND				
I'M NOT GONNA LOSE YOU	BECAUSE I LOVE YOU	JE JODY 2215	250.00	northern
CHUBBY AND THE TURNPIKES				
I KNOW THE INSIDE STORY	I DIDN'T TRY	CAPITOL 5840	250.00	northern
CHUCK AND JOE				
HARLEM SHUFFLE	I WISH YOU DIDN'T TREAT ME SO	DECCA 31871	15.00	mod
CHURCH, EUGENE				
DOLLAR BILL	U MAKKA HANNA	WORLD PACIFIC 77866	20.00	northern
CHURCH, JIMMY				
RIGHT ON TIME	I DON'T CARE WHO KNOWS	SS7 2559	40.00	northern
THE HURT	ONLY YOU (AND YOU ALONE)	OKEH 7186	100.00	northern
THINKING ABOUT THE GOOD TIMES		PEACHTREE 101	200.00	northern
CHYMES				
MY BABY'S GONE AWAY	WHERE I CAME FROM	DOWN TO EARTH 71	20.00	northern
BRING IT BACK HOME	LET'S TRY IT AGAIN	OKEH 7246	40.00	northern
CINDERELLAS				
BABY, BABY (I STILL LOVE YOU)	PLEASE DON'T WAKE ME	DIMENSION 1026	40.00	northern
CINCINNATIANSDO WHAT YOU WANNA DO	MAGIC GENIE	ROOSEVELT LEE 16115	75.00	northern
DO WHAT YOU WANNA DO	MAGIC GENIE	EMERALD 16115	50.00	northern
CISSEL, CHUCK				
DON'T TELL ME YOU'RE SORRY	FOREVER	ARISTA 499	10.00	70's
CITATIONS				
HEY, MR. LOVE	TWO FOR THE ROAD	SOLID SOUL 210	20.00	group
KEEP THE FAITH	I WILL STAND BY YOU	BALLAD 7101	25.00	northern
CITY LIMITS				
LOVE IS EVERYWHERE	UNCLE JAMES	TSOP 4761	10.00	70's
CLARK, ALICE				
YOU HIT ME	HEAVEN'S WILL	WARNER BROS 7270	100.00	northern
CLARK, BILLY				
TOO BAD - TOO SAD	YOU'LL NEVER MAKE IT ALONE	GAMA 949	75.00	northern
CLARK, CHRIS				
I LOVE YOU	I WANNA GO BACK THERE AGAIN	V.I.P. 25041	15.00	motown
DO RIGHT BABY DO RIGHT	DON'T BE TOO LONG	V.I.P. 25031	15.00	motown
FROM HEAD TO TOE	THE BEGINNING OF THE END	MOTOWN 1114	15.00	motown
LOVE'S GONE BAD	PUT YOURSELF IN MY PLACE	V.I.P. 25038	15.00	motown
WHISPER YOU LOVE ME BOY	THE BEGINNING OF THE END	MOTOWN 1121	15.00	motown
CLARK, CLAUDINE				
THE TELEPHONE GAME	WALKIN' THROUGH A CEMETERY	CHANCELLOR 1124	50.00	northern
CLARK, CONNIE				
MY SUGAR BABY	SAME: INSTRUMENTAL	JOKER 716	300.00	**northerB**
CLARK, DEE				
DON'T WALK AWAY FROM ME	YOUR TELLING OUR SECRETS	VEE JAY 409	10.00	northern
I'M A SOLDIER BOY	SHOOK UPOVER YOU	VEE JAY 487	10.00	northern
HOT POTATO	I DON'T NEED	CONSTELLATION 165	10.00	northern
I CAN'T RUN AWAY	SHE'S MY BABY	CONSTELLATION 155	15.00	northern

CLARK, ??? (continued)

- I'M GOIN' HOME
- IN MY APARTMENT
- IN THESE VERY TENDER MOMENTS
- THAT'S MY GIRL
- WARM SUMMER BREEZES

CLARK, DELORES
- LIVIN' TO PLEASE

CLARK, DORISETTA
- YOU LOVE ME (YOU LOVE ME NOT)

CLARK, ISAAC
- FLIP FLOP THE DUCK

CLARK, JIMMEY SOUL
- (COME ON AND BE MY) SWEET DARL
- I'LL BE YOUR WINNER
- TELL HER
  - 2400

CLARK, LEE
- ALL ALONE IN MY LONELY ROOM
- ALL ALONE IN MY LONELY ROOM

CLARK, LUCKY
- LET ME BE THE FOOL

CLARKE, STANLEY
- STRAIGHT TO THE TOP

CLARKE, TONY
- THE ENTERTAINER
- THE FUGITIVE KIND
- (THEY CALL ME) A WRONG MAN
- JOYCE ELAINE
- LANDSLIDE

CLASS MATES
- YOU CAN DO ME SOME GOOD

CLASSETTS
- THE GUY'S IN LOVE WITH YOU
- YOU'RE GONNA NEED ME

CLASSIC EXAMPLE
- HEY THERE LITTLE GIRL

CLASSIC SULLIVANS
- A RING DON'T MEAN A THING WITH
- PAINT YOURSELF IN THE CORNER
- SHAME, SHAME, SHAME

CLASSICS
- LOOKING FOR A LOVE (OF MY OWN)
- SO GLAD THAT I FOUND YOU

CLASSMEN
- DOIN' ME RIGHT

CLASS-SET
- MY STYLE

CLAY, JUDY
- LONELY PEOPLE DO FOOLISH THING
- HAVEN'T GOT WHAT IT TAKES
- YOU BUSTED MY MIND

CLAY, OTIS
- MESSING WITH MY MIND
- THE ONLY WAY IS UP
- I TESTIFY
- YOU HURT ME FOR THE LAST TIME
- A LASTING LOVE
- I PAID THE PRICE
- IT'S EASIER SAID, THAN DONE
- SHOW PLACE

CLAY, SONGEE (SONJI)
- I CAN'T WAIT (UNTIL I SEE MY BABY'S FACE)
- NOBODY
- DEEPER IN MY HEART
  - MAKER 8003

CLAY, TOM
- NEVER BEFORE

CLAY, VERNA RAE
- HE LOVES ME, HE OVES ME NOT

CLAYTON, PAT
- SOMEONE ELSE'S TURN

CLAYTON, WILLIE
- LOVE PAINS
- LOVE YA ONE MORE TIME

CLEAR
- EQUAL LOVE OPPORTUNITY

CLEFTONES
- THERE SHE GOES

Title	Label	Price	Genre
OLE FASHUN LOVE	CONSTELLATION 173	10.00	northern
I AIN'T GONNA BE YOUR FOOL	CONSTELLATION 142	15.00	northern
LOST GIRL	COLUMBIA 44200	20.00	northern
IT'S RAINING	CONSTELLATION 113	30.00	northern
HEARTBREAK	CONSTELLATION 132	10.00	northern
HE'S GONE	ANTARES 101	100.00	northern
IT WOULD MEAN SO MUCH TO ME	MERCURY 71253	200.00	motown
DON'T ABUSE MY LOVE	FINGER TIPS 100	30.00	funk
(SOMEBODY) STOP THAT GIRL	SOULHAWK 1	15.00	**northerB**
A GIRL'S WORLD	SOULHAWK 3	150.00	northern
HOLD YOUR HORSES	MOIRA 104	10.00	northern
AS LONG AS YOU'RE IN LOVE WITH	REJO 100	30.00	northern
AS LONG AS YOU'RE IN LOVE WITH	ATCO 6266	10.00	northern
FEELING OF LOVE	CHESS 1806	25.00	northern
THE FORCE OF LOVE	EPIC 2697	10.00	70's
THIS HEART OF MINE	CHESS 1924	8.00	northern
POOR BOY	CHESS 1935	8.00	northern
NO SENSE OF DIRECTION	M-S 206	150.00	northern
YOU'RE A STAR	CHESS 1944	20.00	northern
YOU MADE ME A V.I.P.	CHESS 1979	25.00	northern
I'M SOLD ON YOUR LOVE	BRIGHT STAR 501	20.00	northern
I DON'T WANT NOBODY ELSE	ULTRA-CLASS 1111	30.00	northern
I'VE GOT TO SPACE	ULTRA-CLASS 104	10.00	group
THAT'S GROOVY	GSF 6875	20.00	northern
RIGHT BEFORE MY EYES	KWANZA 7715	10.00	70's
I DON'T WANT TO LOSE YOU	KWANZA 7678	8.00	70's
WE CAN MAKE IT	MASTER KEY 3	75.00	70's
I'M JIMMY MACK	WISE WORLD 62728	200.00	northern
ONE DANCE	YANG-G 4665	1500.00	northern
THE THINGS WE DID LAST SUMMER	PEARCE 5818	150.00	northern
JULIE	MOD-ART 1075	15.00	70's
I'M COMING HOME	SCEPTER 1281	10.00	ballad
WAY YOU LOKK TOGNIGHT	SCEPTER 12135	15.00	northern
HE'S THE KIND OF GUY	SCEPTER 12157	15.00	**northerB**
CHECK IT OUT	ECHO 2002	10.00	70's
SPECIAL KIND OF LOVE	ECHO 2003	30.00	70's
I'M SATISFIED	ONEDERFUL 4841	10.00	northern
BABY JANE	DAKAR 610	50.00	northern
GOT TO FIND A WAY	ONEDERFUL 4850	10.00	northern
TIRED OF FALLING	ONEDERFUL 4837	10.00	northern
A FLAME IN MY HEART	ONEDERFUL 4846	10.00	northern
THAT'S HOW IT IS	ONEDERFUL 4848	10.00	northern
GENTLE ON MY MIND	SONGEE 1002	75.00	northern
HERE I AM AND HERE I'LL STAY	SONGEE 1001	20.00	northern
WHAT NOW MY LOVE	AMERICAN MUSIC	15.00	northern
MARRY ME	CHANT 103	50.00	motown
I'VE GOT IT BAD	SURE SHOT 5001	15.00	northern
YOU'VE GOTTA SHARE	SILVER TIP 1007	100.00	northern
RUNNING IN & OUT MY LIFE	KIRSTEE 22	10.00	70's
WHERE HAS LOVE GONE	KIRSTEE 1005	10.00	ballad
SAME: INSTRUMENTAL	DT 5799	15.00	70's
LOVER COME BACK TO ME	GEE 1079	20.00	northern

CLIFF, JIMMY				
WATERFALL	WONDERFUL WORLD BEAUTIFUL PEOPLE	A&M 1146	8.00	northern
CLIFF, ZELMA				
I DON'T BELIEVE	GOOD NIGHT MY LOVE	BATTLE 45916	30.00	northern
CLIFFORD, LINDA				
MARCH ACROSS THE LAND	A LONG LONG WINTER	PARAMOUNT 269	15.00	70's
CLIMATES				
BREAKING UP AGAIN	NO YOU FOR ME	SUN. 404	20.00	northern
CLINTON, LARRY				
SHE'S WANTED	IF I KNEW	DYNAMO 300 DJ	1000.00	northern
SHE'S WANTED	IF I KNEW	DYNAMO 300 stock	1500.00	northern
CLOUD, MICHEAL				
CHECK YOUR DIRECTION	DON'T LET NOBODY TURN YOU AROU	HOMARK 3	30.00	70's
CLOUDBURST				
I'M LOVIN' YOU	NEVER LET ME GO	STORMY MONDAY 771076	300.00	70's
CLOVERS				
TRY MY LOVIN' ON YOU	SWEET SIDE OF A SOULFUL WOMAN	JOSIE 997	20.00	northern
COALITIONS				
INSTEAD ..HOW ARE YOU	I DON'T MIND DOING IT	REDUN 5	10.00	group
COASTERS				
CRAZY BABY	BELL BOTTOM SLACKS AND A CHINE	ATCO 6379	60.00	**northerB**
LOVE POTION NUMBER NINE	D.W.WASHBURN	KING 6385	10.00	northern
COATES, GOLDIE				
FISHERMAN	LOVE IS A TREASURE	COURTLAND 102	40.00	northern
COBB, JOHNNY				
FORGET HIM	LOVE DOESN'T PAY	JAGUAR 468	15.00	northern
COBBLESTONE				
TRICK ME, TREAT ME	SHE'S LOVES ME (SHE LOVES ME NOT)	MERCURY 73051	100.00	northern
COBRA KINGS				
BIG LIMAS	TRAGEDY	BLACK GOLD 300	20.00	mod
TO HOT TO HANDLE	NIGHT WALK	BLACK GOLD 200	15.00	mod
COCHRAN, WAYNE				
I'M IN TROUBLE	GOIN' BACK TO MIAMI	MERCURY 72623	15.00	northern
CODAY, BILL				
RIGHT ON BABY		CRAJON 48203	250.00	northern
C.O.D'S				
MICHEAL	CRY NO MORE	KELLMAC 1003	10.00	northern
PRETTY BABY	I'M A GOOD GUY	KELLMAC 1005	10.00	northern
I'LL COME RUNNING BACK TO YOU	I'M LOOKING OUT FOR ME	KELLMAC 1008	40.00	northern
SHE'S FIRE	IT MUST BE LOVE	KELLMAC 1010	3000.00	northern
COMING BACK GIRL	IT MUST BE LOVE	KELLMAC 1012	200.00	northern
GIMME YOUR LOVE	FUNKY DISCO	MAGIC TOUCH 8003	10.00	northern
COE, JAMIE				
I CRIED ON MY PILLOW	MY GIRL	ENTERPRISE 5050	30.00	northern
I WAS THE ONE	GOOD ENOUGH FOR A KING	ENTERPRISE 5055	20.00	northern
COEFIELD, BRICE				
AIN'T THAT RIGHT	JUST ONE MORE NIGHT	OMEN 10	200.00	northern
COFFEY, DENIS				
GETING IT ON '75	CHICANO	SUSSEX 631	8.00	funk
THEME FROM BLACK BELT JONES	LOVE THEME FROM BLACK BELT JONES	WB 7769	100.00	funk
THEME FROM ENTER THE DRAGON	JUNCTION FLATS	SUSSEX 511	15.00	funk
COIT, JAMES				
BLACK POWER	PHILLANDRINE	PHOOF 101	10.00	**northerB**
COLBERT, CHUCK AND VIEWPOINT				
STAY	A FOOL SUCH AS ME	CAILLIER 102	30.00	funk
COLBERT, GODOY				
I WANNA THANK YOU	BABY I LIKE IT	REVUE 11037	40.00	northern
COLBERT, PHIL				
THE EDGE OF HEAVEN	TOMORROW MAY NEVER COME	PHILIPS 40361	20.00	northern
WHO'S GOT TE ACTION		PHILIPS 40313	100.00	northern
COLD FOUR				
LOVE AND CARE	LOW RIDEN	DRELLS 889	40.00	70's
COLE, BENNIE				
I DON'T WANT TO CRY		RAYNARD 104	75.00	funk
COLEMAN, DAVID				
DROWN MY HEART	MY FOOLISH HEART	BARRY 1013	30.00	northern
COLEMAN, JIMMY				
CLOUDY DAYS	DON'T SEEM LIKE YOU LOVE ME	SIR-RAH	50.00	ballad
CLOUDY DAYS	DON'T SEEM LIKE YOU LOVE ME	REVUE 11002	15.00	ballad
COLEMAN, MICHEAL				
ELECTRIC TWIST		PECO NO#	100.00	funk
COLEMAN, SUSAN				
THE AGE OF THE WOLF	HEY GIRLS	REMMIX 4422	20.00	**northerB**
COLLIER, MITTY				
I HAD A TALK WITH MY MAN	FREE GIRL	CHESS 1907	8.00	northern
NO FAITH, NO LOVE	TOGETHER	CHESS 1918	8.00	ballad

YOU HURT SO GOOD	I CAN'T LOSE	PEACHTREE 121	8.00	ballad
YOUR SIGN IS A GOOD SIGN	MAMA HE TREATS YOUR DAUGHTER M	PEACHTREE 128	10.00	ballad
I'D LIKE TO CHANGE PLACES	SAME:	PEACHTREE 122 DJ	10.00	funk
HELP ME	FOR MY MAN	CHESS 1942	10.00	northern
MY PARTY	I'M SATISFIED	CHESS 1964	10.00	northern
PAIN	LET THEM TALK	CHESS 1889	50.00	northern
COLLINS AND COLLINS				
TOP OF THE STAIRS	PLEASE DON'T BREAK MY	A&M 2233	100.00	70's
COLLINS, ALBERT				
COOKIN' CATFISH	TAKING MY TIME	20th. CENTURY	15.00	mod
COLLINS, BOB AND THE FABULOUS FIVE				
INVENTORY ON HEARTACHES	MY ONE AND ONLY GIRL	MAIN LINE 1367	200.00	northern
COLLINS, EUNICE				
AT THE HOTEL	AT THE HOTEL PT.2	MOD-ART 601	30.00	70's
COLLINS, KEANYA				
I'LL GET OVER IT	IT AIN'T NO SECRET	BLUE ROCK 4072	15.00	northern
AS MUCH YOURS, AS HE IS MINE	YOU DON'T OWN ME	ITCO 103	15.00	northern
LOVE BANDIT	I CALL YOU DADDY	KEANYA 1	40.00	northern
COLLINS, LA SHAWN				
WHAT YOU GONNA DO NOW	GIRL CHOOSES THE BOY	SINCERE 1003	250.00	northern
COLLINS, LYN				
WIDE AWAKE IN A DREAM	ROCK ME AGAIN & AGAIN	PEOPLE 641	15.00	70's
MAMA FEELGOOD	FLY ME TO THE MOON	PEOPLE 618	10.00	funk
THINK (ABOUT IT)	AIN'T NO SUNSHINE	PEOPLE 608	10.00	funk
COLLINS, RODGER				
SHE'S LOOKING GOOD	I'M SERVING TIME	GALAXY 750	8.00	northern
COLLINS, ROMONA				
YOU'VE BEEN CHEATING	NOW THAT YOU'VE GONE	CLARK'S 346	600.00	northern
COLLINS, TERRY				
I L.O.V.E. Y.O.U.	ACTION SPEAKS LOUDER THAN WORD	KWANZA 7739	10.00	70's
COLLINS, TOMMY				
I WANTA THANK YOU	OH WHAT I'D GIVE	VERVE 10565	15.00	northern
I WANTA THANK YOU	OH WHAT I'D GIVE	T.N.T 1036	20.00	northern
COLLINS, WILL AND WILLPOWER				
ANYTHING I CAN DO	SAME:	BAREBACK 531 DJ	250.00	70's
COLMAN, DONNA				
YOUR LOVES TOO STRONG	IF YUOU WANT ME	AVIN 100	150.00	northern
COLON, WILLIE				
THE HUSTLER	GUAJIRO	FANIA 468	20.00	mod
WILLIE BABY	JAZZY	FANIA 444	20.00	mod
COLT 45'S				
LADY, LADY	I KNOW I LOVE YOU	JERRY 119	400.00	northern
COLTON, TONY				
I STAND ACCUSED	FURTER ON DOWN THE TRACK	ABC 10705	100.00	northern
COMBINATIONS				
I'M GONNA MAKE YOU LOVE ME	THE GODDESS OF LOVE	KIMTONE 1001	1000.00	northern
LIKE I NEVER DID BEFORE	WHAT YOU GONNA DO	KELLMAC 1011	4000.00	northern
WHILE YOU WERE GONE	THE FEELING IS FINE	SOLID ROCK 70592	100.00	northern
WHY	COME BACK	KELLMAC 1007	300.00	northern
COMBINATIONS INC.				
DIRTY DEAL	WHAT WOULD HAPPEN	ARC LARK 601	150.00	northern
COMMANDS				
A WAY TO LOVE ME	TOO LATE TO CRY	DYNAMIC 123	70.00	northern
I'VE GOT IT BA FOR MY BABY	A WAY TO LOVE ME	DYNAMIC 123	50.00	northern
CHAIN GANG	MUST BE ALRIGHT	DYNAMIC 114	20.00	group
DON'T BE AFRAID TO LOVE ME	AROUND THE GO GO	DYNAMIC 111	60.00	northern
HEY IT'S LOVE	NO TIME FOR YOU	DYNAMIC 104	50.00	northern
HEY IT'S LOVE	NO TIME FOR YOU	BACK BEAT 570	30.00	northern
COMMITTEE				
GIVE IN TO THE POWER OF LOVE	YOU'RE MY WONDER FULNESS	NMI 7008	100.00	70's
COMMUNICATORS AND THE BLACK EXPERIENCE				
IS IT FUNKY ENOUGH	ONE CHANCE	DUPLEX 1304	40.00	funk
THE ROAD	HAS TIME REALLY CHANGED	TRI OAK 4	100.00	funk
COMPACTS				
WHY CAN'T IT BE	THAT'S HOW MY WORLD BEGAN	CARLA 718	150.00	northern
COMPANIONS				
BE YOURSELF	HELP A LONELY GUY	GENERAL	20.00	northern
AMERICAN 711				
COMPLIMENTS				
THE TIME OF HER LIFE	EVERYBODY LOVES A LOVER	CONGRESS 252	75.00	northern
COMPOSERS				
LET'S GET TO THE POINT	CHANCES GO ROUND	COMPLEX 3 1	20.00	70's
CONGENIAL FOUR				
YOU PLAYED THE PART (OF A LOSER)	FREEDOM SONG	CAPITOL 2927	30.00	group
CONN, BENNIE				
FORGIVE ME	I'M SO GLAD TO BE BACK HOME	MAGNUM 741	15.00	ballad
HAVE YOU HAD A LOVE	I DON'T HAVE	SOULTOWN 107	40.00	ballad

CONN, BILLY
I SHOULD HAVE KNOWN	I PROMISE YOU (I WON'T MENTION	FEDERAL 12500	75.00	northern

CONNELLY, EARL
MAKE UP YOUR MIND	THE DEVIL IN YOU	MAYCON 119	10.00	70's
PLEASE MAKE UP YOUR MIND	TELL ME WHY	MAYCON 121	20.00	70's
DON'T LET ME GO	MY LOVE IS STRONG	MAYCON 110	20.00	northern

CONNOR, BUDDY
WHEN YOU'RE ALONE 1003	SAME: (60's Version)	BREAKTHROUGH	100.00	northern
WHEN YOU'RE ALONE 1004	SAME: (70's remix)	BREAKTHROUGH	50.00	70's

The above was later relesed and credited to "The World's Funkiest Band".

CONNOR, JIMMY
LET'S GET MARRIED	THE REALITY OF LIFE	SHELLY 10604	40.00	northern

CONQUEST, JUNE
ALL I NEED	TAKE CARE	WINDY C 606	20.00	northern
ALMOST PERSUADED	PARTY TALK	FAME 6406	10.00	northern
WHAT'S THIS I SEE	NO ONE ELSE	CURTOM 8543	15.00	northern

CONQUISTADORS
CAN'T STOP LOVING YOU	YOU'VE BEEN GOOD	ACT IV 13	300.00	northern
SADNESS AND MADNESS	LONELY WAS I	SIGNETT 9609	150.00	northern

CONRAD, CHARLES
YOU GOT THE LOVE	ISN'T IT AMAZING	SHANDY 4001	25.00	northern

CONSERVATIVES
HAPPINESS (TAKE YOUR TIME)	THEME FROM HAPPINESS	ON TIME 100	20.00	group

CONSTELLATIONS
SPECIAL LOVE	I CAN'T TURN YOU LOOSE	SONDAY 700	10.00	northern
I DIDN'T KNOW HOW TO	POPA DADDY	GEMINI STAR 30005	50.00	northern
I DON'T KNOW ABOUT YOU	EASY TO BE HARD	GEMINI STAR 30008	200.00	northern
TEAR IT UP BABY	DOO DOO DA DEM	SMASH 1923	15.00	northern

CONSTRUCTION
HEY LITTLE WAY OUT GIRL	MY HEART WOULD SING	SYNC 6 924	300.00	northern

CONTACTS
YOU GONNA PAY	WHY LITTLE GIRL	QUADRAN 40002	300.00	northern

CONTEMPLATIONS
ALONE WITH NO LOVE	SAME: INSTRUMENTAL	DONTEE 101	500.00	northern

CONTENDERS
(YOU GOTTA) DO WHAT U GOTTA DO	MOON JERK	EDGE 506	15.00	northern
LOVELY LOVER	I LIKE IT LIKE THAT	JAVA 103	30.00	northern

CONTESSAS
I KEEP ON KEEPING ON	THIS IS WHERE I CAME IN	E RECORDS 402	20.00	northern

CONTINENTAL FOUR
THE WAY I LOVE YOU	I DON'T HAVE YOU	JAY WALKING 9	15.00	northern

CONTINENTAL SHOWSTOPPERS
NOT TOO YOUNG	NEVER SET ME FREE	SEVENTY 7 107	30.00	70's

CONTINENTALS
FUNKY FOX	STRAIGHT AHEAD	BLUE FOX 101	20.00	funk

CONTOURS
GONNA WIN YOU BACK	LOOK OUT FOR THE STOP SIGN	MOTOR CITY 4503	10.00	70's
I'M A WINNER	MAKES ME WANNA COME BACK	ROCKET 41192	15.00	70's
I'M A WINNER	MAKES ME WANNA COME BACK	SOLID GOLD 554	25.00	70's
CAN YOU DO IT	I'LL STAND BY YOU	GORDY 7029	10.00	motown
CAN YOU JERK LIKE ME	THAT DAY WHEN SHE NEEDED ME	GORDY 7037	10.00	motown
DETERMINATION	JUST A LITTLE MISUNDERSTANDING	GORDY 7052	10.00	motown
DO YOU LOVE ME	MOVE MR. MAN	GORDY 7005	15.00	motown
DON'T LEDT HER BE YOUR BABY	IT MUST BE LOVE	GORDY 7016	10.00	motown
FIRST LOOK AT THE PURSE	SEARCHING FOR A GIRL	GORDY 7044	10.00	motown
FUNNY	THE STRETCH	MOTOWN 1012	300.00	motown
IT'S SO HARD BEING A LOSER	YOUR LOVE GROWS MORE PRECIOUS	GORDY 7059	15.00	motown
PA I NEED A CAR	YOU GET UGLY	GORDY 7019	15.00	motown
SHAKE SHERRY	YOU BETTER GET IN LINE	GORDY 7012	10.00	motown
WHOLE LOTTA	WOMAN COME ON AND BE MINE	MOTOWN 1008	200.00	motown

CONTRAILS
FEEL SO FINE	MAKE ME LOVE YOU	MILLAGE 104	50.00	northern

CONTRIBUTORS OF SOUL
YOU CAN'T HELP BUT FALL IN LOV	SAME:	VENTURE 628 DJ	10.00	northern

CONWELL, JAMES
THE TROUBLE WITH GIRLS	I KNOW I'M SURE (I'M IN LOVE)	4J RECORDS 511	75.00	northern

CONWELL, JIMMY
CIGARETTE ASHES	SECOND HAND HAPPINESS	MIRWOOD 5530	20.00	**northerB**
TO MUCH	LET IT ALL OUT	GEMINI. 1003	75.00	**northerB**

COOK, JERRY
FUNKY WAGON	HEY MRS JONES	TROYX 101	20.00	funk
I HURT ON THE OTHER SIDE	TAKE WHAT I'VE GOT	CAPITOL 5981	75.00	**northerB**

COOK, JOE
PLEASE DON'T GO	FIND A NEW GIRL	TOP-TOP 1001	20.00	group

COOK, LITTLE JOE

MEET ME DOWN IN SOULSVILLE	YOU MAKE ME WANT TO CRY	OKEH 7211	15.00	ballad
HOLD ON TO YOUR MONEY	DON'T YOU HAVE FEELINGS	LOMA 2026	10.00	northern
HOLD ON TO YOUR MONEY	DON'T YOU HAVE FEELINGS	TWO JAY 1001	15.00	northern
I'LL NEVER GO TO A PARTY AGAIN	THE TROLLEY SONG	20th. CENTURY 420	20.00	northern
I'M FALLING IN LOVE WITH YOU B	DOODLE PICKLE	HOT 1003	200.00	**northerB**

COOK, RONNIE

ONLY THE LONELY	WAY OUT	DORE 721	20.00	group

COOKE, CAROLYN

I DON'T MIND	TOM, DICK & HARRY	RCA 8553	25.00	northern

COOKE, SARAH

PLEASE DON'T GO	HEY HEY (TRHE SUNS GONNA SHINE	BIG TOP 519	200.00	northern

COOKIE V

QUEEN OF FOOLS	YOU GOT THE WRONG GIRL	CHECKER 1222	10.00	northern

COOL SOUNDS

RAG DOLL	WHERE DO WE GO FROM HERE	SOUL TOWN 103	50.00	group
RAG DOLL	MY REQUEST	PICK-A-HIT 103	30.00	group
RAG DOLL	COME HOME	PULSAR 2421	50.00	group
BOY WONDER (WHO MADE GOOD)	SAME:	WB 7615 DJ	30.00	70's
WHO CAN I TURN TO	A LOVE LIKE OURS COULD LAST:	WB 7575	50.00	70's
I'LL TAKE YOU BACK (IF YOU PROMISE)	WHERE DO WE GO FROM HERE	WB 7538	25.00	group

COOPER N' BRASS

DOES ANYBODY KNOW WHAT TIME IT	SAME:	AMAZON 7 DJ	10.00	northern

COOPER, BARBARA

WHAT ONE MORE TEAR	THE PLAYGROUND	RCA 9048	30.00	northern

COOPER, CHRISTINE

HEARTACHES AWAY MY BOY	(THEY CALL HIM) A BAD BOY	PARKWAY 983	200.00	**northerB**
S.O.S. (HEART IN DISTRESS)	SAY WHAT YOU FEEL	PARKWAY 971	10.00	northern

COOPER, ED

JUST LIKE A HERO	DON'T LET LIVE GET YOU DOWN	NIMROD 904	75.00	northern

COOPER, EULA

BEGGARS CAN'T BE CHOOSEY	I NEED YOU MORE	NOTE 7208	25.00	northern
TRY	LOVE MAKE ME DO FOOLISH THINGS	TRAGAR 6814	250.00	northern
LET OUR LOVE GROW HIGHER	HAVE FAITH IN ME	SUPER SOUND 702	400.00	**northerB**

COOPER, GENE

GO GO INN	THE KIND OF MAN I AM	HI-Q 5037	20.00	northern

COOPER, WILLIE AND THE WEBS

YOU DON'T LOVE NOBODY	I CAN'T TAKE IT NO MORE	WHIZ 508	100.00	northern
YOU DON'T LOVE NOBODY	I CAN'T TAKE IT NO MORE	DYNAMIC 105	100.00	northern
CAN'T LET YOU GO	TRY LOVING ME	DYNAMIC 106	150.00	northern
DON'T EVER HURT ME	LITTLE GIRL BLUE	DYNAMIC 109	100.00	northern

COOPERETTES

EVERYTHING'S WRONG	DON'T TRUST HIM	BRUNSWICK 55307	20.00	northern
GOODBYE SCHOOL	SAME: INSTRUMENTAL	BRUNSWICK 55296	30.00	northern
SHING- A- LING	(LIFE HAS) NO MEANING NOW	BRUNSWICK 55329	75.00	**northerB**

COPELAND, JOHNNY

SUFFERING CITY	IT'S MY OWN TEARS THAT'S BEING WASTED	ATLANTIC 2542	15.00	northern

COPELAND, VIVIAN

HE KNOWS MY KEY (IS ALWAYS IN THE MAIL BOX)	SO NICE, I HAD TO KISS YOU TWICE	DORO 3500	15.00	70's
I DON'T CARE	OH NO NOT MY BABY	DORO 1006	20.00	northern

COPNEY, BOBBY

LOVE AU-GO-GO	AIN'T NO GOOD	TUFF 414	15.00	northern

CORBY, CHUCK AND THE ENTREES

COMPLETE OPPOSITES	SOUL BROTHER	CHESS 2077	15.00	northern
CITY OF STRANGERS	BRING MY DADDY HOME	SONIC 118 DJ	15.00	group
HAPPY GO LUCKY	MAN LOVES TWO	SOUND 717	40.00	northern
HAPPY GO LUCKY	MAN LOVES TWO	VEEP 1235	20.00	northern

CORLETTS   (also see CARLETTS)

I'M GETTING TIRED	LOST WITH YOUR LOVE	CAPITOL 2775	70.00	northern

CORONADAS

I'M SOLD ON YOUR LOVE	YOU CAN DO ME SOME GOOD	BRIGHT STAR 157	20.00	northern

CORVAIRS

LOVE IS SUCH A FUNNY THING	A VICTIM OF HER CHARMS	SYLVIA 5003	50.00	northern

CORY

TAKE IT OR LEAVE IT	BEYOND THE HURT	PHANTOM 10742	20.00	70's

COSBY, BILL

LITTLE OLE MAN (UPTIGHT)	DON' CHA KNOW	WB 7072	8.00	northern
LITTLE OLE MAN (UPTIGHT)	HUSH HUSH	WB 7072	10.00	northern

COSBY, EARL

OOH HONEY BABY	I'LL BE THERE	MIRA 204	20.00	northern

COSMO

SMALL TOWN GOSSIP	THINGS I'D LIKE TO DO	SS7 2504	25.00	northern
SMALL TOWN GOSSIP	THINGS I'D LIKE TO DO	JAM 105	40.00	northern
SOFT AND PRETTY	YOU GOTTA DANCE	JAM 106	60.00	northern
SOFT AND PRETTY	YOU GOTTA DANCE	SS7 2520	40.00	northern

COTILLIONS

SOMETIMES I GET LONELY	ONE OF THESE DAYS	ABC 10413	25.00	northern
AIN'T NO BIG THING	DO THE THINGS I LIKE	TOMAHAWK 141	50.00	northern

COTTEN, CHAREN

A LITTLE MORE LOVE	TAKE CARE OF BUSINESS AT HOME	PHILOMEGA 801	40.00	70's
A LITTLE MORE LOVE	TAKE CARE OF BUSINESS AT HOME	PERCEPTION 550	30.00	70's

COTTON, HAYES

BLACK WING'S HAVE MY ANGEL	I'LL BE WAITING	RESIST 504	1000.00	northern
LOVE PLAYS FUNNY GAMES	I'LL BE WAITING	CLAIRE 7000	400.00	northern

COUNTRY STORE

CAUGHT WITH MY HEART DOWN	YOUR LOVE (IS THE ONLY LOVE)	T.A. 196	15.00	northern

COUNTS

WHAT'S IT ALL ABOUT	MOTOR CITY	T.M. RECORDS 100	150.00	70's
ASK THE LONELY	IF YOU DON'T LOVE ME	YES 103	300.00	northern
PEACHES BABY	MY ONLY LOVE	SHRINE 117	2000.00	northern
STRONGER THAN EVER	GOSPEL TRUTH	YES 102	300.00	northern

COUNTS (THEE)

SOMEDAY I'M GONNA GET YOU	SO FAR AWAY	DYNAMO 50	100.00	northern
SOMEDAY I'M GONNA GET YOU	S FAR AWAY	HIGHLAND 1171	50.00	northern

COURCY, JOANN

I GOT THE POWER	I'M GONNA KEEP YOU	TWIRL 2026	400.00	northern

COURTIAL with ERROL KNOWLES

DON'T YOU THINK IT'S TIME	LOSING YOU	PIPELINE 2002	75.00	funk

COURTNEY, DEAN

IT MAKES ME NERVOUS	YOU'RE ALL I GOT	PARAMOUNT 214	15.00	70's
(LOVE) YOU JUST CAN'T WALK AWAY	BETCHA CAN'T CHANGE MY MIND	MGM 13776	200.00	northern
I'LL ALWAYS NEED YOU	TAMMY	RCA 9049	60.00	northern
WE HAVE A GOOD THING	MY SOUL CONCERTO	RCA 8919	25.00	northern

COURTNEY, LOU

SOMEBODY NEW IS LOVIN ' YOU	JUST TO LET HIM BREAK YOUR HEA	EPIC 50070	8.00	70's
SKATE NOW	I CAN ALWAYS TELL	RIVERSIDE 4588	8.00	northern
DO THE THING	THE MAN IS LONELY	RIVERSIDE 4589	15.00	funk
HEY JOYCE	I'M MAD ABOUT YOU	POPSIDE 4594	20.00	funk
HOT BUTTER 'N ALL	HOT BUTTER 'N ALL Pt.2	HURDY-GURDY 101	20.00	funk
IF THE SHOE FITS	IT'S LOVE NOW	POPSIDE 4596	15.00	northern
TRYIN' TO FIND MY WOMAN	LET ME TURN YOU ON	BUDDAH 121	20.00	northern
WATCHED YOU SLOWLY SLIP AWAY	I'LL CRY IF I WANT TO	PHILIPS 40287	150.00	northern

COVAY, JULIAN

A LITTLE BIT HURT	SWEET BACON	PHILIPS 40505	20.00	northern

COX, SAM.

LIFE IS LOVE	DESTINATION	RENFRO 1917	200.00	northern

COX, WALLY

COME ON HOME	I FOUND YOU	CORDON 102	40.00	northern
THIS MAN	I'VE HAD ENOUGH	WAND 11233	25.00	**northerB**

C-QUENTS

IT'S YOU AND ME	DEAREST ONE	CAPTOWN 4028	70.00	northern
IT'S YOU AND ME	DEAREST ONE	ESSICA 4	40.00	northern

CRANSTON BAND, LAMONT

TAKIN' A CHANCE	E JAM	WATERHOUSE 15002 PS	75.00	northern

CRAVER, SONNY

I'M NO FOOL		MUSETTE 102	100.00	northern
I WANNA THANK YOU	UH HUH OH YEAH	STANSON 510	300.00	northern
I'M NO FOOL	I WANNA THANK YOU	TERI DE 7	75.00	northern
OUTSIDE OF MEMPHIS	STILL WATERS	DALYA 1895	20.00	northern

CRAWFORD, CAROLYN

FORGET ABOUT ME	DEVIL IN HIS HEART	MOTOWN 1050	75.00	motown
MY HEART	WHEN SOMEONE'S GOOD TO YOU	MOTOWN 1070	50.00	motown
MY SMILE IS JUST A FROWN	I'LL COME RUNNING	MOTOWN 1064	75.00	motown
WHEN SOMEONE'S GOOD TO YOU	MY HEART	MOTOWN 1070	40.00	motown

CRAWFORD, FAYE

WHAT HAVE I DONE	SO MANY LIES	RCA 8555	75.00	northern

CRAWFORD, JAMES

HONEST I DO	HONEST I DO PT.2	OMEN 12	20.00	northern
IF YOU DON'T WORK YOU CAN'T EAT	STOP AND THINK IT OVER	MERCURY 72441	15.00	northern

CREATION

I GOT THE FEVER	SOUL CONTROL	ERIC 5006	8.00	northern

CREATIONS

FOOTSTEPS	A DREAM	ZODIAC 1005	30.00	northern
HOW SWEETLY SIMPLE	LOVIN' FEELIN'	VIRTUE 2522	10.00	group
I'M SO IN LOVE WITH YOU	SAVE THE PEOPLE	VIRTUE 2517	15.00	group
OH BABY!	PLENTY OF LOVE	GLOBE 1000	15.00	group
TIMES ARE CHANGING	I'VE GOT TO FIND HER	GLOBE 103	15.00	group
WE'RE IN LOVE	LADY LUCK	TAKE TEN 1501	15.00	group
THIS IS OUR NIGHT	YOU'RE MY INSPIRATION	MELODY 101	150.00	motown
TAKE THESE MEMORIES	DON'T LET ME DOWN	VIRTUE 101470	25.00	northern

CREATIVE SOURCE

YOU'RE TOO GOOD TO BE TRUE	OH LOVE	SUSSEX 508	10.00	70's

CRE-SHENDOS
| YOU'RE STILL ON MY MIND | THIS MUST BE LOVE | AQUARIUS 822 | 20.00 | northern |

CROCKER, FRANKIE
| TON OF DYNAMITE | CONFESSION OF LOVE | TURBO 0001 | 100.00 | northern |

CROCKETT, HOWARD
ALL THE GOOD TIMES ARE GONE	THE GREAT TITANIC	MELODY 121	10.00	motown
BRINGING IN THE GOLD	I'VE BEEN A LONG TIME LEAVING	MELODY 111	10.00	motown
MY LIL'S RUN OFF	SPANISH LACE AND MEMORIES	MELODY 115	10.00	motown
PUT ME IN YOUR POCKET	THE MILES	MELODY 119	10.00	motown
THE BIG WHEEL	THAT SILVER HAIRED DADDY	MELODY 109 DJ	10.00	motown

CROCKETT, P.C.
| THIS IS MY STORY | PLEASURE | VERVE 10588 | 15.00 | ballad |

CROCKETT, ULYSSES
| FUNKY RESURGENCE | TAMURA'S THEME | TRANSVERSE 3 | 20.00 | funk |

CROOK, ED
| THAT'S ALRIGHT | YOU'LL SEE | TRI-SOUND 601 | 20.00 | **northerB** |

CROOK, GENERAL
IN THE WARMTH OF MY ARMS	FOR SOUL SATISFACTION	CAPITOL 2492	25.00	ballad
WHEN LOVE LEAVES YOY CRYING	HOLD ON I'M COMING	CAPITOL 2720	25.00	ballad
THANKS BUT NO THANKS	I'M SATISFIED	WAND 11281	10.00	70's
DO IT FOR ME	TILL THEN	DOWN TO EARTH 74	10.00	funk
FEVER IN THE FUNKHOUSE	SAME: SAME: INSTRUMENTAL.	WAND 11276	10.00	funk
GIMME SOME	GIMME SOME Pt.2	DOWN TO EARTH 73	10.00	funk
TESTIFICATION	THE BEST YEARS OF MY LIFE	WAND 11260	10.00	funk
WHAT TIME IT IS	WHAT TIME IT IS Pt.2	DOWN TO EARTH 77	10.00	funk

CROSS BRONX EXPRESSWAY
| CROSS BRONX EXPRESSWAY | HELP YOUR BROTHERS | ZELL'S 148 | 50.00 | funk |

CROSSEN JR., RAY
| TRY SOME SOUL | WOULD YOU STILL SAY THAT I'M T | MUSICOR 1246 | 10.00 | northern |

CROSSROADS
| COMING HOME TO YOU BABY | HERE I STAND | ATCO 6765 | 20.00 | northern |

CROSSTOWN EXPRESS
| LET ME TRY | JUST KEEP THE FUNK | PEE ZEE 200 | 15.00 | group |

CROW
| YOUR AUTUMN OF TOMORROW | UNCLE FUNK | INNER EAR 429 | 200.00 | northern |

CROWN FOUR
| LOVE FOR MY GIRL | BIRTH OF A PLAYBOY | LEE JOHN 619 | 20.00 | northern |

CROWN G'S
| I CAN'T STOP WANTING YOU | SAME: INSTRUMENTAL | CROWN G 51771 | 15.00 | northern |

CROWNS
| BETTER LUCK NEXT TIME | YOU MAKE ME BLUE | VEE JAY 546 DJ | 30.00 | northern |

CRUSADERS
| YOU PAY FOR LOVE | BE MY GIRL FRIEND | PHILLY GROOVE | 200.00 | 70's |
| 155 DJ | | | | |

CRYSTAL CLEAR
| STAY WITH ME | SAME: | POLYDOR 2099 DJ | 100.00 | 70's |

CRYSTAL MOTION
| YOU'RE MY MAIN SQUEEZE | YOU'RE MY MAIN SQUEEZE Pt.2 | SOUND GEMS 105 | 20.00 | 70's |

CRYSTALS
| ARE YOU TRYING TO GET RID OF M | I GOT A MAN | UA 994 | 40.00 | northern |

CUMBO, LINDA
| TROUBLE MAKER | | CALLA | 75.00 | northern |
| YESTEDAY, TODAY AND TOMORROW | | SELECT 738 | 75.00 | northern |

CUMMINGS, WILLIAM
| MAKE MY LOVE A HURTING THING | JUST YESTERDAY'S DREAM | BANG BANG 348 | 300.00 | northern |

CUNNINGHAM, DIANE
SOMEDAY BABY	PARTY TIME	NEW BREED 101	40.00	northern
SOMEDAY BABY	PARTY TIME	FONTANA 1601	20.00	northern
CERTAIN KIND OF LOVER	YOU'VE HURT ME NOW	FONTANA 1608	20.00	northern

CUNNINGHAM, SKIP
| HAVE WE MET BEFORE | LIKE TAKING CANDY FROM A BABY | 20th. CENTURY 588 | 25.00 | northern |

CURRY, CLIFFORD
| I CAN'T GET MYSELF TOGETHER | AIN'T NO DANGER | ELF 90013 | 20.00 | northern |

CURRY, GERALDINE AND THE HEARTSTOPPERS
| YOU'RE SO WONDERFUL | NO MATTER HOW HARD I TRY | LONDON HOUSE 656 | 30.00 | northern |
| MARCHING OUT OF YOUR LIFE | COURT IN MAM | ALL PLATINUM 2341 | 10.00 | northern |

CURRY, HELEN
| LOVE HIM IN RETURN | A PRAYER FOR MY SOLDIER | DJO 115 | 20.00 | northern |
| SAD AND BLUE | A PRAYER FOR MY SOLDIER | DJO 110 | 50.00 | northern |

CURRY, LOUIS
CAPTIVATED	YOU'RE SWEETER THAN A CUP OF H	M-S 210	70.00	northern
GOD'S CREATION	I'VE GOT TO GET AWAY FROM HERE	M-S 215	40.00	northern
I'LL TRY AGAIN TOMORROW	A TOAST TO YOU	M-S 203	15.00	northern
YOU'RE JUST PLAIN NICE	DON'T BE MORE WOMAN THEN I'M A	REEL 251	300.00	northern

CURTIS, BENNY
| DIRTY HEARTS | BEFORE YOU GO | RESIST 503 | 30.00 | northern |

CURTIS, CRY BABY				
THERE WILL BE SOME CHANGES MAD	DON'T JUST STAND THERE	JULET 1005	15.00	ballad
CURTIS, DEBBIE				
I CHECK MY MAIL BOX	IT'S A BAD WAY TO BE	JABRO 101	400.00	northern
CURTIS, DON DAY				
DON'T TALK ABOUT ME, BABY	THE BUMBLE BEE	ABC 10459 DJ	20.00	northern
CURTIS, LENNY				
NOTHING CAN HELP YOU NOW	WHO YOU GONNA RUN TO	END 1127	450.00	**northerB**
CURTIS				
HOW CAN I TELL HER	I REMEMBER	CHARM CITY 1879	20.00	70's
CURTISS, KEITH				
MY LOVE I CAN'T HIDE	I GOT TOO KEEP YOU BABY	SMOKE 601	300.00	northern
CUSTER AND THE SURVIVORS				
I SAW HER WALKING	FLAP JACKS	ASCOT 2207	15.00	northern
CUTCHINS, BOBBY				
I DID IT AGAIN	GOOD TREATMENT	LASSO 503	10.00	70's
CUTE-TEENS				
WHEN MY TEENAGE DAYS ARE OVER	FROM THIS DAY FORWARD	ALADDIN 3458	400.00	motown
CYNTHIA				
HEAVENLY LOVE	THE WAY I FEEL	BARRY 1007 DJ	30.00	northern
CYNTHIA AND IMAGINARY THREE				
THAT'S WHAT I AM (WITHOUT YOU)	MANY MOOD (OF A MAN)	BIG HIT 110	300.00	northern
CYNTHIA AND THE IMAGINATIONS				
HEY BOY (I LOVE YOU)	LOVE IS REAL	BLUE ROCK 4074	50.00	northern
THERE'S SOMETHING THE MATTER	IS THERE ANYONE, ANYWHERE	MAGIC CITY 6	30.00	northern

D

D AND JOE (also see DEE & JOE)				
ALONE IN THE CHAPEL		DE - TO 2875	75.00	ballad
D., LITTLE RALPHIE				
TAKE ME BACK	HALF WAY LOVER	20th. CENTURY 6654	15.00	northern
D.C.BLOSSOMS				
HEY BOY	I KNOW ABOUT HER	SHRINE 107	600.00	northern
DACOSTA, RITA				
DON'T BRING ME DOWN	GOLDEN DAYS OF NOW	PANDORA 7050	400.00	northern
DON'T BRING ME DOWN	NO, NO, NO	MOHAWK 703	75.00	northern
DAISES				
COLD WAVE	PUT YOUR ARMS AROUND ME HONEY	CAPITOL 5667	30.00	northern
DALE, JEFF				
WHERE DID YOU GO	COME TO ME GIRL	ATCO 6352	50.00	northern
A SUFFERING PAIN		ATCO 6405	25.00	northern
DALTON BOYS				
I'VE BEEN CHEATED	SOMETHING'S BOTHERING YOU	V.I.P. 25025 stock	100.00	motown
I'VE BEEN CHEATED	SOMETHING'S BOTHERING YOU	V.I.P. 25025 DJ	40.00	motownB
I'VE BEEN CHEATED	TAKE MY HAND	V.I.P. 25025	200.00	motown
DAMON'S EXPRESS, LIZ				
YOU'RE FALLING IN LOVE	1900 YESTERDAY	MAKAHA 503	30.00	northern
YOU'RE FALLING IN LOVE	1900 YESTERDAY	WHITE WHALE	10.00	northern
DAN AND THE CLEAN CUTS				
ONE LOVE, NOT TWO	GOOD MORNING	SCEPTER 1289	15.00	group
CO-OPERATION	WALKIN' WITH PRIDE	SCEPTER 12115	10.00	northern
DANDERLIERS				
ALL THE WAY	WALK ON WITH YOUR NOSE UP	MIDAS 9004	20.00	northern
D'ANDREA, ANN				
DON'T STOP LOOKING	MISTER GOODTIME FRIDAY	JAMIE 1352	20.00	northern
DANFAIR, AZZIE				
YOU'VE GOT EVERYTHING (I WANT)	DON'T BOTHER ME	MELLOW 1003	40.00	northern

DANFAIR, BILLY

I GOT LOVE	TROUBLE, TROUBLE, TROUBLE	NIKE 1018	50.00	northern

DANIEL, J.J.

MR. LONESOME	DEEP DOWN INSIDE	SURE SHOT 5017	20.00	northern

DANIELS, PEACHES (also Peaches on Bumps)

FEELIN' SOMETHING NEW INSIDE	I HATE TO FORGET WHEN I TRY TO	PZAZZ 52	10.00	ballad

DANIELS, TONY.

I WON'T CRY	DRIP DROP	BEVEL 501	300.00	northern
HOW LONELY	SAME: INSTRUMENTAL	SPORT 103 TD	40.00	northern

DANIELS, YVONNE

GOT TO GET CLOSE TO YOU	SUPER SOUL MUSIC	RED LITE 117	15.00	northern
I DON'T WANNA GET AWAY FROM YOUR LOVE	SAME:	STERLING 101	700.00	northern

DANIELS

(I LOST MY HEART IN THE)BIG CITY	FINALLY	LANTAM 1	20.00	northern

DANLEERS

BABY YOU'VE GOT IT	THE TRUTH HURTS	LE MANS 5	25.00	northern

DAPPS

BRINGING UP GUITAR	GITTIN' A LITTLE HIPPER	KING 6147	20.00	funk
THE RABBIT GOT THE GUN	THERE WAS A TIME	KING 6169	15.00	funk
I'LL BE SWEETER TOMORROW	A WOMAN, A LOVER, A FRIEND	KING 6201	25.00	group

DARBY, DALE

LET'S GOT IT TOGETHER	BACK STREET	WESTGATE 204	15.00	70's
PUSH IT UP BABY	TIME IS CHANGING	WESTGATE 202	15.00	70's
PRAISE THE WOMAN	TREAT A WOMAN RIGHT	WESGATE 201	40.00	ballad
HOW CAN I SAY GOODBYE	PUSH IT UP BABY	L.A.CENTRAL 204	15.00	ballad

DARBY, SUE

CAN'T GET ENOUGH OF YOU BABY	CALL ME	ABC 10898	30.00	northern

DARK, TOMMY

WOBBLE LEGS	WOBBLE LEGS	SUGAR 501	15.00	funk

DARLETTES

LOST	SWEET KIND OF LONELINESS	MIRA 1003	25.00	northern

DARLINGS

TWO TIME LOSER	PLEASE LET ME KNOW	MERCURY 72185	20.00	northern
TWO TIME LOSER	PLEASE LET ME KNOW	KAY KO 1002	40.00	northern

DARNELL, BOBBY AND THE DORELLS

TELL ME HOW TO FIND TRUE LOVE	BABY CHECK YOURSELF	BRONZE 101	100.00	ballad

DARNELL, KISSY

YOU JEOPARDIZE MY LIFE	SAME: INSTRUMENTAL	GO GO G.T.O. 6	100.00	northern

DARNELL, LARRY

WITH TEARS IN MY EYES	I'LL GET ALONG SOMEHOW	ANNA 1109	100.00	motown

DARNELLS

TOO HURT TO CRY, TOO MUCH IN LOVE	COME ON HOME	GORDY 7024	40.00	motown

DARRINGTON, WILLIE

NEVER SHOULD HAVE WALKED AWAY	SAME: PT.2	RAV. 30569	10.00	70's
NEVER SHOULD HAVE WALKED AWAY	LAY	RAV. 8198	100.00	70's

DARRIS, DANELLE

DON'T LOVE ME AND LEAVE ME	LET'S DO THE SHOTGUN	COMMERCE 5020	100.00	northern

DARROW, JOHNNY

LOVE IS A NIGHTMARE	POOR BOY	SUE 741	300.00	northern

DAUGHERTY, EDWIN

GROOVY MONDAY	YIOUR LOVE IS SHOWING	SAVERN 105	25.00	funk

DAUGHTERS OF EVE

HEY LOVER	STAND BY ME	USA 1780	30.00	northern
SOCIAL TRAGEDY	A THOUSAND STARS	CADET 5600	15.00	northern

DAVE AND THE SHADOWS

AT THE FAIR	DANCING CHEEK TO CHEEK	CHECK MATE 1016	30.00	motown
HERE AFTER	BLUE DOWN	CHECK MATE 1011	40.00	motown

DAVENPORT SISTERS

YOU'VE GOT ME CRYING AGAIN	HOY HOY	TRI-PHI 1008	30.00	motown

DAVENPORT, CHET

CAN'T GET OVER YOU	THE PRESIDENTIAL SONG	TOEHOLT 1361	150.00	70's
WHAT WOULD I DO	WAR IN THE GHETTO	KING BEE 4002	20.00	ballad

DAVID AND THE GIANTS

SUPERLOVE	ROLLING IN MY SLEEP	CRAZY HORSE 1307	15.00	**northerB**
TEN MILES HIGH	I'M DOWN SO LOW	CRAZY HORSE 1300	25.00	**northerB**

DAVID AND RUBEN

(I LOVE HER SO MUCH) IT HURTS	THE GIRL IN MY DREAMS	WB 7316	75.00	northern
(I LOVE HER SO MUCH) IT HURTS	THE GIRL IN MY DREAMS	RAMPART 662	150.00	northern

DAVID, LEE

TEMPTATION IS CALLING MY NAME	(I FEEL A) COLD WAVE COMING ON	COLUMBIA 44138	60.00	northern

DAVISON, ALFIE

LOVE IS A SERIOUS BUSINESS	KNOCK ON ANY DOOR	MERCURY 76001	50.00	70's

DAVIS JR., SAMMY

DON'T SHUT ME OUT	THE DISORDERLY ORDERLY	REPRISE 322	20.00	northern

DAVIS, BRENDETTA

I CAN'T MAKE IT WITHOUT YOU	UNTIL YOUR GONE	LIBERTY 56056	40.00	northern

DAVIS, CARL				
WINDY CITY THEME	SHOW ME THE WAY TO LOVE	CHI SOUND 904	20.00	70's
DAVIS, COURT				
TRY TO THINK WHAT YOUR DOING		EAST COAST	800.00	northern
DAVIS, G. AND THE TYLER, R.				
HOLD ON, HELP IS ON THE WAY	BET YOU'RE SURPRISED	PARLO 102	50.00	**northerB**
DAVIS, GEATER				
I'VE GOT TO PAY THE PRICE	I'M GONNA CHANGE	LUNA 801	10.00	70's
MY LOVE IS SO STRONG FOR YOU	I CAN HOLD MY OWN	HOUSE OF ORANGE	15.00	northern
2402				
DAVIS, GWEN				
MY MAN DON'T THINK I KNOW	I CAN'T BE YOUR PART TIME BABY	SS7 2557	50.00	northern
DAVIS, HERMAN				
GOTTA BE LOVED	MEMORIES	VENUS V 9680	15.00	70's
DAVIS, J.C.				
BUTTERED POPCORN		NEW DAY	75.00	funk
MONKEY	SWEET SWEET LOVE	CHESS 1858	15.00	mod
DAVIS, JESSE				
GONNA HANG ON IN THERE GIRL		ERA 3189	400.00	northern
THERE'S ROOM FOR ME REVERE	IT'S TOO LATE TO BE SORRY	REVERE 101	800.00	northern
THERE'S ROOM FOR ME REVERE	IT'S TOO LATE TO BE SORRY	REVERE 101 PS	1000.00	northern
DAVIS, JOYCE				
ALONG CAME YOU	HELLO HEARTACHES, GOODBYE LOVE	OKEH 7237	50.00	northern
DAVIS, KING AND THE HOUSE ROCKERS				
BABY YOU SATISFY ME	WE ALL MAKE MISTAKES SOMETIMES	VERVE 10492	15.00	northern
DAVIS, LARRY				
TEARS OF SORROW	POURING WATER ON A DROWNING MAN	TRUE SOUL 11	15.00	ballad
I'VE BEEN HURT SO MANY TIMES	FOR 5 LONG YEARS	KENT 4519	50.00	northern
DAVIS, LUCKY (JAMAL)				
IT'S NOT WHERE YOU START	SAME: INSTRUMENTAL	HIGHLAND 1201 yellow	20.00	70's
IT'S NOT WHERE YOU START	SAME: INSTRUMENTAL	HIGHLAND 1201 orange	10.00	70's
LOVE IS BETTER	VACATE	BIG CITY 2001	150.00	70's
DAVIS, LYNN				
I GOT A NEW LOVE (SENT TO ME F	MY NEW LOVE	FEDERAL 12498	20.00	northern
DAVIS, MARY				
DANGER! (PLAYBOY AT WORK)	TAPS BLOW FOR MY BABY	CONCLAVE 338	300.00	northern
DAVIS, MAXINE				
BEFORE I LEAVE YOU	I REALLY GOT IT BAD FOR MY BAB	GUYDEN 2113	30.00	northern
DAVIS, MELVIN (MEL)				
DOUBLE OR NOTHING	YOU CAN'T RUN AWAY	ROCK MILL 3248	10.00	70's
LET LOVE IN YOUR LIFE	WACKY WORLD	ROCK MILL 5238	10.00	70's
YOU MADE ME OVER	I'M WORRIED	INVICTUS 1259	75.00	70's
I'M WORRIED	JUST AS LONG	INVICTUS 9115	10.00	ballad
FAITH	LOVE BUG GOT A BEAR HUG	MALA 12009	20.00	northern
FIND A QUIET PLACE	THIS AIN'T THE WAY	WHEEL CITY 1003	600.00	**northerB**
I MUST LOVE YOU	STILL IN MY HEART	GROOVESVILLE 1003	300.00	northern
SAVE IT (NEVER TOO LATE)	THIS LOVE WAS MEANT TO BE	MALA 590	20.00	northern
DAVIS, RHONDA				
CAN YOU REMEMBER	LONG WALK ON A SHORT PIER	DUKE 473	100.00	northern
DAVIS, TYRONE (also see TYRONE WONDER BOY)				
I'LL BE RIGHT THERE	JUST BECAUSE OF YOU	DAKAR 618	8.00	northern
LET ME BACK IN	LOVE BONES	DAKAR 621	8.00	northern
TURN BACK THE HANDS OF TIME	I KEEP COMING BACK	DAKAR 616	8.00	northern
YOU KEEP ME HOLDING ON	WE GOT A LOVE NO ONE CAN DENY	DAKAR 626	8.00	northern
ALL THE WAITING IS NOT IN VAIN	NEED YOUR LOVIN' EVERYDAY	DAKAR 609	8.00	northern
CAN I CHANGE MY MIND	A WOMAN NEEDS TO BE LOVED	DAKAR 602	8.00	northern
I'M RUNNING A LOSING GAME	TRIED IT OVER (AND OVER AGAIN)	SACK 4359	40.00	northern
IS IT SOMETHING YOU'VE GOT	UNDYING LOVE	DAKAR 605	8.00	northern
ONE-WAY TICKET	WE GOT A LOVE	DAKAR 624	8.00	northern
YOU CAN'T KEEP A GOOD MAN DOWN	IF I DIDN'T LOVE YOU	DAKAR 615	8.00	northern
DAWN				
BABY' GONE AWAY	GOTTA GET AWAY	ABC 10791	20.00	northern
BABY I LOVE YOU	BRING IT ON HOME	RUST 5128	20.00	northern
IN LOVE AGAIN	BA BA BA DE BA	GAMBLE 4002	20.00	northern
LOVE IS A MAGIC WORD	HOW CAN I GET OFF THIS MERRY-G	UA 50096	20.00	northern
DAWSON, LEAH				
MY MECHANICAL MAN	STRANGE THINGS HAPPEN	MAGIC CITY 001	15.00	**northerB**
DAWSON, ROY				
OVER THE TOP	DON'T IT	COEMANDS 1	15.00	70's
DAY, BOBBY				
DON'T LEAVE ME HANGIN' ON AROUND	WHEN I STARTED DANCIN'	CLASS 705	75.00	northern
PRETTY LITTLE GIRL NEXT DOOR	BUZZ, BUZZ, BUZZ	RCA 8196	100.00	northern
SO LONELY (SINCE YOU'VE BEEN G	SPICKS AND SPECKS	SURE SHOT 5036	15.00	northern
DAY, DANNY				
THIS TIME LAST SUMMER	PLEASE DON'T TURN THE LIGHT OU	V.I.P. 25019	30.00	motown
DAY, EDDIE				
FOR MY GIRL	SUMMERS GONE	ONYX 702	15.00	northern

Title	Flip / Title	Label	Price	Category
DAY, JACKIE				
BEFORE IT'S TOO LATE	WITHOUT A LOVE	MODERN 1028	15.00	northern
NAUGHTY BOY	PHELECTRON 382	1000.00		northern
OH! WHAT HEARTACHES	IF I'D LOSE YOU	MODERN 1032	15.00	northern
DAYE, EDDIE AND 4 BARS				
GUESS WHO LOVES YOU	WHAT AM I GONNA DO	SHRINE 112	800.00	northern
DAYE, JOHNNY				
A LOT OF PROGRESS	YOU'RE ON TOP	PARKWAY 119	10.00	northern
I'LL KEEP LOVING YOU	ONE OF THESE DAYS	BLUE STAR 230	40.00	northern
DAYBREAK				
I NEED LOVE	EVERYTHING MAN	P&P 003	400.00	70's
DAYTON SIDEWINDERS				
FUNKY IN HERE		CARLCO	200.00	funk
GO AHEAD ON		CARLCO N	100.00	funk
DAYLIGHTERS				
WHISPER THE WIND	I CAN'T STOP CRYING	TIP TOP 2007	30.00	northern
WHISPER THE WIND	I CAN'T STOP CRYING	TOLLIE 9018	15.00	northern
D.C. BLOSSOMS				
HEY BOY	I KNOW ABOUT HERE	SHRINE 107	700.00	northern
D.C. MAGNATONES				
DOES SHE LOVE ME	NOT ROOM FOR TWO	D.C.MAGNATONES 216	1000.00	northern
DE COSTA, BARBARA				
NOW I KNOW	THE ONE IN YOUR ARMS	RIC TIC 103	20.00	motown
DE LORY, AL				
RIGHT ON	JESUS CHRISTO	CAPITOL 3196	15.00	northern
TRAFFIC JAM	YESTERDAY	PHI-DAN 5006	20.00	northern
DE SANTO, SUGAR PIE				
SOULFUL DRESS	USE WHAT YOU GOT	CHECKER 1082	10.00	northern
HERE YOU COME RUNNING	NEVER LOVE A STRANGER	CHECKER 1101	10.00	northern
I DON'T WANNA FUSS	I LOVE YOU SO MUCH	CHECKER 1093	10.00	northern
JUMP IN MY CHEST	MAMA DIDN'T RAISE NO FOOLS	CHECKER 1109	10.00	northern
SLIP-IN MULES	MR. & MRS	CHECKER 1073	10.00	northern
BE HAPPY	THE FEELIN'S TOO STRONG	SOUL CLOCK 106	20.00	northern
THE ONE WHO REALLY LOVES YOU	(THAT) LOVIN' TOUCH	BRUNSWICK 55375	10.00	northern
DO THE WHOOPIE	GET TO STEPPIN'	BRUNSWICK 55349	10.00	mod
DE VONNS				
FREDDIE	PUT ME DOWN	PARKWAY 976	15.00	northern
ONE SIDED LOVER	WONDERFUL	REDD 306	15.00	northern
SOMEONE TO TREAT ME	NEVER FIND A LOVE LIKE MINE	KING 6226	25.00	northern
GROVING WITH MY THING	WISE UP AND BE SMART	MR. G 825	20.00	northern
DEACONS				
FAGGED OUT	LUCH BREAK	NEO FO 103	50.00	funk
DEADBEATS				
NO SECOND CHANCE	WHY DID YOU	STRATA 104	850.00	northern
DEAL, HARRY AND THE GALAXIES				
I STILL LOVE YOU	YOU'RE ALWAYS IN MY MIND	ECLIPSE 6000	45.00	northern
DEALERS				
YOU GOT IT	(WE'RE SO) GLAD THAT WE MADE I	BIG BUNNY 507	20.00	northern
DEAN AND JEAN				
LOVINGLY YOURS	GODDESS OF LOVE	RUST 5100	40.00	northern
DEAN AND MARC				
BOOGIE WOOGIE TWIST	BOOGIE WOOGIE TWIST Pt. 2	CHECK MATE 1008	40.00	motown
DEAN, DEBBIE				
BUT I'M AFRAID	ITSY BITY PITY LOVE	MOTOWN 1014	50.00	motown
DON'T LET HIM SHOP AROUND	A NEW GIRL	MOTOWN 1007	45.00	motown
EVERYBODY'S TALKING ABOUT MY B	I CRIED ALL NIGHT	MOTOWN 1025	50.00	motown
STAY MY LOVE	WHY AM I LOVIN' YOU	V.I.P. 25044 DJ	150.00	motown
WHY AM I LOVING YOU	WHY AM I LOVING YOU	V.I.P. 25044 DJ	40.00	motown
WHY AM I LOVING YOU	STAY MY LOVE	V.I.P. 25044	stock	250.00
motown				
DEAN, GARY				
YOU CAN SAY	THE DRUNKARD	YOUNG 1004	400.00	northern
DEAN, SNOOPY				
I CAN'T CONTROL THIS FEELING	BE GOOD TO ME	BLUE CANDLE 1500	20.00	70's
DEANE, JANET				
I'M GLAD I WAITED	ANOTHER NIGHT ALONE	GATEWAY 719	20.00	northern
DEANS				
NO NOT NOW	CATCH THE TRAIN	PANIK 5007 DJ	100.00	northern
DEBANAIRS				
FEEL ALL RIGHT	EVERYTHING I NEED	W-BS 2507	15.00	northern
DEBONAIRES				
WOMAN WHY?	STOP LET'S BE UNITED	GALAXY 774	15.00	group
PLEASE DON'T SAY WE'RE THROUGH	EENIE, MEENIE GYPSALEENIE	GOLDEN WORLD 26	10.00	motown
PLEASE DON'T SAY WE'RE THROUGH	A LITTLE TOO LONG	GOLDEN WORLD 17	20.00	motown
HOW'S YOUR NEW LOVE TREATING YOU	C.O.D. (COLLECT ON DELIVERY)	GOLDEN WORLD 44	20.00	northern
HOW'S YOUR NEW LOVE TREATING YOU	BIG TIME FUN	GOLDEN WORLD 38	25.00	northern
HEADACHE IN MY HEART	LOVING YOU TAKES ALL MY TIME	SOLID HIT 102	800.00	northern
HEADACHE IN MY HEART	I'M IN LOVE AGAIN	SOLID HIT 104	100.00	northern

49

DEBONAIRS

PLEASE COME BACK BABY

	UNTRUE WOMAN	SOUL CLICK 8097	350.00	northern

DEBRA

WHAT'S IT GONNA BE

	CAN YOU REMEMBER	GREE-JACK 461	15.00	northern

DECEPTIONS

OF ALL THE HEARTS

	PEOPLE	BROOKS 323	15.00	group

DECISIONS

I CAN'T FORGET ABOUT YOU

	IT'S LOVE THAT REALLY COUNTS	SUSSEX 214	10.00	northern

DECKER, BOBBY

WHERE QUIET WATERS FLOW

	WHERE I LONG TO BE	NEBO 750	100.00	northern

DECKER, CHARMEL

UP JUMPED THE DEVIL

	LOVER'S LAND	CORSICAN 201	50.00	northern

DECRESCENDOS

ONE OF THE CROWD

	WATER OF LOVE	PRISM 1941	100.00	northern

DEDICATIONS

I AIN'T A BIT SORRY

	TOY BOY	BELL 611	30.00	northern

DEE AND JOE

WHO IS IT GONNA BE

WHO IS IT GONNA BE

	I FOUND A LOVE	JUBILEE 5670	20.00	northern
	I FOUND A LOVE	BIG SIX 101	100.00	northern

DEE, JEANNIE

SHAKE A HAND

	THREE FOOLS	HUDD 42969	30.00	funk

DEE, JOEY

BABY DON'T YOU KNOW (I NEED U)

FEELL GOOD ABOUT IT

GOOD LITTLE YOU

PUT YOUR HEART IN IT

	HALF MOON	JANUS 220	20.00	70's
	PT.2	JUBILEE 5532	15.00	northern
	DANCING ON THE STREET	JUBILEE 5539	25.00	northern
	YOU CAN'T SIT DOWN	JUBILEE 5566	20.00	northern

DEE, LITTLE JIMMY

I SHOULD HAVE LISTENED

	I WENT ON	INFINITY 10	50.00	northern

DEES, SAM

COME BACK STRONG

FRAGILE HANDLE WITH CARE

EASIER TO SAY THAN DO

MY WORLD

I'M SO VERY GLAD

LONELY FOR YOU BABY

	WORN OUT BROKEN HEART	ATLANTIC 3205	10.00	70's
	SAVE THE LOVE AT ANY COST	ATLANTIC 3287	40.00	70's
	SAME:	LO LO 2306	20.00	ballad
	SAY YEAH	POLYDOR 14455	15.00	ballad
	CLAIM JUMPING	CLINTONE 10	15.00	northern
	I NEED YOU GIRL	SSS INTER. 732	150.00	northern

DEES, SAM AND SWANN, BETTYE

JUST AS SURE

	STORYBOOK CHILDREN	BIG TREE 16054	30.00	70's

DEIRDRE-WILSON TABAC

ANGEL BABY

	GET BACK	RCA 215	20.00	northern

DEL CAPRIS

HEY LITTLE GIRL

HEY LITTLE GIRL

	FOREVER MY LOVE	RONJERDON 39	15.00	northern
	FOREVER MY LOVE	KAMA SUTRA 235	15.00	northern

DEL CHONTAYS

BABY I NEED YOU

	THE HUSTLE	STEELTOWN 2467	200.00	northern

DEL COUNTS

WITH ANOTHER GUY

	WHAT IS THE REASON	SOMA 1465	40.00	northern

DEL LARKS.

JOB OPENING (FOR AN EXPERIENCED HEART MENDER)

	SAME: INSTRUMENTAL	QUEEN CITY 2004	2,000.00	northern

DEL ROYALS

MAN OF VALUE

	SAME:	MERCURY 72970 DJ	75.00	northern

DELACARDOS

I KNOW I'M NOT MUCH

SHE'S THE ONE I LOVE

	YOU DON'T HAVE TO SEE ME	ATLANTIC 2389	20.00	northern
	GOT NO ONE	ATLANTIC 2368	15.00	northern

DEL-CHORDS

EVERYBODY'S GOTTA LOSE SOMEDAY

	YOUR MOMMY LIED TO YOUR DADDY	MR. GENIUS 401	50.00	group

DELCOS

ARABIA

ARABIA

	THOSE THREE LITTLE WORDS	SHOWCASE 2501	25.00	northern
	THOSE THREE LITTLE WORDS	DELTA 100	10.00	northern

DELEGATES OF SOUL

I'LL COME RUNNING BACK

	WHAT A LUCKY GUY I AM	UPLOOK 51470	60.00	northern

DELEGATES.

THE PEEPER

THE PEEPER

88120

	PIGMY Pt.1	AURA 88120	10.00	funk
	PIGMY PT. 1	PACIFIC JAZZ	10.00	funk

DELETTS

LOOK AT ME

	WHAT'S THE USE	BLUE ROCK 4043	100.00	northern

DELFONICS

HE DON'T REALLY LOVE YOU

I TOLD YOU SO

LOVING HIM

DON'T THROW YOUR LOVE AWAY

	WITHOUT YOU	MOON SHOT 6703	15.00	northern
	SEVENTEEN AND IN LOVE	PHILLY GROOVE 182	8.00	70's
	YOU GOT YOURS AND I'LL GET MIN	PHILLY GROOVE 157	8.00	70's
	I DON'T CARE WHAT PEOPLE SAY	ARISTA 0308	75.00	group

DEL FI'S (see also DEL PHI'S)

NO MORE

	THE MAGIC OF YOU LOVE	CADETTE 8010	100.00	motown

DELICATES

STOP SHOVIN' ME AROUND

STOP SHOVING ME AROUND

	COMIN' DOWN WITH LOVE	CHALLENGE 59304	20.00	northern
	HE GAVE ME LOVE	SOULTOWN 101	40.00	northern

50

Artist / Title	Title	Label	Price	Genre
YOU SAY YOU LOVE ME	I GOT A CRUSH ON YOU BOY	PULSAR 2413	40.00	northern
DE-LITES				
LOVER	TELL ME WHY	CUPPY 101	1000.00	northern
DELL KINGS featuring Carl Henderson				
JUST REMEMBER	THE BIGGEST MISTAKE	RENCO 3002	400.00	northern
DELL, FRANK				
HE BROKE YOUR GAME WIDE OPEN	I'LL GO ON LOVING YOU	VALISE 6900 red	100.00	northern
HE BROKE YOUR GAME WIDE OPEN	I'LL GO ON LOVING YOU	VALISE 6900 orange	300.00	northern
BABY YOU'VE GOT IT	NEED	VALISE 6901	15.00	northern
DELLS				
CLOSER	GIVE MY BABY A STANDING OVATIO	CADET 5696	8.00	70's
IT'S ALL UP TO YOU	OH MY DEAR	CADET 5689	10.00	70's
YOUR SONG	PASSIONATE BREEZE	20th. CENTURY 2475	20.00	70's
WEAR IT ON OUR FACE	PLEASE DON'T CHANGE ME NOW	CADET 5599	8.00	northern
GOOD-BYE MARY ANN	AFTER YOU	ARGO 5456	30.00	northern
HEY SUGAR (DON'T GET SERIOUS)	POOR LITTLE BOY	VEE JAY 712	10.00	northern
INSPIRATION	YOU BELONG TO SOMEONE ELSE	CADET 5563	15.00	northern
MAKE SURE	DOES ANYBODY KNOW I'M HERE	CADET 5631	8.00	northern
RUN FOR COVER	OVER AGAIN	CADET 5551	30.00	northern
THERE IS	SHOW ME	CADET 5590	8.00	northern
THERE IS	O-O, I LOVE YOU	CADET 5574	10.00	northern
THINKIN' ABOUT YOU	THE CHANGE WE GO THROUGH	CADET 5538	50.00	northern
DELORENGO, JOEY				
WAKE UP TO THE SUNSHINE GIRL		MI VAL 101	00.00	northern

Of dubious origin?? I reserve judgement on value until the next price guide.

Artist / Title	Title	Label	Price	Genre
DEL-PHIS				
I'LL LET YOU KNOW	IT TAKES TWO	CHECK MATE 1005	70.00	motown
DELPHS, JIMMY				
ALMOST	DON'T SIGN THE PAPER	KAREN 1538	10.00	northern
AM I LOSING YOU	LOVE I WANT YOU BACK	KAREN 1550	10.00	northern
DANCING A HOLE IN THE WORLD	SAME: INSTRUMENTAL	CARLA 1904	1,000.00	northern
DEL-RAYS				
FORTUNE TELLER	LIKE I DO	ATCO 6348 DJ	20.00	northern
DELRAYS INC.				
DESTINATION UNKNOWN	CRYING IN MY SLEEP	TAMPETE 5444	30.00	northern
MY HEART IS NOT A TOY	COMING HOME	AMERICAN 1	600.00	northern

Artist / Title	Title	Label	Price	Genre
DELTAS				
HEY GIRL JUST LIKE YOU	DO WHAT COMES EASY	NEW CHICAGO SOUND 69730	30.00	northern
DEL-TOURS				
SWEET AND LONELY	BLIND GIRL	STARVILLE 1206	1500.00	northern
DEL-VONS				
GONE FOREVER	ALL I DID WAS CRY	WELLS 1001	30.00	ballad
DEMAIN, ARIN				
SILENT TREATMENT	YOU DON'T HAVE TO CRY ANYMORE	BLUE STAR 1000	750.00	northern
DEMOTRONS				
I DON'T WANT TO PLAY NO MORE	I WANT A HOME IN THE COUNTRY	ATLANTIC 2589	10.00	northern
DEMURES				
RAINING TEARDROPS	HE'S GOT YOUR NUMBER	BRUNSWICK 55284	250.00	northern
DENNIS, BILL				
I'LL NEVER LET YOU GET AWAY	POOR LITTLE FOOL	SHRINE 113	800.00	northern
DENNIS, ERIC				
TOO MANY LOVE PAINS	THE NEXT BEST THING TO LOVE	P-COLA 101	15.00	70's
DENTON, MICKEY				
MI AMORE	AIN'T LOVE GRAND	IMPACT 1002	15.00	group
KING LONELY THE BLUE	HEARTACHE IS MY NAME	IMPACT 1101	30.00	northern
DEPENDABLES				
IT'S INCOMPLETE	OUT ON THE STREETS AGAIN	VESTPOCKET 2	30.00	northern
DEREK AND RAY				
INTERPLAY	DRAGNET '67	RCA 9111	20.00	northern
DESHANNON, JACKIE				
WHAT IS THIS	TRUST ME	IMPERIAL 66370	10.00	northern
DESIRES				
SMILE	BABY WE CAN MAKE IT	TAMBOO 2004 DJ	200.00	northern
DETERMINATIONS				
ONE STEP AT A TIME	WHO BROKE THE BOTTLE	EVENT 253	20.00	northern
BING BONG	GIRL, GIRL, GIRL	KING 6297 DJ	25.00	northern
YOU CAN'T HOLD ON TO LOVE	THAT'S WHAT I LIKE	IMPORTANT 1010	100.00	northern
DETROIT CITY LIMITS				
NINETY EIGHT CENTS PLUS TAX	HONEY CHILE	OKEH 7308	25.00	mod
DETROIT EMERALDS				
I'LL KEEP ON COMING BACK	TAKE ME THE WAY I AM	RIC TIC 141	8.00	motown
SHADES DOWN	ODE TO BILLY JOE	RIC TIC 138	8.00	motown
SHOW TIME	SAME: INSTRUMENTAL.	RIC TIC 135	8.00	motown
HOLDING ON	THINS ARE LOOKING UP	WESTBOUND 147	25.00	northern

Artist	A-side	B-side	Label	Price	Category
DETROIT EXECUTIVES					
	COOL OFF	SHO-NUFF HOT PANTS	PAMELINE 2010 green	300.00	northern
	COOL OFF	SHO-NUFF HOT PANTS	PAMELINE 2010 orange	30.00	northern
DETROIT LAND APPLES					
	I NEED HELP	PRECIOUS MEMORIES	SHOTGUN 203	70.00	**northerB**
DETROIT ROAD RUNNERS					
	SWINGIN' CAMELS	NEW KIND OF LOVE	ABC 11117	10.00	northern
DETROIT SOUL					
	ALL OF MY LIFE	MISTER HIP	MUSIC TOWN 502	30.00	**northerB**
	DOES YOUR MIND GO WILD	LOVE WITHOUT MEANING	MUSIC TOWN 207	15.00	northern
DE'VIGNE, JOHNNY					
	I SMELL TROUBLE	THINGS AIN'T THE SAME	DE-LITE 518	75.00	northern
DEVILS					
	THE X-SORCIST	HIP HUG-HER	PEOPLE 637	20.00	funk
DEVORE, FLORENCE					
	KISS ME NOW (DON'T KISS ME LAT	WE'RE NOT OLD ENOUGH	PHI-DAN 5000	40.00	**northerB**
DEVOTIONS					
	DO DO DE DOP	CAN YOU EXPLAIN IT	NATION 61165	1000.00	northern
	SAME OLD SWEET FEELIN'	DEVIL'S GOTTEN INTO MY BABY	TRI-SOUND 501 yellow	10.00	northern
	SAME OLD SWEET LOVIN	DEVIL'S GOTTEN INTO MY BABY	TRI-SOUND 501 gold	20.00	northern
DEXTER AND WANDA					
	HOW CAN I SHOW YOU	PAST, PRESENT AND FUTURE	CARESS 81739	15.00	70's
DEY AND KNIGHT					
	SAYIN' SOMETHING	OOH DA LA DA LAY	COLUMBIA 43693	20.00	northern
DEZEL, NEICE					
	IT DOESN'T MATTER	LAST NIGHT	J&S 8718	10.00	70's
DIABOLICS					
	I BET YOU NEVER KNEW	NIGGERS WILL BE NIGGERS	TOGETHERNESS 1001	10.00	group
DIALTONES					
	IF YOU DON'T KNOW YOU JUST DON	DON'T LET THE SUN SHINE ON ME	DIAL 4054	20.00	northern
DIAMOND JOE					
	HURRY BACK TO ME	DON'T SET ME BACK	SANSU 460	15.00	northern
	IT DOESN'T MATTTER ANYMORE	GOSSIP GOSSIP	SANSU 475 D	15.00	northern
	WAIT A MINUTE BABY	HOW TO PICK A WINNER	SANSU 454	15.00	northern
DIAMOND UPRISERS					
	DIAMOND JERK (NEW KIND OF JERK)	SAME: INSTRUMENTAL	RILEYS 850	40.00	northern
DIAMOND, BOBBY					
	STOP!	USUALLY YOU	COLUMBIA 43943	25.00	northern
DIAMOND, GENE					
	LONELY DRIFTER	TILL THE END OF TIME	MOTHERS 1302	15.00	northern
	MISS TALL AND SLENDER	I TOLD YOU SO	TRC 1009	20.00	northern
DIAMOND, GERRI					
	ONLY YOU	COUNTERPART	2588	150.00	northern
	GIVE UP ON LOVE	MAMA, YOU FORGOT	HBR 458	10.00	northern
DIAMOND, HANK					
	SOUL SAUCE	EVERYTHING IS WHERE IT BELONGS	WORLD PACIFIC 77812	20.00	mod
DIAMOND, TONY					
	I DON'T WANT TO LOSE YOU	YOU MEAN EVERYTHING TO ME	CAPITOL 2418	25.00	ballad
	DON'T TURN AWAY	YOU'RE THE SWEETEST YET	BLUE ROCK 4019	125.00	northern
DIAMONETTES					
	DON'T BE SUPRISED	RULES ARE MADE TO BE BROKEN	DIG 257	15.00	northern
DICKERSON, CLYDE					
	LOVE BANDIT	YOU ARE A LOVE BANDINO	JONETTA 400	30.00	mod
DICKSON, RICHARD					
	A THOUSAND MILES AWAY	ONE LAST CHANCE	KEYMEN 112	500.00	group
DIFFERENCES					
	FIVE MINUTES	THAT WAS THE DAY	MONCA 1783	400.00	northern
DIFFERENT SHADES OF BROWN					
	LABEL ME LOVE	LIFE'S A BALL (WHILE IT LASTS)	TAMLA 54219	20.00	70's
DIFFERENT STROKES					
	SING A SIMPLE SONG	EVERYDAY PEOPLE	OKEH 7326	15.00	funk
DIFOSCO					
	SUNSHINE LOVE	YOU SAVED ME FROM DESTRUCTION	EARTHQUAKE 2	30.00	70's
DILLARD AND JOHNSON					
	HERE WE GO, LOVING AGAIN	SAME: INSTRUMENTAL	PIEDMONT 76	20.00	70's
DILLARD, MOSES (AND THE AND THE TEX TOWN DISPLAY)					
	I PROMISE TO LOVE YOU	WE GOTTA COME TOGETHER	SHOUT 253	40.00	ballad
	I'VE GOT TO FIND A WAY	I'VE GOT TO FIND A WAY Pt.2	CURTOM 1950	20.00	ballad
	OUR LOVE IS TRUE	SAME:	CURTOM 1958	8.00	ballad
	I'LL PAY THE PRICE	THEY DON'T WANT US TOGETHER	MARK V 4796	400.00	northern
	PRETTY AS A PICTURE	GO AWAY BABY	MARK V 4026	400.00	northern
DILLARD, MOSES AND MARTHA STARR					
	CHEATING, TEASING AND MISLEADING	YOU CAN'T LAUGH IT OFF	SHOUT 248	30.00	70's
	CHEATING, TEASING AND MISLEADING	YOU CAN'T LAUGH IT OFF	AWAKE 101	60.00	70's
DINOS					
	BABY, COME ON IN	THIS IS MY STORY	VAN 3265	100.00	northern

DION, DEBRA

DON'T BUG ME BABY	I WANT TO KNOW	SUE 103	20.00	northern

DIPLOMATS

CARDS ON THE TABLE	UNCHAINED MELODY	AROCK 1000	200.00	northern
HONEST TO GOODNESS	DON'T BUG ME	MINIT 32006	25.00	northern
THERE'S STILL A TOMORROW	SO FAR AWAY	WAND 174	25.00	northern

DIRTY D

DIRTY D	YOU TOLD ME A LIE	POWER FUNK 10006	15.00	funk

DISCIPLES OF SOUL

THAT'S THE WAY LOVE GOES	TOGETHER	PHANTOM 2755	100.00	northern

DISCO DUB BAND

FOR THE LOVE OF MONEY	SAME:INSTRUMENTAL	DOWNSTAIRS 201	15.00	funk
FOR THE LOVE OF MONEY	SAME:INSTRUMENTAL	MOVERS 1	15.00	funk

DISTANTS

COME ON	ALWAYS	NORTHERN 3742	200.00	motown
COME ON	ALWAYS	WARWICK 546	100.00	motown
OPEN YOUR HEART	ALL RIGHT	WARWICK 577	100.00	motown

DISTORTIONS

GIMME SOME LOVIN'	LET'S SPEND THE NIGHT TOGETHER	CAPITOL 2223	15.00	mod

DISTRICTS

ONE LOVER (JUST WON'T DO)	LIKE CLOUDS	NILE 40	150.00	northern

DITALIANS

PHILLY DOG NEW BREED	EGYPT LAND	SAXONY 1011	30.00	mod
I GOTTA GO	EGYPT LAND	TRIP. 1926	150.00	northern

DIVINES

I GOTTA MAKE IT	LOVER'S LAND	A.O.A. 832	50.00	northern

DIXON, HOLLIS

YOU MAKE ME CRY	PAPER BOY	COMA 901	20.00	northern

DIXON, JOHNNY

WHERE ARE YOU	SAME: INSTRUMENTAL	BOSS 103	40.00	northern

DIXON, WYLIE

GOTTA HOLD ON	WHEN WILL IT END	TODDLIN TOWN 105	25.00	ballad

D'NUNZIO, SONNY

THAT'S HOW MUCH I LOVE MY BABY	CALIFORNIA'S STILL ON MY MIND	UNITAL 710	20.00	70's

DOCKERY, JAMES

MY FAITH IN YOU HAS ALL GONE	GIVING YOU THE LOVE YOU NED	SOUL CRAFT 1 red	400.00	northern
MY FAITH IN YOU HAS ALL GONE		SOUL CRAFT 1 blue	15.00	northern

DODDS, MALCOLM.

COME SEE THE SUN	I WANT TO MAKE YOU GLAD	PARAMOUNT 202	20.00	70's

DODDS, NELLA

FINDERS KEEPERS, LOSERS WEEPER	A GIRL'S LIFE	WAND 171	10.00	northern
COME BACK BABY	DREAM BOY	WAND 187	15.00	**northerB**
COME SEE ABOUT ME	YOU DON'T LOVE ME ANYMORE	WAND 167	10.00	northern
HONEY BOY	I JUST GOTTA HAVE YOU	WAND 1136	300.00	northern
P'S & Q'S	LOVE YOU BACK	WAND 178	10.00	northern

DODDS, TROY

COUNT OF LOVE	I'M SO IN LOVE WITH YOU	DAYTONA 2101	20.00	northern
THE EARTHQUAKE	THE BOSSA NOVA CHA CHA CHA	BEECHWOOD 201	25.00	northern
TRYING TO FIND MY BABY	THE EARTHQUAKE	BAYTOWN 40012	25.00	northern
TRY MY LOVE	THE REAL THING	EL CAMIRO 701	450.00	northern

DODSON, TOMMY

CO-OPERATE	YOU DON'T KNOW HOW MUCH I LOVE YOU	MAIN SOUND 501	200.00	northern
ONE DAY LOVE	MIND READER	UPTOWN 709	75.00	northern

DOGS

SOUL STEP	DON'T TRY TO HELP ME	TREASURE 1	350.00	northern

DOLLS

THE AIRPLANE SONG	A LOVER'S STAND	MALTESE 107	850.00	northern
THE REASON WHY	AND THAT REMINDS ME	LOMA 2036	20.00	northern

DOLLY AND THE FASHIONS

ABSENCE MADE MY HEART GROW FON	WAITING FOR MY MAN	TRI DISC 111	30.00	northern
JUST ANOTHER FOOL	THE RIGHT ONE	IVANHOE 5019	15.00	northern

DOMINO, FATS

IT KEEPS RAININ'	I JUST CRY	IMPERIAL 5753	10.00	northern
IF YOU DON'T KNOW WHAT LOVE IS	SOMETHING YOU GOT BABY	ABC 10545	25.00	northern

DOMINO, RENALDO

DON'T GO AWAY	JUST SAY THE WORD	BLUE ROCK 4061	15.00	northern
YOU DON'T LOVE ME NO MORE	I'M HIP TO YOUR GAME	SMASH 2160	15.00	northern

DOMINO, VERBLE

I'VE BEEN FOOLED BEFORE	FADED MEMORY	TOI 920	40.00	northern

DON AND JUAN

ALL THAT'S MISSING IS YOU	WHAT'S YOUR NAME	TERRIFIC 5002	100.00	northern
THE HEARTBREAKING TRUTH	THANK GOODNESS	MALA 509	300.00	northern
WHAT I REALLY MEANT TO SAY	MAGIC WAND	BIG TOP 3121	25.00	northern

DON AND RON

I'M SO SO SORRY	GIRL I HOPE TO FIND	WHITE CLIFFS 214	400.00	northern

DON AND THE DOVES

TOGETHER	I NEED YOU	DYNAMICS 107	150.00	northern

DONAYS
DEVIL IN HIS HEART	BAD BOY	BRENT 7033	75.00	northern

DONNER, RAL
MR. MISERY	WAIT A MINUTE NOW (Green Vinyl)	STARFIRE 121	40.00	northern
MR. MISERY	WAIT A MINUTE NOW (Yellow Vinyl)	STARFIRE 121	30.00	northern
MR. MISERY	WAIT A MINUTE NOW (White Vinyl)	STARFIRE 121	20.00	northern
MR. MISERY	WAIT A MINUTE NOW (Black Vinyl)	STARFIRE 121	10.00	**northerB**
MR. MISERY	WAIT A MINUTE NOW	TWILIGHT 1006 DJ only	150.00	northern

DONTELLS
I CAN'T WAIT	GIMME SOME	AMBASSADOR 3346	40.00	northern
IN YOUR HEART (YOU KNOW I'M Right)	NOTHING BUT NOTHING	VEE JAY 666	15.00	northern

DOONE, LORNA
DANGEROUS TOWN	WHO KNOWS IT	RCA 8532	30.00	northern

DORANDO
DIDN'T I	LISTEN TO MY SONG	MUSIC CITY 894	30.00	group

DORIS AND KELLEY
GROOVE ME WITH YOUR LOVIN'	YOU DON'T HAVE TO WORRY	BRUNSWICK 55327	20.00	northern

DOSWELL, KITTIE
JUST A FACE IN THE CROWD	THIS COULD ONLY HAPPEN TO ME	HES 2468	150.00	northern

DOT AND THE VELVELETTES
SEARCHING FOR MY MAN	FOR AS LONG AS U WANT ME	TEEK 4828	20.00	motown

DOTSON, JIMMY
GRAPE VINE'S TALKING	SHE TOLD ME SO	NICETOWN 5027	40.00	ballad
HEARTBREAK AVENUE	BABY TURN YOUR HEAD	MERCURY 72801	70.00	ballad
I USED TO BE A LOSER	I WANNA BE GOOD	VOLT 4013	40.00	northern

DOTTIE AND RAY
LA LA LOVER	I LOVE YOU BABY	LE SAGE 701	15.00	northern

DOUGLAS, CARL
LEAN ON ME	MARBLE AND IRON	BUDDAH 212	25.00	northern
SOMETHING FOR NOTHING	LET THE BIRDS SING	OKEH 7287	25.00	northern
CRAZY FEELING	KEEP IT TO MYSELF	OKEH 7268	25.00	northern

DOUGLAS, JOE
CRAZY THINGS	SOMETHING TO BRAG ABOUT	PLAYHOUSE 1000	85.00	northern

DOUGLAS, RON
NEVER YOU MIND	FIRST TIME AROUND	SMASH 2206	30.00	northern
LOVE IS HERE	I'M IN LOVE	EXCELLO 2319	50.00	group

DOVALE, DEBBIE
HEY LOVER	THIS WORLD WE LOVE IN	ROULETTE 4521	30.00	northern
HEY LOVER	THIS WORLD WE LOVE IN	RICKY	50.00	northern

DOVALLE, JOAN
LET ME GO	NO BETTER FOR YOU	SPORT 102	700.00	northern

DOVE, GLENDA
IT'S IMPOSSIBLE	IT'S GOTTA BE SOMETHING ELSE	LUCKY DOVE 1001	30.00	northern

DOVE, RONNIE
CHAINS OF LOVE	IF I LIVE TO BE A HUNDRED	DIAMOND 271	15.00	northern

DOWDELI, PEARL
IT'S ALL OVER	GOOD THINGS	SAADIA 916	200.00	northern

DOWNBEATS
TOGETHER	SAY THE WORD	DAWN 4531	100.00	funk
DARLING BABY	PUT YOURSELF IN MY PLACE	V.I.P. 25029 stock	200.00	motown
PUT YOURSELF IN MY PLACE	DARLING BABY	V.I.P. 25029 DJ	150.00	motown
REQUEST OF A FOOL	YOUR BABY'S BACK	TAMLA 54056	75.00	motown
YOUR BABY'S BACK	REQUEST OF A FOOL	TAMLA 54026 NI	300.00	motown
I CAN'T HEAR YOU NO MORE	SOUL FOOD	DOWNBEATS 3069	30.00	northern

DOZIER, GENE AND THE BROTHERHOOD
A HUNK OF FUNK	ONE FOR BESS	MINIT 32026	10.00	mod
MUSTANG SALLY	I WANNA TESTIFY	MINIT 32031	10.00	mod
FUNKY BROADWAY	SOUL STROLL	MINIT 32041	10.00	mod

DOZIER, GENE AND THE UNITED FRONT
THE BEST GIRL I EVER HAD	GIVE THE WOMEN WHAT THEY WANT	MERCURY 73603	20.00	70's

DOZIER, LAMONT
BREAKING OUT ALL OVER	FISH AIN'T BITING	ABC 11430	8.00	70's
WE DON'T WANT NOBODY TO COME BACK	TRYING TO HOLD ON TO MY WOMAN	ABC 11407	8.00	70's
DEAREST ONE	FORTUNE TELLER TELL ME	MELODY 102	100.00	motown

DRAIN, CHARLES
I'M GONNA STAY	WHAT GOOD IS A LOVE SONG	RCA 10594	10.00	70's
IS THIS REALLY LOVE	SAME:	RCA 10186	10.00	70's
LIFETIME GUARANTEE OF LOVE	JUST AS LONG	RCA 10521	10.00	70's
HERE I AM	SHE'S GONE	CHECKER 1175	20.00	northern
STOP AND THINK ABOUT IT BABY	SO GLAD	TOP TRACK 1	200.00	northern

DRAKE, KENT
BOSS THING TOGETHER	WITHOUT A LADY'S HAND	WAND 11239	30.00	70's

DRAKE, MIGHTY JOE
TRY, TRY, TRY	GET OUT OF MY LIFE WOMAN	KAPP 2014	30.00	northern

DRAKE, TONY
LET'S PLAY HOUSE	SHE'S GONE	MUSICOR 1357	15.00	ballad
SUDDENLY	IT HURTS ME MORE	BRUNSWICK 55437	85.00	northern

Artist / A-side	B-side	Label	Price	Genre
DRAKE AND THE EN-SOLIDS				
PLEASE LEAVE ME	I'LL ALWAYS BE THERE	ALTEEN 8652	75.00	northern
DRAMATICS				
IF YOU HAVEN'T GOT LOVE	ALL BECAUSE OF YOU	SPORT 101	50.00	northern
INKY DINKY WANG DANG DO	BABY I NEED YOU	WINGATE 22	10.00	northern
TOY SOLDIER	HELLO SUMMER	CRACKERJACK 4015	200.00	northern
DRAPERS				
(I KNOW)YOR LOVE HAS GONE AWAY	YOU GOT TO LOOK UP	GEE 1081	75.00	northern
DREAM MERCHANTS				
STOP (YOU'RE BREAKING MY HEART	GIVE UP (ALL I'VE GOT)	RENEE 5002	20.00	northern
DREAMLOVERS				
BLESS YOUR SOUL	THE BAD TIMES MAKE THE GOOD TIMES	MERCURY 72595	15.00	northern
DREW, PATTI				
HE'S THE ONE	WHICH ONE SHOULD I CHOOSE	CAPITOL 4789	15.00	northern
STOP AND LISTEN	MY LOVER'S PRAYER	CAPITOL 5969	15.00	northern
DREW-VELS				
IT'S MY TIME	EVERYBODY KNOWS	CAPITOL 5145	15.00	northern
I'VE KNOWN	CREEPIN'	CAPITOL 5244	15.00	northern
TELL HIM	JUST BECAUSE	CAPITOL 5055	10.00	northern
DRIFTERS				
THE OUTSIDE WORLD	FOLLOW ME	ATLANTIC 2292	10.00	northern
YOU GOT TO PAY YOR DUES	BLACK SILK	ATLANTIC 2746	30.00	northern
DRIGGERS, HAL				
BROWN BAGGIN'	BLACK PEPPER	CHEECO 663	15.00	mod
DRIPPERS				
HONEY BUNCH	HONEY BUNCH PT.2	MOONSHOT 6701	20.00	mod
DRUMMONETTES				
FUNKY SOUL	DROP ME A LINE	BRADLEY 1410	15.00	funk
DRY WELL				
GYPSY	TRY A LITTLE TENDERNESS	LAUREN 2515	40.00	northern
DUBLIN, SONNY				
PIGIMY GRIND Pt.2	PIGIMY GRIND Pt.1	CUB 9152 DJ	15.00	mod
DUCKETT, GEARLENE				
PLEASE DON'T MAKE ME CRY	MY HEART YEARNS	CARRIE 38	75.00	northern
DUCKY AND THE GLOWLIGHTERS				
OVER & OVER	WATCH YOUR GIRL	UPTOWN 2300	1000.00	northern
DU-ETTES				
EVERY BEAT OF MY HEART	SUGAR DADDY	MARVLUS 6003	15.00	northern
PLEASE FORGIVE ME	LONELY DAYS	ONEDERFUL 4827	10.00	northern
DUFF, BRENDA				
LOVE AIN'T NEVER HURT NOBODY	LEFT IN LOVE ALONE	BLUE ROCK 4083	30.00	northern
DUHON, JAMES (KELLY)				
GRAVE YARD CREEP	COLOR ME SOUL	JETSTREAM 810	15.00	funk
IN SCHOOL	HEART BREAKER (CHILD MAKER)	JUDE 741	20.00	70's
IN SCHOOL	HEART BREAKER (CHILD MAKER)	MAINSTREAM 5564	15.00	70's
PUSHER MAN	DRIFTER	JUDE 753	30.00	funk
DUKAYS				
EVERY STEP	COMBINATION	VEE JAY 491	15.00	northern
I FEEL GOOD ALL OVER	I NEVER KNEW	VEE JAY 460	15.00	northern
I'M GONNA LOVE YOU SO	PLEASE HELP	VEE JAY 442	15.00	northern
DUKE AND LEONARD				
JUST DO THE BEST YOU CAN	YOU'VE LOST YOUR SOUL	STOMP TOWN 101	100.00	northern
DUKE OF EARL (also see GENE CHANDLER)				
WALK ON WITH THE DUKE	LONDON TOWN	VEE JAY 2387	15.00	northern
YOU LEFT ME	I'LL FOLLOW YOU	VEE JAY 455	20.00	northern
DUKE, BOBBY				
SMOTHERING LOVE	I GOTTA BE WITH YOU	VERVE 10487	15.00	northern
DUKES, BOBBY				
JUST TO BE WITH YOU	SAME:INSTRUMENTAL	SARU 1225	30.00	northern
JUST TO BE WITH YOU	SAME:INSTRUMENTAL	CALLA 184	15.00	northern
DUMAS, GRACIE				
SONG OF A WOMAN	SEEKING	J GEMS 1046	200.00	northern
DUNCAN BROTHERS				
MAKE ME WHAT YOU WANT ME TO BE	I GOT MY NEEDS	CAPITOL 5711	20.00	northern
SATISFACTION GUARENTEED	THINGS GO BETTER WITH LOVE	CAPITOL 5620	15.00	northern
DUNN, JOYCE				
TURN AWAY FROM DARKNESS	THE PUSH I NEED	BLUE ROCK 4081	15.00	ballad
A NEW CHANGE OF ADDRESS	SAME:	MERCURY 73003	30.00	funk
DUPONTS				
CROSS MY HEART	WHY DON'T YOU FALL IN LOVE WITH ME	ATCO 6918	20.00	70's
DUPREE, LEONTINE				
COLOR ME FOOLISH	STANDING ON HIS WORD	NATION 7861	50.00	northern
DUPREE, LILLIAN				
SHIELD AROUND MY HEART	HIDE & SEEK	D-TOWN 1051	75.00	northern
DUPREES				
DELICIOUS	THE SKY'S THE LIMIT	RCA 10407	10.00	70's

Artist / Title	B-side	Label	Price	Genre
DURAIN, JOHNNY				
I'LL SHOW YOU	SOMEDAY I'LL GET OVER YOU	BIG CITY 301	25.00	northern
PEOPLE WILL TALK	ABOUT TOLOSE MY MIND	BIG CITY 300 DJ	100.00	northern
DURALCHA				
GHET-TO FUNK		MICROTRONICS NO#	50.00	funk
DURANTE, PAULA				
IF HE WERE MINE	WITHOUT MY GUY	GJM 503	30.00	northern
YOUR NOT MY KIND	YOU'RE MY BABY	GJM 501	20.00	**northerB**
DURETTES				
SWEET SWEET LOVE	TIDAL WAVE	SVR 1006	100.00	northern
SWEET SWEET LOVE	I LOVE YOU MY LOVE (cr. Perfections)	SVR 1006	75.00	northern
DU-SHELLS				
YOUR MY MAIN MAN	WHERE ARE YOU	PAREE NO.#	800.00	northern
DUSHON, JEAN				
IT WON'T STOP HURTING ME	LOOK THE OTHER WAY	LENOX 5568	40.00	northern
SECOND CLASS LOVER		OKEH	75.00	northern
DUSHONS				
YOU BETTER THINK IT OVER	TAKE THESE CHAINS (FROM MY HEART)	GOLDEN GATE 70	50.00	northern
YOU BETTER THINK IT OVER	TAKE THESE CHAINS (FROM MY HEART)	DOWN TO EARTH 70	30.00	northern
DYKE AND THE BLAZERS				
FUNKY BROADWAY	FUNKY BROADWAY PT.2	ARTCO 101	100.00	funk
DYNAMIC ADAM				
FORGIVE ME	SHE'S GONE	ANLA 113	40.00	funk
DYNAMIC CONCEPTS				
FUNKY CHICKEN	NOW THAT YOU LEFT ME	DYNAMIC SOUNDS 802	200.00	funk
DYNAMIC HEARTBEATS				
IT AIN'T NO SECRET	DANGER	P.S. 1780	20.00	northern
DYNAMIC SUPERIORS				
ONE-NIGHTER	DECEPTION	MOTOWN 1365	15.00	70's
DYNAMIC THREE				
YOU SAID YEAH	I HAVE TRIED	DEL VAL 1004	1,250.00	northern
DYNAMIC TINTS				
PACKAGE OF LOVE	PACKAGE OF LOVE Pt.2	TWINIGHT 123	20.00	70's
DYNAMICS				
WOMAN	BECAUSE I LOVE YO	BRAINSTORM 122	30.00	northern
BINGO	SOMEWHERE	WINGATE 18	15.00	motown
I NEED YOUR LOVE	LOVE ME	RCA 9084	200.00	northern
I WANNA KNOW	AND THAT'S A NATURAL FACT	BIG TOP 516 DJ	100.00	northern
YES, I LOVE YOU BABY	SOUL SLOOPY	TOP TEN 100	150.00	northern
WHEN EVER I'M WITHOUT YOU	LOVE TO A GUY	TOP TEN 9409	100.00	northern
YOU MAKE ME FEEL GOOD	LIGHTS OUT	RCA 9278	40.00	northern
YOU MAKE ME FEEL GOOD	LIGHTS OUT	RCA 9278 PS	40.00	northern
DYNAMITE, JOHNNY				
THE NIGHT THE ANGELS CRIED	SAME:	MINARET 141 DJ	75.00	**northerB**
THE NIGHT THE ANGELS CRIED	EVERYBODY'S CLOWN	MINARET 141	150.00	northern
DYNAMITES				
I KNOW SHE'S MINE	LET'S TRY	PAY 209	10.00	group
DON'T LEAVE ME THIS WAY	WEDDINGS BELLS ARE RINGIN'	DOLORES 109	15.00	northern
DYNASONICS				
YOU GOT IT	SOUL BUG	DYNAMICS 1014	25.00	northern
DYNATONES				
THE FIFE PIPER	AND I ALWAYS WILL	HBR 494	10.00	northern
THE FIFE PIPER	AND I ALWAYS WILL	ST. CLAIR 117	20.00	northern
DYNELS				
C'MON LITTLE DARLIN'	JUST A FACE IN THE CROWD	NATURAL 7001	25.00	northern
DYNELLS				
LET ME PROVE THAT I LOVE YOU	SUMMERTIME GROOVE	BLUEBERRY 1002	100.00	northern
CALL ON ME	SAME: INSTRUMENTAL	VENT	200.00	northern
LET ME PROVE THAT I LOVE YOU	CALL ON ME (VOCAL)	ATCO 6638	150.00	northern
DYNETTES				
NEW GUY	WITNESS TO A HEARTBREAK	CONSTELLATION 150	15.00	northern
DYSON, RONNIE				
LADY IN RED	CUP (RUNNETH OVER)	COLUMBIA 10211	15.00	70's
WE CAN MAKE IT LASD FOREVER	JUST A LITTLE LOVE FROM ME	COLUMBIA 46021	8.00	70's

E

Artist / Title	B-side	Label	Price	Category
E.J. AND THE ECHOES				
PUT A SMILE ON YOUR FACE	PEOPLE SAY	DIAMOND JIM 8787	15.00	northern
TREAT ME RIGHT	IF YOU JUST LOVE ME	DIAMOND JIM 8789	30.00	northern
YOU'RE GONNA HURT	I HAD A HARD TIME	DIAMOND JIM 3	300.00	northern
E.K.G.				
GIVE ME LOVE	FOOLISH THING	ROADRUNNERS	40.00	70's
31004				
EADY, ERNESTINE				
LET'S TALK IT OVER	MOONLIGHT IN VERMONT	PHIL LA SOUL 302	2,000.00	northern
THE CHANGE	THAT'S THE WAY IT GOES	JUNIOR 1007	100.00	northern
THE CHANGE	THAT'S THE WAY IT GOES	SCEPTER 12102	100.00	northern
EALY, DELORES AND THE KENYATTES				
IT'S ABOUT TIME I MADE A CHANGE		VELVET 101	50.00	funk
THE HONEYDRIPPER		DUPLEX	150.00	funk
TWO SIDES TO EVERY COIN	I'VE BEEN LOOKING	VELVET 102	75.00	northern
COME INTO MY BEDRROM	BIG SUURPRISE	DUPLEX 1301	20.00	funk
EARL, ROBERT				
SAY YOU'LL BE MINE	LOVE WILL FIND A WAY	CAROL 103	30.00	**northerB**
EARLES INC:				
LET'S TRY IT AGAIN	WHAT WOULD YOUR DADDY SAY	TEE-TI 802	25.00	70's
DOES YOUR MOTHER KNOW	CLOSE TO YOU	ZUDAN 5018	10.00	group
EVERYBODY'S GOT SOMEBODY	SOMEDAY BABY	TEE TI 11264	300.00	northern
I LOVE YOU TOO	TILLIE	TEE TI 15628	40.00	northern
JUST AN ILLUSION	AFRO-WORK	ZUDAN 5017	20.00	northern
EARLS				
MY LONELY LONELY ROOM	IT'S BEEN A LONG TIME COMING	ABC 11109	20.00	group
EASON GAIL				
LOVE'S GONNA FIND YOU	AH MY SISTER	A&M 1751	15.00	70's
EAST COAST CONNECTION				
SUMMER IN THE PARKS	SUMMER IN THE PARKS (PT.2)	NEW DIRECTIONS 7401	10.00	northern
EASTON, BILLY				
I WAS A FOOL	WHY CAN'T THIS TIME	DISPO 700	30.00	northern
EATON, BOBBY				
FEVER, FEVER, FEVER	WE GONNA DO OUT THING	GALAXY 767	30.00	northern
EBONEY ESSENCE				
LET ME IN	UNSATISFIED MAN	GOODIE TRAIN 61	50.00	70's
EBONY JAM				
RIDE ON	SAME: INSTRUMENTAL	AMOS 122	10.00	northern
EBONY RHYTHM BAND				
SOUL HEART TRANSPLANT	DRUGS AIN'T COOL	LAMP NO#	300.00	funk
EBONYS				
I'M SO GLAD I'M ME	DO YOU LIKE THE WAY I LOVE	PIR 3514	15.00	70's
LIFE IN THE COUNTRY	HOOKED UP AND GET DOWN	PIR 3548	8.00	group
CAN'T GET ENOUGH	SAME:	SOUL CLOCK 108	15.00	northern
ECHOES				
MILLION DOLLAR BILL	MY BABY'S GOT SOUL	PULSE 2077	50.00	northern
ECKSTINE, BILLY				
I WONDER WHY (NOBODY LOVES ME)	I'VE BEEN BLESSED	MOTOWN 1105	100.00	northern
EDDIE AND ERNIE				
I'M GOIN' FOR MYSELF	THE CAT	EASTERN 606	10.00	ballad
DOGGONE IT	FALLING TEARS	COLUMBIA 44276	15.00	northern
I CAN'T DO IT (JUST CAN'T LEABVE YOU)	LOST FRIENDS	EASTERN 609	15.00	northern
OUTCAST	I'M GONNA ALWAYS LOVE YOU	EASTERN 608	10.00	northern
WE TRY HARDER	I BELIEVE SHE WILL	CHESS 1984	15.00	northern
WE TRY HARDER	I BELIEVE SHE WILL	SHAZAM 1004	100.00	northern
WE TRY HARDER	I BELIEVE SHE WILL	NIGHTINGALE	75.00	northern
EDEE				
MAKE IT LAST	WHEN HE CALLS ME	ICA 22	20.00	70's
EDMUND JR., LADA				
THE LARUE	SOUL A GO GO	DECCA 32007	200.00	northern
EDWARD, LEE AND THE CONTINENTALS				
(ON THE) REBOUND	(I TRIED 2DO) THE BEST I COULD	LANTIC GOLD 102	15.00	northern
EDWARDS, CHUCK				
BULLFIGHT # 2	PICK IT UP BABY	RENE. 20013	50.00	funk
DOWNTOWN SOULVILLE	I NEED YOU	PUNCH 11001	15.00	northern
EDWARDS, DEE				
(I CAN) DEAL WITH THAT	POSSESS ME	DE TO 2285	100.00	70's
ALL WE NEED IS A MIRACLE	NO LOVE, NO WORLD	RCA 1030	15.00	70's
LOVING YOU IS ALL I WANT TO DO	NO LOVE NO WORLD	COTILLION 45000	10.00	70's

TOO CARELESS WITH MY LOVE	HE TOLD ME LIES	D-TOWN 1024	25.00	northern
HIS MAJESTY MY LOVE	TIRED OF STAYING HOME	D-TOWN 1048	25.00	northern
ALL THE WAY HOME	LOVE, LOVE, LOVE	D-TOWN 1063	40.00	**northerB**
WHY CAN'T THERE BE LOVE	SAY IT AGAIN WITH FEELING	BUMP SHOP 128	20.00	northern
WHY CAN'T THERE BE LOVE	HURT A LITTLE EVERYDAY	GM 716	20.00	northern
YOU SAY YOU LOVE ME	TIRED OF STAYING HOME	TUBA 1706	20.00	northern

EDWARD, DENNIS

JOHNNIE ON THE	I DIDN'T HAVE TO (BUT I DID)	INTERNATIONAL SOULSVILLE 100 1000.00		northern B

EDWARDS, GLORIA

(NEED NOBODY TO HELP ME) KEEP	ANYTHING YOU WANT	KING 6400	20.00	70's
REAL LOVE	ENOUGH OF A WOMAN	DELUXE 138	20.00	northern
REAL LOVE	BLUES PART 2	PACEMAKER 802	40.00	northern

EDWARDS, JACKIE

COME BACK GIRL	TELL HIM YOU LIED	VEEP 1266	10.00	northern

EDWARDS, JOHN

THE LOOK ON YOUR FACE	IT'S THE LITTLE THINGS THAT CO	BELL 45205	300.00	northern

EDWARDS, JUNE

HEAVEN HELP ME	MY MAN (MY SWEET MAN)	SOUTH CAMP 7001	30.00	northern

EDWARDS, LITTLE JIMMY

SLAPPIN' SOME SOUL ON ME		KEY-LOC NO#.	100.00	funk

EDWARDS, LOU

TALKIN' 'BOUT POOR FOLKS	I GOT TO BE ME	COLUMBIA 45611	30.00	northern

EDWARDS, MILL

DON'T FORGET ABOUT ME	I FOUND MYSELF	CUTLASS 8143	15.00	70's

EDWARDS, SHIRLEY

DREAM MY HEART	IT'S YOUR LOVE	SHRINE 110	500.00	northern

EDWARDS, TYRONE

CAN'T GET ENOUGH OF YOU	YOU TOOK ME FROM A WSORLD OUTS	INVICTUS 1269	10.00	70's

8TH. AVE. EXPRESS

FUNKY HOT PANTS		BEAUTY NO#	100.00	funk

8TH. AVENUE BAND

THE WHOLE THING	JENNIFER	COLUMBIA 45593	20.00	northern

EL COROLS

AIN'T NO BRAG	YOU GOTTA BE AN ANGEL	ROUSER 2954	200.00	northern
CHICK CHICK	YOU GOTTA BE AN ANGEL	ROUSER 2954	20.00	northern

E'LAN

NO LIMIT	NO LIMIT (EXTENDED MIX)	ATL. 1003	20.00	70's

ELBERT, DONNIE

I GOT TO GET MYSELF TOGETHER	CAN'T GET OVER LOSING YOU	RED BULLET 101	10.00	northern
DO WHAT'CHA WANNA	LILY LOU	GATEWAY 748	10.00	northern
LITTLE PIECE OF LEATHER	DO WHAT'CHA WANNA	GATEWAY 757	10.00	northern
YOUR RED WAGON (YOU CAN PUSH IT)	NEVER AGAIN	GATEWAY 761	10.00	northern

ELDEES

DON'T BE AFRAID TO LOVE	YOU BROKE MY HAPPY HEART	DYNAMICS 1013	30.00	northern

ELDORADOS

YOU MAKE MY HEART SING	IN OVER MY HEAD	TORRID 100	25.00	northern
LOOKING IN FROM THE OUTSIDE	SINCE YOU CAME INTO MY LIFE	PAULA 3547	20.00	group

ELECTRIC FUNK

THE SHOVEL	BEWARE OF THE SHOVEL	STRAN 111	20.00	funk

ELECTRIC INDIAN

LAND OF A 1000 DANCES	GERONIMO	UA 50613 DJ	10.00	**northerB**
STORM WARNING	RAIN DANCE	UA 50647	10.00	**northerB**

ELECTRIFYING CASHMERES

WHAT DOES IT TAKE	OOH I LOVE YOU	SS7 1500	30.00	70's

ELECTRODES

GO AWAY	I LOVE TOO	FRANTIC 200	75.00	northern

ELECTRONS

IT AIN'T NO BIG THING	IN THE MIDNIGHT HOUR	DATE 1575	10.00	northern
IT AIN'T NO BIG THING	IN THE MIDNIGHT HOUR	SHOCK 289	30.00	northern

ELEGANTS

HYPNOTIZED	GHETTO SLIDE	REAL MUSIC 6003	20.00	group

ELEMENTS

JUST TO BE WITH YOU	SON IN LAW	SARU 1224	25.00	northern

ELGINS (also see THE DOWNBEATS)

DARLING BABY	PUT YOURSELF IN MY PLACE	V.I.P. 25029	15.00	motown
HEAVEN MUST HAVE SENT YOU	STAY IN MY LONELY ARMS	V.I.P. 25037	10.00	motown
IT'S BEEN A LONG, LONG TIME	I UNDERSTAND MY MAN	V.I.P. 25043	10.00	motown
YOU FOUND YOURSELF ANOTHER FOO	STREET SCENE	VALIANT 712	50.00	northern

ELIAS, JEAN

HOW LONG CAN I GO ON FOOLING M	YOU MADE ME A ANYBODY'S WOMAN	BACK BEAT 623	20.00	northern
ELLEN AND ThE SHANDELLSGYPSY		LA SALLE 25	30.00	northern

ELLEDGE, JIMMY

YOU CAN'T STOP A MAN IN LOVE	CAN'T TAKE THE LEAVIN'	SONG BIRD 79	20.00	70's

ELLIE, JIMMY PREACHER

I'M GONNA DO IT MYSELF	GO HEAD ON	JEWELL 770	70.00	northern

ELLING, MELVIN
LONELY EYES	LOVE'S ROAD	STRETCH 44	150.00	northern

ELLINGTONS
DESTINED TO BECOME A LOVER	THE AGONY AND THE ECSTASY	CASTLE 102	50.00	**northerB**

ELLIOT, LINDA
FELL IN LOVE WITH YOU BABY	A LITTLE GIRL GREW UP LAST NIG	JOSIE 958	40.00	northern

ELLIOTT, LU
I LOVE THE GROUND YOU WALK ON	HAVE YOU TRIED TO FORGET	ABC 10897	20.00	northern

ELLIOTT, SHAWN
THE JOKER	LITTLE BIRD	ROULETTE 4634	40.00	northern

ELLIS, JIMMY
HAPPY TO BE	LOOKING THROUGH THE EYES OF LOVE	CENTURY CITY 511	200.00	northern

ELLIS, JONAH
I GET HOT	POPCORN CELLAR	VIKING 1007	30.00	funk

ELLIS, LARRY AND THE BLACK HAMMER
FUNKY THING		AL KING NO.#	200.00	funk

ELLIS, SHIRLEY
THE NITTY GRITTY	GIVE ME A LIST	CONGRESS 202	10.00	funk
SOUL TIME	WAITIN'	COLUMBIA 44021	10.00	northern

ELLISON, LORRAINE
DON'T LET IT GO TO YOUR HEAD	I DIG YOU BABY	MERCURY 72472	15.00	northern

ELLISON, WILLIE JOHN
YOU'VE GOT TO HAVE RHYTHM	GIVING UP ON LOVE	PHIL LA SOUL 337	15.00	funk

ELLUSIONS
YOU DIDN'T HAVE TO LEAVE	YOU WOULDN'T UNDERSTAND	LAMON 2003	200.00	**northerB**

EMANON'S ORCHESTRA
BIRD WALKIN 72869	LOOK IN THE WANT ADS	ALL BROTHERS	100.00	**northerB**

EMBERS
IN MY LONELY ROOM	GOOD GOOD LOVIN'	JCP 1008	20.00	northern
A FOOL IN LOVE	GOOD ALL OVER	JCP 1028	30.00	northern
FIRST TIME	I WANA BE	JCP 1034	70.00	northern
AIN'T NO BIG THING	IT AIN'T NECESSARY	JCP 1054	80.00	northern
JUST CRAZY BOUT YOU BABY	WE'VE COME A LONG WAY TOGETHER	EEE 69	100.00	**northerB**
JUST CRAZY BOUT YOU BABY	FAR AWAY PLACES	BMR 2 (bootleg)	10.00	northern
WATCH OUT GIRL	FAR AWAY PLACES	MGM 14167	100.00	northern
WHERE DIOD I GO WRONG	YOU GOT WHAT YOU GOT	ATLANTIC 2627	40.00	northern
AIN'T NO BIG THING	IT AIN'T NECESSARY	BELL 664	20.00	northern

EMBERS, PAT
THAT BOY (SURE GOT YOUR NUMBER	YOU'LL NEVER LEAVE HER	ASCOT 2158	30.00	northern

EMBRACEABLES
LET MY BABY GO	HERE I GO	SIDRA 9010	100.00	northern

EMBRACERS
STOP AND LRET YOURSELF GO	MR. SUNRISE	LUCKY 1000	200.00	northern

EMNSLEY, ART AND THE ECHOES
OPEN THE DOOR TO YOUR HEART	THIS IS THE BEST WAY	SHIPTOWN 202037	50.00	northern

EMORY AND THE DYNAMICS
PRETTY LITTLE SCHOOL GIRL	A LOVE THAT'S REAL	PEACHTREE 120	100.00	group
LET'S TAKE A LOOK AT OUR LIFE	IT SURE WOULD BE NICE	PEACHTREE 107	700.00	northern

EMOTIONS
STEALING LOVE	WHEN TOMORROW COMES	VOLT 4031	10.00	70's
SOMEBODY NEW	BUSHFIRE	TWIN STACKS 126	15.00	northern
DO THIS FOR ME	LOVE OF A GIRL	VARDAN 201	20.00	northern
I CAN'T STAND NO MORE HEARTACHES	YOU BETTER GET PUSHED TO IT	BRAINSTORM 125	8.00	northern

EMPIRE, FREDDIE
LET ME GIVE MY LOVE TO YOU	SAME: INSTRUMENTAL	COCONUT. 1	40.00	70's

EMPIRES
YOU'RE ON TOP GIRL	SLIDE ON BY	CANDI 1033	1300.00	northern
LOVE YOU SO BAD	COME HOME GIRL	CANDI 1026	50.00	group
PUSH PUSH PT.1	PUSH PUSH PT.2	CAROL 62469	15.00	group

EMULATIONS
MOVE A LITTLE SLOWER GIRL	STORY OF MY LIFE	EMULATE 7121	100.00	northern

ENCHANTED FIVE
HAVE YOU EVER	TRY A LITTLE LOVE	CVS 1001	15.00	northern

ENCHANTERS
I PAID FOR THE PARTY	I WANT TO BE LOVED	LOMA 2012	15.00	northern
THERE'S A LOOK ABOUT YOU	ON A LITTLE ISLAND	TEE PEE 4566	200.00	northern
WE GOT LOVE	I'VE LOST ALL COMMUNICATIONS	LOMA 2054	20.00	northern
YOU WERE MEANT TO BE MY BABY	GOD BLESS THE GIRL & ME	LOMA 2035	15.00	northern

ENCHANTING ENCHANTERS
BOSS ACTION	NO ONE IN THIS WORLD	BENMOKEITH 685	150.00	funk

ENCHANTMENT.
CALL ON ME	SAME: SAME: INSTRUMENTAL.	POLYDOR 14287	100.00	70's
HOLD ON	COME ON AND RIDE	DESERT MOON 6403	10.00	70's

ENCHANTMENTS
I'M IN LOVE WITH YOUR DAUGHTER	I'M IN LOVE WITH YOUR DAUGHTER	FARO 620 orangel	75.00	northern
I'M IN LOVE WITH YOUR DAUGHTER	SAME: PT. 2	FARO 620	60.00	northern

59

END PRODUCT

TURN YOU MY WAY	LOVE NEEDS LOVE	PARAMOUNT 84	25.00	70's

ENDEAVORS

SEXY WOMAN	WHO! SHAFT WHERE?	GAMBIT 6	15.00	group
I CAN'T HELP CRYING	BEWARE OF YOUR FRIENDS	EMPIRESTATE	200.00	northern
18798				

ENFORCERS

DOIN' WHAT I WANNA		M AND M	50.00	funk

ENGLISH, BARBARA (JEAN)

(YOU GOT ME) SITTIN' IN THE CORNER	STANDING ON TIP TOE	AURORA 155	150.00	**northerB**
ALL THE GOOD TIMES ARE GONE	ALL BECAUSE I LOVE SOMEBODY	WB 5685	30.00	northern
I DON'T DESERVE A BOY LIKE YOU	EASY COME, EASY GO	MALA 488	25.00	northern
I WANT TO LOVE YOU	DANCING TO KEEP FROM CRYING	ZAKIA 100	10.00	70's

ENJOYABLES

PUSH A LITTLE HARDER	WE'LL MAKE A WAY	CAPITOL 5321	30.00	northern
SHAME	I'LL TAKE YOU BACK	SHRINE 118	500.00	northern

ENTERTAINERS IV

GETTING' BACK INTO CIRCULATION	MY GARDEN OF EDEN	DORE 759	30.00	northern
GETTING' BACK INTO CIRCULATION	WHEN YOUR YOUNG AND IN LOVE	DORE 759	30.00	northern
HEY LADY	CLAIRE DE LOONEY	DORE 788	15.00	group
TEMPTATION WALK	SHAKE, SHAKE, SHAKE	DORE 749	20.00	northern

ENTERTAINERS

BABY BABY	SETBACKS	BREVIT 501	30.00	northern
I WANNA BE (YOU'RE EVERYTHING)	MR. PITIFUL	JCP 1033	50.00	northern
LOVE IN MY HEART	MY PAD	SYMBOL 212	40.00	northern
TOO MUCH	I TRIED TO TELL YOU	CHESS 1951	15.00	northern

ENTERTAINS

LOVE WILL TURN IT AROUND	WHY COULDN'T I BELIEVE THEM	STEEL TOWN 92540	10.00	70's

ENTICERS

CALLING FOR YOUR LOVE	STORYTELLER	COTILLION 44125	15.00	northern

EPITOME OF SOUND

YOU DON'T LOVE ME	WHERE WERE YOU	SANDBAG 101	30.00	**northerB**

EPPS, PRESTON

AFRO MANIA	LOVE IS THE ONLY GOOD THING	JO JO 106	30.00	funk

EPSILONS

MAD AT THE WORLD	I'M SO DEVOTED	SHRINE 106	200.00	northern
MIND IN A BIND	IT'S ALL RIGHT	HEM 1003	150.00	northern

EQUADORS

YOU'RE MY DESIRE	SOMEONE TO CALL MY OWN	MIRACLE 7	300.00	motownB

ERIC AND THE VIKINGS

VIBRATIONS (MADE US FALL IN LOVE)	GET OFF THE STREETS YA'LL	SOULHAWK 10	20.00	group
I'M TRULY YOURS	WHERE DO YOU GO (BABY)	GORDY 7132	40.00	motown
TOO MUCH FOR	MAN TO TAKE TIME DON'T WAIT	GORDY 7116	40.00	motown

ERNIE AND THE TOP NOTES

DAP WALK		FORDOM NO#	100.00	funk

ERVIN SISTERS

DO IT RIGHT	CHANGING BABY	TRI-PHI 1014	30.00	motown
EVERYDAY'S LIKE A HOLIDAY	WHY I LOVE HIM	TRI-PHI 1022	25.00	motown

ESCORTS

LOVE IS LIKE A DREAM	MAKE ME OVER	KNOCKOUT 10145	8.00	70's
THE HURT	NO CITY FOLKS ALLOWED	RCA 8327	20.00	northern

ESKO AFFAIR

SALT AND PEPPER	MORNING DULLS FIRES	MERCURY 72887	20.00	northern

ESQUIRES

AND GET AWAY	EVERYBODY'S LAUGHING	BUNKY 7752	8.00	northern
GET ON UP	LISTEN TO ME	BUNKY 7750	8.00	northern
HOW COULD IT BE	I KNOW I CAN	BUNKY 7756	10.00	northern
LISTEN TO ME	REACH OUT	CAPITOL 2650	10.00	northern
MY SWEET BABY	HENRY RALPH	HOT LINE 103	30.00	northern
PART ANGEL	I DON'T KNOW	WAND 1195	10.00	northern
THE FEELING'S GONE	WHY CAN'T I STOP	BUNKY 7755	8.00	northern
DANCIN' A HOLE IN THE WORLD	THAT AIN'T NO REASON	ROCKY RIDGE 403	15.00	northern
GIRLS IN THE CITY	AIN'T GONNA GIVE IT UP	LAMARR 1001	10.00	northern
YOU SAY	STATE FAIR	BUNKY 7753	10.00	northern
YOU'VE GOT THE POWER	NO DOUBT ABOUT IT	WAND 1193	10.00	northern

ESSENCE

DON'T PRESS YOUR LUCK	THINK ABOUT LOVIN' YOU	INTERSTATE 103	15.00	northern

ESSEX IV

MY REACTION TO YOU	MY HEART JUST CAN'T TAKE IT	WIND MILL 2001	200.00	70's

ESSEX

MOONLIGHT, MUSIC AND YOU	THE EAGLE	BANG 537	15.00	**northerB**

ESTHER, QUEEN

I DON'T WANT YOU TO WANT ME		GUEST 701	100.00	northern

ETHICS

SAD, SAD, STORY	SEARCHING	VENT 1004	10.00	group
I WANT MY BABY BACK	FAREWELL	VENT 1006	20.00	northern
STANDING IN THE DARKNESS	THAT'S THE WAY WAY LOVE GOES	VENT 1008	20.00	northern
THINK ABOUT TOMORROW	LOOK AT ME NOW	VENT 1001	20.00	northern

Artist / Title		Label	Price	Genre
ETTA AND HARVEY				
IF I CAN'T HAVE YOU	MY HEART CRIES	CHESS 1760	15.00	motown
EVALINE				
A LITTLE BIT OF HURT	THE RIGHT TIME	SS7 2518	30.00	northern
EVANS, KARL				
OO WEE LET IT BE ME	HONEY ON MY SHOULDER	SKYWAY 143	30.00	**northerB**
EVANS, MILL				
I'VE GOT TO HAVE YOUR LOVE	THINGS WON'T BE THE SAME	CONSTELLATION 170	15.00	northern
WHEN I'M READY		TOU-SEA NO.#	100.00	northern
WHY, WHY, WHY	RIGHT NOW	KING 6084	20.00	northern
EVANS, NATE AND BOSS				
THE LOOK ON YOUR FACE	THIS TIME WITH FEELING	DPR 3	100.00	northern
EVANS, NATE AND MEAN GREEN				
THE LOOK ON YOUR FACE	THIS TIME WITH FEELING	DPR 3	25.00	northern
EVERETT, BETTY				
MY LOVE TO LEAN ON	HEY LUCINDA	SS7 1520	15.00	70's
I CAN'T SAY	MY BABY LOVING MY BEST FRIEND	ABC 10978	8.00	ballad
THE REAL THING	GONNA BE READY	VEE JAY 683	8.00	northern
THE SHOOP SHOOP SONG	HANDS OFF	VEE JAY 585	8.00	northern
YOU'RE NO GOOD	CHAINED TO YOUR LCVE	VEE JAY 566	8.00	northern
BETTER TOMORROW THAN TODAY	UNLUCKY GIRL	UNI 55219	15.00	northern
I GOT TO TELL SOMEBODY	WHY ARE YOU LEAVING ME	FANTASY 652	10.00	northern
WHAT IS IT	AIN'T NOTHING GONNA CHANGE MY SAME:	FANTASY 658	10.00	northern
KEEP IT UP		FANTASY 738 DJ	10.00	funk
BYE BYE BABY	YOUR LOVE IS IMPORTANT TO ME	ABC 10861	10.00	northern
GETTING MIGHTY CROWDED	CHAINED TO YOUR HEART	VEE JAY 628	10.00	northern
I CAN'T HEAR YOU	CAN I GET TO KNOW YOU	VEE JAY 599	10.00	northern
LOVE COMES TUMBLING DOWN	PEOPLE AROUND ME	ABC 10919	30.00	northern
PLEASE LOVE ME	I'LL BE THERE	ONEDERFUL 4823	15.00	northern
PRINCE OF PLAYERS	BY MY SIDE	VEE JAY 513	20.00	northern
THE SHOOP SHOOP SONG	HANDS OFF	VEE JAY 585 DJ	10.00	northern
TOO HOT TO HOLD	I DON'T HURT ANYMORE	VEE JAY 699	10.00	northern
TROUBLE OVER THE WEEKEND	THE SHOE WON'T FIT	VEE JAY 716	15.00	northern
EVERETT, FRANK				
SPELLBOUND	MY LOVE IS TRUE	BIG SMOKEY 16	20.00	70's
EXCEPTION				
YOU ALWAYS HURT ME	YOU DON'T KNOW LIKE I KNOW	CAPITOL 2120	10.00	northern
EXCEPTIONAL THREE featuring RUBY CARTER				
WHAT ABOUT ME	UNLUCKY GIRL	WAY OUT 101	50.00	northern
EXCEPTIONALS				
WHAT ABOUT ME	UNLUCKY GIRL	GRT 48	20.00	northern
EXCEPTIONS				
THE LOOK IN HER EYES GROOVES 161	BABY YOU KNOW I NEED YOU	GROOVEY	300.00	northern
EXCITERS				
BLOWING UP MY MIND	YOU DON'T KNOW WHAT YOUR MISSI	RCA 9723	25.00	northern
BLOWING UP MY MIND	YOU DON'T KNOW WHAT YOUR MISSI	RCA 1035	15.00	northern
HARD WAY TO GO	TELL HIM	UA 544	10.00	northern
NUMBER ONE	YOU GOT LOVE	SHOUT 205	15.00	northern
WEDDINGS MAKE ME CRY	YOU BETTER COME HOME	BANG 518	10.00	northern
EXCLUSIVES				
IF ONLY	PARKSIDE	HERBART 2279	200.00	northern
EXCUSES				
TRICK BAG	KEEP ON CLIMBING	VIVACE 4501	300.00	northern
EXECUTIVE FORCE				
MIDNIGHT LOVIN'	YOU'RE THE TYPE OF GIRL	NEW AGE 115	300.00	70's
LET ME SHOW YOU THE WAY	DROP THAT BODY	NEW AGE 116	30.00	group
EXECUTIVE FOUR				
I GOT A GOOD THING AND I AIN'T	YOU ARE	LU MAR 202	500.00	northern
EXITS				
ANOTHER SUNDOWN IN WATTS	I'M SO GLAD	KAPP 2028	200.00	northern
YOU GOT TO HAVE MONEY	UNDER THE STREET LAMP	GEMINI 1004	15.00	group
I DON'T WANT TO HEAR IT	SAME: INSTRUMENTAL	GEMINI 1006	75.00	northern
EXOTICS				
LIKE YOU HURT ME	BIG TIME CHARLIE	CORAL 62439	40.00	northern
EXPERIENCE UNLIMITED				
E.U. GROOVE UNLIMITED 18893	ROCK YER BUTT	EXPERIENCE	40.00	funk
EXPERTS				
MY LOVE IS REAL	SHING-A-LING & BOOG-A-LING BIG	JO-BY 500	40.00	northern
MY LOVE IS REAL	SHING-A-LING & BOOG-A-LING BIG	TAG LTD 102	25.00	northern
EXPLOSIONS				
GARDEN OF FOUR TREES		GOLD CUP 4	50.00	funk
HIP DROP	HIP DROP PT.2	GOLDEN CUP 5	75.00	funk
THE SAND	NO LIFE WITHOUT LOVE	LU-BET 101	10.00	group
EXPO				
ROAD TO SUNSHINE	ALWAYS THINKING OF YOU	EUPHONIC 8411	30.00	70's

EXPORTATIONS

I WANT YOU	FIND ANOTHER DAY	VIR-RO 1001	15.00	70's
STRANGE SENSATIONS	SAME: SAME: INSTRUMENTAL.	UA 1169	10.00	70's

EXPRESSIONS

YOU BETTER KNOW IT	OUT OF MY LIFE	FEDERAL 12533	20.00	northern

EXSAVEYONS

SOMEWHERE	I DON'T LOVE YOU NO MORE	SMOKE 600	30.00	northern
WHERE DO I GO FROM HERE	RUNNING WILD	SMOKE 609	50.00	northern

EXTENSIONS

I WANT TO KNOW	MY NEED	SUCCESS 109	20.00	northern

EXTREMES

HOW I NEED YOUR LOVE		4J	1000.00	northern

EYES OF BLUE

SUPERMARKET FULL OF CANS	DON'T ASK ME TO MEND YOUR BROK	DERAM 85003	20.00	northern
HEART TROUBLE	UP AND DOWN	DERAM 85001	20.00	northern

F

FABIANS

WOULD YOU BELIEVE	CONFIDENTIAL	BLUE ROCKET 315	50.00	northern

FABULOUS APOLLOS

SOME GOOD IN EVERYTHING BAD	SAMEINSTRUMENTAL	VALTONE 105	50.00	northern
THE ONE ALONE	DETERMINATION	VALTONE 101	150.00	northern

FABULOUS BALLADS

GOD BLESS OUR LOVE	GOD BLESS OUR LOVE PT.2	BAY VIEW 11326	50.00	group

FABULOUS CAPRICES

MY LOVE	GROOVY WORLD	CAMARO 3442	30.00	70's

FABULOUS CAPRIS

IN THE ALLEY	STAGGER WALK	DOMINO 105	50.00	funk

FANULOUS CAROUSELS

WOULD YOU LOVE ME	GOOD TIME BABY	TOWNE HOUSE 108	40.00	northern

FABULOUS COUNTS

DIRTY RED	SCRAMBLED EGGS	MOIRA 105	15.00	funk

FABULOUS DINO'S

WHERE HAVE YOU BEEN	THAT SAME OLD SONG	MUSICOR 1025	30.00	group
RETREAT	INSTANT LOVE	SABER 105	50.00	northern

FABULOUS DOWNBEATS

LIFE GOES ON	ASK ME	POISON RING 3674	20.00	northern

FABULOUS EGYPTAINS

END OF TIME		CINDY 96749	20.00	northern

FABULOUS EMOTIONS

NUMBER ONE FOOL	FUNKY CHICKEN	NICO 1000	30.00	northern

FABULOUS FIESTAS

ONE HURT DESERVES ANOTHER	KEEP IT IN, THE FAMILY	RCA 364	30.00	ballad

FABULOUS FLAMES

DO YOU REMEMBER	GET TO STEPPING	BAY-TONE 102	15.00	group

FABULOUS FOUR

IF I KNEW	EVERYBODY'S GOT TO HAVE A HEAR	SAINTMO 300	30.00	northern
I'M COMING HOME	EVERYBODY KNOWS	CHANCELLOR 1090	70.00	northern

FABULOUS HOLIDAYS

I'M SO GLAD	TOO MANY TIMES	MARATHON 257	20.00	70's

FABULOUS IMPACS

MY BABY	I'LL BE CRYING	BOMB. 3017	150.00	**northerB**

FABULOUS JADES

COME ON AND LIVE	PLANNING THIS MOMENT	RIKA 111	200.00	**northerB**

I'LL BE SO HAPPY	COLD HEAT	LENNAN 1264	300.00	northern
FABULOUS MARK III				
PSYCHO		TWINK NO#.	250.00	funk
FABULOUS MOONLIGHTERS				
COLD AND FUNKY	COLD AND FUNKY PT.2	BLUE EAGLE 22467	15.00	funk
FOR GRANTED	I'VE LOST AGAIN	BLUE EAGLE 1011	70.00	northern
FABULOUS ORIGINALS				
IT AIN'T FAIR, BUT IT'S FUN		JEWEL	200.00	funk
FABULOUS PEPS				
WHY ARE YOU BLOWING MY MIND	I CAN'T GET IT RIGHT	PREMIUM STUFF 1	15.00	motown
GYPSY WOMAN	WHY AE YOU BLOWING MY MIND	PREMIUM STUFF 7	40.00	northern
SHE'S GOING TO LEAVE YOU	THIS LOVE I HAVE FOR YOU	GE GE 503	50.00	northern
WITH THESE EYES	I'VE BEEN TRYING	WEE 3 1001	20.00	northern
WITH THESE EYES	LOVE OF MY LIFE	WHEELSVILLE 109	40.00	northern
FABULOUS PLAYBOYS				
HONKEY TONK WOMEN	TEARS, TEARS, TEARS	APOLLO. 760	75.00	northern
FABULOUS SHALIMARS				
FUNKY LINE	FUNKY LINE PT.II	RACK 701	20.00	funk
FABULOUS SOULS				
TAKE ME		FABULOUS SOUL	50.00	funk
DEEP IN THE NIGHT	SAME: INSTRUMENTAL	KGBS 3113	30.00	group
FABULOUS TEARS				
SOMEONE'S WAITING		KOKO 730	200.00	group
FABULOUS TRAITS				
LONELY MAN	LOVE IS STRANGE	TELE-PHONIC 1001	15.00	group
FALANA, FLUFFY				
MY LITTLE COTTAGE (BY THE SEA)	HANGOVER FROM LOVE	ALPHA 7	150.00	northern
FALCONS				
JUST FOR YOUR LOVE	THIS HEART OF MINE	ANNA 1110	200.00	motown
THIS HEART OF MINE	ROMANITA	KUDO 661	300.00	motown
(I'M A FOOL) I MUST LOVE YOU	LOVE LOVE LOVE	BIG WHEEL 322	25.00	northern
GOOD GOOD FEELING	LOVE YOU LIKE YOU NEVER BEEN L	BIG WHEEL 1972	75.00	northern
HAS IT HAPPENED TO YOU YET	LONELY NIGHT	LU PINE 124	150.00	northern
LOVE LOOK IN HER EYES	IN TIME FOR THE BLUES	BIG WHEEL 1971	75.00	northern
STANDING ON GUARD	I CAN'T HELP IT	BIG WHEEL 1967	10.00	northern
FALLS, ART				
I WANT YOU BABY	I'LL BE THERE	NAUTILUS 125	250.00	northern
FAME GANG				
GRITS AND GRAVY	SOUL FEUD	FAME 1458	20.00	funk
FAME, HERB				
YOU'RE MESSIN' UP MY MIND	FROM THE SHADOWS TO THE SUN	DATE 1507	15.00	northern
FAMILY OF EVE				
HAVING IT SO BAD FOR YOU	I DON'T WANT TO PAY	FULL SAIL 5172	30.00	70's
I WANT TO BE LOVED BY YOU	PLEASE BE TRUTHFUL	FULL SAIL 751	30.00	70's
FANTAISIONS				
UNNECESSARY TEARS	THAT'S WHERE THE ACTION IS	SATELLITE 2006	20.00	northern
FANTASIONS				
G.I. JOE WE LOVE YOU	WAIT	THOMAS 308	300.00	northern
FANTASTIC EPICS				
LET'S GET TOGETHER	WE DO IT ALL UP IN HERE	KELTON 121	50.00	northern
FANTASTIC FOUR				
I'M FALLING IN LOVE	I BELIEVE IN MIRACLES	EASTBOUND 620	10.00	70's
AS LONG AS I LIVE	TO SHARE YOUR LOVE	RIC TIC 130	8.00	motown
CAN'T STOP LOOKING FOR MY BABY	JUST THE LONELY	RIC TIC 121	100.00	northern
GODDESS OF LOVE	LOVE IS A MANY-SPLENDORED THIN	RIC TIC 136	8.00	motown
I LOVE YOU MADLY	SAME: INSTRUMENTAL	RIC TIC 144	10.00	motown
MAN IN LOVE	NO LOVE LIKE YOUR LOVE	RIC TIC 137	8.00	motown
PIN POINT IT DOWN	I FEEL LIKE I'M FALLING IN LOV	SOUL 35058	10.00	motown
THE WHOLE WORLD IS A STAGE	AIN'T LOVE WONDEFUL	RIC TIC 122	8.00	motown
WIN OR LOSE	I'VE GOT TO HAVE YOU	RIC TIC 139	8.00	motown
YOU GAVE ME SOMETHING	ROMEO & JULIET	RIC TIC 128	8.00	motown
AS LONG AS THE FEELING IS THER	GODDESS OF LOVE	RIC TIC 134	10.00	motown
LIVE UP TO WHAT SHE THINKS	GIRL HAVE PITY	RIC TIC 119	20.00	northern
FANTASTIC PUZZLES				
COME BACK	COME BACK PT.2	NEW MOON 8501	30.00	70's
FANTASTICS				
IN TIMES LIKE THESE	WHERE THERE'S A WILL	IMPRESSARIO 124	300.00	northern
ME AND YOU	HAVE A LITTLE FAITH	SS7 2565	30.00	northern
THAT ONE	HIGH NOTE	SS7 2548	30.00	northern
THAT ONE	HIGH NOTE	COPA 8005	50.00	northern
FARRA, MARYANN AND THE SATIN SOUL				
LIVING IN THE FOOTSTEPS OF ANOTHER MAN	STONED OUT OF MY MIND	BRUNSWICK 55533	15.00	70's
FARRAR, SUSANN				
THE BIG HURT	OUR TOWN	PHILIPS 40564	20.00	northern
FARREN, CHARLES				
YOU'VE CHANGED MY LIFE FOR THE	A GIRL LIKE YOU	HAWK 200	40.00	northern

FARROW, MIKKI

SET MY HEART AT EASE	COULD IT BE	KARATE 524	150.00	**northerB**

FASCINATIONS (also see FASINATIONS)

GIRLS ARE OUT TO GET YOU	YOU'LL BE SORRY	MAYFIELD 7714	15.00	**northerB**
I'M IN LOVE	CAN'T STAY AWAY FROM YOU	MAYFIELD 7716	10.00	northern
SAY IT ISN'T SO	I'M SO LIUCKY (SHE LOVES ME)	MAYFIELD 7711	20.00	northern
YOU GONNA BE SORRY	TEARS IN MY EYES	ABC 10443	30.00	northern

FASHIONEERS

DON'T YOU KNOW	WITHOUT YOU	BLUE ROCK 4025	100.00	northern

FASHIONS

WHEN LOVE SLIPS AWAY	I.O.U. (A LIFETIME OF LOVE)	20th. CENTURY 6703	20.00	northern
A LOVER'S STAND	ONLY THOSE IN LOVE	20th. CENTURY 6710	15.00	northern

FASINATIONS

MAMAM DIDN'T LIE	SOMEONE LIKE YOU	ABC 10387	30.00	northern
YOU'RE GONNA BE SORRY	TEARS IN MY EYES	ABC 10443 DJ	40.00	northern

FATHER AND SONS

SOUL IN THE BOWL	SOUL IN THE BOWL PT.II	MINIT 32004	10.00	northern

FAULK, LITTLE WILLIE

LOOK INTO MY HEART		M&H	600.00	northern

FAULKCON, LAWRENCE

MY GIRL AND MY FRIEND	WHY SHOULD WE HIDE OUR LOVE	CHECK MATE 1004	75.00	motown

FAVORITE, BARBARA

THEN I'LL BE TRUE	TWO-WAY RADIO	BACK BEAT 585	20.00	northern

FAWNS

GIRL IN TROUBLE	BLESS YOU	TEC 3015	10.00	northern
NOTHING BUT LOVE CAN SAVE	WISH YOU WEERE HERE WITH ME	CAP CITY 105	10.00	northern
NOTHING BUT LOVE CAN SAVE ME	WISH YOU WEERE HERE WITH MEQ	NEW FRONTIERS	20.00	northern
4402				

FAYE, RENA AND THE TEDDY BEAR CO.

DO IT	THANK YOU BABY	MELRON 5015	50.00	funk

FEASTER, CHINO

THE GIRL I LOVE	PRETTY BABY	SHIPP 1000	15.00	northern

FEATHERS

TRYING TO GET TO YOU	MY BABY IS SOUL GOOD	TEAM 518	8.00	northern

FELICE TRIO, DEE

NIGHTINGALE		TERRY NO#	200.00	funk

FELLOWS

LET'S MAKE IT LAST	SHE'S ALWAYS THERE	SOLID HIT 110	150.00	northern

FELTON, TERRY

YOU'RE WELCOME BACK	I DON'T WANT TO HAVE TO WAIT	REVILOT 224	30.00	northern

FENWAYS

BE CAREFUL LITTLE GIRL	SAME: INSTRUMENTAL	BEVMAR 402	10.00	northern
1002				

FERGUSON, HELENA

DON'T SPOIL OUR GOOD THING	THE LONLINESS IS COMING AGAIN	COMPASS 7017	8.00	ballad
MY TERMS	WHERE IS THE PARTY	COMPASS 7009	10.00	northern

FERGUSON, LEON

MISS DOLORES FUNK	STOKIN'	GALAXY 737	20.00	mod

FERGUSON, SHELIA

AND IN RETURN	ARE YOU SATISFIED	SWAN 4225	100.00	northern
DON'T (LEAVE ME LOVER)	I WEEP FOR YOU	SWAN 4217	100.00	northern
HEARTBROKEN MEMORIES	SIGNS OF LOVE	SWAN 4234	75.00	northern
HOW DID THAT HAPPEN		LANDA 706	30.00	northern

FERRELL, LEON

PURE UNADULTERATED LOVE	SOMEONE LIKE YOU	NATION 92767	15.00	northern

FERRIS WHEEL

NUMBER ONE GUY	I CAN'T BREAK THE HABIT	PHILIPS 40512	15.00	northern

FESTIVALS

TAKE YOUR TIME	BABY SHOW IT	COLOSSUS 136	10.00	70's
YOU'VE GOT THE MAKINGS OF A LOVER	HIGH WIDE AND HANDSOME	SMASH 2091	15.00	northern
GREEN GROW THE LILACS	SAME:	GORDY 7120	15.00	motown
I'LL ALWAYS LOVE YOU	MUSIC	SMASH 2056	10.00	northern
YOU'VE GOT THE MAKINGS OF A LO	HIGH WIDE AND HANDSOME	SMASH 2091	15.00	northern

FIATS

SPEAK WORDS OF LOVE	BEFORE I WALK OUT THE DOOR	UNIVERSAL 5003	100.00	northern

FIDELS

I WANT TO THANK YOU	BOYS WILL BE BOYS	MAVERICK 1008	20.00	northern
I'M GIVING YOU NOTICE BABY	SAME:	DORE 761	60.00	northern
TRY A LITTLE HARDER	YOU NEVER DO RIGHT	KEYMEN 106	40.00	**northerB**

FIDELTONES

PRETTY GIRL	GAME OF LOVE	ALLADIN 3442	150.00	motown

FIELD, CLAUDIA

TO LOVE SOMEBODY	LOVE IS ALRIGHT	ROULETTE 7207	15.00	70's

FIELDS, LEE

TAKE ME BACK	TYRA'S SONG	ANGLE 3 1009	8.00	70's
LET'S TALK IT OVER	SHE'S A LOVE MAKER	NORFOLK 1000	10.00	ballad
FUNKY SCREW	THE BULL IS COMING	ANGLE 3 1004	75.00	funk

Artist / Song	Song Title	Label	Price	Genre
SHE'S A LOVE MAKER	LET'S TALK IT OVER	LONDON 190	20.00	funk
TAKE IT OR LEAVE IT	HEY SALLIE MAE, GET OFF MY FEE	DESCO 1001	10.00	funk
THE LAST DANCE	THE LAST DANCE PT. II	ANGLE 3 2005	25.00	funk
FIELDS, LILLY				
I'VE GOT TO TELL YOU	MY BASKET	HOLTON 6711	75.00	northern
LOVE HAS SO MANY MEANINGS	SAME:INSTRUMENTAL	SUNBURST 536	8.00	70's
FIELDS, LILY AND LANDS, HOAGY				
SWEET SOUL (BROTHER)	A BOY IN A MAN'S WORLD	SPECTRUM 118 DJ	20.00	northern
FIELDS, RICHARD DIMPLES				
IT'S FINGER LICKIN' GOOD	YOU SEND ME	DAT RICHFIELD KAT 1005	25.00	funk
FIESTAS				
SOMETIMES STORM	I CAN'T SHAKE YOUR LOVE	RESPECT 2509	20.00	70's
SO FINE	LAST NIGHT I DREAMED	OLD TOWN 1062	10.00	northern
THE PARTY'S OVER	TRY IT ONE MORE TIME	OLD TOWN 1140	10.00	group
I GOTTA HAVE YOUR LOVIN'	AIN'T SHE SWEET	OLD TOWN 1189	15.00	motown
I FEEL GOOD ALL OVER	LOOK AT THAT GIRL	OLD TOWN 1127	20.00	northern
THE GYPSY SAID	MAMA PUT THE LAW DOWN	OLD TOWN 1134	15.00	northern
THE RAILROAD SONG	BROKEN HEART	OLD TOWN 1122	15.00	northern
THINK SMART	ANNA	OLD TOWN 1178	150.00	northern
FIFTH AMENDMENT				
I GOT YOU WHERE I WANT YOU	PLEASE DON'T LEAVE ME NOW	N.Y. SOUND CO. 100	10.00	northern
5TH. DIMENSION				
THERE'S NO LOVE IN THE ROOM	I DON'T KNOW HOW TO LOOK FOR LOVE	ARISTA 101	8.00	70's
I'LL BE LOVIN' YOU FOREVER	TRAIN KEEP ON MOVING	SOUL CITY 752	15.00	northern
TOO POOR TO DIE	GO WHERE YOU WANNA GO	SOUL CITY 753	10.00	northern
TOO POOR TO DIE	GO WHERE YOU WANNA GO	SOUL CITY 753 PS	15.00	northern
5 DEGREES FARENHEIT				
JUST LET YOUR HEART BE YOUR GUIDE	BIG BAD RAIN	ABET 9443	10.00	70's
5 OF A KIND				
THE OTHER SIDE	PLEASE TELL ME (THEY WE'RE WRO	SIDRA 9003	30.00	**northerB**
5 WAGERS				
COME AND ASK ME	SAME: INSTRUMENTAL	TIARA 4741	10.00	70's
FIKES, BETTY AND THE PASSIONS				
PROVE IT TO ME	I CAN'T LIE TO MY HEART	SOUTHBOUND 437	300.00	**northerB**
FINAL DECISIONS				
YOU ARE MY SUNSHINE	YOU GOT TO BE MY WOMAN	HI C RECORDS 1	50.00	70's
HOUR OF YOUR NEED	KEEP ON WALKING	BUMPSHOP 162	10.00	group
FINISHING TOUCH				
SECOND BEST (IS NEVER ENOUGH)	YOUR LOVE HAS PUT A SPELL ON M	PHILLY GROOVE 201	10.00	70's
FINLEY, GEORGE				
TOO LATE FOR TEARS	BRONCO	AMBASSADOR 209	40.00	ballad
FIRE				
FLIGHT TO CUBA		BAY TOWN	200.00	funk
FIRE AND RAIN				
HELLO STRANGER	SOMEBODY TO LOVE	MERCURY 73373	40.00	70's
FIREBIRDS				
SOUL SONATA	I JUST DON'T BELIEVE YOU	EXCELLO 2307 DJ	30.00	northern
FIRST CHOICE				
THIS IS THE HOUSE (WHERE LOVE	ONE STEP AWAY	SCEPTER 12347	25.00	northern
FIRST CLASS				
CANDY	DON'T LISTEN TO YOUR FRIENDS	PARK-WAY 1556	40.00	70's
FIRST LOVE				
LOVE ME TODAY	DON'T SAY GOODNIGHT	DAKAR 4566	15.00	70's
FISCHER, JERRY (also see JERRY FISHER)				
I'VE GOT TO FIND SOMEONE TO YOU	I'VE GOT TO BE A SINGING STAR	MUSICOR 1147	75.00	northern
FISHBACK, SONNY				
HEART BREAKING MAN	I WON'T TAKE BACK THESE WORDS	OUT-A-SITE 50008	500.00	northern
BMI Fishback publishing is slightly slower than the Kodel pub.				
HEART BREAKING MAN	I WON'T TAKE BACK THESE WORDS	OUT-A-SITE 50008	600.00	northern
BMI Pub. Cameo Pub. & Kodel Music is a faster version.				
FISHER, ANDY				
HEART'S ARE BEATING STRONG northern	WEE BIT LONGER	FAT FISH	8009	1000.00
FISHER, JERRY				
I'VE GOT TO FIND SOMEONE TO LOVE	I'VE GOT TO BE A SINGING STAR	THREE SPEED 714	75.00	northern
FISHER, JESSE				
WHY	LITTLE JOHN	WAY OUT 106	10.00	ballad
HONEY	I CAN'T STOP LOVING YOU	SOJAMM 106	500.00	northern
MR. SUPER NOBODY	DON'T CHEAT ON ME	WAY OUT 100	10.00	northern
YOUR NOT LOVING A BEGINNER	WAITING	WAY OUT 104 multi	20.00	northern
YOUR NOT LOVING A BEGINNER	WAITING	WAY OUT 104 white/red	30.00	northern
FISHER, MISS TONI				
THE BIG HURT	MEMPHIS BELLE	SIGNETT 275	10.00	northern
FISHER, SHELLEY				
GIRL, I LOVE YOU	OUTSIDE OF MEMPHIS	DALYA 5002	150.00	northern
I'LL LEAVE YOU (GIRL)	SAINT JAMES INFIRMARY	KAPP 2114	100.00	funk

BIG CITY LIGHTS	ELEGY (PLAIN BLACK BOY)	ARIES 5002	15.00	northern
FISHER, SONNY				
I'M GOING (ALL THE WAY)	HURTING	PEACOCK 1947	20.00	northern
FISHER, WILLIE				
PUT YOUR LOVIN' ON ME	TAKE TIME TO KNOW HER	TIGRESS 174	30.00	70's
YOU SAID CALL ME	SAME: SAME: SAME: INSTRUMENTALMENTAL	TIGRESS 453	30.00	70's
FIVE GENTS				
BITTER CANDY		SUNBURST	50.00	northern
FIVE JAYS				
HEY HEY GIRL	YOU GOT LOVE	CHANT 515	30.00	northern
FIVE KEYS				
STOP (WHAT YOUR DOING TO ME)	GODDESS OF LOVE	RAM LANDMARK 101	20.00	70's
FIVE QUAILS				
BEEN A LONG TIME	GET TO SCHOOL ON TIME	HARVEY 114	30.00	motown
GET TO SCHOOL ON TIME	BEEN A LONG TIME	HARVEY 114	30.00	motown
FIVE STAIRSTEPS				
STAY CLOSE TO ME	I MADE A MISTAKE	CURTOM 1933	10.00	northern
LITTLE YOUNG LOVER	WE MUST BE IN LOVE	CURTOM 1945	10.00	northern
THE GIRL I LOVE	OOH, BABY BABY	WINDY C 607	8.00	northern
COME BACK	YOU DON'T LOVE ME	WINDY C 603	8.00	group
AIN'T GONNA REST (TILL I GET YOU BACK)	YOU CAN'T SEE	WINDY C 605	8.00	northern
CHANGE OF PACE	THE TOUCH OF YOU	WINDY C 608	8.00	northern
DON'T WASTE YOUR TIME	YOU WAITED TOO LONG	WINDY C 601	15.00	northern
PLAYGIRL'S LOVE	WORLD OF FANTASY	WINDY C 602	8.00	northern
FIVE STARS				
BLABBER MOUTH	BABY BABY	COLUMBIA 42056	30.00	motown
BLABBER MOUTH	BABY BABY	END 1028	50.00	motown
OOH SHUCKS	DEAD WRONG	MARK-X 7006	100.00	motown
FIVE WAGERS				
UNTIL I FOUND YOU	LUCKY I FOUND YOU	SALEM 1013	10.00	northern
UNTIL I FOUND YOU	YOU'RE MY WORLD	NATION 1013	10.00	northern
FLAIR AND THE FLAT FOOTS				
HEY BOY - HEY GIRL	JOHN FUZZ	S.P.Q.R. 1007	20.00	northern
FLAIRS				
YOU GOT TO STEAL	WHERE YOU LIVE	RAP 7	15.00	northern
FLAMBEAUS				
DARLING I'M WITH YOU	NOBODY KNOWS	OLD TOWN 2001	15.00	northern
FLAME N KING AND THE BOLD ONES				
HO HAPPY DAY	AIN'T NOBODY JIVIN'	N.Y.S.C. 10	30.00	70's
FLAME AND THE LOVELIGHTS				
THE WAY I WANT OUR LOVE	WHY IS LOVE	JABER 7113	20.00	northern
FLAMES				
STAND UP AND BE COUNTED	MY LONELY HOUR	PEOPLE 600	15.00	funk
FLAMING EMBERS				
JUST LIKE CHILDREN	TELL IT LIKE IT IS	RIC TIC 145	15.00	motown
CHILDREN	SAME: INSTRUMENTAL	RIC TIC 143	10.00	motown
BLESS YOU	SAME: INSTRUMENTAL (cr. Al Kent)	RIC TIC 140	8.00	motown
LET'S HAVE A LOVE-IN	HEY MAMA	RIC TIC 132	8.00	motown
LET'S HAVE A LOVE--IN	SAME: INSTRUMENTAL	RIC TIC 129	10.00	motown
FLAMING EMERALDS				
HAVE SOME EVERYBODY	SAME: INSTRUMENTAL	FEE 361	10.00	70's
FLAMINGO, CHUCK				
LOVE, LOVE, LOVE	LITTLE BIT OF THIS	ROJAC 1002	40.00	northern
WHAT'S MY CHANCES	NO ONE TO CALL MY OWN	ROJAC 1001	500.00	northern
FLAMINGOS				
THINK ABOUT ME	SAME: INSTRUMENTAL	WORLDS 103	10.00	70's
I KNOW BETTER	FLAME OF LOVE	END 1121	25.00	northern
NOBODY LOVES ME LIKE YOU	YOU, ME, AND THE SEA	END 1068	15.00	northern
THE BOOGALOO PARTY	THE NEARNESS OF YOU	PHILIPS 40347	10.00	northern
FLANAGAN, STEVE				
I'VE ARRIVED	I NEED TO BE LOVED SO BAD	ERA 3186	150.00	northern
FLAVOR				
DON'T FREEZE UP	SAME: INSTRUMENTAL	BUNKY 711	10.00	70's
DON'T FREEZE UP	SAME: INSTRUMENTAL	JU-PAR 8001	8.00	70's
FLEMING, GARFIELD				
DON'T SEND ME AWAY	YOU GOT DAT RIGHT	BECKET 7	30.00	70's
FLEMING, JOY				
ARE YOU READY FOR LOVE	ALABAHA STAND-BY	PRIVATE STOCK 45076	15.00	70's
FLEMONS, WADE				
I CAME RUNNING (BACK FROM THE PATY)	THAT TIME OF YEAR	VEE JAY 533	20.00	northern
I'LL COME RUNNING	AIN'T THAT LOVIN' YOU BABY	VEE JAY 368	15.00	northern
JEANETTE	WHAT A PROICE TO PAY	RAMSEL 1001	200.00	northern
THAT OTHER PLACE	I KNEW YOU WHEN	VEE JAY 614	100.00	northern
TWO OF A KIND	I KNEW YOU'D BE MINE	RAMSEL 1002	250.00	northern
WATCH OVER HER	WHEN IT RAINS IT POURS	VEE JAY 578	15.00	northern

FLETCHER, DARROW

IT'S NO MISTAKE	TRY SOMETHING NEW	CROSS OVER 980	40.00	70's
RISING COST OF LOVE	SAME:	ATLANTIC 3600 DJ	10.00	70's
THE PAIN GETS A LITTLE DEEPER	MY JUDGEMENT DAY	GROOVY 3001	10.00	northern
I LIKE THE WAY I FEEL	THE WAY OF A MAN	REVUE 11008	10.00	northern
THOSE HANGING HEARTACHES	SAME:	REVUE 11035 DJ	15.00	northern
CHANGING BY THE MINUTE	WHEN LOVE CALLS	UNI 55244	10.00	northern
DOLLY BABY	WHAT IS THIS	UNI 55270	8.00	group
GOTTA DRAW THE LINE	I'VE GOTTA KNOW WHY	GROOVY 3007	15.00	northern
INFATUATION	LITTLE GIRL	JACKLYN 1003	15.00	northern
THE PAIN GETS A LITTLE DEEPER	MY JUDGEMENT DAY	GROOVY 3001 DJ	25.00	northern
WHAT GOOD AM I WITHOUT YOU	LITTLE GIRL	JACKLYN 1006	15.00	northern

FLETCHER, SAM

I'D THINK IT OVER	FRIDAY NIGHT	TOLLIE 9012	200.00	**northerB**
MORE TODAY THAN YESTERDAY	WHAT'LL I DO	VAULT 502	20.00	northern

FLETCHER, TEE

ALL BECAUSE OF YOU	SAME: INSTRUMENTAL	TRAGAR 6810	300.00	northern
HAPPY LOVING YOU	PARDON ME WHILE I CRY	SHURFINE 19	30.00	northern
WOULD YOU DO IT FOR ME	DOWN IN THE COUNTRY	TRAGAR 6802	20.00	northern
THANK YOU BABY	WALK ON OUT	JOSIE 970	25.00	northern

FLIGHT

NO MORE PART TIME LOVIN'	FLYING HIGH	FLY 4 15	100.00	70's

FLINT EMERALDS

IS IT ALL A BAD DREAM	YOU DON'T KNOW THAT I LOVE YOU	COCONUT GROOVE 4021	15.00	70

FLIRTATIONS

CHANGE MY DARKNESS INTO LIGHT	NATURAL BORN LOVER	JOSIE 956	20.00	northern
NOTHING BUT A HEARTACHE	CHRISTMAS TIME IS HERE AGAIN	DERAM 85036	10.00	northern
STRONGER THAN HER LOVE	SETTLE DOWN	FESTIVAL 705	100.00	northerB
STRONGER THAN HER LOVE	SETTLE DOWN	FESTIVAL 705 multi	175.00	northern

FLORES, REE

LOOK INTO MY HEART	GET OUT OF MY LIFE WOMAN	M&H 9343	400.00	northern

FLOWERS, PHIL

GOT TO HAVE HER FOR MY OWN	COMIN' HOME TO YOU	COLUMBIA 43397	20.00	northern
STAY AWHILE	IF YOU REALLY LOVE HIM	ICI INDUSTRIES 1806	100.00	70's
THE MAN, THE WIFE & THE BABY	NOTHING LASTS FOREVER	BELL 928	10.00	northern
DISCONTENTED	CRY ON MY SHOULDER	DOT 17058	15.00	northern
HOW CAN I FORGET HER	IF I COULD HAVE MY WAY	ALMANAC 812	40.00	northern
WHERE DID I GO WRONG	ONE MORE HURT	DOT 17043	15.00	northern
YOU LITTLE DEVIL	THE CLEOPATRA	JOSIE 909	10.00	northern

FLOWERS, PHIL AND THE UNDERDOGS

DISCONTENTED	UNDERDOG	LOFT 103	150.00	northern

FLOWERS

FOR REAL	SAME: INSTRUMENTAL	LAX 101	200.00	70's
WE COULD MAKE IT HAPPEN	PT.2	LAX 102	150.00	70's

FLOYD, BILLY

MY OH MY	TIME MADE YOU CHANGE YOUR MIND	ARCTIC 145	400.00	northern
SWEETER THAN CANDY	ONE CHANCE	20TH. CENTURY 6678	30.00	northern

FLOYD, HOLLIS

BLACK PONCHO IS COMING	EVERYTHING IS EVERYTHING	SILLOH 31775	15.00	mod

FLUORESCENT SMOG

ALL OF MY LIFE		W.G.	500.00	northern

FOLGER, DAN

THE WAY OF THE CROWD		ELF 90004	100.00	northern

FOLLET, JACKIE

I AM WHAT I AM	DON'T CARE TO	VERVE 5065	50.00	northern
THERE'S A MOMENT	THAT'S A GOOD ENOUGH REASON	VERVE 5034	15.00	northern

FONTANA, WAYNE

SOMETHING KEEPS CALLING ME BAC	PAMELA, PAMELA	MGM 13661	8.00	northern

FORD, KEN

OUR LOVE IS FOR REAL	I WANNA DANCE	GOLD MINE 1000	20.00	70's

FORD, MARY

ONE IN A MILLION	WHY CAN'T HE BE YOU	TOWER 279	15.00	northern

FORD, YOUNG HENRY AND THE GIFTS

TWO HEARTS MAKE A ROMANCE	TREAT HER NICE	ROULETTE 4552	10.00	northern

FOREMAN, SYL

BEFORE I LEAVE YOU	THESE PRECIOUS MOMENTS	BIG STAR 7	100.00	northern
BEFORE I LEAVE YOU	THESE PRECIOUS MOMENTS	MANDINGO	150.00	northern

FOREVERS

WHAT GOES AROUND (COMES AROUND	SOUL TOWN	WEIS 3002	15.00	northern
BE AWARE	GOT IT MADE	WEIS 600	20.00	northern

FORMATIONS

LONELY VOICE OF LOVE	LOVE'S NOT ONLY FOR THE HEART	MGM 13963	10.00	northern
AT THE TOP OF THE STAIRS	MAGIC MELODY	MGM 13899	10.00	northern
AT THE TOP OF THE STAIRS	MAGIC MELODY	BANK 1007	25.00	northern

FORMULA 12

WHERE IS SHE	SAME:	CATAMOUNT 133	40.00	northern

FORREST, NICK

LET ME BE	MUSIC MAESTRO PLEASE	TEEN LIFE 10	75.00	motown

FORSTON AND SCOTT				
SWEET LOVER	MY DREAMS OF YOU	PZAZZ 1	750.00	northern
FORT, RUBIEN				
I FEEL IT	SO GOOD	ANNA 1117	25.00	motown
I'LL DO THE BEST I CAN	NOBODY	CHECK MATE 1007	30.00	motown
FORTE, RONNIE				
THAT WAS WHISKEY TALKIN'	NERVOUS BREAKDOWN	TARX 1011	30.00	northern
FORTH SESSION				
SHE'S GONE	WOULD YOU LOVE ME TOO	JAYVILLE 7147	100.00	group
FORTSON, LARRY				
KEEP YOUR LOVE GROWING	LATER	VAL. 12	20.00	ballad
FORTSON, ROBBY				
ARE YOU FOR REAL	AIN'T IT LONELY	PZAZZ 27	40.00	northern
FORTUNE, JEANIE				
KEEP ME	ANGRY EYES	RCA 8914	10.00	northern
ONCE MORE WITH FEELING	OCCASIONAL TEARS	RCA 8704	20.00	northern
FORTUNE, ROB				
CRAZY FEELIN	SWEETHEART OF MINE	PARAMOUNT 300	20.00	northern
CRAZY FEELIN'	SWEETHEART OF MINE	NOW. 2	10.00	northern
FOSTER BAND, AL				
THE NIGHT OF THE WOLF	THE NIGHT OF THE WOLF Pt.2	ROULETTE 7162	50.00	funk
FOSTER, BOBBY				
WHERE DO YOU GO	I'M SO GLAD	SELECTOHITS 105	8.00	70's
IF YOU REALLY NEED A FRIEND	BUILDING UP (FOR A LET DOWN)	SOUND PLUS 2101	15.00	northern
FOSTER, EDDIE				
CLOSER TOGETHER	DON'T MAKE ME CRY	OCAMPO 100	150.00	northern
I NEVER KNEW	I WILL WAIT	IN 6311	150.00	**northerB**
FOSTER, FRANK				
HARLEM RUMBLE	BRING IT ON HOME	TRIODE 120	125.00	northern
FOSTER, LARRY				
FUNKY BELLY	FUNKY BELLY PT.2	BIG BEAT 133	15.00	funk
FOSTER, MILLIE				
OLE FATHER TIME	IT KEEPS ON RAINING TEARS	TCF 4	20.00	northern
FOUNTAIN, CAPT. JESSE				
I'M MARCHIN	WHEN IT RAINS LOVE (IT POURS)	CAMEO 457	10.00	northern
FOUNTAIN, JAMES				
MY HAIR IS NAPPY	BURNING UP FOR YOUR LOVE	PEACHTREE 124 DJ	50.00	funk
SEVEN DAY LOVER	MALNUTRITION	PEACHTREE 127	100.00	**northernB**
FOUR ANDANTES				
HIPPER, THAN ME	THE END OF LOVE	MO DO 1007	500.00	northern
FOUR ARTS				
WHO DO YOU THINK YOU ARE	JUST ONE NIGHT	SHEE 100	400.00	northern
FOUR BELOW ZERO				
E.S.P. (Pt. 1)	E.S.P. (Pt.2)	P&P 1050	100.00	70's
MY BABY'S GOT E.S.P.	MY BABY'S GOT E.S.P. PT.2	ROULETTE 7186	40.00	70's
FOUR BROS.				
LET IT ALL REACH OUT	COOL JERK	CARLA 2538	150.00	northern
FOUR BUDDIES				
JUST ENOUGH OF YOUR LOVE	I WANT TO BE THE BOY YOU LOVE	IMPERIAL 66018	50.00	**northerB**
FOUR CHAPS				
TRUE LOVERS	WILL YOU OR WON'T YOU	CO & CE 231	30.00	northern
FOUR DYNAMICS				
THAT THAT A LADY AIN'T SUPPOSE	THAT'S WHAT GIRL ARE MADE FOR	PEACHTREE 129	1000.00	northern
FOUR EXCEPTIONS				
A SAD GOODBYE	YOU GOT THE POWER	PARKWAY 986	50.00	northern
FOUR FLIGHTS				
ALL I WANT IS YOU	ALL I WANT IS YOU Pt.2	ALMERIA 4002	30.00	70's
FOUR GENTS				
YOUNG GIRLS BEWARE	CHERRY LIPS	ONCORE 83	500.00	northern
TOMORROW MAY NEVER COME	THE DONKEY	ONCORE 85	400.00	northern
I'VE BEEN TRYING	SOUL SISTER	HBR 509	20.00	group
FOUR HAVENS				
WHAT TIME IS IT	LET'S HAVE A GOD TIME BABY	VEEP 1214	30.00	group
FOUR HI'S				
HEARTBREAK RIVER	THE TRAIN (LEAVING FOR MISERY)	VERVE 10549	15.00	northern
PRETTY LITTLE FACE	THE TRAIN (LEAVING FOR MISERY)	VERVE 10450	15.00	northern
FOUR HOLLIDAYS				
DEEP DOWN IN MY HEART	HE CAN'T LOVE YOU	MASTER 3001	200.00	northern
STEP BY STEP	GRANDMA BIRD	MARKIE 109	30.00	northern
FOUR JEWELS				
BABY IT'S YOU	SHE'S WRONG FOR YOU BABY	TEC 3007	15.00	group
FOUR LARKS				
ANOTHER CHANCE	RAIN	TOWER 364	10.00	northern
I STILL LOVE YOU	GROOVIN' AT THE GO GO	TOWER 402	40.00	northern
I'VE GOT PLENTY	CAN I HAVE ANOTHER HELPING	TOWER 450	10.00	northern
YOU AND ME	THAT'S ALL THAT COUNTS	UPTOWN 748	100.00	northern

68

FOUR MINTS
DO YOU REALLY LOVE ME — (I'M GONNA) KEEP ON LOVING YOU — CAPSOUL 27 — 15.00 — group

FOUR OF CLUBS
FUNKITY — IT'S YOUR TURN TO CRY — CYPRESS 101 — 100.00 — funk

FOUR PERFECTIONS
I'M NOT STRONG ENOUGH — I'LL HOLD ON — PARTY TIME 1001 — 200.00 — northern

FOUR PROS
THERE MUST BE A REASON — JUST ANOTHER GIRL — CARLA 2531 — 75.00 — northern

FOUR PRO'S
EVERYBODY'S GOT SOME SOUL — YOU CAN'T KEEP A GOOD MAN DOWN — CARLA 2532 — 40.00 — northern
JUST ANOTHER GIRL — THERE MUST BE A REASON — CARLA 2531 — 30.00 — northern

FOUR PUZZLES
ESPECIALLY FOR YOU — RIGHT OR WRONG — FAT BACK 215 — 50.00 — northern

FOUR REPUTATIONS (also see PRESENTATIONS)
CALL ON ME — SORRY — MILLAGE 105 — 400.00 — northern

FOUR SHADES
SOMETHING SPECIAL — MY WORLD — RONN 61 — 15.00 — group

FOUR SHARPS
THE FIFE PIPER — HAPPINESS IS — CAMEO 426 — 20.00 — mod

FOUR SHELLS
REPUTATION — HOT DOG — VOLT 134 — 15.00 — northern

FOUR SIGHTS
LOVE IS A HURTING GAME THAT I CAN'T WIN — THE DREAMER — SHY-SOUL 101 — 100.00 — northern

FOUR SONICS
IF IT WASN'T FOR MY BABY — THERE'S NO LOVE — JMC 141 — 15.00 — 70's
EASIER SAID THAN DONE — THE GREATEST LOVE — SPORT 111 — 10.00 — northern
TELL ME YOU'RE MINE — LOST WITHOUT YOU — SEPIA 1 — 25.00 — northern
WHERE ARE YOU — BLUE VELVET — TRIPLE B 2 — 40.00 — northern
YOU DON'T HAVE TO SAY YOU LOVE — IT TAKES TWO — SPORT 110 — 10.00 — northern

FOUR TEES
ONE MORE CHANCE — FUNKY DUCK — KENT 4530 — 20.00 — northern
I SAID SHE SAID — LIKE MY BABY — VEE JAY 627 — 15.00 — northern
ONE MORE CHANCE — I COULD NEVER LOVA ANOTHER — KENT 4536 — 15.00 — northern

FOUR TEMPOS
STRANGE DREAM — LONELY PRISONER — RAMPART 664 — 15.00 — group
GOT TO HAVE YOU (CAN'T LIVE WI — COME ON HOME — RAMPART 657 — 15.00 — northern

FOUR THOUGHTS
KISSES & ROSES — WHEN I'M WITH YOU — WOMAR 103 — 300.00 — northern

FOUR TOPS
AIN'T THAT LOVE — LONELY SUMMER — COLUMBIA 41755 — 50.00 — motown
AIN'T THAT LOVE — LONELY SUMMER — COLUMBIA 43356 — 10.00 — motown
DON'T BRING BACK THE MEMORIES — WHAT IS A MAN — MOTOWN 1147 — 10.00 — northern
SHAKE ME, WAKE ME — JUST AS LONG AS YOU NEED ME — MOTOWN 1090 — 8.00 — northern
SOMETHING ABOUT YOU — DARLING I HUM OUR SONG — MOTOWN 1084 — 8.00 — northern
WONDERFUL BABY — IF I WERE A CARPENTER — MOTOWN 1124 — 10.00 — northern

FOUR TRACKS
CHARADE — YOU MEAN EVERYTHING TO ME — NOTE 7212 — 200.00 — northern
LIKE MY LOVE FOR YOU — VOODOO WOMAN — MANDINGO 25 — 600.00 — **northerB**

FOUR VOICES
SUMMER KIND OF LOVE — WE LIVE IN THE GHETTO — VOICE 1113 — 75.00 — northern
YOU LOVE IS GETTING STRONER — WITH A LONELY HEART — VOICE 1112 Green lbl — 800.00 — northern
YOUR LOVE IS GETTING STRONGER — WITH A LONELY HEART — VOICE 1112 Gold lbl — 75.00 — northern

FOUR WONDERS
HAVEN'T WE BEEN GOOD FOR EACH — JUST LOOKING FOR MY LOVE — SOLID FOUNDATION 108 — 30.00 — 70's

FOURCOUNTS
A HOME IN LOVELAND — LOVE IS A SONG OF LOVE — LYNDELL 1009 — 200.00 — northern

FOURTH DAY
YOU TURN ME ON — ON MY WAY UP — DT 104 — 20.00 — 70's

FOX, ANNABELLE
LONELY GIRL — HUMOR ME — SATIN 402 — 300.00 — northern
TOO GOOD TO BE FORGOTTEN — GETTING THROUGH TO ME — SATIN 400 — 15.00 — northern

FOX, DAMON
GOTTA GET MY BABY BACK — BLACK WIDOW SPIDER — CRIMSON 1013 — 10.00 — funk
PACKING UP — BONIE MORONIE — FAIRMOUNT 1021 — 1800.00 — northern

FOX, JOHN
IT'S UP TO YOU — ELECTION DAY — CAPITOL 4451 — 30.00 — 70's

FOX, KENNY
I'M CRAZY 'BOUT YOU BABY — YOU'RE MINE — RCA 9590 — 10.00 — ballad

FOXX, INEZ AND CHARLIE
MOCKINGBIRD — JAYBIRDS — SYMBOL 919 — 8.00 — northern
NO STRANGER TO LOVE — COME BY HERE — MUSICOR 1201 — 10.00 — northern
TIGHTROPE — BABY TAKE IT ALL — DYNAMO 102 — 10.00 — **northerB**

FOXX, INEZ
I SEE YOU MY LOVE — ASK ME — SYMBOL 926 — 10.00 — northern
BROKEN HEARTED FOOL — HE'S THE ONE YOU LOVE — SYMBOL 922 — 10.00 — northern

FOXY AND THE 7 HOUNDS
MIRROR, MIRROR — LISTEN LISTEN — WISE WORLD 1002 — 50.00 — northern

FRAN, CAROL

I'M GONNA TRY

FRANCIS, RUFF AND THE ILLUSIONS

GIVE ME MERCY

FRANCISCANS

WALK TO THE BOTTOM OF THE SEA

FRANKIE AND JOHNNY

I'LL HOLD YOU
TIMES GONE BY

FRANKIE AND ROBERT

SWEET THING

FRANKIE AND THE NORTHERNALS

WHAT SHALL I DO
WHAT SHALL I DO
WHAT SHALL I DO

CRYING IN THE CHAPEL	PORT 3000	25.00	northern
MISERY LOVES COMPANY	ESSICA 2	50.00	funk
MOTHER PLEASE ANSWER ME	JIMBO 2	100.00	northern
(I'M) NEVER GONNA LEAVE YOU	HICKORY 1391	50.00	northerB
SWEET THANG	IA 112	15.00	northern
LOVE (IT'S BEEN SO LONG)	TRAGAR 6805	20.00	northern
I ONLY HAVE EYES FOR YOU	CALLA 127BN	20.00	northern
GOOD-BYE LOVE (HELLO SADNESS)	CALLA 127BN	20.00	northern
I ONLY HAVE EYES FOR YOU	CALLA 127	40.00	northern

First recorded with a spoken intro Calla 127 (withdrawn) .Calla 127 BN was the later release, less the spoken intro.

FRANKIE AND THE DAMONS

I HOPE YOU FIND THE WAY

FRANKLIN, ARETHA

I CAN'T SEE MYSELF LEAVING YOU
ROCK STEADY
(NO NO) I'M LOSING YOU
I CAN'T WAIT UNTIL I SEE MY BABY'S FACE

FRANKLIN, BOBBY (Also as BOBBY FRANKLIN'S INSANITY)

THE LADIES CHOICE
WHAT EVER'S YOUR SIGN
PARADISE
BRING IT ON DOWN TO ME PT.1

FRANKLIN, CAROLYN

REALITY

FRANKLIN, ERMA

IT COULD'VE BEEN ME
ABRACADABRA
GOTTA FIND ME A LOVER
I DON'T WANT NO MAMA'S BOY

FRANKLIN, MARIE

BEING IN LOVE AIN'T EASY

FRASER, JIMMY.

OF HOPES & DREAMS & TOMBSTONES

FRAZIER, BILLY

LET'S FACE REALITY
LET ONE HURT DO
TAKE THE CHAIN OF YOUR BRAIN

FRAZIER, JOE

FIRST ROUND KNOCK-OUT
THE BIGGER THEY COME

FRAZIER, RAY AND THE SHADES OF MADNESS

YOUR EYES
  4267
YOUR EYES
I WHO HAVE NOTHING (AM SOMEBODY)

FRED AND THE AND THE NEW J.B'S

IT'S THE J.B'S MONORAIL

FREDDIE AND THE TURBINES

BERNADINE

FREDDY AND THE JADES

TOO MUCH

FREDDY AND THE KINFOLK

MASHED POTATO, POP CORN
THE GOAT

FREDDY AND SOUNDS OF SOUL

YOUR THE BEAT OF MY HEART

FREDERICK, CAROL

I COULDN'T CARE LESS
MR. LOVE

FREE SPIRIT

LOVE YOU JUST AS LONG AS

FREEDOM NOW BROTHERS

SISSY WALK

FREEDOM.

CAN'T YOU SEE

FREEMAN BROTHERS

MY BABY

FREEMAN, ART

A PIECE OF MY HEART
SLIPPIN' AROUND WITH YOU

MAN FROM SOUL	JCP 1057	150.00	northern
GENTLE ON MY MIND	ATLANTIC 2619	8.00	northern
OH ME OH MY (I'M A FOOL 4U BAB	ATLANTIC 2838	10.00	funk
SWEET BITTER LOVE	COLUMBIA 43333	10.00	northern
ONE STEP AHEAD	COLUMBIA 43241	25.00	northern
THE LADIES CHOICE Pt. 2	FEE 301	15.00	funk
WHAT EVER'S YOUR SIGN	BABYLON 1123	8.00	funk
SAME:	THOMAS 803 DJ	15.00	funk
SAME: PT.2	THOMAS 801 DJ	15.00	funk
IT'S TRUE I'M GONNA MISS YOU	RCA 188	10.00	northern
I JUST DON'T NEED YOU	BRUNSWICK 755424	15.00	northern
LOVE IS BLIND	EPIC 9610	150.00	northern
CHANGE MY THOUGHTS FROM YOU	BRUNSWICK 55403	10.00	northern
HAVE YOU EVER HAD THE BLUES	EPIC 9594	40.00	northern
DON'T HURT ME NO MORE	CASTLE 78102	100.00	70's
SAME: INSTRUMENTAL	COLUMBIA 43407	200.00	northern
STAY RIGHT HERE THIS MORNING	CAPITOL 2717	60.00	70's
COULD THIS BE LOVE	NEEDLE POINT 901	100.00	ballad
BABY YOU SATISFY ME	CAPITOL 2497	15.00	funk
LOOKY, LOOKY (LOOK AT ME GIRL)	MOTOWN 1378	10.00	70's
COME AND GET ME LOVE	CLOVRLAY 100	75.00	northern
GOOD SIDE	CARRIAGE TRADE	50.00	70's
SAME:	CARRIAGE 1001	50.00	70's
LONELINESS	STANSON 204	300.00	funk
SAME: PT 2.	PEOPLE 655 DJ	10.00	funk
	CENCO	2000.00	northern
SEARCHING FOR LOVE	RCA 8708	15.00	northern
LAST TAKE	DADE 2024	15.00	mod
BLABBERMOUTH	DADE 2016	15.00	mod
THAT AIN'T RIGHT	PEARL 8001	15.00	northern
	STONEL 1003	400.00	northern
WHERE I OUGHTA BE	STONEL 1004	200.00	northern
SAME: INSTRUMENTAL	CHESS 2154	10.00	70's
	ALL BROTHERS	300.00	funk
SUNSHINE	FREEDOM 1000	50.00	70's
BEAUTIFUL BROWN EYES	SOUL 35011	20.00	motown
EVERYBODY'S GOT TO CRY SOMETIM	FAME 1012	15.00	ballad
I CAN'T GET YOU OUT OF MY MIND	FAME 1008 black	150.00	nortnern

Artist / Song	Track	Label/Cat	Price	Genre
SLIPPIN' AROUND WITH YOU	I CAN'T GET YOU OUT OF MY MIND	FAME 1008 DJ	100.00	**northerB**
SLIPPIN' AROUND WITH YOU	I CAN'T GET YOU OUT OF MY MIND	FAME 1008 red	150.00	northern
FREEMAN, ARTHUR				
PLAYED OUT PLAY GIRL	HERE I AM	EXCELLO 2322	30.00	northern
YOU GOT ME UPTIGHT	I WANT TO COME HOME	JUMBO 101	600.00	northern
FREEMAN, BOBBY	MIDNIGHT SHACK	TOUCH 101	15.00	70's
EVERYTHING'S LOVE	FRIENDS	AUTUMN 9	10.00	**northerB**
I'LL NEVER FALL IN LOVE AGAIN	I GOT A GOOD THING	LOMA 2080	20.00	northern
LIES				
FREEMAN, GEORGE	DARLING, BE HOME SO	EPIC 10583	15.00	ballad
MY DARLING, MY DARLING	THE QUIVER	VALIANT 6039	200.00	northern
DOWN AND OUT	COME TO ME	VALIANT 6035	15.00	northern
YOU GUESSED IT	ALL RIGHT NOW	OKEH 7333	20.00	northern
YOU LIED, I CRIED, LOVE DIED				
FREEMAN, JUDY AND BLACKROCK	DON'T DO IT ANYMORE	RCA 446	25.00	northern
ALL WE NEED IS A MIRACLE	WALK A MILE IN MY SHOES	RCA 493	75.00	northern
HOLD ON				
FREEMAN, ROGER	ALL SHOOK UP	R RECORDS 1512	15.00	northern
COMIN' BACK FOR MORE				
FREITAS, DICK AND PAUL		BEACON 101	20.00	northern
SIAMESE CAT				
FRENCH FRIES	SMALL FRIES	EPIC 10313	20.00	funk
DANSE A LA MUSIQUE				
FRENCH, BOB		BROADMOOR	75.00	funk
Y'ER COMES THE FUNKY MAN				
FRESH AIR	I CAN'T MAKE IT ANY MORE	LUV 102	15.00	northern
I KNOW				
FRIENDLY PEOPLE	MR. MOONLIGHT	VMP 3	10.00	northern
YOU SEND ME	SAME: SAME: SAME: INSTRUMENTALMENTAL	VMP 13393	20.00	northern
I AIN'T GOT NOTHIN' BUT THE BLUES				
FRIENDS	BIRTHDAY SONG	UP. 1	10.00	70's
NO YOU - NO ME				
FRISCO, DONNA	I LOVE EVERY LITTLE THING	SHOWTIME 2453	300.00	northern
THE SAME THINGS THAT MADE ME L				
FROG, WYNDER K.	DANCING FROG	UA 50156	20.00	northern
GREEN DOOR		UA 50453	15.00	northern
I FEEL SO BAD				
FRONTERA, TOMMY	I HEARD EVERY WORD	HI-LITE 107	150.00	northern
(YOU'RE MY) LEADING LADY	MERRY GO ROUND	PALMER 5015	20.00	northern
STREET OF SHAME				
FUDOLI, RICHARD	BOSSA NOVA JUMPING BEAN	MAESTRO 102067	30.00	funk
GWEEE				
FUGITIVES	RICH MAN POOR MAN	SANDMAN 703	20.00	funk
FUNKY YOU	LOVE COME DOWN	SANDMAN 701	20.00	northern
GOOD LOVIN' IF YOU CAN GET IT	DON'T PLAY THAT SONG	ROULETTE 4779	20.00	northern
HUMAN JUNGLE				
FULLER BROTHERS	SAME: INSTRUMENTAL	GD&L 2004	100.00	northern
GEE-WHIZ BABY	(I WANT HER) BY MY SIDE	KEYMEN 110	30.00	northern
MOANIN', GROANIN' AND CRYIN'	I WANT HER BY MY SIDE	SOUL CLOCK 1002	15.00	northern
STRANGER AT MY DOOR	SAME: INSTRUMENTAL	GD&L 2003	150.00	northern
STRANGER AT MY DOOR	MOANING, GROANING AND CRYING	SOUL CLOCK 105	10.00	**northerB**
TIME'S A WASTING				
FULLER FOUR, BOBBY	MY TRUE LOVE	MUSTANG 3018	20.00	northern
THE MAGIC TOUCH				
FULLER, JERRY	TURN TO ME	CHALLENGE 59329	75.00	northern
DOUBLE LIFE	AM I THAT EASY TO FORGET	CHALLENGE 59279	45.00	northern
I GET CARRIED AWAY	LOVE ME LIKE THAT	CHALLENGE 59307	20.00	northern
WHAT HAPPENED TO THE MUSIC				
FULLILOVE, ARTIE	STRANGERS IN THE NIGHT	MARLU 1002	100.00	northern
THANK YOU	REINDEER WALK	MARLU 1001	50.00	**northerB**
SANTA CLAUS PLEASE LISTEN TO ME				
FULLY GUARENTEED	SPINNING AROUND	APT 26014	10.00	70's
WE CAN'T MAKE IT TOGETHER				
FULSOM, LOWELL	DON'T DESTROY ME	JEWEL 811	15.00	funk
DO YOU FEEL IT	BLUES AROUND MIDNIGHT	KENT 443	15.00	northern
TALKIN' WOMAN	CHANGE YOURS WAYS	KENT 448	15.00	northern
MY ACHING BACK	PICO	KENT456	10.00	mod
TRAMP				
FULTON, SONNY	(NO NO) IT WON'T BE LONG	HIT. 1133	100.00	northern
PARDON ME BABY (DID I HEAR YOU RIGHT)				
FUN COMPANY		FUNCO	200.00	funk
ZAMBEZI				
FUNDAMENTALS	LET ME SHOW IT TO YOU	OKEH 7301	100.00	northern
I WOULDN'T BLAME YA				
FUNKA FIZE	NO WORDS	ROYCE 1000	20.00	funk
BECAUSE YOUR FUNKY				

FUNKY SISTERS

DO IT, TO IT	SOUL WOMAN	AURORA 165	20.00	**northerB**

FURYS

ANYTHING FOR YOU	CAT N'MOUSE	WORLD PACIFIC 386	30.00	northern
BABY YOU CAN BET YOUR BOOTS	THE MAN WHO HAS EVERYTHING	LIBERTY 55692	30.00	northern
I LOST MY BABY	WHAT IS SOUL	MACK IV	20.00	northern
NEVER MORE	ZING! WENT THE STRINGS OF MY	MACK IV 112	15.00	northern
I'M SATISFIED WITH YOU	JUST A LITTLE MIXED UP	KEYMAN 104	40.00	**northerB**
COVER GIRL	WHERE MY MONEY GOES	AURA 395	40.00	northern

FUTURE 2000

SOUL DISCO	SOUL DISCO (Version)	TOBIN 350	20.00	funk

FUTURES

AIN'T NO TIME FA NOTHING	(YOU'RE THE ONE) SOMEONE SPECI	PIR 3674	15.00	70's
IN ANSWER TO YOUR QUESTION	LET'S DANCE TOGETHER	PIR 3747	15.00	70's
STAY WITH ME	LOVE IS HERE	GAMBLE 2502	10.00	70's

FUZZ

I'M SO GLAD	ALL ABOUT LOVE	CALLA 179	8.00	northern

G

G, JERRY AND CO.

SHE'S GONE	THE ROAD OF LIFE	CLEVETOWN 240	20.00	northern

G.P. AND THE SOUL EMISSARIES

THE LONE RANGER N FUNKY TONTO	QUIET WATERS	FAT BACK 412	10.00	funk

G.R.C. FIVE

SAGA OF A SECLUDED SWAMP MONST	MY FELLOW AMERICANS	GRC 1016	15.00	funk

GAHA, SAMMY

THANK YOU, THANK YOU	LEBANON	RIGHT ON 103X	350.00	70's

GAINES, PEGGY

SWEET WAY OF LIVING	JUST TO SATISFY MY BABY	REFOREE 711	15.00	70's

GALES, JODI

YOU GOTTA PUSH	SAME: INSTRUMENTAL	THOMAS 808	15.00	funk

GALLA, TONY AND THE RISING SONS

IN LOVE	GUYS GO FOR GIRLS	SWAN 4275	200.00	northern

GALLAHADS

I'VE GOT TO FIND A WAY	ONCE I HAD A LOVE	BEECHWOOD 5000	700.00	northern

GALORE, MAMIE (P.)

THIS TIME TOMORROW	TONIGHT'S THE NIGHT	IMPERIAL 66306	15.00	northern
YOU GOT THE POWER	BLANK:	THOMAS 309	20.00	northern
IT AIN'T NECESSARY	DON'T THINK I COULD STAND IT	ST. LAWRENCE 1012	10.00	northern
NO RIGHT TO CRY		SACK	800.00	northern
SPECIAL AGENT 34-24-38	I WANNA BE YOUR RADIO	ST. LAWRENCE 1004	10.00	northern
TOO MANY MEMORIES	HAVE FAITH IN ME	ST. LAWRENCE 1008	10.00	northern

GALT, JAMES

A MOST UNUSUAL FEELING	WITH MY BABY	AURORA 158	20.00	northern

GAMBLE, JIM

WHEN YOU MOVE YOU LOSE	THE BLUES (IT'S ALL FOR YOU)	KRIS 8094	15.00	funk
WHEN YOU MOVE YOU LOSE	MOVING ON	HIGHLAND 1201	30.00	funk

GAMBLE, KENNY AND THE ROMEOS

AIN'T IT BABY	SAME: INSTRUMENTAL	ARCTIC 114	40.00	northern
OUR LOVE	YOU DON'T KNOW WHAT YOU GOT UN	COLUMBIA 43132	50.00	northern
THE JOKES ON YOU	DON'T STOP LOVING ME	ARCTIC 123	600.00	**northerB**
CHAINS OF LOVE	KEEP ON SMILIN'	ARCTIC 127	800.00	northern
HARD TO FIND THE RIGHT GIRL	EIGHT DAYS A WEEK	ATCO 6470	20.00	northern

GAMBRELLS

JIVE TALK	FIND A LOVE	PIONEER 2109	75.00	northern
YOU BETTER MOVE		CARLA 2527	250.00	northern

GANEY, JERRY

YOU DON'T LOVE ME	HI HEEL SNEEKERS	MGM 13697	40.00	northern

GANGSTERS

I FEEL YOU WHEN YOU'RE GONE	SMOKE	HEAT 1978	10.00	group

GANT, RAY AND THE ARABIAN KNIGHTS

DON'T LEAVE ME BABY	I NEED A TRUE LOVE	JAY WALKING 14	15.00	northern

GARDENER, GENTLEMAN JUNE

THE JOLLY LITTLE MEGET	HEP ME NO#.		50.00	funk

GARDINER HAPPENING, BORIS

Title	B-side	Label	Price	Genre
GHETTO FUNK		LEAL NO#	150.00	funk

GARDNER, AL

Title	B-side	Label	Price	Genre
WATCH YOURSELF	JUST A TOUCH OF YOUR HAND	SIR-RAH 504	30.00	northern
SWEET BABY		SEPIA	400.00	northern
I'LL GET ALONG		GROOVESVILLE 777	100.00	northern

GARDNER, DON

Title	B-side	Label	Price	Genre
WE'RE GONNA MAKE IT BIG	SAME:	MASTER FIVE 9108	20.00	70's
YOUR LOVE IS DRIVING ME CRAZY	THERE AIN'T GONNA BE NO LOVING	MR. G 824	25.00	northern
AIN'T GONNA LET YOU GET ME DOW	SOMEBODY'S GONNA GET HURT	TRU-GLO-TOWN 505	15.00	northern
CHEATIN' KIND	WHAT NOW MY LOVE	SEDGRICK 3001	3000.00	northern
IS THIS REALLY LOVE	TIGHTEN UP YOUR LOVE BONE	CEDRIC 3003	150.00	northern
MY BABY LIKES TO BOOGALOO	I WANT TO KNOW WHERE DID OUR L	TRU-GLO-TOWN 501	15.00	northern
SON MY SON	YOU UPSET MY SOUL	LUDIX 104	20.00	northern

GARDNER, KENARD

Title	B-side	Label	Price	Genre
DO THE SKIN	DO THE BOUNCE	DORE 793	20.00	**northerB**

GARDNER, LEON

Title	B-side	Label	Price	Genre
THE NATURAL		CALLA 163	300.00	funkTHE FARM
SONG		IGLOO 163	300.00	funk
ADAM AND EVE	ADAM AND EVE Pt.2	VISCOJON 464	30.00	northern

GARLAND, JIMMY

Title	B-side	Label	Price	Genre
YOU MADE A PROMISE	BABY, ONE MORE TIME	FESTIVAL 702	20.00	ballad

GARNER JR., EMMETT

Title	B-side	Label	Price	Genre
CHECK OUT WHAT YOU'VE GOT	SO MUCH BETTER	MAXWELL 802	10.00	70's

GARNER, REGGIE

Title	B-side	Label	Price	Genre
HOT LINE	BLESSED BE THE NAME	CAPITOL 3173	20.00	northern

GARNETT, GALE

Title	B-side	Label	Price	Genre
I'LL CRY ALONE	WHERE DO YOU GO TO GO AWAY	RCA 8549	30.00	northern

GARRETT, BOBBY

Title	B-side	Label	Price	Genre
I CAN'T GET AWAY	SAME: INSTRUMENTAL	MIRWOOD 5508	10.00	**northerB**
MY LITTLE GIRL	BIG BROTHER	MIRWOOD 5511	10.00	northern

GARRETT, ELAINE

Title	B-side	Label	Price	Genre
WHAT ABOUT ME	SAME: INSTRUMENTAL	GREEDY 112	15.00	70's

GARRETT, JO ANN

Title	B-side	Label	Price	Genre
ONE WOMAN	I'M A NOW GIRL (DO IT NOW)	DUO 7450	10.00	northern
CAN YOU DEAL WITH THAT	TELL HIM I LOVE HIM	DUO 7462	20.00	funk
A WHOLE NEW PLAN	STAY BY MY SIDE	CHESS 1957	75.00	northern

GARRETT, KELLY

Title	B-side	Label	Price	Genre
LOVE'S THE ONLY ANSWER	KNOWING WHEN TO LEAVE	SMASH 2195	150.00	**northerB**
THIS HEART IS HAUNTED	I DON'T THINK HE'S COMING	AVA 156	30.00	northern

GARRETT, LEE

Title	B-side	Label	Price	Genre
I CAN'T BREAK THE HABIT	BABY, PLEASE DON'T GO	HARTHON 137	30.00	**northerB**

GARRETT, VERNON

Title	B-side	Label	Price	Genre
DROWNING IN THE SEA OF LOVE	DO WHAT YOU SET OUT TO DO	SAFE 101	15.00	ballad
KEEP ON FORGIVING YOU	I MADE MY OWN WORLD	WATTS USA 54	15.00	ballad
IF I COULD TURN BACK THE HANDS	YOU AND ME TOGETHER	MODERN 1026	10.00	northern
CHRISTMAS GROOVE	MERRY CHRISTMAS BABY	GLOW HILL 1	10.00	funk
DON'T DO WHAT I DO	I'VE LEARNED MY LESSON	WATTS USA 5	30.00	funk
I LEARNED MY LESSON	LOVE JUNKIE	L.A.WEST 1	30.00	funk
WE PEOPLE OF THE GHETTO	YOU BLEW MY MIND	KAPP 2088	20.00	funk
ANGEL DOLL	HOP, SKIP AND JUMP	VENTURE 635	20.00	northern
SHINE IT ON	THINGS ARE LOOKING BETTER	KENT 459	15.00	northern

GARRIGAN, EDDIE

Title	B-side	Label	Price	Genre
I WISH I WAS	MAIL CALL	FONTANA 1575	50.00	**northerB**

GARTRELL, DEE DEE

Title	B-side	Label	Price	Genre
WOULD IT BREAK YOUR HEART	SECOND HAND LOVE	MAVERICK 1006	8.00	ballad
I MUST BE DOING SOMETHING RIGH	IF YOU GOT WHAT IT TAKES	MAVERICK 1010 DJ	10.00	funk
FIGHTING, FIRE WTH FIRE	SEE WHAT YOU DONE, DONE	DEMIN-KALO 3	10.00	northern

GARVIN, REX AND THE MIGHTY CRAVERS

Title	B-side	Label	Price	Genre
EMULSIFIED	GO LITTLE WILLIE	OKEH 7174	15.00	northern
I DON'T NEED NO HELP	I DON'T NEED NO HELP Pt.2	WSJ 103	30.00	**northerB**
I GOTTA GO NOW (UP ON THE FLOOR)	BELIEVEV IT OR NOT	LIKE 302	10.00	northern
QUEEN OF THE GO GO	THE OTHER MAN	TOWER 374	30.00	northern
SOCK IT TO 'EM J.B.	SOCK IT TO 'EM J.B. Pt.2	LIKE 301	10.00	northern

GARY AND GARY

Title	B-side	Label	Price	Genre
THE SOFT, EASY LIFE	CONSIDER YOURSELF LUCKY	HEIDI 105	20.00	northern

GARY, JOHN

Title	B-side	Label	Price	Genre
HANG ON TO ME	SLEEPING BEAUTY	RCA 9119	10.00	northern

GASLIGHT

Title	B-side	Label	Price	Genre
I'M ONLY A MAN	I'M GONNA GET YOU	GRAND JUNCTION 1100	10.00	70's
JUST BECAUSE OF YOU	IT'S JUST LIKE MAGIC	POLYDOR 14276	30.00	70's
I CAN'T TELL A LIE	HERE'S MISSING YOU	GRAND JUNCTION 1001	10.00	group

GASOLINE POWERED CLOCK

Title	B-side	Label	Price	Genre
FOREST FIRE ON MAIN ST	SAME: INSTRUMENTAL	GPC 1001	15.00	northern

GASPARD, EUGENE

Title	B-side	Label	Price	Genre
ON AND ON	HOLDING ON	ROSEMONT 4327	20.00	northern

GATEWAY

Title	B-side	Label	Price	Genre
CAN'T ACCEPT THE FACT	SAME:	COLUMBIA 10402 DJ	15.00	70's

GATTI, MARISA				
YOU'RE GONE NOW	LOVE'S WHAT YOU WANT	POO PAN 101	400.00	northern
GATURS				
A HUNK OF FUNK	YEAH YOU'RE RIGHTYOU KNOW	GATUR 555	15.00	funk
COLD BEAR	THE BOOGER MAN	ATCO 6870	15.00	funk
COLD BEAR	THE BOOGER MAN	GATUR 508	30.00	funk
SWIVEL YOUR HIPS	SWIVEL YOUR HIPS Pt.2	GATUR 556	75.00	funk
GAYE, ERROLL AND THE IMAGINATIONS				
LOVE AND EFFECTION	YOU DON'T WANT MY LOVE	STEEL TOWN 92539	20.00	70's
GAYE, MARVIN				
COME GET TO THIS	DISTANT LOVER	TAMLA 54241	8.00	70's
YOU'RE THE MAN	YOU'RE THE MAN PT.2	TAMLA 54221	10.00	funk
BABY DON'T YOU DO IT	WALK ON THE WILD SIDE	TAMLA 54101	10.00	motown
CAN I GET A WITNESS	I'M CRAZY 'BOUT MY BABY	TAMLA 54087	10.00	motown
CHANGE WHAT YOU CAN	YOU	TAMLA 54160	10.00	motown
HIS EYE IS ON THE SPARROW	JUST A CLOSER WALK WITH THEE	MOTOWN 1128	15.00	motown
HITCHHIKE	HELLO THERE ANGEL	TAMLA 54075	10.00	motown
LET YOUR CONSCIENCE BE YOUR GU	NEVER LET YOU GO	TAMLA 54041 striped	75.00	motown
PRIDE AND JOY	ONE OF THESE DAYS	TAMLA 54079	10.00	motown
SANDMAN	I'M YOURS, YOUR MINE	TAMLA 54055	40.00	motown
SOLDIER'S PLEA	TAKING MY TIME	TAMLA 54063 DJ	40.00	motown
STUBBORN KIND OF FELLOW	IT HURT ME TOO	TAMLA 54068	10.00	motown
THE TEEN BEAT SONG	LORAINE ALTERMAN Interviews Marvin Gaye.)	DETROIT FREE PRESS	150.00	motown
THIS IS THE LIFE	MY WAY	TAMLA 102308 DJ	200.00	motown
THIS LOVE STARVED HEART OF MINE	IT'S A DESPERATE SITUATION	TAMLA 42286 PS	75.00	motown
YOU'RE A WONDERFUL ONE	WHEN I'M ALONE I CRY	TAMLA 54093	10.00	motown
WITCHCRAFT	THE MASQUERADE IS OVER	TAMLA DJ no number	500.00	motown
GAYLES, JOANNE				
MEET ME HALF WAY	DON'T SHAKE MY TREE	BRIGHT STAR 12289	10.00	northern
GAYLORD AND HOLIDAY				
LOVE (WHERE HAVE YOU GONE)	A PLACE TO HIDE AWAY	PALMER 5022	20.00	northern
GAYNOR, GLORIA				
SHE'LL BE SORRY	LET ME GO BABY	JOCIDA 300	15.00	northern
GAYTEN, PAUL				
BEATNIK BEAT	SCRATCH BACK	ANNA 1112	10.00	motown
THE HUNCH	HOT CROSS BUNS	ANNA 1106	15.00	motown
GEARING, FRANKIE				
SPINNING TOP	BLUER THAN BLUE	BEALE ST. 1179	50.00	70's
GEDDES, DAVID				
WISE UP GIRL	THE LAST GAME OF THE SEASON	BIG TREE 16052	10.00	70's
GEE, JOEY				
IT'S MORE THAN I DESERVE	DON'T BLOW YOUR COOL	ABC 10781	150.00	northern
GEE, MARSHA				
BABY, I NEED YOU	I'LL NEVER BE FREE	UPTOWN 704	60.00	**northerB**
GEE'S				
IT'S ALL OVER	LOVE IS A BEAUTIFUL THING	PORT 3011	20.00	northern
GEMINIS				
NO MORE TOMORROW	GET IT ON HOME	RCA 8794	8.00	northern
CAN'T LET YOU GO	I HIRED THE GIRL	RCA 9151	15.00	northern
YOU PUT A HURTIN' ON ME	A FRIEND OF MINE	RCA 8865	10.00	northern
GEMS				
I'LL BE THERE	I MISS HIM	RIVERSIDE 4590	30.00	**northerB**
GENE AND EDDIE				
IT'S A SIN	YOU'VE GOT TO LOVE ME SOMETIME	MONCA 52670	30.00	northern
GENERAL ASSEMBLY				
SENSITIVE MIND	LOVIN' TIME	DESIREE 106	30.00	northern
GENERAL ASSISTENCE				
PLEASING PLUMP	I'M LOOKING FOR MY ROOTS	NORTHERN 1002	20.00	group
GENERATION				
HOLD ON	THE LONELY SEA	MOCKINGBIRD 1010	30.00	northern
GENTLEMAN FOUR				
YOU CAN'T KEEP A GOOD MAN DOWN	IT WON'T HURT	WAND 1184	400.00	northern
GENTRY, ART				
MERRY-GO-ROUND	I CAN'T MAKE IT WITHOUT YOU	ONYX 100	15.00	northern
GENTS				
LOVE IS SUCH A BEAUTIFUL THING	THE BIGGER THE CUSHION	PARAMOUNT 295	20.00	70's
GEORGE AND TEDDY				
IT'S A HEARTACHE	DO WHAT YOU WANNA	PHILIPS 40423	20.00	northern
GEORGE, HERMAN				
WHAT HAVE YOU GOT	MENTAL HIGH	BET ITS A HIT 203120	50.00	70's
GEORGE, ORTHEA				
KEEP ON WRITTIN'	COME TO ME	VOLUME 1110	20.00	northern
NOW THAT YOU'RE GONE	WHAT A GOOD THING YOU HAD IN MIND	CHEX 1008	20.00	northern
GEORGE, ROD				
I'VE GOT TO BE (YOUR NO. ONE M	YOU GO TO MY HEAD	TOWNES 101	40.00	northern
GEORGETTES				
HARD, HARD	WOULD YOU RATHER	YODI 1010	40.00	northern

OH SHUCKS	A GOOD MAN IS HARD TO FIND	SABRE 1003	30.00	northern

GEORGIA PROPHETS (also see PROPHETS)

FOR THE FIRST TIME	LOVING YOU IS KILLING ME	DOUBLE SHOT 138	20.00	northern
I GOT THE FEVER	SOUL CONTROL	ERIC 5009	10.00	northern
MUSIC WITH SOUL	CALIFORNIA	CAPRICORN 8006	20.00	northern

GERMAINE, DENISE

HE'S A STRANGE ONE	TOO-RA-LOO-RA (BYE-BYE-BABY)	ABC 10645	20.00	northern
LITTLE LOST LOVER	PLAYBOY	UA 707 dj	50.00	northern

GERONIMO AND THE APACHES

OH YES BABY I LOVE YOU SO	TOO LATE FOR TEARS	GALIKO 891	10.00	northern

GERRARD, DONNY

HE'S ALWAYS SOMEWHERE AROUND	DARLIN'	GREEDY 114	8.00	70's
HE'S ALWAYS SOMEWHERE AROUND	GREEDY (FOR YOUR LOVE)	GREEDY 107	10.00	70's

GERRY AND PAUL

THE CAT WALK	LITTLE BIT OF SOUL	FAT BACK 411	10.00	northern

GETTO KITTY

STAND UP AND BE COUNTED	HOPE FOR THE FUTURE	STROUD 5505	20.00	funk

GHETTO BOYS

HAND WRITING ON THE WALL	CAN I TELL YOU MORE	TARX 1009	100.00	northern

GHETTO CHILDREN

IT'S NOT EASY TO SAY GOODBYE	DON'T TAKE YOUR SWEET LOVIN' A	ROULETTE 7173	40.00	70's
I JUST GOTTA FIND SOMEONE TO LOVE	SAME:	COLUMBIA 45771 DJ	40.00	group

GI GI

DADDY LOVE	DADDY LOVE Pt.2	SWEET. 1	15.00	funk

GIBBS, DOUG

I'LL ALWAYS HAVE YOU THERE	CLOUDY DAY	OAK 108	15.00	70's

GIBBS, SHERRI AND THE QUOVANS

LET HIM GO	OH MY BABY	PHILLY SOUNDS 108	30.00	group

GIBRALTERS

I WON'T BE YOUR FOOL ANYMORE	SIDE BY SIDE	A&W 100	20.00	northern

GIBSON TRIO, JOHNNY

BEACHCOMBER	SWANKY	TWIRL 1023	15.00	northern

GIBSON, BEVERLY ANN (also see BEVERLY ANN)

A THREE DOLLAR BILL	DO THE MONKEY	JUBILEE 5447	40.00	northern

GIBSON, BILLY

YOU GOT IT, I WANT IT	WHAT I NEED NOW IS LOVE	MGM 13469 DJ	20.00	northern

GIBSON, CINDY (AND THE TIFFANYS)

I'LL ALWAYS LOVE YOU	(A LOVELY) SUMMER NIGHT	GENERAL. 700	40.00	northern
WHISPER YOU LOVE ME BOY	STEP BY STEP	ARCTIC 104	250.00	northern

GIBSON, DELORES

LOVE LAND	I WANT A MAN	KING 5664	30.00	northern

GIBSON, DOUGLAS

RUN FOR YOUR LIFE	I WON'T LEAVE	TRC 969	30.00	northern

GIFTED FOUR

ARE YOU CHOOSING	FALLEN STAR	HAMITO-SEMITICA 104	20.00	70's
ARE YOU CHOOSING	FALLEN STAR	CSC 104	15.00	70's

GIFTS

GIRL I LOVE YOU	TOO LITTLE AND TOO LATE	BALLAD 6005	15.00	northern
YOU CAN'T LOVE IN A BROKEN HEART	GOOD BYE MY LOVE	BALLAD 6003	10.00	northern

GIGI AND THE CHARMAINES

POOR UNFORTUNATE ME	BRAZIL	COLUMBIA 44246	20.00	northern

GIL, ROCKY AND THE BISHOPS

I'M SO CRUEL	DANCING IN THE STREETS	TEAR DROP 3150	8.00	group
IT'S NOT THE END	EVERY DAY OF LIFE	TEAR DROP 3181	600.00	northern

GILBERT, CARL

CRYING HEART	FOOL FOOL FOOL	AUDIO ARTS 60011	150.00	northern

GILES, EDDIE AND THE NUMBER

SEXY LADY	JELLY ROLL	CUSTOM SOUND 201	30.00	70's

GILFORD, JIMMY

HEARTBREAKER	I WANNA BE YOUR BABY	SOLID HIT 103	30.00	northern
I WANNA BE YOUR BABY	MISERY STREET	WHEELSVILLE 101	40.00	northern
NOBODY LOVES ME LIKE MY BABY	TOO LATE TO CRY	THEMLA 501	150.00	northern

GILLETTES

SAME IDENTICAL THING	24 HOURS OF THE DAY	J&S 1391	30.00	northern

GILLIAM, JOHNNY

COME BACK CAROL	IT'S TRUE, IT'S TRUE IT'S ONLY	ICA 7	20.00	70's
BABY TAKE ME BACK	YOU MAKE ME FEEL LIKE SOMEONE	MODERN 1052 DJ	40.00	northern
TELL YOUR FRIEND (IT'S OVER)	PEACE ON EARTH	CANCER 2372	15.00	70's
ROOM FULL OF TEARS	PEACE ON EARTH	CANCER 101	80.00	northern

GILSON, PATTI

DON'T YOU TELL A LIE	PULLING PETALS FROM A DAISY	GOLDEN WORLD 6	200.00	motown

GINO

IT'S ONLY A PAPER MOON	HOME SWEET HOME	GOLDEN CREST 581	60.00	northern

GIRLS

THE HURT'S STILL HERE	MARK MY WORD	MEMPHIS 102	20.00	70's

GIRLS THREE				
THAT'S HOW IT IS	BABY, I WANT YOU	CHESS 1958	30.00	northern
GLADYS				
CAN'T GET YOU OUTTA MY MIND	WILLOW WEEP FOR ME	O-GEE 430	40.00	northern
GLASS, LINDA				
BEFORE LOVE BEATS ME GOING	SOUR GRAPES	VIBRATION 3236	150.00	northern
GLIDERS				
NO TIME	LONELY CITIES AND ONE WAY ST.	ALVA 112	8.00	group
GLOBELITERS				
THE WAY YOU DO	SEE HOW THEY RUN	PHILTOWN 40003	20.00	northern
GLORIA AND THE TIARAS				
I'M SATISFIED	RUNNING OUT OF TIME	BETTY 1204	400.00	northern
GLORIES				
TRY A LITTLE TENDERNESS	THERE HE IS	DATE 1636	10.00	ballad
(I LOVE U BABE BUT)GIVE ME MY FREEDOM	SECURITY	DATE 1571	10.00	northern
I STAND ACCUSED (OF LOVING YOU)	WISH THEY COULD WRITE A SONG	DATE 1553	10.00	northern
I WORSHIP YOU BABY	DON'T DIAL MY NUMBER	DATE 1615	60.00	northern
SING ME A OVE SONG	OH BABY THAT'S LOVE	DATE 1579	15.00	northern
GLORY ROADS				
ROCK ME IN THE CRADLE	NOTHING BUT A HEARTACHE	COURTNEY 202	20.00	northern
GLOVER, CLARENCE				
KEEP YOUR PROMISES	MIDNIGHT TRAIN	LYNDELL 797	40.00	ballad
GLOVER, IRA				
FUNKY WOMAN	I'LL BE LOVING YOU	SOUL HOUSE 13429	40.00	funk
GOGGINS, CURBY				
LEAVE ME IF YOU WANT TO	COME HOME TO YOUR DADDY	CARNIVAL 510	40.00	northern
GOINS, HERBIE				
COMING HOME TO YOU	THE INCRDIBLE MISS BROWN	CAPITOL 5978	15.00	mod
GOLDEN BOND				
I KNOW (IT'S ALL OVER)	MEAN, MEAN WORLD	CAIN 2103	30.00	group
I KNOW (IT'S ALL OVER)	MEAN, MEAN WORLD	DELUXE 116 DJ	15.00	group
GOLDEN HARMONEERS				
I'M BOUND	PRECIOUS MEMORIES	MOTOWN 1015	50.00	motown
GOLDEN TOADSTOOLS				
SILLY SAVAGE	WEEPING RIVER	MINARET 138	30.00	funk
GOLDEN, SANDY				
YOU'RE MY EVERYTHING	GREY CLOUDS	MASTERPIECE 201	800.00	northern
GOLDSBORO, BOBBY				
IT'S TOO LATE	I'M COMING HOME	UA 980	8.00	northern
LONGER THAN FOREVER	TAKE YOUR LOVE	UA 50044	10.00	northern
GOMEZ, YVONNE				
MY MAN A GO GO	EASE THE PAIN	HAWAII 128	50.00	northern
GOOD TIME CHARLIE				
ROVER OR ME	I REMEMBER MINI-GINNY	PZAZZ 29	25.00	funk
GOOD, LEMME B.				
GOOD LOVIN'	WE CAN'T FINISH WHAT WE STARTE	MERCURY 72418	20.00	northern
GOOD, TOMMY				
BABY I MISS YOU	LEAVING HERE	GORDY 7034	40.00	motown
GOODE, JOHNNY				
PAYBACK	SAME: INSTRUMENTAL	SOLID HIT 106	15.00	mod
GOODNIGHT, TERRI				
THEY DIDN'T KNOW	THE FIGHTING IS OVER	PHELECTRON 701	800.00	northern
GOODWIN, OTIS AND THE CASTERNETTS				
I FEEL IT JUST A LITTLE BIT	SOMETIMES	JAZZ. 10	30.00	funk
GORDON, BENNY AND THE SOUL BROTHERS				
GIVE A DAMN	GIVE A DAMN PT. 2	PHIL LA SOUL 351	20.00	funk
A KISS TO BUILD A DREAM ON	IT COMES AND GOES	RCA 9270	15.00	northern
GIVE A DAMN ABOUT YOUR FELLER	PT.2	ESTILL 565	40.00	funk
GORDON, RUSSELL				
DOUBLE BOOTY BUMP		JAY-CEE	100.00	funk
GORDON, SAMMY AND THE HIPP HUGGERS				
UPSTAIRS ON BOSTON ROAD	Pt. 2	ARCHIVES 70	20.00	funk
JUNGLE BUMP	PT.2	LU LU 1000	50.00	funk
GORE, LESLEY				
I'M FALLING DOWN	SUMMER AND SANDY	MERCURY 72683	10.00	northern
MY TOWN, MY GUY AND ME	A GIRL IN LOVE	MERCURY 72475	6.00	northern
WE KNOW WE'RE IN LOVE	THAT'S WHAT I'LL DO	MERCURY 72530	10.00	northern
MY TOWN MY GUY AND ME	A GIRL IN LOVE	MERCURY 72475 PS	15.00	northern
GORGEOUS GEORGE				
BIGGEST FOOL IN TOWN	SWEET THING	STAX 165	50.00	ballad
IT'S NOT A HURTING THING		PEACHTREE	100.00	northern
FON-KIN		HOMARK	25.00	funk
GORMAN, FREDDIE				
LOVE HAS SEEN US THROUGH	ALIVE AGAIN	RENE. 901	15.00	70's
TAKE ME BACK	CAN'T GET IT OUT OF MY MIND	RIC TIC 102	15.00	motown
THE DAY WILL COME	JUST FOR YOU	MIRACLE 11	100.00	motown

IN A BAD WAY	THERE CAN BE TO MUCH	RIC TIC 101	15.00	northern
GORME, EYDIE				
EVERYBODY GO HOME	THE MESSAGE	COLUMBIA 42854	8.00	northern
GOSPEL CLASSICS				
MORE LOVE, THAT'S WHAT WE NEED	YOU NEED FAITH	CHECKER 5050	50.00	northern
GOSPEL STARS				
HAVE YOU ANY TIME FOR JESUS	GIVE GOD A CHANCE	DIVINITY 99006	25.00	motown
HE LIFTED ME	BEHOLD THE SAINTS OF GOD	TAMLA 54037	100.00	motown
GOVAN, JAMES				
UPHILL CLIMB	JEALOUS KIND	ENVELOPE 7002	10.00	70's
GRACIE, CHARLIE				
HE'LL NEVER LOVE YOU LIKE I DO	KEEP MY LOVE NEXT TO YOUR HEAR	DIAMOND 178	25.00	**northerB**
WALK WITH ME GIRL	TENDERNESS	SOCK & SOUL 102	15.00	northern
GRAHAM, JIMMY				
LOVE CAN'T BE MODERNIZED	WE SHALL OVERCOME	REVUE 11065	15.00	northern
A SOUL WALK IN	SOUL WALK	REVUE 11044	20.00	funk
GRAHAM, RALPH				
WHAT DO I HAVE TO DO	MY LOVE GOES WITH YOU	SUSSEX 505	10.00	70's
SHE JUST SITS THERE	YOU HAD TO HURT SOMEONE	UP FRONT 21	700.00	northern
GRAND PRIXS				
ROAR OF THE CROWD	LOST LOVE	TINA 1014	100.00	northern
I SEE HER PRETTY FACE	YOU DRIVE ME CRAZY	BIG MACK 2942	700.00	northern
GRAND, BARRY				
LOOKING BACK	ANNIVERSARY SONG	KARATE 504	15.00	northern
GRANGER, GERRI				
I CAN'T TAKE IT LIKE A MAN	GET IT TOGETHER	BELL 987	20.00	northern
CASTLE IN THE SKY		BIG TOP 3110	75.00	northern
I GO TO PICES (EVERYTIME)	DARLING TAKE ME BACK (I'M SORR	BELL 969	75.00	northern
YOU MUST BE DOING SOMETHING RIGHT	I CRIED	DOUBLE L 734	15.00	northern
GRANT, EARL				
HOUSE OF BAMBOO	TWO LOVES HAVE I	DECCA 31044	10.00	mod
HIDE NOR HAIR	I LOVE YOU YES I DO	DECCA 32093	20.00	northern
GRANT, ESTHER				
LET'S MAKE THE MOST OUT OF LOVE	TAKE ME NOW OR LEAVE ME BE	WILSTONE 1001	2000.00	northern
GRANT, JANIE				
MY HEART, YOUR HEART	AND THATREMINDS ME OF YOU	PARKWAY 982	30.00	**northerB**
GRAVES, JOE				
IT'S GOT TO BE REAL	BABY, IF YOU WERE GONE	RACK 103	15.00	70's
A BOY AND GIRL FALLS IN LOVE	DEBBIE	PARKWAY 103	15.00	northern
SEE SAW	BEAUTIFUL GIRL	PARKWAY 964	15.00	northern
GRAY, DOBIE				
SEE YOU AT THE GO GO	WALK WITH LOVE	CHARGER 107	8.00	northern
THE IN CROWD	BE A MAN	CHARGER 105	8.00	northern
OUT ON THE FLOOR	NO ROOM TO CRY	CHARGER 115	15.00	**northerB**
OUT ON THE FLOOR	MY BABY	THUINDERBIRD 549	25.00	northern
HONEY, YOU CAN'T TAKE IT BACK		WHITE WHALE 342	20.00	northern
WHAT A WAY TO GO		WHITE WHALE NO.#	300.00	northern
GRAY, PEARLEAN				
I DON'T WANT TO CRY	THE LOVE OF MY MAN	GREEN SEA 104	20.00	northern
GRAY, WILLIE CHARLES				
I'M GONNA BE A WINNER	HERE I GO AGAIN	MERCURY 72608	30.00	northern
GRAYSON TRIO, MILES				
YOU WERE WRONG	SWEET BREAD	HILL. 210	20.00	mod
GRAYSON, CALVIN				
IT'S BEEN NICE LOVING YOU	IF YOU GOTTA MAKE A FOOL OF SO	CAPITOL 5462	20.00	northern
LOVE JUST BEGAN	YOU'VE GOT TO BE WILLING	IN 6312	200.00	northern
WHERE DO I BELONG	BIG BROTHER	CAPITOL 5308	20.00	northern
GRAYSON, MILT				
YOU'RE OLD STAND-BY	WAYFARIN' STRANGER	DERBY 1007	150.00	northern
SOMETHING THAT GETS TO ME	HURRY SUNDOWN	MGM 13699 DJ	30.00	northern
GREAT DELTAS				
TRA LA LA	STAND UP AND BE A MAN	ENGLEWOOD 41629	400.00	funk
GREAT LAKES ORCHESTRA				
DIDN'T I TELL YOU	THIS IS THE NIGHT FOR LOVING	GREAT LAKES 101	70.00	70's
GREATER EXPERIENCE				
DON'T FORGET TO REMEMBER	CAROL'S CAROL	COLONY 2572	450.00	northern
GREEN BROTHERS				
SWEET LOVIN' WOMAN	LACK OF ATTENTION	TORTOISE 11130	30.00	70's
GREEN (E) , AL AND THE SOUL MATES				
I'LL BE GOOD TO YOU	A LOVER'S HOLIDAY	HOT LINE MUSIC	10.00	ballad
DON'T LEAVE ME	BACK UP TRAIN	HOT LINE MUSIC	15.00	northern
GET YOURSELF TOGETHER	DON'T HURT ME NO MORE	HOT LINE MUSIC	15.00	northern
I TRIED TO TELL MYSELF	SOMETHING	HI 2322	10.00	70's
DON'T LEAVE ME	HOT WIRE	BELL 45305	8.00	northern
LET ME HELP YOU	GUILTY	BELL 45258	10.00	northern
GREEN, BETTY				
LONELY GIRL	HE PUT ME DOWN	CRACKERJACK 4018	15.00	northern

GREEN, BIRDIE (BYRDIE)

HOW COME	TREMBLIN'	END 1117	40.00	northern
TREMBLIN	MEMORIES ARE MADE OF THIS	END 1122	30.00	northern
DON'T MAKE IT HURT	THE MAGIC OF YOUR LOVE	HALLMARK 334	15.00	northern
GET A HOLD OF YOURSELF	DON'T TAKE YOUR LOVE FROM ME	20th. CENTURY 422	20.00	northern

GREEN, CAL

STORMY	SOMEWHERE IN THE NIGHT	MUTT & JEFF 20	10.00	funk
TRIPPIN'	JOHNNY'S GONE TO VIETNAM	MUTT & JEFF 22	15.00	funk
I'LL GIVE YOU JUST A LITTLE MORE TIME	SPANKY	FILMTOWN 62068	400.00	northern

GREEN, CLAUDIA

SKATE A WHILE BABY	I JUST LOVE THE GUY	ABC 10879	25.00	northern

GREEN, GARLAND

ALL SHE DID (WAS WAVE GOODBYE)	DON'T THINK I'M A VIOLENT GUY	UNI 55188	10.00	70's
DON'T LET LOVE WALK OUT ON US	ASK ME FOR WHAT YOU WANT	RCA 10889	40.00	70's
LET ME BE YOUR PACIFIER	LET'S CELEBRATE	RCA 11126	10.00	70's
SENDIN MY BEST WISHES	SWEET LOVING WOMAN	SPRING 146	8.00	70's
YOU AND I GO GOOD TOGETHER	LET THE GOOD TIMES ROLL	SPRING 151	8.00	70's
IF A DREAM GOES BY	80-90-100 M.P.H.	COTILLION 44159	8.00	ballad
PLAIN AND SIMPLE GIRL	HEY CLOUD	COTILLION 44098	8.00	ballad
YOU CAN'T GET AWAY THAT EASY	GET RICH QUICK	COTILLION 44146	10.00	ballad
ANGEL BABY	YOU PLAYED ON A PLAYER	UNI 55213	15.00	northern
JEALOUS KINDA FELLA	I CAN'T BELIEVE YOU QUIT ME	UNI 55143	8.00	northern
JUST MY WAY OF LOVING YOU	ALWAYS BE MY BABY	COTILLION 44126	15.00	northern
LOVE IS WHAT WE CAME HERE FOR	RUNING SCARCED	COTILLION 44162	15.00	northern
PLAIN AND SIMPLE GIRL	HEY CLOUD	COTILLION 44098	8.00	northern
YOU PLAYED ON A PLAYER	MR. MISERY	REVUE 11020	10.00	northern
AIN'T THAT GOOD ENOUGH	LOVE NOW PAY LATER	REVUE 11030	50.00	northern
GIRL I LOVE YOU	IT RAINED 40 DAYS AND NIGHTS	GAMMA 103	150.00	northern
GIRL I LOVE YOU	IT RAINED FORTY DAYS AND NIGHTS	REVUE 11001	50.00	northern

GREEN, JIMMIE

THE ROBOT	SAME: INSTRUMENTAL	WAND 11254	15.00	funk

GREEN, JUDY

COME OUT OF THE CROWD	I CAN'T GET ALONG WITHOUT YOU	KLONDIKE 2232	20.00	northern

GREEN, SAM

IT'S TIME TO MOVE	FIRST THERE'S A TEAR	GOLDSMITH TCB 19	30.00	northern

GREENE, BARBARA

I SHOULD HAVE TREATED YOU RIGH	YOUNG BOY	VIVID 105	10.00	northern
YOUNG BOY	I SHOULD HAVE TREATED YOU RIGH	RENEE 5001	8.00	northern
LOVER'S PLEA	OUR LOVE IS NO SECRET NOW	RENEE 5004	20.00	northern

GREENE, CHARLES

DOUBLE "E" AGENT	BABY OH BABY	ANLA 108	30.00	northern

GREENE, LAURA

COME ON IN	MEMORIES AND SOUVENIRS	CAPITOL 3300	10.00	northern
MOONLIGHT MUSIC IN YOU	LOVE IS STRANGE	RCA 9164 DJ	40.00	northern

GREENE, SUSAYE

THAT'S THE WAY LOVE IS	PLEASE SEND HIM BACK TO ME	TRU-GLO-TOWN 507	40.00	northern

GREENE, TEDDY

CRY	GOTTA LOVE YOU MORE	CAPITOL 5226	30.00	northern

GREENE, VERNON

LOOK AT ME, LOOK AT ME	AM I EVER GONNA SEE MY BABY	MINIT 32034	75.00	northern

GREENWICH, ELLIE

BABY	YOU DON'T KNOW	RED BIRD 10034	100.00	northern

GREER, CORTEZ

VERY STRONG ON YOU	TAKE WHAT'S COMING TO YOU	VIOLET 4010	20.00	**northerB**

GREGG, BOBBY

THEME FROM THE OTHER SIDE	IF YOU WANT TO BE HAPPY	LAURIE 3358 DJ	10.00	northern

GRESHAM, JAMES

WHAT DID I DO	MR. WIND	DECCA 31832	15.00	northern

GRESHAM, JIMMIE (JIMMY)

THIS FEELIN I HAVE	PUT IT OUT OF MY MIND	TERI DE 5	700.00	northern
BE PREPARED TO PAY	THE PRICE IS TOO MUCH TO PAY	BARBARY COAST 100	250.00	northern

GRESHAM, JIMMY AND THE GIBSON KINGS

AIN'T THAT LOVE	TAKE ME TOO	KITTY 1009	150.00	northern

GRIER BROS.

WEEPING BABY ALL THE TIME	I GOT A WOMAN	MELDOY DISC 101	50.00	northern

GRIER, ROOSEVELT (ROSEY)

C'MON CUPID	HIGH SOCIETY WOMAN	AMY 11015	15.00	northern
IN MY TENEMENT	DOWN SO LONG	RIC. 112	75.00	northern
LOVER SET ME FREE	WHY	BATTLE 45911	25.00	northern
PIZZA PIE MAN	WELCOME TO THE CLUB	D-TOWN 1058	100.00	northern

GRIFFIN, BILL

TRY TO RUN A GAME ON ME	FORBIDDEN FRUIT	NAPTOWN 904	70.00	northern

GRIFFIN, HERMAN

I NEED YOU	I'M SO GLAD I LEARNED TO DO THIS	HOB 112.	20.00	motown
SLEEP (LITTLE ONE)	UPTIGHT	MOTOWN 1028	50.00	motown
TRUE LOVE (THAT'S LOVE)	IT'S YOU	TAMLA 54032 stripes	100.00	motown
ARE YOU FOR ME OR AGAINST ME	GETTIN' BETTER	MAGIC TOUCH 7	15.00	northern
DREAM GIRL	NOTHING BEATS A FAILURE BUT A TRY	MERCURY 72401	50.00	northern

MR. HEARTBREAK	NEVER TRUST YOUR GIRL-FRIEND	DOUBLE L 718	15.00	northern
TRUE LOVE	IT'S YOU	COLUMBIA 41951	30.00	northern

GRIFFIN, HERMAN AND THE MELLO-DEES

HURRY UP AND MARRY ME	DO YOU WANT TO SEE MY BABY	ANNA 1115	20.00	motown

GRIFFIN, HERMAN AND THE , MAURICE KING ORCHESTRA

I NEED YOU	I'M SO GLAD I LEARNED TO DO TH	HOB 112	200.00	motown

GRIFFINS, R.L.

PLAYTHING	GIVE YOUR HEART	RIDE 8261	50.00	northern

GRIFFITH, EMILE

GOIN' GOIN' GONE	THAT'S WHAT I LIKE	TRC 983 DJ	20.00	northern

GRIMES, HERMAN

(I'LL MAKE YOU) SMILE AGAIN	THAT'S JUST HALF THE STORY	BOOT HEEL 105	15.00	northern

GRINER, LINDA

GOOD-BY CRUEL LOVE	ENVIOUS	MOTOWN 1037	250.00	motown
GOOD-BY CRUEL WORLD	ENVIOUS	MOTOWN 1037 DJ	300.00	motown

GRIPPER, FREDDIE

FORGIVE ME	SAME	PARAMOUNT 0264	10.00	70's

GROOVE MERCHANTS

THERE'S GOT TO BE SOMEONE FOR	WE ARE ONLY FOOLING OURSELVES	SUEMI 4557	500.00	funk

GROOVE STICK

IMITATION OF LIFE	I CAN SEE	UPTOWN 765	15.00	northern

GROOVE

LOVE (IT'S GETTING BETTER)	THE LIGHT OF LOVE	20th. CENTURY 6671	20.00	northern
LOVE (IT'S GETTING BETTER)	THE LIGHT OF LOVE	WAND 1163	15.00	northern

GROOVERS

I'M A BASHFUL GUY	JUST GO FOR ME	TERI DE 2	75.00	northern
I'M A BASHFUL GUY	JUST GO FOR ME	MINIT 32010	20.00	northern

GROOVETTES

THINK IT OVER BABY	AIN'T A THING	RENESS 109	800.00	northern

GROUP CALLED (US)

PROMISE ME	AMERICAN GIRL	PATTY 1373	40.00	northern

GROUP FROM QUEENS

YOU SEARCH IS OVER	BOSS MAN	VEEP 1238	40.00	group

GTO'S

GIRL FROM NEW YORK CITY	MISSING OUT ON THE FUN	PARKWAY 108	20.00	northern

GUESS, LENIS

JUST ASK ME	WORKIN' FOR MY BABY	LE GRAND 1042	50.00	northern
JUST ASK ME	WORKIN' FOR MY BABY	S.P.Q.R. 1002	30.00	northern
TOO MANY NIGHTS	THANK GOODNESS GOTTA GOOD WOMA	PEANUT COUNTRY	10.00	northern
1002				

GUITAR RAY

PATTY CAKE SHAKE	NEW TRUE LOVE	HOT LINE 912	75.00	mod
YOU'RE GONNA WRECK MY LIFE		SHAGG 711	300.00	northern

GUNGA DIN

SNAKE PIT	CRABCAKES	VALISE 6903	100.00	funk

GUNTER, CORNELL

LOVE IN MY HEART	DOWN IN MEXICO	TOGETHER. 101	200.00	northern

GUNTER, SHIRLEY

STUCK UP	YOU LET MY LOVE GROW COLD	TRC 949	20.00	northern

GUYS FROM UNCLE

THE SPY	JAMMIN'	SWAN 4240	20.00	northern

GUYTON, HOWARD

I WATCH YOU SLOWLY SLIP AWAY	I GOT MY OWN THING GOING	VERVE 10386	100.00	**northerB**

GWEN AND RAY

BUILD YOUR HOUSE ON A STRONG F	IF IT MAKES YOU FEEL GOOD	BEE BEE 223	400.00	**northerB**

GYPSIES

JERK IT	DIAMONDS RUBIES GOLD AND FAME	OLD TOWN 1180	10.00	northern
IT'S A WOMAN'S WORLD	THEY'RE HAVING A PARTY	OLD TOWN 1184	150.00	**northerB**

HAFNER, DICK

GO 'WAY TEARS	WAKE UP SILLY BOY	VALIANT 6044	20.00	northern

HAINES, CONNIE

WHAT'S EASY FOR TWO IS HARD FO	WALK IN SILENCE	MOTOWN 1092	10.00	motown

HAINES, GARY

KEEP ON GOING	I WANT TO SING	SOUND 110	100.00	northerB
1105 DJ				

HAIRSTON, FOREST

WE GOT TO PIECES	THE SOUND OF THE BELLS	VINEY 1	15.00	northern

HAL AND BRENDA (Holloway)

IT'S YOU	UNLESS I HAVE YOU	MINASA 6714	40.00	motown

HALE, LARRY

ONCE	POLLY WOLLY	DIAMOND 203	20.00	northerB

HALL, BARBARA

CAN I COUNT ON YOU	V.I.P.	INNOVATION 8035	10.00	70's
YOU BROUGHT IT ON YOURSELF	DROP MY HEART OFF AT THE DOOR	INNOVATION 9162	20.00	70's

HALL, C. HENRY

(I PRAY FOR) A MIRACLE	I BELIEVE	MERCURY 72252	40.00	northern

HALL, CARL

WHAT ABOUT YOU	WHO'S GONNA LOVE ME	COLUMBIA 45813	150.00	70's
I DON'T WANT TO BE YOUR USED TO BE	THE DAM BUSTED	LOMA 2098	15.00	northern
IS YOUR LOVE GOING OR GROWING	ROLLOVER CASANOVA	MERCURY 72481	40.00	northern
MEAN IT BABY	YOU DON'T KNOW NOTHING ABOUT L	LOMA 2086	40.00	northern
MY BABY'S SO GOOD	WHAT COME OVER YOU	MERCURY 72396	30.00	northern
YOU'RE SO QUALIFY	HE GETS EVERYTHING HE WANTS	MERCURY 72547	40.00	northern

HALL, DAVE

LOOK AT ME		SOUND 115	500.00	northern

HALL, DELORES

GOOD LOVIN' MAN	W-O-M-A-N	KEYMEN 111	15.00	northern

HALL, DORA

PRETTY BOY	TIME TO SAY GOODBYE	REINBEAU 1302	20.00	northern

HALL, GERRI

WHO CAN I RUN TO	I LOST THE KEY	HOT LINE 905	200.00	northern

HALL, NAT

A BROKEN HEARTED CLOWN	EXPLANATION	TOPSOUL 105	30.00	ballad
WATCH YOURSELF	I'M LOST WITHOUT YOU	SOUL BOSS 201	40.00	northern
WHY (I WANT TO KNOW)		LOOP	300.00	northern

HALL, SIDNEY

THE WEEKEND	I'M A LOVER	SHRINE 109	800.00	northern

HALL, WAYMOND

WHAT WILL TOMORROW BRING	SOUL FUNK-TION	JAMAL 1005	300.00	northern

HALOS

COME SOFTLY TO ME	HE'S JUST TOO MUCH	CONGRESS 262	15.00	northern
DO I	JUST KEEP ON LOVING ME	CONGRESS 244	10.00	northern

HAMBER, KENNY

ANYTHING YOU WANT	AIN'T GONNA CRY (OVER ONE GIRL	ARCTIC 131	350.00	northern
THESE ARMS OF MINE	LOOKING FOR A LOVE	ARCTIC 139	100.00	northern
LET'S DO THE CAMEL WALK		MEAN	200.00	northern

HAMBRIC, BILLY

I FOUND TRUE LOVE	SHE SAID GOODBYE	DRUM 1204	30.00	northern
TALK TO ME BABY	HUMAN	FURY 5000	20.00	northern

HAMBRICK, BILLY

JUST CAN'T TAKE IT NO MORE	SOMEONE TO LOVE	JOVIAL 730	20.00	northern

HAMILTON, CHRIS

I'VE GOT TO HAVE YOUR LOVE	I'VE GOT TO CRY	BELL 663	20.00	northern

HAMILTON, EDWARD AND THE ARABIANS

BABY DON'T YOU WEEP	TELL ME	MARY JANE 1005	85.00	northerB
I'M GONNA LOVE YOU	JUST LET ME KNOW	MARY JANE 6707	30.00	northern
I'M GONNA LOVE YOU	CALL ME	JAMECO 2008	15.00	northern
I'M GONNA LOVE YOU	CALL ME	CARRIE 9	10.00	northerB
MY DARLING BABY	WILLING MIND	MARY JANE 1010	20.00	northern
FOR ME ONLY	TELL ME	MARY JANE 1003	25.00	northern
TELL ME	SCHOOL IS COOL	MARY JANE 1006	10.00	northern
TELL ME	MY DARLIN BABY	MARY JANE 1003	15.00	northern
NOW YOU HAVE TO CRY ALONE	I LOVE YOU SO	LANROD 1605 red	100.00	northern
NOW YOU HAVE TO CRY ALONE	TEMPTATION OF LOVE	LANROD 1605 yellow	150.00	northern

HAMILTON, LITTLE JOHNNY

OH HOW I LOVE YOU	GO	DORE 754	150.00	northern
KEEP ON MOVING	MUDDIE PIE	DORE 760	1000.00	northern

HAMILTON, PATTI
MY BABY LOVES ME	THE WAY THAT U TREAT ME BABY	LOVELITE 3	20.00	northern

HAMILTON, PETER
HEY GIRL	SAME: INSTRUMENTAL	JAMIE 1338	100.00	northern

HAMILTON, ROY
LET GO	YOU STILL LOVE HIM	MGM 13138	10.00	northern
100 YEARS	IT'S ONLY MAKE BELIEVE	GAP 125	10.00	ballad
IT'S ONLY MAKE BELIEVE	SAME:	GAP 125	10.00	ballad
WAIT UNTIL DARK	LET THIS WORLD BE FREE	CAPITOL 2057	10.00	ballad
TORE UP OVER YOU	AND I LOVE HER	RCA 8705	10.00	northern
CRACKIN' UP OVER YOU	WALK HAND IN HAND	RCA 8960	75.00	**northerB**
DON'T COME CRYING TO ME	IF ONLY I HAD KNOWN	EPIC 9492	20.00	northern
EARTHQUAKE	I AM	EPIC 9538	100.00	northern
HANG UPS	ANGELICA	GAP 116	15.00	northern
HEARTACHE (HURRY ON BY)	AIN'T IT THE TRUTH	RCA 8641	20.00	northern
I TAUGHT HER EVERYTHING SHE KNOWS	LAMENT	RCA 9061	10.00	northern
INTERMEZZO	MIDNIGHT TOWN - DAYBREAK CITY	MGM 13157	15.00	northern
SHE'S GOT A HEART	THE IMPOSSIBLE DREAM	RCA 8813	10.00	northern
THE CLOCK	I GET THE BLUES WHEN IT RAINS	EPIC 9390	10.00	northern
THE PANIC IS ON	THRERE SHE IS	MGM 13217	75.00	northern
THE SINNER	THEME FROM V.I.P'S	MGM 13175 DJ	15.00	northern
TORE UP OVER YOU	AND I LOVE HER	RCA 8705	15.00	northern
YOU CAN COUNT ON ME	SHE MAKE ME WANNA DANCE	MGM 13291	75.00	northern
YOU SHOOK ME UP	SO HIGH MY LOVE	RCA 9171	100.00	northern
DON'T COME CRYING TO ME	IF ONLY I HAD KNOWN	EPIC 9492 PS	30.00	northern
EARTHQUAKE	I AM	EPIC 9538 PS	125.00	northern
I'LLL COME RUNNING BACK TO YOU	CLIMB EV'RY MOUNTAIN	EPIC 9520 PS	25.00	northern
THE CLOCK	I GET THE BLUES WHEN IT RAINS	EPIC 9390 PS	25.00	northern

HAMILTON, VERA
BUT I AIN'T NO MORE (GSTSKDTS)	SAME:	EPIC 10875 DJ	30.00	funk

HAMILTON, WILLIE
SHE'S ALRIGHT	CHEER UP	HRP 2	20.00	northern

HAMLIN, BILLY
SOMEBODY PLEASE	THE CONCENTRATION	TOY 110	40.00	northern

HAMMOND, CLAY
DANCE LITTLE GIRL	SHOTGUN WEDDING	DUO DISC 109	15.00	northern
DANCE LITTLE GIRL	TWIN BROTHER	KEYMEN 105	15.00	northern

HAMMOND, LITTLE WALTER
LET YOUR CONSCIENCE BE YOUR GUIDE	WE GO TOGETHER, YES WE DO	DUO DISC 110	30.00	northern

HAMPTON, JOHNNY
NOT MY GIRL	DON'T LEAD ME ON	DOTTY'S 345	800.00	**northerB**

HAMPTON, LIONEL
GREASY GREENS	SUNSHINE SUPERMAN	GLAD HAMP 2038	20.00	funk

HANDY, ROY
ACIDENTAL LOVE	WHAT DID HE DO	MARTON 1001	200.00	northern
BABY THAT'S A GROOVE	MONKEY SEE - MONKEY DO	STEPHANYE 334	20.00	**northerB**

HANEY, JACK AND ARMSTRONG, NIKI
PEACEFUL	THE INTERVIEW (SUMMIT CHANTED	MELODY 107	20.00	motown

HANK AND ROVER
A LOT TO BE DONE	A ROCK DOWN IN MY SHOE	OKEH 7264 DJ	30.00	balladB

HANKS, MIKE AND THE DEL-FI'S
THE HAWK	WHEN TRUE LOVE COMES TO BE	MAHS 3 yellow	40.00	motown
WHEN TRUE LOVE COMES TO BE	THE HAWK	SPARTAN 401	20.00	motown

HANNA, JIMMY AND THE DYNAMICS
LEAVING HERE	SOMEONE SOMEWHERE	SEAFAIR BOLO 752	25.00	northern

HARD COVER
DO YOU CARE (LIKE YOU SAY U D0	I BET SHE DOES IT	SHANTY TOWN 101	75.00	70's

HARDIE, CELEST
THANK YOU LOVE	SAME: INSTRUMENTAL	LOADSTONE 3955	15.00	70's
YOU TOUCHED THE INNER PART OF	SAME: INSTRUMENTAL	LOADSTONE 3961	15.00	70's
YOU'RE GONE	THAT'S WHY I CRIED	REYNOLDS 200	300.00	70's

HARDY, CLARA
I DREAM OF YOU	SAME: INSTRUMENTAL	TUNA 101	1500.00	northern
YOU'RE TOO JEALOUS	THE TOUCH OF LOVE	JACK POT 800	150.00	northern

HARDY, HAL
HOUSE OF BROKEN HEARTS	LOVE MAN	HOLLYWOOD 1116	20.00	northern
TEARS OF JOY	AROUND ABOUT SUNDOWN	DELUXE 104	30.00	northern

HARDY, LAVELL
DON'T LOSE YOUR GROOVE	WOMEN OF THE WORLD	ROJAC 117	20.00	funk

HARGRAVES, SILKY
HURT BY LOVE	GO ON GIRL	D-TOWN 1043	50.00	northern
I'LL KEEP ON TRYING	LOVE, LET'S TRY IT AGAIN	WHEELSVILLE 116	200.00	northern
KEEP LOVING ME (LIKE YOU DO)	YOU'RE TOO GOOD (TO ME BABY)	DEARBORN 563	300.00	northern

HARGROVE, ROSE
WHY AM I LOSING YOU	ONCE A DAY	AFCO 523	75.00	northern

HARMONICS
BE YOUR MAN	SCUM-A-DOOM DOOM (IN THE GHETTO)	SOCK IT 004	30.00	northern

HARNER, BILLY

WHAT ABOUT THE MUSIC	PLEASE SPARE ME THIS TIME	KAMA SUTRA 242	10.00	northern
HOMICIDE DRESSER	LAVENDER ROOM	KAMA SUTRA 238	8.00	northern
I STRUCK IT RICH	WATCH YOUR STEP	OR. 1255	10.00	northern
SALLY SAYIN' SOMETHING	DON'T WANT MY LOVIN'	KAMA SUTRA 226	10.00	northern
I GOT IT FROM HEAVEN	SAME:	SOUND GEMS DJ	500.00	70's

HARPER II, HERMAN H.

HEADED FOR THE STREETS	WAITING UP FOR	LOADSTONE 3960	25.00	70's

HARPER, BUD

MR. SOUL	LET ME LOVE YOU	PEACOCK 1939	20.00	northern
WHEREVER YOU WERE	LET IT RAIN	PEACOCK 1932	150.00	northern

HARPER, JEANETTE

PUT ME IN YOUR POCKET	TO BE LOVED	20th. CENTURY	150.00	northern
6683 DJ				

HARPER, WILLIE

BUT I COULDN'T	NEW KIND OF LOVE	ALON 9000	15.00	northern
YOU, YOU	SODA POP	SANSU 451	20.00	northern

HARRIS, BETTY

RIDE YOUR PONY	TROUBLE WITH MY LOVER	SANSU 480	10.00	northern
12 RED ROSES	WHAT'D I DO WRONG	SANSU 455	10.00	northern
SHOW IT	HOOK LINE AND SINKER	SANSU 479	15.00	northern
RIDE YOUR PONY	TROUBLE WITH MY LOVER	SANSU 480	10.00	northern
TAKING CARE OF BUSINESS	YESTERDAY'S KISSES	DOUGLAS 104	25.00	ballad

HARRIS, BILL

AM I COLD AM I HOT	AM I COLD AM I HOT (long vesion)	RCA 10520	40.00	70's

HARRIS, CHARLIE

ALL OVER TOWN	I'LL NEVER LIE TO YOU	COPA 8009	200.00	northern

HARRIS, DIMPLES

DO I NEED YOU	IT WAS YOU	ROMARK 111	30.00	northern

HARRIS, ERNIE

HOLD ON	BETTY	OKEH 7196	20.00	ballad

HARRIS, GAYLE

AIN'T GONNA LET IT GET ME DOWN	HERE I GO AGAIN	DCP 1144	30.00	northern

HARRIS, JILL

BABY, WON'T YOU TRY ME	OH, BABY	CAPITOL 5220	20.00	northern
YOU REALLY DIDN'T MEAN IT	HIS KISS	CAPITOL 5363	50.00	northern

HARRIS, JOYCE

BABY, BABY, BABY	HOW LONG (CAN I HOLD BACK MY TEARS)	FUN 6053	300.00	northern

HARRIS, JUDY

YOU TOUCHED ME	GLORY TRAIN	SUN. 1117	20.00	**northerB**

HARRIS, KURT

EMPEROR OF MY BABY'S HEART	GO OBN	DIAMOND 158	150.00	northern

HARRIS, MAJOR

CALL ME TOMORROW	LIKE A ROLLING STONE	OKEH 7327	150.00	northern
LOVING YOU MORE	JUST LOVE ME	OKEH 7314	40.00	northern

HARRIS, MARCENE

WORK IT OUT	CHILDREN OF GEORGIA	ROMARK 105	10.00	ballad

HARRIS, PEPPERMINT

WAIT UNTIL IT HAPPENS TO YOU	ANYTIME IS THE RIGHT TIME	JEWEL 772	150.00	northern

HARRIS, TYRONE

AIN'T THAT FUN	NOTHING SEEMS TO GO RIGHT	BARCLAY & THE III 103	20.00	70's

HARRISON BROTHERS

I'LL BE STANDING BY	BEAUTIFUL LIES	ABC 10593	15.00	northern
RUN FOR YOUR LIFE	SAME: INSTRUMENTAL	BOBALOU 1001	200.00	northern
STANDING ON THE CORNER	BABY, I'M COMING HOME TO YOU	EVERLAST 5028	20.00	northern

HARRISON, BOB AND JIM

HERE IS MY HEART	HAND CLAP BLUES	CLOCK 71890	30.00	ballad

HARRISON, EARL

HUMPHREY STOMP	CAN YOU FORGIVE ME	GARRISON 3001	10.00	northern

HARRISON, STERLING

SAD AND LONELY	RIGHT THERE WITH YOU	SMASH 1856	20.00	ballad

HARRISON, WILBERT

NEAR TO YOU	SAY IT AGAIN	SEA-HORN 502	15.00	northern

HARRY AND THE KEYAVAS

IF TIS IS GOODBYE	TEARS	IPG 1011	20.00	northern

HART AND SHORTER

IT'S IN MY MIND	COME HERE BABY	COOL SCHOOL 2001	15.00	northern

HART, CAJUN

GOT TO FIND MY WAY	LOVER'S PRAYER	WB 7258	200.00	northern

HART, DON

SOLDIERS COMING HOME	KEEP ON HOLDING ON	COOL SCHOOL 2002	50.00	northern

HART, DON AND THE SHORTER, JAMES

ALL THE LOVE I GOT	I SHED A TEAR	LA BEAT 6609	15.00	northern

HART, JIMMY.

TEA HOUSE IN CHINA TOWN	SUGAR BABY	MERCURY 72540	300.00	northern

HARTFIELD, PETER
LOVE ME	DARLING TONIGHT	MIRACLE 8	50.00	motown

HARVEY
ANY WAY YOU WANTA	SHE LOVES ME SO	TRI-PHI 1017	50.00	**northerB**
COME ON AND ANSWER ME	MEMORIES OF YOU	TRI-PHI 1024	15.00	motown

HARVEY AND THE PHENOMENALS
SOUL N' SUNSHINE	WHAT CAN I DO	DA-WOOD 7200	150.00	funk

HARVEY AND THE SPINNERS
WHISTLING ABOUT YOU	SHE'S LOVES ME SO	TRI-PHI 1010	15.00	motown

HARVEY AND ANN
WHAT CAN YOU DO NOW	WILL I DO	HARVEY 121	20.00	motown

HARVEY, LEE
MY ASSURANCE	IF I'M DREAMING	KRIS 104	100.00	northern
PROVE IT	ONLY TRUE LOVE	J GEMS 105	15.00	northern

HASKINS, AL
YOU GOT ME	TAME ME	SURE SHOT 5018	20.00	northern

HATCHER, ROGER
CAUGHT MAKING LOVE	SAME:	COLUMBIA 45993	15.00	ballad
WE GONNA MAKE IT	HIGH BLOOD PRESSURE	BROWN DOG 9009	10.00	ballad
SWEETEST GIRL IN THE WORLD	I'M GONNA DEDICATE MY SONG TO	EXCELLO 2297	100.00	northern

HATCHER, WILLIE
TELL ME SO	WHO'S GOT A WOMAN LIKE MINE	EXCELLO 2310	30.00	ballad
HAVE A HEART, GIRL	YOU GOT QUALITY	COTILLION 44014	20.00	northern
GOOD THINGS COME TO THOSE WHO WAIT	SEARCHING	COLUMBIA 44259	50.00	northern
HEAD OVER HEELS	WHO'S GOT A WOMAN LIKE MINE	KING 6360 DJ	15.00	northern

HAVENS, RICHIE
I'VE GOTTA GO	MORNING, MORNING	VERVE FOLKWAYS 5009	10.00	northern
INDIAN ROPE MAN	JUST ABOVE MY HOBBY HORSE'S HE	VERVE 5092	15.00	mod

HAVIOR, JAMES
JUMPIN' WITH POPEYE	GIRL, GIRL, GIRL	CROW. 39	50.00	funk

HAWKINS, NIPPY AND THE NIP-TONES
IT'S GONNA BE TOO LATE	ANGIE	LORRAINE 1001	50.00	northern

HAWKINS, SAM
HOLD ON BABY	BAD AS THEY COME	BLUE CAT 112	10.00	northern
IT HURTS SO BAD (DRIP DROP)	I KNOW IT'S ALRIGHT	BLUE CAT 121	10.00	northern

HAWKINS, SAMMY
STANDING ON THE SIDELINES	WOBBLE MAMA	MAYCON 128	30.00	northern

HAYES, MALCOLM
I CAN'T MAKE IT WITHOUT YOU	BABY PLEASE DON'T LEAVE ME	OKEH 7299	75.00	northern
I GOTTA BE WITH YOU	PUT YOUR LOVE TO THE TEST	FILMWAYS 101	30.00	northern
IT'S NOT EASY	HURRY SUNDOWN	LIBERTY 55943 DJ	20.00	northern
SEARCHIN' FOR MY BABY	SHE'S THE ONE I LOVE	CHATAHOOCHIE	100.00	northern

HAYES, MEL
LADY ARE YOU CRAZY	SAME: INSTRUMENTAL	BOOGIE MAN 225	20.00	70's

HAYWARD, LEON
SHE'S WITH HER OTHER LOVE	PAIN IN MY HEART	IMPERIAL 66123	15.00	northern

HAYWOOD, JOE
I CROSS MY HEART (& HOPE TO DI	IN YOUR HEART YOU KNOW I LOVE	FRONT PAGE 1003	15.00	northern
I LOVE YOU YES I DO	IT TAKES THE DARK TO MAKE YOU	RAMPAGE 1002	10.00	northern

HAYWOOD, LEON
MELLOW MOONLIGHT	TENNESSEE WALTZ	DECCA 32230	10.00	northern
SKATE AWHILE	EVER SINCE YOU WERE SWEET 16	FAT FISH 8008	15.00	northern
IT'S GOT TO BE MELLOW	CORNBREAD AND BUTTERMILK	DECCA 32164	15.00	northern
YOU DON'T HAVE TO SEE ME CRY	I WANT TO TALK ABOUT MY BABY	DECCA 32348	15.00	northern
AIN'T NO USE	HEY HEY HEY	FAT FISH 8001	15.00	northern
AIN'T NO USE	ONE OF THESE DAYS	FAT FISH 8001	20.00	northern
BABY RECONSIDER	GOIN' BACK TO NEW ORLEANS	FAT FISH 8011	150.00	**northerB**
IT'S GOT TO BE MELLOW	CORNBREAD AND MILK	EVEJIM 1941	25.00	northern
IT'S THE LAST TIME	SAME:	DECCA 34520 DJ	10.00	northern
THE TRUTH ABOUT MONEY	WOULD I	FANTASY 581	40.00	northern
ONE WAY TICKET TO LOVELAND	THERE AIN'T ENOUGH HATE AROUND	EVEJIM 1943	8.00	ballad
CONSIDER THE SOURCE	JUST YOUR FOOL	CAPITOL 2584	75.00	northern

HAZELHURST, JAMES
I WON'T DIE	COME TO ME TOGETHER	SWAR 6021	20.00	70's

HEAD, ROY
TREAT HER RIGHT	SO LONG, MY LOVE	BACK BEAT 546	10.00	northern

HEADLINERS
TONIGHT'S THE NIGHT	YOU'RE BAD NEWS	V.I.P. 25011	30.00	motown
WE CALL IT FUN	VOODOO PLAN	V.I.P. 25026	20.00	motown

HEARD, OMA
MR. LONELY HEART	LIFETIME MAN	V.I.P. 25008	200.00	motown

HEARTBREAKERS
I FOUND A NEW LOVER	I'M FALLIN' IN LOVE AGAIN	MIRACLE 101	100.00	northern
I'VE GOT TO FACE IT	HOW DO YOU SAY GOODBYE	DERBY CITY 101	20.00	northern

HEARTS OF STONE
IF I COULD GIVE YOU THE WORLD	YOU GOTTA SACRIFICE	V.I.P. 25064	15.00	northern
IT'S A LONESOME ROAD	YESTERDAY'S LOVE IS OVER	V.I.P. 25058	10.00	motown

HEATHERTON, JOEY

WHEN YOU CALL ME BABY	LIVE AND LEARN	DECCA 31962	75.00	northern
WHEN YOU CALL ME BABY	LIVE AND LEARN	DECCA 31962 PS	150.00	northern

HEBB, BOBBY

I LOVE EVERYTHING ABOUT YOU	SOME KINDA MAGIC	PHILIPS 40448	8.00	northern
TRUE I LOVE YOU	PROUD SOUL HERITAGE	LAURIE 3632	10.00	northern
WOMAN AT THE WINDOW	I WAS A BOY WHEN YOU NEEDED A MAN	CADET 5690	15.00	northern
CRAZY BABY	LOVE ME	PHILIPS 40421	8.00	northern
YOU WANT TO CHANGE ME	DREAMY	PHILIPS 40551	20.00	northern
LOVE LOVE LOVE	A SATISFIED MIND	PHILIPS 40400	8.00	northern
LOVE LOVE LOVE	A SATISFIED MIND	PHILIPS 40400 PS	15.00	northern

HEIGHT, DONALD

I CHOOSE YOU	SOMPIN' AND SOMPIN	DAKAR 4556 DJ	70.00	70's
I'LL NEVER FORGET YOU	CRAZXY LITTLE GIRL	OLD TOWN 1161	10.00	ballad
BABY SET ME FREE	CLIMBING THE POLE	OLD TOWN 1172	30.00	northern
BOW 'N ARROW	CAN'T HELP FALLING IN LOVE	ROULETTE 4644	10.00	northern
I CAN'T GET ENOUGH	WE GOTTA MAKE UP	SHOUT 213	15.00	northern
LOOKING FOR MY BABY	DON'T LET ME DOWN	JUBILEE 5671	10.00	northern
SHE BLEW A GOOD THING	TWELTH OF NEVER	JUBILEE 5681	15.00	northern
TALK OF THE GRAPEVINE	THERE'LL BE NO TOMORROW	SHOUT 200	20.00	northern
THREE HUNDRED AND SIXTY FIVE D	I'M WILLING TO WAIT	SHOUT 208	10.00	northern
YOU CAN'T TRUST YOUR BEST FRIEND	PRETTY GIRL	OLD TOWN 1164	100.00	northern
YOU'RE TOO MUCH	SONG OF THE STREET	ROULETTE 4658	15.00	northern

HELMS, JIMMY

YOUR PAST IS BEGINNING TO SHOW	SON OF MARY	ORACLE 1004	10.00	northern
YOU'RE MINE, YOU	SUSIE'S GONE	SYMBOL 923	75.00	northern

HENDERSON, CARL

I LOVE YOU SO	SADNESS	RENFRO 116	100.00	northern
I'M SCHEMING	GOTTA KEEP ON MOVING	RENFRO 1118	300.00	northern
SEE WHAT YOU HAVE DONE	YOU'RE ALL I NEED	RENFRO 843	100.00	**northerB**
SHARING YOU	PLEASE STOP LAUGHING AT ME	RENFRO 338	15.00	northern
THAT GIRL	YOU'RE ALL I NEED	RENFRO 115	20.00	**northerB**

HENDRIX, MARGIE

ONE ROOM PARADISE		MERCURY 72734	40.00	northern
RESTLESS	ON THE RIGHT TRACK	MERCURY 72701	10.00	northern

HENLEY, CHUCK

BROKEN HEART	STANDING IN THE NEED OF LOVE	COACH 811	100.00	northern

HENLY, FLOYD

BELIEVE IN ME	UNCHAINED MELODY	KAS-MO 1001	10.00	northern

HENRY, ANDREA

I NEED YOU LIKE A BABY	THE GRASS IS GREENER	MGM 13893	250.00	northern

HENRY, EDD

I LOVE ONLY YOU	SAME: INSTRUMENTAL	NU SOUND 180	20.00	northern
YOUR REPLACEMENT IS HERE	CROOKED WOMAN	BIG MACK 1286	100.00	northern

HENRY, JA NEEN

BABY BOY	LOVE IS WHAT YOU MAKE IT	BLUE ROCK	50.00	northern

HENRY, JOHN ROOTMAN

SAY IT	LOVE IS NOT A STRANGER	AMBER ANTIQUE 5501	20.00	70's

HENRY, JOSEPH

WHO'S THE KING (UKNOW THATS ME	I FEEL RIGHT	DESCO 1009	15.00	funk

HENRY, THOMAS

SOME DAY	YOU DON'T WANT MY LOVE	SPAR 766	20.00	northern

HENRY, VIRGIL

I'LL BE TRUE	YOU FOOLED ME	COLOSSUS 102	20.00	70's
YOU AIN'T SAYIN' NOTHIN' NEW	I CAN'T BELIEVE YOU'RE REALLY LEAVING	COLOSSUS 115	150.00	70's
YOU AIN'T SAYING NOTHING NEW	I CAN'T BELIEVE YOU'RE REALLY LEAVING	TAMLA 54212	125.00	70's

HENSLEE, GENE

SHAMBLES	BEAUTIFUL WOMEN	MELODY 110	10.00	motown

HENSON, ANNITA

BIT BY BIT	TALK'S AROUND	SEVENS	500.00	northern
INTERNATIONAL 3				

HERBS

THERE MUST BE AN ANSWER	PUT A HURTIN ON MY HEART	SMOKE 612	10.00	group
NEVER, NEVER (WILL I FALL IN L	QUESTION	SMOKE 602	25.00	northern

HERCULOIDS

GET BACK		HERCULOIDS NO#	100.00	funk
PNEUMONIA		HERCULOIDS NO#.	100.00	funk

HERMAN, BONNIE

HUSH DON'T CRY	HERE THERE AND EVERYWHERE	COLUMBIA 43833	150.00	northern

HERMAN, SONNY

WHAT ABOUT ME	SAME: INSTRUMENTAL	UTOPIA 601	300.00	northern

HERRERA, LITTLE JULIAN

LONELY, LONELY NIGHTS	I WANT TO BE WITH YOU	ESSAR 1012	15.00	group

HESITATIONS

IS THIS THE WAY TO TREAT A GIRL	YES I'M READY	GWP 504	10.00	northern
I'M NOT BUILT THAT WAY	SOUL SUPERMAN	KAPP 790	50.00	**northerB**
SHE WON'T COME BACK	I'LL BE RIGHT THERE	KAPP 822	40.00	northern
WAIT A MINUTE	SOUL KIND OF LOVE	KAPP 810	30.00	northern

YOU CAN'T BY PASS LOVE | YOU'LL NEVER KNOW | KAPP 848 | 20.00 | northern

HESS, FRED
YOU'RE NOT THE SAME NOW | COUNT ME IN | HIT. 213 | 25.00 | northern

HESTOR, TONY
JUST CAN'T LEAVE YOU | WATCH YOURSELF | GIANT 707 | 300.00 | northern
JUST CAN'T LEAVE YOU | WATCH YOURSELF | KARATE 523 | 200.00 | northern

HEWITT
IS IT ME | PT. 2 | WEE 92272 | 15.00 | 70's

HEWITT, LONNIE
I GOTTA KEEP MY BLUFF IN | PT 2. | WEE 484 | 15.00 | northern

HEWITT, WINSTON
I'M FEELIN' GOOD | I'M FEELIN' GOOD PT.2 | BOSS 1075 | 100.00 | 70's

HEYWOOD, ANN
CROOK HIS LITTLE FINGER | EVERYTHING UNDER THE SUN | HONDO 100 | 100.00 | northern

HICKERSON JR., WYETH E.
STOP BLOWING YOUR HORN | | BACHMAN | 50.00 | funk

HICKS, JIMMY
I'M MR. BIG STUFF | TELL HER THAT I LOVE YOU | BIG DEAL 1003 | 20.00 | funk

HICKS, JOE
I GOTTA BE FREE | DON'T IT MAKE YOU FEEL FUNKY | AGC 2 | 300.00 | northern
DON'T IT MAKE YOU FEEL FUNKY | SOUL MEETIN' | AGC 1 | 20.00 | **northerB**

HICKS, MARVA
LOOKING OVER MY SHOULDER | HERE I GO AGAIN | INFINITY 50001 | 15.00 | 70's

HIGH KEYES
QUE SERA, SERA | DADDY OOH LONG LEGS | ATCO 6268 | 10.00 | mod
ONE HORSE TOWN | DON'T LEAVE ME NOW | ATCO 6290 | 45.00 | northern
LIVING A LIE | LET'S TAKE A CHANCE | VERVE 10423 | 100.00 | **northerB**

HIGH SOCIETY
I CAN'T BELIEVE | YOU CAN'T HIDE THE REAL YOU | USA 201 | 20.00 | northern

HIGH VOLTAGE.
COUNTRY ROAD | LOVE HATE | COLUMBIA 45701 | 20.00 | northern

HIGHLITERS
FUNKY 16 CORNERS | | PRP NO# | 300.00 | funk

HI-LITES
THAT'S LOVE | SAME: INSTRUMENTAL | INVICTUS 1274 | 15.00 | 70's
I'M SO JEALOUS | THE MIX MIX SONG | DARAN 222 | 10.00 | northern

HILL SISTERS
HIT AND RUN AWAY | ADVERTISING FOR LOVE | ANNA 1103 | 20.00 | motown
HIT AND RUN AWAY | ADVERTISING FOR LOVE | ANNA 103 NI | 500.00 | motown
JUST IN CASE | MY KIND OF GUY | CHOICE 1001 | 20.00 | northern

HILL, BOBBY
TELL ME YOU LOVE ME | TO THE BITTER END | LOLO 2307 | 100.00 | northern

HILL, CLARENCE
A LOT OF LOVIN' GOIN' ROUND | WHEN SUNNY COMES STROLLIN' HOM | MAINSTREAM 627 | 300.00 | northern

HILL, EDDIE
I CAN HEAR YOU CRYING | I CAN'T HELP IT | GE GE 502 | 25.00 | northern
NOTHING SWEETER (THAN YOU GIRL) | SAME: INSTRUMENTAL | M-S 207 | 150.00 | northern
YOU GOT THE BEST OF ME | BABY I CRIED | THEMLA 105 | 175.00 | northern

HILL, ELAINE
IS IT REALLY WORTH IT | YOU'RE GONNA GET IT | RSVP 1101 | 40.00 | northern

HILL, GLORIA
BE SOMEBODY | | DEEP NO.# | 100.00 | northern

HILL, JACKIE
WON'T YOU COME CLOSER | MY MAN, HE'S EVERYTHING | MARBRIT 301 | 15.00 | northern

HILL, LAINE
TIME MARCHES ON | AIN'T I WORTH A DIME | NEW VOICE 809 | 150.00 | **northerB**

HILL, LONNIE
COLD WINTER IN THE GHETTO | COLD WINTER IN THE GHETTO (alt. Take.) | URBAN SOUND 778 | 40.00 | 70's

HILL, TUTTI
HE'S A LOVER | WHEN THE GOING GETS ROUGH | AROCK 1012 | 15.00 | northern

HILL, Z.Z.
UNIVERSAL LOVE | THAT'S ALL THAT'S LEFT | COLUMBIA 10748 | 10.00 | 70's
AIN'T TOO PROUD TO BEG | SWEET WOMAN BY YOUR SIDE | AUDREY 224 | 8.00 | northern
DON'T MAKE PROMISES (YOU CAN'T | SET YOUR SIGHTS HIGHER | KENT 502 DJ | 10.00 | northern
DON'T MAKE PROMISES (YOU CAN'T | SET YOUR SIGHTS HIGHER | KENT 502 | 10.00 | northern
NO MORE DOGGIN' | THE KIND OF LOVE I WANT | KENT 444 DJ | 15.00 | northern
WHAT MORE | THAT'S IT | KENT 432 | 10.00 | northern
WHERE SHE ATT | BABY I'M SORRY | KENT 464 | 10.00 | northern
YOU JUST CHEAT AND LIE | EVERYBODY NEEDS SOMEBODY | KENT 469 | 15.00 | northern

HILL'S FAMILY AFFAIR, ROBBIE
I JUST WANT TO BE | | SOUL WEST NO# | 100.00 | funk

HILLS, BEVERLEY
I DON'T CARE ANYMORE | EVENING BREEZE | AIR PLAY 1 | 10.00 | northern

HILLSIDERS
YOU ONLY PASS THIS WAY ONE TIM | RAIN IS A LONESOME THING | MELODY 120 | 10.00 | motown

HINES, BILLY
ELEANOR JEAN	BROKEN DOWN UGLY THING	WA-TUSI 1	30.00	northern

HINES, ERNIE
THANK YOU BABY (FOR A LOVE BEYOND)	WE'RE GONNA PARTY	USA 888	30.00	northern

HINES, J. AND THE FELLOWS
FUNKY FUNK	FUNKY FUNK Pt.2	NATION-WIDE 100	15.00	funk
VICTORY STRUT	CAMELOT TIME	DELUXE 150	15.00	funk

HINES, RAY
WHY DON'T YOU GIVE ME A TRY	IS IT SOMETHING YOU GOT	RNH 11073	40.00	northern

HIT PACK
NEVER SAY NO TO YOUR BABY	LET'S DANCE	SOUL 35010	20.00	motown

HIT PARADE
STAND BY ME BABY	LOVIN' YOU	RCA 235	20.00	northern
KISSES NEVER DIE	CAN'T STOP	RCA	20.00	northern
KISSES NEVER DIE	CAN'T STOP	OCEANS 1002	100.00	northern

HITSON, HERMAN
SHE'S A BAD GIRL	SHOW ME SOME SIGN	MINIT 32096	30.00	ballad
YOU CAN'T KEEP A GOOD MAN DOWN	AIN'T NO OTHER WAY	SWEET ROSE 25	500.00	northern
BEEN SO LONG	GEORGIA ON MY MIND	ROYAL. 287147	40.00	ballad
YES YOU DID	BETTER TO HAVE LOVED	MINIT 32072	100.00	northern

HOBBS, WILLIE
'TIL I GET IT RIGHT	SAME:	SS7 1510 DJ	20.00	northern

HOBSON, GEORGE
LET IT BE REAL	A PLACE IN YOUR HEART	SOUND CITY 1001	600.00	northern

HOCKADAY, JOE AND THE SOUL BANDITS
BUMP IT 4794	BUMP IT PT.2	GEORGETOWN	40.00	funk

HOCKADAYS
HOLD ON BABY	FAIRY TALES	SYMBOL 918	40.00	northern

HODGE, ANN
YOU'RE WELCOME BACK	NOTHING BUT THE TRUTH	XL 358	200.00	northern

HODGE, ARCHIE
I REALLY WANT TO SEE YOU GIRL	IF I DIDN'T NEED YOU WOMAN	NARCO 003	1200.00	northern

HODGES, CHARLES
I'LL NEVER GO TO A PARTY AGAIN	IS THIS THE BEGINNING OF THE E	PHILIPS 40171	20.00	northern
THE DAY HE MADE YOU	SAME:	CALLA 171 DJ	20.00	northern
YOU'VE GOT THE LOVE I NEED	WHEN EVER YOU SAY	GENUINE 164	100.00	northern

HODGES, CHARLIE
LOVING YOU (IS BEAUTIFUL)	THE DAY HE MADE YOIU	CALLA 171	40.00	northern

HODGES, EDDIE
SOUL SEARCHER		BARD NO. #	500.00	northern

HODGES, PAT
PLAYGIRL	SURPRISE PARTY	KEYMEN 107	20.00	northern

HODGES, JAMES, SMITH AND CRAWFORD
I'M IN LOVE	NOBODY	MPINGO 14000	15.00	70's

HOLDEN, LORENZO
THE WIG	THE DAYS OF WINE AND ROSES	CEE JAM 1 D	75.00	mod

HOLDEN, RON
I NEED YA	CAN WE TALK	NOW. 6	15.00	funk
I'LL FORGIVE AND FORGET	I TRIED	CHALLENGE 59360	50.00	northern

HOLDER, MARK
WHATEVER'S FAIR	WHY DEAR LORD	COTILLION 44147	15.00	funk

HOLIDAE, SONNY
MY DARKEST HOUR	TIEME	SOUND PATTERNS 113	75.00	northern

HOLIDAY, CHARLES
DON'T LIE	I'M WARNING YOU	PLAYBOY RECORD 99	1000.00	northern

HOLIDAY, CHUCK
JUST CAN'T TRUST NOBODY	I STILL LOVE YOU	GLORIA 113	1500.00	northern

HOLIDAY, JIMMY
WHEN I'M LOVING YOU	IT'S NICE TO SEE YOU AGAIN	CROSS OVER 976	10.00	70's
BABY BOY'S IN LOVE	IF YOU'VE GOT THE MONEY	MINIT 32058 DJ	10.00	northern
I'M GONNA MOVE TO THE CITY	THE TURNING POINT	MINIT 32011	10.00	northern
I'VE BEEN DONE WRONG	I CAN'T STAND IT	DIPLOMACY 23	25.00	northern
SHIELD ALL AROUND	A MAN WITHOUT LOVE	KT 503	30.00	northern
THE BEAUTY OF A GIRL IN LOVE	EVERYTHING IS LOVE	MINIT 32028	8.00	northern
THE NEW BREED	LOVE ME ONE MORE TIME	DIPLOMACY 20	10.00	northern

HOLIDAY, JIMMY AND KING, CLYDIE
READY, WILLING AND ABLE	WE GOT A GOOD THING GOING	MINIT 32021	10.00	northern

HOLIDAY, MARVA
IT'S WRITTEN ALL OVER MY FACE	HANG AROUND	GNP CRESCENDO 411	15.00	northern

HOLIDAYS
LAZY DAY	EGO TRIPPING	MARATHON 18475	10.00	group
GETTING KIND OF SERIOUS	(WHY DO WE) PROCRASTINATE	MARATHON 440	15.00	70's
WATCH OUT GIRL	NO GREATER LOVE	GOLDEN WORLD 47	10.00	motown
I KEEP HOLDING ON	I KNOW SHE CARES	REVILOT 210	20.00	northern
I'LL LOVE YOU FOREVER	MAKIN' UP TIME	GOLDEN WORLD 36	10.00	northern
NEVER ALONE	LOVES CREEEPING UP ON ME	REVILOT 205	20.00	northern

EASY LIVING	I LOST YOU	GROOVE CITY 206	200.00	northern

HOLLAND, BRIANT

(WHERE'S THE JOY) IN NATURE BOY	SHOCK	KUDO 667	350.00	motown

HOLLAND, EDDIE

BABY SHAKE	BRENDA	MOTOWN 1043	20.00	motown
BECUASE I LOVE HER	EVERYBODY'S GOING	UA 191	15.00	motown
CANDY TO ME	IF YOU DON'T WANT MY LOVE	MOTOWN 1063	15.00	motown
IF CLEOPATRA TOOK A CHANCE	WHAT ABOUT ME	MOTOWN 1030	15.00	motown
IF CLEOPATRA TOOK A CHANCE	WHAT ABOUT ME	MOTOWN 1030 PS	20.00	motown
IF IT'S LOVE (IT'S ALRIGHT)	IT'S NOT TOO LATE	MOTOWN 1031	30.00	motown
I'M ON OUTSIDE LOOKING IN	I COULDN'T CRY IF I WANTED TO	MOTOWN 1049	150.00	motown
JAMIE	TAKE A CHANCE ON ME	MOTOWN 1021	20.00	motown
JUST A FEW DAYS MORE	DARLING I HUM OUR SONG	MOTOWN 1036	30.00	motown
JUST AIN'T ENOUGH LOVE	LAST NIGHT I HAD A VISION	MOTOWN 1058	20.00	motown
LEAVING HERE	BRENDA	MOTOWN 1052	15.00	motown
MERRY GO ROUND	IT MOVES ME	TAMLA 102	250.00	motown
MERRY-GO-ROUND	IT MOVES ME	UA 172	20.00	motown
WHY DO YOU WANT TO LET ME GO	THE LAST LAUGH	UA 280	30.00	motown
WILL YOU LOVE ME	MAGIC MIRROR	UA 207	25.00	motown
YOU (YOU YOU YOU YOU)	LITTLE MISS RUBY	MERCURY 71290	150.00	motown
YOU DESERVE WHAT YOU GOT	LAST NIGHT I HAD A VISION	MOTOWN 1026	400.00	motown
JAMIE (Time 2.15")	TAKE A CHANCE ON ME	MOTOWN 1021.	50.00	motown

HOLLAND, JIMMY

BABY DON'T LEAVE ME	AS LONG AS I HAVE YOU	BLUE ROCK 4036	40.00	northern
SUGAR BABY	MORE SUGAR BABY	SYCO 2001	20.00	northern
SUGAR BABY	MORE SUGAR BABY	MARKIE	40.00	northern

HOLLAND - DOZIER

NEW BREED KINDA WOMAN	IF YOU DON'T WANT TO BE IN MY	INVICTUS 1254	15.00	70's
WHAT GOES UP, MUST COME DOWN	COME ON HOME	MOTOWN 1045	25.00	motown

HOLLEY, BOBBY

BABY I LOVE YOU	MOVING DANCER	WEIS 3005	15.00	northern

HOLLINGER, DON

LOVE ON THE PHONE	LOVE ON THE PHONE (RAP)	RED ROOSTER 5	10.00	ballad
UNTIL I FIND YOU	CRUEL WORLD	ATCO 6492	30.00	northern

HOLLIS, SANDY

I'M TEMPTED	TABLES WILL TURN	BIG WHEEL 1968	25.00	northern

HOLLOWAY, BRENDA

I'LL ALWAYS LOVE YOU	SAD SONG	TAMLA 54099	10.00	motown
I'LL BE AVAILABLE	OPERATOR	TAMLA 54115	10.00	motown
TOGETHER 'TIL THE END OF TIME	SAD SONG	TAMLA 54125	10.00	motown
WHEN I'M GONE	I'VE BEEN GOOD TO YOU	TAMLA 54111	10.00	motown
WHEN I'M GONE	I'VE BEEN GOOD TO YOU	TAMLA 54111 PS	40.00	motown
YOU CAN CRY ON MY SHOULDER	HOW MANY TIMES DID YOU MEAN IT	TAMLA 54121	10.00	motown
EVERY LITTLE BIT HURTS	LAND OF A THOUSAND DANCES	TAMLA 54094	10.00	motown
GIVING LOVE	SAME:	BIRTHRIGHT 201	10.00	motown
LET LOVE GROW	SAME	MUSIC MERCHANT 1001	10.00	motown
STARTING THE HURT ALL OVER AGAIN	JUST LOOK WHAT YOU'VE DONE	TAMLA 54148	10.00	motown
WHERE WERE YOU	HURT A LITTLE EVERYDAY	TAMLA 54137	15.00	motown
YOU CAN CRY ON MY SHOULDER	HOW MANY TIMES DID YOU MEAN IT	TAMLA 54121	15.00	motown
YOU'VE MADE ME SO VERY HAPPY	I'VE GOT TO FIND IT	TAMLA 54155	8.00	motown

HOLLOWAY, BRENDA AND THE HARRIS, JESS

GONNA MAKE YOU MINE	I NEVER KNEW YOULOOKED SO GOOD	BREVIT 641	40.00	motown

HOLLOWAY, EDDIE

SOMEBODY SMOOCHING MY LOVE	I AM REALLY LOVES YOU	H&H 311796	100.00	70's
I HAD A GOOD TIME	I'M STANDING BY	GEM CITY 102	10.00	ballad

HOLLOWAY, LOLEATTA

MOTHER OF SHAME	OUR LOVE	AWARE 33	10.00	70's

HOLLOWAY, PATRICE

BLACK MOTHER GOOSE	THAT'S THE CHANCE YOU GOTTA TA	CAPITOL 3265	10.00	northern
LOVE AND DESIRE	ECSTASY	CAPITOL 5778	100.00	northern
STAY WITH YOUR OWN KIND	THAT'S ALL YOU GOT TO DO	CAPITOL 5985	15.00	northern
STOLEN HOURS	LUCKY, MY BOY	CAPITOL 5680	150.00	northern
HE IS THE BOY OF MY DREAMS	STEVIE	V.I.P. 25001	3000.00	motown

HOLLY, SONNY

CHEATING AIN'T NO GOOD	THANK YOU FOR LOVING ME	AN-GEL RECORDS 425	100.00	70's

HOLLYWOOD FLAMES

I'M GONNA STAND BY YOU	I'M COMING HOME	SYMBOL 215	25.00	northern

HOLLYWOOD SPECTRUM

I GOTTA GET BACK TO LOVIN' YOU	L.A. U.S.A.	COTILLION 44070	10.00	northern

HOLMAN, EDDIE

TIME WILL TELL	THIS WILL BE A NIGHT TO REMEMBER	SALSOUL 2026	8.00	70's
I NEED SOMEBODY	CATHY CALLED	ABC 11276	15.00	northern
NEVER LET ME GO	WHY DO FOOLS FALL IN LOVE	PARKWAY 157	20.00	group
EDDIE'S MY NAME	DON'T STOP NOW	PARKWAY 981	20.00	northern
I SURRENDER	I LOVE YOU	ABC 11149	15.00	northern
I'LL CRY 1000 TEARS	I'M NOT GONNA GIVE UP	BELL 712	20.00	northern
SHE'S BEAUTIFUL	LOST	DON-EL 124	30.00	northern
THIS CAN'T BE TRUE	A FREE COUNTRY	PARKWAY 960	10.00	northern
YOU KNOW THAT I WILL	AM I A LOSER (FROM THE START)	PARKWAY 106	15.00	northern

HOLMES, CARL
SOUL DANCE NO.3	CROSSIN' OVER	BLACKJACK 1409	10.00	mod

HOLMES, ELDRIDGE
HUMPBACK	I LIKE WHAT YOU DO	JET SET 1006	15.00	mod
EMPEROR JONES	A TIME FOR EVERYTHING	ALON 9022	40.00	northern
LOVELY WOMAN	WHAT'S YOUR NAME	DEESU 305	150.00	northern
WAIT FOR ME BABY	BEVERLEY	SANSU 477	15.00	northern
WITHOUT A WORD	UNTIL THE END	SANSU 469	15.00	northern
WORRIED OVER YOU	GONE GONE GONE	JET SET 765	20.00	northern

HOLMES, MARVIN
YOU BETTER KEEP HER	KWAMI	BROWN DOOR 6576	10.00	70's
FIND YOURSELF	FIND YOURSELF Pt.2	KIMBERLY 104	20.00	funk
OOH OOH THE DRAGON	OOH OOH THE DRAGON Pt.2	UNI 55111	15.00	funk
THANG	SWEET TALK	UNI 55233	10.00	funk
RIDE YOUR MULE	RIDE YOUR MULE PT.2	REVUE 11026	15.00	funk

HOLMES, MARY
I NEED YOUR LOVIN' 158	I'LL MAKE IT UP TO YOU	PHILLY GROOVE	30.00	northern
SOUL BROTHER	AFTER I SHED A TEAR	NASSAU 100	30.00	funk

HOLMES, NATE
YOU'RE STILL ON MY MIND	SO AM I	ABC 11223	20.00	northern

HOLMES, SHERLOCK
STANDING AT A STANDSTILL	SOONER OR LATER	PART III 101	150.00	northern

HOLT BROTHERS
OPEN UP	DANCE WITH ME	MAE MONTI 32063	20.00	70's

HONEY AND THE BEES
BE YOURSELF	ACADEMY NO. #	NI	500.00	northern
HAS SOMEBODY TAKEN MY PLACE	THAT'S WHAT BOYS ARE MADE FOR	BELL 45217	20.00	northern
TWO CAN PLAY THE SAME GAME	INSIDE O' ME	ACADEMY 114	400.00	northern
I'M CONFESSIN'	ONE TIME IS FOREVER	ARCTIC 114	25.00	northern
LOVE ADDICT	I'LL BE THERE	ARCTIC 149	25.00	northern
DYNAMITE EXPLODED	TOGETHER FOREVER	ARCTIC 152	500.00	northern
BABY, DO THAT THING	SUNDAY KIND OF LOVE	ARCTIC 158	50.00	funkWHY DO U
HURT THE ONE WHO LOVE	(YOU BETTER) GO NOW	ARCTIC 141	40.00	northern
HELP ME (GET OVER MY USED TO B	WE GOT TO STAY TOGETHER	JOSIE 1028	15.00	northern
IT'S GONNA TAKE A MIRACLE	WHAT ABOUT ME	JOSIE 1030	10.00	northern

HONEY BEES
SHE DON'T DESERVE YOU	ONE WONDERFUL NIGHT	FONTANA 1939	20.00	northern

HONEYCUTT, JOHNNY
I'M COMING OVER		TRIODE 111	1250.00	northern

HONOR SOCIETY
CONDITION RED	SWEET SEPTEMBER	JUBILEE 5703	15.00	northern

HOOPER, MARY JANE
I'VE GOT REASONS	TEACH ME	POWER-PAC 2053	25.00	funk

HOPKINS, HAROLD
GLAMOUR GIRL	OOH BABY	SCEPTER 12120	15.00	northern

HOPSON, JOYCE
I SURRENDER TO YOU	THIS TIME	REVUE 1034	30.00	northern

HORN, C.V.
LOVE IS A SITUATION	I DON'T WANT TO WAIT	DELLA 971	50.00	northern

HORNE, JIMMY BO
I CAN'T SPEAK	STREET CORNERS	DADE 235	1250.00	northern
IF YOU WANT MY LOVE	ON THE STREET CORNER	ALSTON 4612	30.00	northern
HEY THERE JIM	DON'T THROW YOUR LOVE AWAY	DIG 901	30.00	funk

HORNETS
GIVE ME A KISS	SHE'S MY BABY	V.I.P. 25004	40.00	motown

HORTON, BILL
I WANNA KNOW	NO ONE CAN TAKE YOUR PLACE	KAYDEN 403	100.00	northern

HOT CHOCOLATES
KEEP MY BABY COOL	WHO DO YOU CALL	DUKE 467 dj	15.00	group

HOT SAUCE
BRING IT HOME (AND GIVE IT TO ME)	ECHOES FROM THE PAST	VOLT 4076	10.00	northern

HOT TAMALES
CHICKEN - BACKS	JOIN IN THE FUN	SUPREME 101	100.00	funk
LOVE'S INTENTIONS	MR. STARLIGHT	DETROIT. 410	75.00	northern
LOVE'S INTENTIONS	MR. STARLIGHT	DETROIT. 101 red	200.00	northern

HOTTINGER, BUDDY
I NEED YOUR LOVING	5TH3E ONE I CAN'T FORGET	TANYA 100	100.00	northern

HOTZOG, DERC
PUPPY LOVE		HAMILTON 101	70.00	northern

HOUSE GUEST RATED X
WHAT SO NEVER THE DANCE		HOUSE GUESTS	75.00	funk

HOUSE GUESTS
MY MIND SET ME FREE		HOUSE GUESTS	75.00	funk

HOUSTON OUTLAWS
AIN'T NO TELLING	UNCLE ED'S BACKYARD	WESTBOUND 179	100.00	northern

HOUSTON, EDDIE
I WON'T BE THE LAST TO CRY	LOVE SURE IS A POWERFUL THING	CAPITOL 2397	40.00	ballad

HOUSTON, FREDDIE
CHILLS AND FEVER	I GOTTA MOVE	OLD TOWN 1153	50.00	northern
IF I HAD KNOWN	ONLY THE LONELY ONE	OLD TOWN 1156	200.00	northern
LOVE, LOVE, LOVE	TRUE	WHIZ-ON 7	200.00	northern
SOFT WALKIN'	TO BE IN LOVE	TOTO 101	30.00	northern

HOUSTON, LARRY
LET'S SPEND SOME TIME TOGETHER	GIVE ME SOMETHING TO GO ON	HFMP 1	8.00	70's

HOUSTON, SISSIE (CISSY)
BRING HIM BACK	WORLD OF BROKEN HEARTS	CONGRESS 268	75.00	northern
DON'T COME RUNNING TO ME	ONE BROKEN HEART FOR SALE	KAPP 814	75.00	northern
I JUST DON'T KNOW WHAT TO DO W	THIS EMPTY PLACE	JANUS 131	30.00	northern

HOUSTON, THELMA
BABY MINE	THE WOMAN BEHIND HER MAN	CAPITOL 5767	60.00	northern

HOWARD, DELORES
FIRST TIME IN LOVE	MY GUY AND I	MASTER 422	300.00	northern

HOWARD, FRANK
DO WHAT YOU WANNA DO	DO WHAT YOU WANNA DO Pt.2	DELUXE 124	15.00	funk
I'M SO GLAD	I'M SORRY FOR YOU	BARRY 1008	75.00	northern
JUDY	SMOKY PLACES	EXCELLO 2291	75.00	northern

HOWARD, JOHNNY
THE CHASE IS ON	I MISS MY LADY	BASHIE 101 DJ	25.00	**northerB**

HOWELL, GLORIA
YOU'D BETTER HURRY UP	HE'S GONE	BIG CITY 101	500.00	northern

HOWELL, REUBEN
YOU CAN'T STOP A MAN IN LOVE	WHEN YOU TAKE ANOTHER CHANCE	MOTOWN 1274	15.00	70's
YOU CAN'T STOP A MAN IN LOVE	WHEN YOU TAKE ANOTHER CHANCE	MOTOWN 1274 PS	20.00	northern

HUDSON, AL
ALMOST AIN'T GOOD ENOUGH	I'M ABOUT LOVING YOU	ATCO 7029	20.00	70's
MY NUMBER ONE NEED	ALONE SHE'S GONE	ATCO 7011	10.00	70's
SPREAD LOVE	LOVE ME FOREVER	ABC 12385	10.00	70's
WHY MUST SAY GOODBYE	I LIKE EVERTHING ABOUT YOU	ABC 12294	10.00	70's

HUDSON, JOHNNY
BETTER LOVE	GIRL, YOU SJHOULD HAVE KNOWN	QUICK SAND 101	15.00	70's

HUDSON, POOKIE.
THIS GETS TO ME	ALL THE PLACES I'VE BEEN	JAMIE 1319	125.00	**northerB**

HUESTON, MEL
TIME AND PATIENCE	DOUBLE CONFUSION	CHANSON 1179	15.00	funk
SEACHING	I NEED SOME LOVING	CEZ VISTA 484	100.00	northern

HUEY, BABY AND THE BABYSITTERS
MIGHTY MIGHTY CHILDREN	MIGHTY MIGHTY CHILDREN Pt.2	CURTOM 1939	10.00	funk
JUST BE CAREFUL	GIRL MESSIN' WITH THE KID	SHANN 73924	200.00	northern
JUST BEING CAREFUL	MESSIN' WITH THE KID	USA 801	60.00	northern

HUEY, CLAUDE BABY
FEEL GOOD ALL OVER	THE WORST THING A MAN CAN DO	EARLY BIRD 49654	30.00	northern
KEEP IT TO MYSELF	DIDN'T WE HAVE SOME GOOD TIMES	M.I.O.B. 1281	40.00	northern
WHY WOULD YOU BLOW IT	WHY DID OUR LOVE GO	GALAXY 768	100.00	northern

HUFF, TERRY
THAT'S WHEN IT HURTS	JUST NOT ENOUGH	MAINSTREAM 5585	20.00	70's

HUGHES, AL
TAKE IT OR LEAVE IT		SCOPE 3027	100.00	northern

HUGHES, FRED
AS LONG AS WE'RE TOGETHER	WALK ON BACK TO YOU	EXODUS 2009	15.00	northern
BABY BOY	WHO YOU REALLY ARE	BRUNSWICK 755419	15.00	northern
DON'T LET ME DOWN	MY HEART CRIES OH	VEE JAY 718	15.00	northern
I KEEP TRYING	WE'VE GOT LOVE	EXODUS 2006	15.00	northern
OO WEE BABY, I LOVE YOU	LOVE ME BABY	VEE JAY 684	8.00	northern

HUGHES, FREDDIE
DON'T YOU LEAVE	SARAH MAE	GREG-UH-RUDY 2	10.00	70's
I JUST FOUND OUT	I'VE GOT MY OWN MIND	JANUS 196	30.00	70's
I GOTTA KEEP MY BLUFF IN	HE'S NO GOOD	WAND 1197	15.00	northern
I GOTTA KEE P MY BLUFF IN	NATURAL MAN	WAND 1192	15.00	northern
MY BABY CAME BACK	LOVE CAN'T BE UNDERSTOOD	WEE 1011	15.00	northern
SEND MY BABY BACK	WHERE'S MY BABY	WAND 1182	10.00	northern
SEND MY BABY BACK	WHERE'S MY BABY	WEE 1006	15.00	northern

HUGHES, JIMMY
IT AIN'T WHAT YOU GOT	UNCLE SAM	ATLANTIC 2554	15.00	northern
LOVELY LADIES	TRY ME	FAME 6403	10.00	northern
MY LOVING TIME	I'M QUALIFIED	GUYDEN 2075	15.00	northern
MY LOVING TIME	I'M QUALIFIED	JAMIE 1280	10.00	northern
NEIGHBOR, NEIGHBOR	IT'S A GOOD THING	FAME 1003	8.00	northern
YOU REALLY KNOW HOW TO HURT A GUY	THE LOVING PHYSICIAN	FAME 6410	8.00	northern

HUGHES, JUDY
FINE, FINE, FINE		VAULT NO.#	500.00	northern
OCEAN OF EMOTION		CRUSADER NO.#	200.00	northern

HUGHES, OSCAR
ONE AND ONLY LOVER	GET DOWN	ETHIOPIA 777	50.00	group

HUGHES, RHETTA

I CAN'T STAND UNDER THIS PRESSURE 1546	YOU'RE DOING IT WITH HER	TETRAGRAMMATON	15.00	70's
ONE IN A MILLION	JUST LOVE ME	COLUMBIA 44073	30.00	northern

HUGHLEY, GEORGE

THAT'S WHY I CRY	YOU'RE MY EVERYTHING	BUDDAH 203	100.00	northern

HUMAN BEINZ

NOBODY BUT ME	SUENO	CAPITOL 5990	8.00	northern

HUMES, ANITA

WHAT DID I DO	CURFEW LOVER	ROULETTE 4542	30.00	northern

HUMES, ANITA AND THE THE ESSEX

EVERYBODY'S GOT YOU	ARE YOU GOING MY WAY	ROULETTE 4750	20.00	northern
WHAT DID I DO	CURFEW LOVER	ROULETTE 4542	40.00	northern

HUMPHREY, AMANDA

POWER OF LOVE	CALL ON ME	USA 840 DJ	30.00	northern

HUMPHREY, DELLA

DON'T MAKE THE GOOD GIRLS GO B	YOUR LOVE IS ALL I NEED	ARCTIC 144	15.00	northern
OVER THE TRACKS	JUST LIKE THE BOYS DO	ARCTIC 155	20.00	northern

HUN'S REVIEW

DON'T MAKE ME LOVE YOU	DANGER ZONE	SORRO 967	50.00	northern

HUNT, CLAY

YOUR LOVE'S GONE BAD	(SAY IT) SWEET AND LOW	BAY SOUND 67005	30.00	northern

HUNT, GERALDINE

NEVER, NEVER LEAVE ME	PUSH, SWEEP	ROULETTE 7068 DJ	10.00	northern
I LET MYSELF GO	I WISHED I HAD LISTENED	CHECKER 1028	20.00	northern
I LET MYSELF GO	I WISHED I HAD LISTENED	KATRON 829	40.00	northern
TWO CAN LIVE CHEAPER THAN ONE	HE'S FOR REAL	BOMBAY 4501	150.00	northern
WINNER TAKE ALL	FOR LOVERS ONLY	ABC 10859	200.00	northern

HUNT, PAT

SUPER COOL	EVERYBODY'S SOMEBODY'S FOOL	EARLY BIRD 9664	30.00	funk

HUNT, TOMMY

I DON'T WANT TO LOSE YOU	HOLD ON	ATLANTIC 2278	15.00	northern
I JUST DON'T KNOW WHAT TO DO WITH MYSELF	AND I NEVER KNEW	SCEPTER 1236	10.00	northern
I NEED A WOMAN OF MY OWN	SEARCHIN' FOR MY BABY	DYNAMO 113	10.00	northern
I'LL MAKE YOU HAPPY		CAPITOL 5621	30.00	northern
JERKIN' AROUND	HUMAN	SCEPTER 21021	10.00	northern
THE BIGGEST MAN	NEVER LOVE A ROBIN	DYNAMO 101	15.00	northern
THE PARADE OF BROKEN HEARTS	HUMAN	SCEPTER 1219	8.00	northern
WORDS CAN NEVER TELL IT	HOW CAN I BE ANYTHING	DYNAMO 105	10.00	northern
YOU MADE A MAN OUT OF ME	IT'S ALL A BAD DREAM	SCEPTER 1275	10.00	northern

HUNT, WILLIAM

WOULD YOU BELIEVE	MY BABY WANTS TO DANCE	STREAMSIDE 100	30.00	northern

HUNTER, HERBERT

I WAS BORN TO LOVE YOU	PUSH AWAY FROM THE TABLE	SPAR 9009	85.00	**northerB**
I WAS BORN TO LOVE YOU	PUSH AWAY FROM THE TABLE	SPAR 9009 DJ	150.00	**northern**
ISN'T IT WONDERFUL TO DREAM	MAKE ME KNOW YOU LOVE ME	PONCELLO 714 DJ	20.00	northern

HUNTER, IVORY JOE

EVERY LITTLE BIT HELPED ME	I CAN MAKE YOU HAPPY	GOLDWAX 307	25.00	northern

HUNTER, SHANE

SWEET THINGS (EVERY NOW AND THEN)	TRY MY LOVE	AWAKE 501	50.00	northern

HUNTER, TY

EVERYTIME	FREE	ANNA 1123	20.00	motown
GLADNESS TO SADNESS	LONELY BABY	CHECK MATE 1015	20.00	motown
MEMORIES	ENVY OF EVERY MAN	CHECK MATE 1002	20.00	motown
ORPHAN BOY	EVERYTHING ABOUT YOU	ANNA 1114	20.00	motown
BAD LOSER	SOMETHING LIKE A STORM	CHESS 1893 DJ	15.00	northern
LOVE WALKED RIGHT OUT ON ME	AM I LOING YOU	CHESS 1881	20.00	northern

HUNTER AND HIS GAMES

HOW YOU GET HIGHER	SAME: INSTRUMENTAL	STACEY 2617	50.00	funk

HUSTLERS

WHAT EVER'S YOUR SIGN	WHAT EVER'S YOUR SIGN Pt.2	EFFIE 201	10.00	funk
BOSTON MONKEY	YOU CHEATED	MUSICOR 1129	200.00	northern

HUTCH, WILLIE

I CHOOSE YOU	BROTHER'S GONNA WORK IT OUT	MOTOWN 1222	8.00	70's
JUST ANOTHER DAY	PARTY DOWN	MOTOWN 1371	8.00	70's
TALK TO ME	LOVE POWER	MOTOWN 1360	8.00	70's
CAN'T FIGHT THE POWER	HOW COME BABY, YOU DON'T LOVE	SOUL CITY 754	15.00	northern
I CAN'T GET ENOUGH	YOUR LOVE HAS MADE ME A	MODERN 1021	20.00	northern
LOVE GAMES	TRAMPIN'	RCA 392	15.00	northern
THE DUCK	LOVE RUNS OUT	DUNHILL 4012	300.00	northern

HUTSON, FRANK AND THE EXPOSURES

OLD MAN ME	BIG MAN	GOODIE TRAIN 10	40.00	group

HUTTON, BOBBY

I'VE GOT MEMORY	I CAN'T STAND A WOMAN TWO TIMI	PHILIPS 40657	15.00	northern
LONELY IN LOVE	YOU'FRE MY WHOLE REASON	PHILIPS 40709	30.00	northern
COME SEE WHAT'S LEFT OF ME	THEN YOU CAN TELL ME GOODBYE	PHILIPS 40601	100.00	northern

HUTTON, HAROLD

LUCKY BOY	IT'S A GOOD THING	CHECKER 1125	30.00	northern

Artist / Song	B-side	Label	Price	Genre
HY BOYS				
BIG DREAMS	SAME: INSTRUMENTAL	BB 4008	30.00	northern
HYMAN, PHYLLIS				
BABY (I'M GONNA LOVE YOU)	DO ME	DESERT MOON 6402	25.00	70's
LEAVIN' THE GOOD LIFE BEHIND	SAME:	PRIVATE STOCK 45034	10.00	70's
UNDER YOUR SPELL	COMPLETE ME	ARISTA 495	8.00	70's
YOU KNOW HOW TO LOVE ME	GIVE A LITTLE MORE	ARISTA 463	8.00	70's
HYMES III, FREDERICK				
TIME AIN'T GONNA DO ME NO FAVOURS	EVERYDAY WILL BE LIKE A HOLIDAY	FAB VEGAS 4526	1000.00	northern
HYMES SISTERS				
WALKING AROUND THE TOWN	NO REASON TO CRY	JER JIM HAN 104	75.00	northern
HYPERIONS				
WHYYOU WANNA TREAT ME THE WAY	BELIEVE IN ME	CHATTAHOOCHEE 669	300.00	northern
HYSONG, DON				
BABY HERE'S MY HEART	I'VE GOT TO GET AWAY	BARD 1013	30.00	northern
SOUL SEARCHER		BARD NO.#	500.00	northern
HYTONES				
BIGGER & BETTER	I'VE GOT MY BABY	A-BET 9415	300.00	northern
YOU DON'T EVEN KNOW MY NAME	TILL YOU BREAK UP	SOUTHERN ARTISTS 2023	400.00	northern
YOU DON'T EVEN KNOW MY NAME	TILL YOU BREAK UP	BELL 627	250.00	northern
HYTOWER, ROY				
IT MUST BE LOVE	LOVE THAT GIRL OF MINE	EXPO 103	15.00	northern

I

Artist / Song	B-side	Label	Price	Genre
ICEMEN				
IT'S TIME YOU KNEW / northern	IT'S GONNA TAKE A LOT TO BRING ME BACK	OLE 9	1007	200.00
ONLY TIME WILL TELL	SUGAR BABY	SAMAR 117	20.00	northern
IDEALS				
I GOT LUCKY (WHEN I FOUND YOU) / 1020	TELL HER I APOLOGIZE	ST.LAWRENCE	10.00	northern
THE MIGHTY LOVER	DANCING IN USA	BOO-GA-LOO 108	75.00	northern
YOU HURT ME	YOU LOST AND I WON	SATELILITE 2007	10.00	northern
IDENTITIES				
WHEN LOVE SLIPS AWAY / 6	HEY BROTHER	HOUSE OF THE FOX	15.00	northern
WHEN YOU FIND LOVE SLIPPING AWAY / 300	SAME:	TOGETHERNESS	20.00	northern
IDLE FEW				
PEOPLE THAT'S WHY	LAND OF DREAMS	BLUE BOOK 1	40.00	**northerB**
IKETTES				
PEACHES "N" CREAM	THE BIGGEST PLAYERS	MODERN 1005	8.00	northern
I'M JUST NOT READY FOR LOVE	TWO TIMIN' DOUBLE DEALIN	UA 51103	15.00	funk
WHAT'CHA GONNA DO	DOWN, DOWN	PHI-DAN 5009	15.00	northern
ILANA				
WHERE WOULD YOU BE TODAY	SAME:	VOLT 4064 DJ	30.00	northern
ILLUSIONS				
THE FUNKY DONKEY	SHAKE YOUR MINI	SHOWTIME 1818	10.00	funk
IMAGE				
FUNKY THING	OH LOVE	GRANDE. 303	8.00	funk
GOING GOING GONE	IS THAT WHY	IMAGE 4343	30.00	funk
SURPRISE	BETCHA DIDN'T KNOW	JANUS 194	10.00	northern
IMAGINATIONS				
LOVE DIET	THERE'S ANOTHER ON YOUR MIND	20th. CENTURY 2117	10.00	70's
I WANT A GIRL	I LOVE YOU, MORE THAN ANYONE	BACON FAT 101	10.00	northern
STRANGE NEIGHBORHOOD	I JUST CAN'T GET OVER LOSING YOU	FRATERNITY 1001 DJ	250.00	northern
IMPACTS				
JERKIN' IN YOUR SEAT	HORSE RADISJH	COUNSEL 101.	75.00	northern
IMPALAS				
SPEED UP	SOUL	CAPITOL 2709	30.00	northern
WHIP IT ON ME	I STILL LOVE YOU	BUNKY 7762	15.00	northern
IMPERIAL C'S				
SOMEONE TELL HER	I'LL LIVE ON	PHIL LA SOUL 308	1,000.00	northern
IMPERIAL WONDERS				
TRYING TO GET TO YOU	WHEN I FALL IN LOVE	BLACK PRINCE 317	10.00	70's
LOVE COMING DOWN	MY (JUST TOLD ME SHE LOVES ME)	MUSICOR 1477	15.00	northern

YOU LIVE ONLY ONCE	TURNED AROUND OVER YOU	SOLID FOUNDATION 101	15.00	**northerB**

IMPLEMENTS

LOOK OVER YOUR SHOULDER	I WISH IT WERE ME	PHILIPS 40473	30.00	northern

IMPOSSIBLES

IT'S ALRIGHT	I WANNA KNOW	ROULETTE 4745	75.00	northern

IMPRESSIONS

I'LL ALWAYS BE THERE	FINALLY GOT MYSELF TOGETHER	CURTOM 1997	8.00	70's
WHEREVER SHE LEADETH ME	AMEN (1970)	CURTOM 1948	8.00	70's
AMEN	LONG, LONG WINTER	ABC 10602	8.00	northern
CAN'T SATISFY	THIS MUST END	ABC 10831	8.00	northern
GYPSY WOMAN	AS LONG AS YOU LOVE ME	ABC 10241	8.00	northern
IT'S ALL RIGHT	YOU'LL WANT ME BACK	ABC 10487	8.00	northern
I'VE BEEN TRYING	PEOPLE GET READY	ABC 10622	8.00	northern
NEVER COULD YOU BE	I NEED YOU	ABC 10710	8.00	northern
WOMAN'S GOT SOUL	GET UP AND MOVE	ABC 10647	8.00	northern
YOU ALWAYS HURT ME	LITTLE GIRL	ABC 10900	10.00	northern
YOU MUST BELIEVE ME	SEE THE REAL ME	ABC 10581	8.00	northern
CAN'T SATISFY	THIS MUST END	ABC 10831	10.00	northern
GYPSY WOMAN	AS LONG AS YOU LOVE ME	ABC 10241	10.00	northern
I'M THE ONE WHO LOVES YOU	I NEED YOUR LOVE	ABC 10386	10.00	northern
MINSTREL AND QUEEN	YOU'VE COME HOME	ABC 10357	15.00	northern
TWIST AND LIMBO	SAD, SAD GIRL AND BOY	ABC 10431	15.00	northern
YOU OUGHT TO BE IN HEAVEN	I CAN'T STAY AWAY FROM YOU	ABC 10964	10.00	northern
YOU'VE BEEN CHEATING	MAN OH MAN	ABC 10750	8.00	northern

IN CROWD

GRAPEVINE	CAT DANCE	BRENT 7046	20.00	northern

INCLINES

PRESSURE COOKER	PRESSURE COOKER PT.2	ATCO 6674	10.00	funk
THE ATLANTA BOOGALOO	THE ATLANTA BOOGALOO PT.2	GIL 101	75.00	funk
THE HIPPIE	THE HUSTLER	GIL 102	75.00	funk

INCOMPARABLE SEVEN

FUNKY GRAND PAW		TOP HIT NO#	20.00	funk

INCREDIBLES

CRYING HEART	I CAN'T GET OVER LOSING YOU	AUDIO ARTS 701	15.00	northern
CRYING HEART	I'LL MAKE IT EASY	AUDIO ARTS 60001 Blue	15.00	northern
I FOUND ANOTHER LOVE	HEART AND SOUL	AUDIO ARTS 60007	10.00	northern
STANDING HERE CRYING	WITHOUT A WORD	AUDIO ARTS 60009	10.00	northern
THERE'S NOTHING ELSE TO SAY	ANOTHER DIRTY DEAL	AUDIO ARTS 60006 blue	30.00	northern
THERE'S NOTHING ELSE TO SAY	ANOTHER DIRTY DEAL	AUDIO ARTS 60006	20.00	**northerB**
Amy MALA Bell distibuted green label				

INFINITY

KEEP IT TO YOURSELF	GET ON THE CASE	FOUNTAIN 1102	10.00	northern

INFORMERS

BABY SET ME FREE	A HARD WAY TO GO	BLACK JACK 1402	300.00	northern

INGRAM, LUTHER

SINCE YOU DON'T WANT ME	MISSING YOU	KOKO 103	15.00	70's
TRYING TO FIND MY LOVE	GET TO ME	KOKO 731	15.00	70's
AIN'T THAT NICE	YOU NEVER MISS YOUR WATER	DECCA 31794	60.00	northern
RUN FOR YOUR LIFE	I NEED YOU NOW	HURDY-GURDY 102	100.00	northern
IF IT'S ALL THE SAME TO YOU BABE	EXUS TREK	HIB 698 styrene	200.00	northern
IF IT'S ALL THE SAME TO YOU BABE	EXUS TREK	HIB 698 DJ	300.00	northern
IF IT'S ALL THE SAME TO YOU BABE	EXUS TREK	HIB 698 Orange lbl	200.00	**northerB**
IF IT'S ALL THE SAME TO YOU BABE	EXUS TREK	HIB 698 green lbl	200.00	**northerB**
IF IT'S ALL THE SAME TO YOU BABE	EXUS TREK	HIB 698 orange lbl 2nd.	30.00	**northerB**

INGRAM, LUTHER AND THE THE G-MEN

(I SPY) FOR THE F.B.I.	FOXEY DEVIL	SMASH 2019	20.00	northern

INMATES

THIS IS THE DAY		KOPIT NO.#	750.00	northern

INNER DRIVE

SMELL THE FUNK	PARTY MAN	ZODIAC 1052	10.00	funk

INNER EAR

YOUR AUTUMN OF TOMORROW	UNCLE FUNK	INNER EAR 429	200.00	northern

INNER SPACE

BREAK THE CHAINS	MAKE IT HAD ON HIM	SWEET FORTUNE 2409	10.00	70's

INNERSECTION

I'M IN DEBT TO YOU	LET ME LOVE YUH	GROUP 5 101	150.00	70's

INNERVISION

HONEY BABY (BE MINE)	WE'RE INNERVISION	PRIVATE STOCK 45015	20.00	70's

INNOCENT BYSTANDERS

FRANTIC ESCAPE	CRIME (DOESN'T PAY)	PAMELINE 302	15.00	northern
FRANTIC ESCAPE	CRIME (DOESN'T PAY)	ATLANTIC 276	10.00	northern

INNOVATIONS

STAY ON THE CASE	WHAT NOW MY LOVE	HIT SOUND 889	100.00	northern
JUST KEEP ON LOVING ME	LOVE AND RESPECT	HIT SOUND 890	15.00	northern

INSIDERS

IF YOU HAD A HEART	MOVIN' ON	RCA 9325	20.00	**northerB**
I'M JUST A MAN	I'M BETTER OFF WITHOUT YOU	RCA 9225	20.00	northern

INSIGHTS

(YOU'RE JUST A) SOMEDAY GIRL	YOU GOT IT MADE	RCA 9555	15.00	northern
I NEED YOUR LONELINESS	IT'S ALRIGHT	PALMETTO ARTISTS 89021	200.00	northern

INSPIRATIONS

TOUCH ME, KISS ME, HOLD ME	FUNNY SITUATION	BLACK PEARL 100	10.00	northern
TOUCH ME, KISS ME, HOLD ME	WHAT AM I GONNA DO WITH YOU	BLACK PEARL 100	15.00	northern
YOUR WISH IS MY COMMAND	TAKE A CHANCE ON YOU	MIDAS 9003	400.00	northern
NO ONE ELSE CAN TAKE YOUR PLACE	BLANK:	BREAKTHROUGH 1001	3000.00	northern

INSTIGATIONS

I DON'T WANT TO DISCUSS IT	S.Y,S.L.J.F.M. (LETTER SONG)	T-BIRD 101	15.00	**northerB**
I DON'T WANT TO DISCUSS IT	S.Y,S.L.J.F.M. (LETTER SONG)	GRT 15	10.00	northern

INTENTIONS

DANCING FAST, DANCING SLOW	MY LOVE SHE'S GONE	KENT 455	30.00	northern
DON'T FORGET THAT I LOVE YOU	THE NIGHT RIDER	PHILIPS 40428	30.00	northern
I JUST CAN'T WIN	FEEL SO GOOD	MONEYTOWN 1209	350.00	northern
I LOSIN' YOUR LOVE	I'LL SEARCH THE WORLD	UP TIGHT 196810	75.00	northern

INTERNATIONAL FIVE

SO IN LOVE WITH YOU	I NEED YOU	STARWAY 1101	30.00	northern

INTERNATIONAL GTO'S

I LOVE MY BABY	IT'S BEEN RAINING IN MY HEART	ROJAC 1007	200.00	**northerB**

INTERNATIONAL KCP'S

EVERYBODY'S GOING WILD	QUITTIN' TIME	WHEELSVILLE 115	50.00	northern

INTERNATIONALS

TOO SWEET TO BE LONELY	BEAUTIFUL PHILOSOPHY	D'OR 105	40.00	70's
PUSH BUTTON LOVE	GIVE A DAMN	D'OR 102	15.00	group

INTERPRETATIONS

AUTOMATIC SOUL PT.1	AUTOMATIC SOUL PT.2	BELL 779	15.00	funk
BLOW YOUR MIND	TRIPPIN'	JUBILEE 5688	40.00	funk
JASON PEW MOSSO	PT 2.	JUBILEE 5714	100.00	funk
SNAP-OUT	SOUL AFFECTION	BELL 757	15.00	funk

INTERTAINS

I SEE THE LIGHT	GOTTA FIND A GIRL	UPTOWN 717	15.00	northern

INTERVAL, JIMMY

SOMEBODY TO LOVE	GOT A DATE WITH ANGEL	COLUMBIA 43616 DJ	15.00	northern

INTICERS

SINCE YOU LEFT	I'VE GOTTA SEE MY BABY	BABY LUV 36	1000.00	northern

INTREPIDS

AFTER YOU'VE HAD YOUR FLING	A DOSE OF YOUR LOVE	COLUMBIA 10163	10.00	70's

INTRIGUES

IN A MOMENT	SCOTCHMAN ROCK	BULLET 1001	15.00	northern
IN A MOMENT	SCOTCHMAN ROCK	YEW 1001	10.00	northern
I GOT LOVE	THE LANGUAGE OF LOVE	YEW 1012	15.00	northern
TUCK A LITTLE LOVE AWAY	I KNOW THERE'S LOVE	YEW 1010	15.00	northern
DON'T REFUSE MY LOVE	GIRL LET'S STAY TOGETHER	PORT 3018	40.00	northern
I'M GONNA LOVE YOU	I GOTTA FIND OUT FOR MYSELF	YEW 1002	15.00	northern

INTROS

STOP LOOK AND LISTEN	CRYSTAL	JAMIE 1350	50.00	northern

INTRUDERS

A NICE GIRL LIKE YOU	TOP BE HAPPY IS THE REAL THING	TSOP	15.00	70's
COWBOYS TO GIRLS	TURN THE HANDS OF TIME	GAMBLE 214	8.00	northern
UP AND DOWN THE LADDER	(WE'LL BE) UNITED	GAMBLE 201	10.00	northern
BEST DAYS OF MY LIFE	PRAY FOR ME	GAMBLE 4014	8.00	northern
(YOU BETTER) CHECK YOURSELF	IT MUST BE LOVE	GAMBLE 204	10.00	northern
ALL THE TIME	GONNA BE STRONG	EXCEL. 101	15.00	northern

INVERTS

LOOK OUT LOVE	LONELY LOVER	TOWER 324	20.00	northern
TIME WILL CHANGE	LONELY LOVER	BROADWAY 406	100.00	northern

INVICTAS

NEW BABE (SINCE I FOUND YOU)	COTTON CANDY LANE	RAMA RAMA 7779	10.00	northern

INVINCIBLES

WOMAN IS THE SOUL OF A MAN	GIT IT	WB 7061	30.00	northern
HEART FULL OF SOUL	I'LL COME RUNNING TO YOU	WB 5495	6.00	group
CAN'T NO ONE MAN	WONDERS OF LOVE	CIRAY 6702	100.00	northern
IT'S THAT LOVE OF MINE	MY HEART CRIES	WB 5636	15.00	northern

INVITATIONS

I DIDN'T KNOW	LIVING TOGETHER IS KEEPING US	SILVER BLUE 809	10.00	70's
LOOK ON THE GOOD SIDE	PT.2	SILVER BLUE 818	15.00	70's
THEY SAY THE GIRL'S CRAZY	FOR YOUE PRECIOUS LOVE	SILVER BLUE 801	10.00	70's
WE DON'T ALLOW (NO SITTING DOW	FUNKY ROAD	RED GREG 211	10.00	70's
GIRL I'M LEAVING YOU	THE SKATE	MGM 13574	20.00	northern
GOT TO HAVE IT NOW	SWINGING ON THE LOVE VINE	DIAMOND 253	10.00	northern
SKIING IN THE SNOW	WHY DID MY BABY TURN BAD	DYNOVOICE 215	200.00	northern
WHAT'S WRONG WITH ME BABY	WHY DID MY BABY TURN BAD	DYNOVOICE 210	40.00	**northerB**
YOU'RE LIKE A MYSTERY	WATCH OUT LITTLE GIRL	MGM 13666	30.00	northern

IRENE AND THE THE SCOTTS

WHY DO YOU TREAT ME LIKE U DO	I'M STUCK ON MY BABY	SMASH 2138	15.00	northern

IRMA AND THE FASCINATIONS

LOST LOVE	JUST A FEELING	SCEPTER 12100	20.00	northern

IRMA AND THE THE LARKS

WITHOUT YOU BABY	DON'T CRY	FAIRMOUNT 1003	20.00	northern
WITHOUT YOU BABY	DON'T CRY	PRIORITY 322	85.00	northern

IRONING BOARD SAM

ORIGINAL FUNKY BELL BOTTOMSQ	TREAT ME RIGHT	STYLETONE 394	20.00	funk

IRWIN, DEE (BIG)

AND HEAVEN WAS HERE	EVERYBODY'S GOT TO DANCE BUT ME	DIMENSION 1001	30.00	northern
YOU SATISFY MY NEEDS	I WANNA STAY RIGHT HERE WITH YOU	ROTATE 851	85.00	northern
AIN'T NO WAY	CHERISH	IMPERIAL 66420	8.00	ballad
I CAN'T STAND THE PAIN	MY HOPE TO DIE GIRL	IMPERIAL 66320	8.00	northern
I ONLY GET THIS FEELING	THE WRONG DIRECTION	IMPERIAL 66295	10.00	northern

ISLEY BROTHERS

VACUUM CLEANER	LAY LADY LAY	T NECK 933	8.00	funk
WORK TO DO	BEAUTIFUL	T NECK 936	8.00	funk
JUST AIN'T ENOUGH LOVE	GOT TO HAVE YOU BACK	TAMLA 54146	8.00	motown
BEHIND THE PAINTED SMILE	ALL BECAUSE I LOVE YOU	TAMLA 54175	8.00	motown
I HEAR A SYMPHONY	I GUESS I'LL ALWAYS LOVE YOU	TAMLA 54135	8.00	motown
I HEAR A SYMPHONY	WHO COULD EVER DOUBT MY LOVEQ	V.I.P. 25020 NI	300.00	motown
JUST AIN'T ENOUGH LOVE	GOT TO HAVE YOU BACK	TAMLA 54146	8.00	motown
ONE TOO MANY HEARTACHES	THAT'S THE WAY LOVE IS	TAMLA 54154	8.00	motown
TAKE SOME TIME OUT FOR LOVE	JUST AIN'T ENOUGH LOVE	TAMLA 54182	8.00	motown
TAKE SOME TIME OUT FOR LOVE	WHO COULD EVER DOUBT MY LOVE	TAMLA 54133	8.00	motown
THIS OLD HEART OF MINE	THERE'S NO LOVE LEFT	TAMLA 54128	8.00	motown
WHY WHEN LOVE IS GONE	TAKE ME IN YOUR ARMS	TAMLA 54164	10.00	motown
WHO'S THAT LADY	MY LITTLE GIRL	UA 714	15.00	northern

ITHACAS

IF YOU WANT MY LOVE	GONNA FIX YOU GOOD	FEE BEE 220	50.00	northern

IVORYS

PLEASE STAY	I'M IN A GROOVE	DESPENZA 12266	200.00	northern
PLEASE STAY	I'M IN A GROOVE	WAND 1152	600.00	northern

IVY JO

I CAN FEEL THE PAIN	I'D STILL LOVE YOU	V.I.P. 25063	150.00	motown
I REMEMBER WHEN (DEDICATED TO	SORRY IS A SORRY WORD	V.I.P. 25055	10.00	motown

IVY, SIR HENRY

HE LEFT YOU STANDING THERE	TWO TIME LOSER	FUTURE DIMENSION 479	30.00	70's

J

J., WILLI AND CO.

BOOGIE WITH YOUR BABY	SAME: INSTRUMENTAL	KI KI 7194	20.00	funk

J.B.'S

EVERYBODY WANNA GET FUNKY ONE	SAME: Pt.2	PEOPLE 664	8.00	funk
GIVIN' UP FOOD FOR FUNK	GIVIN' UP FOOD FOR FUNK PT.2	PEOPLE 610	10.00	funk
MY BROTHER	MY BROTHER Pt.2	PEOPLE 2502	10.00	funk
THANK YOU FOR LETTIN' ME BE MYSELF	ALL ABOARD THE SOUL FUNKY TRAI	PEOPLE 663	10.00	funk
THE GRUNT	THE GRUNT Pt.2	KING 6317	15.00	funk
THE RABBIT GOT THE GUN	GIMME SOME MORE	PEOPLE 602	10.00	funk
THESE ARE THE J.B.'S	THESE ARE THE J.B.'S PT.2	KING 6333	15.00	funk

J.M'S FUNK FACTORY.

GET ON THE CASE		MONTEREY	30.00	funk

J.O.B. ORQUESTRA

DON'T WANT THAT ILLUSION	THE SOUL	OM 101	75.00	70's

JACK AND JILL

TAKE ME FOR WHAT I AM	blank:	ARCTIC 121 DJ	10.00	ballad
TWO OF A KIND	JUST AS YOU ARE	MAXX 330	15.00	northern

JACKIE AND THE TONETTES

THE PROOF OF YOUR LOVE	STEADY BOY	D-TOWN 1059	100.00	northern

JACKIE AND THE UMPIRES

THREE KINDS OF LOVE	COOL PARTY	SEW CITY 107	200.00	northern

JACKSON BROTHERS

I'VE GOTTA HEAR IT FROM YOU	WHAT GOES UP MUST COME DOWN	PROVIDENCE 409	200.00	northern

JACKSON FAMILY, SPENCER

BRING BACK PEACE TO THE WORLD	SAME:PT.2	SCARAB 2	30.00	funk

JACKSON FIVE

BIG BOY	YOU'VE CHANGED	STEEL TOWN 681	50.00	groupB
WE DON'T HAVE TO BE OVER 21	JAM SESSION	STEEL TOWN 682	25.00	group
WE DON'T HAVE TO BE OVER 21	JAM SESSION	DYNAMO 146	20.00	group

JACKSON SISTERS

I BELIEVE IN MIRACLES	DAY IN THE BLUE	PROPHESY 3005	50.00	70's

JACKSON, BARBARA

SECOND BEST	INVITATION TO A WEDDING	VEE JAY 507	20.00	northern

JACKSON, BART (Also see GEORGE JACKSON)

WONDERFUL DREAM	DANCING MAN	SOUND FACTS 2	75.00	northern
WONDERFUL DREAM	DANCING MAN	DECCA 32317	30.00	northern

JACKSON, CHUCK

HOW LONG HAVE YOU BEEN LOVING	SAME: SAME: SAME: INSTRUMENTALMENTAL	CAROLINA 489	10.00	70's
ANY DAY NOW	THE PROPHET	WAND 122	10.00	northern
ANY OTHER WAY	BIG NEW YORK	WAND 141	8.00	northern
BEG ME	FOR ALL TIME	WAND 154	10.00	northern
I DON'T WANT TO CRY	JUST ONCE	WAND 106	8.00	northern
I'VE GOT TO BE STRONG	WHERE DID SHE STAY	WAND 1142	8.00	northern
SHAME ON ME	CANDY	WAND 1166	8.00	northern
TELL HIM I'M NOT HOME	LONELY AM I	WAND 132	8.00	northern
THE BREAKING POINT	MY WILLOW TREE	WAND 115	10.00	northern
WHO'S GONNA PICK UP THE PIECES	I KEEP FORGETTIN'	WAND 126	8.00	northern
GIRLS GIRLS GIRLS	THE MAN IN YOU	MOTOWN 1118	10.00	motown
THE DAY THE WORLD STYOOD STILL	BABY, I'LL GET IT	V.I.P. 25052	10.00	motown
WHAT AM I GONNA DO WITHOUT YOU	HONEY COME BACK	MOTOWN 1152	10.00	motown
IN BETWEEN TEARS	GET READY FOR THE HEARTBREAK	WAND 128	10.00	northern
GOOD THIONG COME TO THOSE WHO	YAH	WAND 1105	10.00	northern
HAND IT OVER	SINCE I DON'T HAVE YOU	WAND 169	10.00	northern
IF I DIDN'T LOVE YOU	JUST A LITTLE BIT OF YOUR SOUL	WAND 188	10.00	northern
SOMEBODY NEW	STAND BY ME	WAND 161	8.00	northern
THE SAME OLD STORY	IN REAL LIFE	WAND 108	10.00	northern
THESE CHAINS OF LOVE	THEME TO THE BLUES	WAND 1129	10.00	northern
TELL HIM I'M NOT HOME	LONELY AM I	WAND 132 PS	15.00	northern

JACKSON, CHUCK AND THE BROWN, MAXINE

BABY TAKE ME	SOMETHING YOU GOT	WAND 181	10.00	northern

JACKSON, CLARENCE

WRAP IT UP	DO IT ALL OVER AGAIN	RR 929	10.00	70's
IF IT DON'T FIT DON'T FORCE IT	WHAT'S SO GOOD TO YOU	VALTONE 106 DJ	25.00	northern
IF IT DON'T FIT DON'T FORCE IT	SAME: INSTRUMENTAL	VALTONE 106	10.00	northern

JACKSON, CLEO

I'M THE REASON	SAME: INSTRUMENTAL	MAR-KEE 717	150.00	northern

JACKSON, COOKIE

LOVE BRINGS PAIN	FIND ME A LOVER	UPTOWN 714	20.00	northern
UPTOWN JERK	GO SHOUT IT ON THE MOUNTAN	UPTOWN 700	10.00	northern
DO YOU STILL LOVE ME	BLIND LOVE	PROGRESS 912	300.00	northern
SUFFER	FRESH OUT OF TEARS	OKEH 7292	20.00	northern
TRY LOVE (JUST ONE MORE TIME)	HOT DOG	PROGRESS 121	300.00	northern
YOUR GOOD GIRL'S GONNA GO BAD	THINGS GO BETTER WITH LOVE	OKEH 7279	20.00	northern

JACKSON, DEON

YOU'LL WAKE UP WISER	WE GOTTA LOVE	CARLA 1903	15.00	70's
OOH BABY	ALL ON A SUNNY DAY	CARLA 2537.	10.00	northern
I CAN'T GO ON	I NEED A LOVE LIKE YOURS	CARLA 1900	20.00	northern
YOU GOTTA LOVE	YOU'LL WAKE UP WISER	CARLA 1903	20.00	northern
COME BACK HOME	NURSERY RHYMES	ATLANTIC 2252	20.00	northern
HARD TO GET THING CALLED LOVE	WHEN YOUR LOVE HAS GONE	CARLA 2533	20.00	northern
LOVE MAKES THE WORLD GO ROUND	YOU SAID YOU LOVED ME	CARLA 2526	8.00	northern
LOVE TAKES A LONG TIME GROWING	HUSH LITTLE BABY	CARLA 2527	10.00	northern
THAT'S WHAT YOU DO TO ME	I CAN'T DO WITHOUT YOU	CARLA 2530	20.00	northern
WHEN YOUR LOVE HAS GONE	HARD TO GET THING CALLED LOVE	CARLA 2533	20.00	northern
YOU SAID YOU LOVED ME	HUSH LITTLE BABY	ATLANTIC 2213	20.00	northern

JACKSON, EARL

SOUL SELF SATISFACTION	LOOKING THROUGH THE EYES OF LOVE	ABC 11142	200.00	northern

JACKSON, GEORGE

A LITTLE EXTRA STROKE	SAM, WE'LL NEVER FORGET YOU	HAPPY HOOKER 1080	10.00	70's
LET THEM KNOW YOU CARE	PATRICIA	HI 2236	10.00	70's
SO GOOD TO ME	I'M GONNA WAIT	HI 2130	10.00	70's
ARETHA, SING ONE FOR ME	I'M GONNA WAIT	HI 2212	8.00	ballad
FIND 'EM, FOOL 'EM AND FORGET	MY DESIRES ARE GETTING THE BES	FAME 1457	8.00	ballad
I'M GONNA HOLD ON	THAT'S HOW MUCH YOU MEAN TO ME	FAME 1468	15.00	ballad
TIMES ARE TOUGH	BRINGIN' IT HOME TO ME	WASHATAW 1001 9801	8.00	ballad
FAST YOUNG LADY	FUNKY DISCO MACHINE	MUSCLE SHOALS	8.00	funk
I DON'T HAVE THE TIME TO LOVE	DON'T USE ME	MERCURY 72782	150.00	northern
THAT LONELY NIGHT	WHEN I STOP LOVING YOU	CAMEO 460	10.00	northern
THAT LONELY NIGHT	WHEN I STOP LOVING YOU	DOUBLE R 248	15.00	northern
TOSSIN' AND TURNIN'	KISS ME	MERCURY 72736	15.00	northern
WHO WAS THAT GUY	WON'T NOBODY CHA CHA WITH ME	PRANN 5003	100.00	northern

JACKSON, H.J.

PLEASE FORGIVE ME	DANCE THE SHING-A-LING	CROSS-TONE 2	25.00	northern

JACKSON, J.J.

COURAGE AIN'T STRENGTH	THAT AIN'T RIGHT	LOMA 2104	8.00	northern
SHO NUFF (GOT A GOOD THING GOI	TRY ME	LOMA 2082	8.00	northern
BUT IT'S ALRIGHT	BOOGALOO BABY	CALLA 119	10.00	northern
COME SEE ME (I'M YOUR MAN)	I DON'T WANT TO LIVE MY LIFE ALONE	LOMA 2096	8.00	northern
DOWN, BUT NOT OUT	WHY DOES IT TAKE SO LONG	LOMA 2090	8.00	northern

JACKSON, JERRI

I CAN ALMOST BELIEVE	LET ME TRY	PARALLAX 402	30.00	northern

JACKSON, JERRY

IT'S ROUGH OUT THERE	I'M GONNA PAINT A PICTURE	PARKWAY 100	200.00	northern
TAKE OVER NOW	MISS YOU	CAPITOL 2112	25.00	northern
WIDE AWAKE IN A DREAM	SHE LIED	KAPP 496	100.00	northern

JACKSON, JIMBO AND THE VIOLATORS

POP CORN PT. 1	POP CORN PT. 2	BRAINSTORM 134	30.00	funk

JACKSON, JOHNNIE AND THE BLAZERS

WHAT YOU GONNA DO	WISDOM OF A FOOL	J-MER 101	30.00	northern

JACKSON, JUNE

I'M NOT SLEEPING	LET'S TRY DANCIN'	BELL 45236	15.00	northern
IT'S WHAT'S UNDERNEATH THAT CO	FIFTY PERCENT WON'T DO	IMPERIAL 66185	45.00	northern
YOU'RE WELCOME		MUSETTE 112	800.00	northern

JACKSON, KELLIE

IN THE MIDDLE OF NOWHERE	THE DIFFERRENCE IS LOVE	COLUMBIA 43877	20.00	northern

JACKSON, LOU

I CAN'T BELIEVE YOU SAID YOU L	OPEACE TO YOU BROTHER	SPRING 110	50.00	70's
COME TO ME ONLY	PEACE TO YOU BROTHER	VIRGO 201	10.00	ballad

JACKSON, MARKE

SINCE YOU'VE BEEN MY GIRL	I'LL NEVER FORGET YOU	JAMIE 1357	30.00	**northerB**

JACKSON, MAURICE

STEP BY STEP	SAME: INSTRUMENTAL	PLUM 30	15.00	70's
LUCKY FELLOW	SAME: INSTRUMENTAL	LAKESIDE 3101	30.00	northern
LUCKY FELLOW	SAME: INSTRUMENTAL	CANDLE LITE 1938	40.00	northern
FOREVER MY LOVE	MAYBE	WEIS 3440	40.00	northern

JACKSON, MCKINLEY AND POLITICIANS

LOVE MACHINE PT.1	LOVE MACHINE PT. 2	HOT WAX 7102	10.00	funk

JACKSON, MILLIE

MY MAN, A SWEET MAN	I GOTTA GET AWAY	SPRING 127	8.00	70's
MY HEART TOOK A LICKING	A LITTLE BIT OF SOMETHING	MGM 14050	30.00	northern

JACKSON, OLLIE

GOTTA WIPE AWAY THE TEARDROPS	THE DAY MY HEART STOOD STILL	MAGNUM 737	300.00	**northerB**
JUST A LITTLE WHILE	THANK YOU NUMBER ONE	PEPPER 436	15.00	northern

JACKSON, OTIS.

GET YOURSELF TOGETHER, GIRL	IT'S ALL THE SAME	GENESIS 82782	30.00	70's

JACKSON, OTIS AND THE COMPROMISERS

TURN OUT THE LIGHTS	YOU BELONG TO ANOTHER MAN	C&F 1001	150.00	northern

JACKSON, PAUL

QUACK QUACK QUACK		HOLLYWOOD NO#	200.00	funk

JACKSON, RALPH

DON'T TEAR YOURSELF DOWN	JAMBALAYA	AMY 11002	20.00	northern

JACKSON, RANDY

HOW CAN I BE SURE	LOVE SONG FOR KIDS	EPIC 50576	20.00	70's

JACKSON, SKIP

PROMISE THAT YOU'LL WAIT	I'M ON TO YOU GIRL	DOT-MAR 324	20.00	northern

JACKSON, WALTER

LET ME COME COME BACK	IT DOESN'T TAKE MUCH	BRUNSWICK 55502	75.00	70's
TOUCHING IN THE DARK	IF I HAD A CHANCE	KELLI ARTS 1006	8.00	70's
THE WALLS THAT SEPARATE US	A FOOL FOR YOU	USA 104	8.00	ballad
A CORNER IN THE SUN	NOT YOU	OKEH 7260	10.00	northern
BLOWING IN THE WIND	WELCOME HOME	OKEH 7219	10.00	northern
DEEP IN THE HEART OF HARLEM	MY ONE CHANCE TO MAKE IT	OKEH 7285	10.00	northern
IT'S ALL OVER	LEE CROSS	OKEH 7204	10.00	northern
AFTER YOU THERE CAN BE NOTHING	MY FUNNY VALENTINE	OKEH 7256	15.00	northern
BLOWIN' IN THE WIND	WELCOME HOME	OKEH 7219 DJ	20.00	northern
EVERYTHING UNDER THE SUN	ROAD TO RUIN	OKEH 7305 DJ	10.00	northern
I DON'T WANT TO SUFFER	THIS WORLD OF MINE	COLUMBIA 42528	30.00	northern
I'LL KEEP ON TRYING	WHERE HAVE ALL THE FLOWERS	OKEH 7229	10.00	**northerB**
IT WILL BE THE LAST TIME	OPPORTUNITY	COLUMBIA 42823	30.00	northern
IT'S ALL OVER	LEE CROSS	OKEH 7204 DJ	15.00	northern
IT'S AN UPHILL CLIMB TO THE BOTTOM	TEAR FOR TEAR	OKEH 7247	15.00	northern
MY SHIP IS COMING IN	A COLD, COLD WINTER	OKEH 7295	10.00	northern
ONE HEART LONELY	FUNNY (NOT MUCH)	OKEH 7236	15.00	northern
SPEAK HER NAME	THEY DON'T GIVE MEDALS	OKEH 7272	10.00	northern
SPECIAL LOVE	SUDENLY I'M ALONE	OKEH 7215	10.00	northern
THAT'S WHAT MAMA SAY	WHAT WOULD YOU DO	OKEH 7189	15.00	northern
THEN ONLY THEN	STARTING TOMORROW	COLUMBIA 42659	75.00	northern
IT'S AN UPHILL CLIMB TO THE BOTTOM	TEAR FOR TEAR	OKEH 7247 PS	40.00	northern c

JACOBS EXCHANGE, EDDY

CAN'T SEEM TO GET YOU OUT OF M	SAME:	COLUMBIA 45174 DJ	100.00	northern
PULL MY COAT	BLACK IS BLACK	COLUMBIA 44821	40.00	funk

JACOBS, EDDY

TIRED OF BEING LONELY	TURN ME LOOSE	CHESS 2014	20.00	northern
WAS I SO WRONG	FRIDAY NIGHT GET TOGETHER	KISS-KISS 221	75.00	northern

JACOBS, HANK

BACON FAT	OUT OF SIGHT	SUE 102 DJ	10.00	mod
HEIDE	PLAYBOY'S PENTHOUSE	SUE 113	10.00	mod

SO FAR AWAY	MONKEY HIP AND RICE	SUE 795	10.00	mod
ELIJAH ROCKIN' WITH SOUL	EAST SIDE	CALL ME 5385	75.00	**northerB**

JACOCKS, BILL

YOU ARE THE ONE	FICKLE FINGER	MAGGIO 375	20.00	70's

JADE

BROWN AND BEAUTIFUL	THE SIESTA IS OVER	CENTURY CITY 901	8.00	70's
BROWN AND BEAUTIFUL	VIVA TIRADO	CENTURY CITY 512	10.00	70's
MUSIC SLAVE	LATELY "I"	PESANTE 50	50.00	funk

JADES

(BABY) I'M BY YOUR SIDE	FOR JUST ANOTHER DAY	VERVE 10385	10.00	northern
AIN'T IT FUNNY WHAT LOVE CAN D	BABY I NEED YOUR LOVE	CAPITOL 2281	20.00	northern
HOTTER THAN FIRE	MOVIN' AND GROOVIN'	CHERRY RED 144	30.00	northern
I KNOW THE FEELIN'	MY LOSS, YOUR GAIN	PONCELLO 7703	30.00	northern
I'M WHERE IT'S AT	MOTHER'S ONLY DAUGHTER	NITE LIFE 70002	300.00	**northerB**
LUCKY FELLOW	AND NOW	MODE. 503	200.00	northern
YOU'RE SO RIGHT FOR ME	THERE'S A KINDER WAY TO SAY GO	MGM 13399	15.00	northern

JAGGED EDGE

BABY YOU DON'T KNOW	DEEP INSIDE	RCA 8880	15.00	northern

JAGGERZ

GOTTA FIND MY WAY BACK HOME	FOREVER TOGETHER, TOGETHER FOR	GAMBLE 226	15.00	northern
BRING IT BACK	(THAT'S WHY) I LOVE YOU	GAMBLE 218	10.00	northern

JAGUARS

THE METROPOLITAN	WANDA, WHY	ALCO 1006	100.00	northern

JAMES, AL AND THE NEW RHYTHM BAND

GIVE ME UP TURN ME LOOSE	LET'S GET INTO IT	ALOCIS 23253	400.00	70's

JAMES, BOBBY

I REALLY LOVE YOU		KAROL 3727	1000.00	northern

JAMES, DENITA

I HAVE FEELINGS TOO	WILD SIDE	FLIP 364	30.00	northern

JAMES, ETTA

SEVEN DAY FOOL	IT'AS TOO SOON TO KNOW	ARGO 5402	25.00	northern
TIGHTEN UP YOUR OWN THING	WHAT FOOLS WE MORTALS ARE	CADET 5664	10.00	funk
BREAKING POINT	THAT MAN BELONGS BACK HERE WI	ARGO 5477	10.00	northern
MELLOW FELLOW	BOBBY IS HIS NAME	ARGO 5485	15.00	northern

JAMES, ETTA AND THE DESANTO, SUGAR PIE

DO I MAKE MYSELF CLEAR	SOMEWHERE DOWN THE LINE	ARGO 5519	10.00	northern
IN THE BASEMENT Pt.1	IN THE BASEMENT Pt.2	CADET 5539	10.00	northern
DO I MAKE MYSELF CLEAR	SOMEWHERE DOWN THE LINE	CADET 5519	10.00	northern

JAMES, JESSE

IF YOU WANT A LOVE AFFAIR	SAME:	20th. CENTURY 220	20.00	70's
IF YOU'RE LONELY	GREEN POWER	20th. CENTURY 6704	15.00	northern
THANK YOU DARLIN'	BRING BACK MY BABY	20th. CENTURY 6700	10.00	northern

JAMES, JESSICA

WE'LL BE MAKING OUT	LUCKY DAY	DYNOVOICE 220	25.00	northern

JAMES, JESSIE

ARE YOU GONNA LEAVE ME	SOMEONE TO LOVE ME	SHIRLEY 119	850.00	northern

JAMES, JIMMY

SHE DON'T KNOW	TIME'S RUNNING OUT	COED 583	100.00	northern
JAMES, JOHNNYI'M ADDICTED TO YOUR LOVE	ALI SHUFFLE	BLACK PAINT 84590	30.00	northern
TELL YOU ABOUT MY GIRL	YOU'LL NEED MY LOVE	CIRCLE M. 19682	750.00	northern

JAMES, LAWSON

I'VE BEEN KISSED BEFORE	THE MENDER OF BROKEN HEARTS	DEL VAL 1013	50.00	northern

JAMES, MARION

I'M THE WOMAN FOR YOU	FIND OUT WHAT YOU WANT	K&J 300	75.00	northern

JAMES, MILTON

MY LONELY FEELING		DORE	1,000.00	northern

JAMES, PHILIP AND THE BLUESBUSTERS

WIDE AWAKE IN A DREAM	YOU'RE NO GOOD	BRA 201	100.00	northern
WIDE AWAKE IN A DREAM	YOU'RE NO GOOD	SOUL 2002	100.00	northern

JAMIE

THE PRICELESS GEM	IT OUGHT TO BE A CRIME	MGM 13736	15.00	northern

JAMISON, GAY

SOME DUES TO PAY	IF HE'S ALONE	CRAIG 101	30.00	northern

JAMMERS

WHERE CAN SHE RUN TO	WHAT HAPPENED TO THE GOOD TIME	LOMA 2072	20.00	northern

JANET AND THE THE JAYS

LOVE WHAT YOU'RE DOING TO ME	PLEADING FOR YOU	HI. 2129j	15.00	northern

JANICE

I NEED YOU LIKE A BABY	I THANK YOU KINDLY	ROULETTE 7083	75.00	northern

JARVIS, PAT

GUESS WHO I'M FOOLING	THE SOUL OF MY MAN	SELECT 741	50.00	northern

JASON AND PAM

SOUL TRAIN	SAME: INSTRUMENTAL	HAPPY FOX 501	20.00	funk

JASON, BOBBY

WALL TO WALL HEARTACHES	YOU DON'T KNOW THE MEANING OF	RANWOOD 813	100.00	**northerB**

JAY, GLORIA

KNOW WHAT YOU WANT	I'M GONNA MAKE IT	STAGE PRODUCTIONS 1008	30.00	70's

JAY, JOHNNY AND THE GANGBUSTERS

YOU GET YOUR KICKS	GANGBUSTERS BLUES	JOSIE 980	20.00	**northerB**

JAY AND THE AMERICANS

GOT HUNG UP ALONG THE WAY	(WE'LL MEET IN THE) YELLOW FOR	UA 50196	15.00	northern
LIVIN' ABOVE YOUR HEAD	LOOK AT ME - WHAT DO YOU SEE	UA 50046	10.00	northern

JAY AND THE SHUFFLERS (also see THE SHUFFLERS)

ALWAYS BE MINE	WHEN THE LIGHTS ARE LOW	CRACKERJACK	60.00	northern
4010				

JAY AND THE TECHNIQUES

THIS WORLD OF MINE	I FEEL LOVE COMING ON	SILVER BLUE 812	15.00	70's
APPLES, PEACHES, PUMPKIN PIE	STRONGER THAN DIRT	SMASH 2086	8.00	northern
DANCIN' MOOD	SAME:	SMASH 36 DJ	15.00	northern
BABY MAKE YOUR OWN SWEET MUSIC	HELP YOURSELF TO ALL MY LOVING	SMASH 2154 PS	10.00	northern
Sleeve				

JAYWALKERS

CAN'T LIVE WITHOUT YOU	NUTS AND BOLTS	SWAN 4266	30.00	northern

JAY-HAWKS

CREEPIN'	AIN'T IT SO	ASSOCIATED	30.00	mod
ARTISTS 1064				

JC AND THE SOUL ANGELS

DANCE PARTY		TAMMY	75.00	funk

JEAN, BARBARA AND THE LYRICS

WHY WEREN'T YOU THERE	ANY TWO CAN PLAY	BIG HIT 107	250.00	northern

JEAN, NORMA

I'VE TAKEN OVER	TEENAGE GIRL	HEP ME 108	200.00	northern

JEAN, RUBY

EMPTY WORDS	ROVING GIRL	MONSTER MASTERS 1	200.00	northern

JEANNE AND THE THE DARLINGS

SOUL GIRL	WHAT'S GONNA HAPPEN TO ME	VOLT 156	15.00	funk

JEEN AND HIM

YOU AIN'T GONNA GET A CHANCE	THE PARTY'S OVER	BOSS 101	200.00	northern

JEFERSON, EDDIE

UH OH (I'M IN LOVE AGAIN)	I DON'YT WANT YOU ANYMORE	STAX 147	30.00	northern

JEFFERIES, FRAN

GONE NOW	I'VE BEEN WRONG BEFORE	MONUMENT 1089	75.00	northern

JEFFERIES, ROME

GOOD LOVE	SAME: INSTRUMENTAL	RAIN RECORDS 251	75.00	70's

JEFFERSON, EUGENE

A PRETTY GIRL DRESSED IN BROWN	HIGH PRESSURE BLUES	OPEN 1617	20.00	northern

JEFFERSON, MORRIS

ONE MORE TIME	IT'S THE LAST TIME AROUND FOR	GOOD LUCK 201	10.00	70's

JEFFREE

TAKE MY LOVE	MR. FIX-IT	MCA 40955	8.00	70's

JEIMENEZ, RAY

I'LL KEEP ON LOVING YOU	LEAVE HER ALONE	COLUMBIA 44287	40.00	northern

JELLY BEANS

YOU DON'T MEAN ME NO GOOD	I'M HIP TO YOU	ESKEE 10001	60.00	northern

JENKINS REVUE, CAL

JENKINS GOT A FUNKY THING	THE CUTOFF	KEF 4449	15.00	funk

JENKINS, DIANE

I NEED YOU	SAME: INSTRUMENTAL	CREATIVE FUNK 12006	40.00	70's
SWEET WINE, MUSIC AND MY IMAGI	I'M A WOMAN	CREATIVE FUNK 12005	10.00	70's
TOW A WAY ZONE	ANNIVERSARY	CREATIVE FUNK 12002	15.00	70's

JENKINS, DONALD AND THE DELIGHTERS

MY LUCKY DAY	MUSIC REVOLUTION	BLACK BEAUTY 12075	10.00	northern
SOMEBODY HELP ME	ADIOS (MY SECRET LOVE)	CORTLAND 112	40.00	northern
HAPPY DAYS	WHOILE LOTTA LOVIN'	DUCHESS 104	75.00	northern

JENKINS, MARVIN

I'VE GOT THE BLUES PT.1	I'VE GOT THE BLUES PT.2	PALOMAR 2208	20.00	northern

JENKINS, NORMA

CAN YOU IMAGINE THAT	LOVE JONES	DESERT MOON 6401	8.00	70's
ME MYSELF AND I	NEED SOMEONE TO LOVE	CARNIVAL 528	20.00	northern

JENKINS, WALT

BACK IN MY LIFE	FUNKY WALK (THE MONKEY WALK)	FADERKAT 302 red lbl	20.00	70's

JENKINS, WALTER

FUNKY WALK (THE MONKEY WALK)	BACK IN MY LIFE	FADERKAT 302 yellow	10.00	funk

JENNINGS, LEE

GOING AND GET IT		DOTTY'S 347	20.00	northern
JUST KEEP ON LOVING ME	SAME: INSTRUMENTAL	STAR TRACK 101	15.00	northern

JENNINGS, LENNY

THE LAST LAUGH	EASY BABY	ROULETTE 4704	10.00	northern

JENNY AND THE JEWELLS

LOVE LIKE AN ITCHING IN MY HEART	IT'S A MAN'S MAN'S WORLD	HIT SOUND 257	15.00	northern

JENSEN, DICK

GROOVE WITH WHAT YOU GOT	GIRL DON'T COME	MERCURY 72888	15.00	**northerB**

JERMS

I'M A TEARDROP	GREEN DOOR	HONOR BRIGADE 1	15.00	northern

JEROME, HENRY

UPTIGHT (EVERYTHINGS ALRIGHT)	SHADOW OF YOU SMILE	UA 50672	10.00	**northerB**

JEROME, PATTI

NO MORE TEARS	BABY LET ME BE YOUR BABY	AMERICAN ARTS 10	20.00	northern

JERRY O

KARATE BOOGALOO	THE PEARL	BOO-GA-LOO 102	15.00	northern
THERE WAS A TIME	FUNKY CHARGE	WHITE WHALE 318	10.00	mod
SCRATCH MY BACK	SOUL PEARL	BOO-GA-LOO 110	15.00	mod
(FUNKY) FOUR CORNERS	SOUL LOVER	BOO-GA-LOO 466	10.00	funk
(FUNKY) FOUR CORNERS	SOUL LOVER	WHITE WHALE 282	8.00	funk
GET A LINE	THE FUNKY CHICKEN YOKE	BOO-GA-LOO 107	15.00	funk
POPCORN BOOGALOO PT.1	POPCORN BOOGALOO PT.2	BOO-GA-LOO 104	10.00	funk
FUNKY BOO-GA-LOO	PUSH PUSH	SHOUT 225	10.00	funk

JERRY AND THE UNIQUES

YES HE WILL		LENNAN 1261	150.00	northern

JESSE AND ANITA

NICKEL TO A DIME TO A QUARTER	THE MAN	MONEY 608	25.00	funk

JESSUP, WALT AND THE PRIMETTES

ROLL ON		PUSSYCAT 500	50.00	motown

JETS

EVERYTHING I DO	I WAS BORN WITH IT	PORT 3016	15.00	northern

JETSONS AND THE TANGIERS

DANCE OF LOVE	ALL SOULED OUT	PUMPKIN 101	50.00	**northerB**

JEWEL

PARADISE	YOU AND I	JEWEL 181	40.00	70's

JEWELL, LEN

BETTIN' ON LOVE	PAINT ME	FONTANA 1599	75.00	northern
BETTIN' ON LOVE	WONDERFUL BABY	TERI DE 4	2000.00	northern
BETTIN' ON LOVE	PAINT ME	TERI DE 11	25.00	northern

JEWELL AND THE RUBIES

KIDNAPPER	A THRILL	LA LOUISIANNE 8041	30.00	northern
KIDNAPPER	A THRILL	ABC 10485	15.00	northern

JEWELLS

WE GOT TOGETHERNESS	I'M FOREVER BLOWING BUBBLES	MGM 13577	30.00	northern

JEWELS

OPPORTUNITY	GOTTA FIND A WAY	DIMENSION 1034	10.00	northern

JHAMELS

A ROAD TO NOWHERE	BABY, BABY, BABY	LIBERTY 55983	10.00	northern
LET'S GO GO	I'M SCARCED	CELESTRIAL 1013	100.00	northern

JIM AND LEE

LOVERS WHEN WE MET	LET GO, BABY	SMASH 2112	8.00	ballad

JIMMY AND EDDIE

STOP THINK IT OVER	NEEDLE IN A HAYSTACK	ONE WAY 801	40.00	funk

JIMMY AND THE ENTERTAINERS

NEW GIRL		TODDLIN TOWN 3182	400.00	northern

JIVE FIVE

(FYVE)SUGAR (DON'T TAKE MY CANDY)	BLUES IN THE GHETTO	MUSICOR 1305	10.00	group
A BENCH IN THE PARK	PLEASE BABY PLEASE	UA 936	10.00	northern
CRYING LIKE A BABY	YOU'LL FALL IN LOVE	MUSICOR 1250	10.00	northern
I'M A HAPPY MAN	KISS, KISS, KISS	UA 853	10.00	northern
PROVE EVERY WORD YOU SAY	UNITED	UA 807	15.00	northern
YOU'LL FALL IN LOVE	NO MORE TEARS	MUSICOR 1270	15.00	northern
YOU'RE A PUZZLE	HA! HA!	UA 50069	50.00	northern
IF I HAD A CHANCE TO LOVE YOU	I WANT YOU TO BE MY BABY	DECCA 32736	30.00	northern

JIVES

LOVE	I WANT YOU	TEAR DROP 3267	25.00	group

JO ANN AND TROY

SAME OLD FEELING	JUST BECAUSE	ATLANTIC 2293	15.00	northern

JO, PATTI

AIN'T NO LOVE LOST	STAY AWAY FROM ME	SCEPTER 12366	25.00	70's
MAKE ME BELIEVE IN YOU	KEEP ME WARM	WAND 11255	25.00	70's

JO, SHIRLEY

TRUST EACH OTHER	I LOVE YOU FOR SENTIMENTAL REA	JAS. 323	10.00	northern

JOANNE AND THE THE TRIANGLES

AFTER THE SHOWERS COME FLOWERS	DON'T BE A CRY BABY	V.I.P. 25003	60.00	motown

JOBELL ORCHESTRA

NEVER GONNA LET YOU GO	NEVER GONNA LET YOU GO (Disco)	JAN. 300	20.00	**northerB**

JOBETTES

NO EXPLANATION	WHAT YOU GONNA DO	KEVIN 2268	40.00	northern

JOCKO, J.

I'M GETTIN' OVER	SAME:	KAMA SUTRA 600	100.00	70's

JOCOBS, ADOLPH

DO IT	GETTIN' DOWN WITH THE GAME	ROMARK 117	30.00	funk

JOE AND EVERYDAY PEOPLE
SLEEP WALK PT.1	SLEEP WALK PT.2	BROOKS 101	100.00	funk

JOE AND MACK
DON'T YOU WORRY	THE PRETTIEST GIRL	ONEDERFUL 4830	40.00	northern

JOE AND GEORGE
NO ONE LOVES YOU	YOUR GONNA MISS ME	NOW. 4 DJ	30.00	northern

JOHN AND THE WIERDEST
NO TIME	CAN'T GET OVER THESE MEMORIES	TIE 101	1000.00	**northerB**

JOHN, BOBBY
LONELY SOLDIER	THE BAD MAN	SONY 111	20.00	northern

JOHN, MABLE
ACTIONS SPEAK LOUDER THAN WORD	TAKE ME	TAMLA 54050	400.00	motown
NO LOVE H632 1A	LOOKING FOR A MAN H633 1A	TAMLA 54040	100.00	motown
NO LOVE	LOOKING FOR A MAN	TAMLA 54040 sripes	100.00	motown
WHO WOULDN'T LOVE A MAN LIKE THAT	SAY YOU'LL NEVER LET ME GO	TAMLA 54081	125.00	motown
WHO WOULDN'T LOVE A MAN LIKE THAT	YOU MADE A FOOL OUT OF ME	TAMLA 54031	100.00	motown

JOHN, SAMMIE
BOSS BAG	LITTLE JOHN	SOFT 1003 DJ	15.00	mod

JOHNETTE
I GOTTA HOLD ON (TO MY MAN)	LIVING WITH THE BLUES	RICH 102	20.00	northern

JOHNNY AND JACKEY
BABY DON'TCHA WORRY	STOP WHAT YOU'RE DOING	TRI-PHI 1019	20.00	motown
DO YOU SEE MY LOVE FOR YOU GRO	CARRY YOUR OWN LOAD	TRI-PHI 1016	20.00	motown
LONELY AND BLUE	LET'S GOT TO A MOVIE BABY	ANNA 1108	20.00	motown
NO ONE ELSE BUT YOU	HOY HOY	ANNA 1120	15.00	motown
SO DISAPPOINTING	CASRRY YOUR OWN LOAD	TRI-PHI 1002	20.00	motown
SOMEDAY WE'LL BE TOGETHER	SHO DON'T PLAY	TRI-PHI 1005	25.00	motown

JOHNNY AND JAKE
I NEED YOUR HELP BABY	IT'S MESS I TELL YA!	MOD 1010	10.00	northern
I NEED YOUR HELP BABY	IT'S MESS I TELL YA!	PHILIPS 40589	10.00	northern

JOHNNY AND LILLY
SUFFERING CITY	SOMEBODY'S BEEN SCRATCHIN'	WET SOUL 2	10.00	northern

JOHNNY AND THE EXPRESSIONS
GIVE ME ONE MORE CHANCE	BOYS AND GIRLS TOGETHER	JOSIE 959	25.00	northern
SHY GIRL	NOW THAT YOU'RE MINE	JOSIE 955	15.00	northern
WHERE IS THE PARTY	SOMETHING I WANT TO TELL YOU	JOSIE 946	15.00	northern

JOHNSON AND COMPANY, SMOKEY
THE FUNKIE MOON		INTREPID	25.00	funk

JOHNSON SETTLEMENT, HERB
DAMPH F'AIN'T		TOXAN 102	150.00	funk

JOHNSON SISTERS
I FOUND MY PLACE	YOU DON'T WANT ME ANY MORE	BROADWAY 400	25.00	northern

JOHNSON, AL
I'VE GOT MY SECOND WIND	PEACEFUL	COLUMBIA 11287	8.00	70's
SITTIN' AROUND	SOUL TIME	BURT 4001	200.00	northern

JOHNSON, CHARLES
GOOD GOOD LOVIN'	DON'T LOSE THE GROOVE	DASH 5065	50.00	70's
NEVER HAD A LOVE SO GOOD	BABY I CRIED CRIED CRIED	ALSTON 3751	200.00	70's
I BET'CHA DON'T KNOW		MIGHTY MO 902	50.00	70's

JOHNSON, CHUCK
COMPETITION	HERE WE GO 'ROUND THE MULBERRY	SYMBOL 921	15.00	northern

JOHNSON, DEENA
I'M A SAD GIRL	I'LL NEVER LET YOU DOWN	SIMPSON 102	20.00	northern
THE BREAKING POINT	MAMA'S BOY	WILD DEUCE 1004	100.00	northern

JOHNSON, DORTHY
IF IT'S NOT LOVE DON'T WASTE MY TIME	SINCE YOU'VE BEEN GONE	ZOT 521	20.00	70's

JOHNSON, ERNIE
BIG MAN CRY	DROWNING IN MISERY	STEPH & LEE 8667	20.00	70's
I CAN'T STAND THE PAIN	THESE VERY TENDER MOMENTS	ARTCO 104	1500.00	northern

JOHNSON, GENERAL
DON'T WALK AWAY	TEMPERATURE RISING	ARISTA 203	8.00	70's

JOHNSON, GINO
I'M AWARE OF YOUR LOVE AFFAIR	THE STORY OF A WOMAN	BAILEY 5676	20.00	northern

JOHNSON, HANK
YOU LOST YOUR THING		SPEAR NO#	300.00	funk

JOHNSON, HAWKINS, TATUM AND DURR
YOU'RE ALL I NEED TO MAKE IT	A WORLD WITHOUT YOU	CAPSOUL 24	15.00	70's
YOUR LOVE KEEPS DRAWING ME CLOSER	YOU CAN'T BLAME ME	CAPSOUL 22	15.00	northern

JOHNSON, HERB AND THE IMPACTS
I'M SO GLAD (I FOUND YOU)	WHERE ARE YOU	TOXAN 101	200.00	northern
DAMPH F'AIN'T		TOXAN 102	500.00	funk
TWO STEPS	TELL ME SO	SWAN 4186	30.00	northern
I'M SO GLAD (I FOUND YOU)	WHERE ARE YOU	BRUNSWICK 55393	50.00	northern
CARFARE BACK		ARCTIC 109	500.00	northern

JOHNSON, IKE AND DEE DEE
THE DRAG	YOU CAKE HAVE YOUR CAKE	INNIS 3002	20.00	mod

JOHNSON, JAY R.				
COME ON BACK	ALWAYS BE YOUR LOVIN' MAN	HAWK PRODUCTION	50.00	northern
209				
JOHNSON, JESSE				
LEFT OUT	A HUNDRED POUNDS OF CLAY	OLD TOWN 1195	350.00	northern
JOHNSON, JIMMIE				
LET'S GET A LINE	LET'S GET A LINE Pt. 2	STUFF 401	20.00	funk
JOHNSON, JOE				
DO UNTO OTHERS	NOTHING LIKE BEING FREE	TEE 1026	250.00	northern
JOHNSON, JULES AND THE DYMNAMICS				
I JUST WANT TO THANK YOU	300 DEGREES FAHRENHEIT	POLYDOR 14232	30.00	group
JOHNSON, L.V.				
I LOVE YOU, I WANT YOU I NEED	I DON'T REALLY CARE	ICA 27	10.00	70's
TRYING TO HOLD ON	PT.2	CHI HEAT 101	500.00	70's
JOHNSON, LOU				
ALWAYS SOMETHING THERE TO REMIND ME	MAGIC POTION (Instrumental)	BIG HILL 552	10.00	northern
IF I NEVER GET TO LOVE YOU	THANK YOU ANYWAY (MR. DJ)	BIG TOP 3115	30.00	northern
IT AIN'T NO USE	THIS NIGHT	HILLTOP 551	10.00	northern
REACH OUT FOR ME	MAGIC POTION	BIG TOP 3153	15.00	**northerB**
THE LAST ONE TO BE LOVED	KENTUCKY BLUEBIRD	BIG HILL 553	10.00	northern
UNSATISFIED	A TIME TO LOVE - A TIME TO CRY	BIG TOP 101	15.00	**northerB**
WALK ON BY	LITTLE GIRL	BIG TOP 104	15.00	northern
WHAT AM I CRYING FOR	ANYTIME	BIG TOP 103	20.00	northern
WOULDN'T THAT BE SOMETHING	YOU BETTER LET HIM GO	BIG TOP 3127	20.00	northern
JOHNSON, MARK				
THE BEAUTIFUL PLACE	ODE TO OTIS REDDING	DIAMOND 237	10.00	northern
JOHNSON, MARV				
(YOU'VE GOT TO) MOVE TWO MOUNTAINS	I NEED YOU	UA 241	15.00	motown
AIN'T GONNA BE THAT WAY	ALL THE LOVE I'VE GOT	UA 226	15.00	motown
ANOTHER TEAR FALLS	HE'S GOT THE WHOLE WORLD	UA 590	15.00	motown
COME ON AND STOP	NOT AVAILABLE	UA 617	15.00	motown
COME TO ME	WHISPER	UA 160	10.00	motown
COME TO ME	WHISPER	TAMLA 101	150.00	motown
CRYING ON MY PILLOW	CONGRATULATIONS YOU'VE HURT ME	UA 463	20.00	motown
EASIER SAID THAN DONE	JOHNNY ONE STOP	UA 386 DJ	15.00	motown
HAPPY DAYS	BABY, BABY	UA 273	15.00	motown
I LOVE THE WAY YOU LOVE	LET ME LOVE YOU	UA 208	10.00	motown
I'M NOT A PLAYTHING	WHY DO YOU WEANT TO LET ME GO	GORDY 7042	10.00	motown
I'VE GOT A NOTION	HOW CAN WE TELL HIM	UA 322	10.00	motown
JUST THE WAY YOU ARE	I MISS YOU BABY	GORDY 7051	15.00	motown
KEEP TELLIN' YOURSELF	EVERYONE WHO'S BEEN IN LOVE WI	UA 556	15.00	motown
LET YOURSELF GO	THAT'S WHERE I LOST MY BABY	UA 483	15.00	motown
MERRY-GO-ROUND	TELL ME THAT YOU LOVE ME	UA 294	10.00	motown
MY BABY-O	ONCE UPON A TIME	KUDO 663	250.00	motown
OH MARY	SHOW ME	UA 359	10.00	motown
RIVER OF TEARS	I'M COMING HOME	UA 175	15.00	motown
UNBREAKABLE LOVE	THE MAN WHO DON'T BELIEVE IN	UA 691	20.00	motown
YOU GOT THE LOVE I LOVE	I'LLPICK A ROSE FOR MY ROSE	GORDY 7077	10.00	motown
JOHNSON, MARV AND THE PAULETTES				
HE GAVE ME YOU	THAT'S HOW BAD	UA 454	25.00	motown
WITH ALL THAT'S IN ME	MAGIC MIRROR	UA 423	40.00	northern
JOHNSON, PAT				
EAST OF THE SUN, WEST OF THE MOON	LOVE BROUGHT YOU HERE	WIN OR LOSE 221	15.00	70's
JOHNSON, PAUL				
THAT I LOVE YOU	RED ROCK	KELLMAC 1009	40.00	northern
JOHNSON, RALPH				
HAVE YOUR FUN	SAME: INSTRUMENTAL	MASTER KEY 01	250.00	northern
JOHNSON, ROCHELE				
PLAYING THE FIELD	GYPSY WAYS	SWAN 4124 DJ	50.00	northern
JOHNSON, RODNEY				
GET IT ON	HIT THE WIND	TRAVELRAMA 72051	15.00	70's
JOHNSON, ROY LEE				
CHEEER UP, DADDY'S COMING HOME	GUITAR MAN	PHILIPS 40509	15.00	ballad
JUST IN TIME FOR THE WEDDING	STORMY FEELING	123 716	50.00	ballad
NOBODY DOES SOMETHING FOR NOTH	BUSYBODY	OKEH 7182	30.00	ballad
TAKE ME BACK AND TRY ME	SHE PUT THE WHAMMY TO ME	PHILIPS 40558	30.00	ballad
TOO MANY TEARS	BLACK PEPPER WILL MAKE YOU SNE	OKEH 7160	30.00	ballad
SO ANNA JUST LOVE ME	BOOGALOO NO. 3	JOSIE 965	15.00	northern
JOHNSON, ROZETTA (ROSETTA)				
WHO YOU GONNA LOVE (YOUR WOMAN	I CAN FEEL MY LOVE COMING DOWN	CLINTONE 3	15.00	ballad
MINE WAS REAL	A WOMAN'S WAY	CLINTONE 1	15.00	northern
CHAINED & BOUND	HOLDING THE LOSING HAND	CLINTONE 6 DJ	30.00	northern
HOW CAN WE LOSE SOMETHING WE NEVER HAD	PERSONAL WOMAN	CLINTONE 008	200.00	northern
THAT HURTS	IT'S NICE TO KNOW	ATLANTIC 2297	40.00	northern
JOHNSON, RUBY				
KEEP ON KEEPING ON	IF I EVER NEEDED LOVE	VOLT 147	10.00	northern
WEAK SPOT	I'LL RUN YOUR HEART AWAY	VOLT 133	20.00	northern
WHY YOU WANT TO LEAVE ME	NOBODY CARE	CAPCITY 511	15.00	northern
WHY YOU WANT TO LEAVE ME	NOBODY CARE	NEB'S 600	20.00	northern

JOHNSON, SERENA

ALL WORK AND NO PLAY	LACK OF CUMMUNICATION	BIG 2 1001	50.00	70's

JOHNSON, STACY

DON'T BELIEVE HIM	CONSIDER YOURSELF	MODERN 1001	20.00	northern
REMOVE MY DOUBTS	DON'T BELIEVE HIM	SONY 113	75.00	northern

JOHNSON, SYL

WE DID IT	ANY WAY THE WIND BLOWS	HI 2229	8.00	70's
I FEEL AN URGE	TRY ME	TWINIGHT 108	15.00	northern
ONE WAY TICKET TO NOWHERE	KISS BY KISS	TWINIGHT 134	15.00	northern
THANK YOU BABY	WE DO IT TOGETHER	TWINIGHT 144	15.00	northern
ANNIE GOT HOT PANTS POWER	ANNIE GOT HOT PANTS POWER PT.2	TWINIGHT 151	10.00	funk
CONCRETE RESERVATION	TOGETHER FOREVER	TWINIGHT 129	10.00	funk
DIFFERENT STROKES	SORRY BOUT THAT	TWINIGHT 103	10.00	funk
DRESSES TOO SHORT	I CAN TAKE CARE OF BUSINESS	TWINIGHT 110	15.00	funk
I TAKE CARE OF HOMEWORK	TAKE ME BACK	TWINIGHT 116	15.00	funk
I'LL TAKE THOSE SKINNY LEGS	ODE TO SOUL MAN	TWINIGHT 106	10.00	funk
IS IT BECAUSE I'M BLACK	LET THEM HANG HIGH	TWINIGHT 125	20.00	funk
DO YOU KNOW WHAT LOVE IS	THE LOVE I FOUND IN YOU	SPECIAL AGENT 200 red	200.00	northern
DO YOU KNOW WHAT LOVE IS	THINGS AIN'T RIGHT	SPECIAL AGENT 201 yellow	250.00	northern
I FEEL AN URGE	TRY ME	TWINIGHT 108	15.00	northern
STRAIGHT LOVE NO CHASER	SURROUNDED	ZACHRON 600	10.00	northern
THAT'S WHY	EVERYBODY NEEDS LOVE	TWINIGHT 155	15.00	northern
TRY ME	COME ON SOCK IT TO ME	TWILIGHT 100	10.00	northern

JOHNSON, TERRY

WHATCHA GONNA DO	SUZIE	GORDY 7095	15.00	northern

JOHNSON, TROY

I WANT YOU	THIS AIN'T THE WAY	SOUL BEAT 001	250.00	70's

JOHNSON, W.RAY

STRETCH OUT YOUR ARMS	GIRL	HARAGE 30	30.00	northern

JOHNSON, WALLACE

BABY GO AHEAD	I'M GROWN	SANSU 476	20.00	northern
IF YOU LEAVE ME	SOMETHING TO REMEMBER YOU BY	SANSU 467	20.00	northern

JOHNSON, WILLIE

WHAT I'M GOING TO DO	IT'S ME	SAVANNAH 1103	50.00	70's
IT'S GOT TO BE TONIGHT	BETWEEN THE LINES	CAT 501	75.00	ballad

JOINT EFFORT

COMING HOME TO YOU BABY	LOVING YOU COULD BE MAGIC	RUBY-DOO 15	30.00	northern

JOKERS

SOUL STOMP		SKOFIELD	400.00	northern

JONATHAN

TRACKIN'	NO PLACE LIKE HOME	CATALYST 1	50.00	funk

JONES BROTHERS

GOOD OLD DAYS	LUCKY LADY	AVI 102	75.00	70's
YOUR GOOD LOVIN'	SO MUCH LOVE	SILVER. 100	40.00	northern
WITHOUT YOUR LOVE	ALL THAT'S OVER BABY	SEEL 100	40.00	northern
WITHOUT YOUR LOVE	ALL THAT'S OVER BABY	BELL 831	20.00	northern

JONES GIRLS

YOU DON'T LOVE ME NO MORE	IF YOU DON'T START NOTHING	PARAMOUNT 279	20.00	70's
WILL YOU BE THERE	INEED YOU	PARAMOUNT 291	20.00	70'S
YOU'RE THE ONLY BARGAIN I'VE GOT	YOUR LOVE CONTROLS ME	MUSIC MERCHANT 1009	10.00	70's
YOU'RE THE ONLY BARGAIN I'VE GOT	COME BACK	MUSIC MERCHANT 1003	15.00	70's

JONES, AL

ONLY LOVE CAN SAVE ME NOW	I'M GONNA LOVE YOU	AMY 11041	40.00	northern

JONES, ALBERT

YOU AND YOUR LOVE	HUSTLE DISCO	CANDY APPLE 742	75.00	70's
FIFTEEN CENT LOVE	YOU MUST BE A BLESSING	KAPP 2112	15.00	northern
I DO LOVE YOU	YOU MUST BE A BLESSING	TRI-CITY 313	50.00	northern
IT'S GOING TO BE A LOVELY SUMMER	MONKEY BOOGALOO	KAPP 2100	15.00	northern
UNITY	HELLO DARLIN'	KAPP 2128	40.00	northern

JONES, BARBARA

TREAT ME RIGHT	OUT OF NOWHERE	PAT 606	40.00	northern

JONES, BARRY

LET'S DO THE FUNKY BOOGALOO	LET'S DO THE FUNKY BOOGALOO PT	DIAL 4073	20.00	funk
TURKEY WALK	I'M A GREAT LOVER	BACK BEAT 618	20.00	funk

JONES, BESSIE

NO MORE TEARS		A-BET 9424	50.00	northern

JONES, BILL "TARZAN"

A MAN SHOULD NEVER CRY	OH JANE	TISHMAN 715	300.00	northern

JONES, BOBBY

I AM SO LONELY	I GOT A HABIT	LIONEL 3216	15.00	northern
TALKIN' 'BOUT JONES	YOU GOTTA HAVE LOVE (IN YOUR H	EXPO 101	15.00	northern
YOU'RE A DEVIL	WE'LL LOVE EACH OTHER	EXPO 105	10.00	northern

JONES, BOBBY AND THE PARA-MONTS

BEWARE A STRANGER	CHECK ME OUT	USA 864	25.00	northern

JONES, BRENDA LEE

YOU'RE THE LOVE OF MY LIFE	THREAD YOUR NEEDLE	RUST 5112	20.00	northern

JONES, BUSTER

BABY BOY	YOU'VE GOT TO LEARN	SURE SHOT 5022	20.00	northern

I'M SATISFIED	YOU KNOW WHAT TO DO	SURE SHOT 5033	20.00	northern

JONES, CAROL

PROBLEM CHILD	DON'T DESTROY ME	MUTT 27320	15.00	northern

JONES, CASEY AND THE FIREMAN

(GET UP OFF YOUR) RUSTY DUSTY	BRING THE SUNSHINE IN	EPI RECORDS 102	15.00	funk

JONES, CHRIS

I'M THE MAN	DESTINATION UNKNOWN	GOODIE TRAIN 8	30.00	funk

JONES, CHUCK AND THE COMPANY

BOO ON YOU	BOOTIES	WAND 11250 DJ	10.00	northern

JONES, DENNIS

IS THERE A REASON	RAINDROPS	PLUG 3225	50.00	northern

JONES, E. RODNEY

RIGHT ON - RIGHT ON (SEX MACHINE)	FOOTBALL	WESTBOUND 160	10.00	funk
THE WHOLE THING	LOOSE BOOTY	BRUNSWICK 55476	8.00	funk
PEACE OF MIND	DO THE THANG	TUFF 421	75.00	northern
R & B TIME	R & B TIME Pt.2	TUFF 418	30.00	**northerB**

JONES, ELAINE AND THE TRI-DELLS

THEY'RE DOING IT	YOUR FRIENDS	ANGEL-TOWN 101	150.00	northern

JONES, ERNEST

I CAN'T LIVE WITHOUT YOU	BROKEN DREAMS	TRA MOR 1923	15.00	northern

JONES, GERALDINE

BABY I'M LEAVING YOU	WHEN YOU GET TIRED OF ME	EASTERN 600	15.00	northern
I'M CRACKING UP	LOOKING THRU MY MEMORY	SONAR 101	15.00	northern

JONES, GLORIA

HEARTBEAT	HEARTBEAT Pt.2	UPTOWN 712	10.00	northern
LOOK WHAT YOU STARTED	WHEN HE TOUCHES ME	MINIT 32051	10.00	northern
COME GO WITH ME	HOW DO YOU TELL AN ANGEL	UPTOWN 732	75.00	**northerB**
TAINTED LOVE	MY BAD BOY'S COMING HOME	CHAMPION 14003	40.00	**northerB**

JONES, HELEN

I WANT HIM TO BE PROUD OF ME	HEY LONELY	JAN-A-BABY 1000	20.00	northern

JONES, JACQUELINE

YOU MAKE MY LIFE A SUNNY DAY	IT'S A BEAUTIFUL WORLD	LOADSTONE 3949	15.00	70's
A FROWN ON MY FACE	MY SWEET LOVER	LOADSTONE 3953	50.00	70's

JONES, JAN

INDEPENDANT WOMAN	INDEPENDANT WOMAN PT. 2	DAY-WOOD 101	50.00	70's

JONES, JIMMY

AIN'T NOTHING WRONG MAKIN' LOVE	TIME AND CHANGES	CONCHILLO 1	8.00	70's
IF I KNEW THEN (WHAT I KNOW NOW)	MAKE BELIEVE EVERYTHING'S ALL	CAPITOL 3849	15.00	70's
SAY, AMEN BROTHER	YOU BROKE A BLIND BOY'S HEART	JODY 9014	30.00	funk
WALKIN'	PARDON ME	ROULETTE 4608	30.00	northern

JONES, JOE BOOGALOO

I FEEL THE EARTH MOVE	INSIDE JOB	PRESTIGE 751	15.00	mod

JONES, JOHNNY AND THE KING CASUALS

IT'S GONNA BE GOOD	CHIP OFF THE OLD BLCOK	BRUNSWICK 755406	8.00	ballad
SOUL POPPIN'	BLUES FOR THE BEROTHERS	PEACHTREE 102	15.00	mod
PURPLE HAZE	HORSING AROUND	BRUNSWICK 55389	15.00	**northerB**

JONES, JUGGY

INSIDE AMERICA	INSIDE AMERICA PT.2	CONTEMPO 2080 UK	8.00	funk

JONES, LARRY

THEY CALL ME MR LONELY	A TIME FOR US	LARI-SHIRL 1701	200.00	northern

JONES, LEE AND THE SOUNDS OF SOUL

THIS HEART IS HAUNTED	ON THE OTHE SIDE	AMY 11008	25.00	ballad

JONES, LETHA

I NEED YOU	I GOT THAT FEELING	ANNA 1113	100.00	motown
I NEED YOU	BLACK CLOUDS	ANNA 1113	125.00	motown

JONES, LINDA

I CAN'T STOP LOVING MY BABY	HYPNOTIZED	LOMA 2070	8.00	northern
I JUST CAN'T LIVE MY LIFE	MY HEART (WILL UNDERSTAND)	WB 7278	100.00	northern
I'M TAKING BACK MY LOVE	TAKE THE BOY OUT OF THE COUNTR	ATCO 6344	150.00	northern
MY HEART NEEDS A BREAK	THE THINGS IVE BEEN THROUGH	LOMA 2091 green	30.00	northern
MY HEART NEEDS A BREAK	THE THINGS I'VE BEEN THROUGH	LOMA 2091yellow	50.00	northern
WHAT'VE I DONE (TO MAKE YOU MAD)	MAKE ME SURRENDER (BABY BABY P	LOMA 2077	10.00	northern
YOU HIT ME LIKE T.N.T.	FUGITIVE FROM LOVE	BLUE CAT 128	100.00	northern
I CAN'T STAND IT	GIVE MY LOVE A TRY	LOMA 2085	8.00	northern

JONES, LINDA AND THE WHATNAUTS

I'M SO GLAD I FOUND YOU	WORLD SOLUTION	STANG 5039	15.00	70's

JONES, LOTTIE JOE

WALK TALL (BABY THAT'S WHAT I	I BELIEVE TO MY SOUL	CAPITOL 5994	20.00	northern

JONES, MARVA

I GOT YOUR NUMBER (634-5789)	WHY WAIT	SKI-HI 4790	50.00	northern

JONES, MATILDA

PART OF THE GAME	WRONG TOO LONG	FUTURE STARS 1002	20.00	ballad

JONES, MINIIE

SHADOW OF A MEMORY	YOU GET TO ME	SUGAR 100	100.00	northern

JONES, PALMER

DANCIN' MASTER	THE GREAT MAGIC OF LOVE	EPIC 10321	15.00	northern

JONES, QUINCY

COMIN' HOME, BABY	JIVE SAMBA	MERCURY 72160	10.00	mod
SOUL BOSSA NOVA	ON THE STREET WHERE YOU LIVE	MERCURY 72041	10.00	mod

JONES, ROSEY

HAVE LOVE WEILL TRAVEL	THINK ABOUT IT BABY	TODAY 1526	15.00	**northerB**

JONES, ROSEY AND THE THE SUPERIORS

ALL I NEED IS HALF A CHANCE	THINK ABOUT IT BABY	WICKETT 61472	500.00	northern

JONES, SAMANTHA

RAY OF SUNSHINE	HOW DO YOU SAY GOODBYE	UA 50173	20.00	northern
THAT SPECIAL WAY	I DESERVE IT	UA 979	10.00	northern

JONES, SAMMY

SHE DIDN'T KNOW	YOU'VE GOT TO SHOW ME	JENESIS 234	10.00	70's
SWEEPING YOUR DIRT UNDER MY RUG	RED HOG	JENESIS 236	15.00	70's
SWEEPING YOUR DIRT UNDER MY RUG	RED HOG	MERCURY 73325	15.00	70's
DON'T TOUCH ME	CINDRELLA JONES	WAND 1158 DJ	10.00	ballad

JONES, SEPTEMBER

NO MORE LOVE	I'M COMING HOME	KAPP 802	200.00	northern

JONES, SUE ANN

I'LL GIVE YOU MY LOVE	MISSING YOU	TCB 778	100.00	northern

JONES, TAMIKO

CROSS MY HEART	SAME:	METROMEDIA 205	30.00	northern
SIDEWINDER	A MAN AND A WOMAN	ATLANTIC 2362	10.00	mod
I'M SPELLBOUND	AM I GLAD NOW	GOLDEN WORLD 40 DJ	100.00	northern
I'M SPELLBOUND	AM I GLAD NOW	GOLDEN WORLD 40	300.00	northern

JONES, THELMA

SECOND CHANCE	MR. FIXIT	BARRY 1024	10.00	northern
NEVER LEAVE ME	STRONGER	BARRY 1010	10.00	northern

JONES, TOM

KEY TO MY HEART	THUNDERBALL	PARROT 9801	8.00	northern
STOP BREAKING MY HEART	I (WHO HAVE NOTHING)	PARROT 40051	8.00	northern

JONES, WADE

I CAN'T CONCENTRATE	INSANE	RAYBER 1001	500.00	motown

JONESES

WHEN IT RAIN IT POURS	WHEN IT RAIN IT POURS PT.2	TERSA 100	40.00	funk

JORDAN HARMONIZERS

DO YOU KNOW HIM	I WON'T MIND	TRI-PHI 1009	40.00	motown

JORDAN, JAY

IF IT WASN'T FOR LOVE	TOBACCO ROAD	VERVE 10585	20.00	northern

JORDAN, ROD

I LIVE IN A CASTLE	DON'T JUDGE ME ON THE OUTSIDE	KAREN 322	50.00	northern

JORDAN, STEVE

AIN'T NO BIG THING	IF YOU LOVE ME LIKE YOU SAY	ARV 5009	50.00	northern

JORDAN, VIVILORE

ALL WORK AND NO PLAY	PUT MY LOVING ON YOU	TASK 8211	50.00	70's
PUT MY LOVING ON YOU	PICKIN UP WHERE SHE LEFT OFF	SOUND GEMS 106	30.00	70's

JOSEPH, MARGIE

COME ON BACK TO ME	HE CAME INTO MY LIFE	ATLANTIC 3445	15.00	70's
ONE MORE CHANCE	NEVER CAN YOU BE	VOLT 4012	30.00	70's
RIDIN' HIGH	COME LAY SOME LOVIN' ON ME	ATLANTIC 2988	10.00	70's
PUNISH ME	SWEETER TOMORROW	VOLT 4046	15.00	northern
WHAT YOU GONNA DO	SAME:	VOLT 4023	15.00	northern
A MATTER OF LIFE AND DEATH	SHOW ME	OKEH 7313	15.00	northern

JOSIE, MARVA

DON'T	I LOVE NEW YORK	UA 888	100.00	northern
I DON'T CARE	HEARTBREAK CITY	SAHARA 5501	150.00	northern
LOVE YOU DON'T KNOW ME	LOLLIPOP	JULMAR 2544	20.00	northern

JOSIE AND THE PUSSYCATS

IT'S ALL RIGHT WITH ME	EVERY BEAT OF MY HEART	CAPITOL 2967	15.00	northern

JOVIALETTS

SAY, HEY THERE	T'AIN'T NO BIG THING	JOSIE 949	20.00	northern

JOY, BOBBY

YOU SWEET DEVIL YOU	LETTER FROM A SOLDIER	TRC 981	20.00	northern
YOU SWEET DEVIL YOU	LETTER FROM A SOLDIER	SENTRY 103	30.00	northern

JOY, OLIVER

KEEP LOVE GROWING		BIG DEAL 133	100.00	northern

JOY, RODDIE

COME BACK BABY	LOVE HIT ME LIKE A WALLOP	RED BIRD 10021	15.00	northern
HE'S SO EASY TO LOVE	THE LA LA SONG	RED BIRD 10031	25.00	northern
IF THERE'S ANYTHING ELSE YOU WANT	STOP	RED BIRD 10037	15.00	northern
WALKIN' BACK	EVERY BREATH I TAKE	PARKWAY 134	25.00	northern

JOY-TONES.

THIS LOVE (THAT I'M GIVING YOU)	I WANNA PARTY SOME MORE	COED 600	40.00	northern
THIS LOVE (THAT I'M GIVING YOU)	MR. FAROUK	TCB 1601	25.00	northern

JR. MOORE'S

BABY BOY CARTRECE	DISCO MAMA	HMM JNR. 1010	50.00	funk

J'S
WHEN DID YOU STOP	SAME: LONG VERSION	DANTE 966	25.00	70's

JUDGE SUDS AND THE SOUL DETERGENTS
THE (ROCKIN') COURTROOM	SHI DANK	RED CAP RC 102	150.00	funk

JUDY AND THE AFFECTIONS
AIN'T GONNA HURT MY PRIDE	PRETTY BOY - PRETTY GIRL	TOP TEN 2001	50.00	northern

JUGGY
OILY	THE SPOILER	SUE 9	20.00	funk
THOCK IT TO ME HONEY	BUTTERED POPCORN	SUE 14	10.00	mod

JULIAN, DON AND THE LARKS
SHORTY THE PIMP	SHORTY THE PIMP PT.2	MONEY 607	15.00	funk

JUNIOR AND THE CLASSSICS
KILL THE PAIN	PLEASE MAKE LOVE TO ME	MAGIC TOUCH 2009	40.00	funk

JUPITER'S RELEASE
NEVER NEVER	GOOD STROKES	OWL 6111	30.00	group

JUST BOBBY
I'M A WINNER	LOVE IS POWERFUL	R R 101	20.00	northern

JUST BROTHERS
SLICED TOMATOES	TEARS AGO	MUSIC MERCHANT 1002	30.00	funk
SLICED TOMATOES	YOU'VE GOT THE LOVE TO MAKE ME	MUSIC MERCHANT 1010	25.00	funk
CARLENA	SHE BROKE HIS HEART	GARRISON 3003	800.00	northern
SHE BROKE HIS HEART	THINGS WILL BETTER	EMPIRE 126214	200.00	northern

JUSTIN
RIGHT NOW	THE PLACE WHERE SORROW HIDES	DOWN EAST 5372	10.00	northern
WHAT CAN I DO	RIGHT ON	DOWN EAST 5341	100.00	northern

K

K, ROGER
GIVE ME THE LOVE (I'M NEEDING)	YOU'LL BE ALONE	BIRTH 102	10.00	northern

KADDO STRINGS
CRYING OVER YOU	NOTHING BUT LOVE	IMPACT 1005	50.00	northern

KADO, SUNNY MAN
MARS IN '75	MARS IN '75 Pt.2	GOLD WEST 3	20.00	mod

KALEIDOSCOPE
I'M A CHANGED PERSON	THANK YOU	TSOP 4770	10.00	70's
WE'RE NOT GETTING ANY YOUNGER	I WANNA	TSOP 4765	10.00	70's

KAMPELLS
NEW LOCK ON MY DOOR	YOU'VE GOT IT BAD	SELECT 736	25.00	northern

KARIM, TY
I AIN'T LYING	ONLY A FOOL	ROACH 102	40.00	northern
LIGHTEN UP BABY	ALL IN VAIN	CAR-A-MEL 1677 pink	500.00	northern
LIGHTEN UP BABY	ALL IN VAIN	CAR-A-MEL 1677 orange	500.00	northern
LIGHTIN' UP	DON'T LET ME BE LONELY TONIGHT	ROMARK 104	500.00	northern
ONLY A FOOL	I AIN'T LYING	ROACH 101	30.00	northern
YOU JUST DON'T KNOW	ALL IN VAIN	ROMARK 113	3000.0	northern
YOU REALLY MADE IT GOOD TO ME	ALL AT ONCE	ROMARK 101	600.00	northern
YOU REALLY MADE IT GOOD TO ME	AIN'T THAT LOVE ENOUGH	EBONY 101 DJ	20.00	northern

KARL, FRANKIEAND THE CHEVRONS
DON'T SLEEP TOO LONG	PUT A LITTLE LOVE IN YOUR HEAR	LIBERTY 56164	30.00	northern
YOU SHOULD'O HELD ON	BOY NEXT DOOR	PHILTOWN 105	500.00	northern

KARMEN, STEVE
BREAKAWAY	BREAKAWAY Pt.2	UA 50451	20.00	**northerB**
MOMENTS	SAME: INSTRUMENTAL.)	UA 50534	10.00	northern

KAROL, SHIRLEY
JUST TO MAKE YOU HAPPY	YOU DON'T WANT ME ANYMORE	DAKAR 1449	40.00	northern
MY BABY'S GONE AWAY	FAITH	DAKAR 606 DJ	30.00	northern

KARR, YOLANDA
IT TAKES TWO HEARTS	LEAVE IT TO ME	RA-SEL 7103	15.00	northern

KATHY AND THE CALENDERS
PLEASE DON'T GO	BACK IN YOUR ARMS	PORT 3023	20.00	northern

KATRELL, KIM
DID YOU SEE HER LAST NIGHT	TOMORROW	TYSON 100	200.00	northern

KATS
THE NEW BUMP AND TWIST		CLE-AN-THAIR NO#	75.00	funk
UNDER THE COVERS	WEAR ME OUT	E&C 1001	75.00	funk

KAVETTES

YOU BROKE YOUR PROMISE	I'M NOT SORRY FOR YOU	OKEH 7194	100.00	northern
I'VE GOT A STORY TO TELL YOU	STAY WITH ME	LEN DRE 101	200.00	northern

KAY, CAROL

THIS TIME YOU'RE WRONG	THAT'S WHEN IT HURTS	WRIGHT-SOUND	25.00	northern
4479				

KAY, JOEY

BUNDLE OF JOY	JOHNNY BOM BONNEY	EMPIRE 502	150.00	northern

KAYLI, BOB

EVERYBODY WAS THERE	TOODLE DOO	GORDY 7004 NI	300.00	motown
EVERYONE WAS THERE	I TOOK A DARE	CARLTON 482	15.00	motown
HOLD ON PEARL	TOODLE DOO	GORDY 7008	50.00	motown
PEPPERMINT (YOU KNOW WHAT TO DO)	NEVER MORE	ANNA 1104	25.00	motown
TIE ME TIGHT	SMALL SAD SAM	TAMLA 54051	40.00	motown

KEEBLE, DENISE

BEFORE IT FALLS APART	CHAIN ON MY THING	PELICAN 1230	30.00	northern

KEENE, BILLY

WISHING AND HOPING	CROSS MY HEART	PAULA 335	15.00	northern
SOMEBODY PLEASE	LOSERS WIN SOMETIMES	DOTTIE 1134	15.00	northern
WISHING AND HOPING	CROSS MY HEART	VAULT 943	25.00	northern

KEITH, GORDON

TELL THE STORY	DON'T TAKE KINDNESS FOR A WEA	STEELTOWN 1981	10.00	70's
LOOK AHEAD	WHERE DO I GO FROM HERE	CALUMET 682	15.00	northern

KEITH, ROD

AND THE LORD SAID	JESUS IS YOUR FRIEND	PREVIEW	400.00	northern

KEITH, RON AND LADYS

GOTTA GO BY WHAT YOU TELL ME	PARTY MUSIC	A&M 1780	75.00	70's
CAN'T LIVE WITHOUT YOU (STICKS	GET IT ON	A&M 1702	15.00	70's

KELLEY, EMORISE

THE BIGGEST FOOL	DISAPPOINTED IN LOVE	PEACOCK 1919	20.00	northern

KELLY AND THE SOUL EXPLOSIONS

GOT A GIG ON MY BACK		DYNAMITE 13206	40.00	funk

KELLY BROTHERS

COMIN' ON IN	THAT'S WHAT YOU MEAN TO ME	EXCELLO 2290	10.00	ballad
WALKIN' BY THE RIVER	STAY WITH MY BABY	SIMS 230	10.00	ballad
YOU PUT YOUR TOUCH ON ME	HANGING IN THERE	EXCELLO 2286	10.00	ballad
CRYSTAL BLUE PERSUASION	SAME:	EXCELLO 2308 DJ	20.00	northern
CRYING DAYS ARE OVER	CAN'T STAND IT NO LONGER	SIMS 293	25.00	northern
HAVEN'T I BEEN GOOD TO YOU	IF IT WASN'T FOR YOUR LOVE	ECXELLO 2295 DJ	15.00	northern
LOVE TIME	FIRST STEP DOWN	SIMS 247	25.00	northern
MY LOVE GROWS STRONGER	I'VE GOT MY BABY	SIMS 287	15.00	northern

KELLY, COLETTE

CITY OF FOOLS	LONG AND LONELY WORLD	VOLT 4018	15.00	northern

KELLY, DENISE AND THE FAME

I'D LIKE TO GET INTO YOU	SAME:	20th. CENTURY	50.00	70's
2385 DJ				

KELLY, PAUL

UPSET	I CAN'T HELP IT	LLOYD 7	100.00	northern
NINE OUT OF TEN TIMES	I NEED YOUR LOVE SO BAD	PHILIPS 40409 PS	20.00	ballad
WE'RE GONNA MAKE IT	CALL ANOTHER DOCTOR	DIAL 4088 DJ	8.00	ballad
CHILLS AND FEVER	ONLY YOUR LOVE	DIAL 4021	10.00	northern
SWEET SWEET LOVIN'	CRYING FOR MY BABY	PHILIPS 40457	10.00	northern

KENARD

WHAT DID YOU GAIN BY THAT	SAME:	DORE 848 DJ	400.00	**northerB**

KENDRICK, NAT

(DO THE) MASHED POTATOES	SAME: Pt. 2	DADE 1804	10.00	mod
DISH RAG	DISH RAG Pt. 2	DADE 1808	10.00	mod

KENDRICK, WILLIE

GIVE ME LOTS OF LOVIN'	YOU CAN'T BYPASS LOVE	RCA 8947	25.00	northern
WHAT'S THAT ON YOUR FINGER	CHANGE YOUR WAYS	RCA 9212	150.00	**northerB**

KENNEBRUEW, DELILAH

BRIGHT LIGHTS	WE'LL BE TOGETHER	LOMA 2049	40.00	northern

KENNEDY, JAYE

I'M FEELING IT TO	IF THIS IS GOODBYE	UA 969 DJ	40.00	northern

KENNEDY, JOE

SLICK TRICK	TODAY AND TOMORROW	BANG 517	20.00	northern

KENNEDY, JOYCE

COULD THIS BE LOVE	PADDLE MY OWN CANOE	FONTANA 1924	20.00	northern
DOES ANYBODY LOVE ME	THE HI-FI ALBUMS AND I	BLUE ROCK 4023	20.00	northern
I'M A GOOD GIRL	DOES ANYBODY LOVE ME	BLUE ROCK 4016	100.00	northern

KENNY AND THE IMPACTS

WISHING WELL	HEARTACHES	DCP 1147	50.00	northern

KENOLY, RON

MOVING ON	THE GLORY OF YOUR LOVEQ	AUDIO ARTS 60020	25.00	northern
YOU'RE STILL BLOWING MY MIND	TAKE IT EASY	AUDIO FORTY 1806	20.00	northern

KENT STYLE, RICHARD

GO GO CHILDREN	NO MATTER WHAT YOU DO	CORAL 62504	40.00	mod

MANSHIPS

3rd EDITION

GUIDE TO:-

Bootlegs
Counterfeits,
Reissues of

NORTHERN
SOUL 45's

Complete & comprehensive
reference for authenticating RARE SOUL
1000's of listings of Matrix Stamps & Master Numbers,
Label Designs, & Release Dates

UK £12.00
USA $15.00

THE WORLDS MOST SOUGHT AFTER SOUL LABELS
SHRINE

THE WORLDS MOST SOUGHT AFTER SOUL LABELS
ARTCO

101

102

103

104

KENT, AL

COUNTRY BOY	YOU KNOW I LOVE YOU	WINGATE 4	15.00	motown
OOH! PRETTY LADY	FINDERS KEEPERS	RIC TIC 133	10.00	northern
THAT'S WHY (I LOVE YOU)	AM I THE MAN	CHECKER 881	100.00	motown
WHERE DO I GO FROM HERE	YOU'VE GOT TO PAY THE PRICE	RIC TIC 127	8.00	northern
THE WAY YOU'VE BEEN ACTING LATELY	SAME: INSTRUMENTAL	RIC TIC 123	10.00	northern
HOLD ME	YOU KNOW YOU	WIZARD 100	150.00	motown

KENT, BILLY

TAKE IT ALL THIS TIME	LOVE ME FOREVER	EXPO 104	250.00	northern

KENT, BILLY AND THE ANDANTES

TAKE ALL OF ME	YOUR LOVE	MAHS 2	30.00	motown

KEYES, TROY

IF I HAD MY WAY	SAME: INSTRUMENTAL	VMP 110	10.00	70's
LOVE EXPLOSIONS	I'M CRYING (INSIDE)	ABC 11027	10.00	northern
YOU TOLD YOUR STORY	NO SAD SONGS	ABC 11060	20.00	northern

KEYS, VALERIE

LISTEN HERE	ONE OF THEM	DOUBLE SHOT 134	30.00	mod

KIBBLE, FRED

HEY GIRL! HEY BOY!	THE GAY ONE	COPA 8003	200.00	northern

KIMBLE, NEAL

IF IT WASN'T FOR CHILDREN		TANGERINE 1021	1500.00	northern

KICKAPOO KIDD AND THE DEPUTIES

KICK-A-POO PT.1	KICK-A-POO PT. 2	SOULVILLE 223	20.00	mod

KICKIN' MUSTANGS

KICKIN'		PLATO	150.00	funk

KILGORE, THEOLA

IT'S GONNA BE ALRIGHT	I CAN'T STAND IT	MERCURY 72564	30.00	northern
THE SOUND OF MY MAN	LATER I'LL CRY	LANDIX 311	30.00	northern

KILLENS, JOHNNY K. AND THE DYNAMITES

I DON'T NEED HELP	FRENCHY THE TICKLER	DEEP CITY 2370	50.00	funk

KINDRICK, WILLIE

FINE AS WINE	STOP THIS TRAIN	GOLDEN WORLD 1	50.00	northern

KING CAIN

DON'T GIVE A DAMN		BIG STAR	300.00	funk

KING COBRAS

THANK YOU BABY	D.J. SONATA	SEN-TOWN 103	500.00	northern

KING FLOYD

WALKIN' AND THINKIN'	YOU DON'T HAVE TO HAVE IT	UPTOWN 719	20.00	northern

KING GEORGE

I'M GONNA BE SOMEBODY SOMEDAY	DRIVE ON JAMES	RCA 8743	10.00	northern
SO LONG JOHNNY	AH HUH	RCA 8846	10.00	northern

KING GEORGE AND FABULOUS SOULS

BABY I'VE GOT IT		AUDIO ARTS NO#	200.00	funk

KING GEORGE AND THE TIMPS

I'M THROUGH LOSING YOU	I CRIED	MIDTOWN 2	50.00	northern

KING HANNIBAL

RERUN	AIN'T NOBODY PERFECT	MIRACLE 1001	40.00	funk

KING OF HEARTS

A LITTLE TOGETHERNESS	WHEN YUOU WISH UPON A STAR	ZEA 50004	15.00	northern

KING SOLOMAN'S ADVISERS

THE TIGHT ROPE	BACK OF MY MIND	GHETTO 001	15.00	funk

KING SOUND INTERPRETERS

HI NOTE	SUMMERTIME	TALENT OF MUSIC 8253	400.00	northern

KING SPORTY

THE MORE THINGS CHANGE		KINGSTON	50.00	funk

KING TUTT (AND THE UNTOUCHABLES)

COMIN' OUT	EVEN THOUGH	TK 1041	8.00	70's
YOU'VE GOT ME HUNG UP	D-A-N-C-I-N'	FUN CITY 461	75.00	70's
LET'S KEEP ON JUKIN'	SAME: INSTRUMENTAL	FUTURE STARS 1007	15.00	funk

KING WILLIAMS

FIGHT FOR YOUR GIRL	PATIENCE BABY	MGM 13259	20.00	northern

KING, ANNA

MAMA'S GOT A BAG OF HER OWN	SALLY	END 1126	30.00	northern
THE BIG CHANGE	YOU DON'T LOVE ME ANYMORE	LUDIX 103	75.00	northern

KING, B.B.

THE HURT	WHOLE LOTTA WOMAN	ABC 10576	20.00	northern

KING, BEN E.

I CAN'T TAKE IT LIKE A MAN	GOODBYE MY OLD GAL	MAXWELL 800	10.00	70's
HERMIT OF MISTY MOUNTAIN	DON'T PLAY THAT SONG	ATCO 6222	10.00	northern
THE RECORD (BABY I LOVE YOU)	THE WAY YOU SHAKE IT	ATCO 6343	10.00	northern
CRY NO MORE	(THERE'S) NO PLACE TO HIDE	ATCO 6371	20.00	northern
FORGIVE THIS FOOL	DON'T TAKE YOUR LOVE FROM ME	ATCO 6571	15.00	northern
HEY LITTLE ONE	WHEN YOU LOVE SOMEONE	ATCO 6666	10.00	northern
I CAN'T BREAK THE NEWS TO MYSE	GOODNIGHT MY LOVE	ATCO 6390	50.00	northern
SEVEN LETTERS	RIVER OF TEARS	ATCO 6328	8.00	northern
TEARS, TEARS, TEARS	A MAN WITHOUT A DREAM	ATCO 6472	10.00	northern

KING, BOBBY AND SILVER FOXX BAND

Title	B-side	Label	Price	Genre
TEENY WEENY LITTLE BIT	KATHRINE	ATCO 6493	10.00	northern
WHAT CAN A MAN DO	SI SENOR	ATCO 6303	10.00	northern

KING, BOBBY AND SILVER FOXX BAND

Title	B-side	Label	Price	Genre
FAT BAG		MOS-BE	75.00	funk

KING, CLYDIE

Title	B-side	Label	Price	Genre
'BOUT LOVE	FIRST TIME, LAST TIME	LIZARD 21007	10.00	northern
I'LL NEVER STOP LOVING YOU	SHING-A-LING	MINIT 32032	15.00	northern
MISSIN' MY BABY	MY LOVE GROWS DEEPER	IMPERIAL 66139	100.00	northern
MY MISTAKES OF YESTERDAY	ONE OF THOSE GOOD FOR CRYING O	MINIT 32025	20.00	northern
NEVER LIKE THIS BEFORE	THE LONG AND WINDING ROAD	LIZARD 21005	8.00	northern
ONE PART, TWO PART	LOVE NOW, PAY LATER	MINIT 32054	10.00	northern
SOFT AND GENTLE WAYS	HE ALWAYS COMES BACK TO ME	IMPERIAL 66172	100.00	northern
THE THRILL IS GONE	IF YOU WERE MY MAN	IMPERIAL 66109	75.00	northern
ONLY THE GUILTY CRY		PHILIPS	100.00	northern
PROMISES	THE BOYS IN MY LIFE	PHILIPS 40001	15.00	ballad

KING, CURTIS

Title	B-side	Label	Price	Genre
BAD HABITS	SO NICE WHILE IT LASTED	COLUMBIA 44096	15.00	northern

KING, DIANA

Title	B-side	Label	Price	Genre
THAT KIND OF LOVE	BOY IN THE RAINCOAT	CLARIDGE 300	40.00	northern

KING, DONNA

Title	B-side	Label	Price	Genre
TAKE ME HOME	BLESS HIS HEART	HOT LINE 906	300.00	**northerB**

KING, EDDIE

Title	B-side	Label	Price	Genre
I TALK TOO MUCH	KINDNESS, LOVE AND UNDERSTANDI	BIG WHEEL 1970	20.00	northern

KING, JAY W.

Title	B-side	Label	Price	Genre
I'M SO AFRAID	I DON'T HAVE TO WORRY	SKYSCRAPER 6001	15.00	ballad

KING, JEAN (IE)

Title	B-side	Label	Price	Genre
DON'T SAY GOODBYE	IT'S GOOD ENOUGH FOR ME	HBR 497	75.00	northern
SOMETHING HAPPENS TO ME	THE NICEST THINGS HAPPEN	HBR 450	20.00	northern
YOU'VE GOT A GOOD THING GOING	EVERYBODY KNOWS	GENERAL AMERICAN 717	20.00	northern

KING, JO ANN

Title	B-side	Label	Price	Genre
LET THEM LOVE AND BE LOVED	DON'T PLAY WITH FIRE	FAIRMOUNT 1008	25.00	northern

KING, JOANNE

Title	B-side	Label	Price	Genre
MY BABY LEFT ME	PLEASE MR. SONGWRITER	CORAL 62463	70.00	northern

KING, JOEY

Title	B-side	Label	Price	Genre
(COME BACK) SUMMERTIME	NUT HOUSE	CHECK MATE 1017	40.00	motown

KING, LEONARD

Title	B-side	Label	Price	Genre
THE BARRACUDA	I'VE BEEN SAVED	INFERNO 2003	20.00	mod

KING, MARTIN LUTHER

Title	B-side	Label	Price	Genre
I HAVE A DREAM	WE SHALL OVERCOME	GORDY 7023	15.00	motown
PRICE OF FREEDOM/I HAVE A DREAM	SEGREGATION IS WRONG/URGENCY	GORDY 906 DJ EP	40.00	motown

KING, RAMONA

Title	B-side	Label	Price	Genre
I CHOOSE YOU	A FEW YEARS LATER	SOUL SET 104	10.00	northern
IT'S IN HIS KISS	IT COULDN'T HAPPEN TO A NICER	WB 5416	10.00	northern

KING, RICARDO

Title	B-side	Label	Price	Genre
ON A HOT SUMMER DAY IN THE BIG CITY	WON'T YOU COME ON HOME	JOKER 712	20.00	northern

KING, ROD AND THE THE SOULS

Title	B-side	Label	Price	Genre
THESE ARMS OF MINE	SOUL FEEL	SPACE. 16	15.00	ballad
DON'T BE AFRAID	HYPNOTIZED	SPACE. 21	20.00	northern
PENNILESS LOVER	MUSIC TO MY EARS	SPACE. 19	30.00	funk

KING, SAMMY

Title	B-side	Label	Price	Genre
YOUR OLD STANDY		MARTHON 101	100.00	northern

KING, SANDRA

Title	B-side	Label	Price	Genre
PLEASE HEART	LEAVE IT TO THE BOYS	BELL 613	40.00	northern

KING, SLEEPY

Title	B-side	Label	Price	Genre
LOST MAN	THE PILLOW	AWAKE 909	40.00	northern

KING, SUSAN

Title	B-side	Label	Price	Genre
(OH! OH! OH!)WHAT A LOVE THIS	TELL HER (OR LET ME GO	MIDTOWN 3501	20.00	northern
BUILDING A WALL AROUND MY HEART	WHERE WILL I FIND HIM	TOY 104	20.00	northern
YOU GOT ME IN A FIX	DRUM RHYTHM	TURNTABLE 711	15.00	northern

KING, WILLARD

Title	B-side	Label	Price	Genre
LADY BE MINE	I'M NOTHING WITHOUT YOUR LOVE	CAPITOL 3644	20.00	70's

KING-PINS

Title	B-side	Label	Price	Genre
A LUCKY GUY	DANCE, ROMEO, DANCE	VEE JAY 494 DJ	30.00	northern

KING'DAVIS HOUSE ROCKERS

Title	B-side	Label	Price	Genre
BABY YOU SATISFY ME	WE ALL MAKE MISTAKES SOMETMES	VERVE 10492	15.00	northern

KIRBY, GEORGE

Title	B-side	Label	Price	Genre
NO MORE	FEELING GOOD	ARGO 5498 PS	10.00	ballad
WHAT CAN I DO	GOOD NIGHT IRENE	CADET 5523	100.00	**northerB**

KIRKLAND, MIKE JAMES

Title	B-side	Label	Price	Genre
GIVE IT TO ME	LOVE INSURANCE	BRYAN 9005	15.00	70's
GIVE IT TO ME	LOVE IS	BRYAN 9003	25.00	70's
THE PROPHET	TOGETHER	ZAY 3000	30.00	funk

KIRTON, LEW

Title	B-side	Label	Price	Genre
COME ON WITH IT	DO WHAT YOU WANT, BE WHAT YOU	MARLIN 3311	10.00	70's
HEAVEN IN THE AFTERNOON	SAME: INSTRUMENTAL	ALSTON 3743	30.00	70's

KITT, EARTHA

ANYWAY YOU WANT IT, BABY	THE LITTLE GOLD SCREW	MUSICOR 1203	25.00	northern
THERE COMES A TIME	ANYWAY YOU WANT IT, BABY	MUSICOR 1220	100.00	northern

KITTENS

HOW LONG (CAN I GO ON)	I'VE GOT TO GET OVER YOU	CHESS 2055	15.00	northern
AIN'T NO MORE ROOM	HEY OPERATOR	CHESS 2027	20.00	northern
I GOTTA KNOW HIM	SHINGDIG	ABC 10619	20.00	northern
IS IT OVER BABY	UNDECIDED YOU	ABC 10783	50.00	northern
IT'S GOT TO BE LOVE	(I'M AFRAID) THE MASQUERADE IS OVER	ABC 10835	75.00	northern
LOOKIE, LOOKIE	WE FIND HIM GUILTY	ABC 10730J	75.00	northern

KITTENS THREE

BABY (I NEED YOU)	I'M COMING APART AT THE SEEMS	NEWARK 215	30.00	northern

KLINE, BOBBY

SAY SOMETHING NICE TO ME	TAKING CARE OF BUSINESS	MBS 1002	400.00	northern

KNIGHT BROTHERS

SHE'S A-1	THAT'LL GET IT	CADET 1153	10.00	northern
TEMPTATION 'BOUT TO GET ME	SINKING LOW	CHECKER 1107	10.00	northern

KNIGHT, CHARLES

ON MY STREET	DRIP, DRIP ON MY PILLOW	KNITE LIFE 3	30.00	northern

KNIGHT, CURTIS

THAT'S WHY	VOODOO WOMAN	GULF 31	50.00	northern

KNIGHT, GLADYS AND THE PIPS

JUST WALK IN MY SHOES	STEPPING CLOSER TO YOUR HEART	SOUL 35023 white/lilac	15.00	motown
STEPPING CLOSER TO YOUR HEART	EVERYBODY NEEDS LOVE	SOUL 35034	8.00	motown
EITHER WAY I LOSE	GO AWAY STAY AWAY	MAXX 331	15.00	northern
STOP AND GET A HOLD OF MYSELF	WHO KNOWS	MAXX 334	20.00	northern
TELL HER YOU'RE MINE	IF I SHOULD EVER FALL IN LOVE	MAXX 335	15.00	northern

KNIGHT, JEAN

WHAT ONE MAN WON'T DO ANOTHER	RUDY BLUE	OPEN 2627	25.00	funk

KNIGHT, LARRY AND THE UPSETTERS

HURT ME	EVERYTHING'S GONE WRONG	GOLDEN WORLD 37	20.00	motown

KNIGHT, MARIE

COME ON BABY (HOLD MY HAND)	WHAT KIND OF A FOOL	OKEH 7147	100.00	northern
COME TOMORROW	NOTHING IN THE WORLD	OKEH 7141	20.00	northern
CRY ME A RIVER	COMES THE NIGHT	MUSICOR 1076	10.00	northern
I DON'T WANNA WALK ALONE	I WAS BORN AGAIN	DIAMOND 136	20.00	northern
MAKE YOURSELF AT HOME	SAME:	DIAMOND 171 DJ	15.00	northern
THAT'S NO WAY TO TREAT A GIRL	SAY IT AGAIN	MUSICOR 1106 DJ	100.00	**northerB**
TO BE LOVED BY YOU	HOPE YOU WON'T HOLD IT	ADDIT 1016	50.00	northern
YOU LIE SO WELL	A LITTLE TOO LONELY	MUSICOR 1128	75.00	northern

KNIGHT, ROBERT

LOVE ON A MOUNTAIN TOP	THE POWER OF LOVE	RISING SONS 708	8.00	northern
DANCE ONLY WITH ME	BECAUSE	DOT 16256	20.00	northern

KNIGHT, VICTOR

CHINATOWN	VELVET MOOD	RON-CRIS 1015	150.00	**northerB**

KNIGHTS AND ARTHUR

DO YOU	SO SWEET, SO FINE	GAMBLE 202	20.00	northern
I WANT TO GO BACK	I CAN TELL THE WORLD	ROULETTE 4606	20.00	northern
I SHALL NOT BE MOVED	LOVIN' YOU BABY	LANDA 709	15.00	ballad

KNIGHTS.

I'VE GOT A FEELING	FORGIVE ME	USA 800	200.00	northern

KOLETTES

WHO'S THAT GUY	JUST HOW MUCH (CAN ONE HEART TAKE)	BARBARA 1004	20.00	northern
WHO'S THAT GUY	JUST HOW MUCH (CAN ONE HEART TAKE)	CHECKER 1094	10.00	northern

KOOL BLUES

CAN WE TRY LOVE AGAIN	I WANT TO BE READY	CAPSOUL 30	75.00	70's
(I'M GONNA) KEEP ON LOVING YOU	WHY DID I GO	CAPSOUL 25	150.00	northern

KOOL, EDDIE

I LOOK IN THE MIRROR		DORE NO.#	100.00	northern

KRYSTAL GENERATION

WANTED DEAD OR ALIVE 8006	EVERY MAN SEEMS TO BE FOR HIMS	MISTER CHAND	10.00	70's
YOU WERE NEVER MINE	WONDERFUL WORLD	CMC RECORDS 301	50.00	70's

KUBAN, BOB AND THE IN-MEN

THE CHEATER 20001	TRY ME BABY	MUSICLAND USA	10.00	northern
THE CHEATER 21000 yellow	TRY ME BABY	MUSICLAND USA	15.00	northern

KUMANO

I'LL CRY FOR YOU	I HEARD IT	PRELUDE 8010	15.00	70's

K.W.

COME BACK	BABY IF YOU WERE GONE	OKEH 7303 DJ only	150.00	northern

L

Artist / Title	B-side	Label	Price	Genre
L, JOE				
(I'M NOT GONNA BE) WORRIED	PLEASE MR. FOREMAN	CLISSAC 3001	20.00	northern
L.A. BARE FAXX				
SUPER COOL BROTHER	THE THINGS YOU DO	WATTS USA 10	200.00	funk
L.A.POWER AND LIGHT				
LET'S SPEND SOME TIME TOGETHER	SAME: Vocal version	WB 7087	10.00	northern
L.C.				
PUT ME DOWN EASY	TAKE ME FOR WHAT I AM	SAR 148	15.00	northern
LA MAR, LA REINE				
THAT'S NOT THE WAY TO LOVE		CLOUD 72322	150.00	northern
LA MAR, TONY				
FUNKY WAH WAH	READY FOR YOUR LOVE	FIVE-FOUR 5450	200.00	funk
COME OUT TONIGHT	PROMISES	DUCO 5001	200.00	group
13040				
LA MONT, REGGIE				
HOW LONELY (CAN ONE MAN BE)	DARLING I'LL GET ALONG	BLUE ROCK 4029	30.00	northern
LA VERN				
IT WON'T WORK OUT BABY	SAME: MONO	MAYHEW 851	25.00	northern
LA VETTES				
NO MATTER WHAT YOU DO TO ME	PRACTICE WHAT YOU PREACH	PHILIPS 40338	15.00	northern
LABAT, VICKIE				
GOT TO KEEP HANGING ON	WHEN YOU'RE IN LOVE	SHAGG 712	800.00	northern
LABELLE, PATTI AND THE BLUEBELLES				
TRUSTIN' IN YOU	SUFFER	ATLANTIC 2712	15.00	northern
I'M STILL WAITING	FAMILY MAN	ATLANTIC 2347	15.00	northern
YOU FORGOT HOW TO LOVE	ALL OR NOTHING	ATLANTIC 2311	20.00	northern
LACKEY, RICHARD				
THE GREATEST GIFT	LOVE SHOPPING	SOLID FOUNDATION 106	700.00	northern
LADREW, JOHN				
WHAT'S THE MATTER WITH ME	YOU'RE JUST WHAT I NEEDED	ROULETTE 4688	15.00	northern
LADY MARGO				
SIMPLY GOT TO MAKE IT	STOP BY	CYNTHIA 1000	10.00	70's
LAMAR, PRETTY BOY				
YOU ARE GONNA BE SORRY	I AM IN LOVE	CYCLONE 124	150.00	northern
LAMAR, TONI				
JUST IN THE NICK OF TIME	IT'S TOO LATE	BUDDAH 10	15.00	northern
LAMARR, CHICO				
HOW ABOUT YOU	WHAT DO YOU THINK I AM	FULLER 1004	200.00	northern
LAMONT, LEE				
HAPPY DAYS	PLEASIN' WOMAN	BACK BEAT 564	10.00	northern
I'LL TAKE LOVE	THE CRYING MAN	BACK BEAT 542	10.00	northern
LAMONT, REGGIE				
HOW LONELY (CAN ONE MAN BE)	DARLING I'LL GET ALONG SOMEHOW	BLUE ROCK 4029 DJ	40.00	northern
LAMP, BUDDY				
I WANNA GO HOME	CONFUSION	WHEELSVILLE 120	10.00	northern
SAVE YOUR LOVE	I WANNA GO HOME	WHEELSVILLE 122	100.00	northern
THE NEXT BEST THING	JUST A LITTLE BIT OF LOVIN'	D-TOWN 1064	40.00	northern
YOU'VE GOT THE LOVING TOUCH	WANNA GO HOME	WHEELSVILLE 113	40.00	northern
LAMPKIN, TONY				
YOU'VE GOT TOO MANY MILES	MAKE 'EM BETTER NOW	SWAR 6020	30.00	70's
LANAY, MICKEY				
I'M GONNA WALK	FORGET YESTERDAY	VULCAN 100	100.00	northern
LANCE, MAJOR				
COME WHAT MAY	COME ON, HAVE YOURSELF A GOOD	COLUMBIA 10488	10.00	70's
I NEVER THOUGHT I'D BE LOSING	CHICAGO DISCO	SOUL 35123	8.00	70's
SINCE I LOST MY BABY'S LOVE	GIRL, COME ON HOME	VOLT 4069	8.00	70's
SINCE I LOST MY BABY'S LOVE	AIN'T NO SWEAT	VOLT 4085	8.00	70's
SWEETER	WILD AND FREE	PLAYBOY 6020	8.00	70's
YOU'RE EVERYTHING I NEED	SAME: INSTRUMENTAL	OSIRIS 1	8.00	70's
DO THE TIGHTEN UP	I HAVE NO ONE	DAKAR 1450	10.00	northern
I'M SO LOST	SOMETIMES I WONDER	OKEH 7209	10.00	northern
RHYTHM	PLEASE DON'T SAY NO MORE	OKEH 7203	10.00	northern
UM, UM,UM, UM, UM, UM	SWEET MUSIC	OKEH 7187	8.00	northern
GYPSY WOMAN	STAY AWAY FROM ME	CURTOM 1953	10.00	northern
I WANNA MAKE UP	THAT'S THE STORY OF MY LIFE	VOLT 4079	10.00	northern
LITTLE YOUNG LOVER	MUST BE LOVE COMING DOWN	CURTOM 1956	10.00	northern
SHADOW OF A MEMORY	SWEETER AS THE DAYS GO BY	DAKAR 612	10.00	northern
SINCE YOU'VE BEEN GONE	FOLLOW THE LEADER	DAKAR 608	10.00	northern
I'VE GOT A GIRL	PHYLISS	MERCURY 71582	100.00	group

AIN'T IT A SHAME	GOTTA GET AWAY	OKEH 7223	15.00	northern
AIN'T NO SOUL (LEFT IN THESE OLD SHOES)	I	OKEH 7266	15.00	**northerB**
COME SEE	YOU BELONG TO ME MY LOVE	OKEH 7216	10.00	northern
DELILAH	EVERYTIME	OKEH 7168	50.00	northern
EVERYBODY LOVES A GOOD TIME	I JUST CAN'T HELP IT	OKEH 7233	15.00	northern
HEY LITTLE GIRL	CRYING IN THE RAIN	OKEH 7181	15.00	northern
INVESTIGATE	LITTLE YOUNG LOVER	OKEH 7250	15.00	**northerB**
IT AIN'T NO USE	GIRLS	OKEH 7197	10.00	northern
MONKEY TIME	MAMA DIDN'T KNOW	OKEH 7175	15.00	northern
THE BEAT	YOU'LL WANT ME BACK	OKEH 7255	15.00	**northerB**
THE MATADOR	GONNA GET MARRIED	OKEH 7191	15.00	northern
TOO HOT TO HOLD	DARK AND LONELY	OKEH 7226	15.00	northern
WITHOUT A DOUBT	FOREVER	OKEH 7298	30.00	northern
THINK NOTHING ABOUT IT		OKEH 7200 NI	1000.00	northern
AIN'T NO SOUL (LEFT IN THESE OLD SHOES)	I	OKEH 7266 PS	25.00	northern
COME SEE	YOU BELONG TO ME MY LOVE	OKEH 7216 PS	25.00	northern
INVESTIGATE	LITTLE YOUNG LOVER	OKEH 7250 PS	30.00	northern
RHYTHM	PLEASE DON'T SAY NO MORE	OKEH 7203 PS	25.00	northern
UM, UM, UM, UM, UM, UM	SWEET MUSIC	OKEH 7187 PS	20.00	northern

LANCE AND THE THE SPIRITS
THE PERFECT COMBINATION	COOKING UP SOME SOUL	GARRETT 1005	15.00	northern

LANCELOT, RICK
HEARTBREAK TRAIN	HOO DOO MAN	RCA 8564 DJ	20.00	northern

LANCERS
DOING THE SNATCH	BASSOLOGY	BLUE ROCK 4021	50.00	mod

LANDLORDS AND TENANTS
BACK UP PT.1	BACK UP PT.2	BUDDAH 301	25.00	funk
SAGITTARIUS PT.1	SAGITTARIUS PT.2	COACH 11	60.00	funk

LANDS, HOAGY
WHY DIDN'T YOU LET ME KNOW	DO YOU KNOW WHAT LIFE IS ALL A	SPECTRUM 122	10.00	northern
THE NEXT IN LINE	PLEASE DON'T TALK ABOUT ME WHE	LAURIE 3381	20.00	**northerB**

LANDS, LIZ
HE'S GOT THE WHOLE WORLD IN HIS HANDS	MAY WHAT HE LIVED FOR LIVE	GORDY 7026	10.00	motown
MIDNIGHT JOHNNY	KEEP ME	GORDY 7030	70.00	motown

LANDSLIDES
MUSIC PLASE MUSIC	WE DON'T NEED NO MUSIC	HUFF PUFF 1001	20.00	funk

LANE, JEFF
I SURE DO WANT SOMEONE		DOUBLE ZERO NO.#	250.00	northern
YOU PUT THE HURT ON ME INTERNATIONAL	THE DAY THAT YOU LEFT ME	UNITED	75.00	northern

LANE, LINDA
LONELY TEARDROPS	CANCEL THE CELEBRATION	CUB 9124	50.00	northern

LANE, MICKEY LEE
HEY SAH LO NEY	OF YESTERDAY	SWAN 4222	15.00	northern

LARK, FRANCES
HOLD BACK THE DAWN	GET UP AND DANCE	DORE 730	75.00	northern

LARK, TOBI
TWENTY FOUR HOURS	SHAKE A HAND	COTILLION 44025	8.00	ballad
HAPPINESS IS HERE	TALKIN' ABOUT LOVE	TOPPER 1011	75.00	northern
CHALLENGE MY LOVE	SWEEP IT OUT THE SHED	TOPPER 1015	60.00	northern
I'LL STEAL YOUR HEART	TALK TO AN ANGEL	PALMER 5000	200.00	northern
LOTS OF HEART		USD NO.#	400.00	northern

LARKS
THE JERK	FORGET ME	MONEY 106	10.00	northern
COME BACK BABY	THE SKATE	MONEY 127	20.00	northern
SOUL JERK	MICKEY'S EAST COAST JERK	MONEY 110	10.00	northern
THE JERK	FORGET ME	MONEY 106	10.00	northern

LARRY AND THE LARKS
TELL ME	THE GIRL I LOVE	VEEP 1251	20.00	northern

LAS VEGAS CONNECTION
CAN'T NOBODY LOVE ME LIKE YOU	RUNNING BACK TO YOU	HEP ME 169	30.00	70's
GIVE ME YOUR LOVE	DANCING WITH MY LOVE BONES	HEP ME 169	10.00	70's

LASALLE, DENISE
I'M TRIPPING ON YOU	I'LL GET YOU SOME HELP	MCA 51046	8.00	70's
HEARTBREAKER OF THE YEAR	HUNG UP STRUNG OUT	PARKA 2302	15.00	northern
HEARTBREAKER OF THE YEAR	HUNG UP, STRUNG OUT	WESTBOUND 162	8.00	northern
TOO LATE TO CHECK YOUR TRAP	THE RIGHT TRACK	PARKA 2301	15.00	northern
TOO LATE TO CHECK YOUR TRAP	HEARTBREAKER OF THE YEAR	CRAJON 48201	15.00	northern
A LOVE REPUTATION	ONE LITTLE THING	CHESS 2005	25.00	northern
A LOVE REPUTATION	ONE LITTLE THING	TARPON 6603	60.00	northern

LASALLES
LA LA LA LA LA	THIS IS TRUE	V.I.P. 25036	20.00	motown

LASHANNON, RONNIE
WHERE HAS OUR LOVE GONE	SAME: SHORT VERSION	BRUNSWICK 55532	10.00	70's

LASHONS
LITTLE SISTER BEWARE	MONKEY AGE	VENDED 105	100.00	northern

LASKEY, EMANUEL
I'D RATHER LEAVE ON MY FEET	SAME: LONG VERSION	DT 100	100.00	70's
JUST THE WAY (I WANT HER TO BE)	RIGHT NOW (WIT IT)	MUSIC NOW 2880	15.00	70's

DON'T LEAD ME ON	WHAT DID I DO WRONG	THEMLA 106	40.00	northern
SWEET LIES	I'M A PEACE LOVING MAN	THEMLA 108	40.00	northern
TOMORROW	I NEED SOMEBODY	THELMA 94494	20.00	northern
WELFARE CHEESE	CRAZY	THEMLA 100	20.00	northern
WELFARE CHEESE	THE MONKEY	THEMLA 100	40.00	northern
MORE LOVE (WHERE THAT CAME FROM)	A LETTER FROM VIETNAM	WESTBOUND 143	15.00	northern
TOMORROW	I NEED SOMEBODY	NPC 303	30.00	group
I NEED SOMEBODY	TOMORROW	THEMLA 2282.	30.00	northern
LUCKY TO BE LOVED BY YOU	OUR WORLD	THELMA 103 NI	150.00	northern
LUCKY TO BE LOVED BY YOU	OUR WORLD	WILD DUECE 829	40.00	northern
DON'T LEAD ME ON	YOU BETTER QUIT IT	THELMA 115	15.00	northern

Previously unissed and wrongly credited to Emanuel Laskey, this is in fact Billy Kennedy singing.

LASTER, LARRY
GO FOR YOURSELF	HELP YOURSELF	LOMA 2043	100.00	northern
THAT'S JUST WHAT YOU DID	IT WILL BE	DUO-VIRGO 100	150.00	northern

LATELY, JAMES
LOVE FRIENDS AND MONEY	TEARS RUNNING AND FALLING MY EYES	TEMPLE 2082	1000.00	northern

LATHAM, GERALDINE
LAZY LOVER	MR. FIXIT	WINNER 7 11 101	10.00	northern

LATIMORE, BENNY
I'LL BE GOOD TO YOU	LIFE'S LITTLE UPS AND DOWNS	DADE 2025	40.00	northern
GIRL I GOT NEWS FOR YOU	AIN'T CRY NO MORE	DADE 2013	30.00	northern
IT WAS SIO NICE WHILE IT LASTE	THERE SHE IS	DADE 2014	40.00	northern
RAIN FROM THE SKY	I CAN'T GO ON ANYMORE	BLADE 701	400.00	northern

LATIN BREED
I TURN YOU ON		GC	200.00	funk

LATTER, GENE
SIGN ON THE DOTTED LINE	I LOVE YOU	LIBERTY 56117	10.00	northern

LATTIMORE, ALMETA
THESE MEMORIES	SAME:	MAINSTREAM 5575	200.00	70's

LATTIMORE, CHARLES
DO THE THING	WE TRY HARDER	SHOUT 219	20.00	funk

LAVANT, JACKIE AND THE FfASHIONS
I DON'T MIND DOIN' IT	WHAT GOES UP	PHIL LA SOUL 354	10.00	northern

LAVERNE, TELMA
BABY DON'T LEAVE ME	HE'S A LUCKY GUY	NORTHERN DEL-LA 502	800.00	northern

LAVETTE, BETTY
YOU MADE A BELIEVER OUT OF ME	THANK YOU FOR LOVING ME	EPIC 50143	40.00	70's
LET ME DOWN EASY	WHAT I DON'T KNOW	CALLA 102	10.00	northern
YOU'LL WAKE UP WISER	HEART OF GOLD	ATCO 6891	15.00	northern
HEY LOVE	A LITTLE HELP FROM MY FRIENDS	KAREN 1545	10.00	northern
I'M HOLDING ON	TEARS IN VAIN	BIG WHEEL 1969	15.00	northern
ONLY YOUR LOVE CAN SAVE ME	I FEEL GOOD (ALL OVER)	CALLA 104	15.00	northern
WHAT CONDITION MY CONDITION IS IN	GET AWAY	KAREN 1544	15.00	northern
ALMOST	LOVE MAKES THE WORLD GO ROUND	KAREN 1540	15.00	northern
WITCH CRAFT IN THE AIR	YOU KILLED THE LOVE	LU PINE 123	10.00	northern
SHUT YOUR MOUTH	MY MAN-HE'S A LOVIN' MAN	ATLANTIC 2160	15.00	northern
YOU'LL NEVER CHANGE	HERE I AM	ATLANTIC 2198	20.00	northern

LAWRENCE AND THE ARABIANS
OOH BABY	COINCIDENCE	SHOUT 215	8.00	group
OOH BABY	COINCIDENCE	HEM 1001	40.00	group
I'LL TRY HARDER	MONEY	HEM 1002	100.00	northern
OOB BABY	COINCIDENCE	HEM 1001	40.00	northern

LAWS, ELOISE
TIGHTEN HIM UP	SAME:	MUSIC MERCHANT 1011	15.00	funk
LOVE FACTORY	STAY WITH ME	MUSIC MERCHANT 1013	20.00	**northerB**

LAWS, LUCKY
WHO IS SHE	BROKEN HEART	ONEDERFUL 4825	15.00	northern

LAWSON, JANET
DINDI	TWO LITTLE ROOMS	UA 50671	20.00	funk

LAWSON, JOYCE
LOVE UPRISING	LOVE UPRISING PT. 2	MUTT & JEFF 42	15.00	70's

LAWSON, ROBBY
BURNING SENSATION	I HAVE SEARCHED	KYSER 2122	850.00	**northerB**

LAWSON, SHIRLEY
ONE MORE CHANCE	THE STAR	BACK BEAT 567	50.00	northern
SO MUCH TO ME	SAD SAD DAY	ENTERPRISE 5040	50.00	northern

LAWTON, LOU
KNICK KNACK PATTY WACK	IT'S THAT TIME OF DAY	WAND 1160	50.00	mod
I AM SEARCHING (FOR MY BABY)	DOING THE PHILLY DOG	CAPITOL 5613	15.00	northern

LAYNE, SANDY
HOW MANY TIMES	PUSH MY LOVE BUTTON	LOMA 2052	20.00	northern

LE TRE FEMME
OPEN UP THE SAFE	YOU BETTER GET BACK	20th. CENTURY 6702	15.00	northern

LEACH, JOHN
PUT THAT WOMAN DOWN	LOVE DON'T TURN YOUR BACK ON ME	LAWN 256	400.00	northern

LEADERS

YOU ARE THE ONE I LOVE	IT'S FUNNY HOW FAST YOU FORGOT	BLUE ROCK 4060	25.00	northern

LEAR, KEVIN KING

(YOU GOT) THE POWER OF LOVE	MR. PEARLY	PAGE ONE 21011	15.00	northern

LEAVILLE, OTIS

A REASON TO BE LONELY	BECAUSE OF YOU	BLUE ROCK 4031	10.00	northern
GLAD I MET YOU	THERE'S NOTHING BETTER	DAKAR 625	10.00	northern
I NEED YOU	I LOVE YOU	DAKAR 614	8.00	northern
I'M AMAZED	JUST A MEMORY	LIMELIGHT 3020	30.00	northern
I'M SO JEALOUS	YOU BROUGHT OUT THE GOOD IN ME	DAKAR 622	8.00	northern
NOBODY BUT YOU	CHARLOTTE	SMASH 2141	15.00	northern
WHEN THE MUSIC GROOVES	LET HER LOVE ME	BLUE ROCK 4002	10.00	**northerB**
WHY, WHY, WHY	GLAD I MET YOU	DAKAR 617	10.00	northern
YOU BROUGHT THE GOOD OUT IN ME	I'M SO JEALOUS	DAKAR 622	10.00	northern
BOOMERANG	TO BE OR NOT TO BE	BLUE ROCK 4015	10.00	**northerB**
CAN'T STOP LOVING YOU	BABY (WHY CAN'T YOU HEAR ME)	BRUNSWICK 55337	50.00	northern
GOTTA RIGHT TO CRY	RISE SALLY RISE	LUCKY 1004	200.00	northern
IT'S THE SAME OLD ME	LET ME LIVE	BLUE ROCK 4063	15.00	northern
KEEP ON LOVING	RIGHT BACK IN LOVE	COLUMBIA 43661	25.00	northern
LOVE UPRISING	I NEED YOU	DAKAR 620	10.00	northern

LEDGENDS

FEAR NOT	GOTTA LET YOU GO	LOCKET 756	40.00	northern
FEAR NOT	GOTTA LET YOU GO	COMMONWEALTH 3014	20.00	northern

LEE AND THE LEOPARDS

COME INTO MY PALACE	TRYING TO MAKE IT	GORDY 7002	45.00	motown

LEE, BYRON AND THE DRAGONAIRES

THE RECORD (BABY I LOVE YOU)	HANG ON SLOOPY	BRA. 901	100.00	northern

LEE, CURTIS

IS SHE IN YOUR TOWN		MIRA. NO.#	100.00	northern

LEE, CURTIS AND THE K.C.P.'s

EVERYBODY'S GOING WILD	GET IN MY BAG	ROJAC 114	10.00	northern

LEE, HAYWARD

OOGALOO	IT'S A SIN TO TELL A LIE	SCAMM 1002	20.00	mod

LEE, JACKIE

OH, MY DARLIN'	DON'T BE ASHAMED	MIRWOOD 5527	10.00	**northerB**
THE DUCK	LET YOUR CONSCIENCE BE YOUR GUIDE	MIRWOOD 5502	8.00	northern
YOUR P-E-R-S-O-N-A-L-I-T-Y	TRY MY METHOD	MIRWOOD 5509	8.00	northern
YOU WERE SEARCHING FOR A LOVE	YOUR SWEETNESS IS MY WEAKNESS	UNI 55259	8.00	northern
BRING IT HOME	GLORY OF LOVE	KEYMEN 109	10.00	northern
DARKEST DAYS	ONE FOR THE ROAD	ABC 11146	30.00	northern
PERSHING SQUARE	25 MILES TO LOUISIANA	CAPITOL 3145	10.00	northern
WOULD YOU BELIEVE	YOU'RE EVERYTHING	MIRWOOD 5519	15.00	northern

LEE, JOE

BOTTOM OF THE BAG		PAPA JOES	75.00	funk

LEE, LAURA

YOUR SONG	SAT-IS-FACTION	FANTASY 865	8.00	70's
I CAN'T HOLD ON MUCH LONGER	I'LL CATCH YOU WHEN I FALL	HOT WAX 7305	10.00	northern
CRUMBS OFF THE TABLE	YOU'VE GOT TO SAVE ME	HOT WAX 7210	8.00	funk
IT'S HOW YOU MAKE IT GOOD	HANG IT YOU	CHESS 2062	8.00	funk
TO WIN YOUR HEART	SO WILL I	RIC TIC 111	20.00	**northerB**

LEE, LEONARD

I'M A POOR BOY (WITH MILLIONS)	SINCE YOU'VE BEEN GONE	BROADMOOR 102	20.00	northern

LEE, MAMIE

I CAN FEEL HIM SLIPPING AWAY	THE SHOW IS OVER	MGM 13850	30.00	northern

LEE, MARVA

IF YOU CAN'T BE TRUE	TOO BAD, TOO SAD	ATCO 6367	30.00	northern

LEE, NORA

YOU MUST BELIEVE ME	FORGET IT	WESTWOOD 1421	100.00	northern

LEE, OTIS

HARD ROW TO HOE	THEY SAY I'M A FOOL	QUAINT 1-1	400.00	northern

LEE, PERK

THE DOCKS	PEANUT BUTTER SANDWICH	BOSS 2125	200.00	northern
THE DOCKS	PEANUT BUTTER SANDWICH	USA 748	150.00	northern

LEE, RUBY

I BELIEVE IN YOU	I'M GONNA PUT A WATCH ON YOU	POPTONE 1901	15.00	northern

LEE, SAMMY

IT HURTS ME	NUSERY RHYMES	RAMPART 653	20.00	northern
WHAT GOES AROUND		PROMCO NO.#	75.00	northern

LEE, T.C. AND THE BRICKLAYERS

UP AND DOWN THE HILL	GET AWAY FROM HERE	KING 6135	700.00	northern

LEE, TOMMIE

THAT'S THE WAY I WANT TO LIVE	DELTA QUEEN	CAPITOL 6662	40.00	70's

LEE, WARREN

MAMA SAID WE CAN'T GET MARRIED	A LADY	DEESU 302	100.00	funk

LEE, WILLIE

SWEET THING	MAN THAT I AM	GATUR 511	20.00	funk

LEE'S GROUNDHOGS, JOHN

I'LL NEVER FALL IN LOVE AGAIN	OVER YOU BABY	PLANET 104	20.00	mod

LEGEND, TOBI

NO GOOD TO CRY	HEARTBREAKER	MALA 12003	30.00	northern
TIME WILL PASS YOU BY	HEARTBREAKER	MALA 591	100.00	northern

LEGENDS

HIDEOUT	TELL ME BABY (DO YOU NEED LOVE)	MICKAYS 3008	100.00	northern

LEMON TWISTERS

HEY LITTLE BABY		ARLINGTON 8607	30.00	northern

LEMONS, GEORGE

FASCINATING GIRL	SAME: INSTRUMENTAL	GOLD SOUL	1000.00	northern

LEN AND THE PA'S

SOUL BLOCK		RUSH	100.00	funk

LENA AND THE DELTANETTES

TURN AROUND BABY	I'VE GOT THE WHOLE WORLD IN MY HANDS	UPTOWN 721	25.00	northern

LENOIR, PATTIE AND THE HI STANDS

TRY IT YOU'LL LIKE IT	I HAD A LOVE	C.J. 660	50.00	northern
I'M ON THE RUN		C.J. 663	100.00	northern

LENTON, VAN

YOU DON'T CARE	GOTTA GET AWAY	SMASH 2007	10.00	northern

LEON AND THE METRONOMES

I'LL CATCH YOU ON THE REBOUND	BUY THIS RECORD FOR ME	CARNIVAL 515	40.00	northern

LEON AND THE BURNERS

CRACK UP	WHIPLASH	JOSIE 945	20.00	funk

LEONARD, BILLY

TELL ME DO YOU LOVE ME	TEARS OF LOVE	FAIRMOUNT 1007	20.00	northern

LEONARD, CHARLES

A FUNKY DRIVER ON A FUNKY BUS	SAME: Pt.2	LOADSTONE 3948	15.00	funk

LEONARD, JOY

DON'T FEEL SORRY FOR ME	BABY I WANNA BACKTRACK	HERCULES 102	150.00	northern

LEROY AND THE THE DRIVERS

THE SAD CHICKEN	RAINY NIGHT IN GEORGIA	DUO 7458	150.00	funk
L-O-V-E	BLOW WIND	CORAL 62515	50.00	group

LES CHANSONETTES

DON'T LET HIM HURT YOU	DEEPER	SHRINE 114	600.00	northern

LESLIE, DICK

HARLEM TRAIN	LUCKY MAN	G-L 3368	50.00	northern

LESTER, BOBBY

HANG UP YOUR HANG UPS	SWEET GENTLE NIGHTIME	COLUMBIA 45081	20.00	northern

LESTER, KETTY

PLEASE DON'T CRY ANYMORE	ROSES GROW WITH THORNS	RCA 8371	20.00	northern
SOME THINGSARE BETTER LEFT UNSAID	THE HOUSE IS HAUNTED	RCA 8331	40.00	northern
WEST COAST	I'LL BE LOOKING BACK	TOWER 166	15.00	northern

LEVERETT, CHICO

SOLID SENDER	I'LL NEVER LOVE AGAIN	TAMLA 54024.	600.00	motown

LEVINE, HANK

IMAGE	IMAGE PT. 2	VOGUE 112	10.00	mod

LEVON, TAMMY

SHOW ME THE WAY	A SCHOOL GIRL'S DREAM	NATION 2166	10.00	northern

LEWIS SISTERS

HE'S AN ODDBALL	BY SOME CHANCE	V.I.P. 25018	30.00	motown
YOU NEED ME	MOONLIGHT ON THE BEACH	V.I.P. 25024	30.00	motown

LEWIS, ARTIE

FALLING (IN LOVE WITH YOU)	AIN'T NO GOOD	LOMA 2073	20.00	northern

LEWIS, BARBARA

I'M SO THANKFUL	ROCK AND ROLL LULLABY	REPRISE 1146	20.00	70's
YOU MADE ME A WOMAN	JUST THE WAY YOU ARE TODAY	ENTERPRISE 9012	15.00	70's
DON'T FORGET ABOUT ME	IT'S MAGIC	ATLANTIC 2316	8.00	northern
IF YOU LOVE HER	STRAIGHTEN UP YOUR HEART	ATLANTIC 2200	10.00	northern
PUSHIN' A GOOD THING TOO FAR	COME HOME	ATLANTIC 2255	10.00	northern
SOMEDAY WE'RE GONNA LOVE AGAIN	SPEND A LITTLE TIME	ATLANTIC 2227	10.00	**northerB**
ASK THE LONELY	WHY DID IT TAKE SO LONG	ENTERPRISE 9027	15 .00	northern
LOVE MAKES THE WORLD GO ROUND	I'LL MAKE HIM LOVE ME	ATLANTIC 2400	10.00	northern
THANKFUL FOR WHAT I GOT	SHO-NUFF	ATLANTIC 2482	15.00	northern
DON'T FORGET ABOUT ME	IT'S MAGIC	ATLANTIC 2316	15.00	northern
FOOL, FOOL, FOOL	ONLY ALL THE TIME	ATLANTIC 2413	8.00	northern
HELLO STRANGER	THINK A LITTLE SUGAR	ATLANTIC 2184	10.00	northern
I REMEMBER THE FEELING	BABY WHAT DO YOU WANT ME TO DO	ATLANTIC 2361	15.00	northern

LEWIS, DIANE

I THANK YOU KINDLY	PLEASE LET ME HELP YOU	WAND 1183	10.00	northern
MY DARLIN'	PLEASE LET ME HELP YOU	LOVE 101	10.00	northern

LEWIS, GARY AND THE PLAYBOYS

MY HEART'S SYMPHONY	TINA	LIBERTY 55898	8.00	northern

LEWIS, GUS THE GROOVE

LET THE GROOVE MOVE YOU		TOU-SEA 131	30.00	funk

LEWIS, HERMAN

THINK TWICE BEFORE YOU WALK AW	SAME:	MERCURY 73002 DJ	25.00	northern
WHO'S KISSING YOU TONIGHT	THINK BEFORE YOU WALK AWAY	MERCURY 73002	800.00	northern
WHO'S KISSING YOU TONITE	RIGHT DIRECTION	STONE BLUE 101	1000.00	northern

LEWIS, J.G.

DANCE LADY DANCE	THAT'S HER (THAT'S THE GIRL FO	AL & THE KID 105	20.00	70's
WHAT AM I GOING TO DO	SAME:INSTRUMENTAL	IX CHAINS 7018	15.00	70's

LEWIS, JAMES AND THE CASE OF TYME

MANIFESTO	SOME CALL IT LOVE	LEGEND 1014	30.00	**northerB**

LEWIS, JIMMY

IS THAT ANY WAY TO TREAT A LADY	THERE AIN'T NO MAN THAT CAN'T	HOTLANTA 301	10.00	70's
I'M JUST DOING TO YOU WHAT YOU	STRING BEAN	BUDDAH 255	25.00	funk
I QUIT, YOU WIN	I CAN'T GET NO LOVING NOWHERE	TRC 1000	20.00	northern
LET ME KNOW	THE GIRLS FROM TEXAS	MINIT 32017	20.00	northern

LEWIS, JUNIOR

ALL ABOUT LOVE	WHY TAKE IT OUT ON ME	MGM 13728	15.00	northern
FORTY DAYS AND FORTY NIGHTS	THE ONLY GIRL	COLUMBIA 42361	30.00	northern

LEWIS, KENI

AIN'T GONNA MAKE IT EASY	WHAT'S YOUR SIGN	DE-VEL 6753	30.00	70's
WHAT'S HER NAME	DRUG TRAFF'C	BUDDAH 191	100.00	northern

LEWIS, LITTLE GRADY AND THE SOUL SMOKERS

SOUL SMOKIN PT.1	SOUL SMOKIN PT.2	WAND 11231	20.00	funk

LEWIS, LOUISE

WEE OO I'LL LET IT BE YOU BABE	MATCHES	SKYWAY 144	50.00	**northerB**

LEWIS, MARTY

I CAN'T DO WITHOUT YOU	DON'T LEAVE ME BABY	BIG DEAL 135	100.00	northern

LEWIS, MORRIS

ONE HUNDRED PERCENT OF YOUR L	THE ENCHZATRESS	C.J. 686	20.00	70's

LEWIS, PAT

I CAN'T SHAKE IT LOSE	LET'S GO TOGETHER	GOLDEN WORLD 42	15.00	northern
LOOK AT WHAT I ALMOST MISSED	NO BABY, NO	SOLID HIT 101	25.00	northern
WARNING	I'LL WAIT	SOLID HIT 105	30.00	northern
NO ONE TO LOVE	(I OWE) YOU SOMETHING	SOLID HIT 109	850.00	northern

LEWIS, RAY

TOO SWEET TO BE LONELY	SITTIN' AT HOME WITH MY BABY	DAR 101	20.00	70's

LEWIS, RAY

GIVE MY LOVE A TRY	GETTING OVER YOU	FAIRMOUNT 1013	40.00	northern

LEWIS, RAYMOND

SMOOTH OPERATOR	GOOD-BYE MY LOVE	SANSU 470	10.00	ballad

LEWIS, RUSS

BRAND NEW RECIPE	LOVE MADE ME BLUE	SHARP 6040	10.00	northern

LEWIS, RUTH

HURTING EACH OTHER	THAT SPECIAL WAY	RCA 8859	15.00	northern

LEWIS, TAMALA

YOU WON'T SAY NOTHING	IF YOU CAN STAND BY ME	MARTON 1002	800.00	**northerB**

LEWIS, VERMA

YOU DO	SOMEBODY HELP ME	GOLD TOKEN 103	200.00	northern

LIFE

TELL ME WHY	SAME: Stereo version	REPRISE 1185 DJ	40.00	**northerB**

LIGGINS, MICHEAL

LOADED TO THE GILLS	LOADED TO THE GILLS Pt.2	MIGHTY 7001	100.00	funk

LIGHT DRIVERS

DREAMS OF A SHOESHINE BOY	OPERATOR	GEMINI 1021	30.00	northern

LIGHTS OF DARKNESS

JUST GOT TO FIND THE WAY	SO GLAD THAT I MET YOU	BAZAR 1004	40.00	northern

LIL BUCK and THE TOP CATS

MONKEY IN A SACK		LA LOUISIANNE	100.00	funk

LIL' SOUL BROTHERS

I'VE GOT HEARTACHES	WHAT CAN IT BE	D-TOWN 1069	50.00	northern
I'VE GOT HEARTACHES	WHAT CAN IT BE	WHEELSVILLE 111	40.00	northern
I'VE GOT HEARTACHES northern	WHAT CAN IT BE	WEE 3	1000	40.00

LIL WILLIE

TELL ME WHY	A MAN DON'T LAST TOO LONG	GOLDEN 117	50.00	ballad

LIME

LOVE A GO GO	HEY GIRL	CHESS 2045	15.00	northern

LIMELIGHTS

DON'T LEAVE ME BABY	YOU DON'T LOVE ME ANYMORE	UNCLE 1441	800.00	northern

LIMITATIONS

HOLD ON TO IT	ALL BECAUSE OF YOU	VOLT 4057	15.00	northern
I'M LONELY, I'M TROUBLED	MY BABY	BACONE 101	50.00	northern

LINDA and THE VISTAS

BAD APPLE	SHE WENT AWAY	SHRINE 100	150.00	northern

LINDA and THE PRETENDERS

BELIEVE ME	IT'S NOT MY WILL	ASSAULT 1879	600.00	northern

LINDSEY, THELMA				
WHY WEREN'T YOU THERE	PREPARED TO LOVE YOU	MAGIC CITY 005	100.00	**northerB**
LINDSEY, THERESA				
I'LL BET YOU	DADDY-O	GOLDEN WORLD 43	20.00	northern
GOTTA FIND A WAY	WONDERFUL ONE	CORREC-TONE 5840	10.00	northern
IT'S LOVE	GOOD IDEA	CORREC-TONE 1053	150.00	northern
LITTLE ALFRED				
EVEN THOUGH	WALKING DOWN THE AISLE	JEWEL 744	15.00	group
LITTLE ANN				
GOING DOWN A ONE WAY STREET	I'D LIKE TO KNOW YOU BETTER	RIC TIC 142	15.00	motown
LITTLE ANTHONY and THE IMPERIALS (also see ANTHONY & THE IMPERIALS)				
NOTHING FROM NOTHING	RUNNING WITH THE WRONG CROWD	PURE GOLD 101	30.00	70's
SHIMMY, SHIMMY KO-KO POP	I'M STILL IN LOVE WITH YOU	END 1060	10.00	northern
NEVER AGAIN	HURT	DCP 1154	10.00	northern
BETTER USE YOUR HEAD	THE WONDER OF IT ALL	VEEP 1228	10.00	northern
GONNA FIX YOU GOOD	YOU BETTER TAKE IT EASY BABY	VEEP 1233	10.00	northern
NOBODY BUT ME	YOU'RE MY ONE AND ONLY	SHOW ART 102	150.00	northern
BETTER USE YOUR HEAD	THE WONDER OF IT ALL	VEEP 1228 **PS**	25.00	northern
LITTLE BEAVER				
LISTEN TO MY HEARTBEAT	WE THREE	CAT 2006	8.00	70's
LITTLE BEN and THE THE CHEERS				
BEGGAR OF LOVE	ROLL THAT RIGG	LAREDO 2518	20.00	group
BROWN EYED GIRL	BEGGAR OF LOVE	RUSH 601	15.00	group
LITTLE CAESAR and THE THE EMPIRE				
EVEREYBODY DANCE NOW	SAME: INSTRUMENTAL	PARKWAY 152	20.00	northern
LITTLE CHARLES and THE SIDEWINDERS				
YOUR LOVE IS ALL I NEED	TOO MUCH PRIDE	GEMINI STAR 1001	10.00	ballad
PLEASE OPEN UP THE DOOR	SHANTY TOWN	BOTANIC 1001	10.00	northern
GUESS I'LL HAVE TO TAKE WHAT'S	GIVE ME A CHANCE	JEWEL 752	20.00	northern
HELLO HEARTBREAKER	I GOT MY OWN THING GOING	DRUM 1202	20.00	northern
TALKIN' ABOUT YOU, BABE	A TASTE OF THE GOOD LIFE	DECCA 32095	30.00	northern
IT'S A HEARTACHE	DECCA	31980	30.00	northern
TWICE AS MUCH FOR MY BABY	SWEET LORENE	DECCA 32321	15.00	northern
PLEASE OPEN UP THE DOOR	YOU'RE A BLESSING	RED SANDS 701	20.00	northern
LITTLE CURTIS and THE THE BLUES				
PLEASE KEEP ME	SOUL DESIRE	VANCO 219	400.00	northern
LITTLE DOC, SENSATIONAL				
LOOKING FOR MY BABY	SAME:INSTRUMENTAL	MUSIC-GO-ROUND 1	30.00	70's
LITTLE DONDI				
I'VE FORGOT TO GET MYSELF TOGE	LOVE ME DARLING	RAINES 4500	100.00	northern
LITTLE DOOLEY				
(IT'S GOT TO BE) NOW OR NEVER	MEMORIES	NORTH BAY 308	8.00	70's
IT'S GOT TO BE NOW OR NEVER	MEMORIES	RED RUBY 1	10.00	70's
IF EVER NEEDED YOU	YOU BETTER BE READY	KOKO 742	100.00	northern
YOU BETTER BE READY	RUNNIN' WILD	KOKO 742	50.00	northern
SHE'S SO FINE	I LOVE YOU	BAYLOR 101	50.00	northern
LITTLE EDITH				
I COULDN'T TAKE IT	I BELIEVE IN YOU	JESSICA 405	10.00	northerB
LITTLE EVA				
TAKE A STEP IN MY DIRECTION	EVERYTHING IS BEAUTIFUL ABOUT	VERVE 10529	20.00	northern
LITTLE FOXES				
LOVE MADE TO ORDER	SO GLAD YOUR LOVE DON'T CHANGE	OKEH 7312	75.00	northern
LITTLE GIGI				
I VOLUNTEER	SAVE OUR LOVE IN TIME	DECCA 31760	40.00	northern
LITTLE HANK				
TRY TO UNDERSTAND	I GOT THE FEELIN'	SS7 2551	150.00	northern
MISTER BANG BANG MAN	DON'T YOU KNOW	SS7 2566	15.00	northern
LITTLE HAROLD				
BABY BABY JUST A LITTLE MORE SOUL	WHAT'S WRONG WITH ME BABY	DAMON 114	400.00	northern
LITTLE HELEN				
THE RICHEST GIRL (AIN'T GOT NO MONEY)	MORE AND MORE	SOULTOWN 103	15.00	ballad
MORE AND MORE	WHAT ABOUT ME BOY	SOULTOWN 106	15.00	northern
MORE AND MORE	WHAT ABOUT ME BOY	AMOS 141	10.00	northern
LITTLE HERMAN				
I'M GONNA PUT THE HURT ON YOU	GOTTA KEEP ON WALKING	GINA 751	30.00	northern
ONE OUT OF A HUNDRED	IT'S ALL RIGHT PARTNER	ARLEN 749	20.00	northern
I'M GONNA PUT THE HURT ON YOU	GOTTA KEEP ON WALKING	ARLEN 751	20.00	northern
LITTLE HOOKS				
GIVE THE DRUMMER SOME MORE	I DON'T WANT TO LEAVE YOU	UA 50932	25.00	funk
LITTLE IVA and HER Band				
WHEN I NEEDED YOU	CONTINENTAL STRUT	MIRACLE 2	1000.00	motown
LITTLE JEANETTE				
CRAZY CRAZY	PLEASE COME BACK AGAIN	GREEN LIGHTS 40	100.00	northern
LITTLE JOE and THE LATINAIRES				
BRING IT UP	LOVE IS A HURTIN' THING	TOMI 122 DJ	30.00	mod
AIN'T NO BIG THING	IN CROWD	TOMI 113	60.00	northern

LITTLE JOHN

MY LOVE IS GONE	LOOKING FOR MY PICTURE	NEAL 1236	200.00	ballad
HEART BREAKIN' TIME	DO THE DIP	MARTAY 4508	50.00	northern
JUST WAIT AND SEE	ASK ME	GOGATE 2	1300.00	northern

LITTLE KENNETH and THE RHYTHMAKERS

YOU CAN GO ON HOME	WHAT MORE CAN I SAY	CARL. 506	300.00	northern

LITTLE LISA

PUPPET ON A STRING	HANG ON BILL	V.I.P. 25023	20.00	motown

LITTLE MILTON

LET ME BACK IN	LET YOUR LOSS BE YOUR LESSON	STAX 229	8.00	70's
YOU OUGHT TO BE HERE WITH ME	DON'T LEAVE HER	GOLDEN EAR 2285	8.00	70's
GRITS AIN'T GROCERIES	I CAN'T QUIT YOU BABY	CHECKER 1212	10.00	northern
WHO'S CHEATING WHO	AIN'T NO BIG DEAL ON YOU	CHECKER 1113	8.00	northern
I KNOW WHAT I WANT	YOU MEAN EVERYTHING TO ME	CHECKER 1194	10.00	northern
SO BLUE (WITHOUT YOU)	POOR MAN	CHECKER 1221	10.00	northern
SOMETIMEY	WE GOT THE WINNING HAND	CHECKER 1132	10.00	northern
YOU COLORED MY BLUES BRIGHT	FEEL SO BAD	CHECKER 1162	10.00	northern

LITTLE NATALIE and HENRY

TEARDROPS ARE FALLING	THE UNCLE WILLIE	ROULETTE 4540	15.00	northern

LITTLE OTIS

I OUT-DUKED THE DUKE	BABY I NEED YOU	TAMLA 54058	40.00	motown

LITTLE RICHARD

NEVER GONNA LET YOU GO	DON'T DECIEVE ME	OKEH 7278	8.00	ballad
I NEED LOVE	THE COMMANDMENTS OF LOVE	OKEH 7262	8.00	northern
POOR DOG (WHO CAN'T WAG HIS OWN TAIL)	WELL	OKEH 7251	10.00	**northerB**
A LITTLE BIT OF SOMETHING	MONEY	OKEH 7286	15.00	**northerB**
I DON'T WANT TO DISCUSS IT	HURRY SUNDOWN	OKEH 7271	15.00	**northerB**

LITTLE RICHARD III

SHE BROKE DOWN	THE GIG	DPG 101	20.00	funk

LITTLE RITCHIE

JUST ANOTHER HEARTACHE	I WISH I WAS A BABY	SS7 2554	400.00	northern
JUST ANOTHER HEARTBREAK	I WISH I WAS A BABY	SS7 2554	500.00	northern
ONE BO-DILLION YEARS	I CATCH MYSELF CRYING	SS7 2567 DJ	60.00	northern

LITTLE ROYAL

RAZOR BLADE	JEALOUS	TRIUS 912	10.00	funk
YOU KNOW (YOU MADE ME LOVE YOU)	I CAN TELL	CARNIVAL 531	20.00	northern

LITTLE RUBEN

IN THE NAME OF LONELINESS	SAME: INSTRUMENTAL	NOW RECORDS 602	200.00	70's

LITTLE RUDY D.

WHEN I FALL IN LOVE	KISSING	APOLLO 11 5008	20.00	ballad

LITTLE SAMSON

DON'T TAKE YOUR LOVE	HEALTH CONSCIOUS	EL D 1001	300.00	northern

LITTLE SHERMAN

THE PRICE OF LOVE	Pt 2	ABC 11233	10.00	northern
THE PRICE OF LOVE	THE PRICE OF LOVE Pt.2	SAGPORT 105	20.00	northern

LITTLE SISTERS

JUST A BOY	FIRST YOU BREAK MY HEART	DETROIT SOUND 229	75.00	northern

LITTLE SONNY

LET'S HAVE A GOOD TIME	ORANGE PINEAPPLE CHERRY BLOSSO	WHEELSVILLE 103	10.00	ballad
WADE IN THE WATER	THEY WANT MONEY	ENTERPRISE 9021	15.00	mod
WE GOT A GROOVE	SONNY'S BAG	REVILOT 227	10.00	mod

LITTLE SOUL

PROBLEMS	LONELY STRANGER	SOLID SOUL 39	200.00	northern

LITTLE STANLEY

OUT OF SIGHT LOVING	WANTED	VANCE 111	750.00	northern
THE STRAN	WANTED	VANCE 126	500.00	northern

LITTLE TOMMY

BABY CAN'T YOU SEE	I'M STILL HURT	SOUND OF SOUL 104	600.00	northern
I'M HURT	LOV'H	SOUND OF SOUL 100	20.00	northern

LITTLE TOMMY and THE ELGINS

I WALK ON	NEVER LOVE AGAIN	ABC 10358	100.00	northern

LITTLE TONY and THE HAWKS

THE TEARS	SWEET LITTLE GIRL	RENFRO 314	30.00	ballad
CRY CRY CRY	DO WHAT YOU DID	ORIGINAL SOUND 63	15.00	northern
DON'T TRY TO FIGHT IT	MY LITTLE GIRL	RENFRO 817	15.00	northern

LITTLE WOODEN SOUL-DIERS

LITTLE WOODEN SOLDIER	I CAN SEE	PAM-O 102	40.00	northern

LITTLE, LITTLE ROSE

YOU'VE GOT THE LOVE	INTO SOMETHING FINE	ROULETTE 4747	20.00	northern
GET A HOLD OF YOURSELF	LIE TO ME	BLUE ROCK 4003	40.00	northern

LITTLES, HATTIE

BACK IN MY LOVING ARMS	IT'S LOVE	GORDY 7004 NI	300.00	motown
HERE YOU COME	YOUR LOVE IS WONDERFUL	GORDY 7007	40.00	motown

LIVIN' PROOF

YOU AND I	YOU AND I PT. 2	JU-PAR 532	8.00	group

LIVING COLOR

THANK THE LORD FOR LOVE	GOTTA STRANGE FEELING	MADHATTER 4391	50.00	northern

117

LIVING SOULS				
DROP IT ON ME	SOUL SEARCHIN'	REVUE 11013 DJ	30.00	mod
LIVINGSTON, PAT				
YOU BET I WOULD (IF I COULD)	SAME: INSTRUMENTAL	MONEY 606	30.00	northern
TAKE ME NOW OR LEAVE ME FOR EVER		WILSTONE 1069	100.00	northern
I'VE GOT MY BABY	PLAYIN' WITH FIRE	DIMENSION 1044	25.00	northern
LIZZMORE, MICHEAL				
PROMISE THAT YOU'LL WAIT	TRY A LITTLE TENDERNESS	CAPITOL 3480	50.00	70's
LLOYD, BETTY				
I'M CATCHING ON	YOU SAY THINGS YOU DON'T MEAN	BSC 401	150.00	northern
LLOYD, LINDA				
BREAKAWAY	LITTLE THINGS LIKE THAT	COLUMBIA 43486	100.00	northern
LOADING ZONE				
DANGER HEARTBREAK DEAD AHEAD	DON'T LOSE CONTROL	RCA 9538	10.00	northern
LOCATIONS				
MISTER DIAMOND MAN	HE'S GONE	RON PAUL 101	1000.00	northern
LOCK, MARK				
AIN'T THAT ENOUGH TO MAKE A MAN CRY	OUR LOVE WILL GROW	POST 1	40.00	northern
LOCK STOCK and BARREL				
WHERE CAN SHE BE	LOVE AND SUNSHINE	BULLET RECORDS	100.00	northern
1001				
LOE and JOE				
LITTLE OLE BOY - LITTLE OLE GI	THAT'S HOW I AM WITHOUT YOU	HARVEY 112	15.00	motown
LO-KALS				
YOU LIED	SOMEWHERE YOU'VE GOT A FRIEND	DROCER 1003	50.00	northern
LOLITA and THE EXOTICS				
PUT A LOTTA LOVIN TO IT	TOO, TOO GOOD TO BE TRUE	LIBRA. 102	20.00	northern
LOLLIPOPS				
CHEATING, IS TELLING ON YOU	SAME:	V.I.P. 25051 DJ	20.00	motown
NEED YOUR LOVE	CHEATIN IS TELLING ON YOU	V.I.P. 25051	100.00	motown
LOVE IS THE ONLY ANSWER	DON'T MONKEY WITH ME	RCA 8390	20.00	northern
BUSY SIGNAL	I WANT YOU BACK AGAIN	RCA 8494	20.00	northern
LOVING GOOD FEELING	STEP ASIDE BABY	IMPACT 1021	75.00	northern
LOMAX, ERIC				
SEVEN THE LOSER	LIVE FAST DIE YOUNG	COLUMBIA 44918	30.00	northern
LONAS, KENNY				
WOULD YOU BELIEVE	LOVE YOU	COLUMBIA 43888	20.00	northern
LONDON, PAUL and THE THE KAPERS				
SUGAR BABY	NEVER LIKE THIS	CHECK MATE 1006	50.00	motown
LONETTE				
BLUE JEANS		M-S 211	500.00	northern
VEIL OF MYSTERY	STOP!	M-S 208	15.00	northern
LONG, BARBARA				
WE CALL IT LOVE	TAKE IT FROM ME	JET SET	150.00	northern
LONG, BOBBY and THE DEALERS				
I GOTTA HAVE LOVE TOO	HEARTBREAK AVENUE	OLD TOWN 2003	50.00	northern
LONG, EDDIE				
IT DON'T MAKE SENSE BUT IT SUR	DID YOU EVER DREAM LUCKY	SKYE 4522	30.00	funk
LONG, EMMITT				
CALL ME	YOU'RE PUZZLING ME	DONOYIA 101	300.00	70's
LONG, LYNN				
DON'T LET ME DOWN	DO I BABY	MERCURY 72454	20.00	northern
LONG, MAURICE				
I DON'T LOVE YOU ANYMORE	A LOVER'S QUESTION	CYCLONE 75000	15.00	70's
A CHANGE IS GONNA COME	NO MAN IS AN ISLAND	CYCLONE 75008	10.00	northern
LONG, NORWOOD				
I'D LIKE TO HAVE YOU	SHE BELONGS TO ME	GROOVEY GROOVES 166	200.00	northern
LONG, SHORTY				
CHANTILLY LACE	YOUR LOVE IS AMAZING	SOUL 35031	15.00	motown
DEVIL WITH THE BLUE DRESS	WIND IT UP	SOUL. 35001	10.00	motown
FUNCTION AT THE JUNCTION	CALL ON ME	SOUL 35021	15.00	motown
I'LL BE HERE	TOO SMART	TRI-PHI 1015	15.00	motown
I'LL BE THERE	BAD WILLIE	TRI-PHI 1006	20.00	motown
IT'S A CRYING SHAME	OUT TO GET YOU	SOUL 35005	20.00	motown
NIGHT FO' LAST	(SAME: IINSTRUMENTAL	SOUL 35040	10.00	motown
WHAT'S THE MATTER	GOING MY WAY	TRI-PHI 1021	20.00	motown
LORD LUTHER				
MY MISTAKE	HOUSE OF THE RISING SUN	SCHIRECK 101	200.00	northern
LORDS				
SINCE I FELL FOR YOU	ONLY A MAN	MIKIM 1501	20.00	group
LORELEI				
S.T.O.P. (STOP)	I'LL NEVER LET YOU DOWN	COLUMBIA 45629	8.00	northern
LOREN, DONNA				
NINETY DAY GUARENTEE	TEN GOOD REASONS	CAPITOL 5337	20.00	northern
LORI and LANCE				
I DON'T HAVE TO WORRY	ALL I WANT IS YOU	FEDERAL 12548	100.00	northern

LORNETTES
HIS WAY WITH THE GIRLS	DOWN THE BLOCK AND UP TO HEAVE	GALLIO 110	20.00	northern
I DON'T DENY IT GIRL	STANDING THERE ALL ALONE	GALLIO 105	10.00	northern

LORRAINE and THE DELIGHTS
BABY I NEED YOU	I JUST COULDN'T SAY	BARRY 1002	100.00	**northerB**

LORRI, MARY ANN
I WANNA THANK YOU INTERNATIONAL	ONE MORE TEAR	UNITED	50.00	northern

LOS CANARIOS
GET ON YOUR KNEES	3-2-1-AH	CALLA 156	15.00	northern

LOS STARDUSTERS
ALL NIGHT WORKER	FOREVER	TEAR DROP 3106	20.00	mod

LOST FAMILY
BLOW MY MIND	PRETTY FACE	INT. MUSIC BAG 1101	8.00	70's

LOST GENERATION
YOU ONLY GET OUT OF LOVE	PRETTY LITTLE ANGEL EYES	BRUNSWICK 55492	15.00	70's
YOUR MISSION (IF U DECIDE TO ACCEPT IT)	PT.2	INNOVATION 8002	15.00	70's
YOU'RE SO YOUNG BUT YOU'RE SO TRUE	THE SLY, SLICK AND THE WICKED	BRUNSWICK 55436	15.00	northern

LOST SOUL
A SECRET OF MINE	MINDS EXPRESSWAY	RAVEN 211	350.00	northern
I'M GONNA HURT YOU	FOR YOU	RAVEN 2032	250.00	northern

LOST SOULS
IT WON'T WORK OUT BABY	GIVE ME YOUR LOVE	GLASCO 101	20.00	northern

LOU, BETTI and THE ADAMS, BOBBY
DR. TRUELOVE	WHY DID I DECIDE TO GET MARRIE	TRA-X 16	350.00	northern

LOVE and BROTHERHOOD
SUGAR PIE HONEY	YOU'RE WHAT'S BEEN MISSING	CHESS 2121	8.00	northern

LOVE AFFAIR
TO MAKE YOU LOVE ME	I CAN'T STOP LOVING YOU	UA 396	50.00	70's

LOVE KITTENS
I LIKE EVERYTHING ABOUT YOU	KEEP IT UP	MOS-LEY 5202	15.00	northern

LOVE MACHINE
TELL ME	DUNLOP SONG	EFFORT 1001	100.00	70's

LOVE POTION
THIS LOVE	MOBY BINKS	KAPP 979	30.00	northern

LOVE, C.P.
NEVER BEEN IN LOVE BEFORE	I FOUND ALL THESE THINGS	CHIMNEYVILLE 438	15.00	70's

LOVE, CANDACE
NEVER IN A MILLION YEARS	I WANT TO GET BACK	AQUARIUS 4012	15.00	northern
WONDERFUL NIGHT	UH UH BOY THAT'S A NO NO	AQUARIUS 4010	15.00	northern
PEACE LOVIN' MAN	SOMETHING GONNA HAPPEN	AQUARIUS 4050	15.00	northern

LOVE, CYNDY
YOU NEVER KNEW	GAMES GUYS PLAY	SPACE 14	20.00	northern

LOVE, DARLENE
LORD, IF YOU'RE A WOMAN	JOHNNY BABY	WARNER SPECTOR 10	10.00	northern
TOO LATE TO SAY YOU'RE SORRY	IF	REPRISE 534	150.00	northern

LOVE, DAVE
BABY HARD TIMES	YOU PAINTED ME BLUE	WORLDS 101	10.00	northern
COLALINED BABY	SAME: INSTRUMENTAL	SOLID SOUL 722	20.00	**northerB**

LOVE, DEVOTION and HAPPINESS
JOY SWEET JOY	YESTERDAYS FOOL	P.E.U. JADAN 101	50.00	70's

LOVE, FREDDIE
CRAZY GIRL		ANLA NO.#	50.00	funk
EVERYBODY'S DOING IT	SEA OF LOVE	ANLA 123	20.00	funk

LOVE, J.B.
NO ONE ELSE BUT YOU	I AM A HEART	CONGRESS 239	50.00	northern
THEN ONLY THEN	I WOULDN'T HAVE IT ANY OTHER W	KAPP 603 DJ	100.00	northern

LOVE, JIMMY
TWO SIDES TO EVERY STORY		JOSIE 944	40.00	northern

LOVE, JOHNNY
CHILLS AND FEVER	NO USE PLEDGING MY LOVE	STARTIME 5001	100.00	northern

LOVE, KATIE and THE FOUR SHADES
IT HURT SO GOOD	DON'T LET IT GO TO YOUR HEAD	SCEPTER 12304	20.00	70's
IT HURTS SO GOOD	DON'T LET IT GO TO YOUR HEAD	MUSCLE SHOALS SOUND 100	30.00	70's

LOVE, MARIAN
CAN'T FORGET ABOUT YOU, BABY	TRY A LITTLE TENDERNESS	CAPITOL 2642	60.00	northern
WALK PROUD AND PRETTY	ANOTHER RAINY DAY	CAPITOL 2177	15.00	northern

LOVE, MARTHA JEAN
NICE GUY	TALKIN' 'BOUT MY MAN	ABC 10689	20.00	northern

LOVE, MARY
LAY THIS BURDEN DOWN	THINK IT OVER BABY	MODERN 1029	15.00	northern
YOU TURNED MY BITTER INTO SWEET	I'M IN YOUR HANDS	MODERN 1006	10.00	northern
THE HURT IS JUST BEGINNING	IF YOU CHANGE YOUR MIND	JOSIE 999	10.00	northern
THE HURT IS JUST BEGINNING	IF YOU CHANGE YOUR MIND	HILL 430	20.00	northern
LET ME KNOW	MOVE A LITTLE CLOSER	MODERN 1020	10.00	northern

LOVE, PEACE and HAPPINESS

STRIP ME NAKED	UNBORN CHILD	RCA 584	15.00	70's

LOVE, PRESTON

CISSY POPCORN		HUDSON 2011	100.00	funk

LOVE, RONNIE

NOTHING TO IT	LET'S MAKE LOVE	ALMERIA 4001	15.00	70's
CHILLS AND FEVER	NO USE PLEDGING MY LOVE	DOT 16144	30.00	northern

LOVE, WILSON

FUNNY MONEY	SAME: INSTRUMENTAL	NAT.SOUL 35001	250.00	70's

LOVEABLES

JUST BEYOND MY FINGERTIPS	ANYMAN	TOOT 604	10.00	northern
YOU CAN'T DRESS UP A BROKEN HEART	WE GOT A NEED FOR EACH OTHER	TOOT 600	20.00	northern

LOVEHORN

IF	PART 2	ZODIAC 10312	30.00	ballad

LOVEJOY, JOY

IN ORBIT	UH HUM	CHECKER 1188	15.00	northern

LOVELETTES

I CAN'T FORGET ABOUT YOU	DON'T FORGET POOR ME	CAP CITY 117	10.00	northern

LOVELITES (also see PATTI and THE LOVELITES)

OH MY LOVE	WHO YOU GONNA HURT NOW	UNI 55222	15.00	70's
MY CONSCIENCE	MAN IN MY LIFE	LOVELITE 1	15.00	northern
THIS LOVE IS REAL	OH MY LOVE	UNI 55242	15.00	northern
(WHEN) I GET SCARED	MALADY	PHI-DAN 5008	30.00	northern
GET IT OFF MY CONSCIENCE	OH WHAT A DAY	LOVELITE 1500	20.00	northern
I FOUND ME A LOVER	YOU BETTER STOP IT	BANDERA 2515	15.00	northern

LOVELLS

HERE COME THE HEARTACHES	MY TIME TO CRY	BRENT 7073	20.00	northern

LOVELY, IKE

FOOL'S HALL OF FAME	LITTLE MISS SWEET THING	WAND 11266	15.00	70's

LOVEMAKER, JIMMY

FOXY DEVIL	SOUL	DECCA 31720	25.00	northern

LOVEMAKERS

WHEN YOU'RE NEXT TO ME	MY GIRL IS REALLY DYNAMITE	ISLAND 39	15.00	70's

LOVEMASTERS

PUSHIN' AND PULLIN'	LOVE TRAIN	JACKLYN 1009	10.00	northern

LOVENOTES

BABY, BABY, YOU	BEG ME	CAMEO 409	75.00	northern

LOVERS

DO THIS FOR ME	SOMEONE	PHILIPS 40353	10.00	northern
IN MY TENEMENT	CARAVAN OF LONELY MEN	AGON 1001	15.00	northern
WITHOUT A DOUBT	ONE AY TO LOVE	FRANTIC 2133	600.00	northern

LOVETTES

I NEED A GUY	I'M AFRAID (TO SAY I LOVE YOU)	CARNIVAL 530	50.00	northern
LITTLE MISS SOUL	LONELY GIRL	CARNIVAL 518	40.00	**northerB**

LOWE, FREDDE

I'M SLOWLY LOSING MY MIND	I'M SLOWLY LOSING MY MIND	POLYDOR 14150	20.00	ballad
WE AIN'T AS TIGHT AS WE USED TO BE	I'VE GOT TO FIND SOMEONE TO LO	POLYDOR 14145	20.00	ballad
DECISIONS		SIROCCO 1000	200.00	70's

LOWE, JANICE

(IS IT ALL) IN VAIN	BE MINE	DALLAS GROOVE 200	20.00	70's

LOWE, ROBERT

BACK TO FUNK		EASTBOUND 624	30.00	funk

LOWERY, FRED and THE ARROWS

WORK WITH ME ANNIE	DADDY'S BABY	GAY SHELL 7868	20.00	northern

LOWMAN, PHIL

ROCK ME TIL 'I WANT NO MORE	LONG DUSTY ROAD	PALOS 312	40.00	**northerB**

LOWNLY CROWD

SHADOWS AND REFLECTIONS	SAME: INSTRUMENTAL	MGM 13740	15.00	northern

LUCAS, BILL

CAUSE I KNOW YOUR MINE	I DON'T WANNA EVER LOVE AGAIN	DIONN 502	50.00	**northerB**

LUCAS, CHARLIE and THE THRILLERS

WONDERFUL FEELING	SOUL FOR SALE	WATERBIRD 1	100.00	funk

LUCAS, ERNIE

WHAT WOULD I DO WITHOUT YOU	LOVE THIEF	OKEH 7315	15.00	northern

LUCAS, GLORIA

YOU WON'T BE TRUE		FLODAVIEUR 807	100.00	northern

LUCAS, MATT

BABY YOU BETTER GO-GO	MY TUNE	KAREN 2524	1000.00	northern

LUCIEN, JOHN

WHAT A DIFFERENCE LOVE MAKES	L.A. (LOS ANGELES)	COLUMBIA 44077	50.00	northern

LUCIFER

IT TAKES SOUL	AFTER YOU	NICO 105	30.00	northern

LUDAWAY, RUDY

WHAT'S WRONG BABY		GALICO 102	75.00	northern
WHAT'S WRONG BABY		UA 50590	50.00	northern

LUCKY CHARMS
TIED TO YOUR HEART	LOVE IS A MEMORY	SUGARHILL 102	400.00	northern

LUMLEY, RUFUS
I'M STANDING	LET'S HIDE AWAY	HOLTON 5001	30.00	**northerB**

LUMPKIN, HENRY
I'VE GOT A NOTION	WE REALLY LOVE EACH OTHER	MOTOWN 1005	60.00	motown
MO JO HANNA	BREAK DOWN AND SING	MOTOWN 1029	30.00	motown
WHAT IS A MAN (WITHOUT A WOMAN)	DON'T LEAVE ME	MOTOWN 1013	40.00	motown
I'M A WALKING	MAKE A CHANGE	PAGEANT 605	40.00	northern
SOUL IS TAKING OVER	IF I COULD MAKE MAGIC	BUDDAH 22	15.00	northern
HONEY HUSH		BUDDAH	8.00	northern

LUNAR FUNK
MR. PENGUIN	MR. PENGUIN PT.2	BELL 45172	10.00	funk
SLIP THE DRUMMER ONE	SPACE MONSTER	BELL 45214	30.00	funk

LUNDI, PAT
PARTY MUSIC	SAME: INSTRUMENTAL	VIGOR 1723	8.00	70's

LUNDY, BRAD
BREAKING POINT	I LOVE YOU	LUNDY 6222	30.00	**northerB**

LUNDY, PAT
ANY DAY NOW	NOTHING BUT TEARS	COLUMBIA 44155	15.00	northern
SOUL AIN'T NOTHING BUT THE BLUES	ANOTHER RAINY DAY	COLUMBIA 44312	15.00	northern
THE THRILL IS GONE	CITY OF STONE	COLUMBIA 44773	20.00	northern

LUPPER, KENNY
PASSION FLOWER	SAME:	TAMLA 54294 DJ	15.00	70's

LUSCIOUS THREE
TAKE ME AS I AM	SAY WHAT YOU MEAN	TSUGA RAYS 300	10.00	70's

LUTHER
DON'T WANNA BE A FOOL	THIS CLOSE TO YOU	COTILLION 44216	50.00	70's

LUV BUGS
MAMA'S GONNA WHIP YOU	SOUL IN THE GHETTO	WAND 11234	20.00	northern

LYLE, JAY
HOW GOOD CAN IT GET	HEARTACHES BY THE NUMBER	ANGEL CITY 1	30.00	northern

LYNCH, FRANK
YOUNG GIRL	PEOPLE WILL MAKE YOU SAY THING	MY RECORD 2101	50.00	northern

LYNDELL, LINDA
I DON'T KNOW	WHAT A MAN	VOLT 4001	20.00	funk
BRING YOUR LOVE BACK TO ME	HERE AM I	VOLT 161	20.00	**northerB**

LYNDON, FRANK
DON'T GO AWAY BABY	LISA	UPTOWN 758	25.00	**northerB**

LYNN, BARBARA
I'M STILL THE SAME	SAME: INSTRUMENTAL	JAM STONE 104	8.00	70's
MOVIN' ON A GROOVE	DISCO MUSIC	JETSTREAM 829	100.00	70's
TRYING TO LOVE TWO	SUGAR COATED LOVE	ICHIBAN 142	40.00	70's
YOU MAKE ME SO HOT	IT AIN'T GOOD TO BE TOO GOOD	ATLANTIC 2931	10.00	70's
OH! BABY (WE GOT A GOD THING GOING)	UNFAIR	JAMIE 1277	8.00	northern
THIS IS THE THANKS I GET	RING TELEPHONE RING	ATLANTIC 2450	15.00	northern
CLUB A GO GO	WATCH THE ONE	TRIBE 8322	10.00	northern
I'M A GOOD WOMAN	RUNNING BACK	TRIBE 8316	30.00	northern
NICE AND EASY	YOU BETTER QUIT IT	JETSTREAM 811	10.00	northern
NICE AND EASY	I'M A ONE MAN WOMAN	ATLANTIC 2853	8.00	northern
TAKE YOUR LOVE AND RUN	(UNTIL THEN) I'LL SUFFER	JETSTREAM 804	15.00	**northerB**
TAKE YOUR LOVE AND RUN	(UNTIL THEN) I'LL SUFFER	ATLANTIC 2812	10.00	northern
YOU LEFT THE WATER RUNNING	UNTIL I'M FREE	TRIBE 8319 DJ	25.00	northern
YOU'LL LOSE A GOOD THING	LONELY HEARTACHES	JAMIE 1220	8.00	northern
YOU'RE LOSING ME	WHY CAN'T YOU LOVE ME	ATLANTIC 2513	20.00	northern
I DON'T WANT A PLAYBOY	NEW KIND OF LOVE	TRIBE 8324	50.00	northern

LYNN, BOBBI
JUMP BACK IN THE ARMS OF LOVE	SO IN LOVE WITH YOU	LOOK 5033	20.00	**northerB**

LYNN, CINDY
MEET ME AT MIDNIGHT	SIR GALLAHAD	IN SOUND 402	75.00	northern

LYNN, DELORES
THE BIG SEARCH IS ON	JUST TELL IT LIKE IT IS	JUNIOR 1008	15.00	northern

LYNN, DONNA
DON'T YOU DARE	IT'S RAINING	PALMER 5016	20.00	northern

LYNN, MICKI
I'VE GOT THE BLUES	SOME OF THIS AND SOME OF THAT	CAPITOL 5495	20.00	northern

LYNN, SANDRA
PROVE IT	I CAN'T ESCAPE	LEMAY 1002	15.00	northern
WHERE WOULD I BE	SOMETIME	CONSTELLATION 140	30.00	northern

LYNN, TAMI
I'M GONNA RUN AWAY FROM YOU	ONE NIGHT OF SIN	COTILLION 44123	8.00	northern
I'M GONNA RUN AWAY FROM YOU	THE BOY NEXT DOOR	ATCO 6342	10.00	northern

LYNN, VARNADO
WASH AND WEAR LOVE	TELL ME WHAT'S WRONG	GATOR 1202	600.00	**northerB**
SECOND HAND LOVE	GOODBYE AND GOOD SPEED	YUMIE 1000	300.00	**northerB**

LYNNE, GLORIA
SOMETIMES IT BE'S THAT WAY	SPEAKING OF HAPPINESS	FONTANA 1538	15.00	mod

YOU DON'T HAVE TO BE A TOWER OF STRENGTH	I WILL FOLLOW YOU	EVEREST 19428	30.00	northern

LYONS, MARIE "QUEENIE"

SEE AND DON'T SEE	DADDY'S HOUSE	DELUXE 123	25.00	funk
I'LL DROWN I MY OWN TEARS		DELUXE 101	15.00	northern

LYRICS

KEEP CLOSER TO YOUR HEART	YOU'LL ALWAYS BELONG TO ME	J.W.J. 22925	50.00	northern
SO GLAD	MY SON	GNP CRESCENDO	75.00	northern

LYYLE, JOHNNY

THE SNAPPER	SCREAMIN' LOUD	TUBA 2007	20.00	mod

M

M.V.P.'S

TURNIN' MY HEARTBEAT UP	SAME:	BUDDAH 262 DJ	100.00	northern
TURNIN' MY HEARTBEAT UP	EVERY MAN FOR HERSELF	BUDDAH 262	200.00	northern

M-3'S

FUNNY CAFE	SO GIVE ME LOVE	ABC 10772	20.00	northern

MABRY, BETTY

IT'S MY LIFE	LIVE, LOVE, LEARN	COLUMBIA 44469	25.00	northern

MAC AND BARB

HOLD ME TIGHTER	WHAT'S YOUR BUSINESS ROUND HERE	PYRAMID 63928	75.00	northern

MAC, BOBBY

KEEP ON	WALKIN' TOGETHER	ORIGINAL SOUND 68	10.00	northern
KEEP ON	WALKIN' TOGETHER	MOONGLOW 5019	15.00	northern
SHY GUY	HOW WAS YOUR WEEKEND	VENDED 104	500.00	**northerB**

MACEO and THE ALL THE KINGSMEN

FUNKY WOMEN	SOUTHWICK	HOUSE OF THE FOX 10	15.00	funk
GOT TO GET'CHA	(I REMEMBER) MR. BANKS	HOUSE OF THE FOX 1	10.00	funk
THANK YOU FOR LETTING ME BE MY	SAME Pt .2	HOUSE OF THE FOX 8	10.00	funk

MACEO and THE MACKS

CROSS THE TRACK (WE BETTER GO BACK)	THE SOUL OF A BLACK MAN	PEOPLE 647	20.00	funk

MACK, ANDY

LATER THAN YOU THINK	DO YOU WANTA GO	CHESS 1910	40.00	northern

MACK, BILLY

I CAN'T SLEEP	SON OF A LOVER	MISS BETTY 34	25.00	ballad

MACK, JIMMY

BE GOOD TO THE ONE	LOVE JUNKIE	PAWN 3808	10.00	ballad
MY WORLD IS ON FIRE	GO ON	PALMER 5019	500.00	northern
WOMAN IS HARD TO UNDERSTAND	HARD TO UNDERSTAND	HAMSTER 4541	40.00	northern

MACK, ONE'SY

I'LL NEVER GO AWAY	I DID IT ALL FOR THE RIGHT REA	GODA 101	25.00	northern
NEVER LISTEN TO YOUR HEART	A PART OF A FOOL	GHETTO 17	25.00	northern

MACK, OSCAR

I'M GLAD IT'S OVER	PUT OUT THE FIRE (AND LET ME GO)	AMY 11007	30.00	ballad
YOU NEVER KNOW HOW MUCH I LOVE	DREAM GIRL	STAX 152	20.00	northern

MACKEY, LINDA

YOURS FOR THE ASKING	GOTTA FIND MY MAN	VJ INTERNATIONAL	75.00	northern c

721 PSMAD DOG and THE PUPS

WHY DID YOU LEAVE ME GIRL	SAME: INSTRUMENTAL	MAGIC CITY 12	20.00	northern

MAD LADS

DID MY BABY CALL	LET ME REPAIR YOUR HEART	VOLT 4080	15.00	70's
TRYING TO FOGET ABOUT YOU	YOU BLEW IT	EXPRESS 3985	10.00	70's

MADE IN JAPAN Band

WHAT IT IS		CENCO	75.00	funk

MADISON, ROSALIND

NEIGHBORHOOD GIRL	NO OTHER LOVE	LIBERTY 55795	100.00	northern

MADISONS

BECAUSE I GOT YOU	BAD BABOON	LIMELIGHT 3018	30.00	northern

MAESTRO, JOHNNY

HEARTBURN	TRY ME	PARKWAY 987	10.00	northern
I'M STEPPING OUT OF THE PICTUR	AFRAID OF LOVE	SCEPTER 12112	500.00	northern

MAGIC BAND

FALBALA	TICO TICO	GNP CRESCENDO 492	10.00	northern

MAGIC DISCO MACHINE

SCRATCHIN'	CONTROL TOWER	MOTOWN 1362	15.00	funk

MAGIC NIGHT
IF YOU AND I HAD NEVER MET	LOST AND LONELY BOY	ROULETTE 7153	15.00	northern

MAGIC SAM
SAM'S FUNCK	I'LL PAY YOU BACK	BRIGHT STAR 1037	15.00	funk

MAGIC TONES
IT'S BETTER TO LOVE	TOGETHER WE SHALL OVERCOME	MAHS 1037	15.00	northern
LOOK AWAY	GREAT DAY	RAM-BROCK 2001	15.00	northern

MAGICIANS
WHY DO I DO THESE FOOLISH THINGS	IS IT ALL GONE	VILLA. 704	75.00	group
WHY MUST YOU CRY (I DEEPLY LOVE YOU)	KEEP YOUR HANDS OF MY BABY	VILLA. 706	30.00	group

MAGICTONES
GOT TO GET A LITTLE CLOSER	ME AND MY BABY	WHEELSVILLE 106	45.00	northern
HAPPY DAYS	TRYING REAL HARD (TO MAKE THE	WESTBOUND 145	15.00	northern
HOW CAN I FORGET YOU	ME AND MY BABY	WHEELSVILLE 114	200.00	northern

MAGNETIC FORCE
IS IT WRONG	THROUGH THE PAIN	PICKIN POST 978	30.00	70's

MAGNETICS
I HAVE A GIRL	LOVE AND DEVOTION	RA-SEL 7104	1300.00	**northerB**
LADY IN GREEN	HEART YOU'RE MADE OF STONE	BONNIE 107374	1300.00	**northerB**
WHEN I'M WITH MY BABY	COUNT THE DAYS	SABLE 102	1200.00	**northerB**

MAGNIFICENT 7
NEVER WILL I MAKE MY BABY CRY	OOH, BABY BABY	DIAL 4074	30.00	northern
SHE'S CALLED A WOMAN	SINCE YOU'VE BEEN GONE SO LONG	EASTERN 611	100.00	northern

MAGNIFICENT MEN
ALL YOUR LOVIN'S GONE TO MY HEAD	PEACE OF MIND	CAPITOL 5608	15.00	northern
FOREVER TOGETHER	BABE, I'M CRAZY ABOUT YOU	CAPITOL 2062	20.00	northern
I FOUND WHAT I WANTED IN YOU	ALMOST PERSUADED	CAPITOL 2202	10.00	northern
MUCH MUCH MORE OF YOUR LOVE	STORMY WEATHER	CAPITOL 5812	10.00	northern
TIRED OF PUSHING	BY THE TIME I GET TO PHEONIX	CAPITOL 2134	10.00	northern

MAGNIFICENTS
MY HEART IS CALLING	WHERE DO I GO FROM HERE	DEE GEE 3008	60.00	northern
WHERE DO I GO FROM HERE	ON MAIN STREET	DEE GEE 3008	40.00	northern
MY HEART IS CALLING	ON MAIN STREET	DEE GEE 3008	50.00	northern

MAGNUM
FUNKY JUNKY	COMPOSITION SEVEN	PHOENIX 314 DJ	15.00	funk

MAGNUM FORCE
SHARE MY LOVE WITH YOU	ARE YOU READY FOR THE WEEKEND	KELLI-ARTS 1000	15.00	group

MAHAN, BENNY
SHE KNOWS HOW	WHAT YOU NEVER HAD	SCRATCH 5882	50.00	northern
SHE KNOWS HOW	WHAT YOU NEVER HAD	POMPEII 66690	30.00	northern

MAHOANEY, SKIP
RUNNING AWAY FROM LOVE	THIS IS MY LAST TIME	ABET 9468	10.00	70's
JANICE (DON'T BE SO BLIND TO LOVE)	DON'T STOP ME NOW	SALSOUL 2120	40.00	70's

MAIN CHANGE
SUNSHINE IS HER WAY	LIFE	NEBULA 1	175.00	northern

MAIN EVENTS
DON'T LEAVE (BABY DON'T GO)	GIRL, I WANT YOU TO REMEMBER	GOLDEN BIRD 501	15.00	70's
DON'T LEAVE (BABY DON'T GO)	GIRL, I WANT YOU TO REMEMBER	MIRACLE MILE 501	10.00	70's
DON'T LEAVE (BABY DON'T GO)	GIRL, I WANT YOU TO REMEMBER	UA 50810	8.00	70's

MAJESTICS
TURN BACK THE HANDS OF TIME	Y VOLVERE	LADY 31741	100.00	70's
FUNKY CHICK	COMING ON	MORSOUND 1001	500.00	funk
DOIN THE BEST I CAN	FEELS!	MALA 574	40.00	group
(I LOVE HER SO MUCH) IT HURTS	GIRL OF MY DREAMS	LINDA 121	200.00	northern

MAJJESTEES
TAKE BACK ALL THOSE THINGS	LET HER GO	MUTT 18382	40.00	northern

MAJOR IV
ALL OF MY LOVE	I DON'T BELIEVE IN LOSING	VENTURE 608	25.00	northern
SUGAR PIE	DOWN IN THE GHETTO	VENTURE 606	25.00	northern
THIS LITTLE GIRL OF MINE	JUST ANOTHER LONELY NIGHT	VENTURE 619	40.00	northern

MAJOR, EARL and JIMMY
CHASE IT AWAY	QUIET AS IT'S KEPT	PULSAR 2418	25.00	funk

MAJORS (also see MAJOR IV)
DOWN IN THE GHETTO	SUGAR PIE	VENTURE 606	30.00	northern
LOST IN THE CITY	SAY YOU'LL BE MINE	BIG THREE 403	25.00	northrn

MALIBUS
A BROKENM MAN	IT'S ALL OVER BUT THE SHOUTING	WHITE WHALE 289	10.00	northern
GEE BABY (I LOVE YOU)	WHAT'S THIS COMING	SURE SHOT 5028	30.00	**northerB**
I JUST CAN'T STAND IT	THE ROBOT	DUKE 457	10.00	northern

MALLETT, SAUNDRA and THE VANDELLAS
CAMEL WALK	IT'S GONNA BE HARD TIMES	TAMLA 54067	700.00	motown

MALLORY, WILLIE
YOU WENT BACK ON WHAT YOU SAID	I'LL BE YOUR JIM	LANOR 539	40.00	northern

MALONE, CINDY
IS IT OVER BABY	IT'S UP TO YOU	CAPITOL 5629	30.00	northern

MALONE, J.J.
IT'S A SHAME	DANGER ZONE	GALAXY 784 DJ	15.00	funk

MALT

GIVE LOVE A SECOND CHANCE	TELL ME	CHI-WEST 7	10.00	group

MANCHA, STEVE

DID MY BABY CALL	WHIRL POOL	WHEELSVILLE 102	800.00	northern
DON'T MAKE ME A STORY 1005	I WON'T LOVE YOU AND LEAVE YOU	GROOVESVILLE	15.00	northern
HATE YOURSELF IN THE MORNING	A LOVE LIKE YOURS	GROOVE CITY 204	30.00	northern
I DON'T WANT TO LOSE YOU 1002	I NEED TO BE NEEDED	GROOVESVILLE	20.00	northern
JUST KEEP ON LOVING ME 1007	SWEET BABY (DON'T EVER BE UNTRUE)	GROOVESVILLE	30.00	northern
YOU'RE STILL IN MY HEART 1001	SHE'S SO GOOD	GROOVESVILLE	20.00	northern

MANDARINS

THAT OTHER GUY	BETTER WATCH OUT GIRL	COMMERCE 5014	100.00	northern

MANDELLS

HOW TO LOVE A WOMAN	I CAN'T GET ENOUGH OF YOUR STU	TRANS WORLD 711	20.00	northern
THERE WILL BE TEARS	THERE WILL BE TEARS Pt.2	TRANS WORLD 701	15.00	funk
NOW I KNOW	DON'T TURN YOUR BACK ON ME	HOURGLASS 4	10.00	group
WHAT CAN YOU DO FOR ME	SAME: INSTRUMENTAL	MONEYTOWN 4522	10.00	group
I JUST CAN'T WIN		MONEY TOWN	300.00	group
I MISS YOU BABY	THINK BACK	TRANS WORLD 222	20.00	northern

MANDOLF, MARGARET

SOMETHING BEAUTIFUL	I WANNA MAKE YOU HAPPY	PLANETARY 106	200.00	**northerB**

MANDOLPH, BOBBY

GOTTA GET YOU BACK	TELL ME TOMORROW	VAULT 949	20.00	northern

MANDRILL

MY KIND OF GIRL (MY GIRL)	SAME:	ARISTA 490 DJ	10.00	70's
TOO LATE	SAME:	ARISTA 375 DJ	30.00	70's
NEVER DIE	LOVE SONG	POLYDOR 14214	15.00	northern

MANHATTANS

BABY I'M SORRY	WHEN WE'RE MADE AS ONE	CARNIVAL 529	10.00	northern
I BETCHA (COULDN'T LOVE ME)	SWEET LITTLE GIRL	CARNIVAL 522	20.00	northern
LATER FOR YOU	WHAT SHOULD I DO	AVANTI 1601	50.00	northern
ALL I NEED IS YOUR LOVE	OUR LOVE WILL NEVER DIE	CARNIVAL 526	15.00	northern
LOVE IS BREAKIN' OUT (ALL OVER)	I DON'T WANNA GO	CARNIVAL 542	10.00	northern
THERE GOES A FOOL	CALL SOMEBODY PLEASE	CARNIVAL 506	15.00	northern

MANLEY, LORENZO

(I'M GONNA) SWOP DOWN ON YOU	TO PROVE MY LOVE	ORIGINAL SOUND 60	20.00	northern

MANN, CHARLES

I CAN FEEL IT	SAY YOU LOVE ME TOO	ABC 11347	10.00	70's
LOVING YOU IS CHANGING ME	SAME:	ABC 11434	10.00	70's
SHONUFF NO FUNNY STUFF LOVE	SAME: INSTRUMENTAL	LA. 70	20.00	70's
IT'S ALL OVER	VERY LONELY	ABC 11384	20.00	northern

MANN, CLARENCE

COME WHAT MAY	SAME: INSTRUMENTAL	BAMA 30002	10.00	70's
COME WHAT MAY	SAME: INSTRUMENTAL	SUZIE Q 336	20.00	70's
SHOW ME GIRL	SHOW ME GIRL PT.2	CALIFORNIA GOLD	20.00	70's
MAN'S TEMPTATION	HAVE FAITH IN ME	T&M	30.00	ballad

MANN, DONNY

NO MORE CHILD'S PLAY	TREAT ME LIKE A STRONGER	AVALANCHE 36014	15.00	70's
TRY ME	I'M A WEAK MAN	WOODEN NICKEL 10107	15.00	northern

MANN, REV COLUMBUS

JESUS LOVES	THEY SHALL BE MINE	TAMLA 54047	40.00	motown

MANZEL

SPACE FUNK	JUMP STREET	FRATERNITY 3401	50.00	funk

MAR VELLS

GO ON AND HAVE YOURSELF A BALL	HOW DO I KEEP THE GIRLS AWAY	ANGIE 1005	20.00	northern

MARBOO

WHAT ABOUT LOVE	I REMEMBER SUNDAY MORNING	MIDLAND INT. 10540	8.00	70's

MARCEL, EDDIE

I GO CRAZY		GLAD HAMP 2034	200.00	northern

MARCEL, VIC

FUNKY LOVER	I'VE TRIED	RCA 317	15.00	70's
WON'T YOU COME AND FLY WITH ME	THIS BITTER EARTH	RCA 9750	20.00	northern

MARCELLE, LYDIA

EVERYBODY DANCE	I'VE BEEN HURT LIKE THIS BEFOR	ATCO 6366	30.00	mod
IT'S NOT LIKE YOU	IMITATION LOVE	MANHATTAN 809	70.00	**northerB**

MARCH, PEGGY

FOOL FOOL FOOL	TRY TO SEE IT MY WAY	RCA 9033	15.00	northern
FOOLIN' AROUND	THIS HEART WASN'T MADE TO KICK	RCA 9283	10.00	northern
IF YOU LOVED ME (SOUL COAXING)	THINKING THROUGH MY EYES	RCA 9494	20.00	northern
LOSIN' MY TOUCH	WHY CAN'T HE BE YOU	RCA 8534	40.00	northern
YOUR GIRL	LET HER GO	RCA 8605	15.00	northern

MARCHAN, BOBBY

EVERYTHING A POOR MAN NEEDS	THERE'S SOMETHING ABOUT MY BAB	CAMEO 405	15.00	northern

MARCHAND, RAY

YOUR SHIP OF FOOLS	HOLDING HANDS	DORE 763	600.00	northern

MARCUS, B.K.
DOES SHE CARE ABOUT ME	HIPPIE OF THE CITY	GAMBLE 4013	50.00	northern

MARGIE and THE FORMATIONS
SAD ILLUSION	BETTER GET WHAT GOES FOR YOU	COED 601	60.00	northern

MARIE, ANN
A GIFT OF LOVE	GOD BLESS SON	FAM-LEE 1001	15.00	northern

MARIE, VONDA
I FEEL COMPLETE	OPEN ARMS CLOSED HEART	PHIL L.A. SOUL 319	20.00	northern

MAR - J'S
GOT TO FIND A WAY OUT	FOREVER THERE'LL BE A SUMMER NIGHT	MAGIC TOUCH 2008	200.00	northern

MARK III TRIO
G'WAN (GO ON)	GOOD GREASE	WINGATE 15	15.00	mod
TRES LOBOS	ALL THE THINGS YOU ARE	ATCO 6451	10.00	mod

MARK IV
IF YOU CAN'T TELL ME SOMETHING	TAKE THIS LOVE	BRITE LITE 2001 12"	200.00	70's
IF YOU CAN'T TELL ME SOMETHING	TAKE THIS LOVE	BRITE LITE 2001	1000.00	70's
SIGNS OF A DYING LOVE	SIGNS OF A DYING LOVE PT 2	OTB 1007	75.00	70's
YOU'RE JUST LIKE A DREAM	WHY DO YOU WANT TO HURT ME	MERCURY 73427	10.00	70's

MARKETTS
A TOUCH OF VELVET-A STING OF BRASS	THE AVENGERS	WB 5814	15.00	northern
BELLA DELENA	OUTER LIMITS	WB 5391	10.00	northern
STIRRIN' UP SOME SOUL	TARZAN	WB 5857	20.00	northern

MARKHAM, PIGMEAT
HERE COMES THE JUDGE	THE TRAIL	CHESS 2049	10.00	funk
PIG'S POPCORN	WHO GOT THE NUMBER	CHESS 2087	15.00	funk
SOCK IT TO 'EM JUDGE	THE HIP JUDGE	CHESS 2059	10.00	funk

MARKS, RICHARD
FUNKY FOUR CORNERS	SAME: INSTRUMENTAL	ROULETTE 7034	20.00	funk
FUNKY FOUR CORNERS	SAME: INSTRUMENTAL	TUSKA 101	30.00	funk
I'M THE MAN FOR YOU		TUSKA	100.00	funk

MARKS, TOMMY
CRAZY CRAZY		ZEL 40	150.00	northern

MARLAND, CLETUS
EVERY NOW AND THEN	KEEP ON LOVING	GENEVA 109	20.00	northern
EVERY NOW AND THEN	KEEP ON LOVING	TERRY 109	30.00	northern
YOU'RE GONNA MISS ME	YESTERDAY	TERRY 110	15.00	northern

MARLBORO MEN
(RIDE ON) IRON HORSE	NEVER WILL YOU MEET A GUY LIKE	NITE BEAT 1001	50.00	funk

MARLYNNS
MY HEART IS YOURS	THE BREAK	TOWER 103163	100.00	northern

MARRS, TROY and THE DYNAMICS
RHYTHM MESSAGE	RHYTHM MESSAGE Pt.2	SURE SHOT 5019	30.00	mod

MARS, MARLINA
HEAD AND SHOULDERS	I'VE GOTTA PLEASE HIM	MGM 13361	25.00	northern
I'M GONNA HOLD ON (TO YOUR LOVE)	INSIDE I'VE DIED	MGM 13404	25.00	northern
PUT MY LOVE ON STRIKE	GIVE YOUR LOVE TO ME	MGM 13482	25.00	northern
JUST ANOTHER DANCE	IT IS LOVE THAT REALLY COUNTS	OKEH 7213	200.00	northern
JUST FOR THE BOOK	I THOUGH I KNEW ME	CAPITOL 4997	25.00	northern
THE CORRECT FORM	JOHNNY'S HEART	CAPITOL 4922	30.00	ballad

MARSHALL and THE CHI-LITES
PRICE OF LOVE	BABY IT'S TIME	DAKAR 600	15.00	northern

MARSHALL, BOB and THE CRYSTALS
GIMME SOME LOVIN'	SAME: INSTRUMENTAL	L-REV 22770	15.00	mod
I'M GOING TO PAY YOU BACK	YOU GOT ME CRYING	L-REV 968	40.00	northern

MARSHALL, DONOVAN, BROOMFIELD
SINCE I FOUND MY BABY	LET ME DOWN BABY	AUGUSTA. 100	30.00	70's

MARSHALL, STEVE
MAINTAIN	CREATIVE HAPPINESS	REYNOLDS 200.	20.00	70's

MARSHALL, WAYNE and THE MEMBERS
HER FINAL LETTER	TELL ME WHO	JOSIE 937	30.00	ballad

MARTELLS
WHERE CAN MY BABY BE	TEARS ON MY PILLOW	A LA CARTE 239	450.00	**northerB**

MARTHA and THE VANDELLAS
COME AND GET THESE MEMORIES	JEALOUS LOVER	GORDY 7014	10.00	motown
I'LL HAVE TO LET HIM GO	MY BABY WON'T COME BACK	GORDY 7011	15.00	motown
IN MY LONELY ROOM	A TEAR FOR THE GIRL	GORDY 7031	15.00	motown
LOVE, GUESS WHO	I SHOULD BE PROUD	GORDY 7098	10.00	motown
HEARTLESS	TAKING MY LOVE AND LAEVING ME	GORDY 7094	8.00	motown
ONE WAY OUT	LOVE BUG LEAVE MY HEART ALONE	GORDY 7062	10.00	motown

MARTIN JR'S REVUE, FRED
I WANT ANOTHER CHANCE	COME TO THE CITY	MELRON 5020	20.00	northern

MARTIN, BOBBI
FOR THE LOVE OF HIM	I THINK OF YOU	UA 50602	15.00	northern

MARTIN, BOBBY
MAN WAS MADE TO LOVE WOMAN	DON'T BE DOWN ON ME	GREEN MENU 10052	8.00	70's

MARTIN, CLEVELAND
I DON'T WANT TO SLIP AWAY	SOUL TRAIN THAT'S IT	SINGLE B 120	20.00	70's

MARTIN, CLOE				
IT COMES TO MY ATTENTION	LIFE RACE	GENEVA 509	10.00	70's
MARTIN, DAVID				
YOU'RE MIGHTY RIGHT	YOU'RE MIGHTY RIGHT 2	REKORD 702 blue	50.00	70's
MARTIN, DEREK				
DADDY ROLLING STONE	DON'T PUT ME DOWN LIKE THIS	CRACKERJACK 4013	10.00	mod
IF YOU GO	COUNT TO TEN	SUE 143	20.00	northern
SLY GIRL	SOUL POWER	VOLT 160	10.00	**northerB**
SLY GIRL	SOUL POWER	TUBA 2010	15.00	northern
YOU BETTER GO	YOU KNOW	ROULETTE 4631	15.00	northern
YOU BLEW IT BABY	MOVING HANMDS OF TIME	BUTTERCUP 9	15.00	northern
MARTIN, JAY D.				
BY YOURSELF	HOLD ON TO YOUR YOUR HEART	TOWER 403 DJ	60.00	**northerB**
MARTIN, KENNY				
HEART STORM	LOVIN' MAN	BIG TOP 3053	50.00	northern
MARTIN, LELA and THE SOUL PROVIDERS				
YOU CAN'T HAVE YOUR CAKE	SHY GUY	MELATONE 1032	100.00	northern
MARTIN, PAUL				
I'VE GOT A NEW LOVE	SNAKE IN THE GRASS	ASCOT 2172	20.00	northern
MARTIN, RODGE				
WASTED NIGHTS	CLOSE MY EYES (AND OPEN UP MY	NEWARK 213	20.00	ballad
THEY SAY	I'M STANDING BY	DOT 16394	25.00	northern
MARTIN, SHANE				
I NEED YOU	YOU'RE SO YOUNG	EPIC 10384	40.00	northern
ONE AND ONE	TROUBLE IS MY MIDDLE NAME	COLUMBIA 44222	15.00	northern
MARTIN, TONY				
ASK ANY MAN	SPANISH ROSE	MOTOWN 1088	10.00	motown
THE BIGGER YOUR HEART IS	THE TWO OF US	MOTOWN 1082	10.00	motown
MARTIN, TRADE				
MOANIN'	TAKE ME FOR A LITTLE WHILE	RCA 9112	20.00	northern
SHE PUT THE HURT ON ME	SON OF A MILLIONAIRE	STALLION 1003	150.00	**northerB**
WORK SONG	SO THIS IS LOVE	RCA 8926	20.00	northern
MARTINELLS				
I DON'T CARE	BABY THINK IT OVER	SUCCESS 110	10.00	northern
MARTINEZ, VAL				
SOMEONE'S GONNA CRY	THEY	RCA 8140	30.00	northern
MARTINIS				
BULLSEYE	HOLIDAY CHEER	USA 893	40.00	mod
HUNG OVER	LATE LATE PARTY	BAR 101	20.00	mod
MARVELETTES				
GODDESS OF LOVE	HE'S A GOOD GUY (YES HE IS)	TAMLA 54091	15.00	motown
MY BABY MUST BE A MAGICIAN	I NEED SOMEONE	TAMLA 54158	8.00	motown
PLAYBOY	ALL THE LOVE I'VE GOT	TAMLA 54060	10.00	motown
PLEASE MR.POSTMAN	Group Info:Meet Marvelettes	TAMLA 54046 paper disc	40.00	motown
AS LONG AS I KNOW HE'S MINE	LITTLE GIRL BLUE	TAMLA 54088	10.00	motown
STRANGE I KNOW	TOO STRONG TO BE STRUNG A LONG	TAMLA 54072	10.00	motown
THAT'S HOW HEARTACHES ARE MADE	RAINY MOURNING	TAMLA 54186	8.00	motown
TOO MANY FISH IN THE SEA	A NEED FOR LOVE	TAMLA 54105	8.00	motown
YES HE IS	BLANK:	TAMLA 54091 DJ	30.00	motown
I'LL KEEP HOLDING ON	NO TIME FOR TEARS	TAMLA 54116	15.00	northern
MARVELLOS				
IN THE SUNSHINE	DOWN IN THE CITY	MODERN 1054	15.00	northern
LET ME KEEP YOU SATISFIED	DON'T PLAY WITH MY HEART	WB 7011	15.00	northern
PIECE OF SILK	YES I DO	WB 7054	20.00	northern
SOMETHING'S BURNIN'	WE GO TOGETHER	LOMA 2045	40.00	northern
YOU'RE SUCH A SWEET THING	WHY DO YOU WANT TO HURT THE ON	LOMA 2061	15.00	northern
MARVELLS				
TOMORROW	I'M A FOOL FOR LOSING YOU	FINER ARTS 2026	40.00	northern
MARVELOUS RAY				
WHIRLPOOL	TEARS	ABNER 1004	70.00	northern
MARVELOWS (also see MIGHTY MARVELOWS)				
I DO	MY HEART	ABC 10629	10.00	northern
DO IT	I'VE GOT MY EYES ON YOU	ABC 10756	15.00	northern
YOUR LITTLE SISTER	THE SHIM SHAM	ABC 10708	40.00	northern
YOU'VE BEEN GOING WITH SALLY	FADE AWAY	ABC 10820	15.00	northern
I'M SO CONFUSED	I'M WITHOUT A GIRL	ABC 11073	10.00	northern
HET, HEY GIRL	WAIT BE COOL	ABC 11139	8.00	northern
MARVELS				
MR. SOFT TOUCH	SAME:	MERCURY 72992 DJ	40.00	northern
MARVIN and THE THE UPTIGHTS				
OOMPH	DOUBLE DOSE OF SOUL	SPOTLIGHT 703	30.00	funk
MARX, MELINDA				
IT HAPPENS IN THE SAME OLD WAY	WHAT	VEE JAY 689	20.00	northern
MASEKELA, HUGH				
GETTIN' IT ON	10,000 MILES TO MEMPHIS	UNI 55130	15.00	funk
MASKMAN and THE AGENTS				
I WOULD'NT COME BACK	ROACHES	LOOP 711	20.00	northern
IT'S THE THING	(IN A) CROWDED STATION	LOOP 701	20.00	northern

THERE'LL BE SOME CHANGES	NEVER WOULD HAVE MADE IT	DYNAMO 118	10.00	northern

MASON, AL

GOOD LOVIN'	COLOR HER WOMAN	BUNKY 2587	10.00	70's

MASON, BARBARA

DEDICATED TO YOU	TROUBLE CHILD	CRUSADER 111	10.00	ballad
I DON'T WANT TO LOSE YOU	DEDICATED TO THE ONE I LOVE	ARCTIC 140	8.00	ballad
TROUBLE CHILD	DEDICATED TO YOU	CRUSADER 111 DJ	8.00	ballad
YOU GOT WHAT IT TAKES	IF YOU DON'T (LOVE ME TELL ME	ARCTIC 112	8.00	ballad
YOU NEVER LOVED ME	TAKE IT EASY (WITH MY HEART)	ARCTIC 148	8.00	ballad
BED AND BOARD	YES IT'S YOU	BUDDAH 296	8.00	northern
YOU BETTER STOP IT	HAPPY GIRL	ARCTIC 154 DJ	20.00	northern
AIN'T GOT NOBODY	OH, HOW IT HURTS	ARCTIC 137	20.00	northern
BOBBY IS MY BABY	I NEED LOVE	ARCTIC 120	20.00	northern
DON'T EVER GO AWAY	I'M NO GOOD FOR YOU	ARCTIC 146	10.00	northern
DON'T EVER WANT TO LOSE YOUR LOVE	IS IT ME	ARCTIC 116	20.00	northern
HELLO BABY	POOR GIRL IN TROUBLE	ARCTIC 126	10.00	northern
KEEP HIM	YES, I'M READY	ARCTIC 105	10.00	northern

MASON, JAE

WOMAN (YOU'VE GOTTA BE THERE)	SAME:	BUDDAH 466 DJ	15.00	70's

MASON, TONY

(WE'RE GONNA) BRING THE COUNTRY BACK TO THE CITY LOVELY WEEKEND		RCA 8938	15.00	northern
TAKE GOOD CARE	SEEING IS BELIEVING	RCA 9104	30.00	northern

MASON, WILLIE and ALL THE KINGS MEN

WHY	KNOCK ON WOOD	KA LA MA 2773	400.00	northern

MASQUADERS

IT'S THE SAME THING	TALK ABOUT A WOMAN	SOUL TOWN 201	1000.00	northern

MASQUERADERS

NOW THAT I'VE FOUND YOU	WAKE UP FOOL	HI. 2264	10.00	70's
SWEET SWEETING	THE TRAVELING MAN	ABC 12157	10.00	70's
A FAMILY	A FAMILY Pt.2	LA BEAT 6605	8.00	group
SAY IT	THE GRASS WAS GREEN	GAP 114	8.00	group
DO YOU LOVE ME BABY	LET'S FACE FACTS	WAND 1168	10.00	northern
I DON'T WANT NOBODY TO LEAD ME ON	SWEET LOVIN' WOMAN	WAND 1172	175.00	northern
BE HAPPY FOR ME	SAME: INSTRUMENTAL	LA BEAT 6701	10.00	group
ONE MORE CHANCE	TOGETHER THAT'S THE ONLY WAY	LA BEAT 6702	100.00	northern
ONE MORE CHANCE	TOGETHER THAT'S THE ONLY WAY	LA BEAT 6704	100.00	northern
I AIN'T GONNA STOP	I'M JUST AN AVERAGE GUY	GAP 108	20.00	northern
I GOT THE POWER	TOGETHER THAT'S THE ONLY WAY	LA BEAT 6704	100.00	northern
HOW	I'M GONNA MAKE IT	LA BEAT 6606	150.00	northern

MASTEKEYS

IF YOU HAVEN'T GOT LOVE	WEAK AND BROKENHEARTED	SPORT 109	50.00	northern

MASTER FORCE

HEY GIRL	DON'T FIGHT THE FEELING	RAIN FOREST 1	30.00	70's

MASTER FOUR

LOVE FROM THE FAR EAST	IT'S NOT THE END	TAYSTER 6012	75.00	northern
LOVE FROM THE FAR EAST	IT'S NOT THE END	TAYSTER 6024	50.00	northern
LOVE HAS TAKEN WINGS	WHERE HAVE YOU BEEN	TAYSTER 6015	300.00	northern

MASTERKEYS

IF YOU HAVEN'T GOT LOVE	WEAK AND BROKEN HEARTED	SPORT 109	40.00	northern

MASTERS OF SOUL

PLEASE WAIT FOR ME	LOVE LOVES LOVE	CAPITOL 2255	10.00	group
SHOULD I JUST READ THE SIGNS	I HATE YOU (IN THE DAYTIME AND	DUKE 478	10.00	group
DO YOU REALLY LOVE ME	BY THE TIME I GET TO PHEONIX	OVIDE 241	10.00	northern
COUNT THE TIMES	I NEED YOU	OVIDE 247	10.00	group
NO DOUBT ABOUT IT	DO DA ELECTRIC TWIST	CAPITOL 2483	8.00	group
SAD FACE	LORD BLESS MY WOMAN	OVIDE 253	10.00	group
THE VOW	RIGHT ON	OVIDE 251	8.00	group

MASTERS, LINDA

YOU CAN'T IMAGINE	YOU ARE DRIVING ME CRAZY	DOUBLE HH 115	100.00	northern

MASTERS.

PARTY TIME		MASTERS	100.00	funk
(I'M) JUST A MAN IN LOVE	I'VE MADE A MISTAKE	DELLWOOD 1	300.00	northern
I NEED YOUR LOVE	NOT MY BABY	CRIMSON 1008	75.00	northern

MATADORS

SAY YES BABY	CARMEN I WISH YOU WERE HERE	CHAVIS 1034	500.00	northern
YOU'D BE CRYING TOO	MY FOOLISH HEART	KEITH 6504	150.00	northern

MATEO, GIA

IF YOU CAN'T SAY ANYTHING NICE	JUANITO	RCA 9138	40.00	northern

MATHIS, ALDER RAY

I WANT TO GET MARRIED	TAKE ME BABY	JETSTAR 122	15.00	ballad

MATHIS, JODI

DON'T YOU CARE ANY MORE	MAMA	CAPITOL 3180	15.00	northern

MATTHEWS, JOE

LITTLE ANGEL (THAT'S WHAT YOU	I HAD A MOAN	NEW MOON 1	20.00	northern
AIN'T NOTHING YOU CAN DO	(YOU BETTER) CHECK YOURSELF	KOOL KAT 1001	500.00	**northerB**
SHE'S MY BEAUTY QUEEN	IS IT WORTH IT ALL	THEMLA 104	200.00	northern
SORRY AIN'T GOOD ENOUGH	YOU BETER MEND YOUR WAYS	THEMLA 107	25.00	northern
WE GOT A GOOD THING GOING	SORRY AIN'T GOOD ENOUGH (Alt. Take)	THEMLA 114	15.00	northern
YOU BETTER MEND YOUR WAYS	SORRY AIN'T GOOD ENOUGH	THEMLA 107	60.00	northern

MATTHEWS, JOHNNIE MAE

GOT - TO BE ON	YOU'RE THE ONE	ART 3	200.00	northern
HERE COMES MY BABY	BABY WHAT'S WRONG	BLUE ROCK 4001	15.00	northern
I CAN'T LIVE WITHOUT YOU	MY MAN (SWEETEST MAN IN THE WORLD)	BLUE ROCK 4011	15.00	northern
ITTY BITTY HEART	WORRIED ABOUT YOU	KAREN 4002	30.00	northern
ITTY BITTY HEART	WORRIED ABOUT YOU	SPOKANE 4008	15.00	northern
LONELY YOU'LL BE	CUT ME LOOSE	ATCO 6528	40.00	northern
LONELY YOU'LL BE	CUT ME LOOSE	ART 002	75.00	northern
LONELY YOU'LL BE	CUT ME LOOSE	JAM	60.00	northern
BABY WHAT'S WRONG	HERE COMES MY BABY	BLUE ROCK 4001 PS	20.00	northern
I HAVE NO CHOICE	THAT'S WHEN IT HURTS	BIG HIT 105	800.00	northern

MATTHEWS, MILT

ALL THESE CHANGES	WHEN KIDS RULE THE WORLD	BRYAN 1007	8.00	70's
TRUST ME	OH I CAN'T BELIEVE YOUR GONE	H&L 4692	10.00	70's

MATTHEWS, SHIRLEY

(YOU CAN) COUNT ON ME	BIG-TOWN BOY	ATLANTIC 2210	20.00	northern
(YOU CAN) COUNT ON ME	BIG-TOWN BOY	TARAMAC 602	75.00	northern

MAURICE and MAC

AIN'T NO HARM TO MOAN	USE THAT GOOD THING	BROWN SUGAR 103	10.00	70's
YOU LEFT THE WATER RUNNING	YOU'RE THE ONE	CHECKER 1197	10.00	northern

MAURICE and THE RADIANTS

BABY YOU'VE GOT IT	I WANT TO THANK YOU BABY	CHESS 1954	15.00	northern

MAX INFINITY

YOU GOT ME GOING, GOING	SAME: PT. 2	M-I-C 1	75.00	70's

MAXIMILIAN

THE SNAKE	THE WANDERER	BIG TOP 3068	30.00	mod
YOU'D BETTER	BUTTER BALL	MAGIC CIRCLE 4226	100.00	northern

MAXWELL, HOLLY

NEVER LOVE AGAIN	WINTER GO AWAY	SMIT-WHIT 400	15.00	northern
PHILLY BARRACUDA PT. 1	PHILLY BARRACUDA PT. 2	STAR 100	10.00	mod
DON'T SAY YOU LOVE ME UNTIL YOU	BLUEBERRY HILL	STAR 101	150.00	northern
ONE THIN DIME	IT'S IMPOSSIBLE	CONSTELLATION 152	30.00	northern
ONLY WHEN YOU'RE LONELY	LET HIM GO FOR HIMSELF	CONSTELLATION 162	150.00	**northerB**

MAY, ANITA

WHEN IT'S DARK	TARNISHED ANGEL	AUDIO ARTS 60013	40.00	northern

MAYBERRY MOVEMENT

I THINK I'M IN LOVE	IT'S SO GOOD TO KNOW	EVENT 214	40.00	70's

MAYBERRY, EDDIE

BREAK IT DOWN TO ME	A LOSING BATTLE	CHRIS. 1030	15.00	funk

MAYE, CHOLLI

YOU WILL NEVER GET AWAY	CRY FOR ME	GOLD. 212	40.00	northern

MAYE, LEE

I CAN'T PPLEASE YOU	HALF WAY	LENOX 5566	15.00	northern
IF YOU NEED ME	THE GREATEST LOVE I'VE EVER KNOWN	ABC 11028 DJ	20.00	northern
TOTAL DISASTER		PIC 1	200.00	northern

MAYE, MARSHA

THE SUN SHINES AT NIGHT	YOU WERE NEAR ME	RCA 9260	10.00	northern

MAYER, NATHANIEL

I WANT LOVE AND AFFECTION	FROM NOW ON	FORTUNE 567	30.00	northern
WELL, I'VE GOT NEWS (FOR YOU)	MR. SANTA CLAUS	FORTUNE 550	30.00	northern

MAYES, JIMMY and THE SOUL BREED

DRUMS FOR SALE	PLUCKIN'	PORT 3014 DJ	30.00	funk

MAYFIELD SINGERS

I'VE BEEN TRYING	IF	MAYFIELD 7712	20.00	group

MAZE with FRANK BEVERLEY

COLOR BLIND	WHILE I'M ALONE	CAPITOL 4392	10.00	funk

MCALLISTER, MAURICE and THE RADIANTS

SHY GUY	I'M IN LOVE	CHESS 1872	15.00	northern

MCCAIN, RONNIE

THIS TIME I'M GONE	TOO MUCH OF A GOOD THING	TRIODE 116	20.00	northern

MCCALL, JOHNNY

YOU CAN'T GET AWAY	LET'S CALL IT A DAY	SATELLITE 2001	200.00	northern

MCCALL, TOUSAINT

NOTHING TAKES THE PLACE OF YOU	SHIMMY	RONN 3	15.00	northern

MCCANN, LES

BUCKET O' GREASE	ALL	LIMELIGHT 3077	10.00	mod
BURNIN' COAL	WITH THESE HANDS	ATLANTIC 2615	10.00	mod
RIVER DEEP, MOUNTAIN HIGH	SUNNY	MERCURY 72612	10.00	mod

MCCANNON III, GEORGE

SEVEN MILLION PEOPLE	YOU CAN'T GROW PEACHES ON A CH	PHI-DAN 5007	25.00	northern

MCCANTS, JUNIOR

THE BOY NEEDS A GIRL	HELP MY LOVE	KING 6076	15.00	northern
TRY ME FOR YOUR NEW LOVE	SHE WROTE IT - I READ IT	KING 6106	2000.00	northern

MCCARTHY, BOBBY JAY

SPOON ME UP YOUR HONEY	SEARCHING FOR THE HIGH ROAD	123 1719	15.00	northern

McCLEOD, GLENDA

NO STRANGER TO LOVE	SAME: INSTRUMENTAL	HGEI 14423	75.00	**70'sB**

MCCLURE, BOBBY

BEGGING YOU BABY	I GOT A WOMAN	VANESSA 5123	20.00	70's
NEVER LET YOU GET AWAY	HAVE A LITTLE MERCY	SEDGRICK 3002	75.00	northern
HIGH HEEL SHOES	TO GET WHAT YOU GOT	HI 78512	15.00	70's
I GOT A GOOD WOMAN	BEGGING YOU BABY	VANESSA 5123	20.00	70's
WAS IT SOMETHING I SAID	LOVE TRAP	HI 2307	20.00	70's
YOU BRING OUT THE LOVE IN ME	SURVIVAL KIT	ISLAND 6	20.00	70's
YOU NEVER MISS YOUR WATER	IT FEELS SO GOOD TO BE BACK HO	EDGE 5 12	10.00	70's
BABY, YOU DON'T LOVE ME	DON'T GET YOUR SIGNALS CROSSED	CHECKER 1169	10.00	northern
YOU GOT ME BABY	PEAK OF LOVE	CHECKER 1152	15.00	northern

MCCOY STRINGS, VAN

SWEET AND EASY	IF I COULD MAKE YOU MINE	SHARE 102 blue	10.00	northern
SWEET AND EASY	IF I COULD MAKE YOU MINE	SHARE 102 yellow	12.00	northern
SWEET AND EASY	IF I COULD MAKE YOU MINE	SHARE 102 multi color	15.00	northern

MCCOY, FREDDIE

SPIDER MAN	HAV' MERCY	PRESTIGE 398	10.00	mod
SOUL YOGI	SALEM SOUL SONG	PRESTIGE 462	20.00	mod

MCCRACKLIN, JIMMY

THE WALK	I'M TO BLAME	CHECKER 885	10.00	northern
LET THE DOOR HIT YOU	THIS THING	MINIT 32018	15.00	northern

MCCRAE, GEORGE

TAKE IT ALL OFF	PLEASE HELP ME FIND MY BABY	SOUL CITY 456	15.00	northern

MCCRAE, GWEN

90% OF ME IS YOU	IT'S WORTH THE HURT	CAT 1992	12.00	70's
ALL THIS LOVE THAT I'M GIVING	MAYBE I'LL FIND SOMEBODY NEW	CAT 2015	10.00	70's
LEAD ME ON	LIKE YESTERDAY OUR LOVE IS GON	COLUMBIA 45214	25.00	**northerB**

MCCRAKEN, HUGH

WHAT I GOTTA DO TO SATISFY YOU	RUNNIN' RUNNIN'	CONGRESS 261 DJ	75.00	northern

MCCREA, DARLEN

MY HEART'S NOT IN IT		TOWER 104	50.00	northern

MCCULLERS, MICKEY

SAME OLD STORY	I'LL CRY A MILLION TEARS	TAMLA 54064	85.00	motown
WHO YOU GONNA RUN TO	SAME OLD STORY	V.I.P. 25009	25.00	motown

MCCURN, GEORGE

YOU SAY YOU WANT ME	TOO MANY TEARS	REPRISE 479	15.00	northern

MCDANIELS, GENE

A HUNDRED PUNDS OF CLAY	COME ON TAKE A CHANCE	LIBERTY 55308	10.00	northern
'CAUSE I LOVE YOU SO	SOMETHING BLUE	COLUMBIA 43800	15.00	northern
IT'S A LONELY TOWN	FALSE FRIENDS	LIBERTY 55597	10.00	northern
POINT OF NO RETURN	WARMER THAN A WHISPER	LIBERTY 55480	10.00	northern
SPANISH LACE	SOMEBODY'S WAITING	LIBERTY 55510	8.00	northern
WALK WITH A WINNER	A MIRACLE	LIBERTY 55805	50.00	northern
HANG ON		LIBERTY 55834	25.00	northern

MCDONALD, MIKE

GOD KNOWS	IF YOU WON'T, I WILL	RCA 405	25.00	northern

MCDOUGAL, WILLIE

DON'T TURN AWAY	I CAN'T WAIT	KINARD 2318	50.00	northern

MCELROY,SOLLIE

ANGEL GIRL	PARTY TIME	JA-WES 101	60.00	northern

MCFARLand, JIMMY

LONELY LOVER	LET ME BE YOUR MAN	RPR 108	200.00	northern

MCGEEE, BERNARD

BACK UP GROOVE	CALIFORNIA BREEZE	ROSEMOUNT 82101	20.00	funk

MCGILL, CONNIE and THE VISIONS

A MILLION YEARS	FOR A GREAT DAY	TOY 107	20.00	group
I COULD NEVER LOVE ANOTHER	FOR THAT GREAT DAY	SUPER 102	20.00	group
WEEK ENDS	I'M SO HAPPY I FOUND YOU	CAMILLE 130	20.00	group
I CAN'T STOP MY LOVE	FOR THAT GREAT DAY	SUGAR 501.	15.00	northern
TAKE IT LIKE A MAN	MY LOVE WILL NEVER CHANGE	EDGE 502	50.00	northern

MCGOWAN, SAM

LOVE POWER	WE CAN HELP EACH OTHER	SMASH 2175	10.00	northern

MCGOWAN, SYNG

LONELINESS IS A PLEASURE	JUST IN THE NICK OF TIME	HOPE 553	30.00	northern
LONELINESS IS A PLEASURE	JUST IN THE NICK OF TIME	HOPE 2052	50.00	northern
THAT'S WHAT I WANT	PEGGY DID	HOPE 551	30.00	northern

MCGREGOR, BILLY

MR. SHY	FALL ON MY KNEES	FLASH 6601	10.00	northern

MCGRIFF, JIMMY

ALL ABOUT MY GIRL	M.G. BLUES	SUE 777	10.00	mod
THE WORM	KEEP LOOSE	SOLID STATE 2524	10.00	mod
I'VE GOT A WOMAN	I'VE GOT A WOMAN PT.2	SUE 770	10.00	northern
5003				

MCKAY, BEVERLY

BABY YOU'RE SO RIGHT	YOU BETTER BELIEVE ME	OLD TOWN 1135	30.00	northern
HE'LL NEVER CHANGE	NO NO I CAN'T HELP YOU	SUE 127	15.00	northern
CONSCIENCE		OLD TOWN 1159	50.00	northern

MCKEE, LONETTE

DO TO ME	SAVE IT (DON'T GIVE IT AWAY)	SUSSEX 624	15.00	70's

129

MCKENZIE, DON
WHOSE HEART (ARE YOU GONNA BREAK)	I'LL CALL YOU	MIRACLE 10	75.00	motown

MCKINLEY, FLASH
I'LL RESCUE YOU		BOMBAY 4105	800.00	northern

MCKINNEY, LEE AND THE MAGNETICS
I'LL KEEP HOLDING ON		SABLE 104	800.00	northern

MCKINNIES, MAURICE
SOCK A POO POO	SOCK A POO POO PT.2	BLACK & PROUD 1000	20.00	funk

MCKNIGHT, BUDDY
EVERYTIME PT. 1	EVERYTIME PT.2	RENFRO 125	30.00	northern

MCLOLLIE, OSCAR
NURSERY RHYME	IGNORE ME	SHOW TIME 600	20.00	northern

MCMAHAN, SHARON
GOT TO FIND ANOTHER GUY		KAREN	200.00	northern
HERE COMES THE BOY I LOVE	LOVE IS WONDERFUL	KAREN 319	100.00	northern

MCNAIR, BARBARA
EVERYTHING IS GOOD ABOUT YOU	WHAT A DAY	MOTOWN 1099	10.00	motown
FANCY PASSES	YOU COULD NEVER LOVE HIM (LIKE	MOTOWN 1133	10.00	motown
YOU COULD NEVER LOVE HIM	SAME:	MOTOWN 1133 DJ	10.00	motown
YOU'RE GONNA LOVE MY BABY	THE TOUCH OF TIME	MOTOWN 1087	50.00	motown
I WAS NEVER LIKE THIS	WANTED	WB 5633	75.00	northern

MCNEAL, LANDY
STAND UP AND BE COUNTED (ONE BY ONE)	COUNTING ON YOU BABY	COLUMBIA 44938	25.00	northern

MCNEALY, TIMOTHY
SAGITTARIUS BLACK		SHAWN	400.00	funk

MCNEIL, AARON
THEN YOU'LL KNOW	SO HIGH SO LOW	UPTOWN 737	8.00	ballad

MCNEIR, RONNIE
WENDY IS GONE	GIVE ME A SIGN	SETTING SUN 101	10.00	70's
WENDY IS GONE	GIVE ME A SIGN	PRODIGAL 614	8.00	70's
GOOD SIDE OF YOUR LOVE	DIFFERENT KIND OF LOVE	TORTOISE 11381	100.00	northern
SITTING IN MY CLASS	ISN'T SHE PRETTY	DE TO 2878	400.00	**northerB**

MCPHATTER, CLYDE
BOOK OF MEMORIES	I'LL BELONG TO YOU	DECCA 32719	10.00	ballad
A SHOT A RHYTHM AND BLUES	I'M NOT GOING TO WORK TODAY	AMY 968	15.00	mod
BABY YOU'VE GOT IT	BABY I COULD BE SO GOOD AT LOVE	DERAM 8503	15.00	northern
CRYING WON'T HELP YOU NOW	I FOUND MY LOVE	MERCURY 72407	20.00	northern
DEEP IN THE HEART OF HARLEM	HAPPY GOOD TIMES	MERCURY 72220	15.00	northern
EVERYBODY LOVES A GOOD TIME	LITTLE BIT OF SUNSHINE	AMY 950	15.00	northern
IN MY TENAMENT	SECOND WINDOW, SECOND FLOOR	MERCURY 72253	15.00	northern
LAVENDER LACE	SWEET AND INNOCENT	AMY 975	15.00	northern
LONELY PEOPLE CAN AFFORD TO CR	I DREAMT I DIED	AMY 993	60.00	northern
ONLY A FOOL	THANK YOU LOVE	DERAM 85032	20.00	northern
WHY CAN'T WE GET TOGETHER	THE MIXED UP CUP	DECCA 32753	10.00	northern

MCRAE, JOHNNY
YOU'RE ANYBODY'S GIRL	I LIKE THAT GIRL	DC. 1967	300.00	northern

MEADE, KENT
FUNKY TO ME	THE BAD ONE	MAGIC CARPET 6000	15.00	northern

MEADOWS BROTHERS
GET ON DOWN (LIKE SOUL FOLKS D	I WANNA DO IT	HIP SPIN 144	20.00	funk

MEASURES
GIRLS ARE EVIL	CAN YOU HANDLE IT	DESPENZA 503	20.00	northern

MEGATONS
SHIMMY, SHIMMY WALK	SHIMMY, SHIMMY WALK PT.2	DODGE 808	30.00	mod

MELLOW FELLOWS
MY BABY NEEDS ME	ANOTHER SLEEPLESS NIGHT	DOT 17135	20.00	northern

MELLOW SOUL
I GOT MY PRIDE	WE CAN MAKE IT	MELLO NO.#	2000.00	northern

MELODICS
I NEVER THOUGHT I'D LOSE YOU	AIN'T THAT SHARING MY LOVE	M.O.C. 674	40.00	northern

MELVIN, HAROLD AND THE BLUE NOTES
WHAT CAN A MAN DO	GO AWAY	ARCTIC 135	50.00	northern
PRAYIN'	YOUR LOVE IS TAKING ME ON A JOURNEY	SOURCE 13950	15.00	70's
GET OUT (AND LET ME CRY)	YOU MAY NOT LOVE ME	LANDA 703	30.00	**northerB**
GET OUT (AND LET ME CRY)	YOU MAY NOT LOVE ME	PHIL LA SOUL 372	8.00	northern

MELVIN, KIM
DOIN' THE POPCORN	KEEP THE FAITH	HI. 2160	15.00	mod

MEMBERS OF STAFF
STOP THE BELLS	I WANNA THANK YOU	EVE-JIM 1944	25.00	group

MEMPHIANS
SLIDIN' IN AND OUT	WHO WILL THE NEXT FOOL BE	PAWN 3801	15.00	funk

MEMPHIS BLACK
HANG 'EM HIGH		ASCOT	40.00	funk

MEMPHIS MEN
OH WHAT A NIGHT	ACT NATURALLY	MIRAMAR 109	100.00	northern

MENDES, SERGIO
LOVE MUSIC	SAME:	BELL 45335	20.00	northern

MERCED BLUE NOTES

DO THE PIG	DO THE PIG PT.2	SOUL 35007 NI	250.00	motown
MIDNITE SESSION	MIDNITE SESSION PT. 2	TRI-PHI 1011	25.00	motown
THUMPIN'	DO THE PIG	SOUL 35007 NI	250.00	motown
WHOLE LOTTA NOTHING	FRAGILE	TRI-PHI 1023	30.00	motown

MERCER, BARBARA

HEY	CAN'T STOP LOVING YOU BABY	GOLDEN WORLD 21	10.00	motown
HUNGRY FOR LOVE	THE THINGS WE DO TOGETHER	GOLDEN WORLD 27	60.00	motown
NOBODY LOVES YOU LIKE ME	DOIN' THINGS TOGETHER WITH YOU	GOLDEN WORLD 28	15.00	motown
CALL ON ME	SO REAL	SIDRA 9012	25.00	northern
CALL ON ME	SO REAL	CAPITOL 2059	25.00	northern

MERCER, SANDY

PLAY WITH ME	YOU ARE MY LOVE	H&L 4694	8.00	70's

MERCURY, ERIC

LOVE IS ON OUR SIDE	TAKE ME GIRL I'M READY	COLUMBIA 10729	30.00	70's
POURS WHEN IT PAINS	COLOUR YESTERDAY	MERCURY 73679	10.00	70's
LONELY GIRL	LONELY GIRL PT.2	SAC 01	2000.00	northern

MERIDIANS

HE CAN'T DANCE	BLAME MY HEART	PARNASO 120	500.00	northern

MERIWEATHER, BILL

THAT'S LOVE	NO STRONGER LOVE	FEE 1868	15.00	70's

MERRITT,JIMMY

LONELY BATTLE	I'LL FORGET ABOUT YOU	CRACKERJACK	150.00	northern
4007				

MESSIAH

ALPHA WAVE	EASY LIVIN'	MAGIC MINSTREL	20.00	funk
3001				

MESSINA, J.C.

TIME WON'T LET ME	NICE AND EASY	TOM KING 7507	30.00	**northerB**

METELIKO, GEOFFREY

GOT TO FIND A WAY	SI' I'OFA	HAPPY TIGER 4760	30.00	northern

METRICS

WISHES	I FOUND YOU	CHADWICK 101	150.00	northern

METROS

WHERE WERE YOU	NOW THAT YOU'VE GONE	RA-SEL 9106	20.00	group
SINCE I FOUND MY BABY	NO BABY	RCA 9159	50.00	northern
SWEETEST ONE	TIME CHANGES THINGS	RCA 8994	10.00	northern
WHAT'S WRONG WITH YOUR LOVE	SHE'S JUST NOT EVERYBODY'S GIR	SOUL KING 401	10.00	northern

MEYER, BOB

BEHOLD	YOU'VE GOT TO TELL ME	LAWN 238	20.00	northern

MEZA, LEE

ONE GOOD THING LEADS TO ANOTHE	IF IT HAPPENS	JUBILEE 5555	25.00	northern

MFALME

NUKU PENDA	DANSER ET CHANTER	ASANTE 1	15.00	funk

MICHEAL AND RAYMOND

MAN WITHOUT A WOMAN	WALKING THE DOG	RCA 9244	50.00	**northerB**

MICHEAL AND THE CONTINENTALS

LITTLE SCHOOL GIRL	RAIN IN MY EYES	AUDIO FIDELITY 139	100.00	northern

MICHEALS, CODY

SEVEN DAYS FIFTY TWO WEEKS	OPEN THE DOOR	MERBEN 504	75.00	northern

MICHEALS, JERRI

GIVE IT ALL TO ME	LIKE A MADNESS	CAMEO 414	30.00	northern

MICHEALS, KELLY

I NEED HIM	FOGGY DAYS	CARLA 2537	100.00	northern

MICHEALS, TONY

I LOVE THE LIFE I LIVE	PICTURE ME AND YOU	GOLDEN WORLD 41	50.00	northern

MICHELS, LLOYD

LIFE IS A SONG WORTH SINGING	LIVING FOR THE CITY	FUSION 1	10.00	northern

MICKEY AND THE HIS MICE

CRACKER JACK	ABRAHAM, MARTIN AND JOHN	MARTI 402	15.00	funk

MICKEY AND THE SOUL GENERATION

FOOTBALL	JOINT SESSION	MAXWELL 806	15.00	funk
GET DOWN BROTHER	HOW GOOD IS GOOD	MR. G 1005	700.00	funk
IRON LEG	CHOCOLATE	MAXWELL 803	25.00	funk
SOUTHERN FRIED FUNK		OMEGA	75.00	funk

MIDDLETON, BARBARA

COME ON BACK TO ME	I WONDER WHY	TRC 980	50.00	northern

MIDDLETON, GENE

NO ONE TO LOVE ME	DON'T LET THE GREEN GRASS FOOL	FUNK FACTORY	20.00	northern
5506				
YOU CAN GET IT NOW	A MAN WILL DO ANYTHING	SOUL TOWN 1	250.00	northern

MIDDLETON, TONY

ROTA ROOTA GRIND	SAME: INSTRUMENTAL	COTTON 1	10.00	funk
KEEP ON DANCING	ANGELA	A&M 1084	15.00	northern
YOU SPOILED MY REPUTATION		ABC 10695	100.00	northern
MY HOME TOWN	PLEASE TAKE ME	ALFA 113	20.00	northern
PARIS BLUES	OUT OF THIS WORLD	MALA 544	200.00	northern

Title	B-side	Label	Price	Category
SPANISH MAIDEN		SPEED 1005	25.00	northern
TO THE ENDS OF THE EARTH	DON'T EVER LEAVE ME	MGM 13493	100.00	northern

MIDNIGHT MADNESS
Title	B-side	Label	Price	Category
GUT FUNKY	FEELINGS	C.R.S. 9	25.00	funk

MIDNIGHT MOVERS UNLTD.
Title	B-side	Label	Price	Category
FOLLOW THE WIND	FOLLOW THE WIND PT 2	RENEE 3004	10.00	funk
PUT YOUR MIND IN YOUR POCKET	TRUCK IN	RENEE 3005	10.00	funk

MIDNITERS (THEE)
Title	B-side	Label	Price	Category
EVIL LOVE	WHITTIER BLVD.	CHATTAHOOCHEE 684	15.00	northern
YOU'RE GONNA MAKE ME CRY	MAKING ENDS MEET	WHITTIER 511	750.00	northern
IT'LL NEVER BE OVER FOR ME		WHITTIER 501	30.00	northern
IT'LL NEVER BE OVER FOR ME		WHITTIER 501 PS	75.00	northern

MIGHTY ELEGANT
Title	B-side	Label	Price	Category
I FIND MYSELF (FALLING IN LOVE)	I DON'T KNOW WHAT IT IS	JABER 7115	30.00	group
I FIND MYSELF (FALLING IN LOVE)	I DON'T KNOW WHAT IT IS	WESTBOUND	15.00	group

MIGHTY HANNIBAL
Title	B-side	Label	Price	Category
JERKIN' THE DOG	I FOUND A WAY	SHURFINE 11	20.00	mod
JERKIN' THE DOG	I FOUND A WAY	DECCA 31876	15.00	mod

MIGHTY LOVERS
Title	B-side	Label	Price	Category
MIGHTY LOVER	SOUL BLUES	BOOGALOO 468 yellow	50.00	northern

MIGHTY MARVELLOWS
Title	B-side	Label	Price	Category
YOU'RE BREAKING MY HEART	THIS TOWNS TOO MUCH	ABC 11189	10.00	group
I'M SO CONFUSED	I'M WITHOUT A GIRL	ABC 11073	10.00	northern
TALKIN' BOUT YA, BABY	IN THE MORNING	ABC 11011	10.00	northern

MIGHTY MUSTANGS
Title	B-side	Label	Price	Category
FIRST LOVE	A CHANGE	SURE SHOT 5004	20.00	northern

MIGHTY POPE
Title	B-side	Label	Price	Category
HEAVEN ON THE SEVENTH FLOOR 45157	TOWER OF STRENGTH	PRIVATE STOCK	10.00	70's
IF YOU WANT A LOVE AFFAIR	MANY RIVERS TO CROSS	RCA 50250	100.00	70's

MIGHTY SAM
Title	B-side	Label	Price	Category
IN THE SAME OLD WAY	SILENT TEARS	AMY 990	10.00	ballad
PAPA TRUE LOVE	I WHO HAVE NOTHING	AMY 11044	25.00	northern
NEVER TOO BUSY	MR. & MRS UNTRUE	MALAco 1011	20.00	northern

MIGHTY-KIN-EXPLOSION
Title	B-side	Label	Price	Category
I WANT YOU TO REALIZE	DANCIN'	MUSIC MKE 333	20.00	70's

MIKE AND BILL
Title	B-side	Label	Price	Category
SOMEBODY'S GOTTA GO (SHO AIN'T ME)	SAME:INSTRUMENTAL	ARISTA 139	8.00	70's
THINGS WON'T ALWAYS BE THIS BAD	SAME:INSTRUMENTAL	ARISTA 180	10.00	70's
WHERE DO I STAND	WRONG FAMILY	YORK. 8501	40.00	70's

MIKE AND IKE
Title	B-side	Label	Price	Category
SAX ON THE TRACK (I'S RATHER B	YA YA	ARCTIC 117	30.00	northern

MIKE AND RAY
Title	B-side	Label	Price	Category
IF ONLY YOU KNEW	PRIVATE WORLD OF MY OWN	GIANT 706.	400.00	northern

MIKE AND THE CENSATIONS
Title	B-side	Label	Price	Category
DON'T SELL YOUR SOUL	BABY WHAT'RE GONNA DO	HIGHLAND 1189	15.00	group
THERE IS NOTHING I CAN DO ABOU	DON'T MESS WITH ME	HIGHLAND 1181	15.00	group
YOU'RE LIVING A LIE	SPLIT PERASONALITY	REVUE 11041	10.00	group
DON'T MESS WITH ME	THERE IS NOTHING I CAN DO	HIGHLAND 1181	20.00	northern

MIKE AND THE MODIFIERS
Title	B-side	Label	Price	Category
I FOUND MYSELF A BRAND NEW BAB	IT'S TOO BAD	GORDY 7006	25.00	motown

MILBURN, AMOS
Title	B-side	Label	Price	Category
MY BABY GAVE ME ANOTHER CHANCE	I'LL MAKE IT UP TO YOU	MOTOWN 1038	30.00	motown
MY DAILY PRAYER	I'LL MAKE IT UP TO YOU SOMEHOW	MOTOWN 1046	50.00	motown

MILEM, PERCY
Title	B-side	Label	Price	Category
CALL ON ME	CRYING BABY BABY	GOLDWAX 315	20.00	northern

MILESTONES
Title	B-side	Label	Price	Category
THE JOKEY	JUICIE BRUCIE	ANDRE 706	200.00	northern
THE JOKER	JUICIE BRUCIE	ANDRE 706	100.00	northern

MILLER, BOBBY
Title	B-side	Label	Price	Category
I'M FOR THE GIRLS	LOVE TAKE THE CASE	CONSTELLATION 134	25.00	northern

MILLER, BONNIE
Title	B-side	Label	Price	Category
WHAT ARE YOU TRYING TO DO	SUNDAY	ASTRO 10005	20.00	northern

MILLER, FLORENCE
Title	B-side	Label	Price	Category
I BELIEVE IN LOVE	I'M COMING BACK TO LIFE AGAIN	P&P 555	100.00	northern
THE GROOVE I'M IN		P&P 3131	50.00	northern

MILLER, GENE
Title	B-side	Label	Price	Category
SHO IS GOOD	THE GOODEST MAN	HI. 2121	30.00	funk

MILLER, HAL
Title	B-side	Label	Price	Category
ON MY OWN TO FEET	I STILL CARE	MALA 909	150.00	northern
A BLESSING IN DISGUISE	CRY LIKE THE RAIN	MALA 920	150.00	northern

MILLER, JIMMY
Title	B-side	Label	Price	Category
ON A BACK STREET	BREAK MY HEART BREAK	COUNTERPOINT 9001	100.00	northern

MILLER, LESLEY
Title	B-side	Label	Price	Category
(YOU GOT A WAY OF) BRINGING OUT MY TEARS	HE WORE A GREEN BERET	RCA 8786	20.00	northern
(YOU GOT A WAY OF) BRINGING OUT MY TEARS	I TALK TO YOUR PICTURE	RCA 8600	30.00	northern

MILLER, LISA (LITTLE LISA)

LONELIEST CHRISTMAS TREE	LOVE IS	CANTERBURY 519	10.00	motown

MILLER, RONNIE

LISTEN TO THE MUSIC	I OWE YOU LOVE	JAR-VAL 16	20.00	northern

MILLIONAIRES

IT AIN'YT NO ACHIEVEMENT	LOVE IS STRANGE	SPECIALTY 719	15.00	northern
AND THE RAINS CAME	COFFEE AND DONUTS	SPECIALTY 694	15.00	northern
BREAKDOWN	I NEVER KNOW WHEN TO LEAVE	BIG BUNNY 508	30.00	northern
CHERRY BABY	I THOUGHT ABOUT YOU	BUNNY 506	20.00	northern
IT AIN'T NO ACHIEVEMENT	LOVE IS STRANGE	SPECIALITY 719	20.00	northern
NEVER FOR ME	IF I HAD YOU BABE	PHILIPS 40477	15.00	northern
YOU'VE GOT TO LOVE YOUR BABY	GOOD LOVE IS WORTH WAITING FOR	CASTLE 101	75.00	**northerB**

MILLS, BARBARA

QUEEN OF FOOLS	(MAKE IT LAST) TAKE YOUR TIME	HICKORY 1323	25.00	**northerB**

MILNER, REGGIE

HELLO STRANGER	SOUL MACHINE	VOLT 4048	30.00	northern
SHE'S ALRIGHT	SOMEBODY HELP ME	RONS 2	30.00	northern
HABIT FORMING LOVE	SAME:	VOLT 4028	10.00	northern

MILSAP, RONNIE

AIN'T SOUL LEFT IN THESE OLE S	ANOTHER BRANCH	SCEPTER 12161	15.00	northern
TOTAL DISASTER	IT WENT TO YOUR HEAD	WB 5405	75.00	northern
TOTAL DISASTER	IT WENT TO YOUR HEAD	PRINCESS	100.00	northern
WHEN IT COMES TO MY BABY	1000 MILES FROM NOWHERE	SCEPTER 12127	10.00	northern

MILTON, JACKIE

YOU'LL NEVER KNOW	WILL YOU LOVE ME TOMORROW	DE-VEL 6755	15.00	70's

MILTON, REGINALD

CLAP YOUR HANDS		MILTON	200.00	funk

MIMMS, GARNET

CAN YOU TOP THIS	WE CAN FIND THAT LOVE	VERVE 10624 DJ	10.00	northern
HAPPY LANDING	TAKE ME	VERVE 10642 DJ	10.00	northern
IT WAS EASIER TO HURT HERE	SO CLOSE	UA 848	10.00	northern
LOOK AWAY	ONE WOMAN MAN	UA 773	10.00	northern
LOOKING FOR YOU	MORE THAN A MIRACLE	UA 951	50.00	northern
PROVE IT TO ME	I'LL TAKE CARE OF YOU	UA 995	10.00	northern
STOP AND THINK IT OVER	I CAN HEAR MY BABY CRYING	VERVE 10596	10.00	northern

MIND AND MATTER

UNDER YOUR SPELL	SUNSHINE LADY	M&N	1500.00	northern

MINITS

STILL A PART OF ME	LOVER BOY	MGM SOUNDS OF MEMPHI S 706	100.00	northern

MINNER, PRENTICE

IF YOU	THANK GOD HE GAVE ME YOU	M.L 19731	20.00	70's

MINOR, DIANE

I'M GONNA WALK (RIGHT OUT OF YOUR LIFE)	EVEN THE BAD TIMES ARE GOOD	ISLE CITY 4447	75.00	northern

MINTZ, CHARLES

I'LL COME RUNNING BACK	LUCKY GUY	UPLOOK 42671	250.00	northern

MIRACLE WALKERS

LOVE IN MY SOUL	STRANGERS TO LOVE	SCAMM 1003	200.00	northern

MIRACLES

AIN'T IT BABY	THE ONLY ONE I LOVE	TAMLA 54036	20.00	motown
ALL I WANT	I NEED A CHANGE	CHESS 1768	40.00	motown
BAD GIRL	I LOVE YOUR BABY	CHESS 1734 blue&silver	30.00	motown
BROKEN HEARTED	MIGHTY GOOD LOVIN'	TAMLA 54044	20.00	motown
CAN YOU LOVE A POOR BOY	DEPEND ON ME	TAMLA 540. bootleg	25.00	motown
COME SPY WITH ME	THE LOVE I SAW IN U WAS JUST A MIRAGE	TAMLA 54145	8.00	motown
EVERYBODY'S GOTTA PAY SOME DUES	I CAN'T BELIEVE	TAMLA 54048	20.00	motown
GOT A JOB	MY MAMA DONE TOLD ME	END 1016	30.00	motown
I CAN TAKE A HINT	A LOVE SHE CAN COUNT ON	TAMLA 54078	10.00	motown
I CARE ABOUT DETROIT	blank:	STANDARD GROOVE 13090	100.00	motown
I CRY	MONEY	END 1029	40.00	motown
I GOTTA DANCE TO KEEP FROM CRYING	SUCH IS LOVE, SUCH IS LIFE	TAMLA 54089	10.00	motown
IF YOUR MOTHER ONLY KNEW	WAY OVER THERE	TAMLA 54069	30.00	motown
I'LL TRY SOMETHING NEW	YOU NEVER MISS A GOOD THING	TAMLA 54059	10.00	motown
MICKEY'S MONKEY	WHATEVER MAKES YOU HAPPY	TAMLA 54083	10.00	motown
SAVE ME	(COME ROUND HERE)I'M THE ONE YOU NEED	TAMLA 54140	8.00	motown
THE FEELING IS SO FINE	YOU CAN DEPEND ON ME	TAMLA 54028 globe	350.00	motown
THE FEELING IS SO FINE	YOU CAN DEPEND ON ME	TAMLA 54028 stripe	500.00	motown
THE MAN IN YOU	HEARTBREAK ROAD	TAMLA 54092	10.00	motown
WAY OVER THERE	DEPEND ON ME	TAMLA 54028 stripe	30.00	motown
WAY OVER THERE	DEPEND ON ME	TAMLA 54028 globe	15.00	motown
WAY OVER THERE (with strings)	DEPEND ON ME	TAMLA 54028 (T3)	200.00	motown
WHAT'S SO GOOD ABOUT GOODBYE	I'VE BEEN GOOD TO YOU	TAMLA 54053	15.00	motown
WHOLE LOT OF SHAKING GOING ON	OH BE MY LOVE	TAMLA 54134	8.00	motown
YOU GOTTA PAY SOME DUES	I CAN'T BELIEVE	TAMLA 54048 mis-spelt	75.00	motown
YOU'VE REALLY GOT A HOLD ON ME	HAPPY LANDING	TAMLA 54073	15.00	motown

MIRANDA, BILLY

COUNT YOUR TEARDROPS	YOU COULD'VE HAD A GOOD THING	QUEENS 721	400.00	northern

MIRETTES

HE'S ALRIGHT WITH ME	YOUR KIND AIN'T NO GOOD	MIRWOOD 5514	15.00	northern
NOW THAT I FOUND YOU BABY	HE'S ALRIGHT WITH ME	MIRWOOD 5531	15.00	northern

MISS MADELINE
LONELY GIRL	BEHAVE YOURSELF	MARVLUS 6019	10.00	northern

MITCHELL, DAVE
THE TRIP	HANG IN THERE	MET 2768	20.00	**northerB**

MITCHELL, GROVER
I WILL ALWAYS HAVE FAITH IN U	SOMEONE'S KNOCKING AT MY DOOR	DECCA 31747	10.00	ballad
MIDNIGHT TEARS	LOVING YOU	DECCA 31714	15.00	ballad
I GOTTA KEEP MOVIN'	LIE LIPS LIE	DECCA 31909	30.00	northern
TAKE YOUR TIME AND LOVE ME	SWEETER AS THE SAYS GO BY	JOSIE 961	20.00	northern
THAT'S A GOOD IDEA	LONELY WITHOUT YOUR LOVE	VEE JAY 429	25.00	northern
WHAT HURTS	SUPER HEROES	VANGUARD	40.00	70's

MITCHELL, JOCK
NOT A CHANCE IN A MILLION	I GOT TO KNOW	IMPACT 1023	300.00	**northerB**
YOU MAY LOSE THE ONE YOU LOVE	WORK WITH ME ANNIE	IMPACT 1004	40.00	northern

MITCHELL, JOCK AND THE FABULOUS AGENTS
NO MAD WOMAN	FREE AT LAST (GREAT DAY COMING	GOLDEN HIT 103	150.00	northern

MITCHELL, LEE
THE ECONOMY	IS IT YOU OR IS IT I	ROLL 1	15.00	northern

MITCHELL, MCKINLEY
THE TOWN I LIVE IN	NO LOVE LIKE MY LOVE	MIDAS 2030	15.00	northern
GYPSY	THIS PLACE AIN'T GETTING NO BE	SANDMAN 702	20.00	northern

MITCHELL, PHILLIP
THE WORLD NEEDS MORE PEOPLE LIKE YOU	I'M GONNA BUILD CALIFORNIA ALL	SHOUT 246	25.00	70's
THERE'S ANOTHER IN MY LIFE	IF WE GET CAUGHT I DON'T KNOW	EVENT 223	10.00	70's
FREE FOR ALL	FLOWER CHILD	SHOUT 244	20.00	northern

MITCHELL, PRINCE PHILIP
I'M SO HAPPY	IF IT AIN'T LOVE IT'LL GO AWAY	ATLANTIC 3587	75.00	70's
ONE ON ONE	ONLY SMOKE REMAINS	ATLANTIC 3480	15.00	70's

MITCHELL, STANLEY
GET IT BABY	QUIT TWISTIN' MY ARM	DYNAMO 111	300.00	**northerB**

MITCHELL, WILLIE
THAT DRIVING BEAT	EVERYTHING IS GONNA BE ALRIGHT	HI. 2097	8.00	northern
BAREFOOTIN'	MISTY	HI. 2119 DJ	8.00	northern
PERCOLATIN'	EMPTY ROOMS	HI. 2066	8.00	northern
TAKE FIVE	30-60-90	HI. 2154	8.00	northern
WADE IN THE WATER	TAILS OUT	HI. 2181	8.00	mod
MERCY	STICKS AND STONES	HI. 2112 DJ	8.00	northern
SECRET HOME	20-75	HI. 2075	8.00	northern

MITCHISON, LEON
MITCH'S GROOVE		MITCHITONE NO#	75.00	funk
STREET SCENE		MITCHITONE NO#.	75.00	funk

MIXED EMOTIONS
GOLD OF MY LIFE	CAN YOU FEEL THE FUNK	ROCK-WAY 5709	25.00	70's

MIXON, LITTLE JOE
WHAT YOU SEE IS WHAT YOU GET	SAME: INSTRUMENTAL	DUO 7461	20.00	funk

MOB
I'D LIKE TO SEE MORE OF YOU	GIVE IT TO ME	COLOSSUS 134	10.00	70's
I DIG EVERYTHING ABOUT YOU	LOVE HAS GOT A HOLD ON ME	COLOSSUS 130	10.00	northern
DISAPEAR	I WISH YOU'D LEAVE ME ALONE	MERCURY 72791	10.00	northern
OPEN THE DOOR TO YOUR HEART	I WISH YOU'D LEAVE ME ALONE	DAYLIGHT 1000	75.00	**northerB**

MOD MODS
THE GREATEST STORY	HEAVEN'S DOOR	REP RECORDS 102	20.00	northern

MOD SQUAD
CHARGE	MOD SQUAD YOU ALL	TRC 1004	50.00	funk

MODERN REDCAPS
I COULDN'T CARE LESS	DONE BEING LONELY	SMASH 1768	20.00	northern
NEVER KISS A GOOD MAN GOOD-BY	FREE	PENNTOWNE 101	15.00	northern
NEVER TOO YOUNG	GOLDEN TEARDROPS	SWAN 4243	20.00	northern
EMPTY WORLD	OUR LOVE WILL NEVER BE THE SAME	LAWN 254	100.00	northern

MODERN SOUL TRIO
YOU'RE NO GOOD	THAT'S WHER IT'S AT	YOUNGSTOWN 606	300.00	northern

MODS
DRY MY EYES	ROSALIE	FONA 126595	100.00	northern

MODULATIONS
WORTH YOUR WEIGHT IN GOLD	I'LL AWAYS LOVE YOU	BUDDAH 497	10.00	70's
SHARE YOUR LOVE	WHO'S GOING TO LOSE	MOZEL 101	10.00	group

MOFFETT, JOHNNY
I FOUND JOY	SEND HER HOME TO ME	CANTERBURY 518	15.00	northern
YOU'RE THE ONE	COME ON HOME	CANTERBURY 510	30.00	northern

MOHAWKS
THE CHAMP	SOUND OF THE WITCH DOCTORS	COTILLION 44002	25.00	funk
BABY HOLD ON	BABY HOLD ON PT.2	COTILLION 44037	10.00	mod

MOKIE, J.J. AND R.O.B.
COME TOGETHER IN LOVE	YOU'RE SO REAL	SUN MOON STARS 10067	10.00	70's
YOU'RE SO REAL	COME TOGETHER IN LOVE	SUN, MOON STARS 10068	15.00	70's

MOMENTS
BABY, I WANT YOU	PRAY FOR ME	HOG 1000	1000.00	northern

YOU SAID	LOVE YOU CAN'T YOU HEAR	DEEP 001	300.00	northern

MOMIE-O

YOU'RE WELCOME, STOP ON BY	ONCE YOU GET STARTED	I DENTIFY 8004	20.00	70's

MONDAY, ARTHUR

WHAT GOES AROUND COMES AROUND		STAGE MUSIC	800.00	funk

MONDAY, DANNY

BABY, WITHOUT YOU	GOOD TASTE OF LOVE	MODERN 1025	300.00	northern

MONDAY, JOHNNY

DON'T PUT THE HURT ON ME	IF I HAD IT	20th. CENTURY 569	100.00	northern

MONEY'S BIG ROLL BAND, ZOOT

BIG TIME OPERATOR	ZOOT'S SERMON	EPIC 10077	15.00	mod

MONIQUE

NEVER LET ME GO	I WOULDN'T BELIEVE	MAURCI 108	250.00	northern
IF YOU LOVE ME		MAURCI 104	500.00	northern

MONITORS

NUMBER ONE IN YOUR HEART	GREETINGS (THIS IS UNCLE SAM)	V.I.P. 25032	15.00	motown
SAY YOU	ALL FOR SOMEONE	V.I.P. 25028	15.00	motown
SINCE I LOST YOU GIRL	DON'T PUT OFF TOMORROW WHAT YO	V.I.P. 25039	15.00	motown
STEP BY STEP (HAND IN HAND)	TIME IS PASSING BY	SOUL 35049	8.00	motown
THE FURTHER YOU LOOK THE LESS	BRING BACK THE LOVE	V.I.P. 25046	15.00	motown
FENCE AROUND YOUR HEART	HAVE YOU SEEN HER	BUDDAH 278	20.00	northern

MONORAYS

LOVE	YOU'RE NO GOOD	20th. CENTURY 594	75.00	northern

MONROE, BEN

BROKEN HOME	THE MELODY IS FOR MY BABY	DAKAR 4557	20.00	70's

MONSTARS

GROOVY LIFE	FUNNY SAGA	AAVALANCHE 7710	15.00	funk

MONTCLAIRS

UNWANTED LOVE	BEGGIN' IS HARD TO DO	PAULA 375	8.00	northern
COME ON AND HOLD ME	YOUNG WINGS CAN FLY	UNITED	75.00	northern
INTERNATIONAL				
HEY YOU! DON'T FIGHT IT	NEVER ENDING LOVE	ARCH. 1305	800.00	northern
HUNG UP ON YOUR LOVE	I'M CALLING YOU	PAULA 390	15.00	northern
WAIT FOR ME	HAPPY FEET TIME	SUNBURST 106	25.00	northern

MONTE, JOE

HURTIN' MYSELF	PLEASE SEND ME SOMEONE TO LOVE	CAPITOL 5283	20.00	northern

MONTEGO JOE

IT BE'S THAT WAY SOMETIMES	SOUL MAN	NINANDY 1010	10.00	mod

MONTEREYS AND THE GRANDEURS

COME HOME TO ME	FREEDOM TRAIN	CARDINALE 6901	25.00	northern

MONTGOMERY, BOBBY

MAKE ME YOURS	SEEK AND YOU SHALL FIND	HIGHLAND 78	200.00	northern

MONTGOMERY, CHARLES

I DON'T THINK (I'LL TRY THAT A	YOU AND ME	LADERA 192930	20.00	70's

MONTGOMERY, JACK

BEAUTY ISN'T BORN	SAME: INSTRUMENTAL	AUSTONS 1	75.00	70's
BABY, BABY, TAKE A CHANCE ON M	SAME: INSTRUMENTAL	REVUE 11009	50.00	northern
DEARLY BELOVED	DO YOU BELIEVE IT	SCEPTER 12152	100.00	northern
DON'T TURN YOU'RE BACK ON ME	NEVER IN A MILLION YEARS	BARRACUDA 8030	250.00	northern
MY DEAR BELOVED (mispelt title)	DO YOU BELIEVE IT	SCEPTER 12152	125.00	northern

MONTGOMERY, TAMMY

IF I WOULD MARRY YOU	THIS TIME TOMORROW	CHECKER 1072	25.00	motown

MONTICELLOS

DON'T HOLD BACK	I CAN'T WAIT UNTIL I SEE MY BA	RED CAP 102	100.00	northern

MONTRE EL, JACKIE

DOOM	WORSHIP	READY 1009	20.00	northern
DOOMED BY JEALOUSY	I WORSHIP THE GROUND YOU WALK	ABC 11035	15.00	northern

MONZAS

BABY YOU KNOW	WHERE IS LOVE	PACIFIC544	30.00	northern
HEY! I KNOW YOU	FOREVER WALKS THE DRIFTER	WAND 1120 DJ	40.00	northern
HEY! I KNOW YOU	FOREVER WALKS A DRIFTER	PACIFIC 104	20.00	northern

MOODS

HUSTLIN'	KING HUSTLER	REDDOG 4001	20.00	funk
RAINMAKER	LADY RAIN	WAND 11224	15.00	northern

MOODY, JOAN

ANYTHING WORTH HAVING	BIG TIME OPERATOR	SYLVIA 5002	50.00	northern
BIG TIME OPERATOR	DON'T DO ME THAT WAY	SYLVIA 122	10.00	northern
BIG TIME OPERATOR	DON'T DO ME THAT WAY	TCF 122	20.00	northern

MOON AND MARS

BE BY YOUR SIDE	COPPER PENNY	DOOTONE 477	20.00	northern

MOON PEOPLE

LAND OF LOVE	REVOLT	SPEED 3	15.00	funk

MOONLIGHTERS BAND

MORE THAN I CAN STAND	JUST LIKE SHE SAID SHE WOULD	LAMP 82	150.00	northern
LONELY BABY	RIGHT ON BROTHER	LAMP 653	100.00	northern
FUNKY MOON MEDITATION		BLUE EAGLE	30.00	funk

MOORE, BERNIE

OH NO	HURT WORSE	S.S.I. 1003	50.00	70's

MOORE, BOBBY

I CAREFULLY CHECKED YOUR HEART	LET'S PROVE THEM WRONG	KAY-O 107	150.00	northern

MOORE, BOBBY AND THE RHYTHM ACES

CHAINED TO YOUR HEART	REACHING OUT	CHECKER 1180	10.00	northern
SEARCHING FOR MY LOVE	HEY, MR. D.J.	CHECKER 1129	10.00	northern

MOORE, CECELIA

YOU SET MY SOUL ON FIRE	PEEK-A-BOO	EXTRA 719	200.00	northern

MOORE, CURLY

GOODBYE	WE REMEMBER	SANSU 468	30.00	ballad
YOU DON'T MEAN	DON'T PITY ME	SANSU 473	100.00	northern
GET LOW DOWN PT.1	GET LOW DOWN PT. 2	SANSU 457	15.00	ballad

MOORE, CURLEY AND THE KOOL ONES

FUNKY, YEAH	SHELLEY'S RUBBER BAND	HOUSE OF THE FOX	15.00	funk
1934				

MOORE, DANNY

SOMEBODY NEW	HERE COMES SUMMER	ALLRITE 625	150.00	northern

MOORE, DELILAH

IT TAKES LOVE	WRAPPED UP TIGHT	MIDDLE EARTH 1	200.00	70's
I'LL JUST WALK AWAY	I WISH	MONEY 602	20.00	northern
WRAPPED UP TIGHT	OOO-WEE BABY	MONEY 603	20.00	northern

MOORE, DOROTHY.

GIRL OVERBOARD	SPECIAL OCCASION	MALACO 1052	10.00	70's
JUST THE ONE I'VE BEEN LOOKING	CRY LIKE A BABY	GSF 6908	10.00	70's

MOORE, DOROTHY AND THE FLOYD, EDDIE

WE SHOULD REALLY BE IN LOVE	I'LL NEVER BE LOVED	MALACO 1040	8.00	70's

MOORE, JACKIE

BOTH ENDS AGAINST THE MIDDLE	CLEAN UP YOUR OWN BACKYARD	ATLANTIC 2989	8.00	70's
HERE I AM	DEAR JOHN	SHOUT 232	15.00	northern
WHO TOLD YOU	LOSER AGAIN	WAND 11204	20.00	funk

MOORE, JAMES AND THE PRETENDERS

A MAN SHOULD NEVER CRY	TO BE LOVED (FOREVER)	TISHMAN 905	300.00	northern

MOORE, JOE

HANG RIGHT IN THERE	NOBODY LOVES ME	TRU-GLO-TOWN 509	30.00	northern
I AIN'T	I'VE GOT MY SWEET BABY	TRU-GLO-TOWN 510	100.00	northern
I AIN'T	I'VE GOT MY SWEET BABY	VERVE 10566	20.00	northern
I KNOW YOU LIKE A BOOK	I MUST BE IN LOVE	CB 5004	50.00	northern

MOORE, JOHNNY

JUST BE FOR REAL	(I WANNA) SPEND THE REST OF MY	BRUNSWICK 55459	60.00	70's
I'M ONLY HALF A MAN WITHOUT YO	CAN'T LIVE WITH-OUT YOUR LOVE	JARDAN 7740	200.00	northern
SUCH A WONDERFUL FEELING	WITHOUT YOUR LOVE	BLUE ROCK 4053	15.00	northern
THANK YOU BABY	GRANDPA TOLD ME	MERCURY 72908	15.00	northern
YOUR LOVE IS FADING	THERE'LL NEVER BE ANOTHER YOU	MERCURY 72939	20.00	northern
IT MAY BE TEARS OF JOY	YOUR LOVE'S GOT THE POWER	BRIGHT STAR 148	15.00	northern
HAVEN'T I BEEN GOOD TO YOU	A DOLLAR NINETY EIGHT	WAND 1165	10.00	northern
LONELY HEART IN THE CITY	THAT'S WHAT YOU SAID	BLUE ROCK 4070	15.00	northern
WALK LIKE A MAN	IT'S JUST MY WAY OF LOVING YOU	DATE 1562	40.00	**northerB**
WHAT MORE CAN I DO	LET'S GET IT TOGTHER	LARRY O 404	15.00	northern
YOU'RE THE GIRL FOR ME	CALL IT WHAT YOU WANNA	CHI-CITY 777	15.00	northern
YOU'RE THE ONE TO BLAME	SOLD ON YOU	BRIGHT STAR 145	15.00	northern

MOORE, JOSEPH

I STILL CAN'T GET YOU	I'M LOST WITHOUT YOU	MARVLUS 6008	800.00	northern

MOORE, JUDSON

EVERYBODY PUSH AND PULL	CONFIDENCE	CAPRI 109	20.00	northern

MOORE, MELBA

DON'T CRY	DOES LOVE BELIEVE IN ME	MUSICOR 1403	30.00	northern
DON'T CRY SING ALONG WITH THE MUSIC	DOES LOVE BELIEVE IN ME	MUSICOR 1189	40.00	northern

MOORE, MELVIN

RAIN GO AWAY	HOW DIOES IT FEEL TO BE A BIG	BRAINSTORM 1196	15.00	ballad
ALL OF A SUDDEN		SKY HERO	400.00	70's

MOORE, MISTY

LITTLE THINGS	CAN'T BELIEVE YOUR GONE	PZAZZ 10	100.00	northern

MOORE, ROBERT

CAN'T HELP MYSELF	EVERYTHING'S GONNA BE ALL RIGHT	SAADIA 6091	75.00	funk
JIMMIE BO CHARLIE	TEARS OF THE WORLD	BLUE CANDLE 1499	20.00	funk

MOORE, SAMUEL AND THE CHI'S-TNT'S

I'M SO JEALOUS	SAME: INSTRUMENTAL	DJO 3004	10.00	northern

MOORE, W.J. AND THE DYNAMIC UPSETTERS

EVERYTHING GOOD TO YOU	LAST CALL FOR ALCOHOL	GUTTER 85001	20.00	70's
I BELIEVE I'M FALLING IN LOVE	BEACH MUSIC IS SO GOOD FOR YOU	CARDINAL. 45001	20.00	70's

MOORER, BETTY

SPEED UP	IT'S MY THING	WAND 11202	25.00	northern

MORESE, GINO

LIVED A GOOD LIFE	SAME: INSTRUMENTAL	SMOKE 300	50.00	northern

MORGAN, CHRIS

NOW I TASTE THE TEARS	WHO AM I	BELL 798 DJ	40.00	norhern

MORGAN, J.E.
BY MY SIDE	BY MY SIDE Pt.2	THEODA 518	20.00	northern

MORGAN, JANE
MAYBE	WALKING THE STREETS IN THE RAIN	EPIC 9819 PS	40.00	northern

MORGAN, JOANNE
JUST HOW LOUD	TAKE ME BACK	MGM 13659	20.00	northern
JUST HOW LOUD	TAKE ME BACK	MGM 13659 PS	30.00	northern

MORGAN, LEE
SIDEWINDER	SIDEWINDER PT.2	BLUE NOTE 1911	10.00	mod

MORISETTE, JOHNNIE
I'M HUNGRY		J&J	200.00	funk
MEET ME AT THE FUNK HOUSE	SAME: PT 2	ICEPAC 301	15.00	funk

MORRELL, MIA
I HAVE A MIND OF MY OWN	SUNSHINE AND ROSES	ABC 10951 DJ	75.00	northern

MORRIS, DAVID
SNAP CRACKLE POP	GONE IS THE LAUGHTER	PLUSH 206	50.00	70's
(EVERYTHING IS) HUNKY FUNKY	TWO HEARTS ONE SUMMER DAY	PHILIPS 40534	10.00	northern

MORRIS, ELMORE
BEFORE YOU TURN YOUR BACK ON M	IT SEEMED LIKE HEAVEN TO ME	CRACKERJACK 4006	20.00	northern

MORRIS, FLOYD
A MELLOW MOOD	BEE QUE	BBS 578	20.00	funk

MORRISON, DOROTHY
I CAN'T DO WITHOUT YOU	I CAN'T DO WITHOUT YOU PT.2	BROWN DOOR 6580	100.00	70's

MORRISON, KIM
ONE IN A MILLION	HOLLYWOOD AND VINE	MALACO 1053	30.00	70's

MORRISON, VAN
DOMINO	SWEET JANNIE	WB 7434	10.00	northern

MORROCCO MUZIK MAKERS
PIG KNUCKLES	BACK TO SCHOOL AGAIN	MOTOWN 1047	150.00	motown

MORROW, TEDDY
WHAT'S YOUR SIGN	PEACE, LOVE AND TOGETHERNESS	SEIBU 1010	10.00	group

MORTIMER, AZIE
PROVE IT	I DON'T CARE	OKEH 7337	10.00	ballad
TELLING A LIE	HAUNTED	BLOOMIE 101	75.00	northern
(I GET THE FEELING)YOU'RE ASHAMED OF ME	THE OTHER HALF OF ME	UA 847	40.00	northern
HAUNTED	COOL IT	NUMBER ONE 7501	15.00	northern
LITTLE MISS EVERYTHING	THE BEST YEARS	RCA 8985	15.00	northern
PUT YOURSELF IN MY PLACE	BRING BACK YOUE LOVE	SWAN 4158	15.00	northern
YOU CAN'T TAKE IT AWAY	A ONE WAY LOVE	OKEH 7336	10.00	northern

MORTON, JAY
ALLIGATOR STRUT	DID YOU GET THE MESSAGE	BUDDAH 157	20.00	funk

MOSELY, ERNEST
STUBBORN HEART	KEEP ON LOVING ME	LA CINDY 225	400.00	**northerB**

MOSES, LEE
REACH OUT, I'LL BE THERE	DAY TRIPPER	MUSICOR 1227	10.00	funk

MOSES
I GOT MY MIND TOGETHER	IF YOU DON'T MEAN IT, DON'T TO	PIEDMONT 75	15.00	70's
SWEETEST LOVE	SUNDAY AFTERNOON	PURE SILK 45001	15.00	70's

MOSLEY, TOMMY
EXIT LONELINESS ENTER LOVE	SO THIS IS LOVE	ERA 3184	30.00	northern
YOU LIED, I CRIED, LOVE DIED		UPTOWN 706	30.00	northern

MOST, SAM
PLOP-PLOP BOOM	JUNGLE FANTASY	BELL 955	100.00	funk

MOTIVATIONS
THE SLOW FIZZ	THE SQUEEZE	DYNOVOICE 216	15.00	mod

MOULTRIE, MARY
THEY'RE TRYING TO TEAR US APART	LAST YEAR, SENIOR PROM	KING 6038	75.00	northern

MOULTRIE, SAM
I'LL ALWAYS LOVE YOU	I FOUND LOVE	SOUTHBOUND 102	50.00	northern
I'LL ALWAYS LOVE YOU	DO YOUR OWN THING	WARREN 108	30.00	**northerB**
THE PROMISED LAND	FUNKY JERK	ROULETTE 7038	15.00	northern

MOUSIE AND THE TRAPS
IT'S ALL IN THE WAY	HOW ABOUT YOU	TODDLIN TOWN 8204	150.00	northern

MOVEMENTS
YOU DON'T KNOW	LET'S GET INVOLVED	PEANUT COUNTRY 1002	30.00	group

MR. CALDWELL
LOVE BANDIT	LOVE HAS THE POWER	SCORPIO. 104	40.00	northern

MR. D. AND THE HIGHLIGHTS
EVERY NOW AND THEN	NOSE FULL OF WHITE	JAS. 316	30.00	ballad

MR. FLOODS PARTY
COMPARED TO WHAT	UNBREAKABLE TOY	GM 714	20.00	northern

MR. JIM AND THE RHYTHM MACHINE
(DO THE) HOT PANTS	MIDNIGHT IN MADRID	WIZDOM 1984	10.00	funk

MR. LUCKY
I WAS BORN TO LOVE YOU		STARDOM	1000.00	northern

MR. PITIFUL				
GIRL CAN'T HELP IT	ONE DOLLAR MAN	JOSIE 987	15.00	northern
MR. SOUL, BOBO				
HITCHHIKE TO HEARTBREAK ROAD	SHE'S MY WOMAN	HI. 2225	8.00	70's
HITCH HIKE TO HEARTBREAK ROAD	SHE'S MY WOMAN	OVIDE 258	15.00	northern
H.L.I.C.	ANSWER TO THE WANT ADS	OVIDE 252	10.00	funk
MR. SOUL.				
WHAT HAPPENED TO YESTERDAY	YOU'RE TOO GOOD	GENUINE 150	1500.00	northern
MR. TEARS				
DON'T LEAD ME ON	EXCUSE ME BABY	4J 509	40.00	northern
MR. WIGGLES				
WASH MY BACK	HOME BOY	GOLDEN TRIANGLE 100	20.00	ballad
FAT BACK	FAT BACK PT. 2	PARKWAY 104	25.00	mod
MUHAMMAD, IDRIS				
I'M A BELIEVER	RYTHM	PRESTIGE 756	75.00	70's
EXPRESS YOURSELF	SUPER BAD	PRESTIGE 743	15.00	mod
MULLINS, DEE				
LOVE MAKES THE WORLD GO ROUND	COME BACK (AND BE MY LOVE AGAIN)	MELODY 117	10.00	motown
MURPHY, DONNIE AND THE AMBASSADORS				
EVERYTHING I DO	MY LOVE FOR YOU	RED BUG 5	200.00	northern
MURPHY, JOE				
SO BLUE (WITHOUT YOU)	IT'S A WEAKNESS	VIVID 106	20.00	northern
MURRAY JONES, JUGGY				
INSIDE AMERICA	INSIDE AMERICA Pt.2	JUPITER 902	8.00	funk
MURRAY, BILL AND COPELAND, GEORGE				
THE BIG TIME SPENDER	SAME: PT.2	ANNA 1121	40.00	motown
MURRAY, CLARENCE				
DON'T TALK LIKE THAT	POOR BOY	SSS INTER. 756	10.00	northern
MURRAY, JO JO AND THE TOP FLIGHT				
YOUR LOVE	I'M IN LOVE	IB 7809	15.00	70's
MURRAY, JUGGY				
BUILT FOR SPEED	BUILT FOR SPEED PT.1&2	PONY 1	8.00	funk
MURRAY, MICKEY				
LITTLE BITTY BODY	LITTLE BITTY BODY PT.2	PEPCO 101	40.00	funk
MURRAY, TIM				
THINKING OF YOU	STREET PEOPLE	DETROIT TRAKS 501825	50.00	**northerB**
MURRAY, VIRGIL				
I STILL CARE	SUMMER DREAMIN'	AIRTOWN 15	40.00	northern
I STILL CARE	SUMMER DREAMIN'	KOOL KAT	100.00	northern
MUSIC CITY SOUL BROTHERS				
LET OUR LOVE GO ON	EVERY NIGHT I SEE YOUR FACE	MUSIC CITY 856	25.00	northern
MUSIC CITY TWO IN ONE				
SNAG NASTY	SILLY SONG	MUSIC CITY 890	40.00	funk
MUSTANGS				
TURN BACK THE HANDS OF TIME	HOW FUNKY CAN YOU GET	JETSTAR 120	15.00	funk
MYLES, BIG BOY				
SHE'S SO FINE	THE FLAME	V-TONE 232	30.00	northern
MYLESTONES				
SEXY LADY	LOVE ME GIRL	HAWK SOUND 102	20.00	**northerB**
MYSTIC MOODS				
COSMIC SEA	THE AWAKENING	WB 7686	15.00	funk
HONEY TRIPPIN'	MIDNIGHT SHACK	SOUNDBIRD 5002	8.00	funk
ASTRAL TRIP	DRIFTING PROPHET	WB 7743	20.00	northern
MYSTICS				
JEALOUS OF YOU	COPP AND BLOW	MARQUETTE	100.00	group

N

N GROUP				
KEEP ON RUNNIN'	WORDS OF LOVE	WES MAR 1021	20.00	northern
N AND THE WT 14 KARAT BLACK				
STOP LISTENIN'	AIN'T NOTHING BUT A HABIT	LUNA 802	20.00	funk
NABAY				
BELIEVE IT OR NOT	SAME: INSTRUMENTAL	IMPACT 1032	1000.00	northern

NABBIE, JIM

LOOK HEAR GIRL	REMEMBER ME	RPI 1008	40.00	northern

NAKED TRUTH

THE SHING A LING THING	THE STRIPPER	RCA 9327	15.00	**northerB**

NAOMI AND HARRIS

COME ON BABY AND HURT ME	WE BELONG TOGETHER	ATCO 6543	15.00	northern

NASH, JOHNNY

(I'M SO) GLAD YOU'RE MY BABY	STORMY	MGM 13805	10.00	northern
BIG CITY	SOMEWHERE	ATLANTIC 2344	10.00	northern
I'M LEAVING	OH MARY DON'T YOU WEEP	GROOVE 30	30.00	northern
I'M MOVIN' ON	CIGARETTES, WHISKEY & WILD WIL	WB 5336 DJ	15.00	northern
LOVE AIN'T NOTHING	TALK TO ME	ARGO 5471	20.00	northern
MOMENT OF WEAKNESS	DON'T TAKE AWAY YOUR LOVE	WB 5270	15.00	northern
OL' MAN RIVER	MY DEAR LITTLE SWEETHEART	WB 5301	10.00	northern
STRANGE FEELING	SPRING IS HERE	ARGO 5492	15.00	northern
TOWN OF LONELY HEARTS	IT'S NO GOOD FOR ME	GROOVE 26	30.00	**northerB**
WHAT KIND OF LOVE IS THIS	DEEP IN THE HEART OF HARLEM	GROOVE 21	60.00	northern
YOU'LL NEVER KNOW	GOOD GOODNESS	MGM 13683	10.00	northern
WHAT KIND OF LOVE IS THIS	DEEP IN THE HEART OF HARLEM	GROOVE 21 PS	75.00	northern

NATURA'ELLES

SHOW ME THE WAY	SO MUCH IN NEED	VENTURE 633	15.00	northern

NATURAL FACTS

GIRL DON'T CRY	WHAT TIME IS IT	LUCKY LOU 813	200.00	northern

NATURAL FOUR

LOVE'S SO WONDERFUL	WHAT'S HAPPENING HERE	CURTOM 104	10.00	70's
YOU BRING OUT THE BEST IN ME	YOU CAN'T KEEP RUNNING AWAY	CURTOM 2000	8.00	70's
WHY SHOULD WE STOP NOW	YOU DID THIS FOR ME	BOOLA BOOLA 6084	20.00	group
HANGING ON TO A LIE	TWELVE MONTHS OF THE YEAR	BOOLA BOOLA 1001	400.00	northern
I THOUGHT YOU WERE MINE	YOU DID THIS FOR ME	BOOLA BOOLA 2082	200.00	northern
I THOUGHT YOU WRE MINE	HURT	ABC 11253	150.00	northern
THE DEVIL MADE ME DO IT	GIVE A LITTLE LOVE	CHESS 2119	8.00	northern

NATURAL IMPULSE

SHE WENT AWAY	TIME IS RIGHT	NATURAL IMPULSE	1500.00	northern

NATURALS

DA DA DA DA DA (I LOVE YOU)	THIS LONELINESS	QUADRAN 4443	40.00	northern
DONT' JUST STAND THERE	MAKE IT MOVE	PATH. 5563	75.00	northern

NATURE BOYS

WATCH YOURSELF	DO THE TEMPTATION	UPTOWN 725	30.00	northern

NATURELLES

LOVE HAS JOINED US TOGETHER	SOW ME THE WAY	VENTURE 609	15.00	northern

NAVARRO, TOMMY

I CRIED MY LIFE AWAY	CLUB OF BROKEN HEARTS	DE JAC 1253	100.00	**northerB**

NAYLOR, JERRY

CITY LIGHTS	LIFE	TOWER 162	100.00	northern

NAZTY

I GOT TO MOVE	MAYBE YOUR BABY	MANKIND 12026	10.00	funk

NEAL, ROBERT

I'M SO GLAD	GOOD-BYE NOW	PORT 3020	20.00	northern

NEAL, TOMMY

GOIN' TO A HAPPENING	TEE TA	VAULT 938	15.00	northern
GOIN' TO A HAPPENING	TEE TEA	PAMELINE 100 yellow	75.00	northern
GOIN' TO A HAPPENING	TEE TEA	PAMELINE 100 pink	100.00	northern
GOIN' TO A HAPPENING	TEE TEA	PALMER 5024	200.00	northern

NEIL, TRACY

DON'T HURT ME NO MORE	DO IT NOW	SINCERE 1001	200.00	northern

NELSON, FRANK AND THE BEAT STRINGS

DOMINICA	BLACK PEARLS	MIRA 233	15.00	northern

NELSON, GRANT

MY HEART CAN'T UNDERSTAND	BILLY AND SUE	WAND 1126	20.00	ballad

NELSON, NATE

ONCE AGAIN	TELL ME WHY	PRIGAN 2001	100.00	northern

NELSON, ROY

ELEVATOR MAN	ITCHY TWITCHY LOVE	RANARD 12196	20.00	northern

NELSON, SANDY

SOCK IT TO 'EM J.B.	THE CHARGE	IMPERIAL 66193	15.00	mod

NEPTUNES

GIRL THAT'S AN AWFUL THING TO	TURN AROUND	GEM 100	100.00	northern
HOUSE OF BROKEN HEARTS	MAKE A MEMORY	INSTANT 3255	20.00	northern
I DON'T CRY ANYMORE	I'M COMING HOME	VICTORIA 102	75.00	northern

NERO, FRANCES

KEEP ON LOVIN' ME	FIGHT FIRE WITH FIRE	SOUL 35020 multi	50.00	motown
KEEP ON LOVIN' ME	FIGHT FIRE WITH FIRE	SOUL 35020 lilac/ & white	75.00	motown

NESBARY, SHERM

DON'T MAKE ME SORRY	ALL MY LIFE ALL MY LOVE	CHERI 500	15.00	70's

NESBIT, CHARLIE

SOUL TRAIN	TRIPLE-O SOUL	SALVADOR 888 DJ	15.00	mod

Artist / Title	B-side	Label	Price	Category
NESBIT, SAM				
BLACK MOTHER GOOSE	CHASE THOSE CLOUDS AWAY	AMOS 154	200.00	northern
NEVILLE, ART				
YOU WON'T DO RIGHT	SKEET SCAT	INSTANT 3256	10.00	northern
NEVILLE, IVAN				
DANCE YOUR BLUES AWAY	SWEET HONEY DRIPPER	COOKIE 8032	50.00	70's
NEVILLES, GAIL				
HE CAN'T DO WITHOUT ME	TAKING MY MIND OFF LOVE	STAR-TRACK 350	800.00	northern
HE CAN'T DO WITHOUT ME	TAKING MY MIND OFF LOVE	DOTTY'S 350	800.00	northern
NEVILLES, LARRY				
THIS TIME IT'S REAL	CERTAINLY LOVE	LARAY 101	15.00	70's
NEW ARRIVALS				
SOMEBODY ELSE	BIG TIME GIRL	PALMER 5004	40.00	northern
NEW CONCEPTS				
GIVE ME ANOTHER CHANCE	OVER THE RAINBOW	PHILIPS 40570	20.00	northern
NEW CYMBALS				
I WILL ALWAYS LOVE YOU	PLEASE BABY PLEASE	DE-LITE 554	10.00	70's
NEW FOUNDATIONS				
DARLING (YOU'RE ALL I NEED)	YOU TOOK MY OVE	ATLANTIC 3225	15.00	group
NEW GROUP				
LOVE CAN'T BE MODERNIZED	THERE'S THAT MOUNTAIN	GEMINI. 1005	25.00	northern
NEW HOLIDAYS				
MY BABY AIN'T NO PLAYTHING	MAYBE SO MAYBE NO	WESTBOUND 157	15.00	northern
NEW IMAGE AND THE CHARLES RUSSELL				
IT AIN'T EASY	I RODE TOO HIGH	BIONIC 1001	10.00	70's
NEW JERSEY CONNECTION				
LOVE DON'T COME EASY	SAME: INSTRUMENTAL	CARNIVAL 580	8.00	70's
NEW JERSEY QUEENS				
PARTY (AND DON'T WORRY ABOUT)	SAME: PT 2	MAGNET 2	50.00	funk
NEW PEOPLE				
TILL THE END OF THE TIME	I'M LOSING YOU	ALL STAR 42170 .	15.00	group
NEW PERSPECTIVE				
STONE OUTTA MY HEAD	IT WILL NEVER BE THE END	MAXWELL 807	10.00	northern
NEW PHASE				
LOE IS THE NAME OF THE GAME	PT.2	GAYTIME EAST 1003	50.00	70's
NEW SILHOUETTES				
WE BELONG TOGETHER	CLIMB EVERY MOUNTAIN	JAMIE 1333	40.00	northern
NEW WANDERERS				
AIN'T GONNA DO YOU NO HARM	LET ME RENDER MY SERVICE	READY 1002	1500.00	northern
THIS MAN IN LOVE	ADAM - AND EVE	READY 1006	50.00	northern
NEW WAY				
HOLDING ON	SAME: INSTRUMENTAL	PRESTIGE 109	75.00	70's
NEW WORLD				
THE WORLD TODAY	J.R.	VIRTUE	100.00	funk
NEW YORKERS				
AIN'T THAT NEWS	THERE'S GOING TO BE A WEDDING	TAC-FUL 102	25.00	northern
DON'T WANT TO BE YOUR FOOL	YOU SHOULD HAVE TOLD ME	RADIO CITY 101	350.00	northern
YOU SHOULD HAVE TOLD ME	THERE'S GOING TO BE A WEDDING	RADIO CITY 101	20.00	northern
DON'T WANT TO BE YOUR FOOL	YOU SHOULD HAVE TOLD ME	TAC-FUL 101	250.00	northern
NEW YOUNG HEARTS				
THE YOUNG HEARTS GET LONELY TO	WHY DID YOU HAVE TO GO	ZEA 50001	15.00	group
A LITTLE TOGETHERNESS	YOUNG HEARTS GET LONELY TO	SOULTOWN 10	20.00	northern
NEWBAG, JOHNNY				
GOT TO GET YOU BACK	THE POORER THE MAN	ATLANTIC 2355	50.00	northern
SWEET THING	LITTLE SAMSON	PORT 3008	60.00	northern
NEWBEATS				
TOO SWEET TO BE FORGOTTEN	SHAKE HANDS (AND COME OUT CRYI	HICKORY 1366	8.00	northern
CRYING MY HEART OUT	SHORT ON LOVE	HICKORY 1387	15.00	northern
DON'T TURN ME LOOSE	YOU AND ME AND HAPPINESS	HICKORY 1485	10.00	northern
I'M A TEARDROP	SHE WON'T HANG HER LOVE OUT	HICKORY 1569 DJ	8.00	northern
RUN, BABY RUN (BACK INTO MY ARMS)	MEAN WOOLY WILLIE	HICKORY 1332	8.00	northern
NEWBY, DIANE				
EVERYHING'S WRONG	THE BOY DON'T STAND A CHANCE	KAPP 716	30.00	northern
WHAT YOU'RE PUTIING ME THROUGH	SAY IT AGAIN	KAPP 692	30.00	northern
NEWCOMERS				
THE WHOLE WORLD'S A PICTURE SHOW	TOO MUCH GOING TO SAY GOODBYE	TRUTH 3213	15.00	70's
NEWDAY				
WAIT A MINUTE	JUST ANOTHER REASON	ON TOP 4207	25.00	northern
NEWLYWEDS				
THE QUARREL	LOVE WALKED OUT	FAT FISH 8002	400.00	group
THE QUARREL	LOVE WALKED OUT	HOMOGENIZED SOUL	800.00	group
NEWMAN, DAVEMAKE UP YOUR MIND	CAN'T TAKE NO FOR AN ANSWER	LOOK 5011	100.00	**northerB**
NEWMAN, TONY				
SOUL THING	LET THE GOOD TIMES ROLL	PARROT 40031	10.00	mod
NEWSOME, FRANKIE				
WE'RE ON OUR WAY	SAME:	WB 8056 DJ	20.00	70's

140

NEWSON, FRANKIE				
TAUNTING LOVE	IT'S A SHAME	USA 911	100.00	northern
NEWSOUND				
BET YOU NEVER THOUGHT ABOUT IT	JUST ONE TIME	SCORPION 1001	15.00	northern
NEWTON, BOBBY				
DO THE WHIP	SAME: INSTRUMENTAL	MERCURY 72894	15.00	mod
DON'T FIGHT THE FEELING	ALONE AND LONELY NIGHTS	LORRAINE 1401	20.00	northern
NEWTON, BOBBY AND THE BLOUNT, TINA				
YOUR LOVE GETS SWEETER EVERYDAY	HOW CAN I THANK YOU	INTREDPID 75014	15.00	northern
NIALATIONS				
I'LL TAKE YOU JUST AS YOU COME	SAME:	BRC 105 DJ	8.00	group
NICHOLS, BILLY.				
DIAMOND RING	MY WOMAN	WEST END 1226	15.00	70's
NICHOLS, BILLY AND THE FUNK				
TREAT YOUR NEIGHBOR	EXPRESSWAY TO YOUR HEART	MERCURY 73024	15.00	funk
NICK AND THE JAGUARS				
ICHI-I-BON #1	COOL AND CRAZY	TAMLA 5501	500.00	motown
NICKY NEWARKERS				
WOMAN	LEAVE ME OR LOVE ME	MERCURY 73812	200.00	70's
NIGHT RIDERS				
GIRLS IN THE CITY	SUPER LADY	ECLIPSE 35451	50.00	70's
NIGHT WATCH				
LIPS TO YOUR HEART	CLOUD TIME	ABC 10862	30.00	northern
NIGHTS				
(WHEN U DROP YOUR GUARD) LOVE	LET THERE BE LOVE	LITTLE STAR 1577	10.00	70's
LET THERE BE LOVE	COUNTRY GIRL	LITTLE STAR 1527	8.00	70's
9TH. STREET EXIT				
LET'S MAKE SWEET HARMONY	LET'S MAKE SWEET HARMONY Pt.2	SOLID FOUNDATION	10.00	70's
103				
NITE DREAMERS				
LATER FOR YOU	COUNT DOWN TO SLOW DOWN	ALWIN 103	100.00	northern
NITE TRAIN				
TO THE BITTER END	LET ME BABY YOU BABY	ROULETTE 7077	20.00	northern
NITE-LITERS				
AFRO-STRUT	(WE'VE GOT TO) PULL TOGETHER	RCA 591	8.00	funk
CON-FUNK-SHUN	DOWN AND DIRTY	RCA 374	8.00	funk
K-JEE	TANGA BOO GONK	RCA 461	8.00	funk
NITRO, BILLY				
AS SWEET AS YOUR LOVE FOR ME	MYSTIC LOVER	RESIST 110	300.00	ballad
NIVEN, DAVID				
YOU'RE FOR ME	WHAT YA WANNA DO	PARDNER 1000	100.00	70's
N-JOYS				
THE GIRL'S GOT A NEW STYLE	SHARE YOUR LOVE WITH ME	GRAY SOUNDS 4	100.00	group
NOBLE KNIGHTS				
SING A SIMPLE SONG	MOVIN' PART IV	COTILLION 44030	15.00	funk
NOBLE, BEVERLEY				
WHY MUST I CRY	YOU CHEATED	SPARROW 100	15.00	group
NOBLE, JOHNNY				
YOU'RE SO SMOOTH	NO USE CRYIN'	VEEP 1249	20.00	northern
NOBLES, CLIFF				
THIS FEELING OF LONLINESS	WE GOT OUR THING TOGETHER	ROULETTE 7142	15.00	northern
IS IT THE WAY	THE HORSE 1971	J-V 109	50.00	northern
MY LOVE IS GETTING STRONGER	TOO FOND OF YOU	J-V 1034	150.00	northern
MY LOVE IS GETTING STRONGER	TOO FOND OF YOU	ATLANTIC 2352	100.00	northern
YOUR LOVE IS ALL I NEED	EVERYBODY IS WEAK FOR SOMEBODY	ATLANTIC 2380	30.00	northern
NOEL, DIDI				
LET THE MUSIC PLAY	NO MORE TEARS TO CRY	BLUE CAT 129	15.00	northern
NOMADS				
SOMETHIN'S BAD	TELL HER NO LIES	MO-GROOVE 78240	500.00	northern
NORFOLK				
YOU ARE MY DOLL BABY	YOU ARE MY DOLL BABY PT.2	MIDNIGHT LOVE 1	40.00	70's
NORMAN, JIMMY				
I WANNA MAKE LOVE TO YOU	I'M FALLING IN LOVE:	BUDDAH 504	15.00	70's
GANSTER OF LOVE	GANGSTER OF LOVE Pt.2	JOSIE 994	15.00	funk
FAMILY TREE	IT'S BEAUTIFUL WHEN YOU'RE FAL	MERCURY 72658	15.00	northern
LOVE IS WONDERFUL	WHAT'S THE WORD, DO THE BIRD	LITTLE STAR 126	10.00	northern
THIS I BEG OF YOU	CAN YOU BLAME ME	SAMAR 116	10.00	northern
NORMAN, OLIVER				
DON'T MAKE PROMISES	REACH OUT	DECCA 32354	20.00	northern
DROWNING IN MY OWN DESPAIR	YOUR LOVE COUNTS	DECCA 32209	20.00	northern
NORTH, FREDDIE				
THE HURT	IT'S NO GOOD FOR ME	RIC. 119	100.00	northern
NORTH, PENNY				
THOUGHT I HAD A GOOD THING	SATISFIED	LUAU 5590	20.00	northern
NORVELLS				
WITHOUT YOU	WHY DO YOU WANT TO MAKE ME SAD	JANIS 6366	10.00	northern

Artist / Title	B-side	Label	Price	Category
WITHOUT YOU	WHY DO YOU WANT TO MAKE ME SAD	PENNY 107	15.00	northern
NOTATIONS				
SUPERPEOPLE	IT ONLY HURTS FOR A LITTLE WHILE	GEMIGO 103	10.00	funk
AT THE CROSSROADS	A NEW DAY	TWINIGHT 148	10.00	group
TRYING MY BEST TO FIND HER	GONNA GET READY	TAD 205	150.00	northern
NOTEABLES				
FUNKY FROG	GET READY	SOUND CITY 001	25.00	funk
NOVA'S NINE				
WHY LISTEN	PAIN	ABC 11127	15.00	northern
NOW				
CHAINED	DESPERADO	HIT CITY 9	10.00	70's
GIRL YOU SURE TURN ME ON	SAME: PT.II	FEE 303	10.00	70's
NU LUVS				
HELLO LOVER	BABY YOU BELONG TO ME	CLOCK 2003	20.00	northern
NUE SPECTRUM				
JUST A LITTLE LOVE (GOES A ONG	A MESSAGE	FLO-JAY 101	20.00	group
NUMONICS				
FOREVER AND A DAY	YOU LIED	HODISH 6	10.00	70's
FOREVER AND A DAY	TIME BRING'S ABOUT CHANGES	HODISH 000	20.00	70's
NU-RONS				
ALL MY LIFE	I'M A LOSER	NU-RON 1060	800.00	northern
NU-SOUND EXPRESS LTD				
AIN'T IT GOOD ENOUGH	I'VE BEEN TRYING	SILVER DOLLAR 152	10.00	funk
ONE MORE TIME YOU ALL	A ROSE FOR THE LADY	SILVER DOLLAR	10.00	funk

O

Artist / Title	B-side	Label	Price	Category
O, LE FRANK				
KEEP ON GETTIN' DOWN	SAME Pt. 2	M M-M GOLD 500	30.00	70's
OBJECTIVES				
LOVE WENT AWAY	OH MY LOVE	JEWEL 751	20.00	northern
OBOE				
TRYING TO MAKE IT	I'M JUST THAT KIND OF FOOL FOR	GOLDWAX 304	15.00	ballad
O'BRIEN, BETTY				
SHE'LL BE GONE	LOVE OH! LOVE	LIBERTY 55365	200.00	**northerB**
OBSESSION				
WHAT DO YOU THINK ABOUT THAT B	MUSIC TO MY HEART	HAPPY TIGER 531	10.00	northern
OCCASIONS				
THERE'S NO YOU	BABY DON'T GO	BIG JIM 3273	15.00	group
OCEANLINERS				
CUTTING ROOM		BLUE CANDLE	150.00	funk
OCEANS, SONNY				
PITY ME	I'M HER LOVER MAN	COLUMBIA 43422	20.00	northern
PITY ME	I'M HER LOVER MAN	COLUMBIA 43422 PS	25.00	northern
ODD SQUAD				
JUST TO SEE YOUR FACE	SOUL POWER	MINIT 32088	30.00	northern
ODDIS, RAY				
HAPPY GHOUL TIDE	RANDY, THE NEWSPAPER BOY	V.I.P. 25012	25.00	motown
ODDS AND ENDS				
LET ME TRY	FOOT TRACK	TODAY 1001	15.00	70's
O'DELL, BROOKS				
WALKIN' IN THE SHADOW OF LOVE	IT HURTS ME TO MY HEART	BELL 612	20.00	ballad
I'M YOUR MAN	SHIRLEY, REMEMBER ME	GOLD 216	10.00	northern
STANDING TALL	THE LIVELY ONES	COLUMBIA 43664	50.00	northern
WATCH YOUR STEP	WALK ON BY	GOLD 214	10.00	northern
YOU BETTER MAKE UP YOUR MIND	SLOW MOTION	BELL 618	20.00	northern
ODOM, JOE				
BABY	SAME:	CAPITOL 3311	8.00	ballad
ODYSSEY				
OUR LIVES ARE SHAPED BY WHAT WE KNOW	BROKEN ROAD	MOWEST 5022	30.00	70's
OFFENBACH				
JUDY IN DISGUISE	NO LETTER TODAY	PAULA 293	10.00	northern
O'HARA, CHARLOTTE				
WHAT ABOUT YOU	DAYDREAMS	AVA 126	50.00	northern

O'HENRY, LENNY

ACROSS THE STREET	SATURDAY ANGEL	ATCO 6291	20.00	northern
MR.MOONLIGHT	BURNING MEMORIES	SMASH 1800	30.00	northern

OHIO PLAYERS

VAREE IS LOVE	WALT'S FIRST TRIP	WESTBOUND 208	10.00	group
IT'S A CRYING SHAME	I'VE GOT TO HOLD ON	COMPASS 7018	15.00	northern
YOU DON'T MEAN IT	TRESPASSIN'	COMPASS 7015	15.00	northern

O'JAHS

ROADSIDE 75	LET IT ALL HANG OUT	SS7 2599	20.00	mod

O'JAYS

JUST TO BE WITH YOU	NOW HE'S HOME	LITTLE STAR 1401	20.00	70's
LOOKY LOOKY (LOOK AT ME GIRL)	LET ME IN YOUR WORLD	NEPTUNE 31	8.00	northern
BRANDED BAD	YOU'RE THE BEST THING SINCE CANDY	NEPTUNE 18	8.00	northern
CAN'T TAKE IT	MIRACLES	APOLLO 759	15.00	northern
HOLD ON	WORKING ON YOUR CASE	MINIT 32015	10.00	northern
I DIG YOUR ACT	I'LL BE SWEETER TOMORROW	BELL 691	15.00	northern
I WON'T HURT	I'LL NEVER LET YOU GO	IMPERIAL 66145	15.00	northern
I'LL NEVER FORGET YOU	PRETTY WORDS	IMPERIAL 66162	85.00	northern
I'M SO GLAD I FOUND YOU	LOOK OVER YOUR SHOULDER	BELL 704	10.00	northern
LIPSTICK TRACES	THINK IT OVER, BABY	IMPERIAL 66102	15.00	northern
LOOKY LOOKY (LOOK AT ME GIRL)	LET ME IN YOUR WORLD	NEPTUNE 31 DJ	10.00	northern
NO TIME FOR YOU	A BLOWING WIND	IMPERIAL 66177	20.00	northern
OH, HOW YOU HURT ME	GIRL MACHINE	IMPERIAL 66076	10.00	northern
ONE NIGHT AFFAIR	THERE'S SOMEONE	NEPTUNE 12	8.00	northern
WHIP IT ON ME BABY	I'VE CRIED MY LAST TEAR	IMPERIAL 66121	10.00	northern

O'KAYSIONS

LOVE MACHINE	DEDICATED TO THE ONE I LOVE	ABC 11153	8.00	northern
GIRL WATCHER	DEAL ME IN	NORTH STATE 1001	30.00	northern
GIRL WATCHER	DEAL ME IN	ABC 11094	10.00	northern
WATCH OUT GIRL	HAPPINESS	COTILLION 44089	10.00	northern
GIRL WATCHER	DEAL ME IN	NORTH STATE 1001	30.00	northern

OLENN, JOHNNY

GOTTA KEEP MOVIN		DEE DEE 2000	40.00	northern

OLIVER, BENNY C.

MAKE IT NOW	BEFORE YOU GO	OJOBCO 1	75.00	northern

OLIVER, FRAN

YOU WION'T GET AWAY	TOMORROW MAY NEVER COME	BBS 579	25.00	northern

OLIVER, WES

KEEP THE FAITH	I CONFESS	STAR FIRE 19671	100.00	northern

OLLIE AND THE THE NIGHTINGALES

GIRL, YOU HAVE MY HEART SINGIN	I GOT A SURE THING	STAX 245	10.00	northern

OLYMPICS

BABY, DO THE PHILLY DOG	WESTERN MOVIES	MIRWOOD 5523	8.00	northern
HULLY GULLY	BIG BOY PETE	MIRWOOD 5533	8.00	northern
GIRL, YOU'RE MY KIND OF PEOPLE	PLEASE, PLEASE PLEASE	WB 7369	15.00	northern
PAPA WILL	I FEEL YOUR LOVE (COMING ON)	MAC WINN 102	50.00	funk
NO MORE WILL I CRY	BABY I'M YOURS	LOMA 2017	40.00	northern
OLYMPIC SHUFFLE	GOOD LOVIN'	LOMA `2013	10.00	northern
THE DUCK	THE BUNCE	CRESTVIEW 20010	10.00	northern
THE SAME OLD THING	I'LL DO A LITTLE MORE	MIRWOOD 5529	10.00	northern
WE GO TOGETHER	SECRET AGENTS	MIRWOOD 5504	15.00	northern

OMNI

KEYS TO THE CITY	DON'T BE SELFISH	FOUNTAIN 100	8.00	70's

ONCOMING TIMES

IF YOU HAD MY LOVE	WHAT IS LIFE WITHOUT LOVE	DUO 7459	40.00	northern

ONE G PLUS THREE

SUMMERTIME	POQUITO SOUL	GORDO 705	15.00	funk

125TH. ST.CANDY STORE

PIECE BY PIECE	IS IT LOVE	UPTITE 13	20.00	70's
LOVING YOU BABY IS SO VERY HAR	PIECE BY PIECE	UPTITE 10	20.00	70's
LOVING YOU BABY IS SO VERY HAR	TRIBUTE TO JUDY	UPTITE 16	15.00	northern

ONE HUNDRED YEARS TIME

IF IT'S FEELING YOU WANT (WE G	TAKE CARE OF MY LOVE	V.I.P. 100	20.00	funk

ONEDERFUL BAND

HONEY IN THE BEE-BO	BLACK IS BEAUTIFUL	ONEDERFUL 4853	15.00	funk

ONENESS

THANK YOU	THE BOSS	BOTH SIDES 15173	15.00	group

ONES

HAPPY DAY	YOU HAVEN'T SEEN MY LOVE	SPIRIT 1 DJ	15.00	motown
YOU HAVEN'T SEEN MY LOVE	HAPPY DAY	MOTOWN 1117	10.00	motown

ONLY THREE

DIG IT	(DOWN TO THE SOUL BROTHERS) DJ BALL	WALANA 101	100.00	northern

ONYX

YOU NEVER FAIL TO AMAZE	SOMETHING YOU'RE TRYING TO HID	YEW 1008	40.00	northern

OPALS

DOES IT MATTER	TENDER LOVER	OKEH 7188	75.00	northern
I'M SO AFRAID	RESTLESS DAYS	OKEH 7224	75.00	northern
YOU'RE GONNA BE SORRY	YOU CAN'T HURT ME NO MORE	OKEH 7202	75.00	northern

ORACLES
I AIN'T GOT TIME	LOVE IN MY HEART	O-M 1967	700.00	northern

ORANGE COLOURED SKY
HELP	PRESS A ROSE	PEOPLE 1007	10.00	northern

ORDELLS
SIPPIN' A CUP OF COFFEE	BIG DOM	DIONN 505	20.00	group

ORGANICS
FOOT STOMPING	GOOD THING GOING	COMPOSE 126	50.00	funk

ORIENTALS
SOUL AIN'T YOU THRILLED	MISTY SUMMER NIGHT	NEW DAWN 413	60.00	northern

ORIGINAL BREED
THE PROPHET	I'M SOMEBODY	KAROL 725	30.00	northern

ORIGINAL CADILLACS
I'LL NEVER LET YOU GO	WAYWARD WANDERER	JOSIE 915	40.00	northern

ORIGINAL LARKS (also see DON AND THE DOVES)
TOGETHER	I NEED YOU	SHAZAM 1001	100.00	northern

ORIGINAL SOUL PATROL
SOUL PATROL		MAR-KEE	100.00	funk

ORIGINALS
GOOD LOVIN' IS JUST A DIME AWAY	NOTHING CAN TAKE THE PLACE	MOTOWN 1355	8.00	70's
I'M SOMEONE WHO CARES	ONCE I HAVE YOU (I'LL NEVER LET YOU GO)	SOUL 35093	8.00	70's
OOH YOU (PUT A CRUSH ON ME)	TOUCH	SOUL 35117	8.00	70's
OOH YOU (PUT A CRUSH ON ME)	GAME CALLED LOVE	SOUL 35113	8.00	70's
BABY, I'M FOR REAL	MOMENT OF TRUTH	SOUL 35066	8.00	motown
GOOD NIGHT IRENE	NEED YOUR LOVING (WANT YOU BACK)	SOUL 35029	15.00	motown
I LIKE YOUR STYLE	WE CAN MAKE IT BABY	SOUL 35074	8.00	motown
KEEP ME	A MAN WITHOUT KNOWLEDGE	SOUL 35085	8.00	motown

ORLONS
THE WAH-WATUSI	HOLIDAY HILL	CAMEO 218	10.00	northern
DON'T THROW YOUR LOVE AWAY	BON-DOO-WAH	CAMEO 287	10.00	northern
DON'T YOU WANT MY LOVIN'	I CAN'T TAKE IT	CAMEO 372	15.00	northern
ENVY	NO LOVE BUT YOUR LOVE	CAMEO 384	40.00	northern
ONCE UPON A TIME	KISSIN' TIME	ABC 10948	10.00	**northerB**
SPINNING TOP	ANYONE WHO HAD A HEART	CALLA 113	20.00	northern
IT'S NO BIG THING	CROSSFIRE!	CAMEO 273 PS	15.00	northern
NOT ME	MY BEST FRIEND	CAMEO 257 PS	15.00	northern

ORSI, PHIL
LOVE IS SLIPPING AWAY	CALIFORNIA SUN	BLUE SOUL 9877	100.00	northern

ORTIZ, PETER
OH MY DARLING	LOSER	R CADE 101	15.00	northern

OSBORN, RICHETTA
MY SWEET BABY	CALIFORNIA SOUND	BLUE RIVER 226	300.00	northern

OSBORNE, KELL
QUICKSAND	THE LONELY BOY SONG	TITANIC 5008	350.00	northern
YOU CAN'T OUTSMART A WOMAN	THAT'S WHATS HAPPENING	LOMA 2023	30.00	northern
LAW AGAINST A HEARTBREAKER		HIGHLAND	1000.00	northern
SMALL THINGS (MAKE A DIFFERENC	NOTHING FROM NOTHING LEAVES NO	NEW BAG 101	750.00	northern
YOU CAN'T OUTSMART A WOMAN	THAT'S WHAT'S HAPPENING	LOMA 2023	30.00	northern

OTHER BROTHERS
BRING IT HOME TO ME GIRL	MINI DRESS	AMY 11005	50.00	group
NO CLASS		PET NO#	100.00	funk
IT'S BEEN A LONG TIME BABY	HOLE IN THE WALL	MODERN 1027	20.00	northern
LET'S GET TOGETHER	LITTLE GIRL	AMY 11033 DJ	15.00	northern

OTHER ONES (also see PLAYERS IV)
THE TWO OF US	THE GIRL IN THE SHADE	KNOLL 500	150.00	northern

OTIS, CHARLES
I SEE LOVE GIRL	I WONDER WILL YOU ALWAYS LOVE	CARALJO 2	150.00	northern

OTISETTES
EVERYTHING YOU SAID CAME TRUE	SITTING ALONE (IN MY LONELY RO	EPIC 10879	10.00	northern

OUR BROTHERS KEEPER
YOU BEEN A LONG TIME CMOIN'	SAME:	COLUMBIA 45239	25.00	northern

OUR LADIES OF SOUL
DON'T MAKE IT IMPOSSIBLE	LET'S GROOVE TOGETHER	KELTON 2002	25.00	northern

OUT CROWD
GET YOURSELF TOGETHER	PT.3	OMEN 11	15.00	mod

OUT OF SIGHTS
MY WOMAN'S LOVE	I WAS WRONG	SARU 1618	40.00	northern
FOR THE REST OF MY LIFE	YOU MADE ME BEG	SARU 1610	400.00	northern
I CAN'T TAKE IT	BABY YOU GOT IT	SARU 1612	20.00	group
TEARS DON'T CARE WHO CRY	I'VE GOT TO BE ME	SARU 1615	100.00	group

OUTER LIMITS
JUST ONE MORE CHANCE	HELP ME PLEASE	DERAM 7508	20.00	northern

OUTSIDERS
TIME WON'T LET ME	WAS IT REALLY REAL	CAPITOL 5573	8.00	northern

OVATIONS
I'M IN LOVE	DON'T SAY YOU LOVE ME (IF YOU	MGM 14705	10.00	70's
ONE IN A MILLION	SO NICE TO BE LOVED BY YOU	MGM SOUNDS OF MEMPHI S 717	10.00	70's

144

DON'T BREAK YOUR PROMISE	TOUCHING ME	MGM SOUNDS OF MEMPHIS 708	10.00	northern
I'M LIVING GOOD	RECIPE FOR LOVE	GOLDWAX 117	8.00	group
RECIPE FOR LOVE	I'M LIVING GOOD	GOLDWAX 117	10.00	group
QUALIFICATIONS	I BELIEVE I'LL GO BACK HOME	GOLDWAX 306	15.00	northern
ROCKIN' CHAIR	HAPPINESS	GOLDWAX 341	30.00	northern
THEY SAY	ME AND MY IMAGINATION	GOLDWAX 314	10.00	**northerB**
SWEET THING	TILL I FIND SOME WAY	XL 120	10.00	70's

OVERTON, C.B.

SUPERSTAR LADY	WHEN IT RAINS IT POURS	SHOCK 13	15.00	70's

OVERTON, CHUCK

I'M SO THANKFUL	IS IT POSSIBLE	KAPP 2101	20.00	northern
I'M SO THANKFUL	IS IT POSSIBLE	MOONVILLE	20.00	northern

OWENS, DANNY

I CAN'T BE A FOOL FOR YOU	WHAT AM I LIVING FOR	MANHATTAN 804	600.00	northern

OWENS, GARLAND

I WANT TO KNOW IF YOU LOVE ME	DANCING WITH TEARS IN MY EYES	LEMONDE 1502	40.00	northern

OWENS, GWEN.

YOU BETTER WATCH OUT	EVERYBODY NEEDS LOVE	CASABLANCA 808	8.00	70's
JUST SAY YOU'RE WANTED	STILL TRUE TO YOU	VELGO 2	1500.00	**northerB**
MAKE HIM MINE	ONE MORE DAY	LAU-REEN 1002	200.00	northern
MYSTERY MAN	SOMEONE TO LOVE	ONCORE 84	700.00	northern
KEEP ON LIVING	IT AIN'T HARDLY OVER	JOSIE 1009 DJ	10.00	northern
I'LL BE CRYING	I LOST A GOOD THING	VELGO 1 green	100.00	northern
I'LL BE CRYING	I LOST A GOOD THING	VELGO 1 black	100.00	northern
LIES	RAIN	MEL-ADY 100	10.00	northern

OWENS, TONY

I NEED, I NEED YOUR LOVE	I'M A FOOL FOR LOVIN' YOU	SOULIN 147	40.00	northern
WISHING, WAITING, HOPING	SAME:	SOULIN 146	25.00	northern
ALL THAT MATTERS	I DON'T WANT NOBODY BUT MY BABY	BUDDAH 471	30.00	70's
YOU GOT TO PAY THE PRICE	ONE MAN'S WOMAN ANOTHER MAN'S	LISTENING POST 101	20.00	northern
THIS HEART CAN'T TAKE NO MORE	I GOT SOUL	SOUL SOUND 145	15.00	northern

OXFORD NIGHTS

I'M SUCH A LONELY ONE	JUST GIVE US TIME	DELPHI 16	1500.00	northern

OZZ AND THE SPERLINGS

CAN YOU QUALIFY	DADDY ROLLIN' STONE	GOLDENWAY 501	300.00	northern
DANCE (HOLES IN YOUR SHOES)	I CAN'T JERK	VILLA. 702	40.00	northern
SOMEBODY TO LOVE	A STRONG SHOULDER TO CRY ON	M.I.O.B. 1282	40.00	northern

P

P.G. (also see GENE PITNEY)

SHE'S A HEARTBREAKER	CONQUISTOR	MUSICOR 1306 DJ only	15.00	northern

P.J.

T.L.C. (TENDER LOVING CARE)	IT TAKES A MAN A TEACH WOMAN H	TAMLA 54215	10.00	70's

PACE SETTERS

MY SHIP IS COMING IN (TOMORROW)	VICTIM OF LONELINESS	MICA 503	100.00	northern

PACE, ROGER

BETTER KNOW WHAT YOU'RE DOING	LET THIS CRAZY WORLD GO BY	TWIRL 2023	25.00	northern
THE MINUTE MY BACK WAS TURNED	HEY HEY MY BABY'S GONE	SELECT 744	75.00	northern

PACESETTERS

THE MONKEY WHIP	SAME: INSTRUMENTAL	CORREC-TONE 3476	15.00	northern
FREEDOM AND JUSTICE	PUSH ON JESSIE JACKSON	KENT 4565	15.00	funk

PACETTES

DON'T READ THE LETTER	YOU DON'T KNOW BABY	REGINA 306	15.00	northern

PACKERS

HOLE IN THE WALL	GO 'HEAD ON	PURE SOUL MUSIC 1107	10.00	mod
JUICY LUCY	COME HERE MY LOVE	MARK II 102	10.00	mod
STEAL AWAY	STEAL AWAY PT. 2	SOUL BABY 1	10.00	mod

PAGE, PATTI

YOU DON'T NEED A HEART	BOY FROM THE COUNTRY	COLUMBIA 44989	40.00	northern

PAGE, PRISCILLA

I'M PRETENDING	THROW THE POOR DOG	TOPPER 1010	25.00	northern

PAGE, RICKIE

I CRY INSIDE	I'M HIS GIRL	EPIC 9841	50.00	northern

PAGEANTS

ARE YOU EVER COMING HOME	I'M A VICTIM	RCA 8601	20.00	northern
SHE IS YOUR GIRL	MAKE IT LAST	GROOVE 56	20.00	northern

PAGES
HEARTACHES & PAIN	MACK	SUNSTRUCK 1001	30.00	**northerB**

PAIGE, RAY
DON'T STOP NOW	AIN'T NO SOUL LEFT IN THESE OLD SHOES	RCA 9047	40.00	northern

PAIGE, WESLEY
I'VE GOT TO FIND OUT FOR MYSELF	BETTER DAYS ARE COMING	ROJAC 113	10.00	northern
YOU TURN ME AROUND	BLAME IT ON YOUR LOVE	ROJAC 125	20.00	northern
YOU TURNED ME AROUND	OH MY GOODNESS	ROJAC 1008	50.00	northern

PAINE, JACKIE
GO GO TRAIN	I'LL BE HOME	JETSTREAM 725	10.00	mod
NO PUPPY LOVE		JETSTREAM 729	20.00	northern
NO PUPPY LOVE		JETSTREAM 737	15.00	northern

PAIR EXTRAORDINAIRE
PATIENCE BABY	FIGHT FOR YOUR GIRL	LIBERTY 55748	20.00	northern

PALLBEARERS
MUSIC WITH SOUL	LOVE IS A MANY SPLENDOUR THING	DELPHI 11	50.00	northern
MUSIC WITH SOUL	LOVE IS A MANY SPLENDOUR THING	FONTANA 1603	20.00	northern
GETTING' FIRED UP	EVERY MAN NEEDS A WOMAN	FONTANA 1624	15.00	northern

PAMOJA
OOOH, BABY	ONLY THE LONELY KNOW	KEIPER 60848	50.00	northern

PANDORAS
CALL ME	SWEETHEART, SWEETHEART	OLIVER 2003	15.00	northern

PANE, DIANE
WHAT SIDE YOUR BREAD IS BUTTER	WISHING IT WAS YOU	LOGO 501	100.00	northern

PANIC BUTTONS
COME OUT SMOKIN'	BAD KARMA	GAMBLE 236	20.00	funk
O-WOW	SAME:	GAMBLE 230	10.00	funk
O-WOW	LISA	CHALOM 102	15.00	funk

PAPA BEAR AND THE CUBS
YOU'RE SO FINE	SWEETEST THING THIS SIDE HEAVE	SMS 1002	40.00	northern

PAPA'S RESULTS
SISTER SHEILA	SAME: INSTRUMENTAL	SAL WA 1002	10.00	funk

PARADISE
TELL HER	WE BELONG TOGETHER	PHIL LA SOUL 385	100.00	70's

PARAGONS
OH LOVIN' YOU	CON ME	BUDDAH 478 DJ	100.00	70's

PARAMOUNTS
COME GO WITH ME	I DON'T WANT TO LOSE YOU	OLE 101	25.00	northern
I WON'T SHARE YOUR LOVE	GIRLS WITH THE BIG BLACK BOOTS	MERCURY 72429	40.00	northern
UNTIL I MET YOU	ALL I WANT TO DO IS WAIT	CABELL 114	100.00	northern
UNDER YOUR SPELL	TIME WILL BRING ABOUT A CHANGE	MAGNUM 722	50.00	northern

PARAMOUNT FOUR
YOU DON'T KNOW	I'VE MADE UP MY MIND	SOUTHERN CITY 1114	30.00	northern

PARFAYS
YOU GOT A GOOD THING GOIN' BOY	IN THE BEGINNING	FONTANA 1526	30.00	northern

PARIS
SLEEPLESS NIGHTS	WISHING WELL	DOC 102	700.00	**northerB**

PARIS SISTERS
LONG AFTER TONIGHT IS ALL OVER	SOME OF YOUR LOVIN'	REPRISE 548	30.00	northern

PARIS, BOBBY
NIGHT OWL	TEARS ON MY PILLOW	CAMEO 396	100.00	**northerB**
PER-SO-NAL-LY	TRAGEDY	TETRAGRAMMATON 1504	15.00	**northerB**
I WALKED AWAY	KANSAS CITY	CAPITOL 5929	100.00	northern

PARIS, FREDDIE
FACE IT, BOY, IT'S OVER	LITTLE THINGS CAN MAKE A WOMAN	RCA 9358 DJ	20.00	northern
TAKE ME AS I AM	IT'S O.K. TO CRY NOW	RCA 9232	20.00	northern

PARIS, HARI
YOU HIT MY LOVE	SAME:INSTRUMENTAL	CAREDAJA 1956	10.00	70's

PARISIANS
TWINKLE LITTLE STAR	THE COCKROACH	DEMON HOT 1	130.00	northern

PARKER, BRENDA
HELP ME FIND MR. GOOD MAN	SAME: INSTRUMENTAL.	BLACK FALCON 19104	15.00	70's

PARKER, EDDIE
BODY CHAINS	SAME: INSTRUMENTAL	PRODIGAL 617	10.00	70's
CRYING CLOWN	I NEED A TRUE LOVE	TRIPLE B 1	15.00	northern
I'M GONE	CRYING CLOWN	AWAKE 502	1200.00	**northerB**
LOVE YOU BABY	SAME: INSTRUMENTAL	ASHFORD 1	20.00	**northerB**
BUT IF YOU MUST GO		MIKO 803	700.00	ballad

PARKER, ELBIE
PLEASE KEEP AWAY FROM ME	LUCKY GUY	VEEP 1246	200.00	northern

PARKER, ELMA
GOING TO LOUISIANA		RARE BIRD	75.00	funk

PARKER, GLORIA
IF YOU'VE EVER LOVED SOMEONE	HELLO BABY - GOODBYE TOO	LLP 104	15.00	ballad
THE BEST THING FOR YOU BABY	HEADED IN THE RIGHT DIRECTION	SAMAR 118	25.00	northern
WHY CAN'T WE GET TOGETHER	I'M IN YOUR CORNER	LLP 102	8.00	northern

PARKER, HANK
DON'T LEAVE ME		TUBA 1700	100.00	northern

PARKER, JUNIOR
I'M SO SATIFIED	AIN'T GONNABE NO CUTTING LOOSE	BLUE ROCK 4080	15.00	northern
YOU CAN'T KEEP A GOOD MAN DOWN	EASY LOVIN'	BLUE ROCK 4088	15.00	northern
THESE KIND OF BLUES	SAME: Pt 2.	DUKE 394	10.00	northern

PARKER, MILTON
WOMEN LIKE IT HARDER	ANYHOW	CLOSET 3101	600.00	northern

PARKER, PAULETTE
(GIMME BACK) MY LOVE	SHOULD I LET HIM GO	DUKE 451	20.00	northern

PARKER, RICHARD
GOT TO FIND A WAY	YOU'RE ALL i NEED	COMMONWEALTH 3013	10.00	northern
SUGAR LOVE	YOU'RE ALL I NEED	RIGHT ON 106	15.00	northern

PARKER, ROBERT
BAREFOOTIN'	LET'S GO BABY (WHERE THE ACTIO	NOLA 721	8.00	northern
TIP TOE	SOUL KIND OF LOVING	NOLA 729	8.00	northern
I CAUGHT YOU IN A LIE	HOLDIN' OUT	NOLA 738	20.00	northern

PARKER, WILLIE
DON'T HURT THE ONE YOU LOVE	THE TOWN I LIVE IN	M-PAC 7237	20.00	northern
SALUTE TO LOVERS	DON'T HURT THE ONE YOU LOVE	M-PAC 735	30.00	northern
I'VE GOT TO FIGHT IT		M-PAC 7233	20.00	northern

PARKER, WINFIELD
I WANNA BE WITH YOU	MY OVE FOR YOU	P&L 62142	40.00	70's
I'M ON MY WAY	S.O.S. (STOP HER ON SIGHT)	SPRING 116	10.00	70's
OH MY LOVE	SHE'S SO PRETTY	RU-JAC 22	15.00	ballad
TRUST ME	BABY DON'T GET HOOKED ON ME	GSF 6883	30.00	northern
I LOVE YOU JUST THE SAME	MY LOVE	RU-JAC 17 blue	250.00	northern
I LOVE YOU JUST THE SAME	MY LOVE	RU-JAC 17 yellow	20.00	northern
SWEET LITTLE GIRL	WHAT DO YOU SAY	ATCO 6474	20.00	northern
SWEET LITTLE GIRL	WHAT DO YOU SAY	RU-JAC 20	40.00	northern
WILL THERE EVER BE ANOTHER LOVE		WAND 11218	100.00	northern

PARKINSON, DOUG *Australian only release*
I'LL BE AROUND	RIFF RAFF	SOUTHERN STAR 7309	60.00	70's

PARKS, GINO
BLIBBER BLABBER	DON'T SAY BYE BYE	MIRACLE 3 NI	200.00	motown
FIRE	FOR THIS I THANK YOU	TAMLA 54066	45.00	motown
MY SOPHISTICATED LADY	TALKIN' ABOUT MY BABY	GOLDEN WORLD 32	10.00	motown
SAME THING	THAT'S NO LIE	TAMLA 54042	50.00	motown
SOMETHING WILL HAPPEN TO YOU	THAT'S NO LIE	TAMLA 54108	400.00	motown
NERVES OF STEEL	HELP ME SOMEBODY	CRAZY HORSE 1303	60.00	northern

PARLIAMENTS
THE GOOSE (THAT LAID THE GOLDEN EGG)	LITTLE MAN	REVILOT 214	10.00	funk
TIME	GOOD OLE MUSIC	REVILOT 223	10.00	funk
I'LL GET YOU YET	YOU'RE CUTE	SYMBOL 917	50.00	group
(I WANNA) TESTIFY	I CAN FEEL THE ICE MELTING	REVILOT 207	10.00	northern
A NEW DAY BEGINS	I'LL WAIT	ATCO 6675	15.00	northern
A NEW DAY BEGINS	I'LL WAIT	REVILOT 228 NI	100.00	northern
CRY NO MORE	SWEET NOTHIN	CABELL 112	300.00	northern
DON'T BE SORE AT ME	ALL YOUR GOODIES ARE GONE	REVILOT 211	15.00	**northerB**
HEART TROUBLE	THAT WAS MY GIRL	GOLDEN WORLD 46	100.00	northern
LOOK AT WHAT I ALMOST MISSED	WHAT YOU BEEN GROWING	REVILOT 217	10.00	northern

PARRIS, FRED AND THE RESTLESS HEARTS
LAND OF BROKEN HEARTS	BRING IT HOME DADDY	ATCO 6439	10.00	northern
DARK AT THE TOP OF THE STAIRS	BENEDICTION	BIRTH 101	15.00	northern
I'LL BE HANGING ON	I CAN REALLY SATISFY	GREEN SEA 107	20.00	northern
BLUSHING BRIDE	GIVING MY LOVE TO YOU	GREEN SEA 106	20.00	northern

PARRISH, DEAN
TELL HER	FALL ON ME	BOOM 60012	15.00	**northerB**
SKATE	SKATE PT.2	BOOM 60038	15.00	mod
BRICKS BROKEN BOTTLES & STICKS	I'M OVER EIGHTEEN	MUSICOR 1099	100.00	northern
DETERMINATION	TURN ON YOUR LOVELIGHT	BOOM 60016	20.00	**northerB**
I'M ON MY WAY	WATCH OUT	LAURIE 3418	20.00	**northerB**

PARRISH
YOUR SMILE	FREE TO GO	UPTITE 22	20.00	northern

PARTNERSHIP
NOT FOR LOVE NOR MONEY	BABY, IF I HAD YOU	MGM 13854	15.00	northern
SEARCHIN' FORTY FLOORS	I MISS YOU DIXIE	RCA 9226	10.00	northern

PARTY BROTHERS
DO THE GROUNDHOG	NASSAU DADDY	REVUE 110047	10.00	northern

PARTY FAVORS
CHANGED DISPOSITION	YOU'RE NOT THE MARRYING KIND	RSVP 1109	60.00	northern

PASSION
DON'T BRING BACK MEMORIES	MIDNIGHT LOVERS	PRELUDE 8008	8.00	70's

PASSIONETTS
I'M NOT IN LOVE ANYMORE WITH YOU	MY LIFE DEPENDS ON YOU	SOUL BURST 501	40.00	northern

PASSIONS
BABY, I DO	MAN ABOUT TOWN	BACK BEAT 573	10.00	group
IF YOU SEE MY BABY	RUNNING OUT OF TEARS	EL VIRTUE	600.00	northern
TO MANY MEMORIES	THE REASON	FANTASTIC 79	15.00	northern

TO MANY MEMORIES	THE REASON	UNIQUE 79	10.00	northern
WITHOUT A WARNING	I CAN SEE MY WAY THROUGH	TOWER 443	15.00	northern

PASTELS

BEEN SO LONG	SAME: INSTRUMENTAL	QUALITY SOUND 1	25.00	group

PAT AND THE BLENDERS

DON'T SAY YOU LOVE ME (UNLESS	(THEY CALL ME) CANDY MAN	GAMBLE 2504	15.00	group
(ALL I NEED IS YOUR)GOOD GOOD LOVING	JUST BECAUSE	FAST EDDIE 102	200.00	northern
JUST BECAUSE	SAME: INSTRUMENTAL	FAST EDDIE 102	40.00	northern

PATCHES

I'M GONNA MAKE THIS WORLD A BE	SAME: INSTRUMENTAL	PHAX 2002	10.00	70's

PATIENCE

THIS IS ALL I CAN SAY	SHAME ON YOU	SOUNDS ON SOLID	40.00	northern
GROU 1002				

PATTEN, ALEXANDER

A LIL LOVIN SOMETIMES	NO MORE DREAMS	CAPITOL 5677	100.00	**northerB**

PATTERSON TWINS

GONNA FIND A TRUE LOVE	SAME:	COMMERCIAL 42 DJ	300.00	70's

PATTERSON, BOBBY AND THE MUSTANGS

I GET MY GROOVE FROM YOU	WHAT GOES AROUND COMES AROUND	PAULA 386	40.00	70's
TAKE TIME TO KNOW THE TRUTH	IT TAKES TWO TO DO WRONG	PAULA 379	8.00	ballad
MY THING IS YOUR THING	KEEPING IT IN THE FAMILY	JETSTAR 115	15.00	funk
BUSY, BUSY BEE	SWEET TASTE OF LOVE	JETSTAR 113	10.00	northern
DON'T BE SO MEAN	THE GOOD OL DAYS	JETSTAR 112	15.00	northern
I'M IN LOVE WITH YOU	MARRIED LADY	JETSTAR 121	40.00	northern
MY BABY COMING BACK TO ME	GUESS WHO	JETSTAR 117	10.00	northern
MY BABY'S COMING BACK TO ME	WHAT A WONDERFUL NIGHT FOR LOVE	JETSTAR 116	10.00	northern
THE KNOCK OUT POWER OF LOVE	THE TRIAL OF MARY MAGUIRE	JETSTAR 118	15.00	northern
TILL YOU GIVE IN	LONG AGO	JETSTAR 108	10.00	northern
WHAT A WONDERFUL NIGHT FOR LOV	T.C.B. OR T.Y.A.	JETSTAR 114	10.00	northern
I MET MY MATCH	BROADWAY AIN'T FNKY NO MORE	JETSTAR 111	10.00	ballad

PATTERSON, KELLE

I'M GONNA LOVE YOU JUST A LITT	YOU ARE SO BEAUTIFUL	SHADY BROOK 21	40.00	70's

PATTI AND THE EMBLEMS

MIXED UP SHOOK UP GIRL	ORDINARY GUY	HERALD 590	10.00	northern
IT'S THE LITTLE THINGS	EASY COME, EASY GO	CONGRESS 263	150.00	northern
TRY IT YOU WON'T FORGET IT	LET HIM GO LITTLE HEART	KAPP 791	15.00	northern
ALL MY TOMORROW'S ARE GONE	PLEASE DON'T EVER LEAVE ME BABY	KAPP 850	15.00	northern
I'LL CRY LATER	ONE MAN WOMAN	KAPP 870	15.00	northern
I'M GOONA LOVE YOU A LONG LONG TIME	MY HEART'S SO FULL OF YOU	KAPP 897	150.00	**northerB**

PATTI AND THE LOVELITES

LOVE BANDIT	I'M THE ONE THAT YOU NEED	COTILLION 44145	15.00	northern
LOVE SO STRONG	OH MY LOVE	LOVELITE 1008	15.00	northern

PATTON, ALEXANDER

MAKE THE BEST OF WHAT YOU GOT	I KNEW IT WAS WRONG	DUO DISC 113	20.00	ballad

PAUL, BUNNY

I'M HOOKED	WE'RE ONLY YOUNG ONCE	GORDY 7017	45.00	motown

PAULETTE

LOVE YOU BABY		CONTACT	300.00	northern

PAXTON, PEGGY

IT AIN'T WHAT I DO (IT'S THE W	I FEEL LIKE CRYING	PAULA 229	70.00	northern

PAYNE, FREDA

SAD SAD SEPTEMBER	YOU'VE LOST THAST LOVING FEELING	MGM 13509	30.00	northern

PAYTON, LAWRENCE

TELL ME YOU LOVE ME (LOVE SOUN	SAME	ABC 15014	10.00	70's

PAZANT BROTHERS

FEVER	GROOVIN'	RCA 117	20.00	funk
JUICY LUCY	WORK SONG	GWP 506	15.00	funk
MBOGA-CHAKULA (GREASY GREENS)	CHICK A BOOM	VIGOR 711	15.00	funk
SKUNK JUICE	TOE JAM	RCA 9634	20.00	funk
BACK TO BEAUFORT	WATER FRONT BLUES	PRISCILLA 1002	20.00	funk
DRAGON FLY	DIXIE ROCK	VIGOR 1713	10.00	funk

PEACEMAKERS

DON'T PUSH YOUR LUCK		STAR 100	100.00	funk

PEACHES AND HERB

I NEED YOUR LOVE SO DESPERATELY	FOR YOUR LOVE	DATE 1563	8.00	northern
WE'RE IN THIS THING TOGETHER	LET'S FALL IN LOVE	DATE 1523	10.00	northern

PEACHES

MUSIC TO MY EARS	BABY THINK IT OVER	CONSTELLATION 171	15.00	northern
PLEASE DON'T TAKE MY MAN	I'M LIVING IN A DREAM	BUMP'S 1503	400.00	northern

PEARLS

SHOOTING HIGH	CAN I CALL YOU BABY	LAMP 653	300.00	northern

PEARLY QUEEN

QUIT JIVE' IN		SOUND TRIANGLE	200.00	funk

PEEBLES, ANN

IF THIS IS HEAVEN	WHEN I'M IN YOUR ARMS	HI. 77502	8.00	70's

PEEK, PAUL

I'M MOVIN' UPTOWN	THE SHADOW KNOWS	COLUMBIA 43771	20.00	northern

PENDULUM SWINGERS

NEVER SHOULD HAVE LOVED YOU BABY	NEVER HAPPENED BEFORE	PENDULUM1	50.00	70's
NEVER SHOULD HAVE LOVED YOU BABY	NEVER HAPPENED BEFORE	GWS 2800	30.00	northern

PENETRATIONS

SWEET, SWEET BABY	CHAMPAGNE (SHING-A-LING)	TERI DE 006	250.00	northern
SWEET, SWEET BABY	CHAMPAGNE (SHING-A-LING)	HIGHLAND 1183	150.00	northern

PENETTS

IF I NEVER SEE YOU AGAIN	THAT'S NO WAY TO SPEND YOUR LIFE	BECCO 0001	150.00	northern

PENN, DAN

I NEED SOME ONE	WILLIE AND HAND JIVE	MGM 13458	20.00	northern
I'M YOU PUPPET		MGM	30.00	ballad
LET THEM TALK	CLOSE TO YOU	FAME 6402	20.00	ballad

PENNY

NOW THAT I FOUND YOU	COME SEE BOUT ME	KELTON 3003	25.00	northern

PENNY AND THE EKO'S

GIMME WHAT YOU GOT	SHARE YOUR LOVE	ARGO 5295	200.00	motown

PENNY, BILL AND THE PACEMAKERS

I CAN'T STAY	STICK WITH IT	TEMPO 125936	150.00	northern

PENTAGONS

I WONDER (IF YOUR LOVE WILL EVER)	SHE'S MINE	JAMIE 1201	25.00	northern
GONNA WAIT FOR YOU	FOREVER YOURS	SUTTER	200.00	northern

PEOPLE IN THE NEWS

MISTY SHADE OF PINK		KNAP TOWN	50.00	funk

PEOPLES CHOICE

EASE THE PAIN	HOT WIRE	PALMER 5009	10.00	ballad
EASE THE PAIN	HOT WIRE	GRANDLAND 414	15.00	ballad
JUST LOOK WHAT YOU'VE DONE	KEEP ON HOLDING ON	PHILIPS 40653	15.00	northern
LOST AND FOUND	KEEP ON HOLDIN' ON	PHILIPS 40615	20.00	northern
SAVIN' MY LOVIN' FOR YOU	EASY TO BE TRUE	PALMER 5020	500.00	northern
SAVIN' MY LOVIN' FOR YOU	EASY TO BE TRUE	PALMER 5031	400.00	northern

PEPP, GEORGE

THE FEELING IS REAL	BLOW BETSEY BLOW	COLEMAN 80	1500.00	northern

PEPS

MY LOVE LOOKS GOOD ON YOU(219 mix)	SPEAK YOUR PIECE	D-TOWN 1065	45.00	northern
MY LOVE LOOKS GOOD ON YOU(689 mix)	SPEAK YOUR PEACE	D-TOWN 1065	75.00	northern
YOU NEVER HAD IT SO GOOD	DETROIT, MICHIGAN	D-TOWN 1049	100.00	northern
THIS I PRAY	THINKING ABOUT YOU	D-TOWN 1060	15.00	ballad

PERCY AND THEM

LOOK IN THE MIRROR OF MY EYES	TRYING TO FIND A NEW LOVE	ROULETTE 7202	75.00	70's

PERCY AND THE IMAGE BAND

CATCH A FALLING STAR	STAR OF THE SHOW	COUNT. 1	8.00	group

PEREZ, REUBEN

HOMEMADE		JUDNELL NO#	100.00	funk

PERFECTIONS

CAN THIS BE REAL	TILL I GET HOME	CALGAR 5	100.00	70's
THE RIGHT TO CRY	WOMAN	AGC 3	150.00	northern
DON'T TAKE YOUR LOVE FROM ME	SINCE I LOST MY BABY	DRUMHEAD 100	20.00	northern
GIRL YOU BETTER HURRY	GET ON DOWN	TRI-CITY 328	40.00	northern
SOMEWHERE OVER THE WATER	TO YOU, MY LOVE	ARCHIVES 71	15.00	group
I LOVE YOU, MY LOVE	AM I GONNA LOSE YOU	SVR 1005	125.00	northern
MR. PERFECTION	NO MORE LOVE FOR YOU	PAM-O 101	75.00	northern
SO LONELY	BABY DON'T YOU GO	BIG B. 800	700.00	northern

PERFORMERS

JUST DANCE	LOVE IS THE ANSWER	ABC 10777 DJ	15.00	northern
LITTLE ANGEL	NIGHTMARES	SIR GRAHAM 101	100.00	northern
SET ME FREE	THAT DAY WHEN SHE NEEDED ME	MIRWOOD 5536	20.00	northern
THE DAY WHEN SHE NEEDED ME	SET ME FREE	MIIRWOOD 5536	15.00	northern
I'LL ALWAYS LOVE YOU	DARLING I'M SO THANKFUL	VILLA 707	150.00	ballad

PERIGENTS

LOVE ON THE RAMPAGE	BETTER KEEP MOVIN' ON	MALTESE 106	30.00	northern
LET'S GET INTO SOMETHING	BETTER KEEP MOVIN' ON	MALTESE 101	15.00	nortern

PERKINS, AL

YES, MY GOODNESS YES	I FALL IN LOVE AGAIN	BUDDAH 575	30.00	70's
NEED TO BELONG	AIN'T NOTHING IMPOSSIBLE WITH	ATCO 6820	10.00	group
NOTHING IS IMPOSSIBLE	SNAP YOUR FINGERS	ATCO 6734	15.00	northern

PERKINS, GEORGE

I'M SO GLAD YOU'RE MINE	POOR ME	ROYAL SHIELD 155661	40.00	70's
KEEP ON LOVING ME	BABY I LOVE YOU	ROYAL SHIELD 101	15.00	70's
WE NEED A HELPING HAND	SAME. PT.2	SECOND LINE 001	8.00	ballad
GROOVE MAKING	HOW CAN A BROKE MAN SURVIVE	GOLDEN EAR 114	20.00	funk

PERRELL, EDDIE

LISTEN	ONE FOR MY BABY	QUETTE 101	30.00	northern

PERRIN, SUE

CANDY STORE MAN	RECIPE FOR LOVE	GOLDEN WORLD 2	20.00	motown

PERRY, ANN

THAT'S THE WAY HE IS	SAME: INSTRUMENTAL	THEODA 120 vinyl	40.00	nothernB
THAT'S THE WAY HE IS	SAME: INSTRUMENTAL	THEODA 201 styrene	200.00	nothernB

PERRY, CHARLES

HOW CAN I (KEEP FROM CRYING)	MOVE ON LOVE	MAGNUM 728	30.00	northern
HOW CAN I (KEEP FROM CRYING)	MOVE ON LOVE	MGM 13621	20.00	northern
HOW CAN I (KEEP FROM CRYING)	MOVE ON LOVE	MUTT & JEFF 16	25.00	northern

PERRY, GREG

IT TAKES HEART	THE GETAWAY	ALFA 7016	20.00	70's
VARIETY IS THE SPICE OF LIFE	COME ON DOWN	CASABLANCA 817	8.00	70's
HEAD OVER HEELS (IN LOVE)	LOVE CONTROL	CHESS 2032	15.00	northern

PERRY, JEFF

CALL ON ME	SAME: INSTRUMENTAL	EPIC 50372	30.00	70's
LOVE DON'T COME NO STRONGER	I'VE GOT TO SEE YOU RIGHT AWAY	ARISTA 51	10.00	70's

PERRY, LINDA

I NEED SOMEONE	SAME: INSTRUMENTAL	MAINSTREAM 5550	10.00	70's

PERRY, OSCAR

GIMMIE SOME	COME ON HOME TO ME	PERI-TONE 101874	15.00	70's
HE SENT ME YOU	MOTHER! CAN YOUR CHILD COME HO	MERCURY 73408	30.00	70's
I GOT WHAT YOU NEED	COME ON HOME TO ME	PERI-TONE 101674	30.00	70's
MAIN STRING	I WAS RIGHT	PERI-TONE 1001	15.00	70's
TEASIN' ME	I WANNA THANK YOU	RED SUN 112	15.00	70's
WIND ME UP	I DIDN'T PLAN IT THIS WAY	YELLOW HOR. 242101	30.00	70's
DANGER ZONE	LOVE EVERYTHING ABOUT YOU	JETSTREAM 900	8.00	ballad
PEOPLE ARE TALKING	HAS ANYONE SEEN HER	JETSTREAM 833	8.00	ballad
WE CAME A LONG WAYS	LAY YOUR LOVING ON YOU	PERI-TONE 101574	15.00	ballad
CAN'T MEND A BROKEN HEART (SAM	ONCE IN A WHILE	MERCURY 73363 DJ	40.00	northern
FOOL FROM THE STICKS	LIKE IT WAS THE LAST TIME	BACK BEAT 614	30.00	northern
FACE REALITY		FERON NO.#	300.00	northern

PERSIANS

I ONLY HAVE EYES FOR YOU	THE SUN'S GOTTA SHINE IN YOUR	ABC 11145	20.00	group
(WHEN YOU SAID) LET'S GET MARRIED	(LET'S MONKEY) AT THE PARTY	MUSIC WORLD 102	60.00	northern
I CAN'T TAKE IT ANYMORE	DETOUR	GRAPEVINE 201	10.00	northern
THAT GIRL OF MINE	DON'T LET ME DOWN	SIR RAH 501	40.00	northern

PERSIONETTES

CALL ON ME	IT HAPPENS EVERYDAY	STRATA 102	150.00	northern
CALL ON ME	IT HAPPENS EVERYDAY	OPEN 1256	40.00	northern
CALL ON ME	IT HAPPENS EVERYDAY	OR. 1256	25.00	northern

PERSONAL TOUCH

IT AIN'T NO BIG THING PT.1	IT AIN'T NO BIG THING PT.2	P&P 001	15.00	70's

PERSONATIONS AND ORGANIZATIONS

FUTURE		CURRI CANE	100.00	funk

PERSUADERS

ANOTHER TIME ANOTHER PLACE	I'M SO GLAD, I GOT YOU	BRUNSWICK 55553	10.00	70's
PLEASE STAY	BAD BOLD & BEAUTIFUL GIRL	ATCO 6919	10.00	70's
TRYIN' TOLOVE TWO WOMEN	THE QUICKEST WAY OUT	CALLA 3007	10.00	70's

PERSUASIONS

ONE THING ON MY MIND	DARLIN'	A&M 1698	10.00	70's
IT'S BETTER TO HAVE LOVED AND	PARTY IN THE WOODS	MINIT 32067	10.00	group

PETALS

THE WINDOWS OF YOUR HEART	UP AND DOWN	MERCURY 72661	40.00	**northerB**

PETERMAN, PAT

LOVE THE WAY YOU DO YOUR THING	YOU GONNA REAP IT	123 1727j	40.00	northern

PETERS, HOWARD

TELL ME IT'S ALRIGHT	TIGHTEN UP THE SLACK	CORAL 62533	40.00	ballad

PETERS, NANCY

CRY, BABY HEART	DON'T WORRY ME NO MORE	KUDO 664	300.00	motown

PETERS, PRESTON

GOT TO HAVE PEACE OF MIND	BAD NEWS	MARKHAP 6467	20.00	northern

PETERSON, KRIS (CHRIS)

I'LL GET EVEN WITH YOU	I LOVE YOU	HI-LITE 111	75.00	northern
JUST AS MUCH	UNBELIEVABLE	TOP DOG 102	30.00	northern

PETERSON, LEON

NOW YOU'RE ON YOUR OWN	PARTY CRASHIN' TIME	SKYLARK 501	500.00	northern

PETS

I SAY YEAH	WEST SIDE STORY	CARNIVAL 511	150.00	funk
WHAT KIND OF GIRL	NOBODY (KNOWS HOW MUCH I LOVE	MGM 13324	40.00	northern

PETTIS, RAY

TOGETHER FOREVER	THINK IT OVER	DEE DEE 73173	15.00	northern
IF I FOUND LOVE	QUESTION AND ANSWER	SALEM 1005	15.00	northern

PEYTON, BOBBY

KEEP CALLING ME (BABY LOVE)	SLIDE AND JERK	HILTON 651	50.00	northern

PFB FEATURING LADY

BETCHA I CAN (MAKE YA FEEL GOO	SAME: INSTRUMENTAL	PHILADELPHIA FUNK 100	20.00	funk

PHANTOM

COME BACK TO ME	UH HUH, OHYEAH	KARISMA 5022	300.00	northern

PHARAOHS

IS THAT BLACK ENOUGH FOR YOU	TRACKSA OF MY TEARS	CAPITOL 3072	25.00	funk

PHASE FOUR

IT TAKES MORE THAN AMOMENT	I'M SO GLAD	CLINTONE 2	15.00	northern

PHASE II
THE FIRST SHOT	HAPPINESS IS	OSIRIS 3	10.00	70's

PHASES
ANYTHING YOU WANNA BE	SING YOUR SONG	CAPITOL 2684	40.00	70's

PHELPS, BOOTSEY
FUN IN YOUR THANG	Pt.2	GENERAL AMERICAN 321	75.00	funk

PHELPS, JAMES
WASTING TIME	LA DE DA, I'M A FOOL IN LOVE	ARGO 5509	10.00	ballad
I'LL DO THE BEST I CAN	LOVE IS A 5 LETTER WORD	ARGO 5499	10.00	northern
THE LOOK ON YOUR FACE	YOU WERE MADE FOR LOVE	APACHE 2007	500.00	northern

PHENOMENONS
WITHOUT YOUR LOVE	YOU GAVE ME HAPPINESS	AVI 191	30.00	70's

PHILHARMONICS
I NEED, I NEED YOUR LOVE	WILL YOU MARRY ME GIRL	SOULIN 149	25.00	70's

PHILIPS, DOUG AND THE NOW CONCEPTS
YOU REALLY KNOW HOW TO HURT A GUY	IN AND OUT OF MY LIFE	RAY-PHI 102	100.00	northern
YOU REALLY KNOW HOW TO HURT A GUY	IN AND OUT OF MY LIFE	ATCO 6692	30.00	northern

PHILIPS, ESTHER (LITTLE)
HOME IS WHERE THE HATRED IS	TIL MY BACK AIN'T GOT NO BONE	KUDU 904	15.00	70's
NOBODY BUT YOU	TOO MUCH OF A MAN	ROULETTE 7059	30.00	northern
CATCH ME I'M FALLING	A WOMAN WILL DO WRONG	ATLANTIC 2783	10.00	northern
JUST SAY GOODBYE	I COULD HAVE TOLD YOU	ATLANTIC 2324	40.00	northern
WHILE IT LASTED	WHY SHOULD WE TRY ANYMORE	LENOX 5570	10.00	northern

PHILLIPS, JOE
WITHOUT YOU	THE SWEETHEART TREE	OMEN 18	30.00	northern
CAN'T HELP BUT TO LOVE YOU	I JUST CAN'T HELP THINKING ABOUT YOU	OMEN 6	40.00	northern

PHILLIPS, LAROSE
WANTED	DON'T TAKE ME AWAY FROM YOU	GOLDISC 1005	70.00	northern

PHILLIPS, MISS D.D.
HEY LITTLE GIRL	NOW	EVOLUTION 1008	50.00	**northerB**

PHILLIPS, PHIL
IT TAKES MORE	PYRAMID GAME PYRAMID GAME	HARD BOILED 101	20.00	70's

PHILLIPS, SANDRA
I WISH I HAD KNOWN	HOPING YOU'LL COME BACK	OKEH 7310	100.00	northern
WORLD WITHOUT SUNSHINE	OKI	BROADWAY 403	40.00	northern
YOU SUCCEEDED	WHEN MIDNIGHT COMES	BROADWAY 402	15.00	northern

PHILLIPS, SAUDRA
MISS FATBACK	SAME:	BROWN DOG 9004	20.00	funk

PHILLIPS, SUSAN
KEY IN THE MAILBOX	JUST HOW LONG	ALL PLATINUM 2335	40.00	70's

PHILLY DEVOTIONS
I JUST CAN'T SAY GOODBYE	COME OVER ON THE LOVIN' SIDE	DON DE 127	10.00	70's

PHOENIX
EVERY NOW AND THEN I CRY	LOVE HAVE MERCY	P.I.. 12391	200.00	northern

PHONETICS
DON'T LET LOVE GET YOU DOWN	PRETTY GIRL	TRUDEL 1005	200.00	northern
GHOSTS	IT'S JERKIN' AND TWININ' TIME	TRUDEL 1010	20.00	northern
JUST A BOYS DREAM	DON'T LET LOVE GET YOU DOWN	TRUDEL 1007	800.00	northern
WHAT GOOD (AM I WITHOUT YOU)	DON'T LET LOVE GET YOU DOWN	TRUDEL 1012	300.00	northern

PIC AND BILL
FUNNY HOW TIME SLIPS AWAY	HOW MAN Y TIMES	CHARAY 60	10.00	ballad
SAD WORLD WITHOUT YOU	JUST A TEAR	SMASH 2132	8.00	ballad
YOU CAN NEVER GO BACK	SAME:	BANDIT 12	10.00	ballad
ALL I WANT IS YOU	IT'S NOT YOU	CHARAY 67	15.00	funk

PICKETT, WILSON
HOW WILL I EVER KNOW	THE BEST PART OF A MAN	WICKED 8101	10.00	70's
I WANT YOU	LOVE OF MY LIFE	EMI 8027	10.00	70's
LET ME BE YOUR BOY	MY HEART BELONGS TO YOU	CORREC-TONE 501	60.00	northern
LET ME BE YOUR BOY	MY HEART BELONGS TO YOU	CUB 9113	30.00	northern
LET ME BE YOUR BOY	MY HEART BELONG TO YOU	VERVE 10378	25.00	northern

PICO PETE
CAN'T GO FOR THAT	THE HORSE	GROOMS 312	75.00	northern

PIECES OF EIGHT
COME BACK GIRL	T.N.T.	A&M 879	15.00	northern
STRANGE THINGS ARE HAPPENING	DOUBLE SHOT (OF MY BABY'S LOVE)	ACTION 4	50.00	northern

PIECES OF PEACE
PASS IT ON		TWINIGHT NO#	50.00	funk

PIERCE, BOBBY
MY BABY LOVES ME	MY NIGHT OUT	EXPRESS 10	30.00	mod

PIERCE, DON
THIS FUNKY THING	SPOOK A DELIC	MAJESTY 1041	50.00	funk

PINKERTONES
IT'S NOT THE WAY YOU WALK	IT'S NOT WHO YOU ARE (BUT WHAT	QUEEN-G 1368	400.00	northern

PINKNEY, BILL
MILLIONAIRE	OL' MAN RIVER	GAME 394	20.00	northern

PINKOOSHINS
MAKE IT EASY	SHARE YOUR LOVE	MERCURY 73164	20.00	northern

PINKSTON JR., AL
I LOOK I SEE	YOU'RE NOT THERE	TRA MO. 102	100.00	northern

PIPKINS, JIM AND THE BOSS FIVE
MR. C.C.	I'M JUST A LONELY GUY	EMERGE 1108	30.00	mod

PIRATES
I'LL LOVE YOU 'TIL I DIE	MIND OVER MATTER	MELODY 105	50.00	motown

PITMAN, DONNELL
YOUR LOVE IS DYNAMITE	CANDY LOVE	AFTER FIVE 710	40.00	70's

PITNEY, GENE
SHE'S A HEARTBREAKER	CONQUISTADOR	MUSICOR 1306	10.00	northern

PITTS, BEVERLY
JUST SOME SOUL	UP AND DOWN	SOUL SHOT 6396	30.00	mod

PITTS, GREGG
DEDICATED TO YOU	BACK TO BACK	SOUND PLUS 2177	10.00	ballad

PLATTERS
WASHED ASHORE (ON A LONELY ISLAND)	WHAT NAME SHALL I GIVE YOU MY	MUSICOR 1251	10.00	northern
WITH THIS RING	IF I HAD A LOVE	MUSICOR 1229	10.00	northern
DEVRI	ALONE IN THE NIGHT (WITHOUT YO	MUSICOR 1195	10.00	northern
FEAR OF LOSING YOU	SONATA	MUSICOR 1341	10.00	northern
HARD TO GET THING CALLED LOVE	WHY	MUSICOR 1322	10.00	northern
HEAR NO EVIL, SPEAK NO EVIL, SEE NO EVIL	I LOVE YOU 1000 TIMES	MUSICOR 1166	10.00	northern
SWEET SWEET LOVIN'	SONATA	MUSICOR 1275	10.00	northern
THINK TWICE BEFORE YOU WALK AWAY	SO MANY TEARS	MUSICOR 1302	10.00	northern

PLATTERS '65
RUN WHILE IT'S DARK	WON'T YOU BE MY FRIEND	ENTREE 107	40.00	northern

PLAYER, JAY
LOVE IS THE ANSWER	LOVE IS THE ANSWER PT.2	BEVNIK 556	40.00	70's

PLAYERS
HE'LL BE BACK	I WANNA BE FREE	MINIT 32001	8.00	group
I'M SO ALONE	GET RIGHT	MINIT 32029	10.00	group
THAT'S THE WAY	THER'S GOT TO BE A WAY	MINIT 32019	10.00	group
WHY DID I LIE	I'M SO GLAD I WAITED	MINIT 32012	30.00	northern

PLAYERS IV
THE TWO OF US	THE GIRL IN THE SHADE	KNOLL 500	150.00	northern

PLUMMER, BETTYE JEAN
BABY I WANT YOU BACK	I BELIEVE	SALEM 2000	20.00	northern
YOU DON'T KNOW	I REMEMBER YOU WELL	BELL 45368	100.00	northern

PLUS 4
HAPPIEST GIRL IN THE WORLD	HANG ON (LOVE IS ON THE WAY)	WB 7287	15.00	northern

POETS
A SURE THING	SO YOUNG (AND SO INNOCENT)	SYMBOL 216	10.00	northern
I'M STUCK ON YOU	MERRY CHRISTMAS BABY	RED BIRD 10046	20.00	northern
THE HUSTLER		VEEP 1286	20.00	nothern
I'VE GOT TWO HEARTS	I'M PARTICULAR	SYMBOL 219	40.00	northern
SHE BLEW A GOOD THING	OUT TO LUNCH	SYMBOL 214	10.00	northern
WRAPPED AROUND YOUR FINGER		J-2 1302	800.00	northern

POINDEXTER, ANNETTE
YOU'LL GET IT RIGHT BQACK	SAME: INSTRUMENTAL	BRENA 3608	40.00	northern

POINTER SISTERS
SEND HIM BACK	DESTINATION NO MORE HEARTACHES	ATLANTIC 2893	40.00	**northerB**

POLITICIANS
LOVE MACHINE	FREE YOUR MIND	HOT WAX 7114	10.00	funk

POLK, FRANK
CRACK UP LAUGHING	IN THE RING	CAPITOL 5442	20.00	group
LOVE IS DANGEROUS	I AM YOUR MAN	CAPITOL 5581	30.00	northern
YEARS OF TEARS	DO THE JERK	CAPITOL 5303	20.00	northern

POLK, JAMES AND THE BROTHERS
JUST PLAIN FUNK		TWINK	200.00	funk
POWER STRUGGLE	NEVER GIVE HIM UP	TWINK 711	300.00	funk

POLK, LONNIE
I CAN MAKE YOU HAPPY	I KISS IT AND MAKE IT BETTER	MERCURY 73624 DJ	40.00	70's

POLLARD, RAY
IT'S A SAD THING	ALL THE THINGS YOU ARE	UA 50012	70.00	northern
LIE LIPS LIE	THIS IS MY SONG	DECCA 32111	40.00	northern
THE DRIFTER	LET HIM GO (AND LET ME LOVE YO	UA 916 DJ	75.00	northern
THIS TIME (I'M GONNA BE TRUE)	NO MORE LIKE ME	SHRINE 103	600.00	northern

PONDS, JOE
DON'T LET LOVE P0ASS YOU BY	WHEN WE GET ON CLOUD NINE	SUE 13	20.00	ballad

POODLES
STEP BY STEP		SOUTHERN CITY 1111	40.00	northern

POOKS, EL
I COULD DO THE IMPOSSIBLE		ORIVIOUS	75.00	funk

POOLE, BENNY
PEARL, BABY PEARL	SORRY 'BOUT THAT	SOLID HIT 107	20.00	mod

POOR BOY AND THE THE ORPHANS
I KNOW SHE LOVES ME	SITTING ON TOP OF A GROOVY THI	BUTCHS THANG 1	20.00	northern

POP CORN AND THE MOHAWKS

SHIMMY GULLY	CUSTER'S LAST MAN	MOTOWN 1002	100.00	motown
PRETTY GIRL	YOU'RE THE ONE	NORTHERN 3732	100.00	group
REAL GOOD LOVIN	HAVE I THE RIGHT	MOTOWN 1019	200.00	motown

POPPIES

HE'S GOT REAL LOVE	HE'S READY	EPIC 10019	15.00	northern
LULLABY OF LOVE	I WONDER WHY	EPIC 9893	10.00	northern
DO IT WITH SOUL	HE MEANS SO MUCH TO ME	EPIC 10059	10.00	**northerB**
THERE'S A PAIN IN MY HEART	MY LOVE AND I	EPIC 10086 DJ	50.00	northern
HE'S GOT REAL LOVE	HE'S READY	EPIC 10019 PS	20.00	northern

POPULAR FIVE.

I'M A LOVE MAKER	LITTLE BITTY PRETTY ONE	MINIT 32050	10.00	northern

PORGY AND THE MONACHS

LOVE CHAIN	MAGIC MUSIC MAKERS	VERVE 10597	15.00	northern
MY HEART CRIES FOR YOU	THINK TWICE BEFORE YOU WALK AW	MUSICOR 1221	100.00	**northerB**
Light Brown reissue on Musicor 1221. Is mispressed with "Hey Girl" (previously unissued) on the B-side.			30.00	northern
SOMEBODY SAID (I'D CRY SOMEDAY)	STAY	MALA 462	30.00	northern
THAT GIRL	IF IT'S FOR REAL BABY	MUSICOR 1179	85.00	northern
THATS MY GIRL	(THAT) BOY AND GIRL	VERVE 10609	15.00	northern
THAT'S MY GIRL	THE GIRL AND THE BOY	SYLVES 123	15.00	northern

PORK AND THE PAUL WRIGHT

WATCH YOURSELF	THE COMPANY	PORK A LOT	100.00	70's

PORTEE, ROBERT

CASANOVA	I AM SO PROUD	DIAMOND 151	75.00	northern

PORTER, N.F.

KEEP ON KEEPING ON	DON'T MAKE ME COLOR MY BLACK	LIZARD 1010	10.00	**northerB**

PORTER, NOLAN

IF I COULD ONLY BE SURE	WORK IT OUT IN THE MORNING	ABC 11343	30.00	70's
OH BABY	SINGER MAN	ABC 11367	20.00	northern

PORTER, ROBIE

THAT'S THE WAY LOVE GOES	YESTERDAY YEARS	MGM 13779	10.00	northern
THAT'S THE WAY LOVE GOES	YESTERDAY YEARS	MGM 13779 PS	15.00	northern

POSEY, ART

NO MORE HEARTACHES	NOTHING TAKES THE PLACE OF YOU	SCOPE 126206	40.00	northern

POSSE

FEEL LIKE GIVIN' UP	TAKE SOMEBODY LIKE YOU	V.I.P. 25069	10.00	motown
YOU BEWTTER COME ON OUT AND PL	THAT'S WHAT MAKES US HAPPY	E.J.K. 10	10.00	motown
EVIL	ARE YOU READY	JANUS 133	40.00	northern

POSSESSIONS

YOU AND YOUR LIES	NO MORE LOVE	PARKWAY 930	20.00	northern
YOU AND YOUR LIES	NO MORE LOVE	BRITTON 1004	30.00	northern
YOU AND YOUR LIES	NO MORE LOVE	BRITTON 1003 blue vinyl	50.00	northern

POST COALITION, MIKE

BUBBLE GUM BREAKTHROUGH	NOT A BLADE OF GRASS	WB 7357	15.00	northern

POSTON, A.C.

I'M SO FULL OF LOVE	MY BABY'S STEPPIN' OUT	ODESSA 2010	20.00	northern

POWDRILL, PAT

DO IT	I CAN'T HEAR YOU	DOWNEY 139	50.00	northern
LUCKIEST GIRL IN TOWN	BREAKIN' POINT	REPRISE 286	20.00	northern
TOGETHER FOREVER	THEY ARE THE LONELY	DOWNEY 141	20.00	northern

POWELL, WILLIAM

HEARTACHE SOUVENIRS	CHICKEN SHACK	POWER-HOUSE 101	2000.00	northern

POWER, MIKE

TEENAGE SWEETHEART	I LEFT MY LOVE IN PARIS	ZELMAN 5301	500.00	motown

PRECISIONS

YOU'RE THE BEST (THAT EVER DID HAVE)	NEW YORK CITY	ATCO 6669	15.00	group
A PLACE	NEVER LET HER GO	DREW 1005	8.00	northern
I WANNA TELL MY BABY	MY LOVER COME BACK	D-TOWN 1033	800.00	northern
IF THIS IS LOVE (I'D RATHER BE LONELY)	YOU'LL SOON BE GONE	DREW 1003	10.00	northern
INSTANT HEARTBREAK (JUST ADD TEARS)	DREAM GIRL	DREW 1004	15.00	northern
INTO MY LIFE	DON'T DOUBLE WITH TROUBLE	ATCO 6643	15.00	northern
SUCH MISERY	A LOVER'S PLEA	DREW 1001	30.00	northern
SUGAR AIN'T SWEET	WHY GIRL	DREW 1002	1500.00	northern
WHY GIRL	WHAT I WANT	DREW 1002	10.00	northern
YOU'RE SWEET	MEXICAN LOVE SONG	D-TOWN 1055	20.00	northern
MY SENSE OF DIRECTION IS BLOWN	TAKE A GOOD LOOK	HEN-MAR 4501	30.00	northern

PREE, KAREN

MAKE LOVE LAST FOREVER	SAME:	CASABLANCA 12	30.00	70's

PREE SISTERS

LET'S GET TOGETHER	LOVE AMONG PEOPLE	CAPITOL 3472	15.00	70's

PREMONITIONS

BABY, BABY	IN LOVE TOGETER	JADE 711	100.00	northern

PREPARATIONS

THAT'S WHEN HE REMEMBERS	(I DON'T WANT) NOBODY BUT YOU	MAINSTREAM 720	10.00	funk

153

PREPOSITIONS

SOMETHING DIFFERENT		MOVEMENT	75.00	funk

PRESENT

MANY'S THE SLIP TWIXT THE CUP	I KNOW	PHILIPS 40466	40.00	northern

PRESENTATIONS

CALL ON ME	SORRY	AMERICAN MUSIC	30.00	northern
MAKER 11				

PRESIDENTS

PETER RABBIT	WHICH WAY	DELUXE 127	50.00	funk
SNOOPY	STINKY	DELUXE 120	30.00	mod
SWEET MAGIC	TRIANGLE OF LOVE	SUSSEX 212	15.00	northern

PRESTON, BILLY

BILLY'S BAG	DON'T LET THE SUN CATCH YOU CRYING	VEE JAY 653	10.00	northern
THEGIRL'S GOT "IT"	THE NIGHT	CAPITOL 5611	25.00	northern
IN THE MIDNIGHT HOUR	ADVICE	CAPITOL 5660	10.00	mod
VOLCANO	YOUNG HEARTACHES	CONTRACT 5102	300.00	northern

PRETENDERS

I CALL IT LOVE	IT'S EVERYTHING ABOUT YOU	CARNIVAL 560	60.00	70's
JUST BE YOURSELF	JUST YOU WAIT AND SEE	CARNIVAL 559	30.00	group
HEARTS WERE MADE TO LOVE	FOR THE REST OF MY DAYS	CARNIVAL 556	10.00	group
I CALL IT LOVE	FEELIN' GOOD	CARNIVAL 550	10.00	group
WHAT IS LOVE	SWEET POTATO GRAVY	CARNIVAL 554	15.00	group
I WANNA BE	HEARTS WERE MADE TO LOVE	CARNIVAL 552	15.00	northern
TEMPTATION WALK	`BABY MY LOVE	JERK 202	1000.00	northern

PREYER, RON

IF YOU DON'T WANT MY LOVE	BALTIMORE	SHOCK 10	15.00	70's

PRIDE, FREDDIE

ALL MY LIFE	THE JOY OF CHRISTMAS	DIAMOND JIM 3208	15.00	northern

PRIDE, LOU

I DIDN'T TAKE YOUR WOMAN	GONE BAD AGAIN	CURTOM 601	10.00	70's
LOOK OUT LOVE	YOU'VE GOT TO WORK FOR LOVE	ALBATROSS 2636	250.00	70's
BEEN SUCH A LONG TIME	SAME: INSTRUMENTAL	ONYX 15520	15.00	ballad
VERY SPECIAL	GONE BAD	WMB 16745	8.00	ballad
WE'RE ONLY FOOLING OURSELVES	PHONEY PEOPLE	GEMCO 118	50.00	ballad
I'M COM'UN HOME IN THE MORN'UN	I'M NOT THRU LOV'UN YOU	SUEMI 4567	900.00	northern
YOUR LOVE IS FADING	LONELY ROOM	SUEMI 4569	700.00	northern
IT'S A MAN'S MAN'S WORLD	YOUR LOVE IS FADING	SUEMI 4568	700.00	northern

PRIME MATES

HOT TAMALES PT 1	HOT TAMALES PT.2	SANSU 465	10.00	funk

PRIME MINISTERS

I DON'T KNOW NO MORE	MAKE-UP	RCA 9470	20.00	northern

PRINCE CHARLES AND THE ROYAL TONES

WHAT I LIVE FOR	FAIR WEATHER FRIEND	ONYX 701	50.00	northern

PRINCE ELLA

BABY SUGAR, I LOVE YOU	CUT ME LOOSE	PRINCE 711	150.00	**northerB**

PRINCE GEORGE

WRONG CROWD	I LOVE TOO HARD	DPG 105	100.00	**northerB**

PRINCE HAROLD

BABY, YOU'VE GOT ME	FORGET ABOUT ME	MERCURY 72621	10.00	northern

PRINCE LA LA

SHE PUT THE HURT ON ME	DON'T YOU KNOW LITTLE GIRL	AFO 301	10.00	mod

PRINCE PHILLIP

KEEP ON TALKING	LOVE IS A WONDERFUL THING	SMASH 2152	20.00	northern

PRINCE, BILLY

SOMEBODY HELP ME	ONE SHOT LEFT	VERVE 10462	10.00	mod
SAY IT AGAIN	YOU SHOULD NEVER HAVE LOVED ME	VERVE 10392	30.00	northern

PRINCE, DOROTHY

HEY MISTER	I LOST A LOVE	M-PAC 7208	10.00	ballad

PROBY, P.J.

NIKI HOEKY	GOOD THINGS ARE COMING MY WAY	LIBERTY 55936DJ	10.00	northern
YOU CAN'T COME HOME AGAIN	WORK WITH ME ANNIE	LIBERTY 55974 PS	15.00	northern

PROCTOR, BILLY

I CAN TAKE IT ALL	WHAT IS BLACK	SOUL 35099	20.00	northern

PROCTOR, BILLY AND THE LOVE SYSTEM

KEEPING UP WITH THE JONESES	SAME:	EPIC 50160	20.00	70's

PRODUCERS

LOVE IS AMAZING	LADY LADY LADY	HUFF PUFF 1003	15.00	northern

PRO-FASCINATION

TRY LOVE AGAIN	I WANT TO WRAP YOU IN MY ARMS	MOT. 312	300.00	70's
SOMETHING ON MY MIND	OVERPOWERING LOVE	MOT. 777	50.00	group

PROFESSIONALS

THAT'S WHY I LOVE YOU	DID MY BABY CALL	GROOVE CITY 101	1000.00	northern
MY HEART BELONGS TO YOU	THERE GOES MY BABY	ACTION 707	30.00	group

PROFESSORS

LITTLE RED RIDING HOOD	THE THREE BEARS	OMEN 3	40.00	northern

PROFFESOR LETT AND STUDY

WE OUGHTA GET TOGETHER	THE FUNKY PROFFESOR	BEAN TOWN 115	150.00	funk

PROFILES
GOT TO BE LOVE	YOU DON'T CARE ABOUT ME	BAMBOO 104	10.00	northern
GOT TO BE LOVE (OR SOMETHING)	A LITTLE MISUNDERSTANDING	BAMBOO 115	8.00	northern
IF I DIDN'T LOVE YOU	GOT TO BE YOUR LOVER	DUO 7449	15.00	northern
A LITTLE MISUNDERSTANDING	GOT TO BE LOVE (OR SOMETHING S	BAMBOO 115	15.00	northern
RAINDROPS	WINDSTORM	MUSICLAND USA 20004	100.00	northern
TAKE A GIANT STEP (WALK ON)	THE WATUSI WOBBLE	GOLDIE 1103	75.00	northern

PROFONIX
AIN'T NO SUN	OPEN UP YOUR HEART	DAVEY-PAUL 4023	15.00	northern

PROFOUND IMAGES
UPTITCH	XMAS TIME	KRIS 8096	50.00	funk

PROFS
LOOK AT ME		CUR	500.00	northern

PROLIFICS
GUTS		HEP ME	75.00	funk

PROMATICS
I THINK I'M GONNA LET GO	PART 2	BROWN DOOR 309	150.00	northern
SUGAR PIE HONEY	EVERYBODY'S TALKIN'	JO JO 2201	15.00	northern

PROMINENTS
JUST A LITTLE	YOU'RE GONNA LOSE HER	LUMMTONE 116	100.00	northern

PROMISED LAND
CHEYENNE	NIGHTCRAWLIN'	ERIC 5003	10.00	northern

PROMISES
LIVING IN THE FOOTSTEPS OF ANO	LOVE IS	BRC 104	20.00	70's
THIS LOVE IS REAL	OH BOY	BRC 109 DJ	20.00	70's

PROPHECY
RAIN IN MY LIFE	LET ME KEEP ON WALKING	ALL PLATINUM 2340	15.00	70's
WHAT EVER'S YOUR SIGN	WHAT EVER'S YOUR SIGN Pt.2	MAINSTREAM 5565	8.00	funk
NYA	EVERYBODY WALKING TOGETHER	ALL PLATINUM 2349	10.00	group

PROPHET, BILLY
WHAT CAN I DO	SAD SAM	SUE 133	150.00	**northerB**

PROPHETS
I GOT THE FEVER	SOUL CONTROL	SMASH 2161	8.00	northern
DON'T YOU THINK IT'S TIME	I DON'T LOVE YOU NO MORE BABY	JUBILEE 5596	30.00	northern
IF I HAD (ONE GOLD PIECE)	HUH BABY	SHRINE 116	2000.00	northern
MY KIND OF GIRL	I CAN'T MAKE IT	STEPHANYE 335	15.00	northern
TALK DON'T BOTHER ME	DON'T LOOK BACK	DELPHI 7	50.00	northern
DON'T YOU THINK IT'S TIME	I DON'T LOVE YOU NO MORE BABY	DELPHI	50.00	northern
I GOT THE FEVER	SOUL CONTROL	DELPHI	100.00	northern
TALK DON'T BOTHER ME	DON'T LOOK BACK	JUBILEE 5565	20.00	northern

PROPHETS OF SOUND
SHADE OF RED	WIN MY TIME	MARSI 1011	15.00	northern

PROTO JAYS
YOU COUNTERFEIT GIRL	CAN I SHARE YOUR LOVE	RILEYS 8790	200.00	northern

PRYSOCK, ARTHUR
ALL I NEED IS YOU TONIGHT	WHEN LOVE IS NEW	OLD TOWN 1000	10.00	70's
HURT SO BAD	LOVE MAKES IT RIGHT	OLD TOWN 106 DJ	10.00	70's

PRYSOCK, RED
GROOVY SAX	I HEARD IIT THROUGH THE GRAPEVINE	JUNIOR 1015	75.00	funk
GROOVY SAX	I HEARD IT THROUGH THE GRAPEVINE	CHESS 2042	20.00	mod

PSYCHODELIC FRANKIE
PUTTING YOU OUT OF MY LIFE		HI-SPEED 1670	400.00	northern

PUBLIC SCHOOL 13
RECESS	HELP KICK THE HABIT	JUGGERNAUT 406	15.00	funk

PUFFS
I ONLY CRY ONCE A DAY NOW	MOON OUT THERE	DORE 757	75.00	northern

PULSE
BABY I MISS YOU	SHAKE WHAT YOU GOT	OLDE WORLD 1106	10.00	group

PURDIE, PRETTY
SOUL DRUMS	FUNKY DONKEY	DATE 1568	20.00	funk

PURDY, BERNARD PRETTY
FICKLE FINGER OF FATE	GENUINE JOHN	COLUMBIA 44829	15.00	**northerB**

PURE FUNK
SEARCHING	NOTHING LEFT IS REAL	PLANET EARTH	40.00	funk
1001				

PURE PLEASURE
BY MY SIDE	DANCIN' PRANCIN'	QC 5100	75.00	70's

PURE SOUL BAND
HEADIN' WEST	BROKEN MACHINE	MAM 801	40.00	northern

PURIFY, JAMES AND BOBBY
SHAKE A TAIL FEATHER	GOODNESS GRACIOUS	BELL 669	8.00	northern
I'M YOU PUPPET	EVERYBODY NEEDS SOMEBODY	SPHERE SOUND 101	10.00	northern

PURPLE IMAGE
WHY	(MARCHING TO..) A DIFFERENT DR	DE-LITE 526	10.00	funk

PURPLE MUNDI

STOP HURTING ME BAY	I BELIEVE	CAT 322	500.00	70'S
STOP HURTING ME BABY	MAN FROM THE SKY (cr. Carlos Wright)	CAT 1982	600.00	70's

PURRELL, EDDIE

THE SPOILER	MY PRIDE WON'T LET ME	VOLT 145	15.00	northern

PURSELL, BILL

HEARTBEAT		SPAR 9008	150.00	northern

PUTNEY, MARK

TODAY'S MAN	DON'T COME AROUND HERE ANYMORE	OVIDE 237	15.00	northern
TODAY'S MAN	DON'T COME AROUND HERE ANYMORE	ATLANTIC 2617	15.00	northern

PUZZLES

MY SWEET BABY	I NEED YOU	FAT BACK 216	25.00	northern

PYE, SHERRY

ASK THE GIRL WHO KNOWS	GIMME A BREAK	MATCH 305	10.00	ballad

PYRAMIDS

I'M THE PLAYBOY	CRYIN'	CUB 9112 DJ	15.00	northern
CRYIN'	I'M THE PLAYBOY	SON-BERT 82861	100.00	group

Q

Q, THE

THAT'S THE WAY	STOP THIS FEELING	HOUND 333	75.00	northern

QUADRAPHONICS

BETCHA IF YOU CHECK IT OUT	PROVE MY LOVE TO YOU	INNOVATION 8019	10.00	70's

QUAILS

MY LOVE	NEVER FELT LIKE THIS BEFORE	HARVEY 116	40.00	motown
OVER THE HUMP	I THOUGHT	HARVEY 120 DJ	40.00	motown

QUALITY CONTROLS

GRAPEVINE PT.1	GRAPEVINE PT.2	SURE SHOT 5040	15.00	mod

QUALLS, SIDNEY JOE

HOW CAN YOU SAY GOODBYE	I ENJOY LOVING YOU	DAKAR 4537	10.00	70's
RUN TO ME	SAME:	DAKAR 4546 DJ	15.00	70's
WHERE THE LILLIES GROW	I'M BEING HELD HOSTAGE	DAKAR 4530	10.00	70's

QUARLES, BILLY

BRINGING UP WHAT I'VE DONE	LITTLE ARCHIE	RALLY 501	30.00	northern
QUIT BRINGING UP WHAT I'VE DON	LITTLE ARCHIE	COLUMBIA 43769	20.00	northern

QUARTERMAN, JOE

(I GOT) SO MUCH TROUBLE IN MY MIND	PT. 2	GSF 3	10.00	funk
GET DOWN BABY	GET DOWN BABY Pt.2	MERCURY 73637	10.00	funk
THE WAY THEY DO MY LIFE	FIND YOURSELF	GSF 6893	10.00	funk

QUEEN CITY SHOW BAND

TRUE PATRON OF THE ARTS	ELEANOR RIGBY	POW! 104	15.00	northern

QUEEN YAHNA

AIN'T IT TIME	SAME: INSTRUMENTAL	P&P 1010	20.00	70's

QUEEN, LINDA

I FEEL THE PAIN	WHERE CAN MY BABY BE	ROD 106	100.00	northern

QUESTELL, CONNIE

DON'T LET IT BREAK YOUR HEART	STRAIGHTEN UP	DECCA 31783	50.00	northern
GIVE UP GIRL	WORLD OF TROUBLE	DECCA 31855	100.00	northern
TELL ME WHAT TO DO	THE GIRL CAN'T TAKE IT	DECCA 31986	50.00	northern

QUICKEST WAY OUT

HELLO STRANGER	TICK TOCK BABY (IT'S A QUARTER	KAREN 717	15.00	group

QUIET FIRE

LOST (WITHOUT YOUR LOVE)	YOUR KIND OF LOVE	HIT MACHINE 3977	100.00	70's

QUINTESSENTS

IMAGE OF MAN	MOVIN' ON	VIBRATION 101	150.00	northern

QUOTATIONS

SEE YOU IN SEPTEMBER	SUMMERTIME GOODBYES	VERVE 10261	30.00	group
HAVIN' A GOOD TIME	(FOR ONCE) I CAN HAVE SOMEONE	IMPERIAL 66338	15.00	northern
I DON'T HAVE TO WORRY	IT CAN HAPPEN TO YOU	DIVENUS 107	25.00	northern

QUOVANS

BOOGALOO	BOGALOO PT.2	SYMBOL 217	10.00	mod

R

RADCLIFFE, JIMMY
SO DEEP	LUCKY OLD SUN	SHOUT 202	40.00	ballad
LONG AFTER TONIGHT IS ALL OVER	WHAT I WANT I CAN NEVER HAVE	MUSICOR 1042	25.00	**northerB**
MY SHIP IS COMING IN	GOIN' WHERE THE LOVING IS	AURORA 154	10.00	northern
THROUGH A LONG AND SLEEPLESS NIGHT	MOMENT OF WEAKNESS	MUSICOR 1033	25.00	northern
(THERE GOES) THE FORGOTTEN MAN	AN AWFUL LOT OF CRYING	UA 1024	30.00	northern
DON'T LOOK MY WAY	TWIST CALYPSO	UA 1016	15.00	ballad

RADIANTS
HOLD ON	I'M GLAD I'M THE LOSER	CHESS 2037	8.00	northern
VOICE YOUR CHOICE	IF I ONLY HAD YOU	CHESS 1904	8.00	northern
AIN'T NO BIG THING	I GOT A GIRL	CHESS 1925	8.00	northern
DON'T WANNA FACE THE TRUTH	MY SUNSHINE GIRL	TWINIGHT 153	20.00	northern
FEEL KIND OF BLUE	ANYTHING YOU DO IS ALRIGHT	CHESS 1986	10.00	northern
HEARTBREAK SOCIETY	PLEASE DON'T LEAVE ME	CHESS 1849	75.00	northern
ONE DAY I'LL SHOW YOU (I REALLY LOVE YOU)	FATHER KNOWS BEST	CHESS 1832	100.00	northern
TOMORROW	WHOLE LOT OF WOMAN	CHESS 1939	15.00	northern

RADIATIONS
LOVE BE NOT A STRANGER	HAKING UP THE NATION	VALISE	40.00	group

RAE, DELLA
HAPPY DAY	SOMEONE, SOMETIME	GROOVE 52	15.00	northern

RAELETS
IT'S ALMOST HERE	I WANT TO THANK YOU	TRC 986	10.00	funk

RAFEY, SUSAN
THE BIG HURT	BRING BACK THE LOVE YOU GAVE M	VERVE 10366 DJ	15.00	northern

RAGLAND, LOU
SINCE YOU SAID YOU'D BE MINE	I DIDN'T MEAN TO ,OVE YOU	WB 7734	25.00	70's
WHAT SHOULD I DO	UNDERSTAND EACH OTHER	SMH 71842	70.00	70's
I TRAVEL ALONE	BIG WHEEL	AMY 988	500.00	northern

RAGLAND, LOU AND THE BANDMASTERS
NEVER LET ME GO	PARTY AT LESTER'S	WAY OUT 2605	1000.00	group

RAIN.
OUT OF MY MIND	HERE WITH YOU	BELL 45142	70.00	northern

RAINBOW
DO WHAT YOU WANNA		WILMINGTON HOUSE	200.00	funk

RAINBOWS
HELP ME IF YOU CAN	PEOPLE LIKE TO TALK	CAPITOL 5991	25.00	northern

RAM
LOVE IS THE ANSWER		TUESDAY NO#	50.00	funk

RAMBLERS
SO SAD	COME ON BACK	TRUMPET 102	600.00	northern

RAMON AND COMPANY
THE DUCK WALK		LU SOUND NO#	200.00	funk

RAMRODS
SOUL EXPRESS	SOUL EXPRESS PT.2	RAMPAGE 1003	10.00	funk
SOULTRAIN	PT.2	RAMPAGE 1000	10.00	funk

RAMSEY AND CO.
LOVE CALL		RAMCO	150.00	northern

RAMSEY, ROBERT
TAKE A LOOK IN YOUR MIND	LIKE IT STANDS	KENT 4552	20.00	ballad

RANDAZZO, TEDDY
YOU DON'T NEED A HEART	AS LONG AS I LIVE	DCP 1134	100.00	northern
YOU'RE NOT THAT GIRL ANYMORE	SOUL	DCP 1153	30.00	northern

RANDELL, LYNNE
STRANGER IN MY ARMS	CIAO BABY	EPIC 10147	60.00	northern
STRANGER IN MY ARMS	CIAO BABY	EPIC 10147 PS	100.00	northern

RANDOLF GREAN SOUNDE, RANDOLF
STAR TREK	LOVE THEME FROM "HUSTLE"	RANWOOD 1044	10.00	funk

RANDOLF, BARBARA
CAN I GET A WITNESS	YOU GOT ME HURTING ALL OVER	SOUL 35050	10.00	motown
I GOT A FEELING YOU	GOT ME HURTIN ALL OVER	SOUL 35038	10.00	northerB

RANDOLF, BOOTS
TAKE A LETTER MARIA	C.C. RIDER	MONUMENT 1233	10.00	**northerB**

RANDOLPH, LEROY
(YOU ARE) MY GUIDING LIGHT	KEEP IT FUNKY	RANGLER 152	10.00	northern

RANDOLPH, LORRAINE
IT'S OVER BETWEEN US	YOU'RE WHAT I WANT	GEMINI STAR 8863	15.00	ballad

RAPPERS
KRUNCHBERRY BEAT		ROACH NO#	100.00	funk

RARE FUNCTION				
DISCO FUNCTION		SOUL UNLIMITED	50.00	funk
RAVENETTES				
SINCE YOU'VE BEEN GONE	TALK ABOUT SOUL	SHURFINE 25	20.00	northern
RAVIN MADS				
WHERE IS LOVE	HOW LONG HAS IT BEEN	RAVIN 1000	250.00	northern
RAW SOUL EXPRESS				
THE WAY WE LIVE	THIS THING CALLED MUSIC	CAT 2010	75.00	funk
RAW UMBER				
LOVE ONE ANOTHER	CARRY - ON	VIRGINIA 4075	150.00	70's
RAWLS, LOU				
LOVE IS A HURTIN' THING	MEMORY LANE	CAPITOL 5709	8.00	northern
SOUL SERENADE	YOU'RE GOOD FOR ME	CAPITOL 2172	8.00	northern
THE HOUSE NEXT DOOR	COME ON IN, MR. BLUES	CAPITOL 5160	50.00	northern
YOU CAN BRING ME ALL YOUR HEARTACHES	A WOMAN WHO'S A WOMAN	CAPITOL 5790	10.00	northern
WHEN LOVE GOES WRONG	SHOW BUSINESS	CAPITOL 5941	10.00	northern
RAY AND DAVE				
WRONG, WRONG, WRONG	SIX LONELY DAYS	MICA 501	60.00	northern
RAY AND HIS COURT				
COOKIE CRUMBS		SOUND TRIANGLE	150.00	funk
RAY, ADA				
GIVE OUR LOVE A CHANCE	I NO LONGER BELIEVE IN MIRACLE	ZELLS 252	50.00	northern
RAY, ALDER				
RUN, BABY, RUN	LOVE WILL LET YOU DOWN	REVUE 11014	10.00	ballad
I NEED YOU, BABY	MY HEART IS IN DANGER	MINIT 32005	30.00	northern
RAY, BABY				
THE HOUSE ON SOUL HILL	THERE'S SOMETHING ON YOUR MIND	IMPERIAL 66216	10.00	mod
RAY, CHUCK				
RECONSIDER	I'LL BE THERE	GEMIGO 101	15.00	70's
BABY PLEASE DON'T LET GO	THERE AIN'T A THING YOU CAN DO	BUDDAH 207	30.00	northern
I DON'T MIND	COME ALIVE	TAMBOO 6719	50.00	northern
RAY, DON				
BORN A LOSER	LIVING ON A PRAYER	RCA 9438	100.00	northern
RAY, EDDIE AND COMPANY				
DON'T TAKE YOUR LOVE	I WANT YOUR LOVE	HOT SOX 1002	60.00	ballad
I'VE GOT SOMETHING OF VALUE		TRUE SOUL	200.00	northern
RAY, RICARDO				
NITTY GRITTY	YA YA	ALEGRE 4024	10.00	mod
RAY AND THE CORRUPTERS				
FUNKY TIME	DIPPY FEELING	KWAKU 1	15.00	funk
SOUL EXPLOSION	FANCY FACE	RAMPAGE 1005 DJ	15.00	funk
RAY AND THE THE BEL-AIRES				
THE BLAME IS ON YOU	I WISH I COULD	ARV 5750	100.00	northern
RAYE, ANTHONY				
GIVE ME ONE MORE CHANCE	HOLD ON TO WHAT YOU GOT	IMPACT 1030	40.00	northern
GIVE ME ONE MORE CHANCE	ON THE EDGE OF SORROW	IMPACT 1009	100.00	northern
RAYE, JIMMIE				
LOOK AT ME, GIRL (CRYING)	I TRIED	TUFF 401	20.00	northern
PHILADELPHIA DAWG	WALKED ON, STEPPED ON, STOMPED	KKC 1	20.00	northern
PHILLY DOG AROUND THE WORLD	JUST CAN'T TAKE IT NO MORE	KKC 2	250.00	**northerB**
THAT'LL GET IT	IT'S WRITTEN ALL OVER YOUR FAC	MOON SHOT 6708	40.00	northern
YOU DON'T WANT MY LOVE	I KEPT ON WALKIN'	NIAGARA	25.00	ballad
YOU MUST BE LOSING YOUR MIND	FOR THE SAKE OF LOVE	GARRISON 1007	50.00	northern
YOU MUST BE LOSING YOUR MIND	FOR THE SAKE OF LOVE	JRE 4220	250.00	northern
RAYMOND, RAY				
IT BREAKS MY HEART	SHE'S ALRIGHT	TUFF 409	30.00	northern
RAYS				
LOVE ANOTHER GIRL		MALA 900	40.00	northern
RAYONS				
I'M GIVING UP, BABY	DO YOU LOVE ME	DECCA 732521	50.00	group
RAZZY				
I HATE HATE	SINGING OTHER PEOPLES SONGS	AQUARIAN 601	10.00	70's
R.D.M. BAND				
GIVE UP	CALIFORNIA HERE I COME	VIRTUE 2506	50.00	70's
REACHERS				
I JUST WANT TO DO MY OWN THING	REACH ON BACK	MAGIC DISC 212	30.00	70's
REALISTICS				
BRENDA, BRENDA	HOW DID I LIVE WITHOUT YOU	LOMA 2088	20.00	northern
REASON WHY				
SO LONG LETTER	STEP INSIDE MY WORLD	POLYDOR 14382	40.00	70's
REASONS				
BABY, BABY	MY KINDA GUY	UA 50005 PS	25.00	northern
REAVES, PAULETTE				
DO IT AGAIN	YOUR EYES	DASH 801	10.00	70's
JAZZ FREAK	IT'S HARD TO DANCE	BLUE CANDLE 1526	10.00	70's
LET ME WRAP YOU IN MY LOVE	YOUR REAL GOOD THING IS ABOUT	BLUE CANDLE 1518	10.00	70's

SECRET LOVER	LOVE THE HELL OUT OF ME	BLUE CANDLE 1514	8.00	ballad
RECORD PLAYER				
FREE YOUR MIND	NUSERY RHYMES	GEM CITY 2001	75.00	70's
REDD, BARBARA				
I'LL BE ALL ALONE	DANCING TEARDROPS	S.P.Q.R. 3311	200.00	northern
REDDING, GENE				
(WE'VE GOT) MORE THAN IT TAKES	GOTTA FIND A WAY	HAVEN 7007	8.00	70's
THIS HEART	WHAT DO I DO	HAVEN 7000	8.00	70's
I NEED YOUR LOVIN'	I GOT SOUL	BELL 819	75.00	northern
REDMOND, RAY AND THE GAYLETTES				
YOU DON'T KNOW	YOU SAY YOU LOVE ME	SA-MO 1147	400.00	northern
REDMOND, ROY				
AIN'T THAT TERRIBLE	A CHANGE IS GONNA COME	LOMA 2071	20.00	northern
REED JR., JIMMY				
I AIN'T GOING NOWHERE	DO YOU REMEMBER	MERCURY 726668	200.00	northern
REED, A.C.				
BOOGALOO - TRAMP	TALKING 'BOUT MY FRIENDS	NIKE 2002	15.00	funk
MY BABY'S BEEN CHEATING	MY BABY IS FINE	COOL 50001	75.00	northern
REED, BOBBY				
THE TIME IS RIGHT FOR LOVE	IF I DON'T LOVE YOU	BELL 888	350.00	northern
I'LL FIND A WAY	I WANNA LOVE YOU SO BAD	LOMA 2089	50.00	northern
YOU ARE	I'M NOT COMING BACK	CLAY TOWN 17700	40.00	northern
YOU ARE	I'M NOT COMING BACK	BRUNSWICK 55282	20.00	northern
REED, VIVIAN				
SAVE YOUR LOVE FOR ME	I DIDN'T MEAN TO LOVE YOU	ATCO 6938	150.00	70's
REEDER, ESKEW				
YOU BETTER BELIEVE ME		CROSSTONE 1007	50.00	northern
REEDER, S.Q.				
JUST IN TIME	I WANT TO KNOW	OKEH 7239	20.00	ballad
REEGAN, VALA AND THE VALARONS				
FIREMAN	LIVING IN THE PAST	ATCO 6412	100.00	northern
FIREMAN	LIVING IN THE PAST	BOB CREWE	300.00	northern
REESE AND THE PROGRESSIONS, JAMES				
JODY'S FREEZE		NAJMA N	75.00	funk
REESE AND THE THRILLERS				
TRY IT	ANGRY WOMAN	ONE WAY 109	200.00	northern
REESE, DELLA				
COMPARED TO WHAT	GAMES PEOPLE PLAY	AVCO 4515	10.00	mod
A CLOCK THAT'S GOT NO HANDS	THE BOTTOM OF OLD SMOKEY	RCA 8337	75.00	northern
BLOW OUT THE SUN	I LOVE YOU SO MUCH IT HURTS	RCA 8070	20.00	northern
BLOW OUT THE SUN	I LOVE YOU SO MUCH IT HURTS	RCA 8070 PS	40.00	northern
REESE, JACKSON (JAXON)				
CRY ME A RIVER	PRETTY GIRL	PARKWAY 142	20.00	northern
HURRY SUNDOWN	HOW DO YOU SPEAK TO AN ANGEL	PARKWAY 129	20.00	northern
REESE ,REATHA				
ONLY LIES	THINGS I SHOULD HAVE DONE	DOT 16630	400.00	northern
REEVES, HARRIET				
JUST FRIENDS	COME TO ME	EON 103	40.00	northern
REEVES, MARTHA AND THE VANDELLAS (see Martha & the Vandellas)				
REFLECTIONS				
SHE'S MY SUMMER BREEZE	GIFT WRAP MY LOVE	CAPITOL 4358	15.00	70's
(I'M JUST) A HENPECKED GUY	DON'T DO THAT TO ME	GOLDEN WORLD 16	10.00	motown
(JUST LIKE) ROMEO & JULIET	CAN'T YOU TELL BY THE LOOK	GOLDEN WORLD 9	10.00	motown
COMIN' AT YOU	POOR MAN'S SON	GOLDEN WORLD 20	10.00	motown
GIRL IN THE CANDY STORE	YOUR KIND OF LOVE	GOLDEN WORLD 29	10.00	motown
LIKE COLUMBUS DID	LONELY GIRL	GOLDEN WORLD 12	10.00	motown
OUT OF THE PICTURE	JUNE BRIDE	GOLDEN WORLD 24	10.00	motown
TALKIN' ABOUT MY GIRL	OOWEE NOW NOW	GOLDEN WORLD 15	15.00	motown
WHEELIN' & DEALIN'	DEBORAH ANN	GOLDEN WORLD 22	15.00	motown
YOU'RE MY BABY (AND DON'T YOU	SHABBY LITTLE HUT	GOLDEN WORLD 19	15.00	motown
LIKE ADAM AND EVE	VITO'S HOUSE	ABC 10794	50.00	northern
TALKIN' ABOUT MY GIRL	OOWEE NOW NOW	GOLDEN WORLD 15	10.00	northern
REGAN, EDDIE				
PLAYIN' HIDE AND SEEK	TALK ABOUT HEARTACHES	ABC 10795	50.00	**northerB**
REGAN, JOAN				
DON'T TALK TO ME ABOUT LOVE	I'M NOT A TOY	COLUMBIA 43704	20.00	northern
DON'T TALK TO ME ABOUT LOVE	I'M NO TOY	COLUMBIA 43704 PS	40.00	northernc
REID, CLARENCE				
ALONG CAME WOMAN	SOMETHING SPECIAL ABOUT MY BAB	TAYSTER 6022	15.00	ballad
I'M SORRY BABY	LET THOSE SOUL SOUNDS PLAY	TAYSTER 6013	20.00	ballad
NOBODY BUT YOU BABE	SEND ME BACK MY MONEY	ALSTON 4574	10.00	funk
SEE THROUGH	SAME:	ATCO 7025	15.00	funk
TILL I GET MY SHARE	WITH FRIENDS LIKE THESE	ALSTON 4616	10.00	funk
I REFUSE TO GIVE UP	SOMEBODY WILL	WAND 1106	20.00	northern
I'M YOUR YES MAN		WAND 1121	200.00	northern
PART OF YOUR LOVE	GIMME A TRY	DIAL 4040	15.00	northern

159

RELATIVES
THREE KINDS OF LOVE	SHE'S GOT SOUL	WOW 711	75.00	northern
I'M JUST LOOKING FOR LOVE		ALMONT 306	75.00	northern

RELF, BOB
BLOWING MY MIND TO PIECE	GIRL, YOU'RE MY KIND OF WONDER	TRANS AMERICAN	25.00	**northerB**

REMARKABLES
I CAN'T GIVE UP	YOU WOULDN'T HAVE ANYTHING	AUDIO ARTS 60000	75.00	northern
I CAN'T GIVE UP ON LOSING YOU	LOVE BOUND	AUDIO ARTS 6765	8.00	northern
IS THE FEELING STILL THERE	EASILY MISLED	AUDIO ARTS 700	10.00	northern

REMUS, EUGENE
YOU NEVER MISS A GOOD THING	GOTTA HAVE YOUR LOVIN'	MOTOWN 1001 strings	250.00	motown
YOU NEVER MISS A GOOD THING	GOTTA HAVE YOUR LOVIN'	MOTOWN 1001no strings	200.00	motown
YOU NEVER MISS A GOOD THING	HOLD ME TIGHT	MOTOWN 1001	600.00	motown

RENAULTS
ANOTHER TRAIN PULLED OUT	JUST LIKE MINE	WAND 114	20.00	northern

RENAY, BETTY
YOU'RE THE ONE FOR ME	MONEY HONEY	ULTRA CITY 70391	20.00	northern

RENAY, DIANE
UNBELIEVABLE GUY	NAVY BLUE	20th. CENTURY 456	10.00	northern
CAN'T HELP LOVIN' THAT MAN	IT'S A LOVELY DAY FOR A PARADE	D-MAN 101	150.00	northern

RENE COMBO, GOOGIE
CHICA-BOO	MERCY-MERCY	CLASS 1518	15.00	mod
SMOKEY JOE'S LALA	NEEDING YOU	CLASS 1517	20.00	mod

RENE, DAVE
I'VE BEEN WRONG	TOUCH ME	HELENA 101	20.00	northern

RENE, WENDY
AFTER LAUGHTER	WHAT WILL TOMORROW BRING	STAX 154 DJ.	15.00	ballad
REAP WHAT YOU SOW	GIVE YOU WHAT I GOT	STAX 171	30.00	funk
BAR-B-Q	YOUNG & FOOISH	STAX 159	15.00	**northerB**

REO, RAY
SOUL SENDING	LET'S GO APE	ROUND 1035	20.00	funk

REPARATA AND THE DELRONS
PANIC	SATURDAY NIGHT DIDN'T HAPPEN	MALA 12000	25.00	northern
IT'S WAITING THERE FOR YOU	I BELIEVE	MALA 573	15.00	**northerB**
THE KIND OF TROUBLE THAT I LOVE	BOYS AND GIRLS	RCA 9123	15.00	northern

REVEALERS
THEY HAD A PARTY AT THE WATERGATE	I WANT TO MAKE YOU GLAD	PARAMOUNT 243	200.00	northern

RE-VELLS
I WANT A NEW LOVE	DO I LOVE YOU?	TRENT TOWN 1014	150.00	northern

REVELS
TRUE LOVE	EVERYBODY CAN DO THE NEW DOG B	JAMIE 1318	50.00	northern

REVLONS
WHAT A LOVE THIS IS	DID I MAKE A MISTAKE	TOY 101	30.00	northern

REWIS, SUSAN
AND THE TROUBLE WITH ME IS YOU	I'LL EAT MY HAT	COLUMBIA 43777J	20.00	northern
THEY SAY YOU FOUND A NEW BABY		COLUMBIA 43580	40.00	northern

REYNOLDS, BURNY
TRY ME	IF SHE'S YOUR LOVER	SURKAR 101	20.00	northern

REYNOLDS, JEANIE
YOU AIN'T THE ONLY MAN	I KNOW HELL BE BACK SOMEDAY	CHESS 2150	15.00	70's
UNWANTED COMPANY	PHONES BEEN JUMPING ALL DAY	CASABLANCA 834	15.00	70's

REYNOLDS, L.J.
ALL I NEED	COOKIN' WITH NIXON	LADY 33	20.00	70's
KEY TO THE WORLD	SPECIAL EFFECTS	CAPITOL	20.00	70's

REYNOLDS, LARRY (CHUBBY)
PLEASE DON'T LEAVE ME	THE BELLS OF MY HEART	TRI-SPIN 1005	50.00	northern
SWEET TOOTH	SEARCHIN' AND LOOKING	TRI-SPIN 1006	50.00	northern

REYNOLDS, WILBUR AND THE MASTERS
SWEETE'N	WHO'LL CRY	RESIST 507	75.00	northern
SWEETE'N	TENDERIZER	C.B. RECORDS 1	75.00	northern

RHYTHM MACHINE
FREAKISH LOVE	WHATCHA GONNA DO	RODAN 2436	150.00	funk
THE KICK		LULU 9706	150.00	funk

RHYTHM MASTERS
I CAN DO ANYTHING YOU CAN DO	BLACK CONVERSATION	SUCCESS 100	50.00	funk

RHYTHM RASCALS
WHY DO YOU HAVE TO GO	GIRL BY MY SIDE	ROULETTE 4696	15.00	northern
WHY DO YOU HAVE TO GO	GIRL BY MY SIDE	SONIC 117	30.00	northern

RHYTHM, J.T.
ALL I WANT IS YOU	MY SWEET BABY	PALMER 5021	700.00	northern

RHYTHM, JAY
WOULDN'T IT BE A PLEASURE	SOUL EMOTIONS	LEO 884	25.00	northern

RICE, DENZIL "DUMPY"
DE-FUNKY DUMPY	MARLI	GENERAL	15.00	mod
AMERICAN 319				

RICE, E.J.

WILL YOU BE COMING BACK RECORDS 2	LET ME LOVE YOU (ONE MORE TIME	PLATINUM	150.00	70's

RICE, ROBIN

I'VE HAD IT	WANTED	METRO3	200.00	northern
I'VE HAD IT	WANTED	CRACKERJACK 4016	40.00	northern

RICH, BOBBY

THERE'S A GIRL FOR ME	I CAN'T HELP MYSELF (I'M JUST DREAMING)	SAMBEA 101	1300.00	northern

RICH, CHARLIE

LOVE IS AFTER ME	PASS ON BY	HI 2116	10.00	northern

RICHARDS, DONALD

I CRIED FOR YOUR LOVE	HELLO OPERATOR	CHEX 1003	40.00	northern

RICHARDS, JIMMY

MY NEW FOUND JOY	DON'T FORGET THOSE WHO KNEW YOU	A&M 917	20.00	ballad
(I WON'T BE) RESPONSIBLE	BUTTER BEAN SUZY	A&M 973	20.00	northern
A PENNY FOR YOUR THOUGHTS	PEACE IN THE VALLEY	A&M 1062	30.00	northern

RICHARDS, LISA

TAKE A CHANCE	MEAN OLD WORLD	SURE SHOT 5007	20.00	ballad
LET'S TAKE A CHANCE	MEAN OLD WORLD	JOVIAL 728	40.00	northern

RICHARDSON, DONALD LEE

I'VE LEARNED MY LESSON	YOU GOT ME IN THE PALM OF YOUR	SOULVILLE 1022	30.00	northern

RICHARDSON, GWEN

THAT'S MY BABY	YES I'M SAD	CB 5002	75.00	northern

RICHARDSON, HENRY

SHE LOVES TO PARTY	DANCING GIRL	ELOIS 303	20.00	northern

RICHARDSON, SANDRA

STAY HERE WITH ME	DON'T LET ME DOWN	INTER SOUL 103	10.00	70's

RICK, ROBIN AND HIM

CAUSE YOU KNOW ME	THREE CHORUSES OF DESPAIR	V.I.P. 25035	50.00	motown

RICKETT, NOONEY

TOMORROW IS A BRAND NEW DAY	PLAYER, PLAY ON	IT 107	15.00	**northerB**
WHAT MAKES ADANCE	WHAT MAKES A DANCE PT 2	iT 108	10.00	northern

RICKS, JIMMY

OH! WHAT A FEELING	OL' MAN RIVER	FESTIVAL 703	175.00	northern
THE LONG LONG ARM OF LOVE	WIGGLIN' GIGGLIN'	JUBILEE 5561	20.00	northern
DADDY ROLLIN' STONE	HOMESICK	ATCO 6220	20.00	mod

RICKS, RICKY

CHAINED AND BOUND	WHY DID I	SURE SHOT 5021	40.00	northern

RIDELL, SUNNY

COME OUT IN MY WORLD	DON'T STEAL MY BABY	WHITE CLIFFS 6901	100.00	northern

RIDEOUT

SOMEONE SPECIAL	SAME: INSTRUMENTAL	HOT LICKS 1003	10.00	70's

RIDGLEY, TOMMY

I'M ASKING FORGIVENESS	THERE IS SOMETHING ON YOUR MIN	RIVER CITY 728	20.00	ballad
IN THE SAME OLD WAY	THE GIRL FROM KOOKA MONGA	RIC. 984	20.00	northern
MY LOVE IS GETTING STRONGER	FLY IN MY PIE	INTERNATIONAL CITY 7102	750.00	northern

RIDLEY, SHARON

WHERE DID YOU LEARN TO MAKE LOVE	SCANDAL IN BEDROCK	SUSSEX 229	20.00	70's

RIGHTEOUS BROS. BAND

RAT RACE	GREEN ONIONS	VERVE 10403	15.00	**northerB**

RINGLEADERS

BABY, WHAT HAS HAPPENED TO OUR	LET'S START OVER	M-PAC 7232	150.00	northern

RITA AND THE TIARAS

GONE WITH THE WIND IS MY LOVE	WILD TIMES	DORE 783	400.00	northern

RIVAGE

STRUNG OUT (ON YOUR LOVE)	SITTIN' ON IT	TEMPUS 460	150.00	70's

RIVERA, HECTOR

AT THE PARTY	DO IT TO ME	BARRY 101	8.00	northern
PLAYING IT COOL	I GOT MY EYE ON YOU	BARRY 1012 DJ	20.00	mod

RIVERS, JOHNNY

POOR SIDE OF TOWN	A MAN CAN CRY	IMPERIAL 66205	10.00	northern
POOR SIDE OF TOWN	A MAN CAN CRY	LIBERTY 66205	15.00	northern

RIVIERAS

YOU COUNTER FEIT GIRL	CAN I SHARE YOUR LOVE	RILEYS 369	100.00	northern

RIVINGTONS

POP YOUR CORN	SAME: PT 2.	RCA 301	8.00	funk
YOU MOVE ME BABY	ALL THAT GLITTERS	A.R.E. 100	10.00	group
ALL THAT GLITTERS	YOU MOVE ME BABY	VEE JAY 634	15.00	northern
I LOVE YOU ALWAYS	YEARS OF TEARS	VEE JAY 649 DJ	20.00	northern
JUST GOT TO BE MORE	THE WILLY	VEE JAY 677	20.00	northern
YOU'RE GONNA PAY	I DON'T WANT ANEW BABY	QUAN 1379	40.00	northern

ROAD RUNNERS

EVERY MAN FOR HIMSELF		CUSTOM SOUND	300.00	funk

ROBBINS, JIMMY (also spelt ROBINS)

REPOSSESING MY LOVE	FOR GOODNESS SAKE	ALA 1173	15.00	northern
SHINE IT ON	WAITIN' ON YOU	20th. CENTURY 6667	15.00	northern

ROBINS, JIMMY

Title	B-side	Label	Price	Genre
IT'S REAL	IT'S REAL PT. 2	KENT 487	8.00	ballad
ONCE IN A LIFETIME	LONELY STREET	TRC 995	8.00	ballad
I CAN'T PLEASE HER	I MADE IT OVER	JERHART 207	10.00	northern
I JUST CANB'T PLEASE YOU	I MADE IT OVER	IMPRESSION 108	40.00	northern
IN MY HEART	THERE'S NO NEED TO CRY	JERHART 209	10.00	northern

ROBBINS, ROCK.

Title	B-side	Label	Price	Genre
GOOD LOVIN'	LITTLE GIRL	MY RECORDS 2909	40.00	funk

ROBBINS, SHARON

Title	B-side	Label	Price	Genre
GOOD GRACIOUS BABY	THE REO	JAY-EM 1001	20.00	northern

ROBBINS, SYLVIA

Title	B-side	Label	Price	Genre
DON'T LET YOUR EYES GET BIGGER	FROM THE BEGINNING	SUE 805	20.00	northern
OUR LOVE	I CAN'T TELL YOU	SUE 106	10.00	northern

ROBBINS, TRACIE

Title	B-side	Label	Price	Genre
THIS WORLD WITHOUT YOU	THAT'S WHAT YOU ARE TO ME	BRUNSWICK 55331	40.00	northern

ROBBINSON, LIONEL

Title	B-side	Label	Price	Genre
CANDY	SOMETHING'S WRONG (WITH MY BAB	KNIGHT 304	30.00	funk

ROBERSON, CHUCK

Title	B-side	Label	Price	Genre
I'VE GOT TO HAVE YOUR LOVE	YOU DON'T LOVE ME	BLUESONG 1154	30.00	70's

ROBERTS EXPERIENCE, ROY

Title	B-side	Label	Price	Genre
YOU MOVE ME PT.1	YOU MOVE ME PT.2	HOUSE OF THE FOX 11	15.00	funk

ROBERTS, JOHN

Title	B-side	Label	Price	Genre
TO BE MY GIRL	SOMETHING REMINDS ME	DUKE 429	30.00	northern
I'LL FORGET YOU	BE MY BABY	DUKE 436	10.00	northern

ROBERTS, LOU AND THE MARKS

Title	B-side	Label	Price	Genre
EVERYTHING YOU ALWAYS WANTED TO KNOW MEMPHIS 704	SHE'S NOT MAMA'S LITTLE GIRL	MGM SOUNDS OF	50.00	northern
TEN TO ONE	DON'T COUNT ON ME	MGM 13387	40.00	northerB
YOU FOOLED ME	GETTIN' READY	MGM 13347	40.00	northerB
YOU FOOLED ME	GETTIN' READY	XL	100.00	northern

ROBERTS, ROCKY

Title	B-side	Label	Price	Genre
I WON'T THINK HARD OF YOU	VOLARE	CHESS 2096	15.00	northern

ROBERTS, ROCKY AND THE AIREDALES

Title	B-side	Label	Price	Genre
JUST BECAUSE OF YOU	STASERA MI BUTTO	UA 2804	20.00	northern

ROBERTS, ROY

Title	B-side	Label	Price	Genre
I KNOW WHAT TO DO TO SATISFY YOU	SAME: INSTRUMENTAL	TINA 500	100.00	northern
GOT TO HAVE ALL YOUR LOVE	THE LEGEND OF OTIS REDDING	BQ RO 102	150.00	northern
GOT TO HAVE YOUR LOVE	LEGEND OF OTIS REDDING	NINANDY 1011	75.00	northern

ROBERTS, VIVIAN

Title	B-side	Label	Price	Genre
SO PROUD OF YOU	DON'T SAY GOODBYE	VAULT 921	20.00	northern

ROBERTS,NORA

Title	B-side	Label	Price	Genre
I JUST FLIP	MY LOVE IS YOURS	KICK OFF 189	150.00	northern

ROBERTS,TINA

Title	B-side	Label	Price	Genre
ONE WAY OR THE OTHER	CAN'T STAND TOO MUCH PAIN	SECURITY 1366	1000.00	northern

ROBERTSON, OTHELLO

Title	B-side	Label	Price	Genre
SO IN LOVE	COME ON HOME	BABY LUV 35	200.00	northern
SO IN LUV	COME ON HOME	ERA 3179	100.00	northern

ROBIN, EDE

Title	B-side	Label	Price	Genre
THERE MUST BE A LOVE SOMEWHERE	CHICK N'SLACKS	LE CAM 310	8.00	northerB

ROBINS, ART

Title	B-side	Label	Price	Genre
I CAN'T STAND TO SEE YOU CRY	FOUNTAIN OF LOVE	VANDO 102	20.00	northern

ROBINSON, ANN

Title	B-side	Label	Price	Genre
YOU DID IT 61069	I'M STILL WAITING	ALL BROTHERS	300.00	funk

ROBINSON, BILL AND THE QUAILS

Title	B-side	Label	Price	Genre
DO I LOVE YOU	LAY MY HEAD ON YOUR SHOULDER	DATE 1620	15.00	northern

ROBINSON, BILLY AND THE BURNERS

Title	B-side	Label	Price	Genre
YOU LEFT THE FIRE BURNINHG	I AM A LONELY BLACK BOY	CRAZY HORSE 1305	30.00	northern

ROBINSON, CHUCK

Title	B-side	Label	Price	Genre
LOVE AFFAIR	ARE YOU WOMEN ENOUGH	ALBRADELLA 3000	50.00	70's

ROBINSON, CLEVELAND

Title	B-side	Label	Price	Genre
BOY	SOMEBODY TO LOVE	NOSNIBOR 1011 pink	30.00	northern
BOY	SOMEBODY TO LOVE	NOSNIBOR 1012 green	8.00	northern
LOVE IS A TRAP	A LOAF OF BREAD	NOSNIBOR 1002	600.00	northern
MR.WISHING WELL	TAKE A FOOLS ADVICE	NOSNIBOR 1007	15.00	northern
MY PLACE IN THE WORLD	WOMNAN IN MOTION	NOSNIBOR 1003	15.00	northern
WORK SONG	A MAN GETS TIRED	NOSNIBOR 1004	20.00	northern

ROBINSON, DAVID

Title	B-side	Label	Price	Genre
I'M A CARPENTER		ORBITONE NO#	100.00	funk

ROBINSON, ED

Title	B-side	Label	Price	Genre
I JUST WANNA BE THERE	SAME:	ATCO 6830	15.00	70's

ROBINSON, GERRY

Title	B-side	Label	Price	Genre
SUGAR DUMPLIN'	A MOUNTAIN OUT OF A MOLEHILL	MGM 14350	30.00	northerB

ROBINSON, J.P.

Title	B-side	Label	Price	Genre
LOVE IS NOT A STRANGER	YOU GOT YOUR THING ON A STRING	ALSTON 4577	10.00	ballad
ONLY BE TRUE TO ME	I'VE GOT A LONG WAY TO GO	ALSTON 4570	15.00	ballad
PLEASE ACCEPT MY CALL	SAY IT	ALSTON 4585	10.00	ballad

ROBINSON, JAY AND THE DYNAMICS

I CAN'T LIVE WITHOUT YOU	I DON'T WANT TO BE YOUR PUPPET	MALA 551	30.00	ballad

ROBINSON, JOHNNY

GREEN GREEN GRASS OF HOME	YOU'VE BEEN WITH HIM	OKEH 7328	15.00	ballad
WHEN A MAN CRIES	POOR MAN	OKEH 7317	25.00	ballad
GONE BUT NOT FORGOTTEN	I NEED YOUR SO BAD	OKEH 7307	300.00	northern

ROBINSON, LIONEL

WARNING	ONE WOMAN MAN	KNIGHT 777	50.00	northern

ROBINSON, PRINCE JOHNNY

I FEEL IN LOVE WITH AN ANGEL	I GOT LOVE	MERCURY 73472	15.00	ballad

ROBINSON, ROSCO

WHY ARE YOU AFRAID	DARLING PLEASE TELL ME	SS7 2595	10.00	ballad
THAT'S ENOUGH	ONE MORE TIME	GERRI 1	30.00	northern
THAT'S ENOUGH	ONE MORE TIME	WAND 1125	10.00	northern
WHAT YOU'RE DOING TO ME	A THOUSAND RIVERS	WAND 1149	15.00	northern
YOU DON'T MOVE ME NO MORE	FOX HUNTING ON A WEEKEND	SS7 2610	15.00	northern
DON'T FORGET THE SOLDIERS	TIS YULETIDE	GERRI 2	10.00	ballad
WHY MUST IT END	HOW MANY TIMES MUST I KNOCK	SOUND STAGE 7 2618	15.00	ballad

ROBINSON, RUDY

CLOSE YOUR MOUTH	CLOSE YOUR MOUTH Pt. 2	LAU-REEN 1001	20.00	mod

ROBINSON, SHAUN

MY DEAR HEART	FIND LOVE RIGHT NOW	MINIT 32013 DJ	150.00	northern

ROCK CANDY

ALONE WITH NO LOVE	I DON'T THINK I'LL EVER LOVE ANOTHER	DONTEE 103	20.00	**northerB**

ROCKMASTERS

MY LONELY ONE (WHERE ARE YOU)	A WONDERFUL THING (LOVE)	ONEDERFUL 4820	20.00	northern
RAINING TEARDROPS	GET YO-SELF MARRIED	ROMULUS 3003	200.00	northern

RODGERS MOVEMENT, BUCKS

TAKE IT FROM ME GIRL	L.A.	21ST. CENTURY 603	100.00	northern

RODGERS, JOHNNY AND THE NU TONES

MAKE A CHANGE	SOUL FOOD	AMON 4619	1300.00	northern

RODGERS, TOMMY

I'LL TELL IT TO THE WIND	PASS THE WORD	AJP 1510	20.00	northern

ROECKER, SHERRILL

DON'T SAY NOTHIN' (IF U CAN'T	IT'S ALL OVER	SWAN 4173	20.00	group

ROE-O-TATION

SPECIAL CATEGORY	OLD LOVE	GERIM 1	40.00	northern

ROGER AND THE GYPSIES

PASS THE HATCHET	SAME: PT 2.	SEVEN B 7001	20.00	mod

ROGERS, BIG DADDY

I'M A BIG MAN	BE MY LAWYER	MIDAS 9006	200.00	northern

ROGERS, LEE

GO GO GIRL	I'M A PRACTICAL GUY	D-TOWN 1067	15.00	northern
WALK ON BY	TROUBLES	MAHS 0009	25.00	northern
HOW ARE YOU FIXED FOR LOVE	CRAKED UP OVER YOU	WHEELSVILLE 118	15.00	northern
JUST YOU AND I	BOSS LOVE	D-TOWN 1050	20.00	northern
LOVE AND WAR	HOW ARE YOU FIXED FOR LOVE	WHEELSVILLE 110	100.00	northern
MY ONE AND ONLY	YOU WON'T HAVE TO WAIT	D-TOWN 1062	15.00	northern
SOCK SOME LOVE POWER TO ME	BLANK:	PREMIUM STUFF 6	25.00	northern
THE SAME THINGS THAT MAKE YOU LAUGH	HOW ARE YOU FIXED FOR LOVE	WHEELSVILLE 119	50.00	northern
YOU'RE THE CREAM OF THE CROP	SOMEBODY ELSE WILL	D-TOWN 1041	15.00	northern

ROLESIA AND THE KENYATTAS

KENYATTA IN YOUR TOWN	WHERE WERE YOU	VELVET 15	20.00	funk

ROLLINS, BIRD

NO HEAT NO HOT WATER	NO HEAT NO HOT WATER (LONG VER	MAGNET 7	100.00	funk

ROLLINS, DEBBIE

HE REALLY LOVES ME	SOMEONE	ASCOT 2148	15.00	northern

ROMANS, CHARLIE

TWENTY FOUR HOURS SERVICE	COME BACK HOME	HICKORY 1438	15.00	**northerB**

ROMANS, LITTLE JOE

WHEN YOU'RE LONESOME	YOU'VE GOT THE LOVE	TUFF 419	400.00	**northerB**

ROMEOS

MON PETITE CHOW	CALYPSO CHILI	LOMA 2041	30.00	northern

RON AND BILL

IT	DON'T SAY BYE-BYE	TAMLA 54025	175.00	motown
IT	DON'T SAY BYE BYE	ARGO 5350black	40.00	motown

RON AND CANDY

LOVELY WEEKEND	PLASTIC SITUATION	INNER CITY 173	15.00	70's

RON AND THE EMBRACERS

YOU CAME INTO MY HEART	LATIN BLOOD	SPECTRUM 2	30.00	northern

RONNIE AND JOYCE

ON THE STAGE OF LOVE	YES I'M FALLING IN LOVE	ALPHA 005	15.00	northern

RONNIE AND ROBYN

AS LONG AS YOU LOVE ME (I'LL STAY)	STEP INTO MY HEART	SIDRA 9011	100.00	northern
EACH TIME	AS LONG AS YOU LOVE ME	SIDRA 9006	250.00	northern
SIDRA'S THEME	BLOW OUT THE CANDLE	SIDRA 9007	50.00	northern

RONNIE AND THE PARLEYS
AM I IN LOVE	ROSSI'S SOUND	KERWOOD 1001	200.00	northern

R.P.M.GENERATION
RONA'S THEME	LOVE THEME FROM RONA	ROMAR 702	50.00	**northerB**

ROSARIO, WILLIE
WATUSI BOOGALOO	VIENTO EN POPA	ATCO 6483	20.00	mod

ROSCO AND BARBARA
COULD THIS BE LOVE	IT AIN'T RIGHT	OLD TOWN 1175	20.00	northern

ROSCOE AND THE FRIENDS
BARNYARD SOUL	BROADWAY SISSY	TEC 3012	60.00	funk
WATERMELON MAN	DO WATCHA' KNOW	TEC 3010	50.00	mod

ROSE COLORED GLASS
CAN'T FIND THE TIME	MYSTIC TOUCH	BANG 584	10.00	northern

ROSEBUDS
SAY YOU'LL BE MINE	MAMA SAID	TOWER 105	25.00	northern

ROSIE AND THE ORIGINALS
I DON'T UNDERSTAND	YOU'RE NO GOOD	WAX WORLD 3265	300.00	northern

ROSS, FAYE
FAITH, HOPE & TRUST	YOU AIN'T AIN'T RIGHT	ROUND 1030	15.00	northern
FAITH, HOPE & TRUST	YOU AIN'T AIN'T RIGHT	ROUND 1030 gold lbl	30.00	northern

ROSS, JACKIE
DON'T CHANGE YOUR MIND	WHO COULD BE LOVING YUOU	FOUNTAIN 1101	20.00	70's
HONEY DEAR	WE CAN MAKE IT	CHESS 1940	10.00	northern
NEW LOVER	JERK AND TWINE	CHESS 1920	10.00	northern
SELFISH ONE	EVERYTHING BUT LOVE	CHESS 1903	10.00	northern
KEEP YOUR CHIN UP	LOVE IS EASY TO LOSE	BRUNSWICK 55325	25.00	northern
SHOWCASE	ANGEL IN THE MORNING	MERCURY 73041	20.00	northern
DYNAMITE LOVIN'	YOU REALLY KNOW HOW 2 HURT	CHESS 1929	20.00	northern
GLORY BE	I MUST GIVE YOU TIME	MERCURY 73185	20.00	northern
HASTE MAKES WASTE	WASTING TIME	CHESS 1915	10.00	northern
HONEY DEAR	TAKE ME FOR A LITTLE WHILE	CHESS 1938	10.00	northern
I'VE GOT A SKILL	CHANGE YOUR WAYS	CHESS 1913	10.00	northern

ROSSI, KENNY
DON'T LOSE THIS LOVE	TURN ON YOUR LOVELIGHT	ARCTIC 122	50.00	northern

ROSSI, NITA
SOMETHING TO GIVE	HERE I GO AGAIN	HICKORY 1399	20.00	northern

ROTATIONS
DON'T EVER HURT ME GIRL	I COULD BE LIKE COLUMBUS	LAW-TON 1550	40.00	70's
(PUT A DIME ON) D-9	(SAME: INSTRUMENTAL	FRANTIC 200.	300.00	northern
(PUT A NICKEL ON) D - 9	SAME: INSTRUMENTAL	FRANTIC 200N	400.00	northern
A CHANGED MAN	HEARTACHES	FRANTIC 202	150.00	**northerB**
I CAN'T FIND HER	SEARCHING IN VAIN	DEBROSSARD 111	100.00	northern
TRYING TO MAKE YOU MY OWN	MISTY ROSES	MALA 576	40.00	northern

ROUND ROBIN MONOPOLY
I'D RATHER LOAN YOU OUT	LIFE IS FUNKY	TRUTH 3209	30.00	northern

ROYAL CHESSMEN
YOU MUST BELIEVE ME	BEGGIN' YOU	CUSTOM FIDELITY	300.00	northern

ROYAL ESQUIRES
AIN'T GONNA RUN NO MORE	OUR LOVE USED TO BE (ON THE SUNNY SIDE UP)	HSI PRIX 69001	1500.00	northern

ROYAL FIVE
IT AIN'T AIN'T NO BIG THING	PEACE OF MIND	ARCTIC 160	30.00	northern
MY BABYJUST	CARES FOR ME	COBRA 1128	100.00	northern
SAY IT TO MY FACE	GONNA KEEP LOVIN' YOU	TYLER 200	25.00	**northerB**

ROYAL JESTERS
THAT GIRL	LADY SUNSHINE	OPTIMUM 104	40.00	northern
WHAT LOVE HAS JOINED TOGETHER	WISDOM OF A FOOL	JESTER 102	30.00	northern

ROYAL JOKERS
FROM A TO Z (LOVE GAME)	FROM A TO Z (LOVE GAME) INSTR.	WINGATE 20	10.00	northern

ROYAL PLAYBOYS
ARABIA	BRING IT BACK	DO DE 111	500.00	northern

ROYAL PREMIERS
I CAN MAKE IT IF I TRY	MAKE LOVE TO ME	MBS 105	15.00	northern
WHO AM I WITHOUT YOUR LOVE	I WANNA LOVE LOVE LOVE	TOY 102	30.00	northern

ROYAL ROBINS
HOW HIGH THE MOON	SOMETHING YOU'VE GOT BABY	ABC 10542	20.00	group
SOMETHING ABOUT YOU SENDS ME	ROLLER COASTER	TRU-GLO-TOWN 506	750.00	northern
TURN ME LOOSE	THE COUNTRY FOOL	ABC 10504	25.00	northern

ROYAL, AUDREY
COME ON PLAYBOY	SAME: INSTRUMENTALMENTAL	ALSTON 4575	40.00	northern

ROYAL, BILLY JOE
HEART'S DESIRE	DEEP INSIDE ME	COLUMBIA 43622	20.00	northern

ROYAL, DUKE
MONKEY ON MY BACK		DEBBIE 1003	50.00	northern

ROYALETTES
NEVER AGAIN	I WANT TO MEET HIM	MGM 13405	10.00	northern
ONLY WHEN YOU'RE LONELY	YOU BRING ME DOWN	MGM 13451	15.00	northern
OUT OF SIGHT, OUT OF MIND	IT'S GONNA TAKE A MIRACLE	MGM 13366	10.00	northern

THERE HE GOES	COME TO ME	WB 5439	15.00	northern
ONLY WHEN YOU'RE LONELY	YOU BRING ME DOWN	MGM 13451 PS	25.00	northern

ROYE, LEE

TEARS	WHO AM I	DECCA 32356	75.00	northern

RUBAIYATS

OMAR KHAYYAM	TOMORROW	SANSU 456	20..00	northern

RUBIES

A SPANISH BOY	DEEPER	VEE JAY 596	15.00	northern

RUBIN

YOU'VE BEEN AWAY	BABY, YOUR MY EVERYTHING	KAPP 869	250.00	**northernB**

RUBY.

FEMININE INGENUITY	DECEIVED	GOLD TOKEN 100	250.00	northern

RUBY AND THE ROMANTICS

BABY COME HOME	EVERY DAY'S A HOLIDAY	KAPP 601	15.00	northern
DOES HE REALLY CARE FOR ME	NEVERTHELESS (I'M IN LOVE WITH	KAPP 646	15.00	northern
MUCH BETTER OFF THAN I'VE EVER BEEN	OUR EVERLASTING LOVE	KAPP 578	15.00	northern
TWILIGHT TIME	UNA BELLA BRAZILIAN MELODY	ABC 10911	10.00	northern

RUDOLPH, LORI

DON'T LET THEM TELL ME	GRIEVING ABOUT A LOVE	TRI-PHI 1003	25.00	motown

RUDOLPH, LORRAINE

KEEP COMING BACK FOR MORE	AFTER ALL I'VE BEEN THROUGH	JETSTREAM 817	15.00	northern

RUFFIN, DAVID

ACTION SPEAKS LOUDER THAN WOR	YOU CAN GET WHAT I GOT	CHECK MATE 1003	100.00	motown
I'M IN LOVE	ONE OF THESE DAYS	ANNA 1127	75.00	motown
MR. BUS DRIVER - HURRY	KNOCK YOU OUY (WITH LOVE)	CHECKMATE 1010	50.00	motown
YOU CAN COME RIGHT BACK TO ME	DINAH	MOTOWN 1187	15.00	motown

RUFFIN, JIMMY

DON'T FEEL SORRY FOR ME	HEART	MIRACLE 1	175.00	motown
HOW CAN I SAY I'M SORRY	AS LONG AS THERE IS L-O-V-E	SOUL 35016	15.00	motown
SINCE I'VE LOST YOU	I WANT HER LOVE	SOUL 35002	20.00	motown

RUMBLERS

SOULFUL JERK	HEY DID A DADA	DOWNEY 127	50.00	northern

RUSS, LONNIE

SAY GIRL	SOMETHING FOR MY LOVE	KERWOOD 711	400.00	northern

RUSSELL, JACKIE

IF YOU DON'T WANT ME (LET ME B	DON'T TRADE LOVE FOR MONEY	SOUL KITCHEN 10	100.00	northern

RUSSELL, RICHARD

WISH YOU WERE HERE	NO BODY CAN STOP ME	KASHE 444	15.00	northern

RUSSELL, SAXIE

PSYCHEDLIC SOUL	PSYCHEDELIC SOUL PT.2	THOMAS 1639	75.00	**northerB**

RUSSO, CHARLIE

YOU BETTER BELIEVE IT	HEAVEN KNOWS YOU'RE HERE	LAURIE 3393	20.00	northern

RYAN, ROZ

YOU'RE MY ONLY TEMPTATION	I CAN'T SEE NOTHING BUT THE GO	VOLT 4040	50.00	northern

RYDER, MITCH

BREAK OUT	I NEED HELP	NEW VOICE 811	10.00	northern
DEVIL WITH THE BLUE DRESS	I HAD IT MADE	NEW VOICE 817	8.00	northern
BLESSING IN DISGUISE	WHAT NOW MY LOVE	DYNOVOICE 901	15.00	northern
YOU GET YOUR KICKS	TAKIN' ALL I CAN GET	NEW VOICE 814	15.00	northern
SOCK IT TO ME - BABY	I NEVER HAD IT BETTER	NEW VOICE 820 PS	20.00	northern
YOU GET YOUR KICKS	RUBY BABY	NEW VOICE 830	8.00	northern
SOCK IT TO ME - BABY sleeve	I NEVER HAD IT BETTER	NEW VOICE 820 PS	20.00	northern
TOO MANY FISH IN THE SEA	ONE GRAIN OF SAND	NEW VOICE 822 PS	15.00	northern

S

S.N. AND THE CT'S

THE PLEASURE OF YOUR COMPANY	MARIA (LOVE AND MUSIC)	SUNBURST 771	10.00	northern

S.O.T.

DO THE SPANK	PT.2	SOULAPPLE 3030	15.00	funk

S.O.U.L.

THIS TIME AROUND	ON TOP OF THE WORLD	MUSICOR 1472	8.00	70's
BURNING SPEAR		MUSICOR	100.00	funk
CAN YOU FEEL IT	LOVE, PEACE AND POWER	MUSICOR 1460	10.00	funk
PEACE OF MIND	TO MEND A BROKEN HEART	MUSICOR 1463	15.00	funk
ROPE A DOPE	I NEED SOMEBODY TO LOVE	DYNAMO 6004	10.00	funk

SAAB, CLIFF

THE MULE	MIX IT UP	ROULETTE 7014	15.00	funk

SABLES

I'M ON FIRE	DARLING	RCA 8521	20.00	northern

SADDLER REVUE, REGGIE

JUST WAIT AND SEE	R.R.A.W.J.	DE-LITE 545	20.00	70's
LOVE, YOU CAN'T SHAKE IT	SAME:	DE-LITE 560	20.00	70's
SO LONG SWEET GIRL	I'VE BEEN TRYING	DE-LITE 548	40.00	70's
JUST WAIT AND SEE	RAGGEDY BAG	AQUARIUS 8700	50.00	funk
I CAN'T ACCOUNT TO MY ACTIONS	SAME:	DE-LITE 556 DJ	15.00	70's

SADDLER, JANICE AND THE JAMMERS

MY BABY'S COMING HOME TO STAY	SAME: INSTRUMENTAL	DE-LITE 558	30.00	70's

SADINA

I WANT THAT BOY	WHO AM I KIDDIN'	SMASH 1979	20.00	northern

SAIN, LEE

I CAN'T FIGHT IT	BABY DON'T LEAVE ME	BROACH 6724	15.00	northern
TELL MY BABY	WE'LL MEET AGAIN	GLOW STAR 816	30.00	northern

SAINT, CATHY

BIG BAD WORLD	MR. HEARTBREAK	DAISEY 501	20.00	northern

SAINTS

MIRROR MIRROR ON THE WALL	COME ON LET'S DANCE	REVUE 11069	20.00	group
THE SUN DON'T SHINE (EVERYDAY)	I'VE BEEN TAKE FOR A RIDE	STARDOM	40.00	northern
THE SUN DON'T SHINE (EVERYDAY)	I'VE BEEN TAKE FOR A RIDE	KENT 480	25.00	northern
I'LL LET YOU SLIDE	LOVE CAN BE	WIGWAM	1000.00	northern

SALT

HUNG UP		CHOCTAW NO. #	300.00	funk

SALVADORS

STICK BY ME BABY	I WANNA DANCE	WISE WORLD 301	600.00	**northerB**

SAM AND BILL

I'LL TRY	I FEEL LIKE CRYING	DECCA 32143	15.00	northern
TRYIN' TO GET BACK TO MY BABY	I NEED YOUR LOVE TO COMFORT ME	DECCA 32200	15.00	northern

SAM AND KITTY

I'VE GOT SOMETHING GOOD	LOVE IS THE GREATEST	FOUR BROTHERS 452	30.00	**northerB**
YOUR MONEY - MY LOVE	DON'T HIT ON ME	FOUR BROTHERS 400	15.00	northern

SAMPLE, HANK

I'M SO IN LOVE WITH YOU	YOU'RE BEING UNFAIR TO ME	JAY WALKING 6	20.00	northern

SAMPSON, DON RAY

BABY COME BACK	TAKE IT EASY	E RECORDS 401	50.00	northern

SAMSON AND DELILAH

THERE'S A DJ IN YOUR TOWN	TIME TO PROVE MY LOVE TO YOU	INDIGO 315	15.00	funk
WOMAN	WILL YOU BE READY	ABC 10954	15.00	northern
WOMAN	WILL YOU BE READY	RED CAP 101	25.00	northern

SAN REMO GOLDEN STRINGS

FESTIVAL TIME	JOY ROAD	GORDY 7060	10.00	motown

SAN REMO STRINGS

I'M SATISFIED	BLUEBERRY HILL	RIC TIC 108	10.00	motown
FESTIVAL TIME	JOY ROAD	RIC TIC 112	10.00	northern
HUNGRY FOR LOVE	ALL TURNED ON	RIC TIC 104	8.00	northern

SANDERS, FRANKIE

TAKE ANOTHER LOOK	BLUES TIME IN BIRMINGHAM	JUANA 1953	30.00	70's

SANDERS, NELSON

I HOLD THE KEY	IT'S REAL	SOUL KING 402	10.00	ballad
MOJO MAN	I'M LONELY	RAMBLER 3001	500.00	northern
THIS LOVE IS HERE TO STAY	TIRED OF BEING YOUR FOOL	LA BEAT 6608	30.00	northern

SANDI AND MATUES

THE WORLD		MATUES	200.00	funk

SANDIFER, MCKINLEY

GET UP (IF U WANT 2B SOMEBODY)	SWEET LITTLE WOMAN	USA 907	20.00	funk

SANDPEBBLES

YOU TURN MRE ON	GARDEN OF EDEN	CALLA 160	20.00	northern

SANDPIPERS

LONELY TOO LONG	I REALLY LOVE YOU	GIANT 705	400.00	northern
YOUNG GENERATION	ALI BABA	KISMET 394	30.00	northern

SANDS, EVIE

BILLY SUNSHINE	IT MAKES ME LAUGH	CAMEO 2002	10.00	northern
PICTURE ME GONE	IT MAKES ME LAUGH	CAMEO 413	30.00	northern
RUN HOME TO YOUR MAMA	TAKE ME FOR A LITTLE WHILE	BLUE CAT 118	10.00	northern

SANDS, IDA

RESCUE ME	PROPHESIZE	SHIPTOWN 008	200.00	northern
START ALL OVER AGAIN	DON'T LOSE A GOOD THING	HOW BIG 202129	50.00	northern
YOU CAME ALONG TO RESCUE ME	I PROPHESIZE	CHIEF 103	25.00	northern

SANDS, LOLA

TO WHOM IT MAY CONCERN		BISON 101	150.00	northern

SANDS, TOMMY

THE STATUE	LITTLE ROSITA	LIBERTY 58842	25.00	northern

SANDY AND THE PEBBLES

MY FOOLISH LITTLE HEART	HE'S MY KIND OF FELLOW	MERCURY 72745	20.00	northern

SANDY AND THE STY-LETTS

I'VE GOT TWO LOVERS	WISHING STAR	REM 101	200.00	northern

SANSOM, BOBBY

DON'T LEAVE	HOW'S ABOUT IT BABY	SUBLIME 3	15.00	northern

SANTOS, LARRY

YOU GOT ME WHERE YOU WANT ME	TOMORROW WITHOUT LOVE	EVOLUTION 1007	75.00	**northerB**

SAPPHIRES

WHO DO YOU LOVE	OH SO SOON	SWAN 4162	10.00	northern
EVIL ONE	HOW COULD I SAY GOODBYE	ABC 10693	25.00	northern
GONNA BE A BIG THING	YOU'LL NEVER STOP ME FROM LOVI	ABC 10753 DJ	75.00	northern
GOTTA BE MORE THAN FRIENDS	MOULIN ROUGE (WHERE IS YOUR HE	SWAN 4184	10.00	northern
GOTTA HAVE YOUR LOVE	GEE I'M SORRY BABY	ABC 10639	20.00	northern
I'VE GOT MINE YOU BETTER GET YOU	I FOUND OUT TOO LATE	SWAN 4177	20.00	northern
THE SLOW FIZZ	OUR LOVE IS EVERYWHERE	ABC 10778	30.00	northern

SATANS

WHAT A FOOL	IT MUST BE LOVE	GEM 10	75.00	northern

SATIN

YOUR LOVE'S GOT ME	THE LOOK ON YOUR FACE	SHELL 1004	150.00	northern

SATIN BELLS

BABY, YOU'RE SO RIGHT FOR ME	WHEN YOU'RE READY	SHAMLEY 44002	10.00	northern

SATIN, GINNY

HEY LOVER	WHERE DID ALL THE GOOD TIMES GONE	PHILIPS 40261	50.00	northern

SATIN, LONNIE

WATERMELON MAN	SOUL BOSSA NOVA	SCEPTER 1251	10.00	mod

SATINTONES

ANGEL	A LOVE THAT CAN NEVER BE	MOTOWN 1006	1500.00	motown
GOING TO THE HOP	MOTOR CITY	TAMLA 54026.	500.00	motown
I KNOW HOW IT FEELS	MY KIND OF LOVE	MOTOWN 1010	150.00	motown
MY BELOVED no address	SUGAR DADDY	MOTOWN 1000.	100.00	motown
MY BELOVED no strings	SUGAR DADDY	MOTOWN 1000	200.00	motown
MY BELOVED address on lbl	SUGAR DADDY	MOTOWN 1000	125.00	motown
MY KIND OF LOVE	I KNOW HOW IT FEELS	MOTOWN 1010	150.00	motown
TOMORROW & ALWAYS	A LOVE THAT CAN NEVER BE	MOTOWN 1006	150.00	motown
TOMORROW AND ALWAYS Male lead wth strings	A LOVE THAT CAN NEVER BE	MOTOWN 1006	150.00	motown
ZING WENT THE STRINGS OF MY HE	FADED LETTER	MOTOWN 1020	400.00	motown

SATISFACTIONS

TURN BACK THE TEARS	ONE LIGHT TWO LIGHTS	LIONEL 3205	8.00	70's
OH WHY	WE WILL WALK TOGETHER	CHESAPEAKE 610	50.00	group
TAKE IT OF LEAVE IT	YOU GOT TO SHARE	SMASH 2098	50.00	northern
USE ME	KEEP ON TRYING	SMASH 2131	20.00	northern

SAUNDERS, GARRETT

A DAY OR TWO	EASIER SAID THAN DONE	SEROCK 2001	350.00	northern

SAUNDERS, LARRY

ON THE REAL SIDE	LET ME BE THE SPECIAL ONE	TURBO 38	20.00	northern

SAVOY, RONNIE

LOVING YOU	MEMORIES LINGER	WINGATE 1	10.00	northern
PITFALL		TUFF 416	70.00	northern

SAX, BOBBY AND THE NEW MESSIAH

OUT-HOUSE 73	OUT-HOUSE 73 PT.2	MESSIAH 1000	50.00	funk

SAYLES, JOHNNY

SOMEBODY'S CHANGING (MY SWEET BABY'S MIND)	YOU'RE SO RIGHT FOR ME	DAKAR 607	15.00	70's
MY LOVE AIN'T WITHOUT YOUR LOVE	GOOD GOLLY	BRUNSWICK 55473	15.00	northern
ANYTHING FOR YOU	DEEP DOWN IN MY HEART	MINIT 32003	30.00	northern
DON'T TURN YOUR BACK ON ME	YOU TOLD A LIE	MARVLUS 6000	15.00	northern
I CAN'T GET ENOUGH	HOLD MY OWN BABY	ST. LAWRENCE 1024	20.00	**northerB**
MY LOVE'S A MONSTER	NEVER LET ME GO	CHI-TOWN 3	20.00	**northerB**

SCALES, HARVEY

I CAN'T CRY NO MORE	BROADWAY FREEZE	MAGIC TOUCH 16001	15.00	northern

SCHROEDER ORCH., JOHN

AGENT 00-SOUL	NIGHTRIDER	CAMEO 389	10.00	northern

SCHUMAKER, CHRISTINE AND THE SUPREMES

MOTHER YOU, SMOTHER YOU	SAME:	MOTOWN no.#	250.00	motown

SCHWARTZ, DEDE

FUNNY HOW WE CHANGED PLCES	SAME:	RCA 10605	15.00	70's

SCIENTISTS OF SOUL

BE'S THAT WAY SOMETIMES	BABY BABY I LOVE YOU	KASHE 442	10.00	northern

SCOTT, AL

WHAT HAPPENED TO YESTERDAY	YOU'RE TOO GOOD	GENUINE 150	1500.00	northern

SCOTT BROTHERS

WE LIKE GIRLS	MAGIC WAND	ZACHRON 602	15.00	northern
A HUNK OF FUNK	THEY ALL CAME BACK	TODDLIN TOWN 125	15.00	funk
SIDE TRACKING	GOTTA GET AWAY FROM YOU	CAPRI 111	15.00	funk

SCOTT, BETTYE AND THE DEL-VETTS

GOOD FEELING	DOWN, DOWN, DOWN	TEAKO 747	15.00	northern
GOOD FEELING	DOWN, DOWN, DOWN	ONE WAY 2291	10.00	northern

SCOTT, BILLY AND THE THE PROPHETS

SO GLAD YOU HAPPENED TO ME	EVERY DAY I HAVE TO CRY	3-P 36506	50.00	70's

I'M MOVING ON	DON'T PUSH MY LOVE	ALTO 2012	30.00	northern
SCOTT, CINDY				
I LOVE YOU BABY	IN YOUR SPARE TIME	VEEP 1253	125.00	northern
TIME CAN CHANGE A LOVE	I'VE BEEN LOVING YOU TOO ONG	VEEP 1268	20.00	northern
SCOTT, COOKIE				
YOU LOVE IT WON ME OVER	FUNNY CHANGES	ORR 1007	15.00	northern
YOUR LOVE, IT WON ME OVER	FUNNY CHANGES	ORR 1101	10.00	northern
I DON'T CARE	MISLED	0RR 1016	75.00	northern
MISLED	SAME: INSTRUMENTAL	ORR 1013	30.00	northern
SCOTT, DEAN				
GOTTA HAVE LOSERS YOU	TWO YEARS AGO TODAY	SCEPTER 12137	20.00	northern
SCOTT, EARL				
ALL MIXED UP	MY LOVE IS BURNING	CASH SALES 101	25.00	northern
SCOTT, FREDDIE				
HEY GIRL	THE SLIDE	COLPIX 692 USA	10.00	northern
MR. HEARTACHE	ONE HEARTACHE TOO MANY	COLUMBIA 43112	60.00	northern
SCOTT, GARRETT				
WORKING ON A GROOVY THING	NOW THAT I LOVE YOU	MERCURY 73006	40.00	70's
SCOTT, GLORIA				
JUST AS LONG AS WE'RE TOGETHER	THERE WILL NEVER BE ANOTHER	CASABLANCA 815	10.00	70's
WHAT AM I GONNA DO	SAME: INSTRUMENTAL	CASABLANCA 5	15.00	70's
SCOTT, IRENE				
EVERYDAY WORRIES	YOU'RE NO GOOD	MIDAS 300	30.00	northern
I'M STUCK ON MY BABY	WHY DO YOU TRET ME LIKE YOU DO	SMASH 2138	15.00	northern
SCOTT, JIMMY (LITTLE)				
LOVE LANGUAGE	BE CAREFUL	EARWAX 776	10.00	70's
TAKE A CHANCE ON LOVE	SAME:	BACK BONE 101	15.00	70's
WHAT AM I GONNA DO (ABOUT YOU BABY)	PAIR AND A SPARE	EASTBOUND 610	25.00	funk
IT RAINED 40 DAYS & NIGHTS	DO YOU GET MESSAGE	GIANT 706	225.00	northern
IT RAINED 40 DAYS AND NIGHTS	NOBODY BUT YOU	GIANT 708	200.00	northern
SCOTT, JOHNNY				
LET ME BE A WINNER	I'M COMING OUT FROM UNDER	PORTRA. 10	15.00	70's
SCOTT, KURTIS				
NO, NO BABY	NO PLACE LIKE HOME	SURE SHOT 5020	20.00	northern
SCOTT, LITTLE RENA				
I JUST CAN'T FORGET THAT BOY	SET ME FREE	BLACK ROCK 2000	10.00	northern
I JUST CAN'T FORGET THAT BOY	SET ME FREE	GRAND JUNCTION 1002	8.00	northern
SCOTT, MOODY				
MY LOVELY LADY	I'LL ALWAYS BELONG TO YOU	STRAIGHT AHEAD 12	30.00	70's
(WE GOTTA) BUST OUT OF THE GHETTO	Pt.2	SS7 2660	10.00	funk
SCOTT, RAY AND THE SCOTSMEN				
THE REAL THING	CAN'T GET OVER LOSING YOU	DECCA 32186	20.00	northern
SCOTT, SAM				
A CHANGE IS GONNA COME	DOWN-HEARTED BLUES	OKEH 7258	30.00	ballad
SCOTT, SHARON				
COULD IT BE YOU	I'D LIKE TO KNOW	RCA 8907	75.00	northern
SCOTT, SHIRLEY J.				
GOOSE PIMPLES	LONELY GIRL	STEPHANYE 333	30.00	northern
SCOTT, TOMMY				
PAIN RELIEVER	SAME: INSTRUMENTAL	WISE WORLD 1004	20.00	northern
SCOTT, WALTER				
SOUL STEW RECIPE	FEELIN' SOMETHIONG NEW INSIDE	PZAZZ 26	10.00	funk
SCOTT-HERON, GIL				
LADY DAY AND JOHN COLTRANE	SAVE THE CHILDREN	FLYING DUTCHMAN 26015	15.00	70's
THE BOTTLE	BACK HOME	STRATAEAST 19742	15.00	70's
SEA SHELLS				
QUIET HOME		VILLAGE 1000	250.00	northern
SEAGRAM, RON				
I WANNA SPEND MY WHOLE LIFETIM	GIRLS WERE MADE 2B LOVED	CHOCOLATE MAMA 386	20.00	70's
SEALS, JIMMY				
THE YESTERDAY OF OUR LOVE	SHE'S NOT A BAD GIRL	CHALLENGE 59299 DJ	100.00	northern
SEARS, TOMMY				
GET OUT	SOUL CITY	CHALET 1050 DJ	40.00	northern
SEBASTIAN, JOEL				
ANGEL IN BLUE	BLUE CINDERELLA	MIRACLE 9	50.00	motown
SEBASTION, JOEL *(mispelt artist credit)*				
ANGEL IN BLUE	BLUE CINDERELLA	MIRACLE 9	100.00	motown
2nd. AMENDMENT BAND				
BACKTALK		MONET	300.00	funk
SECOND NATURE				
STILL A LOT OF LOVE	HOW GREAT LIFE CAN BE	JAM. 4572	200.00	70's
SECRETS				
HERE I AM	I FEEL A THRILL COMING ON	OMEN 15	40.00	**northerB**
SEGMENTS OF TIME				
TEARS KEEP FALLING	MEMORIES	SUSSEX 256	30.00	northern

SEMINOLES

I CAN'T STAND IT	IT TAKES A LOT	CHECKMATE 1012	75.00	motown
TROUBLE IN MIND	HAVE YOU GOT A LOVE	HI-LITE 87568	250.00	northern
YOU CAN LUMP IT	FOREVER	ACT IV 94147	250.00	northern
YOU CAN LUMP IT	FOREVER	MID TOWN 101	200.00	northern

SENSATIONS

OH, GIRL	I GUESS THAT'S LIFE	WAY OUT 1003	30.00	northern
I WON'T HURT YOU	GET ON UP MAMA	WAY OUT 1047	15.00	group
TWO CAN MAKE IT	IT'S A NEW DAY	WAY OUT 1005	15.00	group
DEMANDING MAN	GONNA STEP ASIDE	WAY OUT 2005	500.00	northern
LONELY WORLD	GOTTA FIND MYSELF ANOTHER GIRL	WAY OUT 1000	15.00	northern

SENSATIONS AND THE BAKER, YVONNE

I CAN'T CHANGE	MEND THE TORN PEICES	JUNIOR 1010	30.00	northern

SENTIMENTALS

I WANT TO LOVE YOU	THIS TIME	MINT 808	50.00	northern
I;LL MISS THESE THINGS		MINT 807	50.00	northern

SEQUINS

A CASE OF LOVE	YOU'RE ALL I NEED	RENFRO 112	60.00	**northerB**
HE'S A FLIRT		RENFRO 126	400.00	**northerB**
THAT BOY		RENFRO 113	400.00	**northerB**
TRY MY LOVE	HE'S GONNA BREAK YOUR HEART	DETROIT SOUND 500	500.00	northern

SERENADERS

IF YOUR HEART SAYS YES	I'LL CRY TOMORROW	MOTOWN 1046 NI	400.00	motown
I'LL CRY TOMORROW	IF YOUR HEART SAY YES	V.I.P. 25002	75.00	motown
TWO LOVERS MAKE ONE FOOL	ADIOS, MY LOVE	RIVERSIDE 4549	70.00	northern

SERVICEMEN

ARE YOU ANGRY	NEED A HELPING HAND	WIND HIT 100	850.00	**northerB**
CONNIE	SWEET MAGIC	CHRTMAKER 408	400.00	northern
I NEED A HELPING HAND	MY TERMS	PATHEWAY 102 *"Man design label"*	50.00	northern
I NEED A HELPING HAND	MY TERMS	PATHEWAY 102 *"Orange label"*	40.00	northern

7 DWARFS

STOP GIRL	ONE BY ONE	IDEAL 1168	50.00	**northerB**

7 SONS

ON THE RUN	BABY PLEASE COME BACK	VTI 20671	15.00	northern

SEVEN SOULS

I STILL LOVE YOU	I'M NO STRANGER	OKEH 7289	200.00	northern

SEVENS, SAMMY

EVERYBODY CROSSFIRE	WATCH YOUR STEP	SWAN 4159	40.00	northern
YOU ARE A LUCKY SO AND SO	HERE COMES THE BRIDE	SWAN 4146	50.00	northern

7TH. AVENUE AVIATORS

YOU SHOULD 'O HELD ON	BOY NEXT DOOR	CONGRESS 255	300.00	northern

7TH. WONDER

SHE'S MY GIRL	SAME: INSTRUMENTAL	T TOWN 3688	15.00	70's

SEVENTH WONDER

CAPTAIN OF MY SHIP	PHAROH	W.G. 666	20.00	northern

SEXTETTE UNLIMITED

BOOT THAT THING		GERRI	50.00	funk

SEXTON, ANN

I STILL LOVE YOU	COME BACK HOME	SEVENTY 7 114	10.00	funk
YOU'RE LOSING ME	YOU'RE GONNA MISS ME	SEVENTY 7 133	15.00	funk
YOU'VE BEEN GONE TOO LONG	YOU DON'T KNOW WHAT YOU GOT	IMPEL 101	100.00	northern
YOU'VE BEEN GONE TOO LONG	YOU'RE LETTING ME DOWN	SEVENTY 7 104	20.00	**northerB**

SHADES OF BLUE

WITH THIS RING	LONELY SUMMER	IMPACT 1014	8.00	northern
ALL I WANT IS LOVE	HOW DO YOU SAVE A DYING LOVE	IMPACT 1026	20.00	northern
HAPPINESS	THE NIGHT	IMPACT 1015	8.00	northern
OH HOW HAPPY	LITTLE ORPHAN BOY	IMPACT 1007	8.00	northern
PENNY ARCADE	FUNNY KIND OF LOVE	IMPACT 1028	20.00	northern

SHADES OF JADE

IS IT WRONG	AFFECTION	CENCO 114	150.00	northern
WHY DOES IT FEEL SO RIGHT	RAINY SUNDAY	DORE 806	150.00	northern

SHADES OF TIME

CAN YOU DIG IT	POVERTY CHILD	BETTER WORLD 4357	75.00	funk

SHADOWS

MY LOVE IS GONE	NO OTHER LOVE	USA 106	80.00	northern
MY LOVE HAS GONE	NO OTHER LOVE	GOLDEN SOUND 2001	200.00	northern

SHAFFER, BEVERLY

EVEN THE SCORE	WHERE WILL YOU BE BOY	ONEDERFUL 4838	50.00	northern
I SIMPLY LOVE HIM	WHEN I THINK ABOUT YOU	ONEDERFUL 4840	40.00	northern

SHAINE

CALL ME SWEET THINGS	TRY MY LOVE	SUE 16	15.00	northern

SHAKERS

ONE WONDERFUL MOMENT	LOVE, LOVE, LOVE	ABC 10960	20.00	northern

SHALIMARS

STOP AND TAKE A LOOK AT YOURSE	BABY	VERVE 10388	30.00	**northerB**

SHAMETTES

DON'T WASTE YOUR TIME	LOVE ME TOMORROW	GOLD DUST 301	300.00	northern

SHAN-DELLS

I'VE GOT TO LOVE HER	IDLE EXCURSION	BRIDGE SOCIETY 114	150.00	northern

SHANE, JACKIE

ANY OTHER WAY	STICKS AND STONES	SUE 776	10.00	northern
IN MY TENEMENT	COMIN' DOWN	SUE 788	20.00	northern

SHANNON, BOBBY

GET MY GROOVE FROM YOU	YOU'RE AN UPLIFT	TO-MAR 11	100.00	70's

SHA-RAE, BILLY

CRYING CLOWN	DO IT	SPECTRUM 114	8.00	ballad
I'M GONE	LET'S DO IT AGAIN	SPECTRUM 120 mauve	15.00	**northerB**

SHARON AND THE BITS O' HONEY

WAS I REALLY MADE FOR YOU	DON'T PUSH MY LOVECUP ASIDE	PENTHOUSE 1003	75.00	northern

SHARP, DEE DEE

HAPPY 'BOUT THE WHOLE THING	TOUCH MY LIFE	TSOP 4776	10.00	70's
BABY CAKES	GRAVY	CAMEO 219	8.00	northern
GOOD	DEEP DARK SECRET	CAMEO 335	10.00	northern
THERE AIN'T NOTHING I WOULDN'T DO	IT'S A FUNNY SITUATION	CAMEO 382	10.00	northern
(THAT'S WHAT) MY MAMA SAID	LET'S TWINE	CAMEO 357	10.00	northern
HE'S NO ORDINARY GUY	NEVER PICK A PRETTY BOY	CAMEO 329	15.00	northern
STANDING IN THE NEED OF LOVE	I REALLY LOVE YOU	CAMEO 375	15.00	northern
THE NIGHT	RIDE	CAMEO 230	10.00	northern
WHAT KIND OF LADY	YOU'RE GONNA MISS ME	GAMBLE 219	30.00	northern
HE'S NO ORDINARY GUY	NEVER PICK A PRETTY BOY	CAMEO 329 PS	30.00	northern
ROCK ME IN THE CRADLE OF LOVE	YOU'LL NEVER BE MINE	CAMEO 260 PS	20.00	northern
STANDING IN THE NEED OF LOVE	I REALLY LOVE YOU	CAMEO 375 PS	30.00	northern
THE NIGHT	RIDE	CAMEO 230 PS	20.00	northern
WILD!	WHY DONCHA ASK ME	CAMEO 274 PS	15.00	northern

SHARPEES

DO THE 45	MAKE UP YOUR MIND	ONEDERFUL 4835	10.00	northern
DO THE 45	MAKE UP YOUR MIND	KNOCKOUT 4	15.00	northern
I'VE GOT A SECRET	MAKE UP YOUR MIND	ONEDERFUL 4843	10.00	northern
TIRED OF BEING LONELY	JUST TO PLEASE YOU	ONEDERFUL 4839	15.00	northern

SHARPETS

LOST IN THE WORLD OF A DREAM	SAME: INSTRUMENTAL	SOUND CITY 1	250.00	**northerB**

SHAW, CECIL

THIS I'VE GOT TO SEE	PRACTICE WHAT YOU PREACH	BIL-MAR 2501	30.00	70's

SHAW, JAMES

GUILTY OF ADULTRY	I DON'T WANNA GET MARRIED	NATION-WIDE 102	30.00	northern

SHAW, LITTLE JIMMY AND THE STARLETS

LOVE DREAM	DON'T YOU KNOW MY BABY LOVES M	SELMA 1001	40.00	northern

SHAW, MARLENA

LET'S WADE IN THE WATER	SHOW TIME	CADET 5549	25.00	northern

SHAW, PATTI

SOMEBODY PULLED THE SWITCH	AIRWAY TO STARS	CHERRY PRODUCTIONS 106	40.00	70's

SHAW, SHARLOTTE

SAY IT TO ME	HAPPY WITH THE ONE THAT I LOVE	DETROIT ST. SERVICE 76	50.00	northern

SHED, HENRY

SOMETHING DRASTICALLY	SAME:	CREAM 1016	40.00	70's

SHEEN, BOBBY

COME ON AND LOVE ME	LOVE STEALING	CHELSEA 3034	10.00	70's
DR. LOVE	SWEET SWEET LOVE	CAPITOL 5672	40.00	northern
SOMETHING NEW TO DO	I MAY NOT BE WHAT YOU WANT	WB 7662	30.00	**northerB**

SHEFFIELD, CHARLES

IT'S YOUR VOODOO WORKING	ROCK N' ROLL TRAIN	EXCELLO 2200	300.00	northern

SHELDON, SANDI

YOU'RE GONNA MAKE ME LOVE YOU	BABY YOU'RE MINE	OKEH 7277	300.00	**northerB**

SHELTON, ROSCOE

RUNNING FOR MY LIFE	THERE'S A HEARTBREAK SOMEWHERE	SS7 2587	20.00	northern
MY BEST FRIEND	WORRY	BATTLE 45913	15.00	northern

SHEMWELL, SYLVIA

HE'LL COME BACK	FUNNY WHAT TIME CAN DO	PHILIPS 40149	40.00	northern

SHEP

FOOL TO FOOL	I'M SITTING IN	TNT 282	20.00	northern

SHEPARD, KENNY

WHAT DIFFERENCE DOES IT MAKE	TRY TO UNDERSTAND	MAXX 332	175.00	northern

SHEPHERD, WALT "BIG BOY"

NEED YOUR LOVING PT.4	YOU DON'T WANT ME NO MORE	UA 216	50.00	motown

SHEPPARD BOY

MY ANGEL BABY	BABY, I NEED YOU	INTERNATIONAL HITS 1980red	700.00	northern
MY ANGEL BABY	TAKE YOU FROM YOUR GUY	INTERNATIONAL HITS 1142gold	500.00	northern

SHEPPARD, RICK

CAN WE SHARE IT	SAME:	COLUMBIA 10242	75.00	70's
I FALL DEEPER IN LOVE	JUST YOU AND ME	SONIA 1189	30.00	70's
MISERY GET AWAY FROM ME	PRETTY PRETTY GIRL	DORMART 1000	30.00	northern

SHEPPARDS

STUBBORN HEART	HOW DO YOU LIKE IT	MIRWOOD 5534j	100.00	northern

SHERRELL BROS.

THE PRICE	REGGIE'S THEME	CURRISON 908	40.00	northern

SHERRIES (also see SHERRYS)

PUT YOUR ARMS AROUND ME	HAPPY GIRL	HOT 1002.	300.00	northern

SHERRONS

NO MATTER WHAT YOU DO TO ME	SHY GUY	DCP 1139	20.00	northern

SHERRY GROOMS

FOREVER IS A LONG TIME	THAT SAME OLD SONG	ABC 10987	20.00	northern

SHERRY, RUBY

FEMININE INGENUITY	PLEASE DON'T GO	TAKE 6 1002	250.00	northern

SHERRY AND THE INVERTS

I WAS MADE TO LOVE YOU	I'M LOST	TOWER 418	75.00	northern

SHERRYS

PUT YOUR ARMS AROUND ME	HAPPY GIRL	J.J. 1002 1ST.	300.00	**northerB**
PUT YOUR ARMS AROUND ME	HAPPY GIRL	HOT 1002 2nd.	300.00	northern

SHIRELLES

LAST MINUTE MIRACLE	NO DOUBT ABOUT IT	SCEPTER 12198	20.00	**northerB**
TOO MUCH OF A GOOD THING	BRIGHT SHINY COLORS	SCEPTER 12192	10.00	northern
WAIT TILL I GIVE THE SIGNAL	WILD AND SWEET	SCEPTER 12209	25.00	northern

SHIRLEY AND JESSIE

YOU CAN'T FIGHT LOVE	IVORY TOWER	WAND 1116	15.00	northern

SHIRTAILS

I WANT YOU TO STAY WITH ME	SOMETHING'S WRONG WITH OUR LOVE	DATE 1503	30.00	northern
THE CEILING	STAY AWAY FROM THE FOG	PRIME 2715	50.00	northern
I WANT YOU TO STAY WITH ME	SOMETHING'S WRONG WITH OUR LOV	DATE 1503 PS	40.00	northern

SHIVEL, BUNNY

TOP TWENTY	BABY TIME	CAPITOL 5662	20.00	northern
YOU'LL NEVER FIND A LOVE LIKE	THE SLIDE	CAPITOL 5765	20.00	northern

SHIVERS, PAULINE

WON'T YOU COME BACK HOME	YOU'RE A DEVIL	O-PEX 111	15.00	northern
YOU BETTER TELL HIM NO	BOOM BOOM	O-PEX 110	10.00	northern

SHOBEY, EL

NEVER MISSED WHAT YOU GOT	WHOLE THING	SHOUT 251	30.00	70's

SHOOTERS

TUFF ENUFF	SHE'S ALL RIGHT	TRANS WORLD 6980	30.00	ballad
TUFF ENUFF	SHE'S ALL RIGHT	FINER ARTS 2016	15.00	ballad

SHORT KUTS

YOUR EYES MAY SHINE	LETTING THE TEARS TUMBLE DOWN	PEPPER 434	15.00	northern

SHORTER, JAMES

MODERN DAY WOMAN	READY FOR THE HEARTBREAK	LA BEAT 6604	50.00	northern

SHORTY AND THE JUNIOR KOOLS

JAMMING WITH SHORTY		O.W. NO# 8801	200.00	funk

SHOW STOPPERS

WHAT CAN A MAN DO	AIN'T NOTHING BUT A HOUSE PARTY	SHOWTIME 101	8.00	**northerB**
WHAT CAN A MAN DO?	AIN'T NOTHING BUT A HOUSE PARTY	HERITAGE 800	8.00	northern

SHOWMEN

IT WILL STAND	COUNTRY FOOL	MINIT 632	10.00	northern
NEED LOVE	A LITTLE BIT OF YOUR LOVE	JOKERS 3 2146	150.00	northern
NO GIRL	I'LL BE GONE TOMORROW	JEREE 36	150.00	northern
OUR LOVE WILL GROW	YOU'RE EVERYTHING	SWAN 4219	30.00	northern
TAKE IT BABY	IN PARADISE	BB 4015	15.00	northern
TAKE IT BABY	IN PARADISE	SWAN 4213	15.00	northern
THE WRONG GIRL	FATE PLANNED IT THIS WAY	MINIT 643	75.00	northern

SHUFFLERS

ALWAYS BE MINE	WHEN THE LIGHTS ARE LOW	CRACKERJACK 4010	75.00	northern

SIGLER, BENNY

WHO YOU GONNA TURN TO	I CAN GIVE YOU LOVE	PHIL LA SOUL 314	300.00	**northerB**

SIGLER, BUNNY

LET THEM TALK	WILL YOU STILL LOVE ME TOMORROW	DECCA 32183	20.00	ballad
COMPARATIVELY SPEAKING	WILL YOU LOVE ME TOMORROW	DECCA 31947	30.00	northern
FOLLOW YOUR HEART	CAN YOU DIG IT	PARKWAY 6001	15.00	**northerB**
FOR CRYIN' OUT LOUD	EVERYTHING GONNA BE ALL RIGHT	DECCA 31880	75.00	northern
GIRL DON'T MAKE ME WAIT	ALWAYS IN THE WRONG PLACE	PARKWAY 123	20.00	**northerB**
LET THE GOOD TIMES ROLL	THERE'S NO LOVE LEFT	PARKWAY 153	8.00	northern
SUNNY SUNDAY	LOVEY DOVEY	PARKWAY 6000	15.00	northern
SUNNY SUNDAY	LOVEY DOVEY - YOU'RE SO FINE	PARKWAY 6000 PS	20.00	northern

SILHOUETTES

RED SNOW	OH WHAT A DAY	WESTERN WORLD 553	50.00	funk
NOT ME BABY	THE GAUCHO SERENADE	GOODWAY 101	500.00	**northerB**

SILK

FALLING IN LOVE ISN'T EASY	COME OVER HERE	DECCA 32829	30.00	northern
FALLING IN LOVE ISN'T EASY	COME OVER HERE	NATION 7858	50.00	northern

SILVA, RHON

GET IT RIGHT	GOT TO HAVE IT	UPTIGHT 24221	600.00	funk

SILVERS, MARY

THE POWER OF LOVE	I	ONEDERFUL 4816	20.00	northern

SIMMONS, CHARLEY AND THE ROYAL IMPERIALS

DO THE SISSY	WHY SHOULD THEY PAY	PJ RECORDS INC. 107	75.00	funk

SIMMONS, FAY

IF THIS IS GOODBYE	AND THE ANGELS SING	TUFFY 1964	25.00	northern

SIMMONS, RICHARD

BROTHER WHERE ARE YOU	MR. LOVE	MALA 545	30.00	northern

SIMMONS, VESSIE

I CAN MAKE IT ON MY OWN	SAME: PT. 2	SIMCO 62466	15.00	70's

SIMON, JOE

I SEE YOUR FACE	TROUBLES	HUSH 107	50.00	northern
JUST LIKE YESTERDAY		IRRAL 778	15.00	northern

SIMON, MAURICE AND THE PIE MEN

THE GIT-GO	SWEET POTATO GRAVY	CARNIVAL 525	30.00	mod

SIMONE, NINA

SAVE ME	TO BE YOUNG, GIFTED AND BLACK	RCA 269	30.00	mod
IT BE'S THAT WAY SOMETIME	(YOU'LL) GO TO HELL	RCA 9286	10.00	northern

SIMPSON, SARAH

KICK THE HABIT		SOUL-PO-TION	75.00	funk

SIMS, GERALD

YOU'LL BE SORRY	ROCKET	WB 7680 DJ	15.00	70's
COOL BREEZE	THERE MUST BE AN ANSWER	OKEH 7183	40.00	northern
LITTLE ECHO	MOTHER NATURE	OKEH 7199	50.00	northern
MOTHER NATURE	LITTLE ECHO	OKEH 7199	50.00	northern

SIMS, GERALD AND THE DAYLIGHTERS

COOL BREEZE	BABY I LOVE YOU	TIP TOP 2002	60.00	northern

SIMS, MARVIN L.

GET OFF MY BACK	DANGER	REVUE 11038	30.00	northern
HAVE YOU SEEN MY BABY	HAVE YOU SEEN MY BABY PT.2	MELLOW 1004	15.00	northern
HURTING INSIDE	DISILLUSIONED	MELLOW 1005	20.00	northern
NOW I'M IN LOVE WITH YOU	WHAT CAN I DO	MELLOW 1002	40.00	northern

SIMS, MARVIN.

DREAM A DREAM	I CAN'T TURN YOU LOOSE	MERCURY 73288	15.00	70's
LOVE IS ON THE WAY	BLOW AWAY BREEZE	RIVERTOWN 498	50.00	70's

SINCERES

DON'T WASTE MY TIME	GIRL, I LOVE YOU	PZAZZ 007	200.00	northern

SINCLAIR, TERRY

WHAT HAVE YOU HEARD	CLOWN SUIT	DPG 1006	150.00	northern

SINDAB, PAUL

I WAS A FOOL	YEAH, I NEVER KNEW	POWERTREE 144	150.00	northern
I WAS A FOOL	YEAH, I NEVER KNEW	KNOX 144	200.00	northern
I'M UP TIGHT	SINCE I MET YOU	HYPE 1003	20.00	northern
DO WHATCHA WANNA DO	GIVE ME YOUR HEART	HYPE 1007	50.00	northern

On some presses "Give me your heart" is mispressed and plays "You dropped your candy in the sand" value 200.00

SINCE I MET YOU	I'M UP TIGHT	HYPE 104	25.00	northern
SINCE I MET YOU		LUAP 1214	100.00	northern

SINGING PRINCIPAL

WOMAN'S LIB		FLICK	50.00	funk

SIR CEASAR

SHOW ME THE TIME	WHAT ARE THEY LAUGHING ABOUT	RIDE 140	400.00	northern

SIR WALES (also see SIR WALES WALLACE)

WHAT EVER YOU WANT	I WISH I COULD SAY WHAT I WANT	INNOVATION 8045	15.00	70's

SISTER AND BROTHERS

THE JED CLAMPETT	THE JED CLAMPETT Pt.2	UNI 55199	15.00	funk

SISTER SLEDGE

LOVE DON'T GO THROUGH NO CHANG	DON'T YOU MISS HIM	ATCO 7008	10.00	northern

SISTERS LOVE

THIS TIME TOMORROW	SAME	MAN-CHILD 5001	20.00	northern
GIVE ME YOUR LOVE	I COULD NEVER MAKE A BETTER MAN	MOWEST 5041	50.00	funk

SISTERS THREE

YOU CAN FORGET IT	CAN YOU QUALIFY	EARLY BIRD 49655	50.00	northern
KEEP OFF NO TRESSPASSING		MUSTANG	200.00	nortern

6 PAK

MIDNIGHT BREW	THERE WAS A TIME	TRIP UNIVERSAL 15	75.00	northern

1619 B.A.B.

WORLD	FOR YOUR LOVE	BROWN SUGAR	20.00	funk

SKIGGS, PIMBROCK

THAT WAS YESTERDAY	WAKE UP	PZAZZ 49	75.00	northern

SKIPPER, BUDDY

RESTLESS BREED	CANCEL THE RESERVATION	DEESU 319	20.00	northern

SKULL SNAPS

AL'S RAZOR BLADE	AIN'T THAT LOVING YOU	GRILL 301	15.00	funk
IT'S A NEW DAY	MY HANG UP IS YOU	GSF 6891	30.00	funk

SKYE

AIN'T NO NEED (DANCE)	AIN'T NO NEED	ANADA 100	20.00	70's

SKYLINERS

WE GOT LOVE ON OUR SIDE	OH HOW HAPPY	TORTOISE 11243	15.00	70's

A-side	B-side	Label	Price	Genre
EVERYTHING IS FINE	THE LOSER	JUBILEE 5506	10.00	northern

SKY'S THE LIMIT
HUMPING HARD	HUMPING HARD Pt.2	SUPER ATTRACTIONS 1950	50.00	funk

SLEEPLESS KNIGHTS
YOU'RE DRIVING ME CRAZY	DON'T HIDE YOUR LOVE FROM ME	JERROC 1000	20.00	northern

SLO, AUDREY
GONNA FIND THE RIGHT BOY	SAME: INSTRUMENTAL.	SWAN 4262	30.00	northern

SLY, SLICK AND WICKED
READY FOR YOU	SHO NUFF	PEOPLE 625	60.00	70's
TONIGHT'S THE NITE	WE'RE SLY SLICK AND WICKED	BAD BOYS 1006	40.00	70's
YOUR LOVE WAS MEANT FOR ME	IT'S NOT EASY	PARAMOUNT 186	30.00	70's

SLY
BUTTERMILK	BUTTERMILK Pt.2	AUTUMN 14	15.00	mod

SMALL, ELLIOTT
STAY IN MY HEART	GIRLS ARE MADE FOR LOVIN'	BANG 570	10.00	northern
I'M A DEVIL	HATE TO SEE YOU GO	A.B.S. 108	20.00	northern

SMALL, WILLIE
HOW HIGH CAN YOU FLY	SAY YOU WILL	JESSICA 401	15.00	northern

SMALLEY, LEROY
GIRLS ARE SENTiMENTAL	AIN'T IT A SHAME	GOLDEN WORLD 107	50.00	motown

SMILEY, JIMMY
GIRL I LOVE YOU	MORE THAN WORDS CAN SAY	CAMILLE 121	10.00	northern
MORE THAN WORDS AN SAY	GIRL I LOVE YOU	GAIT 4168	15.00	northern

SMITH JR., WILLIE
COMMON TOUCH	SAME: INSTRUMENTAL	WSJR 1027	40.00	funk

SMITH, BARRY
TEENAGE SONATA	THAT';S ALL THAT'S REQUIRED	GSF 6892	50.00	ballad
DON'T GO AWAY GIRL	HOLD ON TO IT	SHANE 1301	15.00	northern
LOOK WHAT YOU'VE DONE	IT'S NOT UNUSUAL	SHANE 6240	15.00	northern

SMITH, BERNARD AND THE JOKERS WILD
NEVER GONNA LET YOU GO	MAN WITHOUT PEACE	SPECTRUM 111	150.00	northern
GOTTA BE A REASON	39-21-46	GROOVE 504	250.00	northern

SMITH, BOBBIE (BOBBY)
HERE COMES BABY	I GET A FEELING, MY LOVE	BIG TOP 3111	30.00	northern
NOW HE'S GONE	YOUR LOVEY DOVEY WAYS	BIG TOP 3129	50.00	northern
WANTED	MR. FINE	BIG TOP 3085	30.00	northern
WALK ON INTO MY HEART	MISS STRONGHEARTED	AMERICAN ARTS 2	60.00	**northerB**

SMITH, BOBBY AND THE SPINNERS
SHE DON'T LOVE ME	TOO YOUNG, TOO MUCH, TOO SOON	TRI-PHI 1018	30.00	motown

SMITH, BUDDY
WHEN YOU LOSE THE ONE	YOU GET WHAT YOU DESEREVE	BRUTE 002	1000.00	northern

SMITH, CURTIS
I LIKE EVERYTHING	SAY YOU WILL	DOMA 101	15.00	northern
THE LIVING END	SAY YOU WILL	ESSICA 404	15.00	northern

SMITH, EDDIE
I DIDN'T REALIZE	ONE HUNDRED YEARS	MELLOTONE 10007	500.00	northern

SMITH, GEORGE
I'VE HAD IT	WHEN LOVE TURNS TO PITY	TURNTABLE 713	200.00	northern
PRETTY LITTLE GIRL	BORN AGAIN	LAURIE 3263	250.00	northern

SMITH, GEORGE E.
DON'T FIND ME GUILTY	HUMAN	CONCLAVE 340	20.00	northern
DON'T FIND ME GUILTY	HUMAN	BOJO 1001	60.00	northern

SMITH, HELENE
SURE THING	TRUE LOVE DON'T GROW ON TREES	DEEP CITY 2375	40.00	northern
SURE THING	WRONG OR RIGHT HE'S MY BABY	DEEP CITY 2380	60.00	northern
THRILLS AND CHILLS	I'M CONTROLLED BY YOUR LOVE	LLOYD 9	30.00	northern
YOU GOTTA BE A MAN	SOME KIND OF MAN	PHIL LA SOUL 325	30.00	funk

SMITH, JAMES WESLEY
TALKING ABOUT A WOMAN		ANGEL TOWN 714	500.00	northern

SMITH, JEFF AND UNIVERSE
THE HIDDEN SECRET	BACK HOME AGAIN	INCENTIVE 401	40.00	70's

SMITH, KENNY
KEEP ON WALKIN' BABY	WE HAVE EACH OTHER	CHESS 1947	75.00	ballad
GO FOR YOURSELF	MY DAY IS COMING	RCA 8850	20.00	northern
LORD, WHAT'S HAPPENING TO YOUR PEOPLE	SAME:	GAR 317 DJ	75.00	**northerB**
LORD, WHAT'S HAPPENING TO YOUR PEOPLE	SAME:	GAR 317 stock copy	125.00	**northerB**
LORD, WHAT'S HAPPENING TO YOUR PEOPLE	SAME:	GOLD SPOT	300.00	northern
EVERYBODY KNOWS I LOVE YOU		KOGEN	0.00	northern
ONE MORE DAY	SINFUL SOUL	FLO-RUE 1113	600.00	northern

SMITH, MARTHA
AS I WATCH YOU WALK AWAY	IT ALWAYS SEEMS LIKE SUMMER	CAMEO 359	15.00	northern

SMITH, MARVIN
HAVE MORE TIME	TIME STOPPED	BRUNSWICK 55299	15.00	**northerB**
LOVE AIN'T NOTHING BUT PAIN	I WANT	BRUNSWICK 55314	15.00	northern
WHO WILL DO YOUR RUNNING NOW	YOU'RE REALLY SOMETHING SADI	MAYFIELD 942	100.00	northern

SMITH, MISS ELSIE
WATERMELON MAN	HI-LOVE	OPEN 2601	15.00	mod

SMITH, MOSES

KEEP ON STRIVING	COME ON, LET ME LOVE YOU	COTILLION 44075	150.00	70's
THE GIRL ACROSS THE STREET	HEY LOVE (I WANNA THANK YOU)	DIONN 508	30.00	**northerB**
THE GIRL ACROSS THE STREET	HEY LOVE (I WANNA THANK YOU)	DIONN 508 DJ	100.00	**northerB**

SMITH, O.C.

LOVE CHANGES	GOT TO KNOW	SOUTH BAY 1003	10.00	70's
I'M YOUR MAN	THAT'S LIFE	COLUMBIA 43525	10.00	northern
ON EASY STREET	BEYOND THE NEXT HILL	COLUMBIA 43809	150.00	northern
DOUBLE LIFE	THE SEASON	COLUMBIA 44151	15.00	northern

SMITH, OTIS

LET HER GO	ALLEY FULL OF TRASH & BOTTLES	PERCEPTION 4	75.00	**northerB**

SMITH, RICHARD

I DON'T WANNA CRY	MAMA SAID	HI-Q 5042	60.00	northern

SMITH, ROY

DON'T GO AWAY	THE PAIN LINGERS ON	ASCOT 2239	20.00	northern
DON'T GO AWAY	THE PAIN LINGERS ON	CHANTAIN 0014	40.00	northern
DON'T GO AWAY	THE PAIN LINGERS ON	CUTLASS	100.00	70's
VERY STRONG ON YOU	IT HAPPENS THE BEST OF US	LIBERTY 55975	15.00	northern

SMITH, SHARON

I'M WAITING	I WANT A MAN	VENUS 100	50.00	northern

SMITH, VERDELLE

IF YOU CAN'T SAY ANYTHING NICE	I DON'T NEED ANYTHING	CAPITOL 5731	8.00	northern
TAR AND CEMENT	A PIECE OF THE SKY	CAPITOL 5632	10.00	northern
WALK TALL	IN MY ROOM	CAPITOL 5567	8.00	northern

SMITH, WASHINGTON

FAT CAT	DON'T TAKE YOUR LOVE FROM ME	OKEH 7275	20.00	northern
FAT CAT	DON'T TAKE YOUR LOVE FROM ME	RAINBOW	30.00	northern

SMITH, YOUNGBLOOD

YOU CAN SPLIT	MR. BRIGHT TIMES	VERVE 10416	100.00	northern

SMITH BROTHERS

THERE CAN BE A BETTER WAY	PAYBACK'S A DRAG	SOUL DIMENSION 5102	200.00	northern

SMOKE SUGAR COMPANY

SAVE A LITTLE LOVE FOR RAINY D	DOIN' IT	TERI DE 10	50.00	70's

SMOKEY AND THE FABULOUS BLADES

JERK, BABY JERK	CHARLIE'S THEME	DORE 723	60.00	**northerB**

SMOKIN' SHADES OF BLACK

GREASE WHEELS	LOVE SHIP	STEM 23	75.00	funk

SNELL, ANETTE

IT'S ALL OVER NOW	SAME:	EPIC 50464 DJ	25.00	70's

SOCIALITES

YOU'RE LOSING YOU'RE TUCH	JIVE JIMMY	WB 5476	15.00	northern

SODD, MARION

PERMANENT VACATION	ENOUGH FOR EVERYONE	MAD 1206	30.00	northern

SOFT SUMMER SOUL STRINGS

I'M DOING MY THING	THEME FROM SOUL STRINGS	COLUMBIA 44844	10.00	northern

SOFT TOUCH

IS THIS THE WAY TO TREAT A GUY	CLOSE TO YOU	SHOUT 259	20.00	70's

SOLARS

HERE'S MY HEART	NOBODY KNOWS BUT MY BABY AND M	KING 6295	30.00	northern

SOLE, GARY

HOLDIN ON	SOUL LIGHT TOUCH	KNIGHT 102-38	150.00	northern

SOLID STATE

I'M GONNA MAKE YOU MINE	I'M GONNA MAKE YOU MINE	MUSIC TOWN 9709	40.00	70's

SOLITAIRES

FOOL THAT I AM	FAIR WEATHER LOVER	MGM 13221	30.00	northern

SOLO, SAM E.

LOVE IS NOT A GAME	TEARS KEEP FALLING	IMPERIAL 66182	30.00	northern
TEARS KEEP FALLING	LOVE IS NOT A GAME	RUBY 5075	40.00	northern

SOMETHING NEW

YOU BABE	WHAT'S THIS I SEE	WAND 11225	30.00	northern

SOMMERS, JOANNE

NEVER THROW YOUR DREAMS AWAY	YOU'VE GOT POSSIBILITIES	COLUMBIA 43567	70.00	northern
DON'T PITY ME	MY BLOCK	WB 5629	150.00	northern

SONATAS

GOING DOWN THE ROAD		HOT LINE 101	100.00	northern

SONNETTES

I'VE GOTTEN OVER YOU	TEARDROPS	KO. 1	25.00	northern

SONNY AND DIANE

THAT'S ENOUGH	LOVE TRAP	EPIC 50280	20.00	70's

SONS OF MOSES

DEVILED EGG	ALPINE WINTER	BIX INTERNATIONAL 102	75.00	funk
SOUL SYMPHONY	FATBACK	CORAL 62549	20.00	**northerB**

SONS OF ROBIN STONE

GOT TO GET YOU BACK	LOVE IS JUST AROUND THE CORNER	ATCO 6929	15.00	70's
LET'S DO IT NOW	IT ONLY HAPPENS IN THE MOVIES	EPIC 50257	20.00	70's

SONS OF SLUM

16 MILES OF PLASTIC GHETTO	THE PUSH AND PULL	GAMMA 100	40.00	funk

SONS OF WATTS

CAN'T YOU TELL I'M LONELY	WHEN YOU LOVE, YOU'RE LOVED TO	BLUE ROCK 4086	40.00	northern

SONTAG, HEDY

HE NEVER CAME BACK	BAD GIRL	PHILIPS 40170	40.00	northern

SOOTHERS

I BELIEVE IN YOU	THE LITTLE WHITE CLOUD	PORT 70041	60.00	northern

SOPHISTICATED LADIES

CHECK IT OUT	GOOD MAN	MAYHEW 532	15.00	70's

SOPHISTICATES

BACK UP BABY	CRY ME A RIVER	SONNY 1001	100.00	northern
I REALLY HOPE YOU DO	LET ME GO	UNDERGROUND SOUND 1002	400.00	northern
I CAN'T STAND IT	I NEED YOU	MUTT 27318	20.00	northern

SO-RARE

PARADISE	HOW DO YOU SPELL RELIEF	NCS 2451	10.00	group

SOUL AGENTS

SHE'S BLOWING MY MIND		HOECUTT NO#	50.00	funk
THE IRON HORSE		DUST BOWL 100	100.00	funk
SOUL BAG	DOUBLE O SOUL IN ACTION	DOUBLE CHECK 49	30.00	group

SOUL ANGELS

THE LADIES CHOICE	IT'S ALL IN YOUR MIND	JOSIE 1002	20.00	funk

SOUL BANDITS

BE GOOD	SAVE IT	GRANDE RIGHT 2	60.00	northern

SOUL BLENDERS

I'M NOT ASHAMED	THE DEAL	VANESSA 101	15.00	group
TIGHT ROPE	DRIVIN' ME MAD	KNIGHT 102	150.00	northern

SOUL BROS. INC.

LOVE SWEET LOVE	THE DEVIL MADE ME	S.B.I. 1000	50.00	northern
PYRAMID	CAPRICORN XL 2	GOLDEN EYE 1001	200.00	northern

SOUL BROTHERS

THAT LOVING FEELING	I SAW FOREVER MY LOVE	COMMONWEALTH 3012	30.00	northern
COME ON AND LOVE ME	PLEASE PASS THE KETCHUP	G-D 1004	50.00	northern
GOTTA GET A GOOD THING GOIN'	GOOD LOVIN' NEVER HURT	MERCURY 72575	10.00	northern
THE PARADE OF BROKEN HEARTS	NOTIFY ME	WAND 125	20.00	northern
WHAT CAN IT BE	HEARTACHES	D-TOWN 1069	60.00	northern

SOUL BROTHERS INC.

ALL THE TIME	DIDN'T WE	BARI 3004	10.00	northern

SOUL BROTHERS SIX

DRIVE	WHAT YOU GOT (IS GOOD FOR ME)	ATLANTIC 2645	20.00	funk
I'LL BE LOVING YOU	SOME KIND OF WONDEFUL	ATLANTIC 2406	30.00	northern
THANK YOU BABY FOR LOVING ME	SOMEBODY ELSE LOVING MY BABY	ATLANTIC 2592	20.00	northern
YOU BETTER CHECK YOURSELF	WHAT CAN YOU DO	ATLANTIC 2456	10.00	northern
YOUR LOVE IS SUCH A WONDERFUL	I CAN'T LIVE WITHOUT YOU	ATLANTIC 2535	10.00	northern
DON'T NEGLECT YOUR BABY	OH I NEED YOU YES I DO	LYNDEL746	50.00	northern

SOUL CHARGES

CHARGE IT UP BABY		AMERICAN	100.00	funk

SOUL CITY

EVERYBODY DANCE NOW	WHO KNOWS	GOODTIME 801	15.00	**northerB**
I SHOT FOR THE MOON	I WILL TAKE CARE OF YOU	MERCURY 72735	50.00	northern

SOUL CLINIC

SO SHARP	NO ONE LOVE ME ANYMORE	BAY SOUND 67006	50.00	funk

SOUL COMBINATION

SOUL COMBINATION	YOU DON'T HAVE TO SHOW ME	INVOLVED 31	30.00	funk

SOUL COMMUNICATERS

THOSE LONELY NIGHTS	PLEASE DON'T GO	FEE BEE 221	200.00	northern

SOUL COMPANY

HUMP THE BUMP	HUMP THE BUMP Pt.2	JUMP OFF 2001	25.00	funk

SOUL CONGRESS

THE BLACK HOUSE	THE PLAYBOY SHUFFLE	BANG 563	30.00	funk

SOUL CREATIONS

CHICKEN HUT		SOUL CLICK	75.00	funk

SOUL CRUSADERS

I SIT IN MY ROOM	THOSE MEMORIES	LU TALL 319	30.00	group

SOUL EXCITEMENT

STAY TOGETHER	SMILE	PINK DOLPHIN 106	300.00	funk

SOUL EXCITERS

SHOOT THE MONKEY	PT 2.	123 1708	10.00	funk

SOUL EXPERIENCE

I'M SO GLAD I FOUND YOU	WHO'S LIPS YOU BEEN KISSING	SMOKE 1002	30.00	70's

SOUL FOUR

MISERY	YOU'RE THE ANGEL	RINGO 4321	25.00	northern

SOUL GENERALS

GRANDMA'S FUNKY POPCORN	GRANDMA'S FUNKY POPCORN PT.2	AHNED 400	500.00	funk

SOUL GENTS

WONDERS OF LOVE	IF I SHOULD WIN YOUR LOVE	FROS-RAY 2707	100.00	northern

SOUL INC.

FUNKY LADY	FUNKY LADY PT 3.	SOCK. 1002	20.00	funk
WHAT GOES UP MUST COME DOWN	GOOD TO THE LAST DROP	EMBLEM 101	200.00	northern

SOUL INVADERS INC:

SO GOOD	CARELESS LOVING	YORKTOWN 543	40.00	group

SOUL LIFTERS

HOT FUNKY & SWEATY		HOUSE OF THE FOX	50.00	funk

SOUL MACHINE

TWITCHIE FEET	BAG OF GOODIES	PZAZZ 21	25.00	mod

SOUL MAJESTICS

MISSING YOU	DONE TOLD YOU BABY	CHICAGO MUSIC BAG	30.00	northern
MISSING YOU	DONE TOLD YOU BABY	AL-TOG 1	15.00	northern

SOUL MATES

TOO LATE TO SAY YOU'RE SORRY	YOUR LOVE	MARINA 7992	300.00	northern

SOUL MEN

THERE WAS A TIME	I REMEMBER	WORLD WIDE 102	300.00	funk

SOUL MERCHANTS

CHEESE AND CRACKERS	AIN'T GONNA GO FOR THAT	ROYAL CREST 155	40.00	funk
TALKING ABOUT YOU GIRL	(T.L.C.) TENDER LOVING CARE	MOONVILLE 1111	40.00	northern

SOUL NOTES

DON'T MAKE ME BEG	HOW LONG WILL IT LAST	WAY OUT 1001	20.00	northern
HOW LONG WILL IT LAST	I GOT EVERYTHING I NEED	WAY OUT 1006	15.00	northern

SOUL ONES

SOUL POT	THIS IS MY PRAYER	DEAL 01	400.00	funk

SOUL PATROL

PETER PAN	DON'T KNOCK THE COP	ZUMA 100A	250.00	funk
PETER PAN	DUSTY	ZUMA 100	300.00	funk
SWEETER THAN THE OTHER SIDE	SWEET THAN THE OTHER SIDE Pt.2	DISCOVERY 1226	15.00	funk
NEED OF LOVE	SAVE YOUR LOVE	HIGHLAND 77	100.00	northern

SOUL PROCEDURES

BUT WHAT IS THIS FEELING	GLAMOUR GIRL	FIVE-O 506	100.00	group

SOUL PUSHERS

WITH A BROKEN HEART	SUNSHINE ON A BLUE BLUE DAY	AMBUSH 6968	30.00	northern

SOUL SEARCHERS

THERE WAS A TIME	PT 2.	AND RAY 4213	100.00	funk
SWEET HOME	LONG TIME AGO	SEARCHER 1	20.00	group

SOUL SENDERS

DESTINATION SOUL	I GOT TO GET A MOVE ON	SOUL-O-MATIC 1001	40.00	funk
SOUL BROTHER'S TESTIFY	SOUL BROTHER'S TESTIFY Pt.2	ANLA 102	20.00	funk

SOUL SET

PIN THE TAIL ON THE DONKEY	HE DON'T LOVE YOU	BB 4006	40.00	mod
WILL YOU EVER LEARN	PLEASE DON'T MAKE ME CRY	BI-ME 7683	700.00	northern

SOUL SEVEN

THE CISSY THANG	MR. CHICKEN	SOULTEX 103	150.00	funk

SOUL SHAKERS

GET HIP TO YOURSELF	THE COLD LETTER	LOMA 2027	40.00	northern
I'M GETTING WEAKER	IT'S LOVE (CAUSE i FEEL IT)	LOMA 2047	150.00	northern
YOU'RE TURNIN'	BIG TRAIN	TERI DE 3	350.00	northern

SOUL SISTERS

GOOD TIME TONIGHT	SOME SOUL FOOL	SUE 10005	10.00	northern
I CAN'T STAND IT	BLUEBERRY HILL	SUE 799	10.00	northern
THINK ABOUT THE GOOD TIMES	THE RIGHT TIME	SUE 130	10.00	northern

SOUL SOCIETY

SIDEWINDER	AFRO-DESIA	DOT 17136	20.00	mod

SOUL STEPPERS

STEPPIN' UP	THE GREAT GREAT GRANDSON	KRIS 8085	20.00	funk

SOUL STOPPERS BAND

BOILING WATER		CAPP MATT	150.00	funk

SOUL SUPERIORS

TRUST IN ME BABY	GOT TO FIND THAT GIRL	SOUL BEAT 107	100.00	northern

SOUL SUSPECTS

FUNKY DROP	HANDLE IT	BLACK PRINCE 319	15.00	funk

SOUL TORANODOES

GO FOR YOURSELF	FUNKY THANG	BURT 4000	15.00	funk
HOT PANTS BREAK DOWN	BOOT'S GROVE	MAGIC CITY 14	100.00	funk
CRAZY LEGS	BOBBY'S MOOD	WESTWOOD 1017	150.00	funk

SOUL TWINS

GIVE THE MAN A CHANCE	QUICK CHANGE ARTIST	KAREN 1533	85.00	**northerB**
JUST ONE LOOK	IT'S NOT WHAT YOU DO..	KAREN 1535	15.00	northern
SHE'S THE ONE	MR. INDEPENDENT	BACK BEAT 599	30.00	northern

SOUL UNLIMITED

SAGITTARIUS		BRUBOON	100.00	funk

SOUL VIBRATIONS

THE DUMP		VIBRANT	150.00	funk

SOUL, JOHNNY

I'M GONNA RAT ON YOU	I CAN'T BUY NO LOVE	SPORT 107	200.00	northern

	A-side	B-side	Label	Price	Genre
	LONELY MAN	COME AND GET IT	SSS INTER. 785	15.00	northern

SOUL, LITTLE NICKY

YOU SAID	I WANTED TO TELL YOU	SHEE 101	500.00	nothern

SOUL, REGGIE

MY WORLD OF ECSTASY	MIGHTY GOOD LOVING	CAPRI 103	50.00	northern

SOUL, SHARON

HIS LOVE IS AMAZING	LET ME GET TO KNOW YOU	CORAL 62487	50.00	northern
HOW CAN I GET TO YOU	DON'T SAY GOODBYE LOVE	WILD DEUCE 1001	40.00	northern
YOU FOUND MY WEAK SPOT	JUST HOW LONG CAN I GO ON	CORAL 62505	50.00	northern

SOUL, TOMMY

I'LL BE RIGHT HERE	I NEED SOMEONE (TO LOVE)	GASLIGHT 12945	400.00	northern

SOULETTES

BRING YOU FINE SELF HOME	LET ME BE THE ONE	SCOPE 126478	800.00	northern

SOUL-FAY

YOUNG GIRL	WHO WILL BE THERE TOMORROW	AUDIO FORTY 1801	150.00	northern

SOULFUL ILLUSION

SEARCHING FOR LOVE	TO GET YOUR LOVE	MERCURY 72754	75.00	northern

SOULFUL STRINGS

BURNING SPEAR	WITHIN YOU WITHOUT YOU	CADET 5576	10.00	northern

SOULFUL TWINS

I CAN'T LET YOU GO	I NEED SOME KIND OF SOMETHING	SABLE 101	40.00	northern

SOULFUL TWO

FI YI DANCE 1108	HAVE MERCY	PURE SOUL MUSIC	50.00	northern

SOULISTICS

JONES'N	COTTON-EYED JOE	LIBERATION 1025	200.00	funk

SOUL-JERS

CHINESE CHECKERS	POOCHUM	RAMPART 648	15.00	mod
GONNA BE A BIG MAN	CRAZY LITTLE THINGS	RAMPART 649	25.00	northern

SOULMASTERS

I'LL BE WAITING HERE	YOU TOOK AWAY THE SUNSHINE	RAVEN 2020	200.00	northern

SOUL-MATES (Brenda Holloway)

I WANT A BOYFRIEND	I GET A FEELING	ERA 3109 DJ	25.00	motown

SOULSATIONS

HERE COMES THE PAIN	HERE COMES THE PAIN PT.2	STE-AL 1001	30.00	northern

SOUL-TEASERS

TWO LOVERS	ON A HOT SUMMER DAY IN THE CIT	JOKER 713	100.00	northern

SOULTONES

YOU AND ME BABY	I WANT WHAT I WANT	VALISE 1900	20.00	northern

SOULVILLE ALL-STARS

IM GONNA GET TO YOU	WON'T YOU PLEASE BE MY GIRL	SOULVILLE 1005	75.00	northern
NOBODY TO BLAME (BUT MYSELF)	NOTHING IN THIS WORLD MATTERS	SOULVILLE 1001	100.00	northern

SOUND INC.

ON THE BRINK	I AM COMING THRU	LIBERTY 55844 DJ	20.00	northern

SOUND MASTERS

LONELY LONELY	II WANT TO BE YOUR BABY	JULET 102	150.00	northern

SOUND OF SOUL

HEY GIRL I STILL LOVE HIM	LOVE IS SUCH A FUNNY THING	JOSIE 962	25.00	northern

SOUND OF VISION

WHAT DO NEVER THE DANCE	WHAT SO NEVER THE DANCE PT.2	HOUSE GUESS 10318	100.00	funk

SOUNDBREAKERS

TRYING TO GET BACK TO YOU	THE JERK IS CATCHING	SYMBOL 220	30.00	northern

SOUNDS FOUR

A MEMORY BEST FORGOTTEN	LOVE TOGETHER	SAINTMO 201	30.00	northern
A MEMORY BEST FORGOTTEN	KEEP ON LOVIN'	SAINTMO 201	30.00	northern
KEEP ON LOVIN'	HEY GIRL	SAINTMO 203	30.00	northern

SOUNDS OF BLACK

MYSTERIES OF BLACK		JULMAR	100.00	funk
SOUNDS OF BLACK		LAKESIDE	50.00	funk

SOUNDS OF DAWN

IF I HAD MY WAY	HOW MANY TIMES	TWIN STACKS 125	20.00	northern
IT'S GOT TO HAPPEN RIGHT NOW	WILL IT EVER STOP	TWIN STACKS 127	30.00	northern

SOUNDS OF LANE

TRACKS TO YOUR MIND	MY MY MAMA (Geoge McCannon)	COBBLESTONE 713	30.00	northern

SOUNDSATIONS

MR. SENSATION	THE MOMENT	BYE 101	150.00	northern

SOUTHERN COMFORT

IT'S IN MY LETTER	SAME: INSTRUMENTAL	SUN CITY No.#	300.00	70's

SOUTHSIDE MOVEMENT

DO IT TO ME	AIN'T GONNAWATCH YOU NO MO'	20th. CENTURY 2167	10.00	70's

SOUTHWIND SYMPHONY

COMING HOME	YOUR LOVE IS FADING	GLOLITE 92	15.00	northern

SPACEARK

DO WHAT YOU CAN DO	WELCOME TO MY DOOR	COLOR WORLD 100	50.00	funk

SPARKELS				
TRY LOVE (ONE MORE TIME)	THAT BOY OF MINE	OLD TOWN 1160	300.00	northern
SPARKZ				
I'LL SHOW YOU	AIN'T NO BIG THING	BELL 793	40.00	ballad
SPECIALS				
I CAN'T FIND ANOTHER	I CAN'T FIND ANOTHER Pt.2	SATCH 515	15.00	funk
YOU STOOD ME UP	EVERYBODY SAY YEAH	SATCH 512	75.00	northern
FOOL FOR YOUR LOVE	BABY YOU NEED ME	SATCH 514	15.00	group
SPELLBINDERS				
HELP ME (GET MYSELF BACK TOGETHER)	DANNY BOY	COLUMBIA 43830	15.00	northern
A LITTLE ON THE BLUE SIDE	CHAIN REACTION	COLUMBIA 43522	15.00	northern
WE'RE ACTING LIKE LOVERS	LONG LOST LOVE	COLUMBIA 43611	10.00	northern
SPELLMAN, BENNY				
FORTUNE TELLER	LIPSTICK TRACES	MINIT 644	15.00	northern
THE WORD GAME	I FEEL GOOD	ATLANTIC 2291	10.00	northern
THE WORD GAME	I FEEL GOOD	ALON 9024	15.00	northern
IF YOU TELL HER	SINNER GIRL	SANSU 462 DJ	20.00	northern
SPENCER				
MY BABY'S COMIN' HOME	WE GOT A LOVE THAT'S OUT OF SIGHT	MIDTOWN 3502	20.00	northern
SEARCHIN' FOR LOVE	YOU DON'T KNOW WHAT YOUR GETTING	MIDTOWN 3503	20.00	northern
1003				
SPENCER, CARL				
COVER GIRL	PROGRESS	RUST 5104	200.00	northern
SPENCER, ELVIN				
LIFT THIS HURT	YOU'RE BEING UNFAIR	TWINIGHT 150	100.00	northern
SPENCER, JAMES				
TAKE THIS WOMAN OFF THE CORNER	I NEED YOUR LOVE	MEMPHIS 101	30.00	funk
IN-LAW TROUBLE	YOU BETTER KEEP AN EYE	TAURUS 725 DJ	30.00	northern
SPENCER, EDDIE				
IF THIS IS LOVE	POWER OF LOVE	ARC 1206 canadian	50.00	**northerB**
SPICE				
SWEET NORMA JONES	CAN'T WAIT TIL THE MORNING COM	SOUND GEMS 101	20.00	70's
SPIDELLS				
HMMM, WITH FEELING DARLING	UNCLE WILLIE GOOD TIME	MONZA 1123	10.00	northern
IF IT AIN'T ONE THING	DON'T YOU FORGET	CORAL 62531	60.00	northern
PUSHED OUT OF THE PICTURE	WITH YOU IN MIND	CORAL 62508	75.00	northern
SPIDELS				
LIKE A BEE	YOU KNOW I NEED YOU	CHAVIS 1035	15.00	northern
SPIEDELS				
DREAM GIRL	THAT'S WHAT I GET	PROVIDENCE 418	40.00	northern
SPINDLES				
TEN SHADES OF BLUE	NO ONE LOVE YOU (THE WAY I DO)	ABC 10850	20.00	northern
TO MAKE YOU MINE	AND THE BAND PLAYED ON	ABC 10802	50.00	northern
SPINNERS				
I JUST WANT TO FALL IN LOVE	HEAVY ON SUNSHINE	ATLANTIC 3765	30.00	70's
(SHE'S GONNA LOVE ME) AT SUNDOWN	IN MY DIARY	V.I.P. 25050	8.00	motown
(SHE'S GONNA LOVE ME) AT SUNDOWN	MESSAGE FROM A BLACKMAN	V.I.P. 25054	8.00	motown
I CROSS MY HEART	FOR ALL WE KNOW	MOTOWN 1109	15.00	motown
I GOT YOUR WATER BOILING BABY	I'VE BEEN HURT	TRI-PHI 1013	25.00	motown
I JUST CAN'T HELP BUT FEEL THE PAIN	BAD, BAD WEATHER	MOTOWN 1136	15.00	motown
I'LL ALWAYS LOVE YOU	TOMORROW MAY NEVER COME	MOTOWN 1078	15.00	motown
LOVE (I'M SO GLAD) I FOUND YOU	SUDBUSTER	TRI-PHI 1004	25.00	motown
SWEET THING	HOW CAN I	MOTOWN 1067	15.00	motown
THAT'S WHAT GIRLS ARE MADE FOR	HEEBIE JEEBIE'S	TRI-PHI 1001	20.00	motown
TRULY YOURS	WHERE IS THAT GIRL	MOTOWN 1093	10.00	motown
WHAT DID SHE USE	ITCHIN' FOR MY BABY	TRI-PHI 1007	20.00	motown
SPITTING IMAGE				
JB'S LATIN		MASAI 99981	100.00	funk
SPLENDORS				
PLEASE DON'T GO	BLUE ALLEY	KARATE 520	50.00	northern
SPLIT DECISION BAND				
WATCHIN' OUT	DAZED	NETWORK 1005	100.00	70's
SPOON, BILL				
LOVE IS ON THE WAY	DON'T PLAY WITH MY LOVE	HIGHLAND 1000	100.00	70's
SPOONER AND THE SPOONS				
WISH YOU DIDN'T HAVE TO GO	HEY, DO YOU WANNA MARRY	FAME 6405	20.00	northern
SPOONER'S CROWD				
TWO IN THE MORNING	I'LL BE YOUR BABY	CADET 5533	50.00	mod
SPOTSWOOD, KENDRA				
STICKIN' WITH MY BABY	JIVE GUY	TUFF 407 DJ	40.00	northern
SPRINGERS				
NOTHINGS'S TOO GOOD FOR MY BABY	WHO DO YOU LOVE	WALE 428	4000.00	northern
ALL TOO SOON WE GROW OLD	STOP HIDING IN THE CLOSET	WALE 429	30.00	group
I KNOW MY BABY LOVES ME SO	I KNOW WHY	WAY OUT 2699	20.00	group
LAST HEARTBREAK	WHY	WAY OUT 2800	15.00	group
YOU CAN LAUGH	IT'S BEEN A LONG TIME	WAY OUT 5696	40.00	northern

SPRINGFIELD RIFLE

THAT'S ALL I REALLY NEED	I LOVE HER	JERDEN 905Q	40.00	northern

SPRINGFIELD, DUSTY

LIVE IT UP	GUESS WHO	PHILIPS 40245	10.00	northern
WHAT'S IT GONNA BE	SMALL TOWN GIRL	PHILIPS 40498	8.00	northern
LIVE IT UP	GUESS WHO	PHILIPS 40245 PS	10.00	
WHAT'S IT GONNA BE	SMALL TOWN GIRL	PHILIPS 40498 PS	10.00	northern

SPURLING, CHARLES

POPCORN CHARLIE	BUDDY BOY	KING 6267	15.00	funk
SHE CRIED JUST A MINUTE	DON'T LET HIM HURT YOU BABY	KING 6115	20.00	northern
WHICH ONE	THAT WOMAN	KING 6142 DJ	20.00	northern
YOU'D BE SURPRISED	MR. COOL.	KING 6077	20.00	northern

SPYDERS

I CAN TAKE CARE OF MYSELF	MAKE UP YOUR MIND	MTA 128	30.00	northern
I CAN TAKE CARE OF MYSELF	MAKE UP YOUR MIND	GOLDEN STATE 106	50.00	**northerB**

SQUIRES

DON'T ACCUSE ME	SO MANY TEARS AGO	GEE 1082	100.00	northern

ST. ANN, EDWARD

MORE LUCK TO YOU BABY	HEY! LITTLE GIRL	USA 773	50.00	northern

ST. ANTHONY ,CHESTER

TOGETHER		A&M 766	30.00	northern

ST. CLAIR, KELLY

DON'T LOOK OVER YOUR SHOULDER	DARKNESS ON YOUR MIND	MILLAGE 1042	20.00	northern
DON'T LOOK OVER YOUR SHOULDER	DARKNESS ON YOUR MIND	MILLAGE 1042 PS	40.00	northern

ST. CLAIR, RENEE

LOOK WHAT I GOT	I'VE GOT A REASON TO CRY	JUBILEE 5576	75.00	northern

ST. CLAIRE, SYLVIA

JUST LOVE ME	IS HE ALL RIGHT	BRUNSWICK 55279 DJ	150.00	northern

ST. GERMAN, TYRONE

I'M STILL HOOKED ON YOU	YOU ARE THE APPLE OF MY EYE	BELSHAZZER no #	15.00	70's
IN A WORLD SO GOLD	DON'T COP NO ATTITUDE	MORNING DOVE 1	20.00	70's

ST. JAMES ,BOBBY

I'VE BEEN TAKEN FOR A RIDE	THE SUN DON'T SHINE EVERY DAY	WATTS REC 901	100.00	northern

ST. JAMES, HOLLY

MAGIC MOMENTS	WAITING FOR MY FRIEND	ABC 11042	15.00	northern
THAT'S NOT LOVE	TWO GOOD REASONS	ABC 10996	300.00	northern

ST. JOHN, ROSE AND THE WONDERETTES

I KNOW THE MEANING	FOOL DON'T LAUGH	VEEP 1231	150.00	northern
MEND MY BROKEN HEART	AND IF I HAD MY WAY	UA 997	50.00	northern

STACKHOUSE, RUBY

PLEASE TELL ME	WISHING	KELLMAC 1001	40.00	northern

STAGEMASTERS

BABY, I'M HERE JUST TO LOVE YO	FREE AT LAST	SLIDE 2101	10.00	northern
BABY, I'M HERE JUST TO LOVE YO	FREE AT LAST	HIT KINGDOM 1801	100.00	northern

STANBERRY, JOHN

I CAN'T BELIEVE (SHE TOOK THE	SUNNY DAY	STANLOS 52573	15.00	70's
YOU CAME INTO MY WORLD	THRU LIFE STEP BY STEP	JAYVILLE 1001	50.00	northern

STANDING ROOM ONLY

ALL IN A DAY	SACRIFICE	LAMAR 27	25.00	70's

STAPLES, GORDON AND THE MOTOWN STRINGS

STRUNG OUT	SOUNDS OF THE ZODIAC	MOTOWN 1180	15.00	funk

STAR, MARTHA

I WANNA BE YOUR GIRL	SWEET LOUIE	THEMLA 113	175.00	northern
LOVE IS THE ONLY SOLUTION	I'M LONELY	THEMLA 112	400.00	northern
NO PART TIME LOVE FOR ME	IT'S TOO BAD BABY	THEMLA 111	50.00	northern

STARR, MARTHA

SWEET TEMPTATION	LITTLE GIRL BLUE	CHARAY 35	1000.00	northern

STARLETS

LOVING YOU IS SOMETHING NEW	MY BABY'S REAL	CHESS 1997	30.00	northern

STARLIGHTS

BOOT LEG	MY SPECIAL ANGEL	TEAR DROP 3099	50.00	funk

STARR, EDWIN

DON'T TELL ME I'M CRAZY	WHO IS THE LEADER OF THE PEOPL	SOUL 35100	15.00	70's
I'LL NEVER FORGET YOU	PAIN	GRANITE 522	15.00	70's
LOVE (THE LONELY PEOPLE'S PRAYER)	YOU'VE GOT MY SOUL ON FIRE	MOTOWN 1276	10.00	70's
STAY WITH ME	PARTY	GRANITE 528	10.00	70's
THERE YOU GO	SAME: INSTRUMENTAL	SOUL 35103	8.00	70's
AGENT DOUBLE OO SOUL	SAME: INSTRUMENTAL	RIC TIC 103	8.00	northern
BAC K STREET	SAME: INSTRUMENTAL	RIC TIC 107	8.00	northern
I WANT MY BABY BACK	GONNA KEEP ON TRYING TILL I WI	GORDY 7066	8.00	northern
MY WEAKNESS IS YOU	I AM THE MAN FOR YOU BABY	GORDY 7071	10.00	northern
TIME	RUNNING BACK AND FORTH	GORDY 7097	8.00	northern
GIRLS ARE GETTING PRETTIER	IT'S MY TURN NOW	RIC TIC 118	10.00	northern
I HAVE FAITH IN YOU	STOP HER ON SIGHT (S.O.S.)	RIC TIC 109	15.00	northern
MY KIND OF WOMAN	YOU'RE MY MELLOW	RIC TIC 120	100.00	northern
SCOTT'S ON SWINGERS	SAME:	RIC TIC 109X DJ only	200.00	northern

STARR, HARRY
ANOTHER TIME ANOTHER PLACE	STEP INTO MY WORLD	END 1129	150.00	northern

STARR, JOHNNY
DON'T BLOCK THE ROAD	DO RE MI FA SO LA TI DO	MALA 12019	25.00	northern
DON'T HOLD BACK	THE SWINGING ORGAN	EASTERN 60001	10.00	northern

STARR, NO NO
PULL YOURSELF TOGETHER	SWING YOUR LOVE MY WAY	MIDAS 301	10.00	northern

STARR, TOMMY
BETTER THINK OF WHAT YOU'RE LOSING	LOVE WHEEL	LOMA 2095	15.00	northern

STAR-TELLS
FALLING IN LOVE WITH YOU GIRL	YOU'RE WRONG ABOUT ME	LAMARR 1002	15.00	northern

STARTONES
LOVIN' YOU BABY	ONE ROSE	BILLIE FRAN 1	400.00	northern

STAR-TREKS
GONNA NEED MAGIC	DREAMIN'	VEEP 1254	50.00	northern

STARVUE
BODY FUSION 6643	LOVE STRUCK	MIDWEST INTER.	30.00	70's

STATEN, MAC AND THE NOMADS
THERE SHE GOES	DO THE FREEZE	PRELUDE 1111	700.00	northern

STATEN, PATINELL
LITTLE LOVE AFFAIR	I LET A GOOD MAN GO	SEPIA 8201	2000.00	northern

STATES AND SON, JOHNNY
BUG EYE		RENDEZVOUS	100.00	funk

STATON, CANDI
NOW YOU'VE GOT THE UPPER HAND	YOU CAN'T STOP ME	UNITY 711	500.00	**northerB**

STEELE, COLE
IT'S FOR YOU	SLEEP IN PUBLIC PLACES	JIM-KO 41095	30.00	northern

STEELE, JOHNNY
I CAN'T GO ON	DANGER ZONE	GOLDEN CITY 1010	30.00	ballad

STEELERS
IT MUST BE LOVE	DANCING GIRL	TRIPLE T 2	30.00	70's
CAN'T STAND THIS PAIN	A THOUSAND TOMORROWS	EPIC 10587	20.00	northern
YOU GOT ME CALLIN'	YOU'RE WHAT'S MISSING FROM MY	EPIC 10773	20.00	northern
CRYING BITTER TEARS	WALK ALONE	GLOW STAR 815	30.00	northern
DISTURBING THOUGHTS	LOVE, LOVE, LOVE LOVE FOR ME	AMG 17	150.00	northern
GET IT FROM THE BOTTOM	I'M SORRY	TORRID	10.00	northern

STEEPLECHASE
NEVER COMING BACK	LADY BRIGHT	POLYDOR 14030	50.00	70's

STEINWAYS
DON'T WONDER WHY	CALL ME	OLIVER 2007 DJ	20.00	northern
YOU'VE BEEN LEADING ME ON	MY HEART'S NOT IN IT ANYMORE	OLIVER 2002	75.00	northern

STEMMONS EXPRESS
WOMAN, LOVE THIEF	LOVE POWER	KARMA 201	200.00	northern
WOMAN, LOVE THIEF	LOVE POWER	WAND 1198	150.00	northern

STEPHENS, SANDRA
IF YOU REALLY LOVE ME	NEVER NO MORE	DARAN 204	250.00	northern
IF YOU REALLY LOVE ME	NEVER NO MORE	JA-WES 203	300.00	northern

STEPTONES
LET THE PEOPLE TALK	DON'T YOU WANT TO FALL IN LOVE	IX CHAINS 7016	8.00	70's
LONELY ONE	STEPIN HIGH	DIAMOND JIM 8794	300.00	northern

STER-PHONICS
DON'T LEAVE ME	YOU KNOW I LOVE YOU	MAS-TOK 65	400.00	northern

STEREOPHONICS
IF YOU DON'T DO RIGHT		ENJOY	300.00	northern

STEREOS
DON'T LET IT HAPPEN TO YOU	THE BEST THING TO BE IS A PERSON	VAL 5672	50.00	northern
MUMBLING WORD	GOOD NEWS	WORLD 1012	30.00	northern

STERLING, SPENCER
JILTED	YOUNG IN YEARS	BIG TOP 3104	75.00	northern

STEVENS, APRIL
WANTING YOU	FALLING IN LOVE AGAIN	MGM 13825	20.00	northern

STEVENS, FLIP FLOP
LET'S DO THAT THING	LET'S DO THAT THING PT.2	SHIPTOWN 10	75.00	funk

STEVENS, LINDY
PENNYGOLD	SOME MORE OF YOUR LOVIN'	DECCA 32971 DJ	20.00	northern

STEVENS, TARI
(YOUR LOVE WAS JUST A) FALSE ALARM	(THEY CALL HIM) A BAD BOY	FAIRMOUNT 1001	75.00	**northerB**

STEVENSON, LITTLE DENISE
WOULD IT BE ME		VOICE 273	100.00	northern

STEWART, BILLY
A FAT BOY CAN CRY	COUNT ME OUT	CHESS 1888	20.00	northern
NO GIRL	HOW NICE IT IS	CHESS 1941	15.00	northern
OL'MAN RIVER	EVERY DAY I HAVE THE BLUES	CHESS 1991	10.00	northern
SUGAR AND SPICE	STRANGE FEELING	CHESS 1868	20.00	northern

STEWART, DARRYL

NAME IT AND CLAIM IT	CROSS MY HEART	WAND 11209	150.00	northern
YOU MUST KNOW MAGIC	A SMART MONKEY DOESN'T MONKEY	MUSICOR 1423	40.00	ballad

STEWART, DELL

DIDN'T I TELL YOU	LOVE THAT GIRL	WATCH 6343	40.00	ballad

STEWART, GWEN

YOU TOOK ME FOR A FOOL	I THOUGHT IT OVER	CALL ME 5388	25.00	northern

STEWART, MARION

I MUST BE LOSING YOU	A HUNDRED YEARS FROM TODAY	R, 1516	300.00	northern
THE MAN I LOVE	I'M THE GIRL	R. 1514	15.00	northern

STEWART, SYLVESTER

HELP ME WITH A BROKEN HEART		G&P 901	150.00	northern

STICKS OF DYNAMITE

IT'S FOOTBALL BABY		SAXTON	75.00	funk

STIMULATION

MAGIC TOUCH OF LOVE	CAN YOU DIG WHERE I'M COMING FROM	HI-STEPPING 754547	100.00	70's
STIMULATORSWARM SUMMER NIGHTS	SAME: INSTRUMENTAL	SOUND-O-RIFFIC 2	500.00	group

STOKES, JIMMY

KEEP ON GOIN'	TELEPHONE STOP RINGING	SIANA 721	85.00	northern

STOKES, JUDY

A REAL MAN	KISS OUR LOVE GOODBYE	SOUL POWER 10	300.00	northern

STOKES, PATTI

IS IT TRUE	GOOD GIRL	MIR-A-DON 1005	30.00	northern

STONE, BOB

FOXY LITTLE MAMA	STONE SOUL	JIVE 1047	25.00	funk

STONE, GEORGE

HOLE IN THE WALL	MY BEAT	MUSICOR 1122	10.00	mod

STOPPERS

COME BACK BABY	THE LA LA SONG	JUBILEE 5528	150.00	northern

STORM

SWEET HAPPINESS	GOING GOING GONE	SUNFLOWER 106	15.00	northern

STORM, BILLY

SHE COMES UP	I DON'YT KNOW WHY	PI KAPPA 500	40.00	70's
EDUCATED FOOL	I CAN'T HELP IT	INFINITY 23J	75.00	northern
PLEASE DON'T MENTION HER NAME	THE WARMEST LOVE	HBR 474	60.00	northern

STORM, TOM AND THE PEPS

THAT'S THE WAY LOVE IS	I LOVE YOU	GE GE 96947	75.00	northern

STORMY

I WON'T STOP TO CRY	THE DEVASTATOR	TWINIGHT 104	200.00	northern

STORMY JAZZMIN

STORMY JAZZMIN'	STORMY JAZZMIN' PT.2	STORM 1	25.00	funk

STORY, ALLEN (BO)

WHY OH WHY	CHUBBY CHUBBY	CHECK MATE 1014	40.00	motown

STRANDS

THE BREEZE FROM THE TREES	OLD MAN RIVER	TARX 1006	150.00	northern

STRANGERS

NIGHT WINDS	THESE ARE THE THINGS I LOVE	WB 5438	50.00	northern

STRATOLINERS

YOUR LOVE	WHAT DO YOU WANT WITH MY LOVE	FEDERAL 12568	25.00	northern

STREET, JUDY

WHAT	YOU TURN ME ON	STRIDER 4	200.00	**northerB**

STREET, RICHARD AND THE DISTANTS

ANSWER ME	SAVE ME FROM THIS MISERYQ	THEMLA NO. #	300.00	motown
ANSWER ME	SAVE ME FROM THIS MISERY	HARMON 1002	150.00	motown

STREISAND, BARBARA

OUR CORNER OF THE NIGHT	HE COULD SHOW ME	COLUMBIA 44474	10.00	northern

STRIBLIN, KAREN

WE'RE NOT TOO YOUNG	JUST A LITTLE GIRL IN LOVE	JABER 7117	200.00	northern

STRICKLAND, HOMER

I'LL GET OVER YOU	MY GRANDPA TOLD ME	JADAN 777	15.00	northern

STRIDEL, GENE

TOMORROW IS A BRAND NEW DAY	THE ZEBRA	ATLANTIC 2500	20.00	northern
TOMORROW IS ANOTHER DAY	THE ZEBRA	ATLANTIC 2500 PS	40.00	northern

STRIDES

I CAN GET ALONG (WITHOUT YOUR	THE STRIDE	M-S 202	150.00	northern
I'M SO GLAD WE'FRE TOGETHER	MAKE YOUR MOVE	M-S 209	50.00	group

STRINGER, BOBBY

BEFORE YOU	YOU'VE GOT TO MANY MILES	SWAR 7125	10.00	70's
PUT YOUR MIND AT EASE	FUNKY BROADWAY	FUN CITY 114	20.00	70's

STRINGFIELD FAMILY

THE SOUND OF DISCO ROCK	THE STRINGFIELD HUSTLE	EASTERN SOUND 58	30.00	70's

STRINGFIELD, SHONA

I NEED A REST	OOH SWEET BABY	RIALTO 2001	15.00	northern

STRIPLIN, SYLVIA

YOU CAN'T TURN ME AWAY	GIVE ME YOUR LOVE	UNO MELODIC 702	40.00	70's

STROGIN, HENRY

Title	B-side	Label	Price	Genre
MISERY	I CRIED LIKE A BABY	HANK 5001	20.00	northern
LOVE INSURANCE	I WANNA	TEN STAR	20.00	northern

STRONG, BARRETT

Title	B-side	Label	Price	Genre
MAN UP IN THE SKY	SAME:	CAPITOL 4223 DJ	15.00	70's
SURRENDER	THERE'S SOMETHING ABOUT YOU	CAPITOL 4120	8.00	70's
LET'S ROCK	DO THE VERY BEST YOU CAN	TAMLA 54021	1250.00	motown
MISERY	TWO WRONGS DON'T MAKE A RIGHT	TAMLA 54043	40.00	motown
MONEY (THAT'S WHAT I WANT)	OH I APOLOGIZE	ANNA 1111	10.00	motown
MONEY (THAT'S WHAT I WANT)	OH I APOLOGIZE	TAMLA 54027	50.00	motown
MONEY (THAT'S WHAT I WANT)	I APOLOGISE (Mix 66220)	TAMLA 54027.	50.00	motown
MONEY AND ME	YOU GOT WHAT IT TAKES	TAMLA 54035	50.00	motown
WHIRLWIND	I'M GONNA CRY	TAMLA 54033	30.00	motown
YES, NO MAYBE SO	YOU KNOWS WHAT TO DO	TAMLA 54029	30.00	motown
YES, NO, MAYBE SO	YOU KNOW WHAT TO DO	ANNA 1116	15.00	motown
MAKE UP YOUR MIND	I BETTER RUN	TOLLIE 9023	30.00	northern

STRONG, ELSIE

Title	B-side	Label	Price	Genre
ASK THE LONELY	THIS IS THE LAST TIME	SOUNDS INTERNATIONAL	40.00	northern
JUST ASK ME	SAME: INSTRUMENTAL	FINALLY 1000	10.00	northern
THE GIRL RATED TRIPLE X	I'M THE REAL THING	LEGRAND 4000	30.00	northern
YOU CUT THE LOVE LINE	GO AWAY GRAY CLOUDS	EMPIRE 50105	400.00	northern

STRONG, MARCELL

Title	B-side	Label	Price	Genre
MUMBLE IN MY EAR	WHAT YOU'RE MISSING SOMEONE'S	FAME 1475	30.00	ballad
TRYING TO MAKE UP		EMERGE 1110	100.00	northern

STROTHER, PERCY

Title	B-side	Label	Price	Genre
CAN'T STAY FOR ANOTHER DAY	OOH BABY	PLS 81710	100.00	70's

STUART, BRAD

Title	B-side	Label	Price	Genre
I WOULDN'T MIND	THAT DAY WHEN SHE NEEDED ME	SIR GRAHAM 391	30.00	northern

STUART, JEB

Title	B-side	Label	Price	Genre
YOU BETTER BELIEVE IT, BABY	BABY LET'S GET TOGETHER TONIGH	ESQUIRE INTERNATIONAL	40.00	70's
CAN'T COUNT THE DAYS	I JUST LOVE YOUR WORK	CLIMAX 22004	25.00	ballad
DON'T STOP GIVING ME LOVE	SUPER STRANG VIBRATIONS	ESQUIRE 9551	30.00	northern

STUBBS, JOE

Title	B-side	Label	Price	Genre
KEEP ON LOVING ME	WHAT'S MY DESTINY	LU-PINE 120	15.00	northern

STUNNERS

Title	B-side	Label	Price	Genre
NOBODY BUT ME	WITHOUT YOU	RENFRO 120	600.00	northern

STYLERS

Title	B-side	Label	Price	Genre
GOING STEADY ANNIVERSARY	PUSHING UP DAISIES	GORDY 7018	45.00	motown

STYLES

Title	B-side	Label	Price	Genre
BABY YOU'RE ALIVE	KNOW YOU KNOW THAT I KNOW	MODERN 1048	40.00	northern

STYLETTES

Title	B-side	Label	Price	Genre
ON FIRE	PACKING UP MY MEMORIES	SAN-DEE 1010	75.00	northern
PACKIN' UP MY MEMORIES	ON FIRE	CAMEO 337	25.00	northern

STY-LETTS

Title	B-side	Label	Price	Genre
TOO FAR TO TURN AROUND	HELLO MY DARLIN'	PILLAR 515	200.00	northern

STYLISTS

Title	B-side	Label	Price	Genre
WHAT IS LOVE	WHERE DID THE CHILDREN GO	V.I.P. 25066	20.00	motown

SUBWAY RIDERS

Title	B-side	Label	Price	Genre
AFTER THE SESSION	ADAM	MOON SHOT 6706	75.00	northern

SUE, CARLETTA

Title	B-side	Label	Price	Genre
YOU KEEP HOLDING BACK ON LOVE	TELL ME EVERYTHINBG YOU KNOW	STRING 2	15.00	70's

SUGAR AND SPICES

Title	B-side	Label	Price	Genre
HAVE FAITH IN ME	TEARDROPS	SWAN 4208	150.00	northern

SUGAR AND SWEET

Title	B-side	Label	Price	Genre
I'VE CHANGED		AUDIO FORTY 1004	100.00	northern
MY LOVER	COOL IT BABY	MORTON 101	100.00	northern

SULL, EDDIE

Title	B-side	Label	Price	Genre
I'M LOOKING FOR MY BABY	TELL THE WHOLE WORLD ABOUT IT	RENEE 115	30.00	northern
I'M LOOKING FOR MY BABY	TELL THE WHOLE WORLD ABOUT IT	MARC 102	40.00	northern

SUMMERS, ED

Title	B-side	Label	Price	Genre
I CAN TELL	PREPARE YOURSELF	SOYA 1001	40.00	70's

SUMMERS, JOHNNY

Title	B-side	Label	Price	Genre
I CAN'T LET GO		YORKTOWN 1009	200.00	northern
I'M STILL YOURS		YORKTOWN	400.00	northern
THE FEELING IS STILL THERE		AUDIO FORTY 1800	200.00	northern

SUMMITS

Title	B-side	Label	Price	Genre
LET ME LOVE YOU AGAIN	IT TAKES TWO	DC INTERNATIONAL	15.00	group
I CAN'T GET OVER LOSING YOU	SAME: INSTRUMENTAL	DONTEE 102	100.00	northern

SUNDAY

Title	B-side	Label	Price	Genre
AIN'T GOT NO PROBLEMS	WHERE DID HE COME FROM	ALTEEN 9631	50.00	northern
AIN'T GOT NO PROBLEMS	WHERE DID HE COME FROM	CHESS 2074	40.00	northern

SUNLINERS

Title	B-side	Label	Price	Genre
ALL ALONE	THE SWINGIN' KIND	GOLDEN WORLD 31	100.00	northern

SUNLINERS BAND

Title	B-side	Label	Price	Genre
SOUL POWER		KEY-LOC	100.00	funk

SUNLOVERS

Title	B-side	Label	Price	Genre
MY POOR HEART	THIS LOVE OF OURS	BREAKTHROUGH 1002	70.00	northern

MY POOR HEART	THIS LOVE OF OURS	MUTT & JEFF 18	50.00	northern
MY POOR HEART	I'LL TELL THE WORLD	MUTT & JEFF 17	60.00	northern
YOU'LL NEVER MAKE THE GRADE	THIS LOVE OF OURS	MUTT & JEFF 18	50.00	northern
I'LL TREAT YOU RIGHT		MUTT & JEFF 21	20.00	group

SUNNY AND THE SUNLINERS

I'M NO STRANGER	WHEN IT RAINS	KEY-LOC 1044	25.00	northern
GET DOWN		KEY-LOC 1059	100.00	funk
IF I COULD SEE YOU NOW	SHOULD I TAKE YOU HOME	RPR 105	20.00	northern
NO ONE ELSE WILL DO	OUT OF SIGHT-OUT OF MIND	TEAR DROP 3027	20.00	northern
TRICK BAG	CHEATIN' TRACES	TEAR DROP 3081	15.00	northern

SUPERBS

HE BROKE A YOUNG GIRLS HEART	GODDESS OF LOVE	DORE 748	20.00	group
HE BROKE A YOUNG GIRL'S HEART	IT'S A MILLION MILES TO PARADIse	DORE 755	20.00	group
MY HEART ISN'T IN IT	AMBUSH	DORE 741	20.00	group
HAPPIEST GIRL IN THE WORLD	LOVE'S UNPREDICTABLE	CATAMOUNT 2122	20.00	northern
I WANNA DO IT WITH YOU BABY	HE BROKE A YOUNG GIRLS HEART	DORE 782	75.00	northern
ONLY FOR LOVERS	YOU DON'T CARE	ALTEEN 3004	30.00	northern
THE WIND IS BLOWING	BETTER GET YOUR OWN ONE BUDDY	DORE 764	150.00	northern
THE WIND IS BLOWING	GO FOR WHAT YOU KNOW	DORE 771	100.00	northern

SUPERIORS

I'D RATHER DIE	HEAVENLY ANGEL	SUE 12	15.00	northern
LET ME MAKE YOU HAPPY	CAN'T MAKE IT WITHOUT YOU	MGM 13503	15.00	northern
WHAT WOULD I DO	TELL ME TO GO	VERVE 10370	20.00	northern

SUPERIORS BAND

THE LADY	THE LADY PT.2	BARVIS 319	50.00	funk

SUPERLATIVES

FORGET ABOUT TOMORROW	DO WHAT YOU WANT TO DO	DYNAMICS 1011	15.00	group
IT'S EASY TO LOVE	COME ON DOWN TO THE GHETTO	WAL-LY 6330	15.00	group
DON'T LET TRUE LOVE DIE	SHE'S MY WONDER WOMAN	DYNAMICS 1017	15.00	northern
DON'T LET TRUE LOVE DIE	SHE'S MY WONDER WOMAN	WESTBOUND 154	15.00	northern
I STILL LOVE YOU	WE'RE SO LONELY	UPTITE 250 yellow	40.00	northern
I STILL LOVE YOU	WE'RE SO LONELY	UPTITE 250 blue	40.00	**northerB**
I STILL LOVE YOU	WE'RE SO LONELY	UPTITE 250 lined	40.00	northern
LONELY IN A CROWD	I DON''T KNOW HOW	WESTBOUND 144	10.00	northern
WON'T YOU PLEASE (BE MY BABY)	DON'T EVER LEAVE ME	DYNAMICS 1012	15.00	northern

SUPREMES

YOU AND ME	GLOW	GROG 500	30.00	group
(HE'S) SEVENTEEN	YOUR HEART BELONGS TO ME	MOTOWN 1027	40.00	motown
A BREATH TAKING FIRST SIGHT SOUL SHAKIN	ROCK AND ROLL BANJO BAND	MOTOWN 1044 long title	50.00	motown
A BREATH TAKING GUY	ROCK ND ROLL BANJO BAND	MOTOWN 1044	20.00	motown
BABY LOVE	ASK ANY GIRL	MOTOWN 1066 PS	20.00	motown
BUTTERED POPCORN	WHO'S LOVING YOU	TAMLA 54045 globe	85.00	motown
BUTTERED POPCORN	WHO'S LOVING YOU	TAMLA 54045 striped	200.00	motown
HE'S ALL I GOT	LOVE IS LIKE AN ITCHING	MOTOWN 1094	10.00	motown
I WANT A GUY	NEVER AGAIN	MOTOWN 1008	1500.00	motown
I WANT A GUY	NEVER AGAIN	TAMLA 54038 stripes	150.00	motown
MY HEART CAN'T TAKE IT NO MORE	YOU BRING BACK MEMORIES	MOTOWN 1040	40.00	motown
NOTHING BUT HEARTACHES	HE HOLDS HIS OWN	MOTOWN 1080 PS	15.00	motown
RUN, RUN, RUN	I'M GIVING YOU YOUR FREEDONM	MOTOWN 1054	20.00	motown
STOP! IN THE NAME OF LOVE	I'M IN LOVE AGAIN	MOTOWN 1074 PS	15.00	motown
THE ONLY TIME I'M HAPPY	SUPREMES INTERVIEW	GEORGE ALEXANDER 1079	25.00	motown
THINGS ARE CHANGING 33 rpm	BLANK:	MOTOWN 3114 DJ PS	100.00	motown
TIME CHANGES THINGS	LET ME GO THE RIGHT WAY	MOTOWN 1034	20.00	motown
TWINKLE TWINKLE LITTLE ME	CHILDREN'S CHRISTMAS SONG	MOTOWN 1085 PS	10.00	motown
WHEN THE LOVELIGHT STARTS SHIN	STANDING AT THE CROSSROADS OF	MOTOWN 1051	10.00	motown
YOU CAN'T HURRY LOVE	PUT YOURSELF IN MY PLACE	MOTOWN 1097 PS	15.00	motown
YOU KEEP ME HANGING ON	REMOVE THIS DOUBT	MOTOWN 1101 PS	15.00	motown

SURGEONS

DON'T TELL ME	YOU KNOW	CEE-JAM 100	200.00	northern

SURRATT, WILLIAM AND THE ESQUIRES

ROCK ME	STANDING IN THE MOONLIGHT	PYRAMID 7022	150.00	northern

SUSPICIONS

SOUL BEAT	A WINTER'S SERENADE	MAGIC TOUCH 2002	30.00	funk

SWANN, BETTYE

I THINK I'M FALLING IN LOVE	DON'T TAKE MY MIND	MONEY 136	15.00	northern
I'M LONELY FOR YOU	MY HEART IS CLOSED FOR THE SEASON	CAPITOL 2263	15.00	northern
MAKE ME YOURS	I WILL NOT CRY	MONEY 126	8.00	northern
MY HEART IS CLOSED FOR THE SEASON	DON'T TOUCH ME	CAPITOL 2382	8.00	northern
THE HEARTACHE IS GONE	OUR LOVE	MONEY 118	10.00	northern
KISS MY LOVE GOODBYE	THE BOY NEXT DOOR	ATLANTIC 3019	100.00	70's
DON'T WAIT TOO LONG	WHAT IS MY LIFE COMING TO	MONEY 108	15.00	northern
FALL IN LOVE WITH ME	LONELY LOVE	MONEY 129	15.00	northern
WHAT CAN IT BE	THE MAN THAT SAID NO	MONEY 113	15.00	northern
YOU GAVE ME LOVE	DON'T LOOK BACK	MONEY 135	15.00	northern

SWANSON, BENICE

LYING AWAKE	BABY I'M YOURS	CHESS 1927	30.00	northern
LYING AWAKE	BABY I'M YOURS	CHESS 1927 PS	100.00	northern

SWEET BOBBY AND HONEY BOY

TELL THE TRUTH	WATCH THE ONE WHO'S TALKING	SOUND O RIFFIC 1	25.00	funk

SWEET CHERRIES

DON'T GIVE IT AWAY	LOVE IS WHAT YOU MAKE IT	T NECK 904	15.00	funk
FROM THE BEGINNING	LOVE IS WHAT YOU MAKE IT	T NECK 910	10.00	northern

SWEET GERALDINE

BRAIN STORM	MAKE LOVE TO ME (BABE)	MAGIC CITY 19	50.00	70's

SWEET MIXTURE

HOUSE OF FUN AND LOVE	I LOVE YOU	BAZAR 1008	40.00	70's

SWEET THINGS.

I'M IN A WORLD OF TROUBLE	BABY'S BLUE	DATE 1522	45.00	northern
DON'T COME LOOKING FOR ME	YOU'RE MY LOVING BABY	DATE 1504 PS	25.00	northern

SWEET THREE

I WOULD IF I COULD	DON'T LEAVE ME NOW	CAMEO 463	25.00	northern
THAT'S THE WAY IT IS	BIG LOVERS COME IN SMALL PACKAGES	DECCA 32005	30.00	northern

SWEET WILLIAM

BRING IT ON HOME	I CAN HEAR MY BABY	JED 11	20.00	mod
MAYBE	BABY	COMPANION 107	75.00	northern

SWEET

BROKEN HEART ATTACK	DON'T DO IT	SMASH 2136	15.00	northern
GOT TO HAVE MORE LOVE	YOU CAN'T WIN AT LOVE	SMASH 2116	15.00	northern

SWEETHEARTS

BEAUTY IS JUST SKIN DEEP	EDDIE MY LOVE	KENT 428	75.00	northern
NO MORE TEARS	THIS COULDN'T BE ME	KENT 442	30.00	northern

SWEETS

MAMA SAW ME	THE RICHEST GIRL	VALIANT 711	25.00	northern
SOMETHING ABOUT MY BABY	SATISFY ME BABY	SOULTOWN 105	500.00	**northerB**

SWINGING TIGERS

SNAKE WALK Pt.1	SNAKE WALK Pt.2	TAMLA 54024	750.00	motown

SWINGMASTERS

SWITCH BLADE	RAINBOW	TRIUS 914	15.00	funk

SWISHER, DEBRA

YOU'RE SO GOOD TO ME	THANK YOU AND GOODNIGHT	BOOM 60001 DJ	15.00	northern

SWISS MOVEMENT

I WISH OUR LOVE WOULD LAST FOR	ONE IN A MILLION	GOLD. 2	100.00	70's

SWOPE, SHERYL

ONE MOMENT	MEET ME	DUO 7456	50.00	northern
RUN TO ME	ARE YOU GONNA DO RIGHT THIS TI	DUO 7453	30.00	northern

SYKES, GARNETT

LONGER THAN FOREVER	GO GO GIRL	MUSETTE 13	200.00	northern

SYMPHONICS

ALL ROADS LEAD TO HEARTBREAK	IT WON'T BE LONG	DEE-JON 1	20.00	group
NO MORE	SHE'S JUST A SAD GIRL	BRUNSWICK 55313	50.00	northern
SILENT KIND OF GUY	(FEET) DON'T FAIL ME NOW	BRUNSWICK 55303	15.00	northern
SILENT KIND OF GUY	FEET (DON'T FAIL ME NOW)	WILSON 100	50.00	northern

T

T.J. AND THE GROUP

BLUES FOR THE B'S		M & M NO#	100.00	funk

T.K.O's

DANCING WITH MY BABY	GETTING INTO SOMETHING	TEN STAR 106	10.00	mod
THE CHARGE	CAN YOU DIG IT	TEN STAR 105	10.00	mod

T.N.J's

DON'T FORGET ABOUT ME	FALLING IN LOVE	CHESS 2155	15.00	70's
I DIDN'T KNOW	SHE'S NOT READY	NEWARK 228	200.00	northern
TWO GIRLS	I GOT IT BAD	LUCKY LOU 812	150.00	northern

TABLE OF CONTENTS

WRAPPED AROUND YOUR FINGER	MICHELLE YOUR MY BABY	LAKE 7052	25.00	70's

TAILFEATHERS

THAT'S THE WAY IT'S GONNA BE	NOW AIN'T THAT LOVE	U[PTITE 252	30.00	group

TALENT, TONY

GOTTA TELL SOMEBODY (ABOUT MY BABY)	HOOKED ON YOU	VANDO 3001	15.00	**northerB**

TAM, TIM AND THE TURN-ONS

WAIT A MINUTE	OPELIA	PALMER 5002	8.00	**northerB**

TAMIKO

DON'T LAUGH IF I CRY AT YOUR P	RHAPSODY	ATCO 6298	60.00	northern

TAMS

A-side	B-side	Label	Price	Genre
UNTIE ME	DISILLUSIONED	ARLEN 11	10.00	northern
BE YOUNG, BE FOOLISH, BE HAPPY	THAT SAME OLD SONG	ABC 11066	10.00	northern
FIND ANOTHER LOVE	MY BABY LOVES ME	GENERAL AMERICAN 714	10.00	northern
HEY GIRL DON'T BOTHER ME	TAKE AWAY	ABC 10573	10.00	northern
SHELTER	GET AWAY (LEAVE ME ALONE)	ABC 10885	10.00	northern
SILLY LITTLE GIRL	WEEP LITTLE GIRL	ABC 10601	10.00	northern
TROUBLE MAKER	LAUGH AT THE WORLD	ABC 11128	10.00	northern

TAN GEERS

A-side	B-side	Label	Price	Genre
WHAT'S THE USE OF ME TRYING	LET MY HEART ANS SOUL BE FREE	OKEH 7319	150.00	northern
THIS EMPTY PLACE	(HE'S) NOT THAT KIND OF GUY	SCEPTER 12282	15.00	northern

TANGENETTS

A-side	B-side	Label	Price	Genre
ANY OLE WAY	YOU'RE THE ONE	RAN 101	75.00	northern

TANNER, AL

A-side	B-side	Label	Price	Genre
DOING OUR OWN THING	LET'S BOOGIE FREAK N' ROCK	TYMO 728	15.00	funk

TANNER, ROBERT

A-side	B-side	Label	Price	Genre
SWEET MEMORIES	BE MY WOMAN	MEGATONE 113	400.00	northern

TANZELL, CONNIE

A-side	B-side	Label	Price	Genre
DON'T KNOCK ME	I WANT HER BY MY SIDE	SOUL CLOCK 100	30.00	northern

TARGET

A-side	B-side	Label	Price	Genre
GIVE ME ONE MORE CHANCE	SAME: INSTRUMENTAL	KAMA 1001	300.00	70's

TARLETON, KARL

A-side	B-side	Label	Price	Genre
ALONG CAME YOU	STAY WITH ME	UNI 55227	30.00	northern

TARTANS WITH KADDO STRINGS

A-side	B-side	Label	Price	Genre
NOTHING BUT LOVE	I NEED YOU	IMPACT 1010	15.00	northern

TARVER, JAMES

A-side	B-side	Label	Price	Genre
MOVING AND GROOVING	ROBOT IT'S GETTING FUNKY	ROACH 804	15.00	funk

TATE

A-side	B-side	Label	Price	Genre
IT TAKES MORE THAN LOVE	FREE	CLOVERSTREET 101	300.00	northern
LOVE SHOP		CLOVERSTREET 102	150.00	northern

TATE, FREDDIE

A-side	B-side	Label	Price	Genre
I DIDN'T BELIEVE YOU	FUNKY COUNTRY	MAGNUM 743	20.00	70's

TATE, HOWARD

A-side	B-side	Label	Price	Genre
BABY, I LOVE YOU	HOW BLUE CAN YOU GET	VERVE 10525	10.00	northern
HALF A MAN	LOOK AT GRANNY RUN RUN	VERVE 10464	10.00	northern
YOU'RE LOOKIN GOOD	HALF A MAN	UTOPIA 511	200.00	northern

TATE, TOMMY

A-side	B-side	Label	Price	Genre
I'M WRAPPED UP	LINGER A LITTLE LONGER	SUNDANCE NO.#	15.00	70's
WHAT GIVES YOU THE RIGHT	IF I GAVE YOU MY HEART	SUNDANCE 5003	15.00	70's
A LOVER'S REWARD	BIG BLUE DIAMONDS	OKEH 7253	50.00	northern
I'M TAKING ON PAIN	ARE YOU FROM HEAVEN	OKEH 7242	200.00	northern

TAURUS AND LEO

A-side	B-side	Label	Price	Genre
GOING OUT THE WORLD BACKWARDS	I AIN'T PLATING BABY	VELVET SOUND 367	20.00	northern

TAX FREE

A-side	B-side	Label	Price	Genre
LOVE IS GONE	LOVE ME	FOX CAR 900	30.00	70's

TAYLOR BROTHERS

A-side	B-side	Label	Price	Genre
YOUR LAST CHANCE	SHOWDOWN	UNITED 98	20.00	northern

TAYLOR, ALEX

A-side	B-side	Label	Price	Genre
SLOWLY TURNING TO LOVE	EARLY MORNING DREAM	BEST 1001	40.00	70's

TAYLOR, BOBBY

A-side	B-side	Label	Price	Genre
IT WAS A GOOD TIME	THERE ARE ROSES SOMEWHERE IN THE WORLD	SUNFLOWER 126	40.00	70's

TAYLOR, BOBBY AND THE VANCOUVERS

A-side	B-side	Label	Price	Genre
DOES YOUR MAMA KNOW ABOUT ME	FADING AWAY	GORDY 7069 PS	15.00	motown
OH, I'VE BEEN BLESSED	BLACKMAIL	V.I.P. 25053	15.00	motown

TAYLOR, CARMEN

A-side	B-side	Label	Price	Genre
YOU'RE PUTTING ME ON	MY SON	KAMA SUTRA 206	10.00	northern

TAYLOR, DEBBIE

A-side	B-side	Label	Price	Genre
I HAVE LEARNED TO DO WITHOUT YOU	CHEAPER IN THE LONG RUN	POLYDOR 14219	30.00	70's
JUST DON'T PAY	I DON'T WANT TO LEAVE	ARISTA 144	10.00	70's
CHECK YOURSELF	WAIT UNTIL I'M GONE	DECCA 32259	10.00	ballad
DON'T LET IT END	HOW LONG CAN THIS LAST	GWP 510	10.00	northern
DON'T NOBODY MESS WITH MY BABY	STOP	GRAPEVINE 202	15.00	northern

TAYLOR, E.G. AND THE SOUNDS OF SOUL

A-side	B-side	Label	Price	Genre
YOU MADE ME MAD	PICK YOURSELF UP	VAL. 1025	20.00	northern

TAYLOR, EMANUEL

A-side	B-side	Label	Price	Genre
YOU REALLY GOT A HOLD ON ME	SOCIETY	BERNARD 788	200.00	70's
YOU'RE THE ONE FOR ME	REMEMBERR ME ALWAYS	BERNARD 77	20.00	70's

TAYLOR, FELICE

A-side	B-side	Label	Price	Genre
IT MAY BE WINTER OUTSIDE	SAME: INSTRUMENTAL	MUSTANG 3024	10.00	northern
I CAN FEEL YOUR LOVE	GOOD LUCK	KENT 483	15.00	northern

TAYLOR, FLORIAN

A-side	B-side	Label	Price	Genre
THINK ABOUT ME	KNOWING (THAT YOU WANT HER)	CADET 5546	50.00	northern
THINK ABOUT ME	KNOWING (THAT YOU WANT HER)	GROOVY 103	100.00	northern

TAYLOR, GERRI

A-side	B-side	Label	Price	Genre
I'M SATISFIED WITH YOUR LOVE	I'M STEPPING OUT	MICA 502 DJ	250.00	northern
EMPTY ARMS AND BITTER TEARS	COME HOME I'M LONELY	CONSTELLATION 154	30.00	northern

TAYLOR, GLORIA

DON'T WANT TO BE A GIRL THAT CRIES	TOTAL DISASTER	MERCURY 73186	50.00	northern
HAD IT ALL THE TIME	WHAT'S YOUR WORLD	SELECTOR SOUND 1976	30.00	northern
YESTERDAY WILL NEVER COME	UNYIELDING	MERCURY 73137	20.00	northern
GROUNDED PT. 1	GROUNDED PT. 2	SILVER FOX 19	10.00	northern
POOR UNFORTUNATE ME	YOU MIGHT NEED ME ANOTHNER DAY	KING SOUL 493	30.00	northern
YOU GOT TO PAY THE PRICE	LOVING YOU AND BEING LOVED BY	SILVER FOX 14	8.00	northern

TAYLOR, HERSEY

LET ME MAKE YOU HAPPY	WE'RE GONNA RUN OUT OF TIME	FUTURE STARS 1001	15.00	70's
AIN'T GONNA SHARE YOUR LOVE	CUT YOU LOOSE	FUTURE STARS 1003	30.00	ballad

TAYLOR, ISAAC

I'M TIRED OF THESE CHANGES	JUST ANOTHER MAN	RONN 80	10.00	northern

TAYLOR, JACKIE

WALKIN' BACK	I'VE BEEN LOVED	JUBILEE 5530	70.00	northern

TAYLOR, JAMES

LOVE WITH HOPE	EVERYTHING ABOUT YOU	OVIDE 242	40.00	northern

TAYLOR, JAY JAY

I'M NOT TIRED YET	TELL ME THE TRUTH	DYNAMITE 8665	10.00	70's
I'M NOT TIRED YET	TELL ME THE TRUTH	JEWEL 848	8.00	70's

TAYLOR, JOHNNIE

WHAT ABOUT MY LOVE	REAGANOMICS	BEVERLY GLEN 2003	15.00	70's
AIN'T THAT LOVING YOU	OUTSIDE LOVE	STAX 209	8.00	northern
CHANGES	I HAD A DREAM	STAX 186	8.00	northern
TOE-HOLD	LITTLE BLUEBIRD	STAX 202	8.00	northern
FRIDAY NIGHT	STEAL AWAY	STAX 68	8.00	northern
ROME (WASN'T BUILT IN A DAY)	NEVER, NEVER	SAR 131	30.00	northern

TAYLOR, JOYCE

WHAT CAN I DO	MEAN MIS-TREATER	WAL-LY 5072	150.00	northern

TAYLOR, LEROY

OH LINDA	NOBODY CAN LOVE YOU	BRUNSWICK 55345	50.00	northern

TAYLOR, LEROY AND THE FOUR KAYS

TAKIN' MY TIME	I'LL UNDERSTAND	SHRINE 101	100.00	northern

TAYLOR, LITTLE EDDIE

I HADF A GOOD TIME	FORGIVE ONE MISTAKE	PEACOCK 1949	300.00	northern

TAYLOR, MARVA W.

NOTHING I'D RATHER BE THAN YOU	HEY, YOU AND YOU AND YOU AND	FORTE 5015	75.00	northern

TAYLOR, MONROE

PROUD GUY	MONKEY JERK	CHESAPEAKE 617	10.00	northern

TAYLOR, R.DEAN

LET'S GO SOMEWHERE	POOR GIRL	V.I.P. 25027	20.00	motown
THERE'S A GHOST IN MY HOUSE	DON'T FOOL AROUND	V.I.P. 25042	25.00	motown

TAYLOR, RANDY

THEATRE OF BROKEN HEARTS	SOUL MACHINE	UPTOWN 718	50.00	northern

TAYLOR, ROBBY

A STOP ALONG THE WAY	THIS IS MY WOMAN	INTEGRA 103	15.00	northern

TAYLOR, ROBERT

PACKING UP YOUR LOVE	A CHANGE GONNA COME	SONIC 8624	15.00	northern
PACKING UP YOUR LOVE	SO MUCH LOVE	ALTEEN 8624	40.00	northern

TAYLOR, ROMEO

WILL YOU COME BACK MY LOVE	FOR YOU	CELESTRIAL 1003	100.00	northern

TAYLOR, RONNIE

WITHOUT LOVE	I CAN'T TAKE IT	REVILOT 212	20.00	ballad

TAYLOR, ROSEMARY

REALLY GOT IT BAD FOR MY BABY	MERCY MERCY	ABC 11083 DJ	15.00	northern

TAYLOR, SAMMY

SOMETHING THE DEVIL'S NEVER DONE	SEND HER BACK	RED LITE 116	30.00	funk

TAYLOR, SEAN

TOO LATE TO TURN BACK NOW	PUT ME DOWN EASY	MAGIC TOUCH 2008	15.00	northern

TAYLOR, SHERRI AND THE WARD, SAMMY

LOVER	THAT'S WHY I LOVE YOU SO MUCH	MOTOWN 1004	75.00	motown

TAYLOR, TED

SOMEBODY'S ALWAYS TRYING	TOP OF THE WORLD	OKEH 7198	40.00	northern

TEACHO AND THE STUDENTS

CHILLS AND FEVER	SAME OLD BEAT	OKEH 7234	20.00	northern

TEARDROPS

EVERY STEP I TAKE	RAISE YOUR HAND	MAX. 234	20.00	northern
TEARS COME TUMBLING	YOU WON'T BE THERE	MUSICOR 1139	15.00	northern

TEARS

SWEET LOVE	FUNK FAMILY	FUNKSHUN 301	30.00	70's
GOOD LUCK MY LOVE	WHAT YOUR DOING TO ME	SMASH 1981	100.00	northern
SHE'S MINE	HURT	ASTRONAUT 5001	50.00	northern

TECHNICS

CAUSE I REALLY LOVE YOU	A MAN'S CONFESSION	CHEX 1012	150.00	northern
HEY GIRL DON'T LEAVE ME	I MET HER ON THE FIRST OF SEPTEMBER	CHEX 1013	100.00	northern

TEDDY AND THE FINGERPOPPERS

SOUL GROOVE PT.1	SOUL GROOVE PT. 2	ARCTIC 143	50.00	northern

TEE N' CEE AND THE LTD'S

TIGHTEN UP WITH SOUL		RISING SOUL NO#	100.00	funk

TEE, JON

CRAZY	ROLL DEM BONES	JAY-TONE 816	300.00	northern
YOU MADE A LOVER OUT OF ME	DON'T-CHA LOOK LIKE THAT AT ME	JAY-TONE 818	500.00	northern

TEE, WILLIE

CONCENTRATE	GET UP	GATUR 8001	20.00	70's
FIRST TASTE OF HURT	FUNKY FUNKY TWIST	GATUR 509	60.00	70's
I'M HAVING SO MUCH FUN	FIRST TASTE OF HURT	GATUR 557	400.00	norhern
I HEARD EVERYTHING YOU SAID	CLOSE YOUR EYES	HOT LINE 910	8.00	ballad
I'M ONLY A MAN	WALK TALL	CAPITOL 2369	40.00	northern
REACH OUT FOR ME	LOVE OF A MARRIED MAN	CAPITOL 2892	40.00	northern
ALWAYS ACCUSED	ALL FOR ONE	AFO 307	30.00	northern
I PEEPED YOUR HOLE CARD	SHE REALLY DID SURPRISE	GATUR 701	300.00	northern
I WANT SOMEBODY	YOU BETTER SAY YES	ATLANTIC 2302	30.00	northern
PLEASE DON'T GO	MY HEART REMEMBERS	NOLA 737	400.00	northern
THANK YOU JOHN	DEDICATED TO YOU	ATLANTIC 2287	10.00	northern
WALKING UP A ONE WAY STREET	TEASIN' YOU	NOLA 708	30.00	northern
WALKING UP A ONE WAY STREET	TEASIN' YOU	ATLANTIC 2273	15.00	northern

TEEN TURBANS

WE NEED TO BE LOVED	DIDN'T HE RUN	LOMA 2066	40.00	northern

TELLER, CHRIS

I'VE BEEN HURT	UNLUCKY GIRL	CIRAY 6703	100.00	northern

TEMPESTS

WHAT YOU GONNA DO	CAN'T GET YOU OUT OF MY MIND	SMASH 2126	10.00	northern
WOULD YOU BELIEVE	YOU (ARE THE STAR I WISH ON)	SMASH 2094	20.00	northern

TEMPLE, RICHARD

THAT BEATIN' RHYTHM	COULD IT BE	MIRWOOD 5532	50.00	northern

TEMPOS

(COUNTDOWN) HERE I COME	SAD SAD MEMORIES	CANTERBURY 504	30.00	northern
(COUNTDOWN) HERE I COME	SAD SAD MEMORIES	CANTERBURY 504 yellow	75.00	northern
I GOTTA MAKE A MOVE	IT WAS YOU	MONTEL MICHELLE 955	250.00	northern
LET STICK TOGETHER	DON'T ACT THAT WAY	RILEY'S 5	30.00	northern
LONELY ONE	LONELY NIGHT	RILEY'S 8782	300.00	northern
SAD, SAD MEMORIES	SAME: INSTRUMENTAL	SOULTOWN 1	75.00	northern

TEMPTATIONS

CHECK YOURSELF	YOUR WONDERFUL LOVE	MIRACLE 12	25.00	motown
DREAM COME TRUE	ISN'T SHE PRETTY	GORDY 7001	25.00	motown
FAREWELL MY LOVE	MAY I HAVE THIS DANCE	GORDY 7020	25.00	motown
GIRL (WHY YOU WANNA MAKE ME BLUE)	BABY, BABY I NEED YOU	GORDY 7035	15.00	motown
I WANT A LOVE I CAN SEE	THE FURTHER YOU LOOK THE LESS	GORDY 7015	25.00	motown
I'LL BE IN TROUBLE	THE GIRLS ALRIGHT WITH ME	GORDY 7032	15.00	motown
LONELINESS MADE ME REALIZE	DON'T SEND ME AWAY	GORDY 7065	10.00	motown
MY GIRL	(TALKIN' ABOUT) NOBODY BUT MY BABY	GORDY 7038 PS	40.00	motown
OH, MOTHER OF MINE	ROMANCE WITHOUT FINANCE	MIRACLE 5	45.00	motown
SLOW DOWN HEART	PARADISE	GORDY 7010	20.00	motown

TEMPTONES

GIRL I LOVE YOU	GOOD-BYE	ARCTIC 130	400.00	northern
SAY THESE WORDS OF LOVE	SOMETHING GOOD	ARCTIC 136	200.00	northern

TENDER LOVING CARE

MY WORLD IS FALLING	TWO FOOLS ARE WE	RENFRO 1	20.00	70's

TENDER TOUCH

YOU WERE NEVER MINE TO BEGIN W	CAN I SEE YOU TOMORROW	PARAMOUNT 252	30.00	70's

TERRELL, FREDDIE

YOU HAD IT MADE	WHY NOT ME	CAPITOL 2728	75.00	northern

TERRELL, PHIL

I'LL ERASE YOU (FROM MY HEART)	I'M JUST A YOUNG BOY	CARNIVAL 513	30.00	northern
LOVE HAS PASSED ME BY	DON'T YOU RUN AWAY	CARNIVAL 523	150.00	northern

TERRELL, TAMMI

COME ON AND SEE ME	BABY DON'TCHA WORRY	MOTOWN 1095	10.00	motown
I CAN'T BELIVE YOU LOVE ME	HOLD ME OH MY DARLING	MOTOWN 1086	10.00	motown
THERE ARE THINGS	WHAT A GOOD MAN HE IS	MOTOWN 1115	100.00	motown
THIS OLD HEART OF MINE	JUST TOO MUCH TO HOPE FOR	MOTOWN 1138	10.00	motown

TER-RELLS

(BECAUSE OF) THREE LITTLE WORD	LONELY	ABC 10994	30.00	northern
I'LL NEVER LET YOU GO	DON'T ASK ME TO STOP LOVING YO	ABC 11046	15.00	northern

TERRIBLE TOM

WE WERE MADE FOR EACH OTHER	SAME:	MAVERICK 1001 DJ	75.00	northern

TERRIFICS

I'LL GET HIM BACK	WE'RE SO YOUNG	DIAMOND JIM 8784	300.00	northern

TERRY AND MARSHA

IT'S A POSSIBILITY	HE	CHAMP 209 multi	15.00	northern
IT'S A POSSIBILITY	HE	CHAMP 209 pink	50.00	northern

TERRY, WILEY

FOLLOW THE LEADER	SAME: PT 2.	USA 793	15.00	funk

TEX, JOE

ALL THE HEAVEN A MAN REALLY NEEDS	LET'S GO SOMEWHERE AND TALK	DIAL 1021	10.00	70's
UNDER YOUR POWERFUL LOVE	SASSY SEXY WIGGLE	DIAL 1154	15.00	70's

AIN'T I A MESS	BABY YOU'RE RIGHT	ANNA 1128	20.00	motown
ALL I COULD DO WAS CRY	ALL I COULD DO WAS CRY PT.2	ANNA 1119	20.00	motown
ALL I COULD DO WAS CRY PT.2	BABY YOU'RE RIGHT	CHECKER 1104	10.00	motown
YOU BETTER BELIEVE IT BABY	I BELIEVE I'M GONNA MAKE IT	DIAL 4033 DJ	8.00	**northerB**

TEX, JOE AND THE VIBRATORS

I'LL NEVERBREAK YOUR HEART	SAME: PT.2	ANNA 1124	20.00	motown

THANO

GIMMIE SOMETHING	WE'VE NEVER MET	VERVE 10399	30.00	northern

THE "US"

LET'S DO IT TODAY		JABER NO#	100.00	funk

THEMES

NO EXPLANATION NEEDED	BENT OUT OF SHAPE	MINIT 32009	30.00	northern

THEO-COFF INVASION

LUCKY DAY	NOCTURNAL FLOWER	DEARBORN 570	75.00	northern

THERON AND DARRELL

IT'S YOUR LOVE		SOLO	75.00	funk

THESE GENTS

YESTERDAY STANDING BY	PT.2	WESTERN WORLD	30.00	group
YESTERDAY STANDING BY	PT.2	SOULVATION ARMY 741	10.00	group

THIEVES

WHY DID YOU DO IT TO ME	I'M NOT THE ONE	BROADWAY 405	300.00	northern

THIRD GUITAR

SAD GIRL	LOVIN' LIES	ROJAC 120	20.00	northern
BABY DON'T CRY	DON'T TAKE YOURB LOVE FROM ME	ROJAC 123	150.00	funk

THIRD PARTY

SUCH A SOUL SAYS	SUCH A SOUL SAY PT. 2	SOULHAWK 2	50.00	funk

THIRD POSITION TRIO

SHE LOVES ME	THE GATOR PARTY	CELE-CAN 100	50.00	group

THIRTEENTH AMENDMENT

THE STRETCH	HARD TO BE IN LOVE	SLAVE 10001	50.00	funk

THOMAS GROUP, JOE

COMIN' HOME BABY	MORE	COBBLESTONE 714	15.00	mod

THOMAS, B.J.

CHAINS OF LOVE	YOU'LL NEVER WALK ALONE	HICKORY 1415	10.00	northern
I DON'T HAVE A MIND OF MY OWN	BRING BACK THE TIME	SCEPTER 12154	10.00	northern
I DON'T HAVE A MIND OF MY OWN	BRING BACK THE TIME	PACEMAKER 234	15.00	northern

THOMAS, CHARLES

THE MAN WITH THE GOLDEN TOUCH	LOOKING FOR LOVE	LOMA 2031	40.00	northern

THOMAS, DANNY BOY

HAVE NO FEAR	MY LOVE IS OVER	GROOVY 3002	25.00	ballad

THOMAS, DAVID

I'LL ALWAYS NEED YOU (BY MY SIDE)	I'M A LONELY MAN	PRIME 2717	750.00	northern
YOU BETTR INVESTIGATE		JETSTREAM 809	50.00	**northerB**

THOMAS, DEENA

STANDING THERE CRYING	PORQUE ESTAS LLORANDO	CLARK 164	100.00	northern

THOMAS, DON

COME ON TRAIN	TRAIN START MOVING	NUVJ 1001	20.00	**northerB**

THOMAS, ELLA AND THE DOLLETTS

THING CALLED LOVE	LOVER BABY	GD&L 2002	300.00	northern

THOMAS, FRANCIENE

I'LL BE THERE	TO BEAUTIFUL TO BE GOOD	TRAGAR 6803	75.00	funk

THOMAS, GERRI

LOOK WHAT I GOT	IT COULD HAVE BEEN ME	WORLD ARTISTS	20.00	**northerB**
1059 DJ				

THOMAS, HERSCHEL

WHAT'S OVER IS OVER	COME BACK WHERE YOU BELONG	LEO TODD 1	40.00	northern

THOMAS, IRMA

MOMENTS TO REMEMBER	TIMES HAVE CHANGED	IMPERIAL 66069	10.00	northern
THE HURT'S ALL GONE	IT'S STARTING TO GET TO ME NOW	IMPERIAL 66120	10.00	northern
TWO WINTERS LONG	SOMEBODY TOLD YOU	MINIT 660	10.00	northern
WHAT ARE YOU TRYING TO DO	TAKE A LOOK	IMPERIAL 66137	15.00	northern

THOMAS, JAMO AND THE PARTY BROTHERS

I SPY (FOR THE F.B.I.)	SNAKE HIP MAMA	THOMAS 303	10.00	northern
ARREST ME	JAMO'S SOUL	THOMAS 304 PS	25.00	northern
I SPY (FOR THE F.B.I.)	SNAKE HIP MAMA	THOMAS 303 PS	30.00	northern

THOMAS, JIMMY

HURRY AND COME HOME	YOU CAN GO	SUE 778	20.00	northern
WHERE THERE'S A WILL	JUST TRYIN' TO PLEASE YOU	MIRWOOD 5522	15.00	**northerB**

THOMAS, LARRY

SOUL BEFORE NEWS	MUHAMMAD ALI	STYLETONE 5905	50.00	funk

THOMAS, LEON

L-O-V-E	BOOM BOOM BOOM	FLYING DUTCHMAN	15.00	northern
26025				

THOMAS, PAT

I CAN'T WAIT UNTIL I SEE MY BABY'S FACE	THE LONG LONG NIGHT	VERVE 10333	20.00	northern
1001				

THOMAS, PRISCILLA
STEP ASIDE	SYMPATHY	WINNER 7 11 102	15.00	northern

THOMAS, ROBERT
CRAZY ABOUT YOUR LOVE	SAME: INSTRUMENTAL	HAWK 2054	10.00	70's
SALVATION	SOUL OF A MAN	CHARAY 87	20.00	northern

THOMAS, ROSCOE
AMERICAN GIRL	SAME: INSTRUMENTAL.	WORLD 1001	30.00	70's
AMERICAN GIRL	SAME:INSTRUMENTAL	SOUND GEMS 109	15.00	70's

THOMAS, SYLVIA
AT LAST	SO WILL I	BAMBOO 101.	20.00	northern

THOMAS, TABBY
ONE DAY		SOUL INTERNATIONAL	75.00	funk

THOMAS, TIMMY
WHAT'S BOTHERING ME	DIZZY DIZZY WORLD	CLIMAX 22001	10.00	70's
HAVE SOME BOOGALOO	LIQUID MOOD	GOLDWAX 320	50.00	mod
IT'S MY LIFE	WHOLE LOTTA SHAKING GOING ON	GOLDWAX 327	30.00	northern

THOMAS, TYRONE
FLY AWAY LOVE BIRD	STUCK ON YOURSELF	SOUL INTERNATIONAL	15.00	70's

THOMPSON BROTHERS
YOU BROUGHT LOVE INTO MY LIFE	I SAW THE LIGHT	WMOT 5353	500.00	70's

THOMPSON, BILLY
BLACK-EYED GIRL	KISS TOMORROW GOODBYE	WAND 1108	125.00	northern
BLACK-EYED GIRL	KISS TOMORROW GOODBYE	COLUMBUS 1043	175.00	northern

THOMPSON, CHERYLE
DON'T WALK AWAY	IT'S THE END	VEE JAY 695	75.00	northern

THOMPSON, HERBIE
UNCLE TOM	UNCLE TOM PT. 2	BIG HIT 112	30.00	funk

THOMPSON, JIMMY
JIMMY'S PLACE Pt.1	JIMMY'S PLACE Pt.2	JIMMY THOMPSON	20.00	northern
30259				

THOMPSON, JOHNNY
GIVEN UP ON LOVE	I AIN'T NO FOOL	JAY-TEE 8	75.00	70's

THOMPSON, MARTY
WHIRLPOOL	WHAT AM I GONNA DO	SIR BEN 1	40.00	northern

THOMPSON, PAT AND THE POWELL, ARCHIE
DARLING DARLING	OOH BABY	MIR-A-DON 1003	25.00	northern

THOMPSON, PAUL
SPECIAL KIND OF WOMAN	WHAT I DON'T KNOW CAN'T HURT ME	VOLT 4042	400.00	northern

THOMPSON, ROY
KEEP ON DANCING	SOMETHING GREATER THAN LOVE	OKEH 7283	20.00	northern
SOOKIE SOOKIE	LOVE YOU SAY	OKEH 7267	20.00	northern

THORNTON SISTERS
BIG CITY BOY	WATCH YOUR STEP	BOBSAN 1000	75.00	northern
I KEEP FORGETTING		CUPPY 102	300.00	northern

THORNTON, BIG MAMA
WADE IN THE WATER	BALL AND CHAIN	ARHOOLIE 520	30.00	mod

THOSE TWO
I CAN'T TREAT HER BAD	IF WE COULD START ALL OVER	MELIC 1	200.00	northern

3 DEGREES
DRIVIN' ME MAD	LOOK IN MY EYES	SWAN 4235	15.00	northern
GOTTA DRAW THE LINE	CLOSE YOUR EYES	SWAN 4224	15.00	northern
ARE YOU SATISFIED	LOVE OF MY LIFE	SWAN 4267	10.00	northern
CONTACT	NO NO NOT AGAIN	WB 7198	40.00	**northerB**
REFLECTIONS OF YESTERDAY	WHAT I SEE	NEPTUNE 23	15.00	northern
WARM WEATHER MUSIC	DOWN IN THE BOONDOCKS	METROMEDIA 109	15.00	northern

THREE JADES
I CARE YOU YOU	MAKES MY WORLD GO ROUND	MAURCI 102.	400.00	northern
MAKES MY WORLD GO WORLD	I CARE FOR YOU	MAURCI 102	300.00	northern
SHOW ME YOUR WAY	COME ON LET'S PARTY	MAURCI 103	25.00	northern

THREE OF US
I'M GOONA LOVE YOU BABY	SAME: INSTRUMENTAL	MOLLY 101	100.00	70's

THREE SHADES OF SOUL
BEING IN LOVE	SMOOTH SAILING	ENJOY 5002	15.00	northern

THREE STRANGERS
FIND MY BABY	BLANK:	FRANTIC 201	100.00	northern

THRILLS
SHOW THE WORLDWHERE IT'S AT	UNDERNEATH MY MAKE-UP	CAPITOL 5871	15.00	northern
WHAT CAN GO WRONG	NO ONE	CAPITOL 5631	20.00	northern

THUNDER, JOHNNY
DEAR JOHN I'M GOING TO LEAVE YOU	SUZIE - Q	DIAMOND 185	10.00	northern
JUST ME AND YOU	BEWILDERED	DIAMOND 206	20.00	northern

THUNDER, LIGHTNING AND RAIN
SUPER FUNKY		SAADIA	100.00	funk

THUNDER, MARGO
THE SOUL OF A WOMAN	SAME:	HAVEN 7001	15.00	70's
EXPRESSWAY TO YOUR HEART	HUSH UP YOUR MOUTH	HAVEN 7008	15.00	funk

Artist / Title	B-side	Label	Price	Genre
THURMON, CHUCKY				
TURN IT OVER		THURMOE BLAST	100.00	funk
THURMOND, DUFF				
NOW THAT YOU LEFT ME	IF YOU LOVED ME BABY	NEW VOICE 816	30.00	northern
TIARAS				
LOVES MADE A CONNECTION	YOU'RE MY MAN	SETON 777	300.00	northern
TI-CHAUNS				
I DON'T WANNA	WHAT YOU WANNA SAY	SONAR 102	150.00	northern
TIFFANIES				
IT'S GOT TO BE A GREAT SONG	HE'S GOOD FOR ME	KR 120	25.00	**northerB**
TIFFANYS				
GOSSIP	PLEASE TELL ME	ATLANTIC 2240	30.00	northern
HAPPIEST GIRL IN THE WORLD	LOVE ME	ARCTIC 101	40.00	northern
I JUST WANNA BE YOUR GIRL	I FEEL THE SAME WAY TO	JOSIE 942	30.00	northern
TIFFE, JERRY				
HEY WHATCHA' DOIN	FANNY JO	SCEPTER 12271	20.00	northern
TIKI'S				
STP LOOK AND LISTEN	CREAM IN MY COFFEE	ASCOT 2186	20.00	northern
TIL, SONNY				
TEARS AND MISERY	I BETTER LEA VE LOVE ALONE	RCA 9759	25.00	northern
HEY! LITTLE WOMAN	IN THE CHAPEL IN THE MOONLIGHT	CP PARKER 212	40.00	northern
NO NOT FOR HER	I GAVE IT ALL UP	CLOWN 3061	150.00	northern
TILLERY, LINDA				
WOMANLY WAY	MARKIN' TIME	OLIVIA 918	50.00	northern
TILLMAN, CHARLOTTA				
BABY I'M SERIOUS	A # 1 LOVER BOY	JOSIE 953	75.00	northern
TIM				
I NEED YOUR LOVE	MY SIDE OF THE TRACK	CELTEX 102	10.00	northern
TIMBERLAKE, BOBBIE LEE				
YOU HURT ME	ANOTHER GIRL'S BOYFREIND	MIRWOOD 5520	50.00	northern
TIMEBOX				
BEGGIN'	A WOMAN THAT'S WAITING	DERAM 85031	15.00	mod
TIMELESS LEGEND				
I WAS BORN TO LOVE YOU	I WAS BORN TO LOVE YOU PT.2	DAWN-LITE 12005	300.00	70's
TIMIKO				
IS IT A SIN	THE BOY FOR ME	CHECKER 1041	40.00	northern
TIMMIE AND THE PERSIONETTES				
THERE COMES A TIME	TIMMY BOY	OLYMPIA 100 DJ	30.00	northern
TINDLEY, GEORGE				
AIN'T THAT PECULIAR	IT'S ALL OVER BUT THE SHOUTING	WAND 11205	10.00	northern
DON'T YOU HEAR THEM LAUGHING	THEY CAN DREAM	ROWAX 801	30.00	northern
I COULDN'T CARE LESS	DONE BEING LONELY	SMASH 1768	30.00	northern
PITY THE POOR MAN	WAN TU WAH ZUREE	WAND 11215	10.00	northern
AIN'T GONNA WORRY ABOUT YOU	SINCE I MET CINDY	DOO-WOPP 101	110.00	northern
TIP TOPS				
A LITTLE BIT MORE	MEETCHA AT THE CHEETAH	ROULETTE 4684	50.00	northern
TIPTON, LESTER				
THIS WON'T CHANGE	GO ON	LA BEAT 6607	1800.00	northern
TJADER, CAL				
SOUL SAUCE	SOMEWHERE IN THE NIGHT	VERVE 10345	15.00	**northerB**
TMG'S				
THE HATCH		SOUL SHAKE	300.00	funk
TOJO				
BLUE LOVER	BROKEN HEARTED LOVER	TEC 3011	50.00	group
TOKAYS				
BABY, BABY, BABY (YOU'RE MY HE	HEY SENORITA	BRUTE 1	500.00	northern
TOLBERT, MOSS				
MONEY IN MY POCKET	DON'T DO IT DARLIN'	VEE JAY 558 DJ	20.00	northern
TOLLIVER, KIM				
I DON'T KNOW WHAT FOOT TO DANCE ON	SAME: INSTRUMENTAL	CASTRO 101	15.00	northern
I GOTTA FIND A WAY	I'LL TRY TO DO BETTER	ROJAC 126	20.00	northern
TOM AND JERRIO				
BOO-GA-LOO	BOOMERANG	JERRY-O 110	20.00	northern
COME ON AND LOVE ME	GREAT GOO-GA-MOO-GA	ABC 10704	15.00	northern
TOMANGOES				
I REALLY LOVE YOU	YOU'VE BEEN GONE SO LONG	WASHPAN 3125	600.00	**northerB**
TOMASETTI, MIKE				
COME SEE WHAT I GOT		USA 836	100.00	northern
TONETTES				
I GOTTA KNOW	MY HEART CAN FEEL THE PAIN	DYNAMIC 103	75.00	northern
TONEY JR., OSCAR				
YOU CAN LEAD YOUR WOMAN TO THE ALTER UNLUCKY GUY		BELL 688	10.00	northern
AIN'T THAT TRUE LOVE	DOWN IN TEXAS	BELL 776	10.00	northern
A LOVE THAT NEVER GROWS COLD	WITHOUT LOVE (THERE IS NOTHING	BELL 699	10.00	northern
AIN'T THAT TRUE LOVE	FOR YOUR PRECIOUS LOVE	BELL 672	15.00	northern

TONI AND THE HEARTS
COME BACK BABY	WOULD YOU LOVE ME	PATH. 5562	15.00	northern

TONI AND THE SHOWMEN
TRY MY LOVE	BEWARE	TEN STAR 103	75.00	northern

TONY AND LYNN
I'M HIP TO YOU BABY	WE'RE SO MUCH IN LOVE	BLUE ROCK 4065	15.00	northern

TONY AND TYRONE
DON'T EVER LEAVE ME	TALKING ABOUT THE PEOPLE	STON-ROC 6711	10.00	northern
PLEASE OPERATOR	APPLE OF MY EYE	ATLANTIC 2458	30.00	northerB

TONY AND THE MOCKIN' BYRDS
WALKIN' THE DUCK	MOCKINGBIRD HILL	ASSOCIATED ARTISTS 1265	40.00	northern

TONY AND THE TECHNICS
HA HA HE TOLD ON YOU	WORKOUT WITH YOUR PRETTY GIRL	CHEX 1010	50.00	northern

TOONE, GENE
EVERY NOW AND THEN	SO GLAD (TROUBLE DON'T LAST)	SIMCO 30003	150.00	ballad
WHAT MORE DO YOU WANT	HOW IT FEELS	SIMCO 6664	800.00	northern

TOOTSIE AND THE VERSATILES
I'VE GOT A FEELING	NOBODY BUT YOU	ELMOR 6000	75.00	northern

TOP NOTES
WAIT FOR ME, BABY	COME BACK, CLEOPATRA	FESTIVAL 1021	20.00	northern

TOP SHELF
DOGGONE BABY I LOVE YOU	YOU'RE HURTING ME	SPECTRUM 124	40.00	northern
NO SECOND THOUGHTS	GIVE IT UP	LO LO 2304	10.00	northern
NO SECOND THOUGHTS	GIVE IT UP	CALLA 2304	10.00	northern

TOPICS
BOOKING UP BABY	GIVING UP	MERCURY 73447	200.00	70's
TRY A LITTLE LOVE	ALL GOOD THINGS MUST END	HEAVY DUTY 3	15.00	70's
WOMAN'S LIBERATION	I'LL UNDERSTAND	CASTLE 1002	15.00	70's
HAVE YOUR FUN	A MAN AIN'T SUPPOSED TO CRY	DREAM 204	1500.00	northern
HEY GIRL (WHERE ARE YOU GOING)	IF LOVE COMES KNOCKING	CHADWICK 102	300.00	northern
SHE'S SO FINE	I DON'T HAVE TO CRY	CARNIVAL 520	40.00	northerB

TORCHES
NO I WON'T	DARN YOUR LOVE	RING-0 1302	20.00	northern

TORME, MEL
COMIN' HOME BABY	RIGHT NOW	ATLANTIC 2165	10.00	mod

TORQUES
BUMPIN'		LEMCO	150.00	funk

TOTAL ECLIPSE
A LOVE LIKE YOURS	YOU TOOK OUR HEART	RIGHT ON 102	15.00	northern

TOUCH
PICK AND SHOVEL	BLUE ON GREEN	LECASVER 1001	30.00	funk

TOUCH OF CLASS
LOVE ME BABY	GOTTA GET OVER	RENFRO 37	15.00	70's

TOWANA AND THE TOTAL DESTRUCTION
WEAR YOUR NATURAL BABY	HELP ME GET THAT FEELING	ROMARK 102	50.00	northern

TOWER OF POWER
THIS TIME IT'S REAL	SOUL VACCINATION	WB 7733	10.00	northern

TOWNSEND, ED
DON'T LEAD ME ON	I WANT TO BE WITH YOU	TRU-GLO-TOWN 504	15.00	northern
I MIGHT LIKE IT		MAXX 325	20.00	northern

TOWNSEND, HONEY
THE WORLD AGAIN	TECHNICOLOR DREAM	MALA 540 DJ	15.00	northern

TOYS
CAN'T GET ENOUGH OF YOU BABY	SILVER SPOON	DYNOVOICE 219	10.00	northern
I GOT MY HEART SET ON YOU	SEALED WITH A KISS	MUSICOR 1319	15.00	northern

TRACEY, WREG
ALL I WANT IS YOU	TAKE ME BACK (I WAS WRONG)	ANNA 1105	15.00	motown
TAKE ME BACK (I WAS WRONG)	ALL I WANT FOR CHRISTMAS	ANNA 1126	20.00	motown

TRADITIONS
MY LIFE WITH YOU	SOMETHING GONE WRONG	BAR CLAY 19678	30.00	northern
OH MY LOVE	GIRLS	BAR CLAY 19671	20.00	northern
ON FIRE	MY HEART	ARTCO 102	2000.00	northern
TWINKLE LITTLE STAR	RUBY TUESDAY	ABET 9435	200.00	northern

TRAFFIC JAM
I CAN'T GET OVER YOU	TRAFFIC JAM	TOEHOLT 14708	150.00	70's

TRAITS
HARLEM SHUFFLE	SOMEWHERE	UNIVERSAL 30494	15.00	northern
HARLEM SHUFFLE	SOMEWHERE	SCEPTER 12169	10.00	northern
TOO GOOD TO BE TRUE	GOTTA KEEP MY COOL	GARRISON 3007	20.00	northern

TRAITS, THE (ORIG.)
NEED LOVE	SOMEDAY SOON	CONTACT 501	30.00	group

TRANELLS
BLESSED WITH A LOVE	TAKE THIS HEART (NEVER BREAK THIS HEART)	FLO-JO 101	1000.00	northern

TRAN-SISTERS
PULL THE COVERS RIGHT UP	YOUR LOVE	IMPERIAL 5983	15.00	northern

TRAVELERS
MY BABY DOESN'T LOVE ME ANYMOR	MARY HAD A LITTLE LAMB	GLAD HAMP 2024	100.00	northern

TRAYNOR, JAY
UP AND OVER	DON'T LET THE END BEGIN	ABC 10845	300.00	northern

TREETOP, BOBBY
SO SWEET SO SATISFYIN'	VALENTINE	TUFF 415	200.00	**northerB**
WAIT TIL I GET TO KNOW YOU	VALENTINE	TUFF 417	175.00	**northerB**

TRELLS
BAD WEATHER	I'M SORRY	PORT CITY 1112	50.00	northern

TRENDS
A NIGHT FOR LOVE	GONNA HAVE TO SHOW YOU	ABC 10817	50.00	northern
CHECK MY TEARS	DON'T DROP OUT OF SCHOOL	ABC 10944	20.00	northern
DANCE WITH ME BABY	(TO BE) HAPPY ENOUGH	SMASH 1914	30.00	northern
GONNA HAVE TO SHOW YOU	A NIGHT FOR LOVE	ABC 10817	50.00	northern
NO ONE THERE	THAT'S HOW I LIKE IT	ABC 10881	60.00	northern
NOT TOO OLD TO CRY	YOU DON'T DIG THE BLUES	ABC 10731	70.00	northern
THANKS FOR A LITTLE LOVIN'	I NEVER KNEW HOW GOOD I HAD IT	ABC 10993	300.00	northern

TRENT SISTERS
A LETTER A DAY	HARD TO GET	GOGATE 1	300.00	northern

TREVOR, VAN
A FLING OF THE PAST	C'MON NOW BABY	VIVID 1004	20.00	northern

TRIBULATIONS
YOU GAVE ME UP FOR PROMISES	MAMA'S LOVE	IMPERIAL 66416	15.00	northern

TRICE, JAMAL
IF LOVE IS NOT THE ANSWER	NOTHING IS TOO GOOD (FOR YOU BABY)	SOUL 35120	25.00	70's

TRIDER, LARRY
CARBON COPY	HOUSE OF THE BLUES	CORAL 62391	100.00	northern

TRILONS
I'M THE ONE	FOREVER	TAG 449	30.00	northern

TRIPLET TWINS
GET IT	PRETTY PLEASE	THOMAS 809	15.00	funk
GONNA CHANGE		MAGIC TOUCH	100.00	northern

TRIPLETS
HEY LITTLE GIRL	(BABY) COME ON HOME	BLUE ROCK 4013	40.00	northern

TRIPLETTES
THAT MAN OF MINE	PATCHING UP THE WOUND	MOLLY-JO 1003	700.00	northern

TRIPPS
HERE COME THOSE HEARTACHES	GIVE IT BACK	VICTORIA 1003	30.00	northern

TRIUMPHS
BURNT BISCUITS	RAW DOUGH	VOLT 100	30.00	funk
WALKIN' THE DUCK	TURN OUT THE LIGHT	VERVE 10422	20.00	**northerB**
I'M COMING TO YOUR RESCUE	THE WORLD OWES ME A LOVING	OKEH 7291	100.00	northern
MEMORIES	WORKIN'	OKEH 7273	40.00	northern
MEMORIES	WORKIN'	OKEH 7273 DJ PS	100.00	northern

TROPICS
HEY YOU LITTLE GIRL	HAPPY HOUR	TOPIC 551	500.00	northern

TROTTER, DON AND THE EIGHTH WONDER
GIVE BACK YOUR LOVIN'	PEACE OF MIND	UTOPIA 602	40.00	northern
LOVELAND	THE APARTMENT	JOSIE 1011	30.00	northern

TROTTER, GERALD
ONE MORE HURT (WONT HURT MUCH)		MO DO 22628	50.00	northern

TROUTMAN, TONY
WHAT'S THE USE	SAME: INSTRUMENTAL	JERRI 102	150.00	**northerB**

TROY
PLEASE AY YOU WANT ME	IT'S JUST NOT THE SAME	COLUMBIA 45616	25.00	ballad
AND TOMORROW MEANS ANOTHER DAY	IF YOU GOTTA BREAK ANOTHER HEAT	COLUMBIA 45748	50.00	ballad

TROY, BENNY
I WANNA GIVE YOU TOMORROW	SAME: DISCO VERSION	DE-LITE 1572	30.00	70's
6699				

TROY, BENNY AND THE MAZE
THINGS ARE LOOKIN' BETTER	I DON'T KNOW ANYMORE	20th. CENTURY	30.00	northern
6699				

TROY, DORIS
FACE UP TO THE TRUTH	HE'S QUALIFIED	CAPITOL 2043	50.00	northern
I'LL DO ANYTHING	HEARTACHES	CALLA 114	20.00	northern

TROY, HELEN
I'LL BE AROUND	I THINK I LOVE YOU	KAPP 446 DJ	150.00	northern

TROY, J.B.
AIN'T IT THE TRUTH	EVERY MAN NEEDS A WOMAN	MUSICOR 1188	25.00	northern
LIVE ON	I'M REALLY THANKFUL	MUSICOR 1210	30.00	northern

TRUE IMAGE
I'M NOT OVER YOU YET	SAME:	SUPER SMASH	700.00	70's

TRUE TONES
HE'S GOT THE NERVE	THAT'S LOVE	JOSIE 1003	15.00	northern
HE'S GOT THE NERVE	THAT'S LOVE	JOSIE 950	20.00	northern
ONE MORE TIME	GIRLS ASRE SENTIMENTAL	LSP 2	60.00	northern

TRUITT, LITTLE JOHNNY (also see LITTLE JOHN on Neal)

DON'T LET ME BE A CRYING MAN	THERE GOES A GIRL	A-BET 9416	15.00	northern

TRUMAINS

RIPE FOR THE PICKING	MR. MAGIC MAN	RCA 11117	75.00	70's

TSU TORONADOES

I STILL LOVE YOU	MY THING IS MOVING THING	OVIDE 243	40.00	northern
WHAT GOOD AM I	GETTING THE CORNERS	ATLANTIC 2579	10.00	northern
A THOUSAND WONDERS	THE TORONADO	OVIDE 223	600.00	northern
GOT TO GET THROUGH TO YOU	THE GOOSE	ATLANTIC 2614	10.00	northern
I STILL LOVE YOU	MY THING IS A MOVING THING	VOLT 4030	30.00	northern
ONLY INSIDE	NOTHING CAN STOP ME	OVIDE 250	20.00	northern
PLEASE HEART DON'T BREAK	AIN'T NOTHING NOWHERE	RAMPART ST. 644	150.00	northern

TUCKER, BOBBY

YOUR LOVE IS ALL I NEED	SAME: INSTRUMENTAL	MALA 12006	20.00	northern

TUCKER, RAYFORD

IF YOU NEED MORE TIME	ONLY THE LONELY	SANDPIPER 10447	15.00	northern

TUCKER, SUNDRAY

IF IT WAS ME	ASK MILLIE	TK 1046	30.00	70's

TUCKER, TOMMY

THAT'S HOW MUCH	THAT'S LIFE	FESTIVAL 704	25.00	northern

TURBINES

WE GOT TO START OVER	WHAT MORE CAN I SAY	CENCO 116	1000.00	northern

TURKS

YOU TURN ME ON	GENERATION GAP	DJO 111	20.00	group
THE BAD BROUGHT THE GOOD	LET IT FLAME	DJO 113	30.00	northern

TURN OF THE CENTURY

MONEY CAN'T	A MAN IN LOVE	BUMP SHOP 125	10.00	northern

TURNAROUNDS

SOUL WALK	SOMEWWHERE IN THE WORLD	TRC 999	15.00	funk
AIN'T NOTHIN' SHAKIN'	RUN AWAY AND HIDE	ERA 3137	40.00	northern
CAN'T TAKE NO MORE	I NEED YOUR LOVIN'	MINIT 32047	40.00	northern

TURNER BROTHERS

I'M THE MAN FOR YOU BABY	MY LOVE IS YOURS TO-NIGHT	CARNIVAL 535	30.00	group

TURNER REBELLION, NAT

TRIBUTE TO A SLAVE	PLASTIC PEOPLE	DELVALIANT 100	30.00	funk

TURNER, BENNY

I DON'T KNOW	GOOD TO ME	M-PAC 7219	20.00	northern

TURNER, BETTY

BE CAREFUL GIRL	STAND BY AND CRY	LIBERTY 55861	150.00	northern
TELL YOURSELF A LIE	COLD LITTLE WORD	CRESCENT 6501	30.00	northern
THE WINDS KEPT LAUGHIN'	LITTLE MISS MISERY	CRESCENT 637	450.00	northern

TURNER, BIG JOE

TWO LOVES HAVE I	SHAKE, RATTLE AND ROLL	BLUESTIME 45001	50.00	northern

TURNER, DUKE

(LET ME BE YOUR) BABY SITTER	PT.2	SPINNING TOP 42170	20.00	northern

TURNER, ERNEST

I STILL LOVE YOU	WHY DON'T YOU WRITE	HOLLYWOOD 1136	30.00	northern

TURNER, IKE

BLACK ANGEL	THINKING BLACK	STERLING AWARD	15.00	funk

TURNER, IKE AND TINA

BOLD SOUL SISTER	THE HUNTER	BLUE THUMB	10.00	funk
BEAUTY IS JUST SKIN DEEP	ANYTHING I WASN'T BORN WITH	TRC 963 DJ	15.00	northern
CAN'T CHANCE A BREAK UP	STAGGER LEE AND BILLY	SUE 139	20.00	northern
DUST MY BROOM	ANYTHING YOU WASN'T BORN WITH	TRC 1019	8.00	northern
DUST MY BROOM	I'M HOOKED	TRC 967	15.00	northern
SOMEBODY NEEDS YOU	JUST TO BE WITH YOU	LOMA 2015	20.00	northern

TURNER, SAMMY

ONLY YOU	RIGHT NOW	MOTOWN 1055	15.00	motown
FOR YOUR LOVE I'LL DIE	THE HOUSE I LIVE IN	20th. CENTURY 610	20.00	northern

TURNER, SPIDER

I'VE GOT TO GET MYSELF TOGETHE	WHEN I SEE YOU BABY	GOOD TIME 1019	200.00	northern

TURNER, SPYDER

I CAN'T MAKE IT ANYMORE	DON'T HOLD BACK	MGM 13692	10.00	northern
RIDE IN MY 225	ONE STOP	FORTUNE 570	25.00	northern
YOU'RE GOOD ENOUGH FOR ME	STAND BY ME	MGM 13617	10.00	northern

TURNER, TITUS

EYE TO EYE	WHAT KINDA DEAL IS THIS	OKEH 7244	20.00	northern

TURNER, TOMMY

LADY	I'LL BE GONE	ELBAM 70	30.00	northern
LAZY	I'LL BE GONE	ELBAM 72	300.00	northern

TURNPIKES

CAST A SPELL	NOTHING BUT PROMISES	CAPITOL 2234	75.00	northern

TUTEN, JAMES BOOTIE

I'LL NEVER LET YOU SAY GOODBYE	THIS IS A LOVE AFFAIR	ULTIMATE 5382	20.00	70's

TWANS

I CAN'T SEE HIM AGAIN	DARLING TELL ME WHY	DADE 1903	600.00	northern

Artist / Title	B-side	Label	Price	Genre
TWENTIE GRANS				
GUILTY	GIVING UP ON LOVE IS LIKE	COLUMBIA 44239	15.00	northern
20th. CENTURY				
HOT PANTS	HOT PANTS Pt.2	SKY DISC 640	20.00	funk
21ST. CENTURY LTD.				
COMING RIGHT BACK	SHADOW OF A MEMORY	DOT 17190	50.00	northern
JUST CAN'T FORGET YOUR NAME	THE THOUGHT OF ME LOSING YOU	JOY 672	50.00	northern
YOUR SMALLEST WISH	WHAT KIND OF WORLD WOULD THIS	BENGEE 110	20.00	northern
YOUR SMALLEST WISH	WHAT KIND OF WORLD WOULD THIS	ATCO 6887	10.00	northern
24 KARAT GOLD				
NEW LOVE	WHAT DOES THE FUTURE HOLD	DESERT BONE 24	15.00	70's
TWILIGHTS				
YOU'RE THE ONE	THAT'S ALRIGHT	AQUA	50.00	northern
SHE'S GONNA PUT YOU DOWN	IT'S BEEN SO LONG	HARTHON 134	50.00	northern
TWISTIN' KINGS				
CONGO	CONGO Pt.2	MOTOWN 1023	40.00	motown
XMAS TWIST	WHITE HOUSE TWIST	MOTOWN 1022	25.00	motown
TWO FELLOWS				
STOP (DON'T GIVE UP YOUR LOVIN	YEA, YEA, YEA, YEA,	MUTT 17793	20.00	northern
TWO PEOPLE				
STOP LEAVE MY HEART ALONE	LOVE DUST	REVUE 11033	70.00	northern
TWO PLUS TWO				
LOVE WILL CONQUER ALL	HIGH RISE	DITTO 102	150.00	northern
TWO THINGS IN ONE				
OVER DOSE	CLOSE THE DOOR	MUSIC CITY 893	20.00	funk
TOGETHER FOREVER	STOP TELLING ME	MUSIC CITY 891	15.00	group
2001:BLACK ESSENCE				
CHANGE IN MY LIFE	WHEN YOU WALK ALONE WITH LOVE	JWJ 5	200.00	northern
2 TIMES 2				
OUTSIDE THE CITY	ACROSS THE SEA	NEW WORLD 2X2	40.00	northern
TWO TONS OF LOVE				
BROWN AND BEAUTIFUL	IT'S A BAD SITUATION IN A BEAUTIFUL	KAPP 2095	10.00	70's
WHAT GOOD AM I WITHOUT YOU	SOY NADA YO SIN TI	PARAMOUNT 56	50.00	70's
TYLER, CHIP				
BECAUSE I LOVE YOU	I LOVE YOU YVONNE	CHICORY 401	150.00	**northerB**
TYLER, HAROLD				
REALITY	A MAN CAN'T LIVE (TWO LIVES)	TYMO 729	40.00	70's
TYMES				
(A TOUCH OF) BABY	HIDDEN SHORES	MGM 13631	10.00	northern
HERE SHE COMES	THE TWELTH OF NEVEDR	PARKWAY 933	20.00	northern
HERE SHE COMES	MALIBU	PARKWAY 924	20.00	northern
STREET TALK	PRETEND	MGM 13536	15.00	northern
THE LOVE THAT YOU'RE LOOKING F	GOD BLESS THE CHILD	COLUMBIA 44799	10.00	northern
THIS TIME IT'S LOVE	THESE FOOLISH THINGS (REMINDS ME OF YOU)	WINCHESTER 1002	15.00	northern
WHAT WOULD I DO	A TOUCH OF BABY	MGM 13631	20.00	northern
HERE SHE COMES	MALIBU	PARKWAY 924 PS	30.00	northern
SO MUCH IN LOVE	ROSCOE JAMES MCCLAIN	PARKWAY 871	10.00	northern
TYNES, MARIA				
THE QUEEN IS ON HER KNEES	CHANGE MY MIND	UPTOWN 743	50.00	northern
TYRELL, STEVE				
A BOY WITOUT A GIRL	YOUNG BOY BLUES	PHILIPS 40150	40.00	northern
TYRONE (WONDER BOY)				
PLEASE CONSIDER ME	YOU MADE ME SUFFER	FOUR BROTHERS 450	15.00	northern
SUFFER	TRY ME	FOUR BROTHERS 447	30.00	northern
TYSON, LITTLE JIMMY				
WHO WILL BE THE NEXT FOOL		CW	300.00	funk

U

Artist / Title	B-side	Label	Price	Genre
U.S.				
I MISS MY BABY	BABY I OWE YOU SOMETHING GOOD	WESTBOUND 197	50.00	group
UFO'S				
EGG ROLL		VIRTUE	300.00	funk
TOO HOT TO HOT		RISING SONS	100.00	funk
UGGAMS, LESLIE				
DON'T YOU EVEN CARE	WHO KILLED TEDDY BEAR	ATLANTIC 2313	20.00	**northerB**

LOVE IS A GOOD FOUNDATION	I JUST CAN'T HELP BELIEVING	SONDAY 6006	25.00	northern

UJIMA

I'M NOT READY	A SHOULDER TO LEAN ON	EPIC 50095	150.00	70's

ULTIMATE TRUTH

TAKE A LITTLE TIME	HOOKED ON LOVE	J CITY 275	15.00	group

ULTIMATES

GIRL, I'VE BEEN TRYING TO TELL YOU	I JUST CAN'T STAND IT	BR-ROMA 101	200.00	northern
JUST BECAUSE YOU'VE GONE AND LEFT ME	NEVER LEAVE ME (THE QUINNS)	CAPITO 2023	75.00	northern

ULTIMATIONS

WOULD I DO IT OVER	WITH OUT YOU	MARVLUS 6020	15.00	northern

UNDERDOGS

LOVE'S GONE BAD	MO JO HANNA	V.I.P. 25040	20.00	motown

UNDERWOOD, CARL

AIN'T YOU LYING	LEAVE ME ALONE	MERGING 858	700.00	northern

UNFORGETTABLES

TOO MUCH TROUBLE	SAD SONG	LOADSTONE 3954	30.00	funk
OH THERE HE GOES	HE'LL BE SORRY	TITANIC 5012	75.00	northern
TRUST YOUR LUCK	GYPSY	SAMONE 100	700.00	northern

UNION

STRIKE		MESA	75.00	funk

UNIQUE BLEND

YES I'M IN LOVE	OLD FASDHIONED WOMAN	EASTBOUND 601	250.00	70's

UNIQUES

I'LL DO ANYTHING	GO ON AND LEAVE	PAULA 289	40.00	northern
NOT TOO LONG AGO	FAST WAY OF LIVING	PAULA 219U	10.00	northern

UNITED FOUR

SHE'S PUTTING YOU ON	GO ON	HARTHON 139	20.00	**northerB**

UNIVERSAL JOINT

LOVE WON'T WEAR OFF (AS THE YEARS WEAR ON)	SAME:INSTRUMENTAL	SNIFF 382	300.00	northern

UNIVERSALS

DIAMONDS AND PEARLS	SPARKLING	COOKING 1112	75.00	northern
NEW LEASE OF LIFE	WITHOUT FRIENDS	MODERN 1057	30.00	northern
WITHOUT FRIENDS	NEW LEASE ON LIFE	OPEN 1250	50.00	northern

UNIVERSOULS

NEW GENERATION		TENER CUSTOM	200.00	funk

UNLIMITED FOUR

I WANNA BE HAPPY	CALLING	CHANSON 1178	15.00	northern

UNLUV'D

AIN'T GONNA DO YOU NO HARM	AN EXCEPTION TO THE RULE	TRUE LOVE 1000	20.00	northern
AN EXCEPTION TO THE RULE	AIN'T GONNA DO YOU NO HARM	PARKWAY 138	15.00	northern

UNTOUCHABLES

RAISIN' SUGAR CANE	DO YOUR BEST	MADISON 147	45.00	northern

UPBEATS

LET'S GET TOGTHER	SOUL DREAMING	D & A 5001	200.00	northern

UPCHURCH COMBO, PHILIP

YOU CAN'T SIT DOWN	YOU CAN'T SIT DOWN PT. 2	UA 329	8.00	mod
YOU CAN'T SIT DOWN	YOU CAN'T SIT DOWN PT .2	BOYD 329	10.00	mod

UPFRONTS

BABY, FOR YOUR LOVE	SEND ME SOMEONE TO LOVE	LUMMTONE 107	200.00	northern

UPTIGHTS

FREE AT LAST	YOU GIT'S NONE OF THIS	SKYE 4525	100.00	ballad
ACADEMY AWARDS OF LOVE	I CAN LOVE YOU FOREVER	MALA 528	15.00	northern
LOOK A LITTLE HIGHER	JUST A DREAM	ALLEY1045	100.00	northern
SHY GUY	HE SAID	COLUMBIA 44243	75.00	northern
UPTONESWEAR MY RING	DREAMING	MAGNUM 714	20.00	group
WEAR MY RING	DREAMING	WATTS 1080	30.00	group

UPTOWNERS

SUCH A LOVE	FROM LOVERS - TO FRIENDS	CAPTOWN 4030	200.00	northern

UTOPIAS

GIRLS ARE AGAINST ME	I WANT TO GO BACK TO MY DREAM WORLD	LASALLE 0072	1000.00	northern

VALADIERS
GREETINGS (THIS IS UNCLE SAM)	TAKE A CHANCE	MIRACLE 6	40.00	motown
GREETINGS (THIS IS UNCLE SAM)	TAKE A CHANCE (H-915)	MIRACLE 6	50.00	motown
I FOUND A GIRL	YOU'LL BE SORRY SOME DAY	GORDY 7013	50.00	motown
WHILE I'M AWAY	BECAUSE I LOVE HER	GORDY 7003	200.00	motown

VALA-QUONS
WINDOW SHOPPING ON GIRL'S AVEN	I WANNA WOMAN	TRC 951	40.00	northern

VALENTIN, BOBBY
BAD BREATH	LOVE ME SO	FANIA 445	30.00	mod
USE IT BEFORE YOU LOSE IT	FUNKY BIG FEET	FANIA 458	30.00	mod

VALENTINE, ALVIN
SWEET SWEET REVENGE	THERE OUGHTA BE A LAW	BRUNSWICK 755409	15.00	northern

VALENTINE, JOE
TRUE LOVE	SHARING YOUR LOVE	TEE-JAY 17380	10.00	70's
ALL THE LOVE I HAVE FOR YOU IS	ONE NIGHT STAND	TEE-JAY 17379	10.00	ballad
I CAN'T STAND TO SEE YOU GO	ONE NIGHT OF SATISFACTION	RONN 14	10.00	ballad
I CAN'T STAND TO SEE YOU GO	ONE NIGHT SATISFACTION	VALERIE 67119	75.00	ballad
SHE'S GONE AGAIN	COMING ON HOME	RACHAN 311	75.00	ballad
I LOST THE ONLY LOVE I HAD	SURELY, I'LL NEVER DO YOU WRON	VAL 7225	600.00	northern

VALENTINE, LEZLI
I WON'T DO ANYTHING	I'VE GOT TO KEEP ON LOVING	ALL PLATINUM 2305	15.00	northern

VALENTINE, PATIENCE
UNLUCKY GIRL	ERNESTINE	SAR 142	15.00	northern
IF YOU DON'T COME	I MISS YOU SO	SAR 119	500.00	norhern

VALENTINE, ROSE
I'VE GOTTA KNOW RIGHT NOW	WHEN THE HEARTACHES END	RCA 9276	50.00	northern

VALENTINE, T.D.
LOVE TRAP	ALISON TOOK ME AWAY	EPIC 10523	20.00	northern

VALENTINES
GOTTA GET YOURSELF TOGETHER	I'M ALRIGHT NOW	SS7 2646	15.00	northern
BREAKAWAY	IF YOU LOVE ME	SS7 2663	40.00	**northerB**
MAMA I HAVE COME HOME	JOHNNY ONE HEART	LUDIX 102	15.00	northern

VALENTINO, MARK
WALKING ALONE	THE PUSH AND KICK	SWAN 4121	20.00	northern

VALENTINOS
BABY, LOTS OF LUCK	SHE'S SO GOOD TO ME	SAR 144	15.00	northern
DARLING, COME BACK HOME	I'LL MAKE IT ALRIGHT	SAR 137	15.00	northern
SWEETER THAN THE DAY BEFORE	LET'S GET TOGETHER	CHESS 1977	100.00	northern
WHAT ABOUT ME	DO IT RIGHT	CHESS 1952	15.00	northern

VALERIE AND NICK
I'LL FIND YOU	LONELY TOWN	GLOVER 3000	15.00	northern

VALERY, DANA
YOU DON'T KNOW WHERE YOUR INTE	HAVING YOU AROUND	COLUMBIA 44004	175.00	northern

VALIANT TRIO
I'LL MAKE HER MINE	YOU LEFT ME	E.V. 97500	150.00	northern

VALIANTS
TELL ME WHAT YOU'RE GONNA DO		DESTINATION	200.00	northern

VALONS
YOU'RE SOMETHING SPECIAL (2.20")	MORE POWER TO YOU (2.10")	MARK III 450	50.00	northern
YOU'RE SOMETHING SPECIAL (2.12")	MORE POWER TO YOU (2:17")	MARK III 450	50.00	northern

VAL-RAYS
IT HURTS DOESN'T IT GIRL	I'M WALKING PROUD	UA 50145	10.00	northern

VAN DYKE, CONNIE
IT HURT ME TOO	OH FREDDY	MOTOWN 1041	50.00	motown
DON'T DO NOTHING I WON'T DO	THE WORDS WON'T COME	WHEELSVILLE 112	200.00	northern

VAN DYKE, EARL
I CAN'T HELP MYSELF	HOW SWEET IT IS TO BE LOVED BY	SOUL 35014	10.00	motown
6 BY 6	THERE IS NO GREATER LOVE	SOUL 35028	10.00	motown
ALL FOR YOU	TOO MANY FISH IN THE FISH	SOUL 35009 NI	1000.00	motown
I CAN'T HELP MYSELF	HOW SWEET IT IS TO BE LOVED BY	SOUL 35014	10.00	motown
SOUL STOMP	HOT 'N TOT	SOUL 35006	20.00	motown
THE FLICK	THE FLICK PT.2	SOUL 35018	15.00	motown

VAN DYKES
NO MAN IS AN ISLAND	I WON'T HOLD IT AGAINST YOU	MALA 520	8.00	group
NO MAN IS AN ISLAND	I WON'T HOLD IT AGAINST YOU	HUE 6501	30.00	group
YOU NEED CONFIDENCE	YOUR SHAKIN' ME UP	MALA 549	10.00	group
SAVE MY LOVE FOR A RAINY DAY	TEARS OF JOY	MALA 584	100.00	northern
WHAT WILL I DO (IF I LOSE YOU)	I'VE GOT TO GO ON WITHOUT YOU	MALA 530	15.00	northern
YOU'RE SHAKING ME UP	YOU NEED CONFIDENCE	MALA 549	10.00	northern

VAN PEEBLES, MELVIN

SWEETBACK'S THEME	HOPPIN JOHN	STAX 97	20.00	funk

VAN, ILA   (also Ila Vann)

CAN'T HELP LOVING THAT MAN OF MINE	I'VE GOT THE FEELING	ROULETTE 4733	30.00	northern

VANCE, FRANKIE

DO YOU HEAR ME BABY	CAN'T BREAK THE HABIT (OF YOUR LOVE)	REVUE 11048	15.00	northern

VANDALS

IN MY OPINION	IN MY OPINION Pt.2	T NECK 923	10.00	70's

VANDIVER, JOE

YOU'RE EVERYTHING	GOT YOU WHERE I WANT YOU NOW	JADE 1002	400.00	northern

VANELLI, JOHNNY

SEVEN DAYS OF LOVING YOU	YOU REALLY KNOW HOW TO HURT SO	PRE-VUE 2770	200.00	**northerB**

VANGUARDS

FALLING OUT OF LOVE	GOTT'A HAVE LOVE	LAMP 92	100.00	70's
GIRL GO AWAY (IT'S WRONG TO LO	MAN WITHOUT KNOWLEDGE	LAMP 81	25.00	northern
GOOD TIMES BAD TIMES	MAN WITHOUT KNOWLEDGE	LAMP 94	150.00	northern
THE THOUGHT OF LOSING YOUR LOVE	IT'S TOO LATE FOR LOVE	LAMP 80	10.00	northern

VANN, ILA

YOU MADE ME THIS WAY	MY MOTHER SAID	P.I.P. 8933	40.00	northern

VANN'S ORCHESTRA, TEDDY

THEME FROM COLOREDMAN	INTRODUCTION TO:	CAPITOL 5878 DJ	25.00	northern

VARIATIONS

I WANNA TAKE YOU UPTOWN	SAME: INSTRUMENTAL	RIGHT-ON 1001	20.00	northern
YESTERDAY IS GONE	EMPTY WORDS	OKEH 7324	25.00	northern

VARIOUS ARTISTS EP

GREETINGS TO TAMLA MOTOWN APPRECIATION SOCIETY	GREETINGS TO UK FANS	HITSVILLE USA 97311 DJ	100.00	motown

VARISCO, PAUL

TELL ME WHERE LOVE GOES	SWEET LORENE	KAPP 883 DJ	100.00	northern

VARNER, DON

HANDSHAKIN'	MORE POWER TO YA	DIAMOND 264	15.00	northern
MASQUERADE	DOWN IN TEXAS	SOUTH CAMP 7003	30.00	northern
TEARSTAINED FACE	MEET ME IN CHURCH	VEEP 1296 NI	1000.00	northern
TEARSTAINED FACE	MOJO MAMA	QUINVY 8002	750.00	**northerB**

VARTAN, SYLVIE

I MADE MY CHOICE	ONE MORE DAY	RCA 8520	25.00	northern

VASHONETTES

A MIGHTY GOOD LOVER	LOVE	CHECKER 1195	75.00	northern

VASHONS

WE'LL BE TOGETHER		DELLE 191	1000.00	northern

VAUGHN, SHIRLEY

STOP AND LISTEN	DOESN'T EVERYBODY	FAIRMOUNT 1023	20.00	northern
YOU DON'T KNOW	CLIMB EVERY MOUNTAIN	FAIRMOUNT 1010	20.00	northern
WATCH OUT MR.LONELY	JUST A LITTLE LOVE	DOUBLE RR 246	10.00	northern

VAUGHN, YVONNE

WHEN YOU GONNA TELL HER ABOUT	LONELY LITTLE GIRL	DOT 16751	10.00	northern

VEDA

WHAT'S IT ALL ABOUT	AIN'T NOTHING BUT A PARTY	WEST SOUNDS 39	20.00	70's
YOU AN LOVE ME AGAIN	GET UP AND GET DOWN	MW 1004	30.00	group
YOU MAKE ME FEEL SO REAL	WE ARE HIS CHILDREN	INSTANT 3333	100.00	70's

VEE

A STONE GOOD LOVER	CHEATING IS A NO NO	MIER 4	30.00	northern

VELASCO, VI

I DON'T WANT TO GO ON	YOU ARE MY SUNSHINE	VEE JAY 655	40.00	northern

VELL, GENE

I'M CALLING MY BABY	SCREAMING ALL NIGHT LONG	WHIZ 502	50.00	northern

VELLS

THERE HE IS (AT MY DOOR)	YOU'LL NEVER CHERISH A LOVE SO TRUE	MELODY 103	50.00	motown

VELOURS

I'M GONNA CHANGE	DON'T PITY ME	MGM 13780	75.00	**northerB**

VELVELETTES

A BIRD IN THE HAND (IS WORTH TWO IN THE BUSH)	SINCE YOU'VE BEEN LOVING ME	V.I.P. 25030	20.00	motown
A BIRD IN THE HAND (IS WORTH TWO IN THE BUSH)	SINCE YOU'VE BEEN LOVING ME	V.I.P. 25021 NI	300.00	motown
HE WAS REALLY SAYING SOMETHING	THROW A FAREWELL KISS	V.I.P. 25013	15.00	motown
LONELY LONELY GIRL AM I	I'M THE EXCEPTION TO THE RULE	V.I.P. 25017	40.00	motown
NEEDLE IN A HAYSTACK	SHOULD I TELL THEM	V.I.P. 25007	15.00	motown
THERE HE GOES	THAT'S THE REASON WHY	I.P.G. 1002	40.00	motown
THESE THINGS WILL KEEP ME LOVING YOU	SINCE YOU'VE BEEN GONE	V.I.P. 25034 NI	300.00	motown
THESE THINGS WILL KEEP ME LOVING YOU	SINCE YOU'VE BEEN LOVING ME	SOUL 35025	15.00	northern

VELVET HAMMER

HAPPY	PARTY HARDY	SOOZI 112	15.00	70's

VELVET SATINS

NOTHING CAN COMPARE TO YOU	UP TO THE ROOFTOP	GENERAL AMERICAN 006	100.00	**northerB**

VELVET, JAMES

BOUQUET OF FLOWERS	WHENI NEEDED YOU	CUB 9111	10.00	motown
BOUQUET OF FLOWERS	WHEN I NEEDED YOU	CORREC-TONE 502	15.00	motown

VELVETONES				
WHAT CAN THE MATTER BE	HAIRY LUMPTY BUMP	VERVE 10514	25.00	northern
VELVETS				
LET THE FOOL KISS YOU	BABY THE MAGIC IS GONE	MONUMENT 961	100.00	northern
LOVIN' ON BORROWED TIME	LOVE IS SLIPPING AWAY	NUMBER ONE111	100.00	northern
VEL-VETS				
I GOT TO FIND SOMEBODY	WHAT NOW MY LOVE	20th. CENTURY	100.00	northern
6676				
VENEESE AND CAROLYN				
JUST A LITTLE SMILE (FROMYOU)	GOODBYE SONG	POLYDOR 14469	50.00	70's
VERDELL, JACKIE				
ARE YOU READY FOR THIS	I'M YOUR GIRL	DECCA 32118	15.00	northern
DON'T SET ME FREE	DOES SHE EVER REMIND YOU OF ME	DECCA 32181	15.00	northern
VERDI, LIZ				
THINK IT OVER	YOU LET HIM GET AWAY	COLUMBIA 43154	150.00	northern
VERNADO, LYNN				
SECOND HAND LOVE	GOODBYE AND GOOD SPEED	YUMIE 1000	300.00	**northerB**
WASH AND WEAR LOVE	TELL ME WHAT'S WRONG WITH THE MEN	GATOR 1202	600.00	**northerB**
VERNEE, YVONNE				
IT'S BEEN A LONG TIME	YOUR TOUCH	SONBERT 3475	50.00	northern
JUST LKE YOU DID ME	I'M IN LOVE	SONBERT 5842	850.00	northern
DOES HE LOVE ME ANYMORE	SO MUCH IN LOVE	CORREC-TONE 3178	150.00	northern
VERNON AND JEWELL				
HOLD MY HAND	HOW ABOUT YOU	KENT 430	40.00	northern
VERSATILES				
CRY LIKE A BABY	LONELY MAN	STAFF 210	30.00	northern
YOU'RE GOOD ENOUGH FOR ME	BYE BYE BABY	BRONCO 2050	20.00	northern
VERSATONES				
WITH A BROKEN HEART	ROLLIN ROLLIN	MAGIC CITY 4	150.00	northern
VE-SHELLES				
PLEDGING MY LOVE	SHING-A-LING	BOOLA BOOLA 200	50.00	group
VESTEL, LENNY				
IT'S PARADISE		SANLA	200.00	northern
VIBRATIONS				
CANADIAN SUNSET	THE STORY OF A STARRY NIGHT	OKEH 7241	10.00	northern
'CAUSE YOU'RE MINE	I TOOK AN OVERDOSE	EPIC 10418	30.00	northern
COME TO YOURSELF	TOGETHER	OKEH 7297	15.00	northern
END UP CRYING	AIN'T LOVE THAT WAY	OKEH 7220	20.00	northern
FINDING OUT THE HARD WAY	MISTY	OKEH 7230	15.00	northern
GONNA GET ALONG WITHOUT U NOW	FORGIVE AND FORGET	OKEH 7249	12.00	**northerB**
IF YOU ONLY KNEW	TALKIN' BOUT LOVE	OKEH 7228	15.00	northern
KEEP ON KEEPING ON	HELLO HAPPINESS	OKEH 7212	15.00	**northerB**
LOVE IN THEM THERE HILLS	REMEMBER THE RAIN	OKEH 7311	10.00	northern
SOUL A GO GO	AND I LOVE HER	OKEH 7257	15.00	northern
SURPRISE PARTY FOR BABY	RIGHT ON BROTHER RIGHT ON	NEPTUNE 28	25.00	**northerB**
YOU BETTER BEWARE	PICK ME	OKEH 7276	15.00	northern
SHAKE IT UP	MAKE IT LAST	CHESS 2151	200.00	70's
VIBRETTES				
HUMPTY DUMP		LUJON 101	25.00	funk
VIC AND JOE				
TO GET YOUR LOVE BACK	WE COULD FIND LOVE	JODA 101 D	15.00	northern
VICTORS				
NOT ONLY A GIRL KNOWS	HURT	PHILIPS 40475	100.00	northern
VILLAGE CALLERS				
HECTOR	I'M LEAVING	RAMPART 659	30.00	funk
HECTOR, PART 2	MISSISSIPPI DELTA	RAMPART 660	20.00	funk
VILLAGE CRUSADERS				
AKIWANA	HASHISHI	TRANS AMERICAN 8	30.00	funk
VILLAGE SOUNDS				
THESE WINDOWS	LOVE IN	ONYX 102	125.00	northern
VINA, JOE				
YOU WALKED (ALL OVER MY HEART)	TAKE THIS HEART	WEBER 101	75.00	northern
VINES				
THAT WALK	HEY HEY GIRLS	SUTTER 10	100.00	northern
V.I.P.ERS				
LITTLE MISS SWEETNESS	SAME OLD VALARIE	DUCHESS 102	15.00	northern
VIRGINIA WOLVES				
STAY	B.L.T.	AMY 966	15.00	**northerB**
VIRTUES				
TAKE ME BACK	MOVIES ARE GROOVEY	VIRTUE 121674	40.00	70's
VISITORS				
I'M IN DANGER	UNTIL YOU CAME ALONG	DAKAR 603	10.00	group
LONELY ONE - ONLY SON	I'M GONNASTAY	DAKAR 613	10.00	group
I'M IN DANGER	UNTIL YOU CAME ALONG	BASHIE 9157	20.00	northern
MY LOVE IS READY AND WAITING	WHAT ABOUT ME	TRC 1003	25.00	northern
NEVER THE LESS	ANYTIME IS THE RIGHT TIME	TRC 1010	25.00	northern

VITO, GENE

UNDISCOVERED COUNTRY	WITH THE DAWN	DECCA 32140	75.00	northern

VITO AND THE SALUTATIONS

I'D BEST BE GOING	SO WONDERFUL	RED BOY 1001	40.00	northern
I'S BEST BE GOING	SO WONDERFUL (MY LOVE)	SANDBAG 103	20.00	northern

VOICE BOX

I WANT IT BACK (YOUR LOVE)	BABY, BABY DON'T YOU KNOW	LOMA 2101	20.00	northern

VOICE MASTERS

IF A WOMAN CATCHES A FOOL	YOU'VE HURT ME BABY	BAMBOO 103	15.00	northern
IF A WOMAN CATCHES A FOOL	DANCE RIGHT INTO MY HEART	BAMBOO 1131	10.00	motown
NEEDED	NEEEDED (FOR LOVERS ONLY)	ANNA 102	75.00	motown
TWO LOVERS	IN LOVE IN VAIN	FRISCO 15235	100.00	northern

VOICES OF EAST HARLEM

WANTED DEAD OR ALIVE	CAN YOU FEEL IT	JUST SUNSHINE 517	20.00	70's
CASHING IN	I LIKE HAVING YOU AROUND	JUST SUNSHINE 510	15.00	northern

VOICES.

FOREVER IS A LONG, LONG TIME	FALL IN LOVE AGAIN	PENNY 105	30.00	northern
CRYING HAS BECOME AN EVERYDAY THING	IMITATION OF LIFE	BLUE SOUL	200.00	northern
BABY YOU'RE MESSING UP MY MIND	AN IMITATION OF LIFE	VICTORIA 1000	100.00	northern

VOLCANOS

(IT'S AGAINST) THE LAWS OF LOVE	SAME: INSTRUMENTAL	ARCTIC 115	30.00	**northerB**
(IT'S AGAINST) THE *RULES* OF LOVE	SAME: INSTRUMENTAL	ARCTIC 115	300.00	northern
HELP WANTED	MAKE YOUR MOVE	ARCTIC 111	15.00	**northerB**
HELP WANTED	A LADY'S MAN	ARCTIC 125	15.00	**northerB**
MAKE YOUR MOVE	BABY	ARCTIC 103	50.00	northern
YOU'RE NUMBER ONE	MAKE YOUR MOVE	ARCTIC 128	50.00	**northerB**
STORM WARNING	BABY	ARCTIC 106	10.00	**northerB**
GOTTA BE A FALSE ALARM	MOVIN' AND GROVIN'	HARTHON 138	30.00	**northerB**

VOLTAIRES

MY MY MY BABY	MOVIN' MOVIN' ON	BACONE 9468	100.00	northern

VOLUMES

AIN'T THAT LOVIN' YOU	I LOVE YOU BABY	INFERNO 5001	30.00	motown
AIN'T GONNA GIVE YOU UP	AM I LOSING YOU	KAREN 101	250.00	northern
GOTTA GIVE HER LOVE	I CAN'T LIVE WITHOUT YOU	ASTRA 1020	100.00	northern
GOTTA GIVE HER LOVE	I CAN'T LIVE WITHOUT YOU	AMERICAN ARTS 6	15.00	northern
I GOT LOVE	MAINTAIN YOUR COOL	TWIRL 2016	100.00	northern
I JUST CAN'T HELP MYSELF	ONE WAY LOVER	AMERICAN ARTS 18	60.00	northern
I'VE NEVER BEEN SO IN LOVE	I'M GONNA MISS YOU	GARU 107	300.00	northern
MY KIND OF GIRL	MY ROAD IS THE RIGHT ROAD	INFERNO 2004	10.00	northern
THAT SAME OLD FEELING	THE TROUBLE I'VE SEEN	IMPACT 1017	100.00	northern
YOU GOT IT BABY	A WAY TO LOVE YOU	INFERNO 2001	15.00	northern

VON, TAWNY

LAST NIGHT (I FOUND THE BOY)	DON'T SAY IT NEVER WAS	ENTRE 1002	75.00	northern

VONDELLS

HEY GIRL, YOU'VE CHANGE		AIRTOWN CUSTOM 12	700.00	northern
LENORA	VALENTINO	MARVELLO 5006	50.00	northern

VONDORS

LOOK IN THE MIRROR	FOOT LOOSE	HOLIDAY 125	75.00	northern

VONETTES

TOUCH MY HEART	YOU DON'T KNOW ME	COBBLESTONE 703	85.00	northern

VONTASTICS

I'LL NEVER SAY GOODBYE	DON'T MESS AROUND	SATELLITE 2002	75.00	northern
LADY LOVE	WHEN MY BABY COMES BACK HOME	MOON SHOT 6702	20.00	northern

VONT CLAIRES

DON'T CHA TELL NOBODY	I'VE GOT TEARS IN MY EYES	DOUBLE R 249	50.00	northern

VOWS

TELL ME	BUTTERED POPCORN	V.I.P. 25016	75.00	motown

VOYAGE

SAME OLD SONG	ONE DAY	DECCA 32265	15.00	northern

WADDY, SANDY
EVERYTHING IS EVERYTHING	SECRET LOVE	S.O.S. 1003	15.00	northern
EVERYTHING IS EVERYTHING	SECRET LOVE	WAND 1169	15.00	northern

WADE AND JAMIE
DON'T PUT OFF 'TILL TOMORROW	SEND FOR ME	PALOMAR 2200	20.00	northern

WADE, BOBBY
I'M IN LOVE WITH YOU	DOWN HERE ON THE GROUND	WAY OUT 103	25.00	northern
FLAME IN MY HEART	CAN'T YOU HEAR ME CALLING	BIG JIM 3275	150.00	northern

WADE, DONALD
WALKING	WOE IS ME	ROJAC 1000	100.00	northern

WADE, LEN AND THE TIKIS
BOSS BEAT	WHICH WAY DO I GO	UA 987	25.00	mod
THE NIGHT THE ANGELS CRIED	DON'T PUT ME DOWN	UA 891	25.00	northern

WADE, ROGER
LITTLE GIRL	I CAN ONLY HURT YOU	THELMA 84946	75.00	motown
LITTLE GIRL	I CAN ONLY HURT YOU	HARMON 1003	75.00	motown

WADE, WILLIE
WHEN PUSH COMES TO SHOVE	COME INTO MY WORLD	NITE LIFE 70001	500.00	northern

WAGNER, CLIFF
EXCEPTION TO THE RULE	LOVE WILL MAKE YOU CRAWL	JEWEL 777	25.00	northern

WAGNER, DANNY
I LOST A TRUE LOST	MY BUDDY	IMPERIAL 66305	50.00	northern

WAGNER, GARY
I CAN'T GO ON WITHOUT YOU	SAVE YOUR LOVE	MAJOR SOUND 101	200.00	northern

WAHLS, SHIRLEY
BECAUSE I LOVE YOU	I DON'T KNOW	CALLA 140	40.00	northern
CRY MYSELF TO SLEEP	PROVE IT EVERYDAY	BLUE ROCK 4059	10.00	northern
WHY AM I CRYING	THAT'S HOW LONG (I'M GONNA LOVE YOU)	KING 6083	40.00	northern

WAITERS, L.J.
IN THE SAME OLD WAY	YOUR LOVE IS SLIIPING AWAY	UNITY 2710	30.00	northern

WAKEFIELD SUN
SING A SIMPLE SONG	THINGS ARE LOOKING UP	ROULETTE 7073	10.00	funk
GET OUT	WHEN I SEE YOU	MGM 14028	15.00	northern
TRYPT ON LOVE	SING A SIMPLE SONG	MGM 14072	25.00	northern

WALES, HOWARD
HUXLEY'S HOWL	MY BLUES	COSTAL 101	200.00	funk

WALKER III, FLETCHER
GUESS I'LL NEVER UNDERSTAND	DIDN'T WE	PARAMOUNT 0065	40.00	70's

WALKER, EDIE
GOOD GUYS	YOUNG TEARS DON'T FALL FOREVER	RISING SONS 713	40.00	northern
I DON'T NEED YOU ANYMORE	DON'T CRY SOLDIER	MEW 102	75.00	northern
YOUR UNUSUAL LOVE	BABY ANGEL	MEW 103	300.00	northern

WALKER, GLORIA
MY PRECIOUS LOVE	PAPA'S GOT THE WAGON	PEOPLE 2504.	20.00	70's

WALKER, JR. AND THE ALL STARS
AIN'T THAT THE TRUTH	SHOOT YOUR SHOT	SOUL 35036	20.00	motown
BRAINWASHER	CLEO'S MOOD	HARVEY 117	20.00	motown
GOOD ROCKIN'	BRAINWASHER PT.2	HARVEY 119	40.00	motown
LEO'S BACK (mispelt title!)	SHAKE AND FINGERPOP	SOUL 35013	10.00	motown
SATAN'S BLUES	MONKEY JUMP	SOUL 35003	20.00	motown
TUNE UP	DO THE BOOMERANG	SOUL 35012 lilac & white	10.00	motown
TWIST LACKAWANNA	WILLIE'S BLUES	HARVEY 113	15.00	motown

WALKER, LITTLE WILLIE
THERE GOES MY USED TO BE	TICKET TO RIDE	GOLDWAX 329	30.00	ballad

WALKER, RANDOLPH
ACHIN' ALL OVER	YOU'LL LOSE YOUR LOVE	MALA 572	20.00	northern

WALKER, ROBERT
STICK TO ME	THE BLIZZARD	RCA 9304	20.00	northern

WALKER, ROBERT AND THE NIGHT RIDERS
EVERYTHING'S ALL RIGHT	KEEP ON RUNNING	DETROIT SOUND 224	200.00	northern

WALKER, RONNIE
MY BABY DOESN'T LOVE ME ANYMOR	I'M SAYING GOODBYE	BELL 651	30.00	ballad
REALLY, REALLY LOVE YOU	AIN'T IT FUNNY	PHILIPS 40470	15.00	group
EVERYTHING IS EVERTHING		VENT 1005	30.00	northern
IT'S A GOOD FEELIN'	PRECIOUS	NICO 1000	50.00	northern
IT'S A GOOD FEELIN'	PRECIOUS	ABC 11215	15.00	northern

WALKER, SPIDER
I'M MAD		S AND M 112	75.00	northern

WALKER, WILLIE				
JERK IT WITH SOUL	DO THE PEOPLE	TASTE 7	50.00	northern
WALL OF SOUND				
HANG ON	YOU HAD TO HAVE YOUR WAY	TOWER 363	15.00	northern
HANG ON	YOU HAD TO HAVE YOUR WAY	BIG BIRD 127	30.00	northern
WALLACE BROTHERS				
WHAT-CHA FEEL IS WHAT-CHA GET		WALBRO NO#	200.00	funk
TRIPLE ZERO	I DON'T THINK (THERE COULD BE)	GRAHAM 802	100.00	northern
WALLACE, JIMMY				
I'LL BE BACK	LET BY GONES BE BY GONES	ALPHA 6	700.00	northern
WALLACE, WALES				
FOREVER AND A DAY	A LOVE LIKE MINE	DAKAR 4505	25.00	70's
SOMEBODY I KNOW	TALK A LITTLE LOUDER	BRC 101	15.00	70's
WHAT EVER YOU WANT	I WISH I COULD SAY WHAT I WANT	INNOVATION 9157	10.00	70's
WHY SHOULD WE STAY TOGETHER	PEOPLE SURE ACT FUNNY	NOW SOUND 101	15.00	70's
THAT AIN'T THE WAY	WE'RE NOT HAPPY	BASHIE 102	50.00	northern
YOU'LL NEVER GET AWAY	I GOTTA HAVE YOU	RENEE 111	50.00	northern
WALLIS, SUZY				
TELL HIM	A TIME FOR US	RCA 8863	20.00	northern
WALLY AND THE KNIGHT				
HANG ON LITTLE MAMA	EVERY MAN HAS A DREAM	TARX 1010	20.00	northern
WALSH GYPSY BAND, JAMES				
CUZ IT'S YOU GIRL	BRING YOURSELF AROUND	RCA 11403	25.00	70's
WALTER AND SISTERS				
HOW LONG	HOW LONG PT.2	STUDIO 10 69	100.00	northern
WALTER B. AND THE UNTOUCHABLES				
I CAN'T STOP LOVING YOU	SHE WAS WRONG	APOLLO. 9	300.00	northern
WALTER AND THE ADMERATIONS				
MAN OH MAN	LIFE OF TEARS	LA CINDY 32769	1500.00	northern
WALTON JR., WILBUR				
TWENTY FOUR HOURS OF LONELINES	FOR THE LOVE OF A WOMAN	123 1703	30.00	northern
WAMMACK, TRAVIS				
SCATCHY	FIRE FLY	ARA 204	8.00	northern
WANDERERS				
SOMEBODY ELSE'S SWEETHEART	SHE WEARS MY RING	CUB 9099	40.00	northern
YOU C\AN'T RUN AWAY FROM ME	I'LL KNOW	UA 648	50.00	northern
WARD, CLARA				
THE RIGHT DIRECTION	TEAR IT DOWN	VERVE 10412	45.00	northern
WARD, HERB				
WRONG PLACE AT THE WRONG TIME	YOU CAN CRY	PHIL LA SOUL 312	40.00	ballad
HANDS OFF SHE'S MINE	IF I PRAY	BUDDY 244	75.00	northern
HONEST TO GOODNESS	IF YOU GOT TO LEAVE ME	RCA 9688	100.00	northern
STRANGE CHANGE	WHY DO YOU WANT LEAVE ME	ARGO 5510	150.00	northern
WARD, PATTIE				
(GIRLS) YOU HAVE TO WAIT FOR L	GET OFF MY STUFF	ROAD 6245	30.00	northern
WARD, ROBERT				
I WILL FEAR NO EVIL	MY LOVE IS STRICTLY RESERVED F	GROOVE CITY 201	30.00	northern
WARD, ROY				
HORSE WITH A FREEZE PT.1	HORSE WITH A FREEZE PT.2	SEVEN B 7020	50.00	funk
WARD, SAM.				
SISTER LEE	STONE BROKE	GROOVE CITY 205	350.00	**northerB**
WARD, SAMMY				
BREAD WINNER	YOU'VE GOT TO CHANGE	SOUL 35004	25.00	motown
WHAT MAKES YOU LOVE HIM	DON'T TAKE IT AWAY	TAMLA 54049	40.00	motown
WARD, SINGING SAMMY				
EVERYBODY KNEW IT	BIG MOE JOE mix 034379	TAMLA 54057.	60.00	motown
EVERYBODY KNEW IT	BIG JOE MOE mix 34309	TAMLA 54057	30.00	motown
SOMEDAY PRETTY BABY	PART TIME LOVE	TAMLA 54071	50.00	motown
WHO'S THE FOOL	THAT CHILD IS REALLY WILD	TAMLA 54030 stripes	100.00	motown
WARE, LEON				
INSIDE YOUR LOVE	HUNGRY	FABULOUS 749	8.00	70's
WHAT'S YOUR NAME	CLUB SASHAY	FABULOUS 748	10.00	70's
WHY I CAME TO CALIFORNIA	CAN I TOUCH YOU THERE	ELEKTRA 69957	20.00	70's
WARM EXCURSION				
FUNK-I-TIS		WATTS USA 52	50.00	funk
HANG UP	HANG UP PT.2	PZAZZ 39	25.00	funk
WARNER, PETE				
I JUST WANT TO SPEND MY LIFE WTH YOU	HANDS	POLYDOR 14278	30.00	70's
WARRIORS				
HERE'S ANOTHER ONE		TIKI	50.00	funk
WARWICK, DEE DEE				
I'M GLAD I'M A WOMAN	SUSPICIOUS MINDS	ATCO 6810	15.00	northern
WE'VE GOT EVERYTHING GOING FOR	DON'T YOU EVER GIVE UP ON ME	MERCURY 72738	20.00	northern
WHEN LOVE SLIPS AWAY	HOUSE OF GOLD	MERCURY 72667	15.00	northern
WHERE IS THAT RAINBOW	I WHO HAVE NOTHING	MERCURY 72966	30.00	northern
DO IT WITH ALL YOUR HEART	HAPPINESS	BLUE ROCK 4008	20.00	northern
DON'T CALL ME ANYMORE	YOU'RE NO GOOD	JUBILEE 5459	15.00	northern

DON'T THINK MY BABY'S COMING BACK	STANDING BY	TIGER 103	50.00	northern
GOTTA GET A HOLD OF MYSELF	ANOTHER LONELY SATURDAY	BLUE ROCK 4032	15.00	northern
I CAN'T GO BACK	I (WHO HAVE NOTHING)	HURD 79	30.00	northern
I WANT TO BE WITH YOU	WE'RE DOING FINE	BLUE ROCK 4027	12.00	northern
MONDAY MONDAY	I'LL BE BETTER OFF WITHOUT YOU	MERCURY 72834	10.00	northern
YOU DON'T KNOW	WE'RE DOING FINE	BLUE ROCK 4027	15.00	northern

WASHINGTON, ALBERT
I'M THE MAN	THESE ARMS OF MINE	FRATERNITY 1002	20.00	northern

WASHINGTON, BABY
THAT'S HOW HEARTACHES ARE MADE	THERE HE IS	SUE 783	10.00	northern
HEY LONELY ONE	DOODLIN	SUE 794	10.00	northern
I CAN'T AFFORD TO LOSE HIM	I DON'T KNOW	COTILLION 44047	10.00	northern
I KNOW	IT'LL CHANGE	SUE 4	10.00	northern
I'M GOOD ENOUGH FOR YOU	DON'T LET ME LOSE THIS DREAM	COTILLION 44086	10.00	northern
IS IT WORTH IT	HAPPY BIRTHDAY	CHESS 2099	10.00	northern
IS IT WORTH IT	HAPPY BIRTHDAY	CHECKER 1105	20.00	northern
IT'LL NEVER BE OVER FOR ME	MOVE ON DRIFTER	SUE 114	20.00	northern
I'VE GOT A FEELING	HUSH HEART	SUE 769	15.00	northern
LEAVE ME ALONE	YOU AND THE NIGHT	SUE 790	15.00	northern
RUN MY HEART	YOUR FOOL	SUE 119 DJ	20.00	northern
THERE HE IS	NO TIME FOR PITY	SUE 137	8.00	northern
THINK ABOUT THE GOOD TIMES	HOLD BACK THE DAWN	VEEP 1297	25.00	northern
YOU ARE WHAT YOU ARE	EITHER YOUR WITH ME	SUE 150	10.00	northern
YOUR FOOL	RUN MY HEART	SUE 119	15.00	northern

WASHINGTON, BILLY
I WANNA COME IN	LATER FOR ROMANCE	TCF 124	30.00	northern
WHAT DID YOU DO (TO MY BABY)	DO YOU REALLY LOVE ME	DORO 1303	50.00	northern

WASHINGTON, ERNIE
LONESOME SHACK	HOW ABOUT YOU	CHATTAHOOCHIE 673	200.00	northern

WASHINGTON, GINO
OH NOT ME	HEY I'M A LOVE BANDIT	ATAC 2878	15.00	ballad
FOXY WALK	IT'S WINTER (BUT I HAVE SPRING	ATAC 2743	50.00	funk
GINO IS A COWARD	PUPPET ON A STRING	RIC TIC 100	20.00	motown
GINO IS A COWARD	PUPPET ON A STRING	SONBERT 3770	50.00	northern
GINO IS A COWARD	PUPPET ON A STRING	CORREC-TONE 503	40.00	northern
I'M SO IN LOVE WITH YOU		ATAC	300.00	northern
LIKE MY BABY	I'LL BE AROUND (WHEN YOU WANT ME)	MALA 12029	100.00	northern
GINO IS A COWARD	LIKE MY BABY (instrumental)	W.M.C. 358	75.00	northern
NOW YOU'RE LONELY	ROMEO	W.I.G. 9005	50.00	northern
RAT RACE	OH NOT ME	WASHPAN 854	20.00	northern
WHAT CAN A MAN DO	SAME: INSTRUMENTAL	WASHPAN 3122	30.00	northern
WHAT CAN A MAN DO	DOING THE POPCORN	ATAC 101	15.00	northern

WASHINGTON, JACKIE
WHY WON'T THEY LET ME BE	MEET ME IN THE BOTTOM	VANGUARD 35036 PS	40.00	northern

WASHINGTON, JEANETTE (BABY)
LET LOVE GO BY	MY TIME TO CRY	ABC 10223	30.00	northern

WASHINGTON, JOE AND WASH
BLUEBERRY HILL	LOOK ME IN THE EYES	WEST SOUNDS	100.00	funk

WASHINGTON, JUSTINE
I CAN'T WAIT UNTIL I SEE MY BABY'S FACE	WHO'S GONNA TAKE CARE OF ME	SUE 797	20.00	northern

WASHINGTON, LEE
LITTLE GIRL	THE U.T.	FAT FISH 8006	30.00	group
LITTLE GIRL	THE U.T.	JERK 909	50.00	group

WASHINGTON, LOU AND THE PROFESSIONALS
WHEN WE MEET AGAIN	ANY OLD TIME	USA 831	400.00	group

WASHINGTON, LOU D.
SMOKEY	THE WAY A ROMANCE SHOULD BE	STEEL TOWN 195	15.00	northern

WASHINGTON, MICHEAL
STAY MINE	SAME: INSTRUMENTAL	CAPCITY 119	15.00	northern

WATKINS, BILLY
THE ICE-MAN	THE BLUE AND LONELY	ERA 3183	100.00	**northerB**

WATKINS, LOVELACE
DREAMS	WHO AM I	SUE 10003	100.00	northern

WATSON, BILLY
GET MYSELF TOGETHER	SO LONG	BARRACUDA 502	50.00	northern

WATSON, CRESA
DEAD	ALPINE WINTER	CHARAY 700	15.00	ballad

WATSON, JOHNNY (GUITAR)
AIN'T GONNA MOVE	BABY DON'T LEAVE ME	JOWAT 118	150.00	northern
BIG BAD WOLF	YOU CAN STAY	MAGNUM 726	400.00	northern
WAIT A MINUTE BABY	OH SO FINE	HIGHLAND 1151	100.00	northern
CRAZY ABOUT YOU	SHE'LL BLOW YOUR MIND	OKEH 7302	15.00	northern
I'D RATHER BE YOUR BABY	SOUL FOOD	OKEH 7290	25.00	northern
SOUTH LIKE WEST	KEEP ON LOVIN' YOU	OKEH 7263	40.00	northern
HOLD ON, I'M COMIN'	WOLFMAN	OKEH 7270 PS	25.00	northern
SHE'LL BLOW YOUR MIND	CRAZY ABOUT YOU	OKEH 7302	15.00	ballad
HOLD ON, I'M COMING	WOLFMAN	OKEH 7270	15.00	mod
I'D RATHER BE YOUR BABY	SOUL FOOD	OKEH 7290	30.00	northern

WATSON, LES

SOUL MAN BLUES	NO PEACE, NO REST	POMPEII 66689	30.00	northern
I'M GONNA CRY	HURT	VESUVIUS 1004	20.00	northern

WATSON, ROMANCE

WHERE DOES THAT LEAVE ME	FROGGY BOTTOM	CORAL 62442	150.00	northern

WATSON AND THE SHERLOCKS

STANDING ON THE CORNER	FUNKY WALK	SOULVILLE 1015	15.00	northern

WATTS, GLENN

MY LITTLE PLAYTHING	MONEY GIVES DIGNITY	BUNKY 7751	20.00	northern

WATTS, WENDELL

GROOVIEST THING THIS SIDE OF H	LOVE BUG	JIMINIE 6002	40.00	70's
YOU GIRL	WILL YOU BE STAYING AFTER SUND	REFOREE 715	100.00	70's

WAYMON, SAM

IF YOU SAY SO	IT BE'S THAT WAY SOMWETIMES	RCA 9770	20.00	northern
LONELY FOR MY BABY	HEY LOVE	RCA 9756	20.00	northern
YOU CAN COUNT ON ME	I LOVE YOU	NINANDY 1012	20.00	northern

WAYNE, TAMMY

HAVE A GOOD TIME	KISSAWAY	BOOM 60004	25.00	northern

WDJ-PRINCE OF SOUL

FUNKY LOVING		GENTS	100.00	funk

WE THE PEOPLE

MAKING MY DAYDREAM REAL	WHATCHA DONE FOR ME, I'M GONNA	LION 164	50.00	70's

WE TWO

WAY DOWN DEEP INSIDE	MAGIC MOMENTS	ABC 10930	30.00	northern

WEAPONS OF PEACE

THIS LIFE'S (ABOUT TO GET ME DOWN)	ROOTS MURAL THEME	PLAYBOY 6101 PS	30.00	70's

WEATHERS, OSCAR

JUST TO PROVE I LOVE YOU	YOUR FOOL STILL LOVES YOU	TOP & BOTTOM 402	15.00	northern

WEAVER, JERRY

I'M SO IN LOVE WITH YOU	I'M IN LOVE	TMI 115	15.00	70's
THAT'S WHEN YOU KNOW WHAT IT F	LOVE DON'T MAKE YOU ACT LIKE T	MGM 14789	15.00	70's
I'M IN LOVE	LOVE SICK CHILD	S.O.B. 110	30.00	northern

WEBB, BETI

I KNOW (YOU COULD BE HAPPY)	I HAVE, I HAVE	MGM 13715	10.00	northern
I KNOW (YOU COULD BE HAPPY)	I HAVE, I HAVE	XL	30.00	northern

WEBB, JOYCE

IT'S EASIER SAID THAN DONE	LAUGHING TO KEEP FROM CRYING	GOLDEN WORLD 108	25.00	motown
YOU'VE GOT A WHOLE LOT OF LIVING	CLOSER TO THE BLUES	RIC TIC 102	20.00	motown

WEBS

LET ME TAKE YOU HOME	DO I HAVE A CHANCE	SOTOPLAY 6	200.00	group
I WANT YOU BACK	WE BELONG TOGETHER	VERVE 10610	10.00	northern
KEEP YOUR LOVE STRONG	LET'S PARTY	ATLANTIC 2415	15.00	northern
TOMORROW	THIS THING CALLED LOVE	POP-SIDE 4593	10.00	northern

WEBSTER, BILLY

GOOD PEOPLE	JAZZ JERK	SILVER TONE 203	20.00	northern

WEBSTER, JOE AND THE ANGLOS

INCENSE	STEPPIN' STONES	CONSTELLATION 153	20.00	northern

WEDGEWORTH, LARRY

NO MORE GAMES	NO MORE GAMES (Long Version)	GROOVEHALL 1	50.00	70's

WEE WILLIE AND THE WINNERS

GET SOME	A PLAN FOR THE MAN	SHOTGUN 1002	20.00	funk
IT'S BETTER TO GIVE THAN TO RE	THREE STAGES OF LOVE	SHOTGUN 1001	20.00	funk

WEEKENDS

CANADIAN SUNSET	YOU'RE NUMBER ONE WITH ME	COLUMBIA 43597	20.00	northern

WEEKS, RALPH

SOMETHING DEEP INSIDE	GUA-JAZZ	4 STARS 1	40.00	northern

WELCH, CHARLIE CHUCK

DESTINATION HEART ACHE	HERE I AM AGAIN	COLUMN 226	150.00	northern

WELCH, LENNY

JUST WHAT I NEED	DON'T START	BIG APPLE 702	10.00	70's
CORONET BLUE	I'M OVER YOU	KAPP 854	10.00	northern
RUN TO MY LOVING ARMS	CORONET BLUE	KAPP 712	10.00	northern
THE RIGT TO CRY	UNTIL THE REAL THING COMES ALO	KAPP 808	10.00	northern
WAIT AWHILE LONGER	DARLING STAY WITH ME	MERCURY 72777	10.00	northern
YOU CAN'T RUN AWAY	HALFWAY TO YOUR ARMS	MERCURY 72866	10.00	northern

WELLS, BARBARA

PRETTY BOY	WHEN A WOMAN'S IN LOVE	CORAL 62386	50.00	northern

WELLS, BILLY

THIS HEART THESE HANDS	TEN TO ONE	SWEET SOUL 3	150.00	northern

WELLS, BOBBY

BE'S THAT WAY SOMETIMES	RECIPE FOR LOVE	ROMUR 1	30.00	**northerB**
LET'S COPP A GROOVE	THE PSYCHEDELIC THEME	ROMUR 11	20.00	northern

WELLS, JEAN

WHAT HAVE I GOT TO LOSE	DROWN IN MY OWN TEARS	CALLA 185	10.00	northern
WHAT HAVE I GOT TO LOSE	BROOMSTICK HORSE COWBOY	CALLA 157	15.00	northern
DON'T COME RUNNING TO ME	LITTLE BOOTS	ABC 10745	40.00	northern
AFTER LOVING YOU	PUTTING THE BEST ON THE OUTSID	CALLA 128	8.00	northern

SHARING YOUR LOVE	SONG OF THE BELLS	QUAKERTOWN 1023	50.00	northern
WITH MY LOVE AND WHAT YOU'VE GOT	HAVE A LITTLE MERCY	CALLA 143	20.00	northern

WELLS, JENNIFER

DINING IN CHINATOWN	FOR SOME	GENUINE 166	200.00	northern

WELLS, JUNIOR

UP IN HEAH	JUNIOR'S GROOVE	BRIGHT STAR 149	15.00	northern
I'M GONNA CRAMP YOUR STYLE	YOU OUGHTA QUIT THAT	BRIGHT STAR 152	15.00	northern
(I GOT A) STOMACH ACHE	SHAKE IT BABY	VANGUARD 35049	15.00	mod

WELLS, KENNY

ISN'T IT JUST A SHAME	I CAN'T STOP	NEW VOICE 812	300.00	northern

WELLS, MARY

AIN'T IT THE TRUTH	STOP TAKING ME FOR GRANTED	20th. CENTURY 544	10.00	northern
HE'S A LOVER	I'M LEARNIN'	20th. CENTURY 590	10.00	northern
NEVER, NEVER LEAVE ME	WHY DON'T YOU LET YOURSELF GO	20th. CENTURY 570	10.00	northern
DIG THE WAY I FEEL	LOVE SHOOTING BANDIT	JUBILEE 5684	10.00	northern
BYE BYE BABY	PLEASE FORGIVE ME	MOTOWN 1003 stripe	15.00	motown
BYE BYE BABY	PLEASE FORGIVE ME	MOTOWN 1003 map	25.00	motown
I'M SO SORRY	I DON'T WANT TO TAKE A CHANCE	MOTOWN 1011	20.00	motown
STRANGE LOVE	COME TO ME	MOTOWN 1016 PS	30.00	motown
DEAR LOVER	CAN'T YOU SEE (YOU'RE LOSING ME)	ATCO 6392	10.00	northern
KEEP ME IN SUSPENSE	SUCH A SWEET THING	ATCO 6423	10.00	northern
ME WITHOUT YOU	I'M SORRY	20th. CENTURY 606	10.00	northern
USE YOUR HEAD	EVERLOVIN' BOY	20th. CENTURY 555	10.00	northern
HE'S A LOVER	I'M LEARNIN'	20th. CENTURY 590 PS	25.00	northern

WELSH, JANIE

I CAN'T STOP THINKING 'BOUT YO	OPEN ARMS-CLOSED HEART	GDC 4004	25.00	northern

WESLEY, JOHNNY AND THE FOUR TEES

LOVE IS A FUNNY THING	STOP THE MUSIC	MELIC 4195	800.00	northern
YOU STILL NEED ME	IT'S THE TALK OF THE TOWN	MELIC 4170	75.00	northern

WEST SIDERS

DON'T YOU KNOW	NO TEARS LEFT FOR CRYING	LEOPARD 5004	60.00	northern
DON'T YOU KNOW	NO TEARS LEFT FOR CRYING	UA 600	50.00	northern

WEST, BARBARA

CONGRATULATIONS BABY	GIVE ME BACK THE MAN I LOVE	RONN 32	30.00	northern

WEST, C.L.

BUMPING TRAVELING MAN	BUMPING TRAVELING MAN Pt.2	DUPLEX 1307	50.00	funk

WEST, DODIE

IN THE DEEP OF THE NIGHT	ROVIN' BOY	CHECKER 1114	20.00	northern

WEST, JOHNNY

TEARS BABY	IT AIN'T LOVE	SOUL 841	400.00	northern

WESTLEY, JOHN

I LOVE YOU	YOU'RE THE ONE	CORSAIR 115	150.00	northern
JUST BELIEVE	DON'T GIVE IT AWAY	RENFRO 114	75.00	ballad

WESTON PRIM

SIMMERIN'		MEMPHIS EXPRESS	75.00	funk

WESTON, KIM

I GOT WHAT YOU NEED	SOMEONE LIKE YOU	MGM 13720	8.00	northern
A LITTLE MORE LOVE	GO AHEAD AND LAUGH	TAMLA 54106 NI	500.00	motown
A THRILL A MOMENT	I'LL NEVER SEE YOU AGAIN	GORDY 7041	40.00	motown
HELPLESS	A LOVE LIKE YOURS	GORDY 7050	15.00	motown
I'M STILL LOVING YOU	GO AHEAD AND LAUGH	TAMLA 54110	40.00	motown
IT SHOULD HAVE BEEN ME	LOVE ME ALL THE WAY	TAMLA 54076	10.00	motown
JUST LOVING YOU	ANOTHER TRAIN COMING	TAMLA 54085	20.00	motown
LOOKING FOR THE RIGHT GUY	FEEL ALRIGHT TONIGHT	TAMLA 54100	20.00	motown
TAKE ME IN YOUR ARMS	DON'T COMPARE ME WITH HER	GORDY 7046	10.00	motown
DANGER, HEARTBREAK AHEAD	I'LL BE THINKIN'	PEOPLE 1001	8.00	northern
THAT'S GROOVY	LAND OF TOMORROW	MGM 13804	10.00	northern
YOU'RE JUST THE KIND OF GUY	NOBODY	MGM 13881	10.00	northern
I GOT WHAT YOU NEED	SOMEONE LIKE YOU	MGM 13720 PS	20.00	northern

WHEELER, ART

THAT'S HOW MUCH I LOVE YOU	WALK ON	CEE-JAM 4	75.00	northern
COMING ATTRACIONS	PAWN SHOP	DOT 17185	10.00	northern

WHEELER, BEVERLY AND THE CAMEROS

DON'T SHAKE MY TREE	SAME: INSTRUMENTAL	BSC 129	20.00	funk

WHEELER, MARY

PROVE IT	FRESH OUT OF TEARS	CALLA 111	40.00	northern

WHEELER, MARY AND THE KNIGHTS

I FEEL IN MY HEART	A FALLING TEAR	ATOM 701	600.00	northern

WHISPERING SHADOW

STOP THE WORLD	(U GOT TO WATCH) THE FOG	MR. D'S 3078	30.00	70's

WHISPERS

FLYING HIGH	THE TIME WILL COME	SOUL CLOCK 107	8.00	northern
I CAN REMEMBER	PLANETS OF LIFE	SOUL CLICK 1001	10.00	northern
I CAN'T SEE MYSELF LEAVING YOU	GREAT DAY	SOUL CLOCK 104	20.00	northern
I'M THE ONE	YOU MUST BE DOING ALL RIGHT	SOUL CLOCK 1005	15.00	northern
NEEDLE IN A HAYSTACK	SEEMS LIKE I GOTTA DO WRONG	SOUL CLOCK 1004	8.00	northern
DOCTOR LOVE	LONELY AVENUE	DORE 751	100.00	northern
NEEDLE IN A HAYSTACK	WALTZ FOR YOUNG LOVERS	DORE 794	40.00	northern
REMEMBER	WHAT WILL I DO	SOUL CLOCK 109	10.00	northern

THE DIP	WIERDO	DORE 735	75.00	northern
THE DIP	IT ONLY HURTS FOR A LITTLE WHILE	DORE 842	50.00	northern
YOU GOT A MAN YOUR HANDS	YOU CAN'T FIGHT WHAT'S RIGHT	DORE 792	75.00	northern

WHITE JR., JOSH

I CAN'T RUN AWAY	THIS CAN'T BE WRONG	MERCURY 72328	40.00	northern

WHITE, ANTHONY

HEY BABY	THERE WILL NEVER BE ANOTHER	PIR 3566	40.00	70's
NEVER LET YOU GET AWAY FROM ME	NEVER REPAY YOUR LOVE	PIR 3574	30.00	70's

WHITE, BOBBY

IT'S A GREAT LIFE	JUST ANOTHER WEEK BEHIND	KENT 491	15.00	northern

WHITE, DANNY

CRACKED UP OVER YOU	TAKING INVNTORY	DECCA 32048	15.00	northern
KEEP MY WOMAN HOME	I'M DEDICATING MY LIFE	ATLAS 1257	15.00	northern
KEEP MY WOMAN HOME	I'M DEDICATING MY LIFE	ATTERU 2000	25.00	northern
MISS FINE MISS FINE	CAN'T DO NOTHING WITHOUT YOU	FRISCO 110	30.00	northern
ONE LITTLE LIE	LOAN ME A HANDKERCHIEF	ABC 10525	20.00	northern
ONE LITTLE LIE	LOAN ME A HANDKERCHIEF	FRISCO 108	40.00	northern

WHITE, E.T. AND THE GREAT POTENTIAL

GOT TO FIND A TRUE LOVE	WALK ON WOMAN	GREAT POTENTIAL 13161	40.00	70's

WHITE, HI-FI

NEED SOMEBODY	SAME: INSTRUMENTAL)	SANDMAN 705	20.00	northern

WHITE, JEANETTE

MUSIC	NO SUNSHINE	A&M 1092	10.00	**northerB**
MUSIC	NO SUNSHINE	VIBRATION 1001	15.00	northern

WHITE,BARRY

TRACY (ALL i HAVE IS YOU)	FLAME OF LOVE	FARO 613	70.00	northern

WHITEHEAD, EDDIE

JUST YOUR FOOL	GIVE THIS FOOL ANOTHER CHANCE	BLACK JACK 711	1000.00	northern

WHITLEY, RAY

I'VE BEEN HURT	THERE IS ONE BOY	DUNHILL 201 DJ	40.00	northern

WHITNEY, MARVA

DON'T LET OUR LOVE FADE AWAY	LIVE AND LET LIVE	EXCELLO 2328	30.00	70's
THIS GIRLS IN LOVE WITH YOU	HE'S THE ONE	KING 6283	40.00	northern
DADDY DON'T KNOW ABOUT SUGAR B	WE NEED MORE	EXCELLO 2321	20.00	funk
GIVING UP ON LOVE	THIS IS MY QUEST	T NECK 922	20.00	funk
I MADE A MISTAKE BECAUSE IT'S	SAME: Pt.2	KING 6268	10.00	funk
THINGS GOT TO GET BETTER	GET OUT OF MY LIFE	KING 6249	10.00	funk
UNWIND YOURSELF	IF YOU LOVE ME	KING 6146	20.00	funk
YOU GOT TO HAVE A JOB	I'M TIRED, I'M TIRED, I'M TIRED	KING 6218	10.00	funk
YOUR LOVE IS GOOD FOR ME	WHAT DO I HAVE TO DO TO PROVE	KING 6202	10.00	funk
YOUR LOVE WAS GOOD FOR ME	WHAT KIND OF MAN	KING 6158	10.00	funk
BALL OF FIRE	IT'S MY THING	KING 6229	15.00	**northerB**
SAVING MY LOVE FOR MY BABY	YOUR LOVE WAS GOOD FOR ME	FEDERAL 12545	20.00	northern

WHITNEY, MARY LEE

THIS COULD HAVE BEEN ME	DON'T COME A KNOCKIN'	LOMA 2044	10.00	group

WIGGINS, JAY

MY LONELY GIRL	FORGIVE THEN FORGET	IPG 1015	20.00	northern
TEARS OF A LOVER	YOU'RE ON MY MIND	SOLID 3001	100.00	northern

WIGGINS, PERCY

LOVE IS A WONDERFUL THING	YOU MAKE ME FEEL LIKE SINGING	RCA 9838	15.00	ballad
IT'S DIDN'T TAKE MUCH (FOR ME	THE WORK OF A WOMAN	RCA 8915	50.00	northern
THAT'S LOVING YOU	LOOK WHAT I'VE DONE (TO MY BABY)	A-BET 9434	75.00	**northerB**

WIGGINS, SPENCER

LONELY MAN	THE POWER OF A WOMAN	GOLDWAX 330	40.00	northern

WILBORN'S PSYCHEDELIC SIX, YORK

FUNKY FOOTBALL		TRUE SOUL NO#.	50.00	funk
PSYCHEDELLIC HOT PANTS		TRUE SOUL NO#	300.00	funk

WILBURN, BOBBY

I'M A LONELY MAN	SAME:	GAMBLE 4015	250.00	northern

WILCHER, WILLIE

HOOPY DOO	SAME: INSTRUMENTAL	MARY JANE 1002	25.00	funk

WILCOX, NANCY

MY BABY	COMING ON STRONG	RCA 9233	30.00	northern

WILD SOUND EXPERIENCE

I KNOW YOU		COLPAR 5272	40.00	northern

WILDWEEDS

CAN'T YOU SEE THAT I'M LONELY	SOMEDAY MORNING	CADET 5572	30.00	northern

WILEY, ED AND THE PANASONICS

YOUNG GENERATION	STRETCHING OUT	NA-CAT 210	50.00	funk

WILEY, MICHELLE

FEEL GOOD	I FEEL SO GOOD AT HOME HERE	20th. CENTURY 2317	45.00	70's

WILLIAMS, AL

THE OTHER SIDE OF YOUR LOVE	GO HEAD ON WITH YOUR GOOD THIN	CRAJON 48206	40.00	70's
I AM NOTHING	BRAND NEW ME	PALMER 5011	1000.00	northern
I AM NOTHING	BRAND NEW ME	LABEAT 6602 DJ	1000.00	northern
I AM NOTHING	BRAND NEW ME	LABEAT 6602	850.00	northern

WILLIAMS, ALBERT
I'M IN YOUR CORNER	TUMBLING	JAM 128	50.00	northern

WILLIAMS, ANDY
THE HOUSE OF BAMBOO	THE HAWAIIAN WEDDING SONG	CADENCE 1358	10.00	mod

WILIAMS, BERNARD
IT'S NEEDLESS TO SAY	FOCUSED ON YOU	HARTHON 136	30.00	**northerB**
EVER AGAIN	NEXT TO YOU	BELL	1750.00	northern

WILLIAMS, BOBBY
FUNKY SUPER FLY	FUNKY SUPER FLY Pt.2	DUPLEX 1302	25.00	funk
SOUL PARTY	SOUL PARTY Pt.2	R.E.W. 3738	10.00	funk
BABY I NEED YOUR LOVE	TRY IT AGAIN	SURE SHOT 5025	30.00	northern
IT'S ALL OVER	WHEN YOU PLAY (YOU GOTTA PAY)	SURE SHOT 5013	30.00	northern
I'VE ONLY GOT MYSELF TO BLAME	I'LL HATE MYSELF TOMORROW	SURE SHOT 5031	100.00	northern
TELL IT TO MY FACE	I'M DEPENDING ON YOU	LU PINE 111	25.00	northern
TRY LOVE	PLAY A SAD SONG	SURE SHOT 5003	15.00	northern

WILLIAMS, BOBBY AND HIS MAR-KING
LET'S JAM		NOR-MAR	50.00	funk
LET'S WORK A WHILE		NOR-MAR	75.00	funk

WILLIAMS, CALVIN
IT WON'T MATTER AT ALL	LONELY YOU'LL BE	ATCO 6399	20.00	northern
IT WON'T MATTER AT ALL	LONELY YOU'LL BE	NORTHERN DEL-LA 501	40.00	northern

WILLIAMS, CHERYL
EVERYBODY'S HAPPY BUT ME	'M YOUR FOOL	BENGEE 1001	150.00	northern

WILLIAMS, CLARENCE
NO REST FOR THE WORRIED	THE SEVENTH SON	THRONE 803	300.00	northern

WILLIAMS, DANNY
FORGET HER, FORGET HER	I WATCH A FLOWER GROW	UA 762	20.00	northern
THE STRANGER	I CAN'T BELIEVE I'M LOSING YOU	UA 959	20.00	northern

WILLIAMS, DAPHINE
I LOVE YOU	I'M YOUR MAN	YODI 16857	100.00	northern

WILLIAMS, DICKY
THAT'S WHERE TRUE LOVE BEGAN	OH DREAMY ME	METRO 8168	100.00	northern

WILLIAMS, DORIE
YOUR TURN TO CRY	TELL ME EVERYTHING YOU KNOW	635 RECORDS 2603	150.00	northern

WILLIAMS, DOROTHY
THE WELL'S RUN DRY	COUNTRY STYLE	GOLDWAX 115	75.00	northern
THE WELL'S RUN DRY	COUNTRY STYLE	BANDSTAND USA 1005	150.00	northern
WATCHDOG	CLOSER TO MY BABY	VOLT 118	15.00	**northerB**

WILLIAMS, FRANK
YOU GOT TO BE A MAN	THE SPANISH FLY	DEEP CITY 2369	30.00	funk
YOU GOT TO BE A MAN	THE SPANISH FLYER	PHIL LA SOUL 304	20.00	funk
GOOD THING	GOOD THING Pt.2	LLOYD 8	30.00	northern

WILLIAMS, FREDDIE
NAME IN LIGHTS	I JUST CAN'T BELIEVE IT	HOLLYWOOD 1114	50.00	northern
I'VE GOT TO LIVE WHILE I CAN	I JUST CAN'T BELIVE IT	HOLLYWOOD 1121	150.00	northern
THINGS ARE LOOKING BETTER	SEA OF LOVE	HOLLYWOOD 1129	15.00	ballad

WILLIAMS, GENE
WHATEVER YOU DO, DO IT GOOD		FORTE	50.00	funk

WILLIAMS, GLORIA
SISTER FUNK	A WOMAN ONLY HUMAN	DOWNTOWN 2	50.00	funk

WILLIAMS, JEANETTE
ALL OF A SUDDEN	MR. SOFT TOUCH	BACK BEAT 568	40.00	**northerB**
SOMETHING'S GOT A HOLD ON ME	LONGING FOR YOUR LOVE	BACK BEAT 587	40.00	northern

WILLIAMS, JERRY (LITTLE)
BABY, BUNNY (SUGAR HONEY)	PHILLY DUCK	CALLA 109	15.00	northern
IF YOU ASK ME (BECAUSE I LOVE)	YVONNE	CALLA 116	50.00	northern
IF YOU ASK ME (BECAUSE I LOVE)	YVONNE	CALLA 116 (1973 issue))	15.00	northern
RUN RUN ROADRUNNER	I'M IN THE DANGER ZONE	MUSICOR 1285	30.00	northern
JUST WHAT DO YOU PLAN TO DO ABOUT	BABY, YOU'RE MY EVERYTHING	CALLA 105	10.00	northern
I'M THE LOVER MAN	THE PUSH PUSH PUSH	LOMA 2005	8.00	northern
I'M THE LOVER MAN	THE PUSH PUSH PUSH	SOUTHERN SOUND 118	10.00	northern

WILLIAMS, JOE
LONELY MAN	I'LL BELONG TO YOU	RCA 8775	30.00	northern

WILLIAMS, JOHN
DO ME LIKE YOU DO ME	BLUES, TEARS AND SORROWS	SANSU 472	40.00	northern

WILLIAMS, JOHN GARY
THE WHOLE DAMN WORLD IS GOING	ASK THE LONELY	STAX 205	50.00	70's

WILLIAMS, JOHNNY
YOU'RE SOMETHING KINDA MELLOW	YOU MAKE ME WANT TO LAST FOREV	BABYLON 1119	8.00	70's
BABY BE MINE	I MADE A MISTAKE	BASHIE 100	15.00	northern
MAGGIE	BREAKING POINT	TWINIGHT 109	20.00	northern
I'D LIKE TO BE WITH YOU	I GOT A FEELING	CUB 9160	10.00	northern
JUST A LITTLE MISUNDERSTANDING	YOUR KOVE CONTROLS MY WORLD	BASHIE 103	10.00	northern
MY BABY'S GOOD	blank:	CHESS 1976	75.00	northern

WILLIAMS, JOYCE
THE FIRST THING I DO IN THE MO	SMILIN'	NICKEL 2	40.00	funk

WILLIAMS, JUAN
I CHECK MY MAILBOX EVERYDAY		BLUE SOUL 102	600.00	northern

WILLIAMS, JUANITA
BABY BOY	YOU KNEW WHAT YOU WAS GETTIN'	GOLDEN WORLD 18	20.00	motown
YOU KNEW WHAT YOU WERE GETTIN'	SOME THINGS YOU NEVER GET USED	WINGATE 8	20.00	northern

WILLIAMS, KEN
COME BACK	BABY IF YOU WERE GONE	OKEH 7303	100.00	northern

WILLIAMS, LARRY
BOSS LOVIN'	JUST BECAUSE	OKEH 7294	15.00	northern
BOSS LOVIN'	CALL ON ME	EL BAM 69	20.00	northern
BOSS LOVIN'	CALL ON ME	SMASH 2035	10.00	northern
YOU ASK ME FOR ONE GOOD REASON	I AM THE ONE	OKEH 7280	60.00	northern

WILLIAMS, LARRY AND THE WATSON, JOHNNY
A QUITTER NEVER WINS	MERCY, MERCY, MERCY	OKEH 7274	15.00	**northernB**
FIND YOURSELF SOMEONE TO LOVE	NOBODY	OKEH 7300	15.00	northern
TOO LATE	TWO FOR THE PRICE OF ONE	OKEH 7281	30.00	**northernB**

WILLIAMS, LAWANDA
COME BACK TO ME	THAT HANDSOME GUY	KEKE 1004	500.00	northern

WILLIAMS, LEE SHOT
LOVE NOW PAY LATER	TIGHTEN UP YOUR GAME	GAMMA 101	100.00	northern

WILLIAMS, LEE AND THE CYMBALS
I'M JUST A TEENAGER	A GIRL FROM A COUNTRY TOWN	RAPDA 2	30.00	northern
I NEED YOU BABY	SHING-A-LING USA	CARNIVAL 538	15.00	northern
I'LL BE GONE	I LOVE YOU MORE	CARNIVAL 521	20.00	northern
LOST LOVE	PEEPIN' (THROUGH THE WINDOW)	CARNIVAL 527	40.00	northern
LOVE IS BREAKIN' OUT (ALL OVER	TIL YOU COME BACK TO ME	CARNIVAL 540	30.00	northern
PLEASE SAY IT ISN'T SO	SHING-A-LING USA	CARNIVAL 532	20.00	northern

WILLIAMS, MAURICE
BEING WITHOUT YOU	BABY, BABY	DEESU 302	30.00	**northerB**
DON'T BE HALF SAFE	HOW TO PICK A WINNER	DEESU 311	20.00	northern
RETURN	MY BABY'S GONE	SEA-HORN 503	75.00	northern

WILLIAMS, MEL
BURN BABY BURN		STAR 704	500.00	northern
PROMISES, PEROMISES, PROMISE		STAR 705	25.00	northern
SWEET LITTLE GIRL OF MINE		BUDDAH 447	250.00	70's
CAN IT BE ME	JET SET	MODERN 1023	30.00	northern
DARLING DON'T	BLUE TEARS	RAMEL 1001	40.00	northern
THAT DON'T MAKE ME MAD	NEVER LOVED A WOMAN (THE WAY I LOVE)	SOUL TIME 713	30.00	northern

WILLIAMS, MIKE
LONELY SOLDIER	IF THIS ISN'T LOVE	ATLANTIC 2339	10.00	northern

WILLIAMS, NATHAN
WHAT PRICE	REACHING HIGHER	UA 50804	750.00	70's
WHAT PRICE	REACHING HIGHER	LIME 101	850.00	70's

WILLIAMS, O.D.
FUNKY BELLY	I'M MOVING ON OUT OF YOUR LIFE	BAR-BARE 1266	15.00	funk

WILLIAMS, PATTI
I'M DONING THE BEST THAT I CAN	THE CLOCK	FORWARD 135	40.00	northern

WILLIAMS, PORGY
LONELY MAN'S HUM (later mix)	JUST A LONELY MAN'S HUM	SYLVES 100 silver	40.00	northern
LONELY MAN'S HUM	LET'S FORM A COMMITTEE	SYLVES 123	10.00	northern

WILLIAMS, RICHARD
WOULDN'T YOU REALLY RATHER HAV	HEAVEN HELP US ALL	QUAD 107	20.00	70's

WILLIAMS, SAM
LOVE SLIPPED THROUGH MY FINGER	LET'S TALK IT OVER	TOWER 367	400.00	northern
YOU TEMPT ME	I CAN'T STAND THE PAIN	MUSIC WORLD 104	100.00	northern

WILLIAMS, SCOTTY
FEAR	I AIN'T NOBODY WITHOUT YOU	MONA LEE 220	100.00	northern
IN THE SAME OLD WAY	I'VE GOT TO FIND HER	JUBILEE 5602	60.00	northern

WILLIAMS, SEBASTIAN
I DON'T CARE WHAT MAMA SAID	GET YOUR POINT OVER	OVIDE 249	20.00	northern
TOO MUCH	HOME TOWN BOY	SOUND OF SOUL	300.00	northern
102				

WILLIAMS, SUNDAY
THAT'S WHAT YOU WANT	YOU'VE HURT ME NOW	RED BALL 2	20.00	northern

WILLIAMS, T.J. AND THE TWO SHADES OF SOUL
BABY, I NEED YOU	SAME:	JOSIE 1000	250.00	northern
MY LIFE	COMING BACK TO MIAMI	JOSIE 995	25.00	northern

WILLIAMS, TIMMIE
COMPETITION		MALA 515	1000.00	northern

WILLIAMS, TOMMY
GOING CRAZY (OVER YOU)	FROM ME	BACK BEAT 561	30.00	northern

WILLIAMS, TONY
HOW COME	WHEN I HAD YOU	PHILIPS 40141	70.00	northern

WILLIAMS, WANDA
I'VE GOT A SECRET	IT'S ALL OVER	FOREST GREEN 4905	75.00	northern

WILLIAMS, WILLIE
IT DOESN'T PAY	JUST BECAUSE	ABC 10958	30.00	ballad

HAVE YOU EVER BEEN PLAYED FOR	WITH ALL OF MY SOUL	ABC 10860	75.00	northern

WILLIE AND THE HANDJIVES

GOTTA FIND A NEW LOVE	RUNNIN' GIRL	VEEP 1227	40.00	northern

WILLINGHAM, DORIS

YOU CAN'T DO THAT	LOST AGAIN	JAY BOY 6001	15.00	northern

WILLIS, BETTY

AIN'T GONNA DO YOU NO GOOD	GONE WITH THE WIND IS MY LOVE	MOJO 102	150.00	ballad

WILLIS, TIMMY

MR. SOUL SATISFACTION	I'M WONDERING	VEEP 1279	10.00	northern
MR. SOUL SATISFACTION	I'M WONDERING	SIDRA 9013	15.00	northern

WILLOWS

MY KINDA GUY	HURTIN' ALL OVER	MGM 13484	20.00	northern

WILLS, VIOLA

I GOT LOVE	LOST WITHOUT THE LOVE OF MY GUY	BRONCO 2051	10.00	northern

WILSON, AL

YOU DID IT FOR ME	DIFFERENTLY	PLAYBOY 6085	10.00	70's
THE SNAKE	GETTING READY FOR TOMORROW	SOUL CITY 767	8.00	northern
HELP ME	SAME: INSTRUMENTAL	WAND 1135	40.00	northern
NOW I KNOW WHAT LOVE IS	DO WHAT YOU GOTTA DO	SOUL CITY 761	15.00	northern
WHO COULD BE LOVIN' YOU	WHEN YOU LOVE, YOU'RE LOVED TO	SOUL CITY 759	8.00	northern

WILSON, BETTY

DON'T GIVE UP	ANYTHING TO PLEASE MY MAN	DAYCO 2109	20.00	northern
I'M YOURS	ALL OVER AGAIN	DAYCO 1631	300.00	northern

WILSON, BOB

SUZY'S SERENADE	AFTER HOURS	SS7 2578	20.00	**northerB**

WILSON, DONALD

I'VE GOTTA GET MYSELF TOGETHER	I STILL REMEMBER YOU	COLUMBIA 45044	75.00	northern

WILSON, DUSTY

BETTER THAN YOU	SILVERY MOON	ZEBRA 90040	200.00	northern
CAN'T DO WITHOUT YOU	LIFE NOT WORTH LIVING	BRONSE 1800	125.00	northern
IT'S GOING TO BE A TRADEDY	WHILE THE WHOLE WORLD LAUGHS	MUTT 15907	1000.00	northern

WILSON, EDDIE

TOAST TO THE LADY	JUST CALL ON ME	TOLLIE 9033	75.00	northern

WILSON, FLORA

DANCING ON A DAYDREAM	SAME: INSTRUMENTAL	SOULVATION	20.00	funk
ARMY 742				

WILSON, FRANK

DO I LOVE YOU (INDEED I DO)	SWEETER AS THE DAYS GO BY	SOUL 35019	8000.00	northern

WILSON, FREDDIE

WHAT WOULD IT BE LIKE	PT.2	GRANDVILLE 101	20.00	funk
WHAT WOULD IT BE LIKE	Pt. 2	SOUL-PO-TION 112	20.00	funk

WILSON, GEORGE

HERE STANDS THE MAN WHO NEEDS	SAME: INSTRUMENTAL	BLACK CIRCLE 6002	15.00	70's

WILSON, GOODIE

THE DOOR BELL RINGS	I STOOD BENEATH THE WINDOW	TITANIC 5	45.00	northern

WILSON, JACKIE

BECAUSE OF YOU	GO-AWAY	BRUNSWICK 55495	20.00	70's
HELPLESS	DO IT THE RIGHT WAY	BRUNSWICK 55418	8.00	northern
I'M THE ONE TO DO IT	HIGHER AND HIGHER	BRUNSWICK 55336	8.00	northern
I'VE LOST YOU	THOSE HEARTACHES	BRUNSWICK 55321	8.00	northern
SOUL GALORE	BRAND NEW THING	BRUNSWICK 55290	8.00	northern
SOUL TIME	DANNY BOY	BRUNSWICK 55277	8.00	northern
THE WHO WHO SONG	SINCE YOU SHOWED ME HOW 2B HAP	BRUNSWICK 55354	8.00	northern
WHISPERS	THE FAIREST OF THEM ALL	BRUNSWICK 55300	8.00	northern
YOU BROUGHT ABOUT A CHANGE IN	FOR ONCE IN MY LIFE	BRUNSWICK 55392	10.00	northern
THIS LOVE IS REAL	LOVE UPRISING	BRUNSWICK 55443	10.00	northern
HAUNTED HOUSE	I'M TRAVELIN' ON	BRUNSWICK 55260	15.00	northern
JUST BE SINCERE	I DON'T WANT TO LOSE YOU	BRUNSWICK 55309	10.00	northern
NO PITY (IN THE NAKED CITY)	I'M SO LONELY	BRUNSWICK 55280	10.00	northern
NOTHING BUT BLUE SKIES	I GET THE SWEETEST FEELING	BRUNSWICK 55381	8.00	northern

"Nothing But Blues Skies" is also entitles "Nothing But Heeartaches" on some releases…same value.

WILSON, JOHN

AIN'T ENOUGH LOVIN'	MOODY FEELING	SWEET CITY 7380	75.00	70's

WILSON, LEE

A LONELY BOY	IF I WOULD LOSE YOU	USA 884	100.00	northern

WILSON, MADELINE

DIAL "L" FOR LONELY	LOVING HIM	SAMAR 115	30.00	northern

WILSON, MICKEY

GEE BABY (YOU'RE DRIVING ME CR	SAME:INSTRUMENTAL	JULET 1004	50.00	northern

WILSON, NANCY

UPTIGHT (EVERYTHING'S ALRIGHT)	YOU'VE GOT YOUR TROUBLES	CAPITOL 5673	10.00	northern
DON'T COME RUNNING TO ME	LOVE HAS MANY FACES	CAPITOL 5340	8.00	northern
DON'T LOOK OVER YOUR SHOULDER	BUT ONLY SOMETIMES	CAPITOL 5935	10.00	northern
THE END OF OUR LOVE	FACE IT GIRL, IT'S OVER	CAPITOL 2136	10.00	northern
WHERE DOES THAT LEAVE ME	GENTLE IS MY LOVE	CAPITOL 5455	10.00	northern

WILSON, NAOMI

GOTTA FIND A WAY	I'M SO YOUNG	SWAN 4227	20.00	northern